MACROECONOMICS

Sixth Edition

914

914

MACROECONOMICS

Sixth Edition

Edwin G. Dolan
Gettysburg College

David E. Lindsey
Deputy Director, Division of Monetary Affairs
Board of Governors of the Federal Reserve System

The Dryden Press
Chicago   Fort Worth   San Francisco   Philadelphia
Montreal   Toronto   London   Sydney   Tokyo

Acquisitions Editor: Jan Richardson
Developmental Editor: Millicent Treloar
Project Editor: Paula Dempsey/Susan Jansen
Art and Design Manager: Alan Wendt
Production Manager: Barb Bahnsen
Permissions Editor: Cindy Lombardo
Director of Editing, Design, and Production: Jane Perkins

Copy Editor: Kathy Pruno
Indexer: Leoni McVey
Compositor: York Graphic Services, Inc.
Text Type: 10/12 Plantin Light

Library of Congress Cataloging-in-Publication Data

Dolan, Edwin G.
    Macroeconomics / Edwin G. Dolan, David E. Lindsey.—6th ed.
      p. cm.
    ISBN 0-03-032892-6
    1. Macroeconomics. I. Lindsey, David Earl. II. Title.
  HB172.5.D65 1991
  339—dc20   90-3201
                                                          CIP

The paper used in this publication meets the minimum requirements
of American National Standard for Information Sciences—Permanence
of Paper for Printed Library Materials, ANSI Z39,48-1984.

Printed in the United States of America
012-032-987654321
Copyright © 1991, 1988 by The Dryden Press, a division of Holt, Rinehart and Winston, Inc.

Address orders:
The Dryden Press
Orlando, FL 32887

Address editorial correspondence:
The Dryden Press
908 N. Elm Street
Hinsdale, IL 60521

The Dryden Press
Holt, Rinehart and Winston
Saunders College Publishing

Cover Source: ©Barbara Kasten, "Diptych I" (left), 1983 Cibachrome, 30″ × 40″.

The Dryden Press Series in Economics

Preface

Change Is the Only Constant

It has been almost two decades since the authors first collaborated on an economics text. Those years have shown that in economics, change is the only constant.

Since our first effort to set forth the principles of economics for beginning students, economists have gained a better understanding of both the world at large and their own discipline. In macroeconomics, more is known about the dynamics of inflation and disinflation, the role of expectations in shaping economic behavior, and the interaction of the domestic economy with the world economy. In microeconomics, the contributions of public choice theory have lent a new perspective to many policy issues; neo-institutionalists have provided new insights on transaction costs, property rights, and the role of information in the economy; the work of the modern Austrian school has brought new emphasis to the role of entrepreneurship; and long-established fields of economics such as antitrust policy, human resources, and income distribution have taken on new life.

But the economy has not stood still in the face of economists' improved understanding. Events have continued to pose new questions. Economists still disagree on such matters as the effects of the federal deficit, the proper strategy for monetary policy, the sources of volatility in securities prices and exchange rates, the reasons for differences in men's and women's average pay, and the effects of antipoverty policies, to name just a few areas of controversy.

The rapid pace of change in economic theory and reality makes teaching economics a challenge. Meeting that challenge requires a textbook that changes too. First, the book must bring the latest policy issues and theoretical topics into the classroom and explain them clearly. Second, the book must emphasize the ways of thinking that all economists use to attack new problems, even where they do not ultimately agree. Finally, the book must reflect ongoing innovation in pedagogical techniques so that the complexities of economics are made accessible to the beginning student.

This sixth edition of *Economics*, like earlier editions, is available in a one-volume hard-cover edition and also separate paperback editions, entitled *Macroeconomics* and *Microeconomics*. Both the hard-cover and paperback versions respond to the need for change with these major features:

1. Feature: Integrated international economics. Topics in international theory and policy are covered in special sections of chapters that discuss related domestic theory and policy—for example, balance of payments accounts together with national income accounts and foreign exchange operations of the Fed together with its domestic open market operations. For maximum flexibility, these sections are self-contained so that those who wish to follow the traditional option of a single international unit at the end of the course may still do so. The special international sections are designated by a world map logo.

Purpose: To show how domestic economic events and policy can best be understood in the context of an integrated world economy.

Benefit: Crucial international issues are no longer crowded into the last days before the final exam.

2. Feature: One-model macro option. The macro chapters offer a one-model option for teaching the theory of income determination. This permits Keynesian and classical theory, fiscal and monetary policy, and the dynamics of inflation and unemployment all to be taught in an aggregate supply and demand framework. The income-expenditure model is covered in an optional chapter, Chapter 9, and an optional section of Chapter 10 for those who prefer to follow the traditional two-model approach. The accelerationist model of inflation, using inflation-adjusted Phillips curves, is found in Chapter 16, which is self-contained and also optional.

Purpose: To unify the teaching of macroeconomics within a single theoretical framework.

Benefit: Less time spent developing models, more time spent on issues and applications, including international topics.

3. Feature: Focus on new microeconomics. A special section of four microeconomic chapters looks at the "new microeconomics"—a set of extensions and modifications of traditional neoclassical analysis that have received wide attention in recent years. The first of these chapters, "Inside the Firm," covers transaction cost theory and the control of agents by their principals, and applies these ideas to the organization of firms and the market in corporate takeovers. The second chapter in the section, "Economics of Information and Uncertainty," covers asymmetric information, risk, speculation, insurance, and auctions. The third chapter in the section, "Entrepreneurship and the Market Process," discusses modern Austrian and other views on entrepreneurship and innovation. The fourth chapter, "Economics of Public Choice," covers resource allocation under democratic government, bureaucracy, and privatization.

Purpose: To keep the microeconomics course lively and up-to-date through coverage of modern extensions of traditional neoclassical theory.

Benefit: Because the "new microeconomics" topics are covered immediately after the traditional neoclassical models, they can be applied in the policy-oriented chapters that follow. Areas in which transaction cost theory, economics of information, entrepreneurship, and public choice theory are applied include antitrust and regulation, environmental policy, labor market policy, poverty, international trade, and Soviet economic reform.

4. Feature: Focus on objectives, constraints on opportunities, and rational choice. A new chapter at the beginning of the microeconomics section introduces objectives, constraints on opportunities, and rational choice as the basic elements underlying economic theories and models. These elements are stressed again and again throughout the micro chapters, whether the discussion concerns the effect of market structure on the constraints of the profit-maximizing firms, the effect of labor-market discrimination on choices made by workers, or the effect of economic regulation on choices made by firms and households.

Purpose: To show that all of the principal problems of microeconomics have a common underlying structure.

Benefit: Unifies the relatively abstract "core theory" chapters (consumer choice, perfect competition, and so on) with the "new economics" chapters and the applied chapters.

5. Feature: State-of-the-art pedagogy. Enhanced teaching and learning aids and a new generic organization of boxed cases mean that the sixth edition of *Economics*, like past editions, defines the state of the art in pedagogy.

Purpose: To help students see the forest as well as the trees.

Benefit: Students who understand economics as a way of thinking rather than just a grab bag of models retain more of what they learn in the principles of economics course.

Keeping a textbook like this up-to-date is not simply a matter of adding new material; the presentation of old material must be revised and reorganized so that each new edition is a harmonious whole. In the sixth edition, this has meant a complete reorganization of the introductory chapters that are common to both the macro and the micro courses:

- A single chapter entitled "The Economic Way of Thinking" introduces basic concepts such as scarcity and choice, markets, and the use of models.

- The appendix on the use of graphs in economics has been substantially expanded and now provides the most thorough coverage of this topic to be found in any text.

- The chapter on elasticity now appears as the third of three chapters common to both the macro and microeconomics courses. Covering elasticity before the macroeconomics chapters permits a more thorough treatment of the microeconomic foundations of macroeconomic models.

- In addition to the streamlined three-chapter introductory section common to both halves of the course, the macro and micro sections each now have an introductory chapter of their own. The macro introduction, "In Search of Stability and Prosperity," discusses the goals of price stability, full employment, and economic growth. The micro introduction, "Economic Theory, Markets, and Government" covers rational choice, objectives and constraints, market failure, and the role of government.

The following pages outline the approach of this book to the changing world of economics in more detail.

Organization of the Book

Macroeconomics

Integration of International Economics. The traditional structure of the macro course calls for teaching fiscal and monetary theory in a closed-economy context and then adding international topics at the end as time permits. In terms of the logic of step-by-step model building, this approach has some appeal. However, it also has a drawback: Increasingly, any newspaper article or TV news report that mentions monetary policy or the budget deficit is likely to mention the balance of payments and exchange rates in the same breath.

If an instructor wants to bring international policy issues into the course from the beginning, the student needs an early introduction to the linkages between the domestic economy and the rest of the world. Five of the chapters in the hard-cover *Economics* and paperback *Macroeconomics* contain special sections that serve this aim. A section in Chapter 5, "The Circular Flow of Income and Product," uses the circular flow model to show the basic linkages between the domestic and world economies. A section in Chapter 6, "Measuring National Income and Product," outlines the balance of payments accounts as a natural extension of the domestic national income accounts. Chapter 9, "The Income-Expenditure Model," includes a section on the net export component of planned expenditure and shows how imports affect the expenditure multiplier. Chapter 12, "Central Banking and Money Creation," adds a section on the Fed's foreign exchange market operations as a follow-up to the usual discussion of its open market operations. A section of Chapter 14, "An Integrated View of Monetary and Fiscal Policy" discusses international implications of fiscal policy and the "twin deficits" phenomenon. These sections provide a series of stepping-stones to Chapter 19, "Foreign Exchange Markets and International Monetary Policy."

Some instructors may, of course, prefer the traditional sequence in which international topics are covered at the end of the macro course. For this reason, the international sections of the various macro chapters are self-contained and clearly identified by a world map logo placed in the margin. It is possible to skip over these sections as the chapters are covered with no loss of continuity. The whole set can then be covered as a unit after Chapter 18 and before proceeding to Chapter 19.

The One-Model Option.   For many years, textbooks relied on a single model for determining the level of real income: the Keynesian income-expenditure model, also known as the "Keynesian cross" or the "45° model." When the issue of inflation rose to importance in the 1970s, it became popular to supplement the income-expenditure model with a flexible-price aggregate supply and demand (AS/AD) model. The Lindsey/Dolan *Basic Macroeconomics* of 1974 was one of the first principles texts to do this. But today an increasing number of instructors take the view that two models for determining real income is one too many. For one thing, it is difficult to give a clean reconciliation of the two models at the principles level. Also, time spent teaching a second income determination model is time taken away from other course objectives, such as integrating international economics more closely into the course.

Unfortunately, almost all texts to date have been written in such a way that the instructor has no choice but to use both models. Not so with this text. Since its fifth edition, this text has taken the logical next step in the evolution of the principles course *by using AS/AD as the core model for macro theory while treating the income-expenditure model as an optional supplement.*

A full-chapter introduction to the aggregate supply and demand model is provided in Chapter 7. The basic income-expenditure model is presented in an optional chapter, Chapter 9. This chapter first presents the standard fixed-price version of the model and then allows prices to vary in order to show the relationship of the income-expenditure and AS/AD models. In addition, an optional section of Chapter 10 applies the income-expenditure model to fiscal policy. In both cases, the income-expenditure material is entirely self-contained. It can be taught in sequence as it appears, preserving the traditional course outline, or omitted without loss of continuity.

But what about the historical importance of Keynes and his work? Taking the one-model option in no way downplays Keynes's contributions to macroeconomic theory and policy. Quite the contrary. Chapter 8 provides a fuller discussion of the Keynesian and classical views of economic stabilization than is given in any competing text. This discussion, presented in the framework of the AS/AD model, presents Keynes's ideas as set forth in his *General Theory* more accurately than the conventional approach used in other texts. By the time students have completed Chapter 8 they will have all the tools they need, including an understanding of the expenditure multiplier, to move directly to the discussion of fiscal policy in Chapter 10.

Continuing Features. Not everything in the macroeconomics chapters is new. Many features that found favor with users of previous editions remain. One is the use of the circular flow model to introduce key macroeconomic concepts and relationships (Chapter 5). Another is the blending of monetary theory, financial institutions, and practical policy issues in Chapters 11 through 14. Still another is the optional, chapter-length treatment of the accelerationist model of inflation (Chapter 16 in this edition). Along the way, many favorite case studies have been retained and a number of new ones added.

Microeconomics

Focus on objectives, constraints on opportunities, and rational choice. The microeconomics section of the text has an all-new introductory chapter that focuses on objectives, constraints on opportunities, and rational choice as unifying elements of microeconomic theory. This introduction serves as a framework for a thorough revision and reorganization of the seven "core theory" chapters that introduce traditional neoclassical price theory.

Each of these seven core chapters now begins by explicitly setting forth the objectives and constraints on opportunities faced by decision makers in firms and households and then proceeds to show how rational choice leads to certain market outcomes. Several topics not covered in previous editions have been added to these chapters, for example, the effects of sunk costs on firms' profit-maximizing choices, long-run equilibrium under monopoly for various assumptions regarding potential competition and competition from substitute products, and allocation over time of nonrenewable natural resources. The organization of the text is tightened by grouping the chapters on pricing in resource markets and markets for capital and natural resources together with the other core theory chapters.

The New Microeconomics. As this text evolved over its previous five editions, more and more elements of the "new microeconomics" found their way into it. Terms such as transaction costs, political rent seeking, and entrepreneurship will be familiar to users of those editions. In preparing this sixth edition, it became clear that it was time to pull these topics together in a more systematic way so that their relation to one another would be made clear and so that they could be applied to a wider variety of policy issues. The result is a four-chapter section that immediately follows the core theory chapters.

The first two chapters are entirely new to this edition. "Inside the Firm" explores the insights of such writers as Ronald Coase and Oliver Williamson regarding transaction costs, opportunism, principal-agent relationships, and the structure of firms. These insights are then applied to current controversies related to takeovers and corporate restructuring. The second of the new chapters deals with the economics of information and uncertainty. Topics covered include the nature of uncertainty, asymmetric information, speculation, hedging, insurance, adverse selection and moral hazard, the "lemons" problem, auctions, and the winner's curse.

The remaining two chapters appeared in a somewhat different form in the fifth edition. One deals with entrepreneurship and market process, emphasizing the contributions of the modern Austrian school. The other covers public choice economics. This chapter appears earlier than in the fifth edition, so that the contributions of public choice theory can be applied to a broader range of policy issues. Also, the chapter has been expanded with new sections on constitutional choice, the median voter theory, and bureaucracy.

Applied Chapters. As in previous editions, a representative range of applied micro topics are covered in the remaining chapters. The chapter on antitrust policy incorporates new material on public choice and modern Austrian perspectives. The chapters on environmental policy and labor-market policy also contain extensive applications of "new economics" topics. The chapter on poverty is completely restructured. In addition to new empirical material on poverty trends, the sections on poverty policy are rewritten to emphasize the importance of constraints on opportunities and choices in determining the economic status of poor households. The chapter on international trade policy covers the latest controversies over competitiveness and protectionism. Finally, the last chapter in the book, which covers Soviet economic reform, is heavily revised to reflect the progress and problems of *perestroika*.

Pedagogy

Many innovative features of earlier editions of *Economics* have become industry standards. An example is multilevel vocabulary reinforcement, with boldface terms, marginal definitions, and an end-of-book glossary. The process of innovation and refinement continues in this new edition of Dolan and Lindsey.

Bracketing

One of the most solidly established techniques of effective pedagogy is that of *bracketing*. Every good classroom lecturer uses bracketing in the form of "Here's what we are going to say; here it is in detail; here is what we just said." The textbook equivalent is chapter preview and review. Sheer volume of preview and review material counts for less than do the care with which the two are tied together and what comes between. Here are the key bracketing techniques used in *Economics:*

- Each chapter opens with a set of *learning objectives* posed in the form of issues to be addressed in the chapter. These are then used in question form to organize the *chapter summary*.

- A list of *key terms from previous chapters* appears at the beginning of each chapter. This is balanced by a list of *newly introduced terms* at the end of the chapter.

- Each chapter begins with a *lead-off case* and ends with a *case for discussion*. The first item in the *problems and topics for discussion* at the end of the chapter asks students to apply what they have learned to issues raised in the lead-off case. The case for discussion is followed by its own set of questions. (Answers to these questions are given in the *Instructor's Manual*.)

Generic Organization of Boxed Cases

Since its first edition, *Economics* has been a leader in the use of case studies as a teaching and learning tool. In addition to the lead-off cases and cases for discussion used to bracket each chapter, numerous *boxed cases* appear within each chapter. A distinctive feature of this text is the organization of these cases into three generic categories, each with a specific purpose:

1. **Economics in the News.** Illustrates an abstract concept raised in the chapter with an actual quoted or paraphrased news item. Example: "Cookie Stores Feel the Bite as Market Shifts."

2. **Applying Economic Ideas.** Uses a tool learned in the chapter for solving a problem drawn from real life. Example: "The Opportunity Cost of a College Education."

3. **Who Said It? Who Did It?** Highlights the contribution of an economist of the past or present to a key idea discussed in the chapter. Example: "Adam Smith on the Invisible Hand."

The Package

A complete support package provides instructors and students with everything they need to teach and learn economics.

Test Bank

Written by Louis Amato and Gaines Liner, both of the University of North Carolina at Charlotte, in collaboration with Edwin G. Dolan, the *Test Bank* includes more than 2,000 items. It is available in two versions, for *Macroeconomics* and *Microeconomics*. The authors have fully class-tested each item, guaranteeing comprehensive, "teacher-friendly" selection. The *Test Bank* contains the following features.

Number and Type of Questions. The *Test Bank* offers over 2,000 multiple-choice and true/false questions. It also contains many graphical questions.

Distribution of Questions by Chapter. Each chapter has an appropriate number of questions based on its content and length. This varies from 40 questions for the first, introductory chapter to 120 for some of the core concept chapters. Some questions appear in alternative forms to permit reuse. Questions are arranged in the approximate order of the chapter coverage of each topic.

Categorization and Coding. All questions are coded according to level of difficulty and cognitive learning type. These are E (easy), M (moderate), D (difficult); and DF (definition or fact), SA (simple analysis), and CI (complex interpretation). This allows the instructor to select a spectrum of questions for testing both recall learning and concept comprehension.

Graphing Emphasis. Many questions ask students to work directly on graphs. Questions are formatted to follow the "hands-on" sample items in the *Study Guide*.

Recordkeeping Aid. The *Test Bank* contains marginal recordkeeping space for the instructor to personalize it with the date each question is used and the percentage of students who correctly answer each question.

Additional Exam and Essay Problems. The *Instructor's Manual* contains two exam and essay problems for each chapter with which to supplement tests. Exam and essay problems typically serve as excellent extra-credit test questions for more proficient students. Answers are included.

Computerized Version. The *Computerized Test Bank* (available for the Macintosh and IBM PC) allows the instructor to create tests tailored to particular requirements. By using the questions stored on disk, both short quizzes and full-length exams can be quickly and easily constructed.

The *Computerized Test Bank* allows instructors to:

- preview questions on the computer screen.
- edit publisher-supplied questions and create personalized questions.
- select exam questions manually or randomly.
- create exam headings and determine the amount of space to be allotted each question.
- scramble questions to create multiple versions of the same test.
- print exams with answer keys and student answer sheets.
- store exams created for future use.
- produce partial hard copy of most graphs that appear in the *Test Bank*.

Direct Service Hotline. For instructors who have any technical difficulties with the *Computerized Test Bank*, The Dryden Press/TEC offers a direct service number: (516) 681-1773, 9 a.m. to 5 p.m. EST.

Instructor's Manual

The *Instructor's Manual* for *Economics* (available in a single, combined version) is intended to help new instructors prepare their first principles course and experienced instructors retailor their course to mesh optimally with the text. With these aims in mind, the *Instructor's Manual* includes the following features.

What's Different Here and Why.   This section, found at the beginning of each chapter, helps convert the course outline and lecture notes from other texts to *Economics*, sixth edition. Changes from the fifth edition of *Economics* are noted. This section also provides technical information on the theoretical models that underlie the book.

Instructional Objectives.   All elements of the *Economics* package—text, *Study Guide*, *Test Bank*, and *Instructor's Manual*—are coordinated by means of specific instructional objectives listed in each chapter of the *Instructor's Manual*. In the text, they are listed for students at the beginning of each chapter. Questions covering every topic on the list of instructional objectives are included in the *Test Bank*.

Lecture Notes and Suggestions.   Each chapter of the *Instructor's Manual* contains a section of lecture notes in outline form. The lecture notes cover the optional appendixes as well as the chapters.

Examination Problems and Essays.   Each chapter contains two or three suggestions for examination problems and essays. These are valuable supplements to the multiple-choice and true/false questions contained in the *Test Bank* where the teaching situation permits grading of problems and essays.

Answers to Selected Problems and Topics for Discussion.   Answers are given to selected items from the "Problems and Topics for Discussion" sections of the text as well as the "Case for Discussion" sections in each chapter. Items that involve library research or ask questions that pertain to students' personal or community situation are omitted.

Study Guide

The *Study Guide* for *Economics*, written by Edwin G. Dolan, provides students with hands-on applications and self-testing opportunities. It is available in two versions, for *Macroeconomics* and *Microeconomics*. It reinforces the text and prepares students for exams. The *Study Guide* contains the following features.

Where You're Going.   All parts of the *Economics* package are tied together by a numbered set of learning objectives for each chapter. These learning objectives, which also appear in the text and the *Instructor's Manual*, are given in the "Where You're Going" section of each chapter of the *Study Guide*. A list of terms introduced in the chapter is also provided.

Walking Tour.   The "Walking Tour" section is a narrative summary of the chapter and incorporates questions on key points. Students work through this material, answering the questions as they go along. Answers to the questions are given in the margins.

Hands On.   This section contains graphical and numerical exercises that give students hands-on experience in working with the concepts covered in the chapter. It is particularly helpful to students who require extra work in order to master difficult graphical material. Complete solutions, including graphs, are given at the end of the chapter.

Economics in the News. Each of these sections takes the form of a brief news item with questions that relate the item to concepts covered in the chapter. Answers are found at the end of the chapter. These items are particularly valuable in preparing for essay-type exam questions. This feature is the *Study Guide* version of the case study approach used in the text and links economics to the real world.

Self Test. This section consists of 15 multiple-choice questions, which are similar in structure to those in the *Test Bank* and act as a final checkpoint before an exam. Annotated answers to the self-test items are given at the end of the chapter.

Don't Make This Common Mistake. These are special boxes, strategically placed throughout the *Study Guide*, that caution students against certain common mistakes made by previous generations of economics students. All of these mistakes are easy to avoid if the student is alerted to them.

Computer Instruction Supplements

EconoGraph II. This supplement, created by Charles Link, Jeffrey Miller, and John Bergman of the University of Delaware, is a computer software package for principles of economics. It consists of nine interactive tutorial lessons. These lessons include the topics students find most difficult to master, including supply and demand, money expansion, AS/AD, Keynesian cross analysis, cost functions, supply under perfect competition, and monopoly.

EconoGraph II is designed for use with IBM PCs with at least 128K of memory, DOS 2.0, and a color graphics card (use with IBM compatibles is possible but not guaranteed). Features include:

1. Intensive instruction in the use of graphs, which are critical in economics.
2. Self-contained 10- to 40-minute lessons.
3. Diagnostic questions and problems in which the computer tells students what they did right or wrong.
4. Graphical manipulations in which students can plot lines and shift curves.
5. Graphs constructed in stages so that each stage can be explained and important aspects highlighted.
6. Self-paced instruction to allow for repetition and review.

Good Graphs! A second computer supplement has been added to the Dolan and Lindsey package for the sixth edition. This supplement, created by Tod S. Porter and Teresa M. Riley of Youngstown State University, goes beyond conventional "spacebar software" that gives students little more than they can read in the text. *Good Graphs!* takes a different approach. Students are presented with the kinds of questions that an instructor might ask on an exam. The program then lets the student actually draw a graph on the computer screen. The answer is evaluated by the program, and, if an error is made, an error message explaining why the graph is incorrect will be displayed. The program gives students a unique opportunity to test how well they understand the graphs used in the course before they get to the exam.

Good Graphs! covers more than 20 topics from both macro and microeconomics sections of the course. These include introduction to graphing, supply and demand, shifts in supply and demand, elasticity, aggregate supply and demand, the Keynesian multiplier, fiscal policy, monetary policy, inflation and unemployment, and international trade and payments.

Good Graphs! requires an IBM personal computer (or 100 percent compatible) with at least 250K memory, a double-sided disk drive, and a copy of DOS 2.0 or some later version. The computer must also be equipped with either a CGA, Hercules, AT&T 6300, EGA, or VGA graphics card.

Transparency Acetates

The two-color transparency acetates are computer generated. This provides maximum accuracy and readability. For complete pedagogical consistency, the color used in the graphics matches that in the text. There are more than 140 acetates of graphs from the text. Each transparency has a complete teaching note to help instructors integrate the transparency into their lectures.

Some Words of Thanks

We wish to thank the following people for their help in revising this edition:

Jack Adams, *University of Arkansas* **Ali Akarca,** *University of Illinois–Chicago* **Charles Bennett,** *Gannon University* **Mary Bone,** *Pensacola Junior College* **Thomas Bonsor,** *East Washington University* **David Brasfield,** *Murray State University* **Donald Bumpass,** *Texas Technical University* **William Carlisle,** *University of Utah* **J. S. J. Charles,** *Southwest Texas State University* **James Clark,** *Wichita State University* **Avi Cohen,** *York University* **C. M. Condon,** *College of Charleston* **James Cover,** *University of Alabama* **J. R. Cowart,** *Mobile College* **James M. Cox,** *DeKalb Community College* **Kenneth DeHaven,** *Tri-County Technical College* **Mary Deily,** *Texas A&M University* **David Edmonds,** *University of Southwestern Louisiana* **Howard Elder,** *University of Alabama* **Charles Ellard,** *Pan American University* **Michael Erickson,** *Eastern Illinois University* **Mohsen Fardmanesh,** *Temple University* **Christopher Fiorentino,** *West Chester University* **Joseph Fosu,** *Western Illinois University* **Nancy Fox,** *St. Joseph's University* **David Fractor,** *California State University, Northridge* **Gary Galles,** *Pepperdine University* **Lynne Gillette,** *Texas A&M University* **Robert Gillette,** *Texas A&M University* **Fred Graham,** *University of Texas, Arlington* **Harish Gupta,** *University of Nebraska* **James Hamilton,** *University of Virginia* **Oskar Harmon,** *University of Stamford* **John Harvey,** *Texas Christian University* **Charles Hegji,** *Auburn University, Montgomery* **Ronald J. Herr,** *Clarke College* **John Holland,** *Iona College* **Peter Huang,** *Tulane University* **R. James,** *James Madison University* **Robert Jerome,** *James Madison University* **James Jonish,** *Texas Technical University* **Ebrahim Karbassioon,** *Eastern Illinois University* **Bruce Kaufman,** *Georgia State University* **Calvin Kent,** *Baylor University* **James Kyle,** *Indiana State University* **Luther Lawson,** *University of North Carolina, Wilmington* **Stephen Lile,** *Western Kentucky University* **Joseph Lin,** *Louisiana State University* **Raymond Lombra,** *Pennsylvania State University* **Franklin Lopez,** *University of New Orleans* **Don Losman,** *National Defense University, Washington* **J. L. Love,** *Valdosta State College* **David MacPherson,** *Pennsylvania State University* **Jay Marchand,** *University of Mississippi* **Benjamin Matta,** *New Mexico State University* **John Mbaku,** *Kennesaw College* **Eugene McKibbin,** *Fullerton College* **Shah Mehrabi,** *Mary Washington College* **Joseph Mesky,** *East Carolina University* **Don Meyer,** *Louisiana Tech University* **Steve Meyer,** *Francis Marion College* **Jefferson Moore,** *Louisiana*

State University **J. M. Morgan,** *College of Charleston* **John Murdoch,** *Northeast Louisiana University* **Kenneth Nowotny,** *New Mexico State University* **Michael Olds,** *Orange Coast College* **James O'Neill,** *University of Delaware* **Pat Papachristou,** *Christian Brothers College* **Judd Patton,** *California State University–San Bernardino* **Carl Pearl,** *Cypress College* **Thomas Peterson,** *Central Michigan University* **John Piscotta,** *Baylor University* **J. M. Pogodzinski,** *Georgia State University* **David Rees,** *Mesa College* **Michael Rendich,** *Westchester Community College* **D. Rogers,** *LeMoyne College* **Donald Schaefer,** *Washington State University* **Bruce Seaman,** *Georgia State University* **Frank Slesnick,** *Bellarmine College* **Phillip Smith,** *Gainesville Junior College* **Ken Somppi,** *Auburn University* **David Spenser,** *Brigham Young University* **Tony Spiva,** *University of Tennessee, Knoxville* **Henry Thomasson,** *Southeastern Louisiana University* **H. Bruce Throckmorton,** *Tennessee Technological University* **Timothy Tregarthen,** *University of Colorado, Colorado Springs* **David Tuerck,** *Suffolk University* **Arienne Turner,** *Fullerton College* **Steven Ullmann,** *University of Miami* **K. T. Varghese,** *James Madison University* **Thomas Vernon,** *Clarion University of Pennsylvania* **Michael Watts,** *Purdue University* **William Weber,** *Illinois State University* **Everett White,** *Loyola University (LA)* **Don Williams,** *Kent State University* **Eugene Williams,** *Northwestern State University* **John Young,** *Riverside Community College* **Edward Zajicek,** *Hope College* **Ernie Zampelli,** *Catholic University of America*

In addition, we would like to thank the staff of The Dryden Press for making this edition possible. They are a truly dedicated, tireless group of professionals.

This edition, like previous editions, represents the collaborative work of Edwin G. Dolan and David E. Lindsey. The views expressed in this book are those of the authors. Nothing in this book should be construed as necessarily reflecting the views of the Board of Governors of the Federal Reserve System or other members of its staff.

Edwin G. Dolan
Great Falls, Virginia

David E. Lindsey
Arlington, Virginia

December 1990

About the Authors

Edwin G. Dolan grew up in the small town of McMinnville, Oregon. He attended Earlham College and then Indiana University, earning a B.A. degree from Indiana. After staying at Indiana to earn an M.A. in economics, he completed his Ph.D. at Yale University. Dolan has taught economics at the University of Connecticut, Dartmouth College, the University of Chicago, George Mason University, and, currently, at Gettysburg College. He has also served as a specialist in transportation regulation, both in the antitrust division of the U.S. Department of Justice and at the Interstate Commerce Commission. His chief research interest is the Soviet economic system. A fluent speaker of Russian, Dolan has been invited to lecture at Moscow State University, the Moscow Financial Institute, and the Russian-American University.

David E. Lindsey comes from the university town of West Lafayette, Indiana. He received his B.A. from Earlham College, where he and Dolan were roommates. He then earned a Ph.D. from the University of Chicago under the direction of Milton Friedman. Lindsey taught economics for several years at Ohio State University and Macalester College. Since 1974 he has been on the staff of the Board of Governors of the Federal Reserve System, where he now serves as Deputy Director of the Division of Monetary Affairs and Associate Economist for the Federal Open Market Committee.

Contents in Brief

Contents

MACROECONOMICS

Sixth Edition

PART ONE

Overview of Economics

CHAPTER

1

The Economic Way of Thinking

After reading this chapter, you will understand:

What economics is all about.

The considerations underlying four fundamental economic choices:

What an economy should produce.

How goods and services should be produced.

Who should do which work.

For whom goods should be produced.

The mechanisms used to coordinate economic choices.

How economists use theory, graphs, and evidence in their work.

Traffic Jam 22,300 Miles Up

A traffic jam 22,300 miles above the earth? Impossible, you say? Think again. The ring of space that circles the earth's equator at that altitude is, in its own way, as crowded as the Indianapolis Motor Speedway on Memorial Day weekend. It's a very special piece of space real estate.

Satellites placed in orbit 22,300 miles above the equator are geosynchronous, which means that their orbital period of 24 hours just matches the earth's rotation. As a result, they appear stationary when viewed from the ground. Geosynchronous satellites are ideal platforms for communications equipment, because they do not periodically pass below the horizon and out of contact, and because antennas used to communicate with them do not have to move to follow the satellite's apparent motion. Their special properties have made them a central component of modern global telecommunications.

Unfortunately, only a limited number of satellites can fit up there. If satellites are placed too close together, radio signals going to or from one satellite interfere with those going to or from its neighbors. Given present technology, about 2 degrees of arc is the closest workable spacing. That means there can be no more than about 180 satellites in geosynchronous orbit at any one time.

However, not all satellite "slots," as the 2-degree parking spaces are sometimes called, are equal. The most sought-after locations are those between 60 and 135 degrees west longitude, which can serve the entire continental United States. Slots at the western end of this arc can also serve Hawaii and Alaska,

Photo source: Courtesy of NASA.

Sources: Joel D. Scheraga, "Establishing Property Rights in Outer Space," *Cato Journal* (Winter 1987): 889–903, and Timothy Tregarthen, "Outer Space: The Scarce Frontier," *The Margin* (September 1987): 8–9.

while those at its eastern end permit direct communication between the continental United States and Europe. Service to other nations in the Western Hemisphere requires use of the same slice of geosynchronous orbit.

Slots in the 60- to 135-degree arc are so handy, in fact, that none are left. They are all either filled with satellites or assigned to users who are scheduled to put equipment in orbit by the end of the 1980s. As far as newcomers are concerned, it's "Sorry, parking lot full."

Given the scarcity of geosynchronous orbital slots, one would at least hope that they are being put to the most effective use possible. But that is not always the case. The slots are occupied by satellites of varying ages and capacities. Some slots have been allocated to users who have held them for some time without putting up any equipment. Meanwhile, some potential users who would dearly like a slot are unable to get one.

A major problem is that those with an urgent need for slots cannot just buy them from their current holders. Property rights do not exist in space. According to the United Nations Outer Space Treaty, which has been ratified by 107 member nations, outer space is "the province of all mankind." Private buying and selling of slots is barred. It's as if the owner of a single-family house on a lot in midtown Manhattan were barred from selling the lot to someone who wants to erect a high-rise that would make more intensive use of the property.

Pessimists foresee increasingly wasteful use of a scarce resource. Optimists hope for a technological reprieve allowing closer spacing of satellites, although at some point the risk of collisions becomes a limiting factor. Meanwhile, the parameters of the geosynchronous orbital ring are fixed by the laws of physics. It is up to us earthlings to use it well or poorly.

Scarcity
A situation in which there is not enough of a resource to meet all of everyone's wants.

Economics
The social science that seeks to understand the choices people make in using scarce resources to meet their wants.

The difficulty of obtaining satellite slots is an example of **scarcity**—a situation in which there is not enough of something to meet everyone's wants. Scarcity and the way people deal with it are the central topics of **economics,** which can be defined as the social science that seeks to understand the choices people make in using scarce resources to meet their wants.

Economics, as the definition makes clear, is a study not of things or money or wealth but of *people*. Economics is about people because scarcity itself is a human phenomenon. Although people work within such physical limits as the laws of orbital mechanics, satellite slots were not scarce until they became the object of human wants. The same is true of all other scarce resources—mozzarella cheese is scarce because people want pizzas, Manhattan real estate is scarce because people want to live and do business on that crowded island, and time is scarce because people have many things they want to do each day.

A second reason that economics is about people is that the choices it studies are made in a social context. That is why economics is considered a social science rather than a branch of operations analysis, engineering, or mathematics. Take, for example, the social context of decisions regarding the use of satellite slots. People want satellite slots because they want to communicate with one another. The decision to use resources to put satellites in orbit reflects a judgment about which human wants should be given priority over others that the same resources could be used to satisfy. United Nations resolutions regarding ownership of orbital slots reflect a debate over the rights of rich and poor nations to control the world's scarce resources.

Of course, satellite slots are a rather exotic example of scarcity and choice. Economic choices are being made every day much closer than 22,300 miles out in space. You make economic choices when you buy clothes or groceries, when you work at a job—even when you choose to fill one of the scarce slots in your class schedule with a course in economics rather than with one in environmental toxicology. Economic choices are made everywhere: in the factory that made the computer this book was typed on, in the government offices that oversee affirmative-action policies, in nonprofit organizations such as churches and student clubs, and in just about any other situation you can think of.

All the examples just given come from the branch of economics known as **microeconomics.** The prefix *micro*, meaning "small," indicates that this branch of economics deals with the choices of small economic units such as households, firms, and government agencies. Although individual units studied by microeconomics are small, its scope can be worldwide. For example, households, firms, and government agencies conduct worldwide trade in such goods as cars, chemicals, and crude oil. That trade and the policies regulating it fall within the scope of microeconomics.

Economics also has another branch, known as **macroeconomics.** The prefix *macro*, meaning "large," indicates that this branch deals with larger-scale economic phenomena. Typical problems in macroeconomics include how to maintain conditions in which people who want jobs can find them, how to protect the economy against the distortions caused by the widespread price changes called inflation, and how to provide for a continued increase in living standards over time. Government policies concerning taxes, expenditures, budget deficits, and the financial system are central concerns of macroeconomics. However, inasmuch as macroeconomic phenomena such as inflation represent the summation of millions of individual choices regarding the prices of particular goods and services, macroeconomics rests on a microeconomic foundation.

Whether one is dealing with microeconomics or macroeconomics, with domestic or international economic relationships, all economic analysis comes down to a special way of thinking about how people choose to use scarce resources. This introductory chapter paves the way toward more specialized material by exploring some of the principles that underlie the economic way of thinking. The first section reviews four key choices that every economy must make. The next section looks at the kinds of social institutions within which choices are made, and the final section covers some important aspects of economic method.

Microeconomics
The branch of economics that studies the choices of small economic units, including households, business firms, and government agencies.

Macroeconomics
The branch of economics that studies large-scale economic phenomena, particularly inflation, unemployment, and economic growth.

1.1   What? How? Who? For Whom?

In every economy certain basic choices must be faced. Among these, the most important are *what* goods should be produced, *how* they should be produced, *who* should do which jobs, and *for whom* the results of economic activity should be made available. Each of these choices is made necessary because of scarcity, and each can be used to introduce key elements of the economic way of thinking.

Deciding What to Produce: Opportunity Cost

The first basic choice is that of what goods to produce. In a modern economy the number of goods and services that could be produced is immense. The essential features of the choice of what goods to produce, however, can be illustrated

Factors of production
The basic inputs of labor, capital, and natural resources used in producing all goods and services.

Labor
The contributions to production made by people working with their minds and muscles.

Capital
All means of production that are created by people, including tools, industrial equipment, and structures.

Natural resources
Anything that can be used as a productive input in its natural state, such as farmland, building sites, forests, and mineral deposits.

Opportunity cost
The cost of a good or service measured in terms of the forgone opportunity to pursue the best possible alternative activity with the same time or resources.

using an economy in which as few as two alternative goods exist, for example, cars and education. For many students, going without a car (or driving a junker instead of the car one wants) is a sacrifice that must be made in order to get a college education. The same trade-off that is faced by an individual student is also faced by the economy as a whole: Not enough cars and education can be produced to satisfy everyone's wants. Someone must choose how much of each good to produce.

The impossibility of producing as much of everything as people want reflects a scarcity of the productive resources that are used to make all goods. Many scarce productive resources must be combined to make even the simplest of goods. For example, making a table requires lumber, nails, glue, a hammer, a saw, the work of a carpenter, that of a painter, and so on. For convenience, productive resources are often grouped into three basic categories, called **factors of production. Labor** includes all of the productive contributions made by people working with their minds and muscles. **Capital** includes all the productive inputs created by people, including tools, machinery, structures, and intangible items such as computer programs. **Natural resources** include anything that can be used as a productive input in its natural state, for example, farmland, building sites, forests, and mineral deposits.

Productive resources that are used to satisfy one want cannot be used to satisfy another at the same time. Steel, concrete, and building sites used for automobile factories cannot also be used for classrooms. People who are employed as teachers cannot spend the same time working on an automobile assembly line. Even the time students spend in class and studying for tests represents use of a factor of production that could otherwise be used as labor in an auto plant. Because production uses inputs that could be used elsewhere, the production of any good entails forgoing the opportunity to produce something else instead. In economic terms, everything has an **opportunity cost.** The opportunity cost of a good or service is its cost in terms of the forgone opportunity to pursue the best possible alternative activity with the same time or resources.

Imagine an economy that has only two goods, cars and education. In such an economy the opportunity cost of producing a college graduate can be stated in terms of the number of cars that could have been produced by using the same labor, capital, and natural resources. For example, the opportunity cost of educating a college graduate might be five Ford Mustangs. Such a ratio (graduates per car or cars per graduate) is a useful way to express opportunity cost when only two goods are involved. More typically, though, we deal with situations in which there are many goods. Having more of one means giving up a little bit of many others.

In an economy with many goods, opportunity costs can be expressed in terms of a common unit of measurement, money. For example, rather than saying that a college education is worth five Mustangs or that a Mustang is worth one-fifth of a college education, we could say that the opportunity cost of a car is $12,000 and that of a college education is $60,000.

Useful as it is to have a common unit of measurement, great care must be taken when opportunity costs are expressed in terms of money, because not all out-of-pocket money expenditures represent the sacrifice of opportunities to do something else. At the same time, not all sacrificed opportunities take the form of money spent. *Applying Economic Ideas 1.1,* which analyzes both the out-of-pocket expenditures and the opportunity costs of a college education, shows why.

Applying Economic Ideas 1.1
The Opportunity Cost of a College Education

How much does it cost you to go to college? If you are a resident student at a typical four-year private college in the United States, you can answer this question by making up a budget like the one shown in Exhibit A. This can be called a budget of out-of-pocket costs, because it includes all the items—and only those items—for which you or your parents actually must pay in a year.

Exhibit A Budget of Out-of-Pocket Costs

Tuition and fees	$ 8,700
Books and supplies	600
Transportation to and from home	600
Room and board	4,350
Personal expenses	1,050
Total out-of-pocket costs	$15,300

Your own out-of-pocket costs may be much higher or lower than these averages. Chances are, though, that these are the items that come to mind when you think about the costs of college. As you begin to think like an economist, you may find it useful to recast your college budget in terms of opportunity costs. Which of the items in Exhibit A represent opportunities that you have forgone in order to

---

Exhibit B Budget of Opportunity Costs

Tuition and fees	$ 8,700
Books and supplies	600
Transportation to and from home	600
Forgone income	12,000
Total opportunity costs	$21,900

---

go to college? Are any forgone opportunities missing? To answer these questions, compare Exhibit A with Exhibit B, which shows a budget of opportunity costs.

Some items are both opportunity costs and out-of-pocket costs. The first three items in Exhibit A show up again in Exhibit B. To spend $8,700 on tuition and fees and $600 on books and supplies, you must give up the opportunity to buy other goods and services—to buy a car or rent a ski condo, for instance. To spend $600 getting to and from school, you must pass up the opportunity to travel somewhere else or to spend the money on something other than travel. Not all out-of-pocket costs are also opportunity costs, however. The last two items in the out-of-pocket budget are examples. By spending $5,400 a year on room, board, and personal expenses during the year, you are not really giving up the opportunity to do something else. Whether or not you were going to college, you would have to eat, live somewhere, and buy clothes. Because these are expenses that you would have in any case, they do not count as opportunity costs of going to college.

Finally, there are some items that are opportunity costs without being out-of-pocket costs. Thinking about what you would be doing if you were not going to college suggests a major item that needs to be added to the opportunity cost budget that does not show up at all in the out-of-pocket budget. If you were not going to college, you probably would have taken a job and started earning money soon after leaving high school. As a high-school graduate, your earnings would be about $12,000 during the nine months of the school year. (You can work during the summer even if you are attending college.) Because this potential income is something that you must forgo for the sake of college, it is an opportunity cost even though it does not involve an outlay of money.

Which budget you use depends on the kind of decision you are making. If you have already decided to go to college and are doing your financial planning, the out-of-pocket budget will tell you how much you will have to raise from savings, parents' contributions, and scholarships to make ends meet. But if you are making the more basic choice between going to college and pursuing a career that does not require a college degree, the opportunity cost of college is what counts.

Out-of-pocket costs and opportunity costs are overlapping categories. Some opportunity costs, such as tuition payments, take the form of out-of-pocket expenditures, while others, such as the income forgone by studying rather than working, do not. Some out-of-pocket expenditures, such as, again, tuition payments, represent opportunity costs of going to college, inasmuch as the funds could be spent for something else if a person decides not to attend college.

Others, such as payments for room and board, are not opportunity costs of going to college, because both students and nonstudents must have somewhere to live and must eat.

The importance of opportunity cost will be stressed again and again in this book. The habit of thinking in terms of opportunity costs is one of the distinguishing features of the economic way of thinking.

Deciding How to Produce: Efficiency and Entrepreneurship

A second basic economic choice is that of how to produce. There is more than one way to produce almost any good or service. Cars, for example, can be made in highly automated factories using a lot of capital equipment and relatively little labor, or they can be built one by one in small shops, using a lot of labor and only a few general-purpose machines. Ford Mustangs are built the first way, Lotuses and Lamborghinis the second way. The same kind of thing could be said about education. Economics can be taught in a small classroom with one teacher and a blackboard serving twenty students, or it can be taught in a large lecture hall where the teacher uses projectors, computers, and TV monitors to serve hundreds of students.

Economic efficiency
A state of affairs in which it is impossible to make any change that satisfies one person's wants more fully without causing some other person's wants to be satisfied less fully.

Efficiency.   Efficiency is a key consideration in deciding how to produce. In everyday speech, *efficiency* means producing with a minimum of expense, effort, and waste. Economists use a more precise definition. **Economic efficiency,** they say, refers to a state of affairs in which it is impossible to make any change that satisfies one person's wants more fully without causing some other person's wants to be satisfied less fully.[1]

Although the language in which the definition of economic efficiency is expressed may be unfamiliar, it is actually closely related to the everyday notion of efficiency. If there is some way to make you better off without making me worse of, it is wasteful (*inefficient*) to pass up the opportunity. If I have a red pen that I am not using, and you need one just for a minute, it would be wasteful for you to buy a red pen of your own. It is more efficient for me to loan you my pen; it makes you better off and me no worse off. If there is a way to make us both better off, it would be all the more wasteful not to take advantage of the opportunity. You loan me your bicycle for the afternoon and I will loan you my volleyball. If I do not ride a bicycle very often and you do not play volleyball very often, it would be inefficient for us both to own one of each item.

Efficiency in production
A situation in which it is not possible, given available knowledge and productive resources, to produce more of one good without forgoing the opportunity to produce some of another good.

The concept of economic efficiency has a variety of applications, of which the question of how to produce is one. **Efficiency in production** refers to a situation in which it is not possible, given available productive resources and existing knowledge, to produce more of one good without forgoing the opportunity to produce some of another good. The concept of efficiency in production, like the broader concept of economic efficiency, includes the everyday notion of avoiding waste. For example, a grower of apples avoids using more than a certain amount of fertilizer per tree. To not do so would be inefficient in the everyday sense that, beyond some point, using more fertilizer does not give the apple

---

[1]Efficiency, defined this way, is sometimes called *Pareto efficiency* after the Italian economist Vilfredo Pareto.

grower any more apples. Better to transfer the extra fertilizer to the production of, say, peaches. That way more peaches can be grown without any reduction in the apple crop.

The economist's definition also includes more subtle possibilities for improving the efficiency of production in cases where the waste of resources is less obvious. For example, it is possible to grow apples in Georgia. It is also possible, by selecting the right tree varieties and using winter protection, to grow peaches in Vermont. Some hobbyists do grow both fruits in both states. However, it would be inefficient to do so on a commercial scale even if growers in both states followed the most careful cultivation practices and avoided any obvious "waste." To see why, suppose that initially apple and peach trees were planted in equal numbers in the two states. Then think of ripping out 500 struggling peach trees in Vermont and replacing them with thriving apple trees. At the same time, tear out 500 heat-stressed apple trees in Georgia and replace them with peaches. Doing so would increase the output of both fruits without increasing the total land, labor, and capital used in fruit production. The original equal distribution of trees was inefficient.

How to increase production potential.   Once efficiency has been achieved, more of one good can be produced only by forgoing the opportunity to produce something else, if productive resources and knowledge are held constant. But over time production potential can be expanded by accumulating more resources and finding new ways of putting them to work.

In the past, discovery of new supplies of natural resources has been an important way of increasing production potential. Population growth has always been, and still is, another source. However, as the most easily tapped supplies of natural resources are depleted and as population growth slows, capital, among the three classical factors of production, will increasingly be the one that contributes most to the expansion of production possibilities.

The act of increasing the economy's stock of capital—that is, its supply of productive inputs made by people—is known as **investment.** Investment involves a trade-off of present consumption for future consumption. To build more factories, roads, and computers, we have to divert resources from the production of bread, movies, haircuts, and other things that satisfy immediate wants. In return, we put ourselves in a better position to satisfy tomorrow's wants.

Increased availability of productive resources is not the only source of economic growth, however. Even more important are improvements in human knowledge—the invention of new technology, new forms of organization, new ways of satisfying wants. The process of looking for new possibilities—making use of new ways of doing things, being alert to new opportunities, and overcoming old limits—is called **entrepreneurship.** It is a dynamic process that breaks down the constraints imposed by existing knowledge and factor supplies.

Entrepreneurship does not have to mean inventing something or founding a new business, although it sometimes does. It may mean finding a new market for an existing product—for example, convincing people in New England that tacos, long popular in the Southwest, make a quick and tasty lunch. It may mean taking advantage of price differences between one market and another—for example, buying hay at a low price in Pennsylvania, where growing conditions have been good in the past year, and reselling it in Virginia, where the weather has been too dry.

Investment
The act of increasing the economy's stock of capital, that is, its supply of means of production made by people.

Entrepreneurship
The process of looking for new possibilities—making use of new ways of doing things, being alert to new opportunities, and overcoming old limits.

Households can be entrepreneurs, too. They do not simply repeat the same patterns of work and leisure every day. They seek variety—new jobs, new foods, new places to visit. Each time you try something new, you are taking a step into the unknown. In this sense you are an entrepreneur.

Entrepreneurship is so important that it is sometimes called the fourth factor of production. The comparison has limited validity, however. Unlike labor, capital, and natural resources, entrepreneurship is intangible and unmeasurable. Although entrepreneurs receive rewards in the marketplace, we cannot speak of a price per unit of entrepreneurship; there are no such units. Also, unlike human resources, which grow old, machines, which wear out, and natural resources, which can be used up, the inventions and discoveries of entrepreneurs are not depleted as they are used. Once a new product or concept such as the transistor, the toothpaste pump, or the limited-partnership form of business has been invented, the required knowledge does not have to be created again (although, of course, it may be supplanted by even better ideas). All in all, it is more helpful to think of entrepreneurship as a process of learning how to better use the three basic factors of production than as a separate factor of production in itself.

Deciding Who Should Do Which Work: The Social Division of Labor

The questions of what should be produced and how to produce it would exist even for a person living in isolation. Even the fictional castaway Robinson Crusoe had to decide whether to fish or hunt birds, and if he decided to fish, he had to decide whether to do so with a net or with a hook and line. In contrast, the economic questions of who should do which work and for whom output should be produced exist only for people living in a human society—another reason economics is considered one of the social sciences.

The question of who should do which work is a matter of organizing the social division of labor. Should everyone do everything independently—be a farmer in the morning, a tailor in the afternoon, and a poet in the evening? Or should people cooperate—work together, trade goods and services, and specialize in one particular job? Economists answer these questions by pointing out that it is more efficient to cooperate. Doing so allows a given number of people to produce more than they could if each of them worked alone. Three things make cooperation worthwhile: teamwork, learning by doing, and comparative advantage.

First consider *teamwork*. In a classic paper on this subject, Armen Alchian and Harold Demsetz use the example of workers unloading bulky crates from a truck.[2] The crates are so large that one worker alone can barely drag them along or, perhaps, cannot move them at all without unpacking them. Two people working independently would take hours to unload the truck. If they work as a team, however, they can easily pick up the crates and stack them on the loading dock. This example shows that even when everyone is doing the same work and little skill is involved, teamwork pays.

[2]Armen A. Alchian and Harold Demsetz, "Production, Information Cost, and Economic Organization," *American Economic Review* (December 1972): 777–795.

A second reason for cooperation applies when there are different jobs to be done and different skills to be learned. In a furniture plant, for example, some workers operate production equipment, others use office equipment, and still others buy materials. Even if all the workers start out with equal abilities, each gets better at a particular job by doing it repeatedly. *Learning by doing* thus turns workers of average productivity into specialists, thereby creating an even more productive team.

A third reason for cooperation comes into play after the process of learning by doing has developed different skills and also applies when workers start out with different talents and abilities. It is the principle of division of labor according to *comparative advantage*. **Comparative advantage** is the ability to do a job or produce a good at a relatively lower opportunity cost than someone else.

> **Comparative advantage**
> The ability to produce a good or service at a relatively lower opportunity cost than someone else.

An example will illustrate the principle of comparative advantage. Suppose two clerical workers, Bill and Jim, are assigned the job of getting out a batch of letters. Jim is a whiz. He can type a letter in 5 minutes and stuff it into an envelope in 1 minute. Working alone, he can finish ten letters in an hour. Bill is clumsy. It takes him 10 minutes to type a letter and 5 minutes to stuff it into the envelope. Alone, he can do only four letters an hour. In summary form:

Jim:	Type 1 letter	5 min.
	Stuff 1 envelope	1 min.
Bill:	Type 1 letter	10 min.
	Stuff 1 envelope	5 min.

Without cooperation, the two workers' limit is fourteen letters per hour between them. Could they do better by cooperating? It depends on who does which job. One idea might be for Jim to do all the typing while Bill does all the stuffing, because that way they can just keep up with each other. But at 5 minutes per letter, that kind of cooperation cuts their combined output to twelve letters per hour. It is worse than not cooperating at all.

Instead, they should divide the work according to the principle of comparative advantage. Even though in absolute terms Bill is the slower typist, he has a *comparative advantage* in that task because the opportunity cost of typing is lower for him: Each 10 minutes he takes to type a letter is equal to the time he needs to stuff two envelopes at 5 minutes each. For Jim, each 5 minutes taken to type a letter could be used to stuff five envelopes at 1 minute each. Thus, for Bill the opportunity cost of typing one letter is to forgo stuffing *two* envelopes, whereas for Jim the opportunity cost of typing one letter is to forgo stuffing *five* envelopes.

Because Bill gives up fewer stuffed envelopes per letter than Jim, the principle of comparative advantage says that Bill should spend all his time typing. If he does, he can produce six letters per hour. Meanwhile Jim can spend 45 minutes of each hour typing nine letters, and the last 15 minutes of each hour stuffing all fifteen letters typed by both. By specializing according to comparative advantage, the two workers can increase their total output to fifteen letters per hour, their highest possible joint productivity.

In this example the principle of comparative advantage points the way toward an efficient division of labor between two people working side by side. The principle also has broader implications. It can apply to a division of labor between firms or government agencies. Perhaps most important, the principle of comparative advantage can apply to the division of labor between countries. In fact, the earliest application of the idea was to the area of international trade (see

Who Said It? Who Did It?   1.1
David Ricardo and the Theory of Comparative Advantage

David Ricardo was born in London in 1772, the son of an immigrant who was a member of the London stock exchange. Ricardo's education was rather haphazard, and he entered his father's business at the age of 14. In 1793, he married and went into business on his own. These were years of war and financial turmoil. The young Ricardo developed a reputation for remarkable astuteness and quickly made a large fortune.

In 1799, Ricardo read Adam Smith's *The Wealth of Nations* and developed an interest in political economy (as economics was then called). In 1809, his first writings on economics appeared. These were a series of newspaper articles on "The High Price of Bullion," which appeared during the following year as a pamphlet. Several other short works added to his reputation in this area. In 1814, he retired from business to devote all his time to political economy.

Ricardo's major work was *Principles of Political Economy and Taxation*, first published in 1817. This work contains, among other things, a pioneering statement of the principle of comparative advantage as applied to international trade. Using a lucid numerical example, Ricardo showed why it is to the advantage of both countries for England to export wool to Portugal and to import wine in return even though both products can be produced with less labor in Portugal, as long as wool can be produced relatively less expensively in England.

But international trade is only a sidelight of Ricardo's *Principles*. The book covers the whole field of economics as it then existed, beginning with value theory and progressing to a theory of economic growth and evolution. Ricardo held that the economy was growing toward a future "steady state." At that point economic growth would come to a halt and the wage rate would be reduced to the subsistence level. This gloomy view and the equally pessimistic views of Ricardo's contemporary, Thomas Malthus, gave political economy a reputation as "the dismal science."

Ricardo's book was extremely influential. For more than half a century thereafter, much of the writing on economic theory published in England consisted of expansions and commentaries on Ricardo's work. Economists as different as Karl Marx, the revolutionary socialist, and John Stuart Mill, a defender of liberal capitalism, took Ricardo's theories as their starting point. Even today there are "neo-Ricardian" and "new classicist" economists who look to Ricardo's works for inspiration.

Who Said It? Who Did It? 1.1). Today comparative advantage remains one of the primary motivations for mutually beneficial cooperation, whether on the scale of the workplace or on that of the world as a whole.

Whatever the scale, the principle of comparative advantage is easy to apply provided one remembers that it is rooted in the concept of opportunity cost. Suppose there are two tasks, A and B, and two parties (individuals, firms, agencies, or countries), X and Y, each capable of doing both tasks, but not equally well. First ask what is the opportunity cost for X of doing a unit of task A, measured in terms of how many units of task B could be done with the same time or resources. Then ask the same question for Y. The party with the lower opportunity cost for doing a unit of task A has the comparative advantage in doing that task. To check, ask what is the opportunity cost for each party of doing a unit of task B, measured in terms how many units of task A could be done with the same time or resources. The party with the lower opportunity cost for doing a unit of task B has the comparative advantage in doing that task.

Deciding for Whom Goods Should Be Produced: Positive and Normative Economics

Together, the advantages of team production, learning by doing, and comparative advantage mean that people can produce more efficiently by cooperating than they could if each worked in isolation. But cooperation raises yet another issue: for whom should goods be produced? The question of the distribution of output among members of society has implications in terms of both efficiency and fairness.

Efficiency in distribution.   Consider first a situation in which production has already taken place and the supply of goods is fixed. Suppose, for example, that thirty students get on a bus to go to a football game. Bag lunches are handed out. Half the bags contain a ham sandwich and a root beer; the other half contain a tuna sandwich and a cola. What happens when the students open the bag? They do not just eat whatever they find—they start trading. Some swap sandwiches; others swap drinks. Maybe there is not enough of everything to give each person his or her first choice. Nevertheless, the trading makes at least some people better off than they were when they started. Moreover, no one ends up worse off. If some of the students do not want to trade, they can always eat what was given to them in the first place.

This example shows one sense in which the "for whom" question is partly about efficiency: Starting from any given quantity of goods, the allocation can be improved through trades that result in better satisfaction of some people's preferences. As long as it is possible to trade existing supplies of goods in a way that permits some people to satisfy their wants without making others worse off, **efficiency in distribution** can be improved even while the total quantity of goods remains fixed.

Incentives and efficiency.   Efficiency in distribution and efficiency in production are two aspects of the general concept of economic efficiency. When both aspects are taken into account, the relationship between distribution and efficiency is not restricted to situations in which the total amount of goods is fixed in advance. That is so because the rules for distribution affect the patterns of production. For example, the rules for distribution affect the supply of productive resources, because most people earn their incomes by providing labor and other factors of production to business firms, and the amount they supply is affected by the wages or other rewards they are promised. Another reason is that rules for distribution affect incentives for entrepreneurship. Some people may work hard to discover new ways of doing things even if they expect no material reward, but that is not true of everyone.

Fairness in distribution.   Efficiency is not the whole story when it comes to the question of for whom goods should be produced. One can also ask whether a given distribution is fair. In practice, questions of fairness often dominate discussions of distribution.

One widely held view judges fairness in distribution in terms of equality. This concept of fairness is based on the idea that all people, by virtue of their shared humanity, deserve a portion of the goods and services turned out by the economy. There are many versions of this concept. Some people think that all

Efficiency in distribution
A situation in which it is not possible, by redistributing existing supplies of goods, to satisfy one person's wants more fully without causing some other person's wants to be satisfied less fully.

income and wealth should be distributed equally. Others think that people have a right to a "safety net" level of income but that any surplus beyond that level may be distributed fairly according to other standards. Still others think that certain goods, such as health care, food, and education, should be distributed equally but that it is fair for other goods to be distributed less equally.

An alternative view, which also has many adherents, judges fairness primarily in terms of the procedures through which a given distribution is carried out. In this view, fairness requires that certain procedural principles be observed, such as respect for private property or nondiscrimination on grounds of race and gender. As long as fair procedures are followed, any resulting distribution of income is viewed as acceptable. Equality of opportunity is emphasized more than equality of outcome.

Positive and normative economics.   Many economists make a sharp distinction between the question of efficiency and that of fairness. Discussions of efficiency are seen as part of **positive economics,** the area of economics that is concerned with facts and the relationships among them. Discussions of fairness, in contrast, are seen as part of **normative economics,** the area of economics that is devoted to judgments about whether particular economic policies and conditions are good or bad.

Normative economics extends beyond the question of fairness in the distribution of output. Value judgments also arise about the fairness of the other three basic choices faced by every economy. In choosing what should be produced, is it fair to permit production of alcohol and tobacco but to outlaw production of marijuana and cocaine? In choosing how to produce, is it fair to allow people to work under dangerous or unhealthy conditions, or should labor under such conditions be prohibited? In choosing who does which work, is it fair to limit access to specific jobs according to age, gender, race, or union membership? Normative issues extend to every corner of economics.

Positive economics, rather than offering value judgments about outcomes, focuses on understanding the processes by which the four basic economic questions are or could be answered. It analyzes the way economies operate, or would operate if certain institutions or policies were changed. It traces relationships between facts, often looking for measurable regularities in economic observations.

Most economists consider positive economics their primary area of expertise, but normative considerations influence the conduct of positive economics in several ways. The most significant of those influences is the selection of topics that are considered important enough to investigate. An economist who sees excessive unemployment as a glaring injustice may study that problem; one who sympathizes with victims of discrimination may take up a different line of research. Also, normative views are likely to affect the ways in which data are collected, ideas about which facts can be considered reliably true, and so on.

At one time it was thought that a purely positive economics could be developed, untainted by normative considerations of values and fairness. Within its framework, all disputes could be resolved by reference to objective facts. Today that notion is less widely held. Nevertheless, it remains important to be aware that most major economic controversies, especially those that have to do with government policy, have normative as well as positive components, and to be aware of the way each component shapes the way we think about those controversies.

Positive economics
The area of economics that is concerned with facts and the relationships among them.

Normative economics
The area of economics that is devoted to judgments about whether economic policies or conditions are good or bad.

1.2   Coordinating Economic Choices

To function effectively, an economy must have some way of coordinating the choices of millions of individuals regarding what to produce, how to produce it, who will do each job, and for whom the output will be produced. This section introduces two ways of achieving coordination: **spontaneous order,** in which independent agents adjust their actions in response to information and incentives from their immediate environment, and **hierarchy,** in which individual actions are guided by instructions from a central authority.

A Noneconomic Example

Let's start with a noneconomic example. Everyone has had the experience of shopping at a supermarket where there are several long checkout lines. In such a situation, you and other shoppers want to get through the checkout process as fast as possible. How should the actions of shoppers be coordinated, keeping this goal in mind? How can a frustrating situation be avoided in which some lines have a long wait for service while the cashiers in other lines stand idle for lack of customers?

One way would be for the store to direct certain customers to certain lines. The store could use a standard rule, such as customers with names starting with A–D to line 1, E–H to line 2, and so on. Instead the store could hire an employee to sit in a special booth and direct shoppers to one line or another. These would be examples of using the principle of hierarchy.

But supermarkets do not work that way. Instead, they leave shoppers to make their own decisions as to what line to join in response to information available from their own observations. As you approach the checkout area, you look first to see which lines are the shortest. You then make allowance for the possibility that some shoppers may have carts that are heaped full, while others have only a few items. Using your own judgment, you head for the line you think will be fastest. If you make a mistake, and another line moves faster than you expected it to, you may switch lines before you reach the cashier.

This approach to the supermarket checkout problem is an example of spontaneous order. It is *spontaneous* in that shoppers make their own decisions in response to cues from their immediate environment; it is *orderly* in the sense that it results in an approximately equal wait for all checkout lines. The lines are equalized even though no shopper has equalization as a specific goal. They all just want to get out of the store as fast as possible.

Spontaneous Order in Markets

In economics, the leading example of spontaneous order is the coordination of decisions through market activities. A **market** is any arrangement people have for trading with one another. Some markets have formal rules and carry out exchanges at a single location, such as the New York Stock Exchange. Other markets, such as the word-of-mouth networks through which teenage babysitters get in touch with people who need their services, are informal and decentralized. Spread out along the organizational spectrum are wholesale and retail markets for consumer goods; labor markets; markets for banking, entertainment, and professional services; and worldwide markets for thousands of goods and

Spontaneous order
A way of achieving coordination in which independent agents adjust their actions in response to information and incentives from their immediate environment.

Hierarchy
A way of achieving coordination in which individual actions are guided by instructions from a central authority.

Market
Any arrangement people have for trading with one another.

services. Despite the wide variety of forms they take, all markets have one thing in common: They provide the information and incentives people need to coordinate their decisions.

Just as shoppers need information on the length of checkout lines to coordinate their efforts, participants in markets need information on the scarcity and opportunity costs of various goods and factors of production. Markets rely primarily on prices to transmit this information. If a good or factor of production becomes more scarce, its price is bid up. The increase in the price signals users to economize in using it, and producers to make greater efforts to increase supplies. Suppose, for example, that discovery of a new use for platinum brings new buyers into the market. Platinum becomes more scarce than before in relation to the newly increased desire to use it. Competition for available supplies then bids up the price of platinum. This sends a message to economize on its use, where possible, and to increase the quantity of platinum mined, where possible. Instead, suppose a new technology reduces the cost of producing platinum. Information about the reduced cost is transmitted by markets through a lower price. People can then consider expanding the quantity of platinum they use, and producers will shift resources to producing other, more urgently needed goods.

In addition to knowing the best use for the resources they control, people must also have incentives to act on that information. Markets, again operating through prices, provide powerful incentives to sell goods and productive resources where they will bring the highest prices and to buy them where they can be obtained at the lowest prices. Profits motivate business managers to improve production methods and to design goods that match customer needs. Workers who stay alert to opportunities and work where they are most productive receive the highest wages. Consumers who stay well informed and spend their money wisely live more comfortably given their budgets.

Adam Smith, who is often considered the father of economics, saw the achievement of spontaneous order through markets as the foundation of prosperity and progress. In a famous passage in *The Wealth of Nations* he called markets an "invisible hand" that nudges people into the economic roles they can play best (see ***Who Said It? Who Did It? 1.2***). To this day, an appreciation of markets as a means of coordinating choices remains a central feature of the economic way of thinking.

Hierarchies and Authority

Important as markets are, they are not the only means of achieving economic coordination. Some decisions are guided by direct authority within hierarchical organizations. The most important examples are decisions made within private firms and those made by government agencies.

In hierarchies, order is maintained not through the spontaneous adaption of independent individuals, but by means of directives issued by managers to their subordinates. Prices typically play a less important role in transmitting information. They are supplemented by a variety of data, reports, instructions, and rules. Material incentives, such as bonuses and raises, play a role in motivating subordinates, but such bonuses are often only loosely linked to market prices. The primary incentive for subordinates to obey managers is that they agreed to do so as a condition of joining the organization and remaining with it.

Who Said It? Who Did It?   1.2
Adam Smith on the Invisible Hand

Adam Smith is considered to have been the founder of economics as a distinct field of study, even though he wrote only one book on the subject: *The Wealth of Nations*, published in 1776. Smith was 53 years old at the time. His friend David Hume found the book such hard going that he doubted that many people would read it. But Hume was wrong—people have been reading it for more than 200 years.

The wealth of a nation, in Smith's view, was not a result of accumulating gold or silver, as many contemporary theorists believed. Rather, it was the outcome of the activities of ordinary people working and trading in free markets. To Smith, the remarkable thing about the wealth produced by a market economy is that it is not a result of any organized plan but the unintended outcome of the actions of many people, each of whom is pursuing the incentives the market offers with his or her own interests in mind. As he put it:

> It is not from the benevolence of the butcher, the brewer, or the baker that we expect our dinner, but from their regard to their own interest. . . . Every individual is continually exerting himself to find out the most advantageous employment for whatever capital he can command. . . .

> By directing that industry in such a manner as its produce may be of the greatest value, he intends only his own gain, and he is in this, as in many other cases, led by an invisible hand to promote an end which was no part of his intention.*

Much of the discipline of economics as it has developed over the past two centuries consists of elaborations on ideas found in Smith's work. The idea of the "invisible hand" of market incentives that channels people's efforts in directions that are beneficial to their neighbors remains the most durable of Smith's contributions to economics.

———————

*Adam Smith, *The Wealth of Nations* (1776), Book 1, Chapter 2.

Markets and Hierarchies in Modern Economics

Although business firms and government agencies are organized internally as hierarchies, they deal with one another through markets. Markets and hierarchies thus play complementary roles in achieving economic coordination. Some economies rely more on markets, others on hierarchies. For example, centrally planned economies such as that of the Soviet Union place relatively heavy emphasis on authority and hierarchies. Market economies such as that of the United States make greater use of spontaneous order. But no economy uses one means of coordination to the exclusion of the other. Both approaches receive extensive attention in both the micro and macro branches of modern economics.

Much of microeconomics focuses on the market linkages among households, firms, and government agencies—how the prices of goods and services are determined and how those prices are affected by changes in market characteristics. In recent years, however, microeconomists have begun to pay more attention to the decision-making processes, often hierarchical, employed within households, firms, and government agencies. This has led to new insights into the ways in which those units interact in markets.

Markets are no less important in macroeconomics. Theories of unemployment require an understanding of labor markets, and theories of inflation focus on changes in the average level of prices of all goods and services traded in markets. Money, interest rates, and other aspects of financial markets are another central concern of macroeconomics. But hierarchies also figure prominently in macroeconomics. Particular attention is paid to the agencies of the federal government that determine government expenditures, taxation, and monetary policy.

In short, wherever one turns in economics, the question of coordination arises. Understanding economic coordination means understanding the complementary roles of markets and authority and of spontaneous order and hierarchies.

1.3   Economic Method

The concepts of scarcity, opportunity cost, efficiency, and spontaneous order that underlie the economic way of thinking are all part of the economic method. This chapter would be incomplete, however, without a few comments on economic method in the narrower sense of the tools and techniques used by economists.

Theories and Models

At the beginning of the chapter we defined economics as the social science that seeks to understand the choices people make in using scarce resources to meet their wants. Later, in discussing positive economics, we noted that understanding something means discovering how its parts are related to one another. In economics, we want to know how each of the four basic types of choices are related to the context in which they are made, and how outcomes are related to choices.

Any representation of the way in which facts are related can be called a **theory** or a **model.** The terms are synonyms, although economists tend to use the term *theory* to refer to more general statements about economic relationships and the term *model* to refer to more particular relationships, especially those that are stated in the form of graphs or mathematical equations.

Theory
A representation of the way in which facts are related to one another.

Model
A synonym for theory; in economics, often applied to theories that are stated in graphical or mathematical form.

Economics needs theories and models because facts do not speak for themselves. Take, for example, the fact that between 1979 and 1981, U.S. motorists cut their use of gasoline by more than 10 percent, from 80.2 billion to 71.7 billion gallons per year. Why did they do that? Economists have a theory. They relate the drop in gasoline consumption to another fact: the 50 percent rise in the retail price of gasoline, from $.86 per gallon to $1.31 per gallon, over the same period. The relationship between the price and consumption of gasoline is seen as a particular instance of a broader theory according to which an increase in the price of any good, other things being equal, tends to decrease the quantity of that good that consumers buy.

The theory as stated is a simple one. It relates quantity purchased to just one other fact, the price of the good. A more complete theory would bring in other factors that influence consumer choice, such as the prices of goods other than gasoline, consumers' incomes, changes in the average fuel economy of cars, and so on. Where does one stop? How much detail does it take to make a good theory?

There is no simple answer to this question because adding detail to a theory involves a trade-off—an opportunity cost, we might say. On the one hand, if essential details are left out, the theory may fail altogether to fit the facts. On the other hand, adding too much detail defeats the purpose of understanding because key relationships may become lost in a cloud of complexity. The only real guideline is that a theory should be just detailed enough to suit the purpose for which it is intended, and no more.

By analogy, consider the models that aircraft designers use. The wind tunnel models made to test the aerodynamics of a new design need to represent the shapes of the wings, fuselage, and control surfaces accurately, but they do not need to include tiny seats with tiny tables and magazine racks. On the other hand, a full-scale model built for the purpose of training flight attendants to work on the new plane would need seats and magazine racks, but it would not need wings.

In much the same way, the theories and models presented in this book are tailored to the purpose of highlighting a few key economic relationships. They are helpful in understanding economics in the same way that experimenting with a hobby-shop plane model is helpful in understanding the basics of flying. Professional economists use more detailed models, just as professional pilots train with complex flight simulators rather than with hobby-shop models. Nevertheless, the basic principles learned from the simple models do not contradict those that apply to the more complex ones. In the simple models, just as in the fancy ones, adjusting the rudder makes the plane turn and adjusting the elevators makes it climb or dive.

The Use of Graphs[3]

The theories introduced so far have been stated in words. Words are a powerful tool for developing understanding, but as the first cave dweller who painted a hunt for wild horses knew, words are even more powerful when they are supplemented by pictures. Graphs are the pictures that economists draw.

Economic graphs vary in purpose. Some simply display data, such as the price of gasoline in various years. Graphs of that kind are familiar to anyone who reads the newspaper or watches the television news. Other graphs go beyond the simple display of data to give a visual representation of theories and models. Such graphs may be less familiar. An example will illustrate how economists use graphs to represent theories.

The production possibility frontier.   Recall our earlier discussion of the trade-off between education and cars. Exhibit 1.1 shows the trade-off in graphical form for a simplified economy in which only those two goods are produced. The horizontal axis measures the quantity of education in terms of the number of college graduates produced per year; the vertical axis measures the production of cars. Any combination of education and cars can be shown as a point in the space between the two axes. For example, production of 10 million graduates and 5 million cars in a given year would be represented by point E.

In drawing the figure, supplies of factors of production and the state of knowledge are assumed to remain constant. Even if all available factors are devoted to education, there is a limit to the number of graduates that can be produced in a year: 20 million. The extreme possibility of producing 20 million

---

[3]Some basic graphical concepts—axes, points and number pairs, slopes, and tangencies—are discussed in the appendix to this chapter.

Exhibit 1.1   Production Possibility Frontier

This figure shows combinations of cars and education that can be produced in a simple economy in which they are the only two products. Quantities of available factors of production and the state of existing knowledge are assumed to be fixed. If all factors are devoted to education, 20 million college graduates can be produced each year (point A). If all factors are devoted to making cars, 18 million cars can be produced each year (point B). Other combinations of the two goods that can be produced using available factors efficiently, such as those represented by points C and D, lie along a curve called a production possibility frontier. The slope of the frontier indicates the opportunity cost of education in terms of cars. Interior points, such as E, represent inefficient use of resources. Beginning from such a point, more of one good can be produced without producing less of the other. Points outside the frontier, such as F, cannot be reached using available factors of production and knowledge.

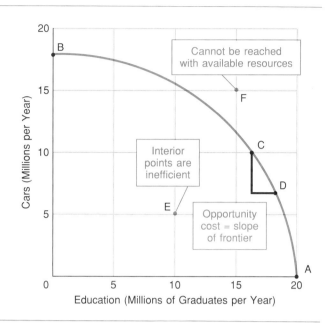

Production possibility frontier

A graph that shows possible combinations of goods that can be produced by an economy given available knowledge and factors of production.

graduates and no cars is shown by point A. Likewise, the maximum number of cars that would be produced if no resources were put into education is 18 million cars, shown by point B. Between those two extremes is a whole range of possible combinations of education and cars. Those intermediate possibilities are shown by points such as C and D, which fall along a smooth curve. The curve is known as a **production possibility frontier.**

Efficiency and economic growth.   The production possibility frontier is a boundary between the combinations of education and cars that can be produced and those that cannot, using given knowledge and quantities of factors of production. As such, it serves nicely to illustrate the concept of efficiency in production. Points inside the frontier, such as point E, represent inefficient production. Beginning from such a point, more cars can be made without cutting the output of education (shown by a move vertically toward the frontier); more education can be produced without cutting the output of cars (a move horizontally toward the frontier); or the output of both goods can be increased (a move up and to the right toward the frontier). Points such as A, B, C, and D that are on the frontier represent efficient production. Starting from any of those points, it is not possible to produce more of one good without producing less of the other. For example, in moving from C to D, output of education is increased but output of cars falls. Points such as F that lie outside the frontier cannot be reached even when the currently available knowledge and factors of production are used efficiently.

Over time, however, economic growth can stretch the production possibility frontier outward so that points such as F become possible. As mentioned earlier, the discovery of new ways of using available factors of production is one source of growth. So are additions to the stock of factors of production, of which growth of the labor force is an example. The case under discussion points to still another source of growth: Over time, the educational process itself improves the quality of the labor force, thus making a given number of people capable of producing more.

Opportunity cost and comparative advantage.   The production possibility frontier can also be used to represent the concept of opportunity cost. As we have seen, once the economy is producing efficiently at a point on the frontier, choosing to make more of one good means making less of the other. For example, suppose we start at point C, where 16 million students graduate each year and 10 million cars are being made. If we want to increase the output of graduates to 18 million per year, we must give up some cars and use the labor, capital, and natural resources freed in this way to build and staff classrooms. In moving from point C to point D, we trade off production of 4 million cars for the extra 2 million graduates. Over that range of the frontier, the opportunity cost of each extra graduate is about two cars. The opportunity cost of graduates, measured in terms of cars, is shown by the slope of the frontier.

As more graduates are produced, moving down and to the right along the frontier, the frontier becomes steeper and the opportunity cost of producing graduates increases. A major reason is that not all factors of production—especially not all workers—are alike. Suppose we start all the way up at point B, where no education is produced, and transfer enough resources to education to open one small college. The first people we would pull off the assembly line to staff the classrooms would be those who have a comparative advantage in teaching. (They may be people who are good production workers but brilliant lecturers, or they may be people who are only competent lecturers but very clumsy production workers.)

By the time enough resources have been transferred to education from the auto industry to reach point D, the most suitable recruits for academic life have already been used. Increasingly, to produce still more education we have to take some of the best production workers from the auto industry with no assurance that they will be especially good teachers. The opportunity cost of increasing the output of education (shown by the slope of the frontier) is correspondingly greater.

Much as the cave dwellers could convey the power and drama of their hunt with a simple drawing, the production possibility frontier shows how many ideas—efficiency, the effects of entrepreneurship and investment, opportunity cost, and comparative advantage—can be conveyed by even a simple graph. We will encounter the production possibility frontier again in later chapters along with many other graphs.

Theory and Evidence

Whether they are simple or complex, represented in words or in graphs, theories are of no use in explaining relationships among facts unless they fit those facts. Theory building is a matter of constantly comparing proposed explanations with evidence gleaned from observations of the actual choices people make—that is, with **empirical** evidence. When empirical evidence is consistent with the relationships proposed in a theory, confidence in the validity of the theory is increased. When evidence is not consistent with the theory, the theory needs to be reexamined. The relationships proposed in it may be invalid, or they may be

Empirical
Based on experience or observation.

valid only under circumstances different from those that prevailed when the observations were made. The theory then needs to be modified by changing the proposed relationships or adding detail.

For example, earlier we noted that the drop in gasoline usage between 1979 and 1981 was consistent with the theory that people will buy less of something when its price goes up, other things being equal. But what about the fact that from 1976 to 1978 gasoline usage rose by 8 percent even though the price of gasoline rose by 11 percent? In seeking an explanation of this observation, an economist would first suggest that probably some of the "other things" were not, after all, equal. A more detailed theory is called for that takes some of those other things into account.

In the case of gasoline usage, such a line of inquiry proves fruitful. In the period from 1976 to 1978, two factors offset the tendency of a rising price to depress gasoline sales. First, the prices of goods and services other than gasoline rose even faster, so that gasoline actually became cheaper relative to the other things consumers bought. Second, consumer incomes rose by a strong 8 percent from 1976 to 1978, which in itself would tend to make people buy more of many goods and services, including gasoline.

From 1979 to 1981, neither of those factors were present. During that period, gasoline prices rose twice as fast as the prices of other goods, and consumer incomes were stagnant, rising less than 1 percent. Thus, both the 1976–1978 and 1979–1981 observations are consistent with a more complete theory that takes gasoline prices, other prices, and consumer incomes into account.

Government agencies and private firms generate mountains of empirical data on economic activity. Economists constantly examine those data in an effort to confirm theories or find inconsistencies that point the way to better theories. Statistical analysis of empirical economic data is known as **econometrics**— literally, the science of economic measurement. In this book we will refer frequently to the results of econometric work. Readers who pursue the study of economics beyond the introductory level will find it useful to take a course in econometric methods.

Econometrics
The statistical analysis of empirical economic data.

Theories and Forecasts

Economic theories can help us understand the past—trends in gasoline consumption in the 1970s, the effects of the tax reforms of the 1980s, and so on. But human nature being what it is, understanding the past is not always enough. People want to know about the future as well. They want forecasts of economic events.

Within limits, economic theory can be useful here, too. Any theory that purports to explain a relationship between events that occurred under circumstances prevailing in the past provides a basis for predicting what will happen under similar circumstances in the future. To put it more precisely, economic theory can be used to make **conditional forecasts** in the form "If A, then B, other things being equal." Thus, an economist might say, "If gasoline prices rise, and if at the same time consumer incomes and the prices of other goods do not change, gasoline purchases will fall," or "If income taxes are cut, consumer spending will increase, assuming no changes in interest rates, total employment, and other relevant factors."

Thousands of economists make a living from forecasting. Decision makers in business and government use economic forecasts extensively. Forecasts are

Conditional forecast
A prediction of future economic events in the form "If A, then B, other things being equal."

not perfect, however, and forecasters sometimes make conspicuous mistakes. There are at least three reasons for the mistakes.

First, insufficient attention is sometimes paid to the conditional nature of forecasts. The news might report, for example, that "economists predict an upturn in inflation," yet inflation might not increase after all. In such a case the news report may have failed to note the forecasters' precautionary comments. The forecasters may have said that the rate of inflation would rise only if business investment continued to increase as it had in the immediate past, but investment may not have increased after all.

Second, a forecast may be invalid because the theory on which it is based is incorrect or incomplete. Economists improve their understanding of economic relationships year by year, but that understanding is still far from perfect, and economists do not always agree on what theory best fits the facts. Some theories give more weight to one fact, others to different facts. The competing theories may imply conflicting forecasts under some conditions. At least one of the forecasts will then turn out to be wrong. Finding out which theories yield better forecasts than others is an important part of the process through which valid theories are distinguished from inadequate ones. Meanwhile, decision makers who chose to rely on a forecast that did not hold up will be disappointed.

Third, economic forecasts can go wrong because some of the things that business managers and government officials most want to know are among the hardest to predict. For example, a competent economist could produce a fairly accurate forecast of gasoline sales, making certain assumptions about incomes and the prices of gasoline and other goods, but only a few specialists would be interested. In contrast, millions of people—including bankers, bond market traders, and families planning to buy homes—would like accurate forecasts of interest rates. Interest rates, however, happen to be among the hardest economic variables to forecast accurately.

This does not mean that economists do not try to forecast interest rates. They do try; they just do not succeed very well. Forecasts of certain other major macroeconomic variables, such as unemployment, inflation, and growth of the national product, do a little better than forecasts of interest rates, but their accuracy remains low relative to the publicity they get.

Most economists take the view that well-founded conditional forecasts, for all their limitations, are a better basis for business and public policy decisions than whims and guesswork. Still, they caution against overreliance on forecasts. For example, in the 1970s many forecasters projected higher energy prices right through the 1980s. When energy prices fell, oil companies, bankers, and even national governments that had relied on the forecasts were in trouble. How best to incorporate forecasts into the policy-making process remains a major issue.

Theory and Policy

Economists are often asked to use their theories to analyze the effects of public policies and forecast the effects of policy changes. The government may, for example, be considering new measures to aid unemployed workers, new approaches to improving air quality, or new measures to regulate international trade. How will the effects of such policies be spread through the economy? How will they affect people's lives?

Economists have their own, characteristic way of thinking about public policy just as they have their own way of thinking about other topics. In particular, economists are concerned with tracing the indirect and unintended consequences of policy as well as the direct and intended consequences. They are also constantly alert to the likelihood that a policy may have long-run consequences that differ from those that appear immediately. The tendency of public policies to have unanticipated effects in addition to those that are intended is sometimes referred to as the **law of unintended consequences.** For example:

Law of unintended consequences
The tendency of public policies to have unanticipated effects in addition to those that are intended.

- Unemployment compensation has the intended effect of aiding unemployed workers, but it also has the unintended effect of increasing the number of workers who are unemployed.

- The requirement that coal-burning electric power plants install very tall smokestacks has the intended effect of reducing local air pollution, but it also has the unintended effect of aggravating the problem of acid rain hundreds of miles downwind from the plants.

- A policy restricting the number of Japanese automobiles that can be imported into the United States each year had the intended short-run effect of aiding U.S. automobile makers, but it had the unintended long-run effect of encouraging Japanese firms to develop new lines of luxury cars that pose a new competitive threat to the U.S. industry.

Economists, by stressing the law of unintended consequences, do not mean to paralyze the process of making public policy. It would be wrong to conclude that the government should never act simply because its actions may do some harm as well as some good. Rather, economists simply urge that policymakers look at the whole picture before they make a decision, not just part of the picture. As Henry Hazlitt once put it, the whole of economics can be reduced to a single lesson: *The art of economics consists in looking not merely at the immediate but at the longer effects of any act or policy; it consists in tracing the consequences of that policy not merely for one group but for all groups.*[4]

Looking Ahead

This chapter has made a number of generalizations about the economic way of thinking and some comments on economic method. Generalizations have their limits, however. The only way really to grasp the economic way of thinking is through putting it to work on specific problems.

The next two chapters begin this process by setting out the model of price determination through supply and demand. That model serves as an appropriate starting point both because it can be applied to many practical problems and provides practice in the use of models and graphical methods. Mastery of the supply-and-demand model will serve as a foundation on which more complex macro- or microeconomic models can be constructed.

---

[4]Henry Hazlitt, *Economics in One Lesson* (New York: Arlington House, 1979), 17.

Summary

1. **What is economics all about?** *Economics* is the social science that seeks to understand the choices people make in using scarce resources to meet their wants.

Scarcity is a situation in which there is not enough of something to meet everyone's wants. *Microeconomics* is the branch of economics that studies choices that involve individual households, firms, and markets. *Macroeconomics* is the branch of economics that deals with large-scale economic phenomena, such as inflation, unemployment, and economic growth.

2. **What considerations underlie the choice of what an economy should produce?** Producing more of one good requires producing less of something else. The reason is that productive resources used to produce one good cannot be used to produce another at the same time. Productive resources are traditionally classified into three groups, called *factors of production*. *Labor* consists of the productive contributions made by people working with their hands and minds. *Capital* consists of all the productive inputs created by people. *Natural resources* include anything that can be used as a productive input in its natural state. The *opportunity cost* of a good or service is its cost in terms of the forgone opportunity to pursue the best possible alternative activity with the same time or resources.

3. **What considerations underlie the choice of how to produce?** Goods and services can be produced in many different ways, some of which are more efficient than others. *Economic efficiency* refers to a state of affairs in which it is impossible to make any change that satisfies one person's wants more fully without causing some other person's wants to be satisfied less fully. *Efficiency in production* refers to a situation in which it is not possible, given the available productive resources and existing knowledge, to produce more of one good or service without forgoing the opportunity to produce some of another good or service. Once efficiency has been achieved, production potential can be expanded by increasing the availability of resources or by improving knowledge. The process of increasing the economy's stock of capital is known as *investment*. The process of looking for new possibilities—making use of new ways of doing things, being alert to new opportunities, and overcoming old limits—is known as *entrepreneurship*.

4. **What considerations underlie the choice of who should do which work?** Although a person can survive apart from all human contact, economic efficiency is greatly enhanced by cooperation with others. Three things make cooperation worthwhile: teamwork, learning by doing, and comparative advantage. Teamwork can enhance productivity even when there is no specialization. Learning by doing improves productivity even when all workers start with equal talents and abilities. Comparative advantage comes into play when people have different innate abilities or, after learning by doing, have developed specialized skills. Having a *comparative advantage* in producing a particular good or service means being able to produce it at a relatively lower opportunity cost than someone else.

5. **What considerations underlie the choice of for whom goods should be produced?** In part, deciding for whom goods should be produced revolves around issues of efficiency. *Efficiency in distribution* refers to a state of affairs in which, with a given quantity of goods and services, it is impossible to satisfy one person's wants more fully without satisfying someone else's less fully. Efficiency is part of *positive economics*, the area of economics that is concerned with facts and the relationships among them. *Normative economics* is the area of economics that is devoted to judgments about which economic conditions and policies are good or bad.

6. **What mechanisms are used to coordinate economic choices?** The two principal ways of coordinating economic choices are *spontaneous order*, in which independent agents adjust their actions in response to information and incentives from their immediate environment, and *hierarchy*, in which individual actions are guided by instructions from a central authority. In economics, the most important mechanisms for achieving spontaneous order are *markets*, by which economists mean any arrangements people have for trading with one another. The mechanism of hierarchy is represented by government and by decision making within firms.

7. **How do economists use theory, graphs, and evidence in their work?** A *theory* or *model* is a representation of the ways in which facts are related to one another. Economists use graphs to display data and make visual representations of theories and models. For example, a *production possibility frontier* is a graph that shows the boundary between combinations of goods that can be produced and those that cannot, using available factors of production and knowledge. Economists refine theories in the light of *empirical* evidence, that is, evidence gleaned from observation of actual economic decisions. The economic analysis of empirical evidence is known as *econometrics*. Economic models are often used to make *conditional forecasts* in the form "If A, then B, other things being equal."

Terms for Review

- scarcity
- economics
- microeconomics
- macroeconomics
- factors of production
- labor
- capital
- natural resources
- opportunity cost

- economic efficiency
- efficiency in production
- investment
- entrepreneurship
- comparative advantage
- efficiency in distribution
- positive economics
- normative economics
- spontaneous order
- hierarchy
- market
- theory
- model
- production possibility frontier
- empirical
- econometrics
- conditional forecast
- law of unintended consequences

Questions for Review

1. Why is economics considered a social science?

2. What is the relationship among scarcity, choice, and opportunity cost?

3. Which of the following are macroeconomic issues? Which are microeconomic issues?
   a. How will an increase in the price of cigarettes affect smoking habits?
   b. What caused the rate of inflation to fall rapidly between 1980 and 1984?
   c. Does a high federal budget deficit tend to slow the rate of economic growth?
   d. How would restrictions on imports of steel affect profits and jobs in industries that use steel as a productive input, such as the automobile and construction industries?

4. What are the three factors of production? Why is entrepreneurship sometimes called a fourth factor of production? In what ways does entrepreneurship differ from labor, capital, and natural resources?

5. What is meant by efficiency in production? By efficiency in distribution? By overall economic efficiency?

6. Under what conditions is it possible to increase the output of one good without decreasing that of some other good?

7. What three considerations make cooperation in production worthwhile?

8. How are the concepts of efficiency and fairness related to those of positive and normative economics?

9. What considerations lead economists to consider a theory or model valid or invalid?

10. What are two ways in which economists use graphs?

11. What is a conditional forecast, and why are economic forecasts not always accurate?

12. Give examples of the law of unintended consequences. Does this law apply only to economic policy?

Problems and Topics for Discussion

1. **Examining the lead-off case.** What are the opportunity costs of building a communications satellite and placing it in geosynchronous orbit? Which of the opportunity costs are out-of-pocket costs to the firm that builds and operates the satellite? Which are not?

2. **Opportunity cost.** Gasoline, insurance, depreciation, and repairs are all costs of owning a car. Which of these can be considered opportunity costs in the context of each of the following decisions?
   a. You own a car and are deciding whether to drive 100 miles for a weekend visit to a friend at another university.
   b. You do not own a car but are considering buying one so that you can get a part-time job located 5 miles from where you live.
   In general, why does the context in which you decide to do something affect the opportunity cost of doing it?

3. **Comparative advantage at the keyboard.** Suppose you learn that because of his extraordinary manual dexterity the great pianist Vladimir Horowitz was also an exceptionally fast and accurate typist. Knowing that, would it surprise you to learn that he hired a secretary to type his correspondence, even though he could do the job more quickly himself?

4. **Comparative advantage in international trade.** Suppose that in the United States a car can be produced with 200 labor hours, while a ton of rice requires 20 labor hours. In Japan, it takes 150 labor hours to make a car and 50 labor hours to grow a ton of rice. What is the opportunity cost of producing rice in each country, stated in cars? What is the opportunity cost of cars, stated in rice? Which country has a comparative advantage in cars? Which in rice?

5. **Efficiency in distribution and the food stamp program.** The federal food stamp program could have been designed so that every low-income family would receive a book of coupons containing so many bread coupons, so many milk coupons, and so on. Instead, it gives the family a book of coupons that can be spent on any kind of food the family prefers. For a given cost to the federal government, which plan do you think would better serve the goal of efficiency in distribution? Why?

Now consider a program that allowed families to trade their food stamps for cash (some such trading does occur, but it is restricted by law) or one in which poor families are given cash, with which they can buy whatever they want. Compare these alternatives with the existing food stamp program in terms of both positive and normative economics.

6. **Spontaneous order in the cafeteria.** Suppose that your college cafeteria does not have enough room for all the students to sit down to eat at once, so it stays open for lunch from 11:30 A.M. to 1:30 P.M. Consider the following three methods of distributing diners over the two-hour lunch period in such a way that everyone can have a seat.

   a. The administration sets a rule: Freshmen must eat between 11:30 and 12:00, sophomores between 12:00 and 12:30, and so on for juniors and seniors.

   b. The lunch period is broken up into half-hour segments, with green tickets for the first shift, blue tickets for the second, and so on. An equal number of tickets of each color is printed. At the beginning of each semester an auction is held in which students bid for the ticket color of their choice.

   c. Students can come to the cafeteria whenever they want. If there are no empty seats, they have to stand in line.

Compare the three schemes in terms of (i) the concepts of spontaneous order and hierarchy; (ii) those of information and incentives; and (iii) that of efficiency.

7. **A production possibility frontier.** Bill Swartz has four fields spread out over a hillside. He can grow either wheat or potatoes in any of the fields, but the low fields are better for potatoes and the high ones are better for wheat. Here are some combinations of wheat and potatoes that he could produce:

Number of Fields Used for Potatoes	Total Tons of Potatoes	Total Tons of Wheat
All 4	1,000	0
Lowest 3	900	400
Lowest 2	600	700
Lowest 1	300	900
None	0	1,000

Use these data to draw a production possibility frontier for wheat and potatoes. What is the opportunity cost of wheat, stated in terms of potatoes, when the farmer converts the highest field to wheat production? What happens to the opportunity cost of wheat as more and more fields are switched to wheat?

Case for Discussion

Growing Rich in Wenjiang County

Wu Xiangtin, a farmer in Wenjiang County, is growing rich—at least by Chinese standards—off the so-called "responsibility system." This is a program in which plots of land have been turned over to farmers for up to 15 years to use in producing goods for consumer markets. Wu earns about $15 a day by selling the eggs produced by his 200 chickens. Last year, he claims, his total income was about 10,000 yuan, or roughly $4,800.

The newly affluent Wu has purchased a new house, a new chicken coop, and a TV set. His next project is to raise rabbits, ducks, and geese. He notes that duck and goose eggs command higher prices than chicken eggs.

Wu's projects are typical of the entrepreneurial energy that was bottled up by Chairman Mao's policies. In 1966, at the start of the Cultural Revolution (a campaign to shape Chinese society along more purely socialist lines), Wu was working as a veterinarian at a nearby commune. The political turmoil made it impossible for him to remain at that job, so he began raising pigs. Local socialist activists, known as Red Guards, denounced him as an "exploiter" and warned, "You will be taking the capitalist road if you raise ducks or chickens."

Wu becomes indignant at the suggestion that the Communist party might someday take away his chickens. "It's the policy of the party," he says. "The party will never take away my 10,000 yuan."

Maybe not. For the time being, local party officials, far from denouncing Wu, are showing him off to foreign visitors as a success story of the new China. Moreover, they say that because of the responsibility system, the average income of the 1,300 people in Wu's production brigade has more than doubled since 1978.

But there are problems that could hinder further change. The most obvious is inequality of income, which could trigger a backlash. Take Wu's neighbor, Li Xiaochuan, who lives in a cramped and dirty house. Li has only four pigs, six chickens, and an income about one-tenth of Wu's. At some point, he and other poor peasants may come to resent their "rich" neighbor and seek a return to what they see as more egalitarian policies.

Source: Adapted from David Ignatius, "China's Capitalistic Road Is Uphill from Here," *The Wall Street Journal*, May 5, 1984, 30. Adapted by permission of *The Wall Street Journal*, © Dow Jones & Company, Inc., 1984. All Rights Reserved Worldwide.

Questions

1. What examples are contained in the story that illustrate the what, how, who, and for whom choices that every economy must make?

2. Under Mao, all Chinese farmers were members of communes. The government gave each commune a plan to produce so many chicken eggs, so many duck eggs, so much rice, and so on. If the commune met the plan, it received a small bonus. If it did not, members earned only just enough to live on. Compare the old system with the system in which Wu now operates in terms of how the choice of what is to be produced is made. How do the two systems differ in terms of information and incentives? In terms of their use of hierarchy and spontaneous order?

3. In what ways does Wu fit the definition of an entrepreneur? How have Wu's actions affected China's production possibility frontier?

4. Compare the Maoist system with the current "capitalist road" in terms of normative economics. With which viewpoint do you sympathize more— the Maoist belief that socialism should strive for equality above all, or the view of China's current leaders, which places a higher priority on efficiency and productivity?

Suggestions for Further Reading

Hazlitt, Henry. *Economics in One Lesson.* New York: Arlington House, 1979.

A classic discussion of the law of unintended consequences as applied to economic policy.

Heilbroner, Robert L. *The Worldly Philosophers.* New York: Simon and Schuster, 1961.

A highly readable account of the major figures and trends in economics since Adam Smith.

McCloskey, Donald N. "The Rhetoric of Economics." *Journal of Economic Literature* (June 1983): 481–517.

A wide-ranging discussion of the methods economists use to persuade one another (and themselves) of the validity of their theories.

Smith, Adam. *The Wealth of Nations.* First published 1776; many modern editions.

Book 1, Chapter 1 begins with Smith's famous account of the division of labor in a pin factory.

Tufte, Edward. *Graphical Presentation of Quantitative Data.*

A definitive discussion of the use and misuse of graphs to present data in the social sciences (mostly economics).

Appendix to Chapter 1
Working with Graphs

Exhibit 1A.1 shows two sets of pictures. Those in the first set are pictures of Hollywood actors of the 1950s. Those in the second set are presidents of the United States. Looking at the two sets of pictures, can you pick out the one actor who was also a president?

Easy, right? Well, if you think it was easy, try explaining how you did it. More challenging yet, try programming a computer to pick out the actor who became president. It would take a top programmer a long time to do that, and a powerful computer to execute the program successfully.

In a series of similar tests of picture recognition, most sixth-graders could beat most computers in speed and accuracy. The reason is that the human brain, although slow at doing some things that computers do quickly (say, dividing one twenty-digit number by another) is preprogrammed to solve other kinds of problems with fantastic speed and accuracy. Picture recognition is one of the areas where the human brain excels. Three key abilities of the human brain give it a

Exhibit 1A.1   Testing Your Visual Skills

Quiz: From the pictures shown here, can you identify the one famous actor who later became president of the United States?

Famous Actors of the 1950s

Presidents of the United States

Top row: Courtesy of the Academy of Motion Picture Arts and Sciences.
Reagan photo: UPI/Bettmann Newsphotos.

comparative advantage over computers where pictures are involved:

1. An ability to store and retrieve vast numbers of visual patterns quickly and accurately. (Think of how many faces you can recognize.)

2. An ability to discard irrelevant detail while highlighting essentials. (That is why you can easily recognize the president/actor from a cartoonist's line drawing.)

3. An ability to see key similarities between patterns that are not exactly the same. (That is why you can match two pictures of a person taken thirty years apart.)

Graphs are an invaluable aid in learning economics precisely because they make use of these three special abilities of the human brain. Graphs are not used to make economics harder, but to make it easier. All it takes to use graphs effectively as a learning tool is the inborn human skill in working with pictures plus knowledge of a few simple rules for extracting the information that graphs contain. This appendix outlines those rules in brief. Additional details and exercises can be found in the *Study Guide* that accompanies this text, available from the publisher.

Pairs of Numbers and Points

The first thing to master is how to use points on a graph to represent pairs of numbers. The table in Exhibit 1A.2 presents five pairs of numbers. The two columns are labeled "x" and "y." The first number in each pair is called the *x value* and the second the *y value*. Each pair of numbers is labeled with a capital letter. Pair A has an x value of 2 and a y value of 3; pair B has an x value of 4 and a y value of 4; and so on.

The diagram in Exhibit 1A.2 contains two lines that meet at the lower left-hand corner; they are called *coordinate axes*. The horizontal axis is marked off into units representing the x value and the vertical axis into units representing the y value. In the space between the axes, each pair of numbers from the table can be shown as a point. For example, point A is found by going two units to the right along the horizontal axis and then three units straight up, parallel to the vertical axis. That point represents the x value of 2 and the y value of 3. The other points are located in the same way.

The visual effect of a graph usually can be improved by connecting the points with a line or a curve. By doing so, the relationship between x values and y values can be seen at a glance: as the x value increases, the y value also increases.

Slopes and Tangencies

Slope
For a straight line, the ratio of the change in the y value to the change in the x value between any two points on the line.

The lines or curves used in graphs are described in terms of their slopes. The **slope** of a straight line between two points is defined as the ratio of the change in the y value to the change in the x value between the two points. In Exhibit 1A.3, for example, the slope of the line between points A and B is 2. The y value changes by six units between these two points, whereas the x value changes by only three units. The slope is the ratio $6/3 = 2$.

Exhibit 1A.2   Number Pairs and Points

Each lettered pair of numbers in the table corresponds to a lettered point on the graph. The x value of each point corresponds to the horizontal distance of the point from the vertical axis; the y value corresponds to its vertical distance from the horizontal axis.

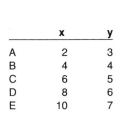

	x	y
A	2	3
B	4	4
C	6	5
D	8	6
E	10	7

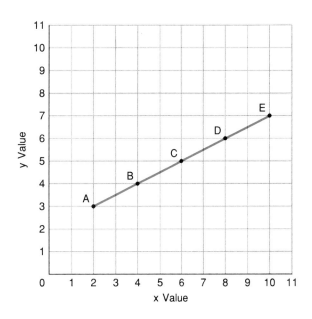

Exhibit 1A.3   Slopes of Lines

The slope of a straight line drawn between two points is defined as the ratio of the change in the y value to the change in the x value between them. For example, the line between points A and B in this exhibit has a slope of $+2$, whereas the line between points C and D has a slope of $-1/2$.

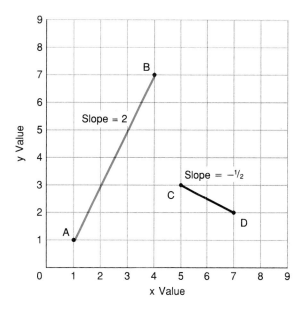

The slope of a line between the points (x_1, y_1) and (x_2, y_2) can be expressed in terms of a simple formula that is derived from the definition just given:

$$\text{Slope} = \frac{(y_2 - y_1)}{(x_2 - x_1)}$$

Applied to the line between points A and B in Exhibit 1A.3, the formula gives the following result:

$$\text{Slope} = \frac{(7 - 1)}{(4 - 1)} = \frac{6}{3} = 2$$

Positive slope
A slope having a value greater than zero.

Direct relationship
A relationship between two variables in which an increase in the value of one variable is associated with an increase in the value of the other.

A line such as that between A and B in Exhibit 1A.3 is said to have a **positive slope,** because the value of its slope is a positive number. A positively sloped line represents a **direct relationship** between the variable represented on the x axis and that represented on the y axis, that is, a relationship in which an increase in one variable is associated with an increase in the other. The relationship of the age of a tree to its height is an example of a direct relationship. An example from economics is the relationship between family income and expenditures on housing.

When a line slants downward, such as the one between points C and D in Exhibit 1A.3, the x and y values change in opposite directions. Going from point C to point D, the y value changes by -1 (that is, decreases by one unit) and the x value changes by $+2$ (that is, increases by two units). The slope of this line is the ratio $-1/2$.

Negative slope
A slope having a value less than zero.

Inverse relationship
A relationship between two variables in which an increase in the value of one variable is associated with a decrease in the value of the other.

When the slope of a line is given by a negative number, the line is said to have a **negative slope.** Such a line represents an **inverse relationship** between the x variable and the y variable, that is, a relationship in which an increase in the value of one variable is associated with a decrease in the value of the other variable. The relationship between the temperature in the room and the time it takes the ice in your lemonade to melt is an example of an inverse relationship. To give an economic example, the relationship between the price of gasoline and the quantity consumers purchase, other things being equal, is an inverse relationship.

The concepts of positive and negative slopes, and of direct and inverse relationships, apply to curves as well as to straight lines. However, the slope of a curve, unlike that of a straight line, varies from one point to the next.[1] We cannot speak of the slope of a curve in general, but only of its slope at a given point. The slope of a curve at any given point is defined as the slope of a straight line drawn tangent to the curve at that point. (A **tangent** line is one that just touches the curve without crossing it.) In Exhibit 1A.4, the slope of the curve at point A is 1 and the slope at point B is -2.

Tangent
A straight line that touches a curve at a given point without intersecting it.

Using Graphs to Display Data

Graphs are used in economics for two primary purposes: for visual display of quantitative data and for visual representation of economic relationships. Some graphs are primarily designed to serve one purpose, some the other, and some a little of both. We begin with some common kinds of graphs whose primary purpose is to display data.

---

[1]Economists try to be consistent, but in talking about lines and curves, they fail. They have no qualms about calling something a "curve" that is a straight line. For example, in Chapter 2 we will encounter "demand curves" that are as straight as a stretched string. Less frequently, they may call something a line that is curved.

Exhibit 1A.4   Slopes of Curves

The slope of a curve at any point is defined as the slope of a straight line drawn tangent to the curve at that point. A tangent line is one that just touches the curve without crossing it. In this exhibit, the slope of the curve at point A is 1 and the slope at point B is −2.

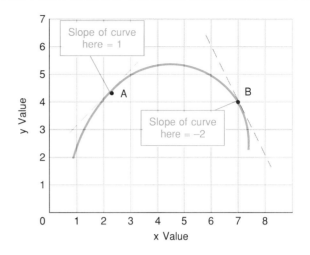

Exhibit 1A.5 shows three kinds of graphs often used to display data. Part (a) is a *pie chart*. Pie charts are used to show the relative size of various quantities that add up to a total of 100 percent. In this case, the quantities displayed are the percentages of U.S. foreign trade accounted for by various trading partners. In the original source, the graph was drawn as part of a discussion of U.S. trade with its neighbors, Canada and Mexico. The author wanted to make the point that trade with these countries is very important—more important even than the more publicized trade with Japan. Note how the graph highlights Canadian and Mexican trade, and at the same time, omits details not relevant to the discussion by lumping together Europe, Africa, the rest of Asia, and many other countries under the heading "rest of the world." In reading graphs, do not just look at the numbers, but ask yourself "what point is the graph trying to make?"

Part (b) of Exhibit 1A.5 is a *bar chart*. Bar charts, like pie charts, are used to display numerical data (in this case, unemployment rates) in relationship to some nonnumerical classification of cases (in this case, countries). Bar charts are not subject to the restriction that data displayed must total 100 percent. What point do you think the author of this graph was trying to make?

Part (c) of Exhibit 1A.5 is an example of a data display graph very common in economics—the *time-series graph*. A time-series graph shows the values of one or more economic quantities on the vertical axis and time (years, months, or whatever) on the horizontal axis. This graph was drawn to make an important point about the manufacturing sector of the U.S. economy: Although the share of U.S. workers employed in manufacturing has fallen steadily in recent decades, the output of manufacturing has not changed much as a percentage of total economic output. Thus the drop in manufacturing employment, sometimes mistakenly seen as a weakness of that sector, instead is an indication of strength. Over the period shown, investment in new equipment, technological progress, and improved training of workers greatly increased the amount of output produced per worker in manufacturing industries.

Note one feature of this time-series graph: the scale on the vertical axis is broken between zero and 18. By spreading out the data points in the range 18 to

Exhibit 1A.5   Using Graphs to Display Data

This exhibit shows three common kinds of data display graphs. The *pie chart* in part (a) is used when the data items sum to 100 percent. The *bar chart* in part (b), like the pie chart, is used when reporting numerical data that are associated with nonnumerical categories (in this case countries). The bar chart does not require data items to sum to 100 percent. The *time-series graph* in part (c) shows the values of one or more economic quantities on the vertical axis and time (in this case, years) on the horizontal axis.

(a)
Shares of U.S. Trade

Note.—Shares are based on the sum of bilateral exports and imports in dollars.

(b)
Unemployment Rates in the Seven Summit Countries

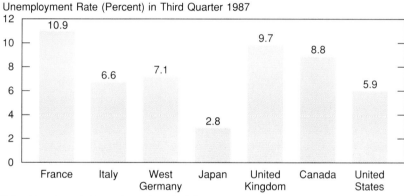

Note.—Unemployment rates used approximate the U.S. concept.

(c)
Real Output and Employment Shares in Manufacturing

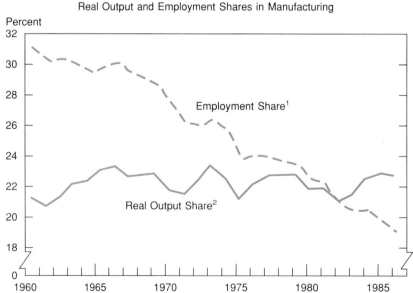

[1]Manufacturing as percent of nonfarm payroll employment.
[2]Manufacturing as percent of real gross domestic product less agriculture, forestry, and fisheries.

Source: U.S. Council of Economic Advisers, *Economic Report of the President* (Washington, D.C.: Government Printing Office, 1988). Part (a), Chart 4-1, 129; part (b), Chart 3-2, 95; part (c), Chart 2-1, 65.

32 percent, the trend of output and employment can be shown in greater detail. The advantage of greater detail has an offsetting danger, however. Careless reading of the graph could cause one to exaggerate the amount by which employment fell. For example, the employment-share line drops about halfway from the top of the diagram to the horizontal axis between 1960 and 1975, but employment did not fall by half in that period. As careful reading of the axis shows, it declined by less than a quarter, from 31 percent of the labor force to 24 percent. The moral of the story: Always examine the vertical and horizontal axes of a graph carefully.

Using Graphs to Display Relationships

Some graphs, rather than simply recording observed facts, attempt to represent relationships among facts, that is, theories and models. Exhibit 1A.6 shows two typical graphs whose primary purpose is to display relationships.

Part (a) of Exhibit 1A.6 is the production possibility frontier that we already encountered in Chapter 1. The graph represents the inverse relationship be-

---

Exhibit 1A.6   Using Graphs to Display Relationships

Relational graphs are visual representations of theories, that is, of relationships among facts. Two typical relational graphs are shown here. Part (a) is the production possibility frontier discussed in Chapter 1. It relates quantities of cars to quantities of education that can be produced with given factors of production and knowledge. Part (b) represents a theory of individual labor supply, according to which an increase in the hourly wage rate, after a point, will cause a person to reduce the quantity of labor supplied. Part (b) is an abstract graph in that it shows only the general nature of the relationship, with no numbers on either axis.

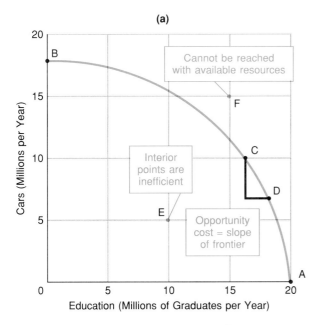

tween the quantity of cars that can be produced and the quantity of education that can be produced, given available knowledge and productive resources.

Part (b) of Exhibit 1A.6 represents a relationship between the quantity of labor that a person is willing to supply (measured in worker-hours per year) and the wage rate per hour the person is paid. According to the theory portrayed by the graph, raising the wage rate will, up to a point, induce a person to work more hours. But beyond a certain point (according to the theory) a further increase in the wage will actually cause the person to work fewer hours. Why? Because the person is so well off, he or she prefers the luxury of more leisure time to the reward of more material goods. The graph could represent the career of the great tennis star Bjorn Borg: As a hungry young athlete, Borg played tournament after tournament, often winning relatively small prizes. As he rose to number-one rank in the world of tennis, his average earnings per tournament soared. His response was to play fewer and fewer tournaments each year, finally retiring completely to live on income from his many investments.

Note one distinctive feature of this graph: It has no numbers on the axes. It is an abstract graph that represents only the qualitative relationships between the hours of labor supplied per year and the wage rate. It makes no quantitative statements regarding how much hours worked will change as the result of any given change in wage rate. Abstract graphs are often used when the point to be made is a general one that applies to many cases, regardless of quantitative differences from one case to another.

Packing Three Variables into Two Dimensions

Anything drawn on a flat piece of paper is limited to two dimensions. The relationships discussed so far fit a two-dimensional framework easily, because they involve just two variables. In the case of the production possibility frontier, the two were the quantity of education (horizontal axis) and the quantity of cars (vertical axis). In the case of the labor supply, they were hours worked per year (horizontal axis) and wage rate per hour (vertical axis). But reality does not always cooperate with geometry. Often three or more variables must be taken into account in order to understand relationships among facts.

A number of methods have been devised to represent relationships involving three or more variables on a piece of paper. For example, a map of the United States might use coordinates of latitude and longitude to indicate position, contour lines to indicate altitude, and shadings of various colors to indicate vegetation. An architect might use a perspective drawing to give the illusion of three dimensions—height, width, and depth—on a flat piece of paper. This section deals with just one simple method of packing three variables into two dimensions. Although the method is a favorite of economists—it will be used in dozens of graphs in this book—we will show its generality by beginning with a noneconomic example.

A noneconomic example.   The example concerns heart disease, the leading cause of death in the United States. In recent years, medical researchers have discovered that the risk of heart disease is closely linked to the quantity of cholesterol in a person's blood. Studies have indicated, for example, that a 25 percent reduction in cholesterol can cut the risk of death from heart attack by nearly 50 percent. Knowing this, millions of people have had their cholesterol levels tested, and if they are found to be high, have undertaken programs of diet, exercise, or drug therapy to reduce their risk of heart disease.

Important though cholesterol is, however, just knowing your cholesterol level is not enough to tell you your risk of dying of a heart attack in the coming year. Other variables also enter into the risk of heart disease, among which one of the most important is age. For example, for men with average cholesterol aged 20 years, the mortality rate from heart disease is only about 3 per 100,000. For men aged 60, the mortality rate rises to over 500 per 100,000, still assuming average cholesterol. We thus have three variables to deal with: mortality, cholesterol, and age. How can we represent these three variables using only two-dimensional graphs?

A possible approach would be to draw two separate graphs. One would show the relationship between age and heart disease for the male population as a whole, without regard to differences in cholesterol counts, as in part (a) of Exhibit 1A.7. The other would show the relationship between cholesterol and heart disease for the male population as a whole, without regard to age, as in part (b) of Exhibit 1A.7. By looking from one diagram to the other, we can get an idea of the three-variable relationship as a whole.

Somehow, though, the side-by-side pair of graphs is clumsy. There must be a better way to represent the three variables in two dimensions, and there is. The better way, shown in part (c) of Exhibit 1A.7, is to use cholesterol and mortality as the x and y axes, and to take age into account by plotting separate lines for men of various ages. That chart is far easier to interpret than the side-by-side pair. If you are a man and know your age and cholesterol count, you just pick out the appropriate line and read off your risk of mortality. If you do not like what you see, you go on a diet.[2]

The multi-curve graph is a lovely invention. One of the great things about it is that it even works for more than three variables. For example, we could easily add a fourth variable, gender, to the graph by drawing a new set of lines in a different color to show mortality rates for women of various ages. Each line for women would have a positive slope similar to the men's lines, but would lie somewhat below the corresponding line for men of the same age, because women, other things being equal, experience lower mortality from heart disease. As we will see in coming chapters, there are many variants on the theme.

Shifts in curves and movements along curves.   Economists use three-variable, multi-curve graphs often enough that it is worth giving some attention to the terminology used in discussing them. How can we best describe what happens to a man as he ages, given the relationship shown in part (c) of Exhibit 1A.7?

One way to describe the effects of aging would be to say, "As a man ages, he moves from one curve to the next higher one on the chart." There is nothing at all wrong with saying that, but an economist would tend to phrase it a bit

---

[2]We could instead have started with the age-mortality chart and drawn separate lines for men with different cholesterol levels. Such a chart would show exactly the same information. We could even draw a chart with cholesterol and age on the axes, and separate contour lines to represent various levels of mortality. The choice often turns on what one wants to emphasize. Here, we emphasize the cholesterol-mortality relationship because cholesterol is something you can do something about. You cannot do anything about your age, so it is given slightly less emphasis by not giving it one of the two axes.

Exhibit 1A.7   Three Variables
in Two Dimensions

This graph shows a common way of representing a three-variable relationship on a two-dimensional graph. The three variables in this case are serum cholesterol (a measure of the amount of cholesterol in the blood), age, and death rate from heart disease for the U.S. male population. In parts (a) and (b), the age-death rate and cholesterol-death rate relationships for all men are shown on separate graphs. The relationship among the three variables is more easily interpreted, however, if all three variables are included in one graph, as in part (c). That is done by drawing separate cholesterol-death rate lines for each age group. As a man ages, his cholesterol-death rate line shifts upward.

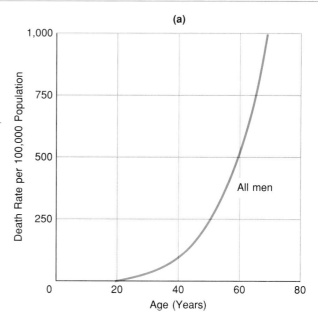

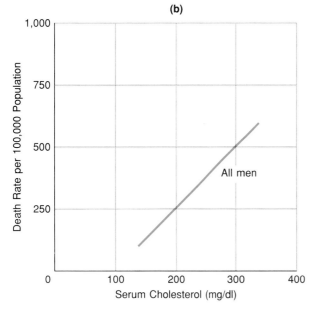

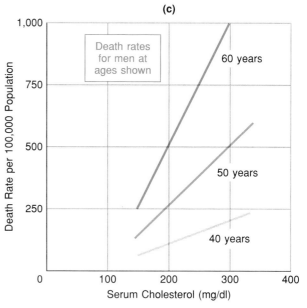

differently, saying "As a man ages, his cholesterol-mortality curve shifts upward." The two ways of expressing the effects of aging have exactly the same meaning. Preferring one or the other is just a matter of habit.

If we express the effects of aging in terms of a shift of the cholesterol-mortality curve, how should we express the effects of a reduction in cholesterol for a man of a given age? An economist would say it this way: "Cutting a man's cholesterol count through diet or exercise will move him down along his cholesterol-mortality curve."

Before you finish this book, you will see the phrases "shift in a curve" and "movement along a curve" a great many times. How can you keep them straight? Nothing could be easier:

- If you are talking about the effect of a change in a variable that is shown on one of the coordinate axes of the diagram, the effect will be shown as a movement along one of the curves.

- If you are talking about the effect of a change in a variable that is not shown on one of the coordinate axes of the diagram, the effect will be shown by a shift in one of the curves.

Forget about cholesterol—students' failure to remember the difference between "shifts in" and "movements along" curves is the leading cause of premature heart attacks among professors of economics!

Study Hints

So much for the basic rules of graphics. Once you master them, how should you study a chapter that is full of graphs?

The first—and most important—rule is to avoid trying to memorize graphs as patterns of lines. In every economics class, at least one student comes to the instructor after failing an exam and exclaims, "But I learned every one of those graphs! What happened?" The reply is that the student should have learned economics instead of memorizing graphs. Following are some hints for working with graphs.

After reading through a chapter that contains several graphs, go back through the graphs one at a time. Cover the caption accompanying each graph, and try to put the graph's picture into words. If you cannot say as much about the graph as the caption does, reread the text. Once you can translate the graph into words, you have won half the battle.

Next, cover each graph and use the caption as a guide. Try to sketch the graph on a piece of scratch paper. How are the graph's axes labeled? How are the curves labeled? What are the slopes of various curves? Are there important points of intersection or tangencies? If you can go back and forth between the caption and the graph, you will find that the two together are much easier to remember than either one separately.

Finally, try going beyond the graph that is shown in the book. If the graph illustrates the effect of an increase in the price of butter, try sketching a similar diagram that shows the effect of a decrease in the price of butter. If the graph shows what happens to the economy during a period of rising unemployment, try drawing a similar graph that shows what happens during a period of falling unemployment. This is a good practice that may give you an edge on your next exam: Making simple variations on graphs that are in the text or lectures is the lazy professor's fast way of creating exam questions.

Making your own graphs.   For some students, the hardest test questions to answer are ones that require original graphs as part of an essay. Suppose the question is "How does a change in the number of students attending a university affect the cost per student of providing an education?" Here are some hints for making your own graph.

1.   Write down the answer to the question in words. If you cannot, you might as well skip to the next question. Underline the most important quantities in

Exhibit 1A.8 Constructing Your Own Graphs

To construct a graph, first put down in words what you want to say: "The larger the number of students at a university, the lower the cost per student of providing them with an education." Second, label the coordinate axes. Third, if you have exact numbers to work with, construct a table. Fourth, draw a curve to represent the relationship in question. Here the curve has a negative slope to indicate that the cost per student goes down as the number of students goes up. For graphs with more than one relationship, repeat these steps.

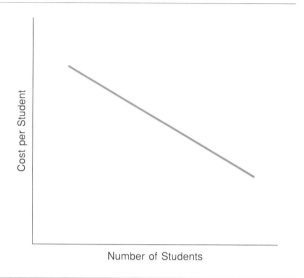

your answer, such as "The larger the number of students who attend a college, the lower the cost per student of providing them with an education, because fixed facilities, such as libraries, do not have to be duplicated."

2. Decide how you want to label the axes. In our example, the vertical axis is labeled "cost per student" and the horizontal axis "number of students" (see Exhibit 1A.8).

3. Do you have specific numbers to work with? If so, the next step is to construct a table showing what you know and use it to sketch your graph. If you have no numbers, you must draw an abstract graph. In this case, all you know is that the cost per student goes down when the number of students goes up. Sketch in a negatively sloped line such as the one in Exhibit 1A.8.

4. If your graph involves more than one relationship between quantities, repeat steps 1 through 3 for each relationship you wish to show. When constructing a graph with more than one curve, pay special attention to points at which you think the curves should intersect. (Intersections occur whenever both the x and y values of the two relationships are equal.) Also note the points at which you think two curves ought to be tangent (which requires that their slopes be equal), the points of maximum or minimum values, if any, and so on.

5. When your graph is finished, try to translate it back into words. Does it really say what you want it to?

A reminder.   As you read this book and encounter various kinds of graphs, turn back to this appendix now and then. Do not memorize graphs as meaningless pictures; if you do, you will get lost. If you can alternate between graphs and words, each one's underlying point will be clearer than if you rely on either one alone. Keep in mind that the primary focus of economics is not graphs; it is people and the ways in which they deal with the challenge of scarcity.

2

Supply and Demand: The Basics

**Before reading this chapter,
make sure you know the meaning of:**

Spontaneous order

Markets

Opportunity cost

Law of unintended consequences

After reading this chapter, you will understand:

How the price of a good or service affects the quantity demanded by buyers.

How other market conditions affect demand.

How the price of a good affects the quantity supplied by sellers.

How other market conditions affect supply.

How supply and demand interact to determine the market price of a good or service.

Why market prices and quantities change in response to changes in market conditions.

How price supports and price ceilings affect the operations of markets.

Price, Health Concerns Boost Chicken's Popularity

Let us say you are having a power lunch. The guy across the table says, "steak, rare." You say, "Chicken breast with lime butter and dill."

You lose—as certainly as if you had ordered cottage cheese. A chicken lacks authority. Cowboys, not chicken farmers, tamed the West.

Yet while Americans cling to a self-image of beef-eating heroes, their diet is actually at a turning point. This year, the government says, the United States will become a nation of bird eaters.

Poultry's recent success springs partly from the same source as Jane Fonda's: the morbid cardiovascular fears of aging baby-boomers. Notwithstanding an occasional salmonella scare, birds are perceived as more healthful than beef (a 100-gram piece of chicken contains 3.7 grams of saturated fat, compared with 20.7 grams of saturated fat in a piece of T-bone steak weighing the same amount, according to the Agriculture Department.)

Chicken is also cheap. Chickens are selling for less today than they did in 1923, when Mrs. Wilmer Steele of Ocean View, Del., sold what chicken historians say was the nation's first flock of commercial broilers (she got 62 cents a pound).

Why is chicken, pound for pound, cheaper than the competition? The answer has to do with the fact that a chicken is highly efficient at converting feed to flesh. To produce a pound of flesh, a chicken consumes less than two pounds of feed, compared with six or seven for a cow and three for a pig.

Also, a chicken doesn't live long. The shorter a creature's life cycle, the quicker its generations can be manipulated genetically. Chicken breeders have steadily developed birds that grow bigger on less feed in less time. (They may be approaching the limits of practicality on this score; modern chickens have "put on so much weight that they have some real problems mating," says Walter Becker, professor emeritus of genetics and cell biology at Washington State University.)

Photo source: Courtesy of Perdue Farms Incorporated.

Source: Timothy K. Smith, "By End of This Year, Poultry Will Surpass Beef in the U.S. Diet," *The Wall Street Journal*, September 17, 1987, 1. Reprinted by permission of *The Wall Street Journal*, © Dow Jones & Company, Inc., 1987. All Rights Reserved Worldwide.

How is it that when you decide you want chicken breast with lime butter for lunch, the chicken appears on the table? Who makes sure supplies of chicken, beef, and pork are adjusted to match consumers' dietary habits? Adam Smith called it the "invisible hand." We call it "spontaneous order." Whatever it is called, the coordinating mechanism is the market.

This chapter outlines a model of economic coordination by means of markets. It is known as the supply-and-demand model. Economists use the term **supply** to refer to sellers' willingness and ability to provide goods for sale in a market. **Demand** refers to buyers' willingness and ability to purchase goods. Once you understand the model introduced in this chapter, you will be unable to read a newspaper article dealing with chicken, beef, or anything else concerning economics without reading "supply" and "demand" between the lines.

Supply
The willingness and ability of sellers to provide goods for sale in a market.

Demand
The willingness and ability of buyers to purchase goods.

2.1 Demand

Just a few years ago compact disk players carried price tags of $1,000 and up. At that price they were a plaything for the rich audiophile—the person who just had to have the best available sound even if it cost the equivalent of a Caribbean vacation. Today discounters sell CD players for as little as $100, and the same flawless sound can be heard booming from dormitory windows on any campus in the country. Is it surprising that when the price fell, more CD players were sold? Hardly—it was simply the law of demand in action.

The **law of demand** can be stated formally as follows: In any market, other things being equal, an inverse relationship exists between the price of a good and the quantity of the good that buyers demand. Thus, the quantity demanded tends to rise as the price falls and to fall as the price rises.

We expect this to happen for two reasons. First, if the price of one good falls while the prices of other goods stay the same, people are likely to substitute the cheaper good for goods that they would have bought otherwise. Second, when the price of one good falls while incomes and other prices stay the same, people feel a little richer. They use their added buying power to buy a bit more of many things, including, in most cases, a little more of the good whose price went down.

Law of demand
The principle that an inverse relationship exists between the price of a good and the quantity of that good that buyers demand, other things being equal.

The terms *demand* and *quantity demanded*, as used in economics, are not the same as *want* or *need*. They combine the notion of willingness with that of ability to buy. I might want a Porsche, but the last time I checked, the sticker price was over $40,000. I do not have that kind of money. Even if I did, there are other things I want more. Thus, the quantity of Porsches I demand at the going price is zero, just as it would be if I were prepared to spend $40,000 on a car but wanted a Lotus rather than a Porsche.

On the other hand, I might *need* dental surgery to avoid losing my teeth. But suppose I am poor. If I cannot pay for the surgery or find a benefactor to pay for it on my behalf, I am out of luck. The quantity of dental surgery I demand, therefore, is zero, however great my need for that service.

The Demand Curve

The law of demand states a relationship between the quantity of a good that people are willing and able to buy, other things being equal, and the price of that good. This one-to-one relationship can be represented in a table or a graph, as shown in Exhibit 2.1.

Exhibit 2.1   A Demand Curve for Chicken

Both the table and the chart show the quantity of chicken demanded at various prices. For example, at a price of $.40 per pound, buyers are willing and able to purchase 2 billion pounds of chicken per year. This price-quantity combination is shown by row A in part (a) and point A in part (b).

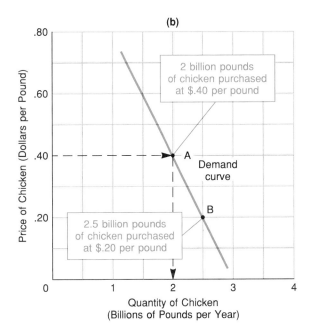

(a)	
Price of Chicken (Dollars per Pound)	Quantity of Chicken Demanded (Billions of Pounds per Year)
.64	1.4
.60	1.5
.56	1.6
.52	1.7
.48	1.8
.44	1.9
A .40	2.0
.36	2.1
.32	2.2
.28	2.3
.24	2.4
B .20	2.5
.16	2.6

Look at the table that forms part (a) of the exhibit. The first row shows that when the price of chicken is $.64 a pound, the quantity demanded per year is 1.4 billion pounds. Reading down the table, we see that as the price falls, the quantity demanded rises. At $.60 per pound, buyers plan to purchase 1.5 billion pounds per year; at $.56, they plan to buy 1.6 billion pounds; and so on.

Part (b) of Exhibit 2.1 presents the same information in graphical form. The graph is called a **demand curve** for chicken. Suppose we want to use the demand curve to find out what quantity of chicken will be demanded at a price of $.40 per pound. Starting at $.40 on the vertical axis, we move across, as shown by the arrow, until we reach the demand curve at point A. Continuing to follow the arrow, we drop down to the horizontal axis. Reading from the scale on that axis, we see that the quantity demanded at a price of $.40 per pound is 2 billion pounds per year. That is the quantity demanded in row A of the table in part (a).

Demand curve
A graphical representation of the relationship between the price of a good and the quantity of that good that buyers demand.

Movements along the Demand Curve

The effect of a change in the price of chicken, other things being equal, can be shown as a movement from one point to another along the demand curve for chicken. Suppose that the price drops from $.40 to $.20 per pound. In the process, the quantity that buyers plan to buy rises. The point corresponding to the quantity demanded at the new, lower price is point B (which corresponds to row B of the table). Because of the inverse relationship between price and quantity demanded, the demand curve has a negative slope.

Change in quantity demanded
A change in the quantity of a good that buyers are willing and able to purchase that results from a change in the good's price, other things being equal; shown by a movement from one point to another along a demand curve.

Economists speak of a movement along a demand curve as a **change in quantity demanded.** Such a movement represents buyers' reaction to a change in the price of the good in question, other things being equal.

Shifts in the Demand Curve[1]

The demand curve in Exhibit 2.1 represents a relationship between two variables: the price of chicken and the quantity of chicken demanded. But changes in other variables can also affect people's purchases of chicken. In the case of chicken, the prices of beef and pork would affect demand. Consumer incomes are a second variable that can affect demand. Changes in expectations about the future are a third, and changes in consumer tastes, such as the increasing preference for foods with a low saturated-fat content, are a fourth. The list could go on and on—the demand for ice is affected by the weather; the demand for diapers is affected by the birthrate; the demand for baseball tickets is affected by the won-lost record of the home team.

How are all these other variables handled when drawing a demand curve? In brief, two rules apply:

1.   When drawing a single demand curve for a good, such as the one in Exhibit 2.1, all other conditions that affect demand are considered to be fixed or constant under the "other things being equal" clause of the law of demand. As long as that clause is in force, the only two variables at work are quantity demanded (on the horizontal axis) and price (on the vertical axis). The effect of a change in price on the quantity demanded thus is shown by a *movement along* the demand curve.

2.   When the "other things being equal" clause is set aside, and there is a change in a variable that is not represented on one of the axes, such as the price of another good or consumer incomes, the effect is shown as a *shift* in the demand curve. In its new position the demand curve still represents a two-variable price-quantity relationship, but it is a slightly different relationship than before because one of the "other things" has changed.

These two rules for graphical representation of demand relationships are crucial to understanding the theory of supply and demand as a whole. It will be worthwhile to expand on them through a series of examples.

Changes in the price of another good.   We have already noted that the demand for chicken depends on what happens to the price of beef as well as what happens to the price of chicken. Exhibit 2.2, which shows demand curves for both goods, provides a closer look at this relationship.

Suppose that the price of beef is initially $1 per pound and then increases to $1.50 per pound. The effect of this change on the quantity of beef demanded is shown in part (a) of Exhibit 2.2 as a movement along the beef demand curve from point A to point B. Part (b) of the exhibit shows the effect on the demand for chicken. With the price of beef higher than before, consumers will tend to buy more chicken *even if the price of chicken does not change.* Suppose the price of chicken is $.40 per pound. When beef was selling at $1 a pound, consumers

---

[1]Before continuing, the reader may want to review the Chapter 1 appendix "Working with Graphs," especially the section entitled "Packing Three Variables into Two Dimensions."

Exhibit 2.2   Effects of an Increase in the Price
of Beef on the Demand for Chicken

An increase in the price of beef from $1 to $1.50 per pound, other things being
equal, causes a movement from point A to point B on the beef demand curve—a
decrease in the quantity of beef demanded. With the price of chicken unchanged
at $.40 per pound, consumers will substitute chicken for beef. That will cause an
increase in the demand for chicken, which is shown as a shift in the chicken
demand curve from D_1 to D_2.

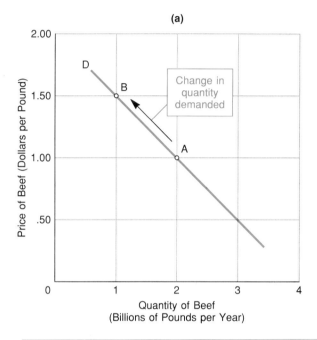
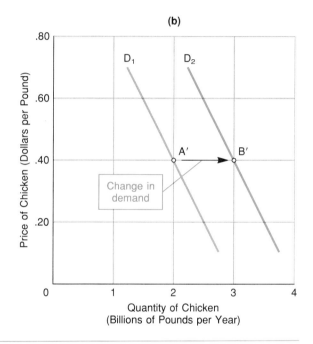

bought 2 billion pounds of chicken a year (point A′ on demand curve D_1). After
the price of beef goes up to $1.50 a pound, they will buy 3 billion pounds of
chicken a year, assuming that the price of chicken does not change (point B′ on
demand curve D_2).

A rise in the price of beef would cause consumers to buy more chicken
regardless of the initial price of chicken. If the price of chicken had started out at
$.60 a pound and remained there while the price of beef went up, consumers
would have increased their chicken consumption from 1.5 billion pounds a year
to 2.5 billion pounds a year. At a price of $.20 a pound for chicken, the quantity
would have risen from 2.5 billion pounds to 3.5 billion pounds, and so on. We
see, then, that a change in the price of beef causes the entire demand curve for
chicken to shift. The "other things being equal" clause of the new demand
curve, D_2, incorporates a price of $1.50 a pound for beef, rather than the price of
$1 a pound assumed in demand curve D_1.

Earlier we explained that economists refer to a movement along a demand
curve as a "change in quantity demanded." The corresponding term for a shift
in a demand curve is a **change in demand.** A change in quantity demanded (a
movement along the curve) is caused by a change in the price of the good in
question (the variable on the vertical axis). In contrast, a change in demand (a

Change in demand
A change in the quantity
of a good that buyers are
willing and able to purchase
that results from a change in
some condition other than
the price of that good;
shown by a shift in the
demand curve.

shift in the demand curve) is caused by a change in some variable other than the price of the good in question (one that does not appear on either axis).

In the example presented in Exhibit 2.2, people bought more chicken when the price of beef went up, replacing one meat with the other in their dinners. Economists call such pairs of goods **substitutes,** because an increase in the price of one causes an increase in the demand for the other—a rightward shift in the demand curve.

Consumers react differently to price changes when two goods tend to be used together. One example is tires and gasoline. When the price of gasoline goes up, people drive less; therefore, they buy fewer tires even if there is no change in their price. An increase in the price of gasoline thus causes a movement upward along the gasoline demand curve and a *leftward* shift in the tire demand curve. Pairs of goods that are related in this way are known as **complements.**

Whether a given pair of goods are substitutes or complements depends on buyers' attitudes toward those goods; these terms do not refer to properties of the goods themselves. Some people might regard cheese and beef as substitute sources of protein in their diets; others, who like cheeseburgers, might regard them as complements.

One more point regarding the effects of changes in the prices of other goods is also worth noting: In stating the law of demand, it is the price of a good relative to those of other goods that counts. During periods of inflation, when the average level of all prices rises, distinguishing between changes in *relative prices* and changes in *nominal prices*—the number of dollars actually paid per unit of a good—is especially important. When the economy experiences inflation, a good can become relatively less expensive even though its nominal price rises, provided that the prices of other goods rise even faster.

Consider chicken, for example. Between 1950 and 1986 the average retail price of a broiler rose by 40 percent, from $.59 per pound to $.83 per pound. Over the same period, however, the average price of all goods and services that consumers bought rose by 350 percent. The relative price of chicken thus fell during the period even though its nominal price rose. The drop in the relative price of chicken had a lot to do with its growing popularity on the dinner table.

Changes in consumer incomes.   The demand for a good can also be affected by changes in consumer incomes. When their incomes rise, people tend to buy larger quantities of many goods, assuming that their prices do not change.

Exhibit 2.3 shows the effect of an increase in consumer incomes on the demand for chicken. Demand curve D_1 is the same as that shown in Exhibit 2.1. Suppose now that consumer incomes rise. With higher incomes, people become choosier about what they eat. They do not just want calories, they want high-quality calories from foods that are tasty, fashionable, and healthful. These considerations have made chicken increasingly popular in the United States as consumer incomes have risen.

More specifically, suppose that after their incomes rise, consumers are willing to buy 3 billion pounds of chicken instead of 2 billion at a price of $.40 per pound. The change is shown as an arrow drawn from point A to point B in Exhibit 2.3. If the initial price of chicken had been $.20 per pound, even more chicken would be bought at the new, higher level of income. At the original income level and a price of $.20, purchases would be 2.5 billion pounds, as

Substitutes
A pair of goods for which an increase in the price of one causes an increase in demand for the other.

Complements
A pair of goods for which an increase in the price of one results in a decrease in demand for the other.

Exhibit 2.3   Effects of an Increase in Consumer Income on the Demand for Chicken

Demand curve D_1 assumes a given level of consumer income. If their incomes increase, consumers will want to buy more chicken at any given price, other things being equal. That will shift the demand curve to the right to, say, D_2. If the prevailing market price at the time of the demand shift is $.40 per pound, the quantity demanded increases to 3 billion pounds (B) from 2 billion (A); if the prevailing price is $.20 per pound, the quantity demanded will increase to 3.5 billion pounds (D) from 2.5 billion (C); and so on.

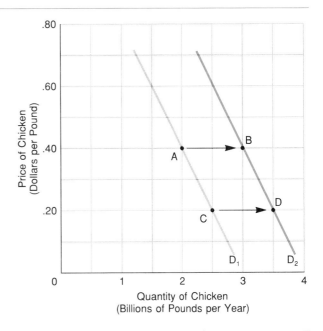

shown by point C. After the increase in incomes, buyers would plan to purchase 3.5 billion pounds, shown by the arrow from point C to point D.

Whatever the initial price of chicken, the effect of an increase in consumer incomes is shown by a shift to a point on the new demand curve, D_2. The increase in demand for chicken that results from the rise in consumer incomes thus is shown as a shift in the entire demand curve. If consumer incomes remain at the new, higher level, the effects of any changes in the price of chicken will be shown as movements along the new demand curve. There is, in other words, a chicken demand curve for every possible income level. Each represents a one-to-one relationship between price and quantity demanded, given the assumed income level.

In the example just given, we assumed that an increase in income would cause an increase in the demand for chicken. Experience shows that this is what normally happens. Economists therefore call chicken a **normal good,** meaning that when consumer incomes rise, other things being equal, people will buy more of it.

There are some goods, however, that people will buy less of when their incomes rise, other things being equal. For example, among your classmates those with higher incomes are likely to go out for pizza more often than those with lower incomes. On nights when they eat pizza, they do not eat in the cafeteria, so the demand for cafeteria food falls as income rises. Similarly, when their incomes rise, people tend to buy less flour for baking at home and to buy more baked goods instead. People tend to buy fewer shoe repair services when their incomes rise; instead, they buy new shoes. Goods such as cafeteria food, flour, and shoe repair services are termed **inferior goods.** When consumer incomes rise, the demand curve for an inferior good shifts to the left instead of to the right. As in the case of substitutes and complements, the notions of inferior-

Normal good
A good for which an increase in consumer incomes results in an increase in demand.

Inferior good
A good for which an increase in consumer incomes results in a decrease in demand.

ity and normality arise from consumer choices; they are not inherent properties of the goods themselves.

Changes in expectations.   Changes in buyers' expectations are a third factor that can shift demand curves. If people expect the price of a particular good to rise relative to those of other goods, or expect something other than a price increase to raise the opportunity cost of acquiring the good, they will step up their rate of purchase before the change takes place.

In a classic case of this type, consumers rushed to buy cars in December 1986 just before a new tax law went into effect. After January 1987, car buyers expected that they would be unable to deduct the sales tax on a new car from their federal income taxes. Depending on the state and the car's price, the change in tax regulations could have been equivalent to a price increase of $200 to $300. After running well above normal in December, new-car sales fell in January. Because more cars were sold in December than would have been sold at the same price if consumers had not expected the tax law to change, buyers' behavior in December can be interpreted as a temporary rightward shift in the demand curve for cars.

Changes in tastes.   Changes in tastes are a fourth source of changes in demand. Sometimes these changes occur rapidly, as, for example, in such areas as popular music, clothing styles, and fast foods. The demand curves for these goods and services shift often. In other cases, changes in tastes take longer to occur but are more permanent. For example, in recent years consumers have been more health conscious than they were in the past. The result has been reduced demand for cigarettes and high-cholesterol foods, along with increased demand for fish, chicken, and exercise equipment.

2.2   Supply

The Supply Curve

We now turn from the demand side of the market to the supply side. As in the case of demand, we begin by constructing a one-to-one relationship between the price of a good and the quantity that sellers intend to offer for sale. Exhibit 2.4 shows such a relationship for chicken.

Supply curve
A graphical representation of the relationship between the price of a good and the quantity of that good that sellers are willing to supply.

The upward-sloping curve in Exhibit 2.4 is called a **supply curve** for chicken. Like demand curves, supply curves are based on an "other things being equal" condition. The supply curve for chicken shows how sellers change their plans in response to a change in the price of chicken, assuming that there are no changes in the prices of other goods, in production techniques, in input prices, in expectations or in any other relevant condition.

Movements along the Supply Curve

Why does the supply curve have a positive slope? Why do sellers, other things being equal, plan to supply more chicken when the prevailing market price is higher than they will when the price is lower? Without going too deeply into a discussion of microeconomic theory, we can consider some commonsense explanations here.

Exhibit 2.4 A Supply Curve for Chicken

Parts (a) and (b) of this exhibit show the quantity of chicken supplied at various prices. As the price rises, the quantity supplied increases, other things being equal. The higher price gives farmers an incentive to raise more chickens, but the rising opportunity cost of doing so limits the supply produced in response to any given price increase.

(a)

Price of Chicken (Dollars per Pound)	Quantity of Chicken Supplied (Billions of Pounds per Year)
.64	2.6
.60	2.5
.56	2.4
.52	2.3
.48	2.2
.44	2.1
A .40	2.0
.36	1.9
.32	1.8
.28	1.7
.24	1.6
B .20	1.5
.16	1.4

(b)

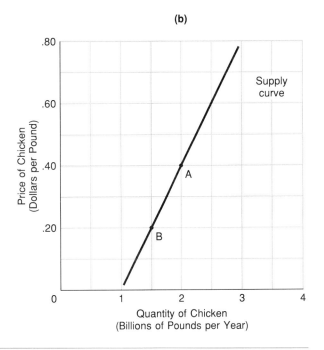

One explanation is that the positive slope of the supply curve represents producers' response to market incentives. When the price of chicken goes up, farmers have an incentive to devote more time and resources to raising chickens. Farmers who raised chickens as a sideline may decide to make chickens their main business. Some people may enter the market for the first time. The same reasoning applies in every market. If parents are finding it hard to get babysitters, what do they do? They offer to pay more. If a sawmill cannot buy enough timber, it raises the price it offers to loggers, and so on. Exceptions to this general rule are rare.[2]

Another explanation is that the positive slope of the supply curve reflects the rising cost of producing additional output in facilities of a fixed size. A furniture factory with a fixed amount of machinery might be able to produce more chairs only by paying workers at overtime rates to run the machinery for more hours. A farmer who is trying to grow more wheat on a fixed amount of land could do so by increasing the input of fertilizer and pesticides per acre, but beyond a certain point each unit of added chemicals yields less additional output.

---

[2]The story of Bjorn Borg's tennis career, reported in the appendix to Chapter 1, suggests that some individuals may respond perversely to increased rewards (see p. 36). Despite such a pattern of choice by some individuals, we would still expect an increase in pay for professional tennis players (relative to other athletes) to attract more participants to the sport.

Exhibit 2.5   The Production Possibility Curve and the Supply Curve

This figure offers an interpretation of the supply curve in terms of the production possibility frontier for an economy in which two goods are produced, tomatoes and chicken. Part (a) shows a production possibility frontier. The slope of the frontier at any point shows the opportunity cost of producing an additional pound of chicken measured in terms of the quantity of tomatoes that otherwise could have been produced using the same factors of production. The frontier curves because some operators have a comparative advantage in producing tomatoes and others a comparative advantage in producing chicken. As more chicken is produced, those with the greatest comparative advantage in producing chicken are the first to switch out of tomatoes. Because the frontier gets steeper as more chicken is produced, the opportunity cost rises, as shown in part (b). The curve in part (b) can be interpreted as a supply curve if it is noted that in order to shift factors of production from tomatoes to chicken, an incentive—in the form of a higher price—is needed to overcome the rising opportunity cost of chicken.

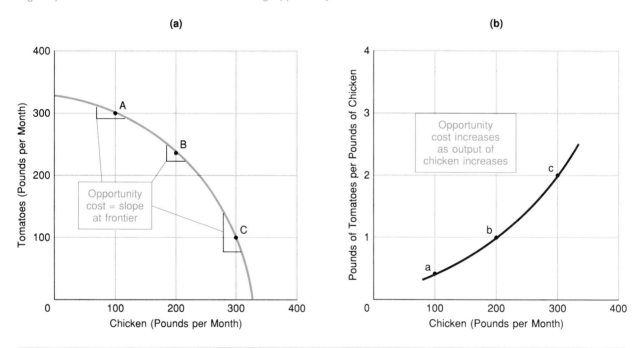

Finally, the positive slope of the supply curve can be explained through the production possibility frontier and the concept of opportunity cost. Imagine an economy in which there are only two goods, tomatoes and chicken. Farmers can choose which product they will specialize in, but some farmers have a comparative advantage in growing tomatoes, others in raising chickens. Beginning from a situation in which only tomatoes are produced, farmers with the strongest comparative advantage in raising chickens—that is, those who are able to produce chicken at relatively the lowest opportunity cost—will switch from tomatoes to chicken even if chicken sells at a low price. As the point of production moves along the frontier, the price of chicken must rise to induce farmers with relatively higher opportunity costs to make the switch. The slope of the frontier at any point represents the opportunity cost of producing more chicken for a farmer who finds it worthwhile to switch from tomatoes to chicken just at that point. In Exhibit 2.5 the slopes at points A, B, and C in part (a) are graphed on a new set of axes in part (b). The graph can be interpreted as a supply curve if it is noted that the price of chicken must rise relative to the price of tomatoes to induce more farmers to switch to chicken as the opportunity cost rises.

Each of these commonsense explanations fits certain circumstances. Together, they provide an intuitive basis for the positively sloped supply curve.

Shifts in the Supply Curve

As in the case of demand, the effects of a change in the price of chicken, other things being equal, can be shown as a movement along the supply curve for chicken. Such a movement is called a **change in quantity supplied.** A change in a condition other than the price of chicken can be shown as a shift in the supply curve. Such a shift is referred to as a **change in supply.** Four sources of change in supply are worth noting. Each is related to the notion that the supply curve reflects the opportunity cost of producing the good or service in question.

Changes in technology.   A supply curve is drawn on the basis of a particular production technique. When entrepreneurs reduce the opportunity costs of production by introducing more efficient techniques, it becomes worthwhile to sell more of the good than before at any given price. Exhibit 2.6 shows how an improvement in production technology affects the chicken supply curve.

Supply curve S_1 is the same as the one shown in Exhibit 2.4. It indicates that farmers will plan to supply 2 billion pounds per year at a price of \$.40 per pound (point A). Now suppose that the development of a faster-growing bird reduces the amount of feed used in raising chickens. With lower costs per unit, farmers will be willing to supply more chicken than before at any given price. They may, for example, be willing to supply 2.6 billion pounds of chicken at \$.40 per pound (point B). The move from A to B is part of a shift in the entire supply curve from S_1 to S_2. Once the new techniques are established, an increase or decrease in the price of chicken, other things being equal, will result in a movement along the new supply curve.

Change in quantity supplied A change in the quantity of a good that suppliers are willing and able to sell that results from a change in the good's price, other things being equal; shown by a movement along a supply curve.

Change in supply A change in the quantity of a good that suppliers are willing and able to sell that results from a change in some condition other than the good's price; shown by a shift in the supply curve.

Exhibit 2.6   Shifts in the Supply Curve for Chicken

Several kinds of changes can cause the supply of chicken to increase or decrease. For example, a new production method that lowers costs will shift the curve to the right, from S_1 to S_2. The shift is to the *right* because, taking into account the new, lower cost of production per unit, producers will be willing to supply more chicken at any given market price. An increase in the price of inputs, other things being equal, will shift the curve to the left, from S_1 to S_3. The shift is to the *left* because, taking into account the new, higher price of inputs, producers will be willing to supply less chicken at any given market price. Changes in sellers' expectations or in the prices of competing goods can also cause the supply curve to shift.

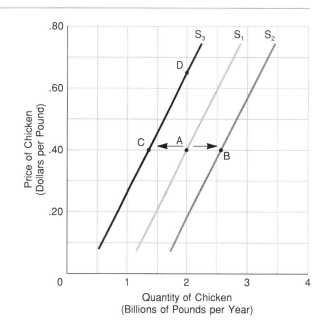

Changes in input prices.   Changes in input prices are a second item that can cause supply curves to shift. An increase in input prices, other things being equal, increases the opportunity cost of producing the good in question, and hence it tends to reduce the quantity of a good that producers plan to supply at a given price. Refer again to Exhibit 2.6. Suppose that starting from point A on supply curve S_1, the price of chicken feed increases and no offsetting changes occur. Now, instead of supplying 2 billion pounds of chicken at $.40 per pound farmers will supply, say, just 1.4 billion pounds at that price (point C). The move from A to C is part of a leftward shift in the supply curve, from S_1 to S_3.

If the price of feed remains at the new level, changes in the price of chicken will cause movements along the new supply curve. For example, farmers could be induced to supply the original quantity of chicken—2 billion bushels—if the price of chicken rose enough to cover the increased cost of feed. As you can see in Exhibit 2.6, that would require a price of about $.65 per pound for chicken (point D).

Changes in prices of other goods.   Changes in the prices of other goods that could be produced using the same factors of production can also produce a shift in the chicken supply curve. In our earlier example, farmers could use available factors of production to raise either chickens or tomatoes. Suppose that the price of tomatoes rises while the price of chicken stays at $.40. The rise in the price of tomatoes gives some farmers who would otherwise have raised chickens an incentive to shift the use of their labor, land, and capital to raising tomatoes. Thus, the effect of an increase in the price of tomatoes can thus be shown as a leftward shift in the chicken supply curve.

Changes in expectations.   Changes in expectations can cause supply curves to shift in much the same way that they cause demand curves to shift. Again we can use farming as an example. At planting time a farmer's selection of crops is influenced not so much by current prices as by the prices expected at harvest time. Expectations over a time horizon longer than one growing season also affect supply. Each crop requires special equipment and know-how. We have just seen that an increase in the price of tomatoes gives farmers an incentive to shift from chicken to tomatoes. The incentive will be stronger if the increase in the price of tomatoes is expected to be long lasting. If it is, farmers are more likely to buy the special equipment needed for that crop and to learn the necessary production techniques.

A Final Word on Shifts in Curves and Movements along Them

The next step in building the supply-and-demand model of markets is to place both the supply and the demand curves on one diagram. Before doing that, however, we should briefly review what has been learned about the two types of curves.

First, for both supply and demand curves, a change in the price of the good in question causes a movement along the curve. The effects of a change in price are built into supply and demand curves when they are drawn. That is why the price of the good is assigned to one of the axes of the graph.

Exhibit 2.7 Sources of Shifts in Supply and Demand Curves

A change in the price of a good, other things being equal, causes a change in quantity demanded or supplied, shown by a movement along a demand or supply curve. Changes in any of the conditions covered by the "other things being equal" clause cause a change in demand or supply, shown by a shift in the demand or supply curve. The table lists some of the most common sources of shifts in demand and supply curves. The list is not exhaustive. Special conditions not listed may affect demand or supply for particular goods, for example, the demand for ice depends on the temperature, the supply of corn depends on rainfall, and so on.

Source of Shift	Direction of Shift
Demand Curve	
Increase in price of a substitute good	Right
Decrease in price of a substitute good	Left
Increase in price of a complementary good	Left
Decrease in price of a complementary good	Right
Increase in consumer income (normal good)	Right
Decrease in consumer income (normal good)	Left
Increase in consumer income (inferior good)	Left
Decrease in consumer income (inferior good)	Right
Change in tastes toward preference for the good	Right
Change in tastes away from preference for the good	Left
Changes in consumer expectations about future market conditions (depending on particular circumstances)	Left or right
Supply Curve	
Increase in prices of inputs (wages, raw materials, etc.)	Left
Decrease in prices of inputs (wages, raw materials, etc.)	Right
Change in technology that lowers cost of production	Right
Increase in price of other goods produced with same productive resources	Left
Decrease in price of other goods produced with same productive resources	Right
Changes in producer expectations about future market conditions (depending on particular circumstances)	Left or right

Because graphs only have two axes, the effects of changes in variables other than price cannot be built into supply and demand curves in the same way. For those other variables, a different graphical technique is used: Any change in a variable covered by the "other things being equal" clause is represented graphically as a shift in the supply or demand curve. The variables in question—prices of other goods, consumer incomes, expectations, and so on—are those that are not assigned to one of the axes of the graph, that is, any variable other than price or quantity.

Exhibit 2.7 summarizes the main variables that shift supply and demand curves. The list is not exhaustive. Almost every good has special factors, not listed in the table, that can shift the supply or demand curve: A rise in temperature increases the demand for ice; the approach of Thanksgiving increases the demand for cranberries; and so on. When conditions are encountered that are not found on the list, use common sense.

2.3   The Interaction of Supply and Demand

Markets transmit information, in the form of prices, to people who buy and sell goods and services. Taking these prices into account, along with other knowledge they may have, buyers and sellers make their plans. As shown by the demand and supply curves, buyers and sellers plan to buy or sell certain quantities of a good at any given price.

Each market has many buyers and sellers, each making plans independently. When they meet to trade, some of them may be unable to carry out their plans on the terms they expected. Perhaps the total quantity of a good that buyers plan to purchase is greater than the total quantity that suppliers are willing to sell at the given price. In that case, some of the would-be buyers must change their plans. Or perhaps planned sales exceed planned purchases at the given price. In that case, some would-be sellers will be unable to carry out their plans.

Sometimes no one is surprised: The total quantity of a good that buyers plan to purchase exactly matches the total quantity that producers plan to sell. When buyers' and sellers' plans mesh when they meet in the marketplace, no buyers or sellers need to change their plans. Under these conditions, the market is said to be in **equilibrium.**

Equilibrium
A condition in which buyers' and sellers' plans exactly mesh in the marketplace, so that the quantity supplied exactly equals the quantity demanded at a given price.

Market Equilibrium

Supply and demand curves, which reflect the plans of sellers and buyers, can be used to give a graphical demonstration of market equilibrium. Exhibit 2.8 uses the same supply and demand curves as before, but this time both curves are drawn on the same diagram. If the quantity of planned sales at each price is compared with the quantity of planned purchases at that price (either the table or the graph can be used to make this comparison), it can be seen that there is only one price at which the two sets of plans mesh. That price—$.40 per pound—is the equilibrium price. If all buyers and sellers make their plans with the expectation of a price of $.40, no one will be surprised and no plans will have to be changed.

Shortages

But what will happen if for some reason people base their plans for buying or selling chicken on a price other than $.40 a pound?[3] Suppose, for example, that they base their plans on a price of $.20. Exhibit 2.8 shows that at that price buyers will plan to purchase chicken at a rate of 2.5 billion pounds per year but

[3]Why might buyers and sellers enter the market expecting a price other than the one that permits equilibrium? It may be, for example, that market conditions have caused the supply or demand curve to shift unexpectedly, so that a price that formerly permitted equilibrium no longer does so. It may be that buyers or sellers expect conditions to change, but they do not change after all. Or it may be that government policy has established a legal maximum or minimum price that differs from the equilibrium price. Later sections of the chapter will explore some of these possibilities.

Exhibit 2.8   Equilibrium in the Chicken Market

This exhibit shows the supply and demand curves for chicken presented earlier in
graphical and numerical form. The demand curve shows how much buyers plan
to purchase at a given price. The supply curve shows how much producers plan
to sell at a given price. At only one price—$.40 per pound—do buyers' and
sellers' plans exactly match. That is the equilibrium price. A higher price causes a
surplus of chicken and puts downward pressure on price. A lower price causes a
shortage and puts upward pressure on price.

(a)

(b)

Price per Pound (1)	Quantity Supplied (Billions of Pounds) (2)	Quantity Demanded (Billions of Pounds) (3)	Shortage (Billions of Pounds) (4)	Surplus (Billions of Pounds) (5)	Direction of Pressure on Price (6)
.64	2.6	1.4	—	1.2	Downward
.60	2.5	1.5	—	1.0	Downward
.56	2.4	1.6	—	0.8	Downward
.52	2.3	1.7	—	0.6	Downward
.48	2.2	1.8	—	0.4	Downward
.44	2.1	1.9	—	0.2	Downward
.40	2.0	2.0	—	—	Equilibrium
.36	1.9	2.1	0.2	—	Upward
.32	1.8	2.2	0.4	—	Upward
.28	1.7	2.3	0.6	—	Upward
.24	1.6	2.4	0.8	—	Upward
.20	1.5	2.5	1.0	—	Upward
.16	1.4	2.6	1.2	—	Upward

Excess quantity demanded (shortage)
A condition in which the quantity of a good demanded at a given price exceeds the quantity supplied.

Inventory
A stock of a finished good awaiting sale or use.

farmers will plan to supply only 1.5 billion pounds. When the quantity demanded exceeds the quantity supplied, as in this example, the difference is an **excess quantity demanded** or, more simply, a **shortage.** In Exhibit 2.8 the shortage is 1 billion pounds of chicken per year when the price is $.20 per pound.

Shortages and inventories.   In most markets the first sign of a shortage is a drop in the **inventory,** that is, in the stock of the good in question that has been produced and is waiting to be sold or used. Sellers plan to hold a certain quantity of goods in inventory to allow for minor changes in demand. When they see inventories dropping below the planned level, they change their plans. Some may try to rebuild their inventories by increasing their output, if they produce the good themselves or, if they do not make it themselves, they may order more from the producer. Some sellers may take advantage of the strong demand for their product to raise the price, knowing that buyers will be willing to pay more. Many sellers will do a little of both. If sellers do not take the initiative, buyers will—they will offer to pay more if sellers will supply more. Whatever the details, the result will be an upward movement along the supply curve as both price and quantity increase.

As the shortage puts upward pressure on price, buyers will change their plans too. Moving up and to the left along their demand curve, they will cut back on their planned purchases. As both buyers and sellers change their plans, the market moves toward equilibrium. When the price reaches $.40 per pound, both the shortage and the pressure to change buying and selling plans will disappear.

Shortages and queues.   In the markets for most goods, sellers have inventories of goods ready to be sold. There are exceptions, however. Inventories are not possible in markets for services—haircuts, tax preparation, lawn care, and the like. Also, some goods, such as custom-built houses and machine tools that are designed for a specialized need, are not held in inventories. Sellers in these markets do not begin production until they have a contract with a buyer.

In markets in which there are no inventories, the sign of a shortage is a queue of buyers. The queue may take the form of a line of people waiting to be served or a list of names in an order book. The queue is a sign that, given the prevailing price, buyers would like to purchase the good at a faster rate than that at which producers have planned to supply it. However, some plans cannot be carried out—at least not right away. Buyers are served on a first-come, first-served basis.

The formation of a queue of buyers has much the same effect on the market as a decrease in inventories. Sellers react by increasing their rate of output, raising their prices, or both. Buyers react by reducing the quantity they plan to purchase. The result is a movement up and to the right along the supply curve and, at the same time, up and to the left along the demand curve until equilibrium is reached.

A reminder.   In this section we have shown in detail how a shortage affects the choices made by buyers and sellers. As you become more proficient in applying the supply-and-demand model, you will begin taking shortcuts in the way you think about its workings. Instead of thinking about people and the choices they make, you will think, "That gap between the curves pushes up the price" or "That change in market conditions shifts the curve." Although such thinking is a sign of familiarity with the model, it carries with it a risk: that of forgetting that economics is about people and the choices they make, not about models and graphs. The graphs do not *do* anything themselves. They are only an aid to thinking about what *people* do when faced with the need to make choices about the use of scarce resources under ever-changing conditions.

Surpluses

Having considered what happens when buyers and sellers initially expect a price below the equilibrium price, we now turn to the opposite case. Suppose that for some reason buyers and sellers expect a price of chicken that is higher than the equilibrium price—say, $.60 per pound—and make their plans accordingly. Exhibit 2.8 shows that farmers will plan to supply 2.5 billion pounds of chicken per year at $.60, but their customers will plan to buy only 1.5 billion pounds. When the quantity supplied exceeds the quantity demanded, there is an **excess quantity supplied,** or a **surplus.** As Exhibit 2.8 shows, the surplus of chicken at a price of $.60 per pound is 1 billion pounds per year.

Excess quantity supplied (surplus)
A condition in which the quantity of a good supplied at a given price exceeds the quantity demanded.

Surpluses and inventories.   When there is a surplus of a product, sellers will be unable to sell all that they had hoped to sell at the planned price. As a result, their inventories will begin to grow beyond the level they had planned to hold in preparation for normal changes in demand.

Sellers will react to the inventory buildup by changing their plans. Some will cut back their output. Others will lower their prices to induce consumers to buy more and thus reduce their extra stock. Still others will do a little of both. The result of these changes in plans will be a movement down and to the left along the supply curve.

As unplanned inventory buildup puts downward pressure on the price of chicken, buyers change their plans too. Finding that chicken costs less than they had expected, they buy more of it. In graphical terms, they move down and to the right along the demand curve. As that happens, the market is restored to equilibrium.

Surpluses and queues.   In markets in which there are no inventories, surpluses lead to the formation of queues of sellers looking for customers. Taxi queues at airports are a case in point. At some times of the day the fare for taxi service from the airport to downtown is more than enough to attract a number of taxis equal to the demand. In some cities drivers who are far back in the queue try to attract riders with offers of cut-rate fares. Often, though, there are rules against fare cutting. The queue then grows until the next rush hour, when a surge in demand shortens it.

Changes in Market Conditions

On a graph, finding the equilibrium point looks easy. In real life, though, it is a moving target. Market conditions—all the items that lie behind the "other things being equal" clause—change frequently. When they do, both buyers and sellers must revise their plans as the point of equilibrium shifts.

Response to a shift in demand.   We will first consider a market's response to a shift in demand. The decline in demand for beef caused by consumers' avoidance of high-cholesterol foods provides a good example. Part (a) of Exhibit 2.9 interprets this case in terms of the supply-and-demand model.

As the figure is drawn, the market is initially in equilibrium at E_1. There the price is $1.25 per pound and the quantity produced is 2.5 billion pounds per year. Now the changed dietary habits of U.S. consumers cause the demand curve to shift to the left, from D_1 to D_2. (There is a shift in the demand curve rather than a movement along it, because a change in tastes is not one of the items found on the axes of the diagram.) What will happen next?

At the original price of $1.25 per pound, there will be a surplus of beef. The supply curve shows that at that price ranchers will plan to produce 2.5 billion pounds per year. However, according to the new demand curve, D_2, consumers will no longer buy that much beef at $1.25 per pound. Instead, given their new tastes, they will buy only 1.5 billion pounds at that price.

But the price does not stay at $1.25 for long. As soon as the demand curve begins to shift and the surplus begins to develop, beef inventories rise above their planned levels, putting downward pressure on the price. As the price falls, ranchers revise their plans. They move down and to the left along their supply curve, reducing the quantity supplied as the price drops. (There is a movement along the supply curve, not a shift in the curve, because the ranchers are responding to a change in the price of beef, the variable shown on the vertical axis. Nothing has happened to change the "other things being equal" conditions, such as technology, input prices, and so on, which could cause the supply curve to shift.)

As ranchers move downward along their supply curve in the direction shown by the arrow in part (a) of Exhibit 2.9, they eventually reach point E_2, where their plans again mesh with those of consumers. At that point the price has fallen to $1.00 per pound and production to 2 million pounds. Although health-conscious consumers would not have bought that much beef at the old price, they will do so at the new, lower price. E_2 thus is the new equilibrium point.

Response to a shift in supply.   The original equilibrium might be disrupted by a change in supply rather than by a change in demand. For example, beginning from a condition of equilibrium, a drought in the corn belt might raise the price of cattle feed. That would shift the supply curve to the left while the demand curve remained unchanged, as shown in part (b) of Exhibit 2.9.

Given the new supply curve, there will be a shortage of beef at the original price. Inventories will decline, and in response, prices will rise. As the price increases, producers will move upward and to the right along their new supply curve, S_2, and consumers will move upward and to the left along their demand curve, D, which remains in its original position. A new equilibrium is established when the price reaches $1.50 per pound.

One of the most frequent mistakes in learning the supply-and-demand model is to think that both curves must shift in order to restore equilibrium. The examples given in Exhibit 2.9 show clearly that this is not the case. In part (a), after the demand curve shifts, a movement along the supply curve is enough to establish the new equilibrium. No shift in the supply curve is needed. Similarly, in part (b), after the supply curve shifts, the demand curve does not need to shift to reach the new equilibrium.

Exhibit 2.9   Effects of Changing Market Conditions in the Beef Market

Part (a) of this figure shows the effects of a decrease in demand for beef caused by a shift in tastes away from high-cholesterol foods. Initially the market is in equilibrium at E_1. The change in tastes causes a shift in the demand curve. At the original equilibrium price of $1.25 per pound, there is a temporary surplus of beef. This causes inventories to start to rise and puts downward pressure on the price. As the price falls, producers move down along their supply curve, as shown by the arrow, to a new equilibrium at E_2. There both the price and quantity of beef are lower than before the shift in demand. Part (b) shows the effects of a decrease in supply caused by a drought, which raises the price of corn used to feed cattle. The shift in the supply curve causes a shortage at the initial price of $1.25 per pound. The shortage puts upward pressure on price. As the price rises, buyers move up and to the left along the demand curve until a new equilibrium is reached at E_2. In each case, note that only one curve needs to shift to bring about the new equilibrium.

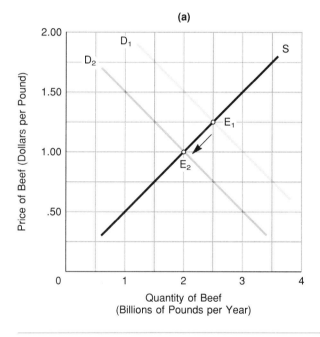

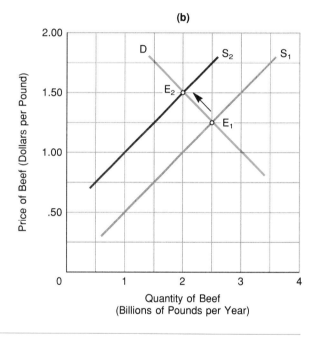

In the turmoil of real-world markets, cases can be found in which both curves shift at once, but that happens only when two separate changes in conditions occur at the same time, one acting on the supply curve and one on the demand curve. An example would be a drought that shifted the supply curve just as the market was already in the process of adjusting to a shift in the demand curve caused by changing tastes. When in doubt as to whether you are dealing with a shift in the curve or a movement along it, refer back to the list of shift factors in Exhibit 2.7. If you cannot point to a specific factor causing a shift in the curve you are dealing with, you probably do not need to shift it.

Equilibrium as Spontaneous Order

The ability of markets to move toward a new equilibrium following a disturbance is an example of economic coordination through spontaneous order. In the case we have been following, the disturbance began either with a change in health consciousness among consumers or with a change in the weather. The challenge: How to coordinate the decisions of thousands of farmers, wholesalers, retailers—the whole chain of supply—to serve consumers' wants under changing conditions.

No commissar of central planning or regulatory bureaucracy is required to accomplish the needed shift in the use of scarce resources. It is all brought about through information and incentives transmitted in the form of changing market prices. To take a real example, in 1988, as the demand for beef lagged and the drought raised the price of feed grains, ranchers culled their herds to 98 million head, down 26 percent from their peak. Meanwhile labor, capital, natural resources, and entrepreneurial energy flowed into chicken production, where booming demand buoyed profit expectations.

The process was remarkably smooth for so vast a shift in resource use. Behind the scenes, surpluses and shortages nudged choices in the needed directions, but at no time did shortages break through in the acute form of empty meat coolers at the supermarket or lines of chicken-hungry consumers stretching down city steets. Similarly, surpluses of beef caused ranchers to cut back their herds, but they did not break through in the form of mountains of rotting beef that had to be dumped into landfills.

Yet no one *intended* this process of adjustment. Equilibrium is not a compromise that a committee of consumers and producers must meet to negotiate. Just as shoppers manage to equalize the length of supermarket checkout lines without central authority, markets move toward equilibrium spontaneously, through the small, local adjustments that people make in their efforts to serve their own interests. As Adam Smith might have put it, we have not the benevolence of Frank Perdue or the Beef Industry Council to thank for our dinner; instead it is their self-love that puts the right food on our table.

Market Adjustment and Entrepreneurship

The supply-and-demand model provides a clear and time-tested account of the process through which markets adjust to equilibrium in response to a change in conditions, yet in an important sense it is incomplete. The behavior of consumers and producers as represented by demand and supply curves is overly mechanical. In the real world, people do not react so passively. As **Economics in the News 2.1** relates, they fight back when their interests are threatened. The examples cited—Rhonda Miller's better steak, Excel's vacuum-wrapped roasts, and Kroger's oven-ready meat loaves—are entrepreneurial responses to the decline in demand for beef. They show that beef producers do not just accept the shift in the demand curve and respond by sliding down the supply curve. Instead, they grab onto the demand curve and try to pull it back.

Taking entrepreneurship into account does not mean that the supply-and-demand model has to be discarded. In fact, the model provides just the framework we need to talk about what entrepreneurs are trying to do. Rhonda Miller's efforts to make a better steak have the effect of nudging the demand curve for beef to the right. Some other entrepreneur might be trying to save on feed costs by developing a genetically engineered steer. If successful, the project would give the supply curve for beef a rightward shove.

Economics in the News 2.1
Beef Producers Fight Consumer Switch to Chicken

Rhonda Miller is building a better steak.

Donning rubber boots, a white coat and a hard hat in Monfort of Colorado Inc.'s chilly packing plant, she mixes up a secret recipe of shredded beef and seaweed extract and pushes it through a stainless steel extruder to make logs of meat.

After the meat binds together in a cooler, she slices it into perfectly shaped, lean strip steaks and seals them in individual packages. "My husband loves these because they're so convenient," says Miller, the company's research director.

The new, tender steak is a radical departure from the unpopular, fatty chuck roasts that roll down conveyor belts

Sources: Marj Charlier, "State of Steak: Beef's Drop in Appeal Pushes Some Packers to Try New Products," *The Wall Street Journal*, August 28, 1985, 1, and "The U.S. Beef Industry Just Can't Seem to Get the Hang of Marketing," *The Wall Street Journal*, January 4, 1989, 1.

at Monfort's plants. Cattlemen are praying that the refabricated steak and other new, easy-to-fix Monfort products will halt the decline in the cattle business.

Another innovative packer is Excel, which sells branded roasts and steaks in vacuum packs, ready for the meat case. The meat has little fat, and the packaging increases shelf life and tenderness, turning most first-time buyers into repeat customers, Excel claims.

Meanwhile, others are pressing ahead on a smaller scale. Kroger Co., one of the nation's largest grocery chains, makes its own oven-ready meat loaves and stuffed cabbages in stores where Excel's case-ready beef has freed up butchers.

Not all packers are as keen on marketing new products as Monfort and Excel. The nation's two largest packers—IBP, Inc. and ConAgra, Inc.—insist they are commodity processors, not marketers. That attitude worries Jens Knutsen, economist at the American Meat Institute. If packers don't help maintain demand for beef, a downward spiral could begin anew: prices would stagnate, losses would be passed back down the industry chain, beef production would fall and cattlemen would cull their herds further.

2.4 Price Floors and Ceilings: An Application

Economics—both macro and micro—encompasses a great many applications of the concepts of supply and demand. Although each situation is unique, each to some extent draws on ideas developed in this chapter. This section, which uses the model to analyze the effects of government-imposed price floors and ceilings, provides some examples. Many more will be added in later chapters.

Price Supports: The Market for Milk

In our earlier example of the market for beef, a decrease in demand caused a surplus, which in turn caused the price to decrease until the surplus was eliminated. Markets are not always left free to respond by adjusting prices, however. The market for milk is a case in point.

Exhibit 2.10 shows the market for milk in terms of supply and demand curves. Suppose that initially the market is in equilibrium at point E_1. The wholesale price of milk is $13 per hundredweight, and production is 110 million hundredweight per year. A trend in taste away from high-cholesterol foods— the same trend that hit the market for beef—shifts the demand curve for milk to the left. As in the case of beef, the result is a surplus, as shown by the arrow in Exhibit 2.10.

Here the similarity between the beef and milk markets ends. In the beef market prices are free to fall in response to a surplus, but in the milk market they are not. Instead, an elaborate set of government-imposed controls and subsidies sets a floor on the price of milk. In the exhibit, the government agrees to pay $13

Exhibit 2.10   Price Supports for Milk

Suppose that initially the market for milk is in equilibrium at E_1. A shift in tastes away from high-cholesterol foods then shifts the demand curve to D_2. If the price were free to fall, there would be a temporary surplus that would push the price down to a new equilibrium at $10 per hundredweight. Instead, the government maintains a support price for milk at a level shown here as $13 per hundredweight. The government buys the surplus milk and stores it in the form of butter and cheese to keep the price from falling.

per hundredweight for all milk that cannot be sold at that price on the open market.

With the demand curve in position D_1, there is no surplus; thus, the government need not buy any milk. But with the demand curve in position D_2, there is a surplus of 40 million hundredweight per year. Under the price support law the government must buy this surplus and store it in the form of cheese, butter, and other products with long shelf lives. Over the years the government has accumulated vast stores of such products. In 1988, the government purchased the equivalent of 9 billion pounds of milk. Dairy farmers have been happy to sell the extra milk, but the cost has been high. Since 1980, the combined costs to consumers and taxpayers has been estimated at more than $1,000 per family—enough to buy each family its own cow.

Without price supports, the shift in demand would cause the price of milk to fall to the new equilibrium price of $10 per hundredweight. When price supports are applied to a product at a level higher than the equilibrium price, however, the result is a lasting surplus condition. This happens because the support price sends misleading messages to consumers and producers. To consumers, the price of $13 says, "Milk is scarce. Its opportunity cost is high. Hold your consumption down." To producers, it says, "All is well. Incentives are unchanged. Feel free to continue using scarce factors to produce milk."

A drop in the price to $10 would send a different set of messages. Consumers would hear: "Milk is cheaper and more abundant. Although it is not cholesterol free, give in to temptation! Drink more of it!" But producers would hear: "The milk market is not what it once was. Look at your opportunity costs. Is there perhaps some better use for your labor, capital, and natural resources?"

From time to time the government has tried to eliminate the milk surplus by shifting the supply curve to the left so that it would intersect the demand curve near the support price. Under one recent program, for example, farmers were encouraged to sell their cows for beef, thereby reducing the size of dairy herds. But such programs have failed to eliminate the milk surplus. The chief reason has been dairy farmers' entrepreneurial response to the high price of milk. The government's efforts to cut the size of herds have been largely offset by increased output per cow as a result of genetic improvements and better farm management practices. For example, some dairy farms in California now have 3,000 and even 4,000 cows, compared with 70 or so on a traditional dairy farm. The cows never see a pasture—they spend their days in a pen munching high-protein alfalfa. Whereas the average Wisconsin cow gives 13,000 pounds of milk a year (a marvel to farmers in much of the world), their California cousins yield over 20,000 pounds a year. To add insult to injury, the alfalfa they eat is grown in fields that are irrigated with government-subsidized water. Meanwhile, the government's vast stocks of butter and cheese continue to grow.

Price Ceilings: The Case of Rent Control

In the milk market, the government maintains a support price that is above the equilibrium price. In other markets, a price ceiling below the equilibrium price is imposed. An example of the latter situation is rent control in housing markets.

Rent control in one form or another exists in several major U.S. cities, including New York, Washington, San Francisco, and Los Angeles. The controls vary from one city to another, but in all cases maximum rents, at least for some categories of apartments, are established by law. The purpose of rent control is to aid tenants by preventing landlords from charging "unreasonably high" rents. What is unreasonably high is determined by the relative political strength of landlords and tenants rather than by the forces of supply and demand.

Intended effects.   Exhibit 2.11 interprets the effects of rent control in terms of supply and demand. For the sake of simplicity it is assumed that the supply of rental housing consists of units of equal size and rental value. Part (a) of the exhibit shows the effects of rent control in the short run. Here the short run means a period that is too short to permit significant increases or decreases in the supply of rental housing. (The short-run supply curve, which is drawn as a vertical line, indicates that a change in price will not result in any change in the quantity of apartments supplied in the short run.[4])

Under the conditions shown, the equilibrium rent per standard housing unit is $500 per month for each of the 100,000 units in the city. Now suppose that a rent ceiling of $250 is imposed. The result is a gain to tenants of $250 per unit per month. The total sum transferred to tenants is $250 per unit times 100,000 units, or $25 million, in all. In graphical terms, that sum is equal to the area of the shaded rectangle in Exhibit 2.11. The benefit to tenants at the expense of landlords is the principal intended effect of rent control.

[4]This is a fairly restrictive assumption. In practice, a small number of housing units can move into or out of the rental market quickly in response to changing conditions. "Mother-in-law apartments" in private homes are an example. If conditions in the rental market are unfavorable, the owners of such units may simply leave them vacant. Allowing for such fast-reaction units means that the short-run supply curve, while still quite steep, would not be vertical. However, a vertical short-run curve simplifies the geometry while capturing the essential features of the situation.

Exhibit 2.11   Effects of Rent Control

Part (a) shows the short-run effects of rent control. In the short run, the supply of
rental apartments is considered to be fixed. The equilibrium rent is $500 per
month. A rent ceiling of $250 per month is then put into effect. One possible
outcome is that landlords will charge disguised rent increases, raising the true
price back to $500 per month. If such disguised increases are prohibited, there
will be a shortage of 50,000 units at the ceiling price. Part (b) shows the long-run
effects when there is time to adjust the number of units in response to the price.
If the ceiling price is enforced, landlords move down their supply curve to E_2. The
shortage then becomes even more severe than in the short run.

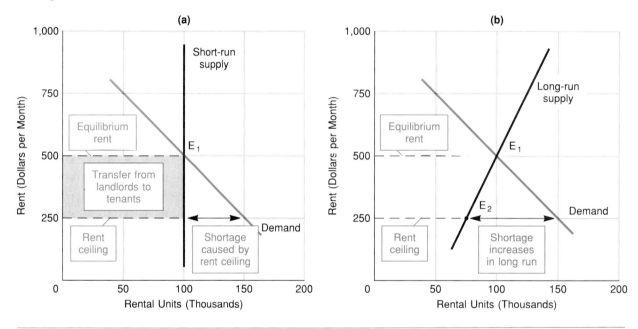

Unintended effects.   The policy of rent control, which does accomplish its goal
of benefiting tenants at the expense of landlords, provides a classic illustration of
the law of unintended consequences. In the short run, when the stock of apartments is fixed, the unintended consequences stem from the apartment shortage
created by the controls. The shortage occurs because the quantity demanded is
greater at the lower ceiling price than at the higher equilibrium price.

The greater quantity demanded has several sources. First, people who
would otherwise own a house or condominium may now want to rent. Second,
people who would otherwise live in non-rent-controlled suburbs may now seek
rent-controlled units in the city. Third, each tenant may want more space, which
results in a demand for more of the standardized units shown in Exhibit 2.11.

The shortage creates a problem for both landlords and tenants: How will the
limited supply of apartments be rationed among those who want them? Both
landlords and tenants devise a number of creative responses—*entrepreneurial*
responses, as an economist would say.

One response on the part of landlords is to seek disguised rent increases.
These may take the form of large, nonrefundable "key deposits" or security
deposits. As an alternative, they may sell old, used furniture or drapes at inflated

prices as a condition for renting the apartment. Finally, the costs of certain maintenance or security services for which the landlord might otherwise have paid may be transferred to tenants.

Tenants too may get into the act. When they decide to move, they may sublet their apartments to other tenants rather than give up their leases. Now it is the tenant who collects the key money or sells the old drapes to the subtenant. The original tenant may have moved to a distant city but maintains a bank account and a post office box for use in paying the rent. The subtenant is instructed to play the role of a "guest" if the landlord telephones. This charade may become quite elaborate and can go on for decades in cities such as New York, where rent control is long established, as illustrated by *Economics in the News 2.2.*

Advocates of rent control view these responses as cheating and often try to outlaw them. If prohibitions are enforced, the landlord will find that there are many applicants for each vacant apartment. In that case the landlord must decide to whom to rent the apartment. In his book *Rent Control: The Perennial Folly*, Charles W. Baird describes the effects as follows:

> People with unconventional life styles will be told to look elsewhere. Families without children will be favored over families with children. Tenants without pets will be favored over tenants with pets. . . . Families whose heads have histories of steady employment will be favored over families whose heads are just beginning employment or frequently change jobs. Landlords know from experience that people with steady employment histories tend to be more dependable in paying their bills.

Economics in the News 2.2
Stalking the Rent-Controlled Tenant

NEW YORK—The landlord wanted to sell the seven-room, 4-1/2 bath apartment overlooking the East River, and Vincent Parco, private eye, agreed to take the case.

The target: a rent-controlled tenant, a.k.a. actress Ann Turkel, who was paying a mere $2,300 a month for an apartment worth at least $1 million on the cooperative market. The objective: To terminate Turkel's lease with extreme prejudice.

Enter the fast-talking Parco, one of a growing breed of housing detectives here. His sleuths found evidence that Turkel spent nine or 10 months a year in Beverly Hills, had a California driver's license and should not be considered a "primary tenant" under New York law.

A housing court judge ruled in Turkel's favor, saying she retained a New Yorker's "state of mind" because she never removed her furs, jewelry, and artwork from the East 58th Street pied-à-terre. But an appeals court overturned the ruling last fall and sent Turkel packing.

Thousands of landlords and tenants are driven to deceptions large and small under New York City's 40-year-old rent-control laws, which have so distorted the housing market here that both sides must engage in a constant form of guerilla warfare.

"We've got plenty of low-income housing in New York," says veteran developer Seymour Durst. "But much of it is occupied by upper-income people."

The rent-control rolls are filled with prominent names like Mia Farrow, Daren McGavin, and fashion designer Arnold Scaasi, who pays $985 for a six-room duplex overlooking Central Park.

Many politicians benefit as well. Mayor Edward I. Koch (D), who earns $110,000 a year, has three rooms in Greenwich Village for $350 a month. Alexander B. Grannis, chairman of the state Assembly's housing committee, lives in a fashionable doorman building on East 87th Street for $870 a month. A similar two-bedroom apartment in a new high-rise three blocks to the north rents for $2,740 a month.

"It's a very, very tough political issue," Grannis said. "Half the tenants in the city are paying 40 or 50 percent of their income for rent, with controls. Otherwise they'd be homeless. But there are also very wealthy people we shouldn't be helping out with regulated apartments. It's a chance system."

Source: Howard Kurtz, "Stalking the Rent-Controlled Tenant," *The Washington Post*, April 5, 1988, A3. © 1988 The Washington Post, reprinted with permission.

If a landlord has applicants for a vacancy who are alike as far as family and job considerations are concerned, he will tend to pick the applicant whose non-economic characteristics — for example, race or religion — are most appealing to him. The other applicants will be put on the waiting list and sent to look elsewhere. People who make decisions based wholly on economic considerations are often accused of being crass, materialistic, and uncaring. However, when people are forbidden to make decisions on the basis of economic criteria, they may well use other criteria that are even more uncharitable.[5]

Unintended effects in the long run.   In the long run, rent control has other unintended effects. The long run in this case means enough time for the number of rental units to grow through construction of new units or shrink through abandonment of old ones (or their conversion to condominiums). Other things being equal, the higher the rent, the greater the rate of construction, and the lower the rent, the greater the rate of abandonment and/or conversion. This is reflected in the positively sloped long-run supply curve in part (b) of Exhibit 2.11.

If rent controls are enforced in such a way that there are no disguised charges by landlords, the number of rental units shrinks and the market moves from E_1 to E_2. At E_2, the unintended effects that appeared in the short run become more pronounced. The intensity of housing discrimination increases relative to the short-run case, because the difference between the number of units available and the number sought by renters increases. Graphically, that difference is shown by the horizontal gap between the supply and demand curves at the ceiling price. In the short run, there is a shortage of 50,000 units; in the long run, the shortage increases to 75,000 units.

Rent controls are often defended as being beneficial to the poor. But when all of the unintended effects of rent control are taken into account, one may question whether poor families really benefit. In cases in which disguised rent increases are possible, the true cost of rental housing is not really decreased. Further, it is hard to believe that landlords' tendency to discriminate against minority group members, single-parent families, and tenants with irregular work histories will benefit the poor. The most likely beneficiaries of rent control are stable, middle-class families who work at the same jobs and live in the same apartments for long periods.

Given the many unintended consequences of rent controls, one might legitimately wonder why the policy retains its popularity in many large cities. Why not replace rent control with some other form of housing assistance for the poor, for example, direct subsidies that would allow poor families to rent apartments at market-determined prices, as is already done in some cities? Some economists explain the popularity of rent control in terms of the political power of the middle-class tenants who are most likely to benefit from rent controls and who see helping the poor as nothing more than a convenient cover for simple self-interest. Some explain their popularity in terms of the short time horizon of government officials: the adverse effect on tenants of ending rent control would appear very quickly, whereas such benefits as increased construction of new apartments would materialize only long after the next election. And some attribute the popularity of rent control to the simple fact that many voters do not give much thought to the policy's unintended consequences.

---

[5]Charles W. Baird, *Rent Control: The Perennial Folly* (Washington, D.C.: The Cato Institution, 1980), 60–61.

Who Said It? Who Did It?   2.1
Alfred Marshall on Supply and Demand

Alfred Marshall, often considered to have been the greatest economist of his day, was born in London in 1842. His father was a Bank of England cashier who hoped the boy would enter the ministry. Young Marshall had other ideas, however. He turned down a theological scholarship at Oxford to study mathematics, receiving his M.A. from Cambridge in 1865.

While at Cambridge, Marshall joined a philosophical discussion group. There he became interested in promoting the broad development of the human mind. He was soon told, however, that the harsh realities of economics would prevent his ideas from being carried out. Britain's economic potential as a country, it was said, could never allow the masses sufficient leisure for education. This disillusioning episode appears to have triggered Marshall's fascination with economics.

At the time, British economics was dominated by the classical school founded by Adam Smith and David Ricardo. Marshall had great respect for the classical writers. Initially he saw his own work as simply applying his mathematical training to strengthen and systematize the classical system. Before long, however, he was breaking new ground and developing a system of his own. By 1890, when he brought out his famous *Principles of Economics*, he had laid the foundation of what we now call the neoclassical school.

In an attempt to explain the essence of his approach, Marshall included the following passage in the second edition of his *Principles:*

In spite of a great variety in detail, nearly all the chief problems of economics agree in that they have a kernel of the same kind. This kernel is an inquiry as to the balancing of two opposed classes of motives, the one consisting of desires to acquire certain new goods, and thus satisfy wants; while the other consists of desires to avoid certain efforts or retain certain immediate enjoyment . . . in other words, it is an inquiry into the balancing of the forces of demand and supply.

Marshall's influence on economics—at least in the English-speaking world—was enormous. His *Principles* was the leading economics text for several decades, and modern students can still learn much from it. As a professor at Cambridge, Marshall taught a great many of the next generation's leading economists. Today his neoclassical school continues to dominate the profession. It has received many challenges, but so far it has weathered them all.

Looking Ahead

This chapter has covered the basics of the supply-and-demand model and described a few applications of that model. There are many more applications in both macro- and microeconomics. In macroeconomics, the supply-and-demand model can be applied to financial markets, labor markets, and the problem of determining the rate of inflation and real output for the economy as a whole. In microeconomics, the model can be applied to product markets, markets for productive resources, and policy issues ranging from pollution to farm policy to international trade, to name just a few. As the great economist Alfred Marshall once put it, nearly all of the major problems of economics have a "kernel" that reflects the workings of supply and demand (see **Who Said It? Who Did It? 2.1**).

When a detailed look is taken at the underpinnings of the model, it appears to fit some kinds of markets more closely than others. The fit is best for markets in which there are many producers and many customers, the goods sold by one producer are much like those sold by others, and all sellers and buyers have good information on market conditions. Markets for farm commodities, such as wheat and corn, and financial markets, such as the New York Stock Exchange, meet these standards reasonably well.

However, even in markets that do not display all of these features, the fit is often close enough so that the supply-and-demand model provides useful insights into what is going on. The rental housing market is an example: Not all rental units are in fact alike, even when measurement is standardized for objective characteristics such as floor space. Nevertheless, most economists would agree that valid conclusions about the effects of rent control can be arrived at by applying the supply-and-demand model to that market. Thus, the supply-and-demand model serves a precise analytical function in some cases and a broader, metaphorical function in others. That flexibility makes the model one of the most useful items in the economist's tool kit.

Summary

1. **How does the price of a good or service affect the quantity of it that buyers demand?** Economists use the term *demand* to refer to the willingness and ability of buyers to purchase goods and services. According to the *law of demand*, there is an inverse relationship between the price of a good and the quantity of it that buyers demand. The *quantity demanded* is the quantity that buyers are willing and able to pay for. The law of demand can be represented graphically by a negatively sloped *demand curve*. A change in the quantity demanded is shown by a movement along the demand curve.

2. **How do other market conditions affect demand?** A change in any of the variables covered by the "other things being equal" clause of the law of demand causes a shift in the demand curve; this is known as a *change in demand*. Examples include changes in the prices of goods that are *substitutes* or *complements* of the good in question as well as changes in consumer incomes, expectations, and tastes.

3. **How does the price of a good affect the quantity supplied by sellers?** *Supply* refers to sellers' willingness and ability to offer products for sale in a market. In most markets an increase in the price of a good will increase the quantity of the good that sellers are willing to supply. This relationship can be shown as a positively sloped *supply curve*. The higher price gives producers an incentive to supply more, but rising opportunity costs set a limit on the amount they will supply at any given price.

4. **How do changes in other market conditions affect supply?** A change in any of the items covered by the "other things being equal" clause of the supply curve will shift the curve. Examples include changes in technology, changes in the prices of inputs, changes in the prices of other goods that could be produced with the same resources, and changes in expectations.

5. **How do supply and demand interact to determine the market price of a good or service?** In a market with an upward-sloping supply curve and a downward-sloping demand curve, there is only one price at which the quantity of a good that sellers plan to supply will exactly match the quantity that buyers plan to purchase. That is known as the *equilibrium* price. At any higher price there will be a *surplus*, and at any lower price there will be a *shortage*.

6. **Why do market prices and quantities change in response to changes in market conditions?** A change in any market condition that shifts the supply or demand curve will change the equilibrium price and quantity in a market. For example, the demand curve may shift to the right as a result of a change in consumer incomes. This causes a shortage at the old price, and the price begins to rise. As the price rises, suppliers move up along the supply curve to a new equilibrium. No shift in the supply curve is required. On the other hand, better technology may shift the supply curve to the right. In that case there is a surplus at the old price, and the price will fall. As the price decreases, buyers will move down along their demand curve to a new equilibrium. No shift in the demand curve is required.

7. **How do price supports and price ceilings affect the operation of markets?** A price support prevents the market price from falling when the demand curve shifts to the left or the supply curve shifts to the right. The result may be a lasting surplus. The government may have to buy and store the surplus to maintain the price, as in the case of milk. A price ceiling prevents the price from rising to its equilibrium level. The result may be a permanent shortage. The total quantity supplied may then be less than the quantity that buyers would like to purchase at the ceiling price or even at the equilibrium price, as in the case of rent control.

Terms for Review

- supply
- demand
- law of demand
- demand curve
- change in quantity demanded
- change in demand
- substitutes
- complements
- normal good
- inferior good
- supply curve
- change in quantity supplied
- change in supply
- equilibrium
- excess quantity demanded (shortage)
- inventory
- excess quantity supplied (surplus)

Questions for Review

1. How does the concept of demand differ from the concepts of want and need?

2. What conditions are covered by the "other things being equal" clause in the law of demand? What effect does a change in any of these conditions have on buyers' plans?

3. Using an example from agriculture or industry, explain why we normally expect the supply curve for a good to have a positive slope. Give examples of events that can cause a supply curve to shift.

4. How do inventories put upward or downward pressure on prices when markets are not in equilibrium? How is equilibrium restored in markets that have no inventories of finished goods?

5. Describe each of the following in terms of shifts in or movements along supply and demand curves: (a) the reaction of a market to an increase in supply; (b) the reaction of a market to a decrease in demand.

6. Will a price support that is lower than the equilibrium price lead to a surplus, a shortage, or neither? What about a price ceiling that is higher than the equilibrium price?

Problems and Topics for Discussion

1. **Examining the lead-off case.** Discuss the process through which chicken has replaced beef as the leading meat item in Americans' diets. Has there been a shift in demand for beef or chicken or both? If so, describe the nature of the shift, citing specific passages in the case. Has there been a shift in the supply curve for beef or chicken, or both? If so, describe the nature of the shift, citing specific passages from the case. Draw a diagram to illustrate the changes that have taken place in the market for chicken. Compare your diagram with those in Exhibit 2.9. Under what conditions does a movement to a new equilibrium involve a shift in just one curve? Under what conditions does it involve a shift in both curves? Which case applies here?

2. **A shifting demand curve.** A vending machine company has studied the demand for soft drinks sold in cans from machines. On a 70-degree day consumers in the firm's territory will buy about 2,000 cans of soda at a price of $.50. For each $.05 rise in price, the quantity sold falls by 200 cans per day; for each 5-degree rise in the temperature, the quantity sold rises by 150 cans per day. The same relationships hold for decreases in price or temperature. Using this information, draw a set of curves showing the demand for soft drinks on days when the temperature is 60, 70, and 85 degrees. Then draw a separate diagram with temperature on the vertical axis and quantity of soda on the horizontal axis. Draw a line representing the relationship between temperature and quantity when the price of soda is $.50. Next draw additional temperature-quantity lines for prices of $.40 and $.60. Do the two diagrams give the same information? Discuss. (Note: If you have any trouble with this exercise, review the Chapter 1 appendix, "Working with Graphs," especially the section entitled "Packing Three Variables into Two Dimensions.")

3. **Demand and the relative price of motor fuel.** In 1979 and 1980 the nominal price of motor fuel rose much more rapidly than the general price level, pushing up the relative price of motor fuel. As we would expect, the quantity sold decreased. In 1981 and 1982 the relative price leveled off and then began to fall, but the quantity sold continued to fall. Which one or more of the following hypotheses do you think best explains the behavior of motor fuel sales in 1981 and 1982? Illustrate each hypothesis with supply and demand curves.

   a. In the 1970s the demand curve had the usual negative slope. However, in 1981 and 1982 the demand curve shifted to an unusual positively sloped position.

   b. The demand curve had a negative slope throughout the period. However, the recession of 1981 and 1982 reduced consumers' real incomes and thus shifted the demand curve.

   c. The demand curve has a negative slope at all times, but the shape depends partly on how much time consumers have to adjust to a change in prices. Over a short period, the demand curve is fairly steep because few adjustments can be made. Over the long term, it has a somewhat flatter slope because further adjustments, such as buying more fuel-efficient cars or moving closer to the job, can be made. Thus, the decreases in fuel sales in 1981 and 1982 were delayed reactions to the price increases that occurred in 1979 and 1980.

4. **Shortages, price controls, and queues.** In 1974 and again in 1979, a decrease in worldwide oil supplies caused long lines of motorists to form at gas stations in the United States but not in European countries. Do you think the lines had anything to do with the fact that the United States had price controls on gasoline but European countries did not? Back up your reasoning with supply and demand curves.

5. **Eliminating queues through flexible pricing.** You are a member of the Metropolitan Taxi Commission, which sets taxi fares for your city. You have been told that long lines of taxis form at the airport during off-peak hours. At rush hours, on the other hand, few taxis are available and there are long lines of passengers waiting for cabs. It is proposed that taxi fares from the airport to downtown be cut by 10 percent during off-peak hours and raised by 10 percent during rush hours. How do you think these changes would affect the queueing patterns of taxis and passengers?

Do you think the proposal is a good one from the passengers' point of view? From the cabbies' point of view? From the standpoint of economic efficiency? Discuss.

6. **Rent control.** Turn to part (b) of Exhibit 2.11 (p. 66), which shows the long-run effects of rent control. If the controls are enforced and there are no disguised rent charges, landlords move down the supply curve to E_2. Buildings are abandoned or converted because of the low rent they bring in. Now consider some alternative possibilities:

   a. Suppose that the controls are poorly enforced so that landlords, through key deposits, furniture sales, or some other means, are able to charge as much as the market will bear. What will the resulting equilibrium price and quantity be, taking both open and disguised rental charges into account?

   b. Now suppose that the controls are enforced so that landlords really cannot collect more than $250 per month. However, the controls are not enforced against tenants who sublet. What will the equilibrium quantity and price be, including both the rent paid to landlords and the disguised rental payments made by subtenants to their sublessors?

Case for Discussion
What's Good for America Isn't Necessarily Good for the Dentists

When Dr. Murray Helfman set up his practice twenty-five years ago, fortune seemed to smile on him. Dentistry, which began as a sideline for barbers, had become a respected profession. Jokes about rich dentists were popular. By the early 1970s dentists' incomes were finally approaching those of physicians.

But after a quarter-century in practice, Helfman, who lives in Rochester, New York, is hardly a rich man. He doesn't drive a Mercedes or own a country home. If his wife didn't help out by managing his office, he would have trouble making ends meet. He moans: "I have three kids in college and a house that I couldn't afford to live in if I hadn't bought it thirteen years ago."

The American Dental Association claims that the average dentist nets $59,530 a year, but that average number hides a lot. Adjusted for inflation, this figure has been shrinking since it peaked about a dozen years ago. Dentists' real net incomes are no higher now, on average, than they were in the early 1960s.

In the late 1960s federal officials decided that Americans were getting inadequate dental care, and the government began spending to encourage dental education. Old dental schools expanded while new ones opened. The result was too many dentists.

On top of this, there are fewer patients coming through the door. Are Americans neglecting their teeth? Hardly. The basic difficulty is simple. Cavity-filling has always been the bread-and-butter business of most dentists. But cavities are going the way of smallpox and polio in the United States. Tooth decay has declined by about 50 percent since the mid-1960s. According to the ADA, one out of three people of college age has never had a cavity. Army dentists, who see a cross section of society, used to tell horror stories about mouths full of rotten teeth. Now they see lots of cavity-free mouths. The reason for this? Better nutrition, for one thing. Fluoridation of drinking water is an even bigger factor.

For many dentists, then, the dream of affluence is fading. Instead of striving for wealth, many young dentists now settle for the security of salaried dentistry. Says Dr. Thomas Ciuchta, a 20-year-old graduate of Temple University School of Dentistry: "I see friends who have their own practices sitting idle two days a week with their expenses building up. I like the security of knowing exactly what I'm making."

Ciuchta gets his regular paycheck from a clinic called Dentalworks located in Hess's department store in Allentown, Pennsylvania. At such facilities (often franchises owned by nondentists), 40-hour weeks, including Saturdays, are the rule and starting salaries may be under $30,000.

Source: Richard Greene, "What's Good for America Isn't Necessarily Good for the Dentists," *Forbes*, August 13, 1984, 79–84.

Questions

1. Draw a supply-and-demand diagram to illustrate the market for dental services. Label the horizontal axis "Dentists per 100,000 People" and the vertical axis "Dentists' Earnings, Constant 1967 Dollars." Draw the supply and demand curves so that the initial equilibrium point is 40 dentists per 100,000 people and the initial earnings are $40,000 per year.

2. Now consider the effect of government-sponsored expansion of dental schools. Would this shift the supply curve for dentists? The demand curve? Both? What would happen to the equilibrium price and quantity?

3. Go back to the initial equilibrium and consider the effect, by itself, of the trend toward less tooth decay. Would this shift the supply curve? The demand curve? Both? How would it affect the equilibrium price and quantity?

4. Put the effects in questions 2 and 3 together on one diagram. Explain the process through which a new equilibrium is reached when both effects act at once.

5. Does the case contain any information about entrepreneurial responses to the changes in market conditions? If so, discuss those responses in terms of their intended effects on supply and demand curves.

Suggestions for Further Reading

Baird, Charles W. *Rent Control: The Perennial Folly.* Washington, D.C.: The Cato Institution, 1980.

This book describes the history and recent practice of rent control in the United States and elsewhere.

Breit, William, and Roger L. Ransom. *The Academic Scribblers.* 2d ed. New York: Holt, Rinehart and Winston, 1982.

Chapter 3 is an essay about Alfred Marshall, the founder of supply-and-demand analysis in its modern form. Chapters 1 and 2 provide useful background.

Campbell, Colin D., ed. *Wage and Price Controls in World War II: United States and Germany.* Washington, D.C.: American Enterprise Institute, 1971.

Vivid descriptions and insightful analysis of what happens when governments overrule the law of supply and demand.

Marshall, Alfred. *Principles of Economics,* various editions.

First published in 1891, this book is still readily understood even by beginning students.

3

Supply, Demand, and Elasticity

Before reading this chapter, make sure you know the meaning of:

Supply and demand (Chapter 2)

Substitutes and complements (Chapter 2)

Normal and inferior goods (Chapter 2)

After reading this chapter, you will understand:

How the responsiveness of quantity demanded to a price change can be expressed in terms of elasticity.

How elasticity applies to situations other than the responsiveness of the quantity of a good demanded to a change in its price.

How elasticity affects the distribution of the economic burden of a tax.

In what ways elasticity is useful for understanding farm policy.

A Bug in the Salad Bowl

WASHINGTON, D.C., JANUARY 1988—There's a bug in America's salad bowl, and it's causing all kinds of pain.

A devastating virus outbreak on farms in California and Arizona, which ship about 10,000 tons of lettuce to market every day in the cold-weather months, has cut production by some 25 percent, impaired quality and boosted the average price by 300 percent in some areas.

The infectious yellows virus, in combination with quirky cold and wet weather, is expected to continue crimping production through January and hold prices well above average until crops from other areas begin moving to market in early spring.

"There's not going to be an overnight cure," said Wade Whitfield, president of the California Iceberg Lettuce Commission at Monterey. "The thing that's hard to see is how long this problem will go on. It was supposed to have ended at the end of the year, but I think it will persist through January."

Although the pinch has squeezed consumers, with lettuce retailing in some Washington supermarkets for nearly $2 a head, Whitfield said the situation "has not been an economic disaster" for farmers. "Most growers have come out okay because the . . . prices were up so much," he said.

The outbreak in the Imperial Valley of California and around Yuma, Arizona—the main winter lettuce areas—has set off a scientific scramble for ways to combat the virus and the sweet potato whitefly that carries it into the fields.

Department of Agriculture scientists have identified wild lettuce strains that appear to be resistant to the virus. But they said it may take years to successfully breed these traits into the domestic types that are grown in the West.

Meanwhile, other scientists are pursuing ways to isolate and eliminate the virus and to persuade farmers to change cultivation techniques that may be contributing to spread of the disease.

Source: Ward Sinclair, "Virus Eats into Lettuce Production; Price Soars," *The Washington Post*, January 6, 1988, A7. © 1988 The Washington Post, reprinted with permission.

In the preceding chapter we saw many examples of supply and demand in action. Now we will shift our focus somewhat. Instead of looking only at the direction of changes that result from changing supply and demand conditions, we will stress the size of the changes.

As the case of the lettuce virus shows, the size of the price change associated with a given change in quantity demanded is crucial. We know that a reduction in supply will cause a rise in price as consumers move up along their demand curve. But how much of a hardship will the poor crop cause for farmers? If the price rises only a little, farmers will be hit hard. But if, as in the case at hand, the price rises sharply enough, the greater price per unit will more than compensate farmers as a group for the reduction in the overall size of the crop. This chapter provides a framework for approaching such questions. The methods introduced here have many applications in both macro- and microeconomics.

3.1   Elasticity

The responsiveness of one economic variable to a change in another can be expressed in many ways, depending on the units of measurement that are chosen. Take the quantity of lettuce demanded by consumers. We could say that each $1 increase in the price *per carton* would reduce the quantity demanded by 100,000 50-pound *cartons per day*. Or we could say that each $1 increase in the price *per ton* would reduce quantity demanded by 437.5 *tons per week*. Although it takes a few minutes with a calculator to verify the fact, these two statements are equivalent; only the units differ.

To avoid confusion arising from the choice of different units of measurement, it is useful to standardize. One common way of doing so is to express all changes as percentages. For example, the news item reports that a 25 percent reduction in quantity was associated with a 300 percent increase in price. These percentages would stay the same regardless of whether the original data were stated in dollars per ton, crates per week, or any other measurement.

The use of percentages to express the response of one variable to a change in another is widespread in economics. The term **elasticity** is used to refer to relationships expressed in this way. Like equilibrium, elasticity is a metaphor borrowed from physics. Much as equilibrium calls to mind a pendulum that has come to rest hanging straight down, elasticity conjures up the image of a rubber band that stretches by a certain percentage of its length when the force applied to it is increased by a given percentage. This chapter introduces several applications of elasticity in economics.

Elasticity
A measure of the response of one variable to a change in another stated as a ratio of percentage changes.

Price Elasticity of Demand

We begin with the relationship between price and quantity demanded. The **price elasticity of demand** is the ratio of the percentage change in the quantity of a good demanded to a given percentage change in its price. Exhibit 3.1 presents five demand curves showing different degrees of price elasticity of demand.

In part (a), the quantity demanded is relatively responsive to a change in price. In this case a decrease in price from $5 to $3 causes the quantity demanded to increase from three units to six. Because the percentage change in quantity demanded is greater than that in price, the drop in price causes total revenue from sales of the good to increase. **Revenue** is the price times the

Price elasticity of demand
The ratio of the percentage change in the quantity of a good demanded to a given percentage change in its price, other things being equal.

Revenue
Price times quantity sold.

Exhibit 3.1 Price Elasticity of Demand

This exhibit shows five examples of demand curves having various degrees of elasticity over the indicated range of variation of price and quantity. The examples illustrate elastic, inelastic, unit elastic, perfectly inelastic, and perfectly elastic demand. For the first three cases, the revenue change associated with a change in price is shown. When demand is elastic, a price decrease causes revenue to increase. When demand is inelastic, a price decrease causes revenue to decrease. When demand is unit elastic, revenue does not change when price changes.

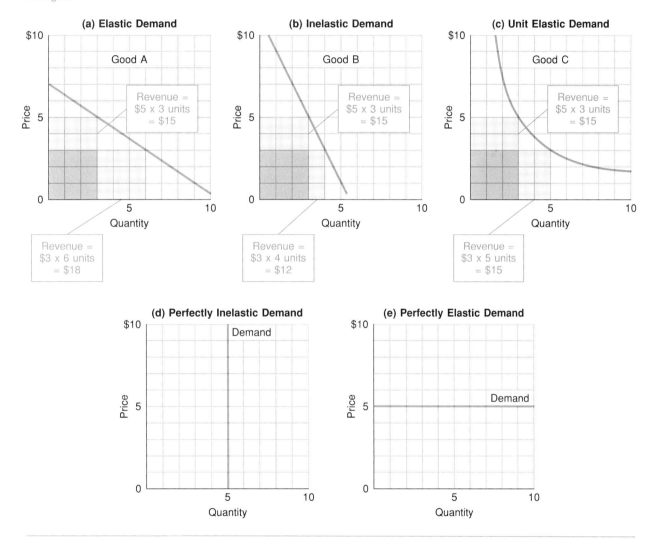

quantity sold. On a supply-and-demand diagram, revenue can be shown as the area of a rectangle drawn under the demand curve, with a height equal to price and a width equal to quantity demanded. In this case comparison of the shaded rectangles representing revenue before the price reduction ($5 per unit × 3 units = $15) and afterward ($3 per unit × 6 units = $18) shows that revenue is

Elastic demand
A situation in which
quantity demanded changes
by a larger percentage than
price and total revenue
therefore increases as price
decreases.

Inelastic demand
A situation in which
quantity demanded changes
by a smaller percentage than
price and total revenue
therefore decreases as price
decreases.

Unit elastic demand
A situation in which price
and quantity demanded
change by the same
percentage and total revenue
therefore remains unchanged
as price changes.

Perfectly inelastic demand
A situation in which the
demand curve is a vertical
line.

Perfectly elastic demand
A situation in which the
demand curve is a horizontal
line.

greater after the price has been reduced. When the quantity demanded changes by a greater percentage than price, so that a price decrease causes total revenue to increase, demand is said to be **elastic.**

Part (b) of Exhibit 3.1 shows a case in which the quantity demanded is relatively unresponsive to a change in price. Here a $2 decrease in price, from $5 to $3 per unit, causes the quantity demanded to increase by just one unit—from three to four. This time the percentage change in quantity demanded is less than that in price. As a result, the decrease in price causes total revenue to fall (again note the shaded rectangles). In such a case demand is said to be **inelastic.**

Part (c) shows a case in which a change in price causes an exactly proportional change in quantity demanded, so that total revenue does not change at all. When the percentage change in quantity demanded equals the percentage change in price, demand is said to be **unit elastic.**

The final two parts of Exhibit 3.1 show two extreme cases. Part (d) shows a vertical demand curve. Regardless of the price, the quantity demanded is five units—no more, no less. Such a demand curve is said to be **perfectly inelastic.** Part (e) shows a demand curve that is perfectly horizontal. Above a price of $5, no units of the good can be sold; but as soon as the price drops to $5, there is no limit on how much can be sold. A horizontal demand curve like this one is described as **perfectly elastic.** The law of demand, which describes an inverse relationship between price and quantity, does not encompass the cases of perfectly elastic and inelastic demand, and we do not expect market demand curves for ordinary goods and services to fit these extremes. Nevertheless, we will see that perfectly elastic and inelastic curves, as limiting cases, sometimes provide useful reference points for theory building even though they are not descriptive of real-world market demand curves.

Calculating Elasticity of Demand

In speaking of elasticity of demand, it is often enough to say that demand is elastic or inelastic, without being more precise. At other times, though, it is useful to attach numerical values to elasticity. This section introduces the most common method used to calculate a numerical value for elasticity of demand.

Percentage changes.   The first step in turning the general definition of elasticity into a numerical formula is to develop a way to measure percentage changes. The everyday method for calculating a percentage change is to use the initial value of the variable as the denominator and the change in the value as the numerator. For example, if the quantity of lettuce demanded is initially 10,000 tons per week and then decreases by 2,500 tons per week, we say that there has been a 25 percent change (2,500/10,000 = .25). The trouble with this convention is that the same change in the opposite direction gives a different percentage. By everyday reasoning, an increase in the quantity of lettuce demanded from 7,500 tons per week to 10,000 tons per week is a 33 percent increase (2,500/7,500 = .33).

Decades ago, economists decided that it would be nice to have a measurement of elasticity that would make a flagpole just as tall from top to bottom as it is from bottom to top. The eminent mathematical economist R. G. D. Allen proposed using the midpoint of the range over which change takes place as the denominator. Allen's midpoint formula is not the only possible one, but it caught on and remains the most popular.

To find the midpoint of the range over which a change takes place, we take the sum of the initial value and the final value and divide by 2. In our example, the midpoint of the quantity range is $(7,500 + 10,000)/2 = 8,750$. When this is used as the denominator, a change of 2,500 units becomes (approximately) a 28.6 percent change $(2,500/8,750 = .286)$. Using Q_1 to represent the quantity before the change and Q_2 to represent the quantity after the change, the midpoint formula for the percentage change in quantity is

$$\text{Percentage change in quantity} = \frac{Q_2 - Q_1}{(Q_1 + Q_2)/2}.$$

The same approach can be used to define the percentage change in price. In our case, the price of lettuce increased from about $250 per ton to about $1,000 per ton. The everyday method would lead to the conclusion that there had been a 300 percent increase, using the starting price as the denominator. Instead, we use the midpoint of the range, or $625, as the denominator ($250 + $1,000/2 = $625). We thus conclude that the $750 increase in price is a 120 percent increase ($750/$625 = 1.2). The midpoint formula for the percentage change in price is

$$\text{Percentage change in price} = \frac{P_2 - P_1}{(P_1 + P_2)/2}.$$

The midpoint formula for elasticity. Defining percentage changes in this way allows us to write a useful formula for calculating elasticities. With P_1 and Q_1 representing price and quantity before a change and P_2 and Q_2 representing price and quantity after, the midpoint formula for elasticity is

$$\begin{array}{c}\text{Price}\\ \text{elasticity}\\ \text{of demand}\end{array} = \frac{(Q_2 - Q_1)/(Q_1 + Q_2)}{(P_2 - P_1)/(P_1 + P_2)} = \frac{\text{Percentage change in quantity}}{\text{Percentage change in price}}.$$

Here is the complete calculation for the elasticity of demand for lettuce when an increase in price from $250 per ton to $1,000 per ton causes the quantity demanded to fall from 10,000 tons per day to 7,500 tons per day:

P_1 = price before change = $250

P_2 = price after change = $1,000

Q_1 = quantity before change = 10,000

Q_2 = quantity after change = 7,500

$$\begin{aligned}\text{Elasticity} &= \frac{(7,500 - 10,000)/(7,500 + 10,000)}{(\$1,000 - \$250)/(\$1,000 + \$250)}\\ &= \frac{-2,500/17,500}{\$750/\$1,250}\\ &= \frac{-.142}{.6}\\ &= -.24\end{aligned}$$

Because demand curves have negative slopes, this formula yields a negative value for elasticity. The reason is that the quantity demanded changes in the direction opposite to that of the price change. When the price decreases, $(P_2 - P_1)$, which appears in the denominator of the formula, is negative whereas $(Q_2 - Q_1)$, which appears in the numerator, is positive. When the price increases, the numerator is negative and the denominator is positive. However, in this book we follow the widely used practice of dropping the minus sign when discussing price elasticity of demand. Thus, the elasticity of demand for lettuce would be stated as approximately .24 over the range studied.

A numerical elasticity value such as .24 can be related to the basic definition of elasticity in a simple way. That definition stated that price elasticity of demand is the ratio of the percentage change in quantity demanded to a given percentage change in price. Thus, an elasticity of .24 means that the quantity demanded will increase by .24 percent for each 1 percent change in price. An elasticity of 3 would mean that quantity demanded would change by 3 percent for each 1 percent change in price, and so on.[1]

Elasticity Values and Terminology

Earlier in the chapter we defined *elastic, inelastic, unit elastic, perfectly elastic,* and *perfectly inelastic* demand. Each of these terms corresponds to a numerical value or range of values of elasticity as calculated using the midpoint formula. A perfectly inelastic demand curve has a numerical value of 0, since any change in price produces no change in quantity demanded. The term *inelastic* (but not perfectly inelastic) *demand* applies to numerical values from 0 up to, but not including, 1. *Unit elasticity,* as the name implies, means a numerical value of exactly 1. *Elastic demand* means any value for elasticity that is greater than 1. *Perfectly elastic* demand, represented by a horizontal demand curve, is not defined numerically; as the demand curve becomes horizontal, the denominator of the elasticity formula approaches 0 and the numerical value of elasticity increases without limit.

Varying- and Constant-Elasticity Demand Curves

The midpoint formula shows elasticity of demand over a certain range of prices and quantities. Measured over some other range, the elasticity of demand for the same good may be the same or different, depending on the shape of the demand curve, as shown in Exhibit 3.2.

A linear demand curve. Part (a) of Exhibit 3.2 shows a demand curve that, like most of those in this book, is a straight line. The elasticity of demand is not

---

[1] As we have said, the midpoint formula (also sometimes called *arc-elasticity*) is not the only one for calculating elasticity. A drawback of this formula is that it can give misleading elasticity values if applied over too wide a variation in price or quantity. Because of this limitation, it is often suggested that the midpoint formula be used only over fairly small ranges of variation in price or quantity. Following this reasoning to its logical conclusion, there is an alternative formula for calculating elasticity for a single point on the demand curve. For a linear demand curve having the formula $q = a - bp$ (with q representing quantity demanded, p the price, and a and b being constants), the *point formula* for elasticity of demand (stated, as elsewhere, as a positive number) is

$$\text{Elasticity} = bp/(a - bp).$$

Exhibit 3.2   Elasticity at Various Points along a Demand Curve

Elasticity varies along a straight-line demand curve, as part (a) of this exhibit illustrates. At the upper end of the curve, where the price is relatively high, a $1 change in price is a relatively small percentage change, and, because the quantity demanded is low, the corresponding quantity change is relatively large in percentage terms. Demand is thus elastic near the top of the demand curve. At the lower end of the curve, the situation is reversed; a $1 change in price is now a relatively large change in percentage terms, whereas the corresponding quantity change is smaller in percentage terms. Thus demand is inelastic. As part (b) shows, a curved demand curve can be drawn such that elasticity is constant for all ranges of price and quantity change.

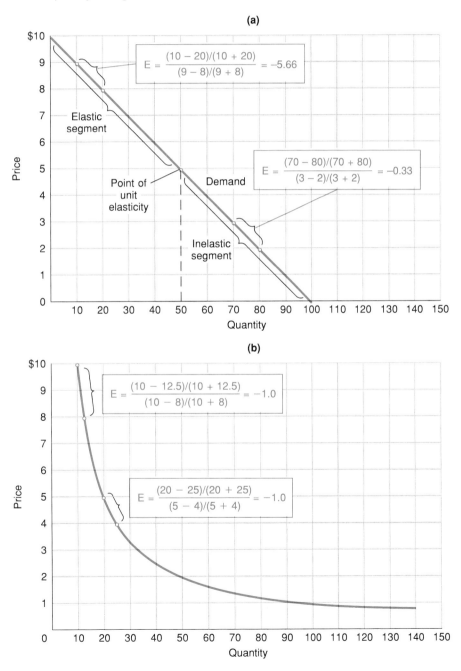

(a)

$$E = \frac{(10 - 20)/(10 + 20)}{(9 - 8)/(9 + 8)} = -5.66$$

$$E = \frac{(70 - 80)/(70 + 80)}{(3 - 2)/(3 + 2)} = -0.33$$

(b)

$$E = \frac{(10 - 12.5)/(10 + 12.5)}{(10 - 8)/(10 + 8)} = -1.0$$

$$E = \frac{(20 - 25)/(20 + 25)}{(5 - 4)/(5 + 4)} = -1.0$$

constant for all ranges of price and quantity along this curve. For example, when measured over the price range $8 to $9, the elasticity of demand is 5.66; when measured over the range $2 to $3, it is .33. (The calculations are shown in the exhibit.)

The calculations illustrate the general rule that elasticity declines as one moves downward along a straight-line demand curve. It is easy to see why. With such a demand curve, a $1 reduction in price always causes the same absolute increase in quantity demanded. At the upper end of the demand curve, a $1 change is a small percentage of the relatively high price, while the change in quantity is a large percentage of the relatively low quantity demanded at that price. At the lower end of the curve, however, the situation is reversed: A $1 change is now a large percentage of the relatively low price, while the increase in quantity is smaller in relation to the relatively larger quantity demanded. Because it is percentages, not absolute amounts, that matter in elasticity calculations, a linear demand curve is less elastic near the bottom than near the top.

A constant-elasticity demand curve.   If the demand curve is not a straight line, other results are possible. There is an important special case in which the demand curve has just the curvature needed to keep elasticity constant over its entire length. Such a curve is shown in part (b) of Exhibit 3.2. As can be seen from the calculations in the exhibit, elasticity is 1.0 at every point on that curve. It is possible to construct demand curves with constant elasticities of any value. Econometric studies of demand elasticity often look for the constant-elasticity demand curve that most closely approximates buyers' average sensitivity to price changes as revealed by market data over time.

Determinants of Elasticity of Demand

The fact that elasticity often varies along the demand curve means that care must be taken in making statements about *the* elasticity of demand for a good. In practice, what such statements usually refer to is the elasticity, measured by the midpoint formula or some alternative method, over the range of price variation that is commonly observed in the market for that good. With this understanding, we can make some generalizations about what makes the demand for some goods relatively elastic and the demand for others relatively inelastic.

Substitutes, complements, and elasticity.   One important determinant of elasticity of demand is the availability of substitutes. When a good has close substitutes, the demand for that good tends to be relatively elastic, because people willingly switch to the substitutes when the price of the good goes up. Thus, for example, the demand for corn oil is relatively elastic, because other cooking oils can usually be substituted for it. On the other hand, the demand for cigarettes is relatively inelastic, because for a habitual smoker there is no good substitute.

This principle has two corollaries. One is that the demand for a good tends to be more elastic the more narrowly the good is defined. For example, the demand for lettuce as a whole tends to be relatively inelastic, as the story at the beginning of the chapter illustrates. Many people are in the habit of eating a salad with dinner and do not think of spinach or coleslaw as completely satisfactory substitutes. At the same time, the demand for any particular variety of lettuce is relatively elastic. If the price of Boston lettuce rises while the prices of iceberg, romaine, and red-leaf lettuce remain unchanged, many people will readily switch to one of the other varieties, which they see as close substitutes.

The other corollary is that demand for the product of a single firm tends to be more elastic than the market demand for the same product, taking all producers into account. As one example, the demand for cigarettes as a whole will be less elastic than the demand for any particular brand, such as Viceroy or Winston. The reason is that one brand can be substituted for another when the price of a brand changes. As another example, the demand for Mrs. Field's cookies is more elastic than the demand for chocolate chip cookies as a whole, because buyers perceive the products of Famous Amos, Smart Cookie, and other firms to be close substitutes. We will return to this point in coming chapters.

The complements of a good can also play a role in determining its elasticity. If something is a minor complement to an important good (that is, one that accounts for a large share of consumers' budgets), demand for it tends to be relatively inelastic. For example, the demand for motor oil tends to be relatively inelastic, because it is a complement to a more important good, gasoline. The price of gasoline has a greater effect on the amount of driving a person does than the price of motor oil.

Time horizon and elasticity.   One of the most important considerations determining the price elasticity of demand is the time horizon within which the decision to buy is made. For several reasons, demand is less elastic in the short run than in the long run.

One reason is that full adjustment to a change in the price of a good may require changes in the kind or quantity of many other goods that a consumer buys. Gasoline provides a classic example. When the price of gasoline jumped in the 1970s, many people's initial reaction was to cut out some nonessential driving; the quantity of gasoline demanded fell only a little. As time went by, though, consumers adjusted in many ways. One important adjustment was to buy more fuel-efficient cars. Another was to base the choice of where to live partly on the length of the drive to work or the availability of public transportation. Gradually, as such adjustments were made, the quantity of gasoline demanded fell more than it had at first.

Another reason elasticity tends to be greater in the long run than in the short run is that an increase in the price of one good encourages entrepreneurs to develop substitutes—which, as we have seen, can be an important determinant of elasticity. To take an example from history, consider the response to what has been called America's first energy crisis, a sharp increase in the price of whale oil, which was used as lamp fuel in the early nineteenth century. At first candles were the only substitute for whale-oil lamps, and not a very satisfactory one. People therefore cut their use of whale oil only a little when the price began to rise. But the high price of whale oil spurred entrepreneurs to develop a better substitute, kerosene. Once kerosene came onto the market, the quantity of whale oil demanded for use as lamp fuel dropped to zero.

A final reason for greater elasticity of demand in the long run than in the short run is the slow adjustment of consumer tastes. The case of beef and chicken, featured in the preceding chapter, provides an example. Chicken, originally the more expensive meat, achieved a price advantage over beef many years ago. But eating lots of beef was a habit, a part of people's life-style, even a part of some people's self-image. Gradually, though, chicken developed an image as a healthy, stylish, versatile food, and finally it overtook beef as the number-one meat dish on the dinner tables of American families.

In later chapters we will see that the relative elasticity of long-run demand plays an important role both in business strategies and in economists' evaluation of the success of markets in meeting consumer needs.

Income Elasticity of Demand

The response of quantity demanded to a change in price is the most common application of the concept of elasticity, but by no means the only one. Elasticity can also be used to express the response of demand to any of the conditions covered by the "other things being equal" assumption on which a given demand curve is based. As we saw in the preceding chapter, one of those conditions is consumer incomes.

The **income elasticity of demand** for a good is defined as the ratio of the percentage change in the quantity of that good demanded to a percentage change in income. In measuring income elasticity, it is assumed that the good's price does not change. Using Q_1 and Q_2 to represent quantities before and after the change in income and y_1 and y_2 to represent income before and after the change, the midpoint formula for income elasticity of demand can be written as follows:

Income elasticity of demand
The ratio of the percentage change in the quantity of a good demanded to a given percentage change in consumer incomes, other things being equal.

$$\begin{matrix}\text{Income} \\ \text{elasticity} \\ \text{of demand}\end{matrix} = \frac{(Q_2 - Q_1)/(Q_1 + Q_2)}{(y_2 - y_1)/(y_1 + y_2)} = \frac{\text{Percentage change in quantity}}{\text{Percentage change in income}}.$$

The numerical value of income elasticity is linked to the concepts of normal and inferior goods. For a normal good, an increase in income causes demand to rise. Because income and demand change in the same direction, the income elasticity of demand for a normal good is positive. For an inferior good, an increase in income causes demand to decrease. Because income and demand change in opposite directions, the income elasticity of demand for an inferior good is negative.

Some of the considerations that determine price elasticity also affect income elasticity. In particular, whether a good is considered to be normal or inferior depends on how narrowly it is defined and on the availability of substitutes. For example, a study by Jonq-Ying Lee, Mark G. Brown, and Brooke Schwartz of the University of Florida looked at the demand for frozen orange juice.[2] Orange juice as a whole is a normal good; people tend to consume more of it as their income rises. However, when the definition is narrowed so that house-brand and national-brand frozen orange juice are treated as separate products, the house-brand product turns out to be an inferior good. As their incomes rise, consumers substitute the higher-quality national brands, which have a positive income elasticity of demand.

[2]Jonq-Ying Lee, Mark G. Brown, and Brooke Schwartz, "The Demand for National Brand and Private Label Frozen Concentrated Orange Juice: A Switching Regression Analysis," *Western Journal of Agricultural Economics* (July 1986): 1–7.

Cross-Elasticity of Demand

Another condition that can cause a change in the demand for a good is a change in the price of some other good. The demand for chicken is affected by changes in the price of beef, the demand for motor oil by changes in the price of gasoline, and so on. Such relationships can be expressed as elasticities: The **cross-elasticity of demand** for a good is defined as the ratio of the percentage change in the quantity of that good demanded to a given percentage change in the price of another good. The midpoint formula for cross-elasticity of demand looks just like the one for price elasticity of demand, except that the numerator shows the percentage change in the quantity of one good while the denominator shows the percentage change in the price of some other good.

Cross-elasticity of demand is related to the concepts of substitutes and complements. Because lettuce and cabbage are substitutes, an increase in the price of cabbage causes an increase in the quantity of lettuce demanded; the cross-elasticity of demand is positive. Because motor oil and gasoline are complements, an increase in the price of gasoline causes a decrease in the quantity of motor oil demanded; the cross-elasticity of demand is negative.

Econometric studies of demand for particular products such as that discussed in **Applying Economic Ideas 3.1** typically look at all three elasticities: price elasticity, income elasticity, and cross-elasticity. To take another example,

Cross-elasticity of demand
The ratio of the percentage change in the quantity of a good demanded to a given percentage change in the price of some other good, other things being equal.

Applying Economic Ideas 3.1
The Demand for Kerosene in Indonesia

Kerosene is a common lighting and cooking fuel in Indonesia. Since it accounts for a substantial fraction of Indonesia's imports (Indonesia exports oil and imports refined oil products such as kerosene), knowing something about the demand is important.

The kerosene demand curve was estimated by Ohio University economists Rajindar Koshal and Vishwa Shukla and by Hasang Rachmany of Indonesia. They reported their results at the May 1978 meeting of the Pan-Pacific conference in Singapore.

The three economists found that a straight-line demand curve for kerosene seemed to fit the data well. They found that the variables that affected the quantity of kerosene consumed in Indonesia were the price of kerosene, the price of electricity, and real per capita income.

All three variables affected the quantity demanded in the usual way. An increase in the price of kerosene reduced the quantity demanded. An increase in the price of elec-

tricity or an increase in income shifted the demand curve to the right.

The economists also found that the demand curve for kerosene was affected by noneconomic developments. Demand shifted to the right over the period 1957 to 1962 as a result of the political instability that accompanied the war to regain West Irian Island from the Dutch. It increased again with the instability that rocked Indonesia during the period of rising energy prices from 1975 to 1979.

Although the quantity of kerosene demanded was affected by price changes, it wasn't affected very much. A 10 percent increase in price, for example, produced only a 2.2 percent reduction in quantity demanded. That corresponds to a price elasticity of demand of .22.

The relationship between the demand for kerosene and the price of electricity suggested that the two are substitutes, but they aren't strong substitutes. A 10 percent increase in the price of electricity was estimated to increase kerosene demand by 1.6 percent, implying a cross-elasticity of demand of .16.

The demand for kerosene increased with increases in income, suggesting that kerosene is a normal good. The economists estimated that a 10 percent increase in income would increase kerosene demand by 9.7 percent, implying an income elasticity of demand of .97. All the percentage responses vary at different points on the demand curve.

Source: Timothy Tregarthen, "The Demand for Kerosene in Indonesia," *The Margin* (September–October 1988): 35. Reprinted with permission.

the previously mentioned study of frozen orange juice found a positive cross-elasticity of demand between house-brand and national-brand juices, indicating that the two are substitutes.

Price Elasticity of Supply

Price elasticity of supply
The ratio of the percentage change in the quantity of a good supplied to a given percentage change in its price, other things being equal.

Elasticity is not confined to demand; it can also be used to indicate the response of quantity supplied to a change in price. Formally, the **price elasticity of supply** of a good is defined as the percentage change in the quantity of the good supplied divided by the percentage change in its price. The midpoint formula for calculating price elasticity of supply looks like the one for determining price elasticity of demand, but the Qs in the numerator of the formula now refer to quantity *supplied* rather than quantity *demanded*. Because price and quantity change in the same direction along a positively sloped supply curve, the formula gives a positive value for the elasticity of supply. Exhibit 3.3 applies the elasticity formula to two supply curves, one with constant elasticity and the other with variable elasticity.

In later chapters we will look in detail at the considerations that determine the elasticity of supply for various products. Two of them are especially important.

One determinant of the elasticity of supply of a good is the mobility of the factors of production used to produce it. As used here, *mobility* means the ease with which factors can be attracted from some other use as well as the ease with which they can be reconverted to their original use. The trucking industry provides a classic example of mobile resources. As a crop such as lettuce or watermelons comes to harvest in a particular region of a country, hundreds of trucks are needed to haul it to market. Shippers compete for available trucks, driving up the price paid to truckers in the local market. Independent truckers throughout the country learn—from their own experience, from trucking brokers, and from CB radios—where they can earn the best rates for hauling produce. It takes only a modest rise in the price for hauling a load of Georgia watermelons to attract enough truckers to Georgia to haul the crop to market. When the harvest is over, the truckers will move elsewhere to haul peaches, tomatoes, or whatever.

In contrast, other products are produced with much less mobile resources. Petroleum provides a good example. In the 1970s, when oil prices rose, producers had an incentive to drill more wells. However, given limited numbers of drilling rigs and other highly specialized equipment, not to mention limited numbers of sites worth exploring, the tenfold increase in oil prices during the decade caused only a slight increase in oil output. Factor mobility in this industry is limited in the other direction also. Once a well has been drilled, the investment cannot be converted to a different use. Thus, in the 1980s, when oil prices fell again, production dropped by a much smaller percentage than price.

A second determinant of elasticity of supply is time. As in the case of demand, price elasticity of supply tends to be greater in the long run than in the short run. In part, the reason is connected with mobility of resources. In the short run the output of many products can be increased by using more of the most flexible inputs—for example, by adding workers at a plant or extending the hours of work. Such short-run measures often mean higher costs per unit for the added output, however, because workers added without comparable addi-

Exhibit 3.3   Calculating Price Elasticity of Supply

This exhibit gives four examples of the way price elasticity of supply is calculated. Price elasticity of supply is shown for two ranges on each of the two supply curves. Supply curve S_1, which is a straight line passing through the origin, has a constant elasticity of 1.0. Supply curve S_2, which is curved, is elastic for small quantities and inelastic for larger ones.

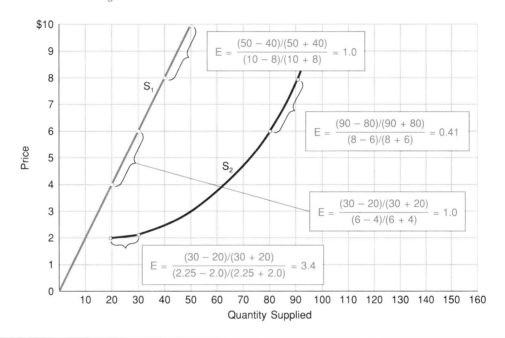

$$E = \frac{(50 - 40)/(50 + 40)}{(10 - 8)/(10 + 8)} = 1.0$$

$$E = \frac{(90 - 80)/(90 + 80)}{(8 - 6)/(8 + 6)} = 0.41$$

$$E = \frac{(30 - 20)/(30 + 20)}{(6 - 4)/(6 + 4)} = 1.0$$

$$E = \frac{(30 - 20)/(30 + 20)}{(2.25 - 2.0)/(2.25 + 2.0)} = 3.4$$

tions in other inputs tend to be less productive. If a firm expects market conditions to warrant an increase of supply in the long run, it will be worthwhile to invest in additional quantities of less mobile inputs of specialized plant and equipment. Once those investments have been made, the firm will find it worthwhile to supply the greater quantity of output at a lower price than in the short-run case because its costs per unit will be lower. In addition, over time the process of learning by doing improves the ability of producers to meet increased demand for a product, thereby making the supply curve more elastic.

3.2   Applications of Elasticity

Elasticity has many applications in both macro- and microeconomics. In macroeconomics, it can be applied to money markets, to the aggregate supply and demand for all goods and services, and to foreign-exchange markets, to name just a few. In microeconomics, elasticity plays a role in discussions of consumer behavior, the profit-maximizing behavior of business firms, governments' regulatory and labor policies, and many other areas. To further illustrate elasticity, we conclude this chapter with applications featuring the problems of tax incidence and farm policy.

Elasticity and Tax Incidence

Who pays taxes? One way to answer this question is in terms of *assessments*—the issue of who bears the legal responsibility to make tax payments to the government. A study of assessments would show that property owners pay property taxes, gasoline companies pay gasoline taxes, and so on. However, looking at assessments does not always settle the issue of who bears the economic burden of a tax—or, to use the economist's term, the issue of **tax incidence.**

Tax incidence
The distribution of the economic burden of a tax.

The incidence of a tax does not always coincide with the way the tax is assessed, because the economic burden of the tax, in whole or in part, often can be passed along to someone else. The degree to which the burden of a tax may be passed along depends on the elasticities of supply and demand. Let's consider some examples.

Incidence of a gasoline tax.   First consider the familiar example of a gasoline tax. Specifically, suppose that the state of Virginia decides to impose a tax of $.50 a gallon on gasoline beginning from a situation in which there is no tax. The tax is assessed against sellers of gasoline, who add the tax into the price paid by consumers at the pump.

Exhibit 3.4 uses the supply-and-demand model to show the effects of the tax. Initially the demand curve intersects supply curve S_1 at E_1, resulting in a price of $1 per gallon. The supply curve is elastic in the region of the initial equilibrium. The elasticity of supply reflects that we are dealing with the gasoline market in just one state; only a slight rise in the price in Virginia is needed to divert additional quantities of gasoline from elsewhere in the nation. The demand for gasoline is less elastic than the supply in the region of the initial equilibrium. Motorists—except those who live near the state line—cannot go

Exhibit 3.4 Incidence of a Tax on Gasoline

S_1 and D are the supply and demand curves before imposition of the tax. The initial equilibrium price is $1 per gallon. A tax of $.50 per gallon shifts the supply curve to S_2. To induce sellers to supply the same quantity as before, the price would have to rise to $1.50. However, as the price rises, buyers reduce the quantity demanded, moving up and to the left along the demand curve. In the new equilibrium at E_2, the price rises only to $1.40. After the tax is paid, sellers receive only $.90 per gallon. Thus, buyers bear $.40 of the tax on each gallon and sellers the remaining $.10. Buyers bear the larger share of the tax because demand, in this case, is less elastic than supply.

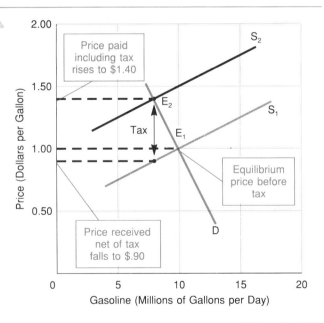

elsewhere to buy gas when the price rises in Virginia. However, they are not entirely unresponsive to a rise in price, because they can decide to drive less or switch to more fuel-efficient cars.

The effect of the tax is to shift the supply curve to the left until each point on the new supply curve is exactly $.50 higher than the point for the corresponding quantity on the old supply curve. (We could instead say that the supply curve shifts *upward* by $.50.) Because sellers must now turn over $.50 to the state government for each gallon of gas sold, they would have to get $1.50 per gallon to be willing to sell the same quantity (10 million gallons per day) as initially. However, when sellers attempt to pass the tax on to motorists, motorists respond by reducing the amount of gas they buy. As the quantity sold falls, sellers move down and to the left along supply curve S_2 to a new equilibrium at E_2.

In the new equilibrium, the price is $1.40 per gallon—just $.40 higher than the original price. The new price includes the $.50 tax, which sellers add on to their net price of $.90 per gallon—a net price that is $.10 less than before. The amount of the tax—$.50 per gallon—is shown by the vertical gap between the supply and demand curves. The economic burden of the tax is divided between buyers and sellers, but in this case it falls more heavily on the buyers.

Incidence of a tax on apartment rents.   In the preceding example, the incidence of the gasoline tax falls more heavily on buyers than on sellers because demand is less elastic than supply. If the elasticities are reversed, the results will also be reversed, as can be seen in the case of a tax on apartment rents.

In Exhibit 3.5 the market for rental apartments in a certain small city is initially in equilibrium at $500 per month. The supply of rental apartments is inelastic. An increase in rents will cause a few new apartments to be built, whereas a reduction will cause a few to be torn down, but in either case the response will be moderate. On the other hand, demand is fairly elastic, because potential renters consider houses or condominiums a fairly close substitute for rental apartments.

Exhibit 3.5   Incidence of a
Tax on Apartment Rents

This exhibit shows the incidence of a tax imposed in a market where supply is less elastic than demand. Initially the equilibrium rent is $500 per month. A $250-per-month tax on apartment rents shifts the supply curve to S_2. The new equilibrium is at E_2. Landlords end up absorbing all but $50 of the tax. If they tried to pass more of the tax on to renters, more renters would switch to owner-occupied housing, and the vacancy rate on rental apartments would rise.

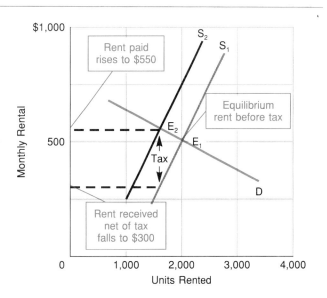

Given this situation, suppose that the local government decides to impose a tax of $250 per month on all apartments rented in the town. This tax, like the gasoline tax, is assessed against landlords, who include the tax payment in the monthly rental they charge to tenants. As in the previous example, the tax shifts the supply curve to the left until each point on the new supply curve lies above the corresponding point on the old supply curve by the amount of the tax. (Again, we could instead say the supply curve shifts upward by the amount of the tax.) After the shift, the market reaches a new equilibrium at E_2. There the rental price paid by tenants rises to only $550 per month—just $50 per month higher than initially. Landlords succeed in passing only $50 of the $250 monthly tax along to tenants. They are forced by supply-and-demand conditions to absorb the remaining $200 of the tax. Their net rental income, after turning over the tax receipts to the town government, is now just $300, down from $500 before imposition of the tax. In this case, because supply is inelastic and demand is elastic, suppliers bear most of the incidence of the tax and buyers only a little.

Measuring the incidence of taxes is not always as easy as it is in these examples. One reason is that it may be hard to get good estimates of the elasticities of supply and demand. Another is that more than two parties may be involved; for example, the burden of a corporate income tax may be shared among the firms' customers, stockholders, and employees. Finally, taxes interact with one another in complex ways. Thus, the incidence of an income tax may depend on the amounts of sales and property taxes that are already being paid.

However, in the more complex cases, as in the simple ones we have examined, it remains true that elasticities are a key determinant of tax incidence. If demand is relatively more price elastic than supply, sellers will bear the bulk of the economic burden of a tax. If supply is relatively more elastic than demand, the burden will fall relatively more heavily on buyers. The considerations that make demand or supply more elastic—more readily available substitutes, greater mobility, more time to adjust—are the considerations that enable the incidence of the tax to be shifted.

Elasticities and Farm Policy

The history of agriculture in the United States has been one of steady technological advances and rising productivity. Yet these breakthroughs have not brought uniform prosperity to the farm economy. Instead, the record has been one of volatile prices and periodic downward pressure on farm incomes. The problems experienced by farmers have led to a system of governmental assistance in the form of subsidies and price supports for farm products. Many aspects of the government's complex farm policy can be explained in terms of elasticities.

Implications of inelastic demand. The demand for many important farm products is inelastic. As illustrated by the case of the lettuce market at the beginning of the chapter, the more inelastic the demand for a product, the more its price will vary in response to changes in output. As the example in part (b) of Exhibit 3.1 showed, when demand is inelastic, a rise in price will result in an increase in revenue and a fall in price will lead to a decrease in revenue. Thus, with inelastic demand, good weather and a large crop will mean a drop in farm revenue; poor weather and a bad crop will mean an increase in revenue.

The historical instability of farm prices is shown in Exhibit 3.6 in terms of the so-called *parity-price ratio*—the ratio of an average of prices that farmers

Exhibit 3.6   The Agricultural Parity-Price Ratio

The basic tools of price supports and output restrictions on which U.S. farm policy is based date back to the Great Depression of the 1930s, when farmers suffered a sharp drop in the prices they received for crops compared with prices of goods that they bought from the rest of the economy. The chart shows the impact of the Depression on farmers in terms of the parity-price ratio, the ratio of an index of prices that farmers receive to an index of prices they pay. As the chart shows, substantial variations in the parity-price ratio have continued to occur despite government attempts to stabilize farm prices.

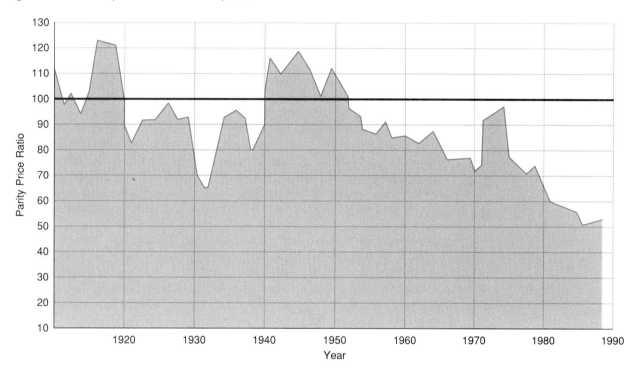

Sources: President's Council of Economic Advisers, *Economic Report of the President* (Washington, D.C.: Government Printing Office, 1977); Bureau of the Census, *Statistical Abstract of the United States, 1984*, 107th ed. (Washington, D.C.: Government Printing Office, 1987), 634; U.S. Department of Commerce, *Survey of Current Business*, various issues.

receive to an average of prices that they pay. (The ratio is multiplied by 100 and stated as a percentage.) The ratio uses the years 1910 to 1914, a time of relative prosperity for farms, as a base period.

As Exhibit 3.6 shows, the parity-price ratio has experienced wide swings, indicating that the prices of farm output are volatile compared with those of farm inputs. In the worst period, from 1929 to 1932, the ratio fell from 93 to 64 in just over three years. The collapse of demand in those early years of the Great Depression pushed all prices down; but because agricultural demand is so inelastic, farmers were hit worse than anyone else. The index of prices paid by farmers dropped a great deal over this period, but the index of prices received fell even more sharply.

Farm prices recovered along with the rest of the economy during World War II. During the 1950s and 1960s farm prices, as measured by the parity-price ratio, declined steadily—but without the sharp fluctuations of earlier periods. Any hope that agricultural markets had become more stable, however, was not borne out by what happened in the 1970s and early 1980s.

In 1973 a combination of factors, ranging from bad weather in the Soviet Union to the failure of the Peruvian anchovy catch, created a worldwide food shortage. Farm prices skyrocketed. The parity-price ratio touched the 100 mark briefly in August 1973, although it averaged below 100 for the year. Many farmers saw this as the beginning of a trend in which U.S. agriculture would increasingly be relied on to feed a hungry and ever more populous world. They responded by borrowing heavily to invest in new equipment and buy land. The price of farmland rose sharply, and farm indebtedness climbed with it.

However, the high prices of the early 1970s proved transitory. The parity-price ratio fell again as quickly as it had risen. By the mid-1980s, before the drought of 1988 caused a new price rise, the ratio hit new lows. The green revolution boosted farm output throughout the world, and even former agricultural basket cases such as India and China became self-sufficient in grain. As prices fell, many farmers found themselves unable to pay off debts they incurred in the 1970s. Thousands of operators were forced out of business, often taking equipment dealers, bankers, and small-town merchants with them.

The nation's farm policies, most of which were conceived in the 1930s, were originally viewed as a way to shield farmers from the hardships created by sharp year-to-year price fluctuations. Through a complex web of price supports and output restrictions, those policies aim to keep farm prices above market equilibrium levels in years when large harvests would otherwise send prices, and hence farm incomes, plunging. As explained in Chapter 2, such artificially high prices mean that farm surpluses accumulate in years of large harvests. In principle, sales of accumulated surpluses were supposed to moderate price increases in years when crops were bad, but that part of the price-stabilization plan has been implemented less often.

Long-term adjustment and income elasticity.   Short-term instability associated with low price elasticity of demand is not the only problem faced by U.S. farm policy. A second problem is long-term adjustment to rising productivity.

The long-term problem has been shaped by the fact that demand for farm products is not only price inelastic but income inelastic as well. As income per person increases, the demand for agricultural output also increases, but not as rapidly as income. The result of slowly growing demand and rapidly improving farm productivity has been a steady decline in the number of farmers needed to meet the demand for agricultural goods. Thus fifty years ago 25 percent of the U.S. population was engaged in farming. Today, the figure is less than 5 percent.

The marketplace has a way of telling people to leave an overcrowded sector: It offers them a lower income in that sector than elsewhere. Throughout the period of declining farm population, income per family member in farm households has been below that in other sectors of the economy. In the 1970s the gap narrowed, so that by some measures farm families caught up with the nonfarm population. However, renewed difficulties in the 1980s pushed relative farm incomes down again.

As the farm population has decreased, the role of the family farm—a farm

Economics in the News   3.1
Farm Subsidies Often Benefit the Strong

In Hollywood and Washington the prevailing image of the American farm portrays a family enterprise passed down from one hardworking generation to the next, one that is now threatened, but is ready to rise strong and healthy again if only it is given a helping hand. However, the reality is more complex. Certainly there are many farms that fit the classic description of the family farm. But much of the $26 billion a year that the federal government spends on farm subsidies (as of 1986) misses farmers in need and ends up in other pockets. Consider the following news items:

- To evade a $50,000-per-farmer cap on government payments, a California rice farm was leased to fifty-six tenants, each of whom qualified for the top payment and then split the $1.5 million income with the landlord. At least eight of the tenants were related to the owner.

- To benefit corn growers by increasing the demand for their crop, the government subsidizes the production of gasohol, a blend of ethanol that is distilled from corn and gasoline. In 1986, $29,230,000 was paid under the program to Archer Daniels Midland, a huge Illinois-based agribusiness that reported record profits for that year. That sum represented 54 percent of total government payments under the program, which critics have christened "corporate food stamps."

- Mohammed Aslam Khan grows rice in Butte City, California. He is a U.S. citizen, but four relatives, passive investors in the farm, are not—they live in Faisalabad, Pakistan. Uncle Sam paid them $152,010 for Khan's 1984 crop.

- In Vincennes, Indiana, Dennis Carnahan's family has pushed corn production costs so low that they could probably turn a profit if the farm program were abolished. But the 33-year-old farmer figures that the program is "the best ball game in town." The Carnahans expect to collect $81,180 from the government for the corn grown on their 3,800-acre farm this year.

The *Des Moines Register* is considered the most influential newspaper in the farm belt. What does it think of the government's programs? "American farm policy is a colossal hoax. It is a hoax on the countryside as well as on urban taxpayers," says the *Register*. Noting that less than one dollar in three spent on farm subsidies goes to a farmer in need, the newspaper suggests limiting payments to a safety net for small and medium-sized farms. Under current policy, "Never before have Americans spent so many tax dollars on agriculture, and never have the results been more destructive to the kind of rural life that Americans profess to want."

Sources: Ward Sinclair, "Loophole Allows Extra Farm Subsidies," *The Washington Post*, January 20, 1987, A3; Michael Isikoff, "Ethanol Producer Reaps 54 Percent of U.S. Subsidy," *The Washington Post*, January 29, 1987, A14; Wendy L. Wall and Charles F. McCoy, "New Farm Law Raises Federal Costs and Fails to Solve Big Problems," *The Wall Street Journal*, June 17, 1986, 1; "Sacred Farmers," *The Wall Street Journal*, March 5, 1987, 28. The quotations from the *Des Moines Register* are as given in "Sacred Farmers."

with sales in the $40,000 to $100,000 range that is the main source of income for the family that owns and operates it—has changed. Farms of this type have shaped most nonfarmers' image of rural life and also have strongly influenced farm policy. Today, however, they are becoming increasingly overshadowed by two other kinds of farms. On the one hand, there are the farms that have sales under $40,000 per year, and whose operators depend on other jobs for most of their incomes; they account for 70 percent of all farms. On the other hand, there are professionally managed farms with sales of $100,000 or more per year. The 12 percent of farms in this category—which tend to be the most productive and technologically advanced—account for about two-thirds of gross farm income.

The decline in the role of the "typical" family farm has caused some observers to call existing farm policies into question. According to these critics, the problem with current policies, which tend to raise farm prices in good as well as bad years, is that they benefit farmers not in proportion to their need but in proportion to their output. As ***Economics in the News 3.1*** shows, often it is the least needy farmers who benefit the most. In this regard, farm policy resembles rent control, which, as we saw in Chapter 2, is sometimes defended in terms of benefits to poor tenants even though middle-class tenants probably benefit more. As in the case of rent control, a full analysis of farm policy, tracing both its intended and unintended effects, would have to take political as well as economic factors into account. It would have to explore the relative political influence of small farmers, large farmers, agro-industry interests, and even environmentalists promoting gasohol as a clean fuel for automobiles. Such an inquiry would take us far beyond the topic of this chapter. But whatever aspect of farm policy one chooses to pursue, the concept of elasticity will prove to be a useful tool.

Summary

1. **How can the responsiveness of quantity demanded to a price change be expressed in terms of elasticity?** *Elasticity* is the responsiveness of quantity demanded or supplied to changes in the price of a good or in other factors, measured as a ratio of percentage changes. The *price elasticity of demand* between two points on a demand curve is computed as the percentage change in quantity demanded divided by the percentage change in the good's price. If the demand for a good is elastic, a decrease in its price will increase total revenue. If it is inelastic, an increase in its price will increase total revenue.

2. **How can elasticity be applied to situations other than the responsiveness of the quantity of a good demanded to a change in its price?** The concept of elasticity can be applied to many situations besides movements along demand curves. The *income elasticity of demand* for a good is the ratio of the percentage change in quantity demanded to a given percentage change in income. The *cross-elasticity of demand* between goods A and B is the ratio of the percentage change in the quantity of good A demanded to a given percentage change in the price of good B. The *price elasticity of supply* is the ratio of the percentage change in the quantity of a good supplied to a given change in its price.

3. **What determines the distribution of the economic burden of a tax?** The way in which the economic burden of a tax is distributed is known as the *incidence* of the tax. The incidence depends on the relative elasticities of supply and demand. If supply is relatively more elastic than demand, buyers will bear the larger share of the tax burden. If demand is relatively more elastic than supply, the larger share of the burden will fall on sellers.

4. **How is elasticity useful for understanding farm policy?** The more inelastic the demand for a good, the more its price will fluctuate in response to a given shift in supply. Also, when demand is inelastic, an increase in quantity will cause a reduction in total revenue.

The instability of farm prices and incomes can be attributed, at least in part, to the inelasticity of demand for many farm products. In addition, demand for many farm products is income inelastic as well as price inelastic. This means that as consumers' incomes have risen, the demand for farm goods has increased only moderately—not enough to keep up with the rate of increase in farm productivity. Thus, a much smaller proportion of the population is engaged in farming now than formerly, and traditional family farms contribute an ever-smaller share of total farm output.

Terms for Review

- elasticity
- price elasticity of demand
- revenue
- elastic demand
- inelastic demand
- unit elastic demand
- perfectly inelastic demand
- perfectly elastic demand
- income elasticity of demand
- cross-elasticity of demand
- price elasticity of supply
- tax incidence

Questions for Review

1. How does revenue change in response to changes in price under conditions of elastic, inelastic, and unit elastic demand?

2. Why is the midpoint of the range of price and quantity variation commonly used in calculating elasticities? Is there an alternative to the midpoint approach?

3. What conditions affect the elasticity of demand? What role do substitutes and complements play? What is the effect of the amount of time consumers have in which to adjust to a change in the price of a good?

4. How is income elasticity of demand related to the concepts of normal and inferior goods?

5. How is cross-elasticity of demand related to the concepts of substitutes and complements?

6. How is elasticity of supply defined? In what way does the midpoint formula for price elasticity of supply differ from that for price elasticity of demand? What conditions affect elasticity of supply?

7. Under what conditions will the economic burden of a tax be divided evenly between buyers and sellers? Under what conditions will it fall more heavily on buyers? On sellers?

8. How have price inelasticity and income inelasticity affected the farm sector of the U.S. economy?

Problems and Topics for Discussion

1. **Examining the lead-off case.** Consider three time horizons: (a) The "very short" run means a period that is too short to allow farmers to change the amount of lettuce that has been planted. No matter what happens to the price, the quantity supplied will be the amount already planted, less the amount destroyed by the virus. (b) The "intermediate" run means a period that is long enough to allow farmers to plant more fields in lettuce, but not long enough to permit them to develop new varieties of lettuce, to introduce new methods of cultivation, or to acquire new specialized equipment. (c) The "long" run means a period that is long enough to allow farmers to develop new varieties and improve cultivation techniques. Discuss these three time horizons in terms of the price elasticity of supply. Sketch a figure showing supply curves for each of the time horizons. Which time horizon or horizons is relevant to the story at the beginning of the chapter?

2. **Calculating elasticity.** Draw a set of coordinate axes on a piece of graph paper. Label the horizontal axis from 0 to 50 units and the vertical axis from $0 to $20 per unit. Draw a demand curve that intersects the vertical axis at $10 and the horizontal axis at 40 units. Draw a supply curve that intersects the vertical axis at $4 and has a slope of 1. Make the following calculations for these curves, using the midpoint formula:

a. What is the price elasticity of demand over the price range $5 to $7?

b. What is the price elasticity of demand over the price range $1 to $3?

c. What is the price elasticity of supply over the price range $10 to $15?

d. What is the price elasticity of supply over the price range $15 to $17?

3. **Elasticity and revenue.** Look at the demand curve given in Exhibit 2.1 (p. 45). Make a third column in the table that gives revenue for each price-quantity combination shown. Draw a set of axes on a piece of graph paper. Label the horizontal axis as in Exhibit 2.1, and label the vertical axis "Revenue" from 0 to $1 billion in increments of $100 million. Graph the relationship between quantity and revenue using the column you added to the table. (You may want to extend the table to show the following additional points: 1 billion units at a price of $.80; 0.5 billion units at a price of $1.00.) Discuss the relationship of your revenue graph to the demand curve, keeping in mind what you know about elasticity and revenue and about variation in elasticity along the demand curve.

4. **Elasticity of demand and revenue.** Assume that you are an officer of your campus film club. You are at a meeting at which ticket prices are being discussed. One member says, "What I hate to see most of all is empty seats in the theater. We sell out every weekend showing, but there are always empty seats on Wednesdays. If we cut our Wednesday night prices by enough to fill up the theater, we'd bring in more money." Would this tactic really bring in more revenue? What would you need to know in order to be sure? Draw diagrams to illustrate some of the possibilities.

5. **Cross-elasticity of demand.** Between 1979 and 1981 the price of heating oil rose by 104 percent. Over the same period use of fuel oil fell slightly while use of LP gas, another heating fuel, rose. Assuming that there was no change in the price of LP gas, what does this suggest about the cross-elasticity of demand for LP gas with respect to the price of fuel oil? Draw a pair of diagrams to illustrate these events. (Suggestion: Draw upward-sloping supply curves for both fuels. Then assume that the supply curve for heating oil shifts upward while the supply curve for LP gas stays the same.)

Case for Discussion
A Novel Sales Ploy: Cut Prices

General Motors Corp. has come up with a plan that might keep its 10-year-old Chevrolet Chevette alive a bit longer.

The plan is simple: cut the price.

To producers of things other than cars, that might seem a fairly obvious tack. But in the auto industry, it is novel, even outlandish.

Chrysler Corp. tried it last spring with its Omni/Horizon models, eight-year-old subcompacts that compete with Chevette. And it worked.

Chrysler knocked $710 off the base price of the Omni/Horizon, added some equipment and the "America" name to the car line, and offered the package for $5,499. The result has been a 26.2 percent increase in sales of cars that were on Chrysler's scrap list. The company sold 165,300 Omni/Horizon models in the first nine months of this year, compared with 130,968 in the same period last year.

GM seems to be taking the same approach with the pricing of its Chevettes for the coming year, auto industry analysts say. GM has trimmed nearly $800 from the price of these rear-wheel-drive, four-cylinder autos, and has made standard some formerly optional equipment. The base price is $4,995.

Still, the days of the oft-maligned, oft-praised Chevette are numbered, GM officials say.

"The car is continuing to sell fairly well, particularly in fleet sales," said Ralph Kramer, Chevrolet's director of public relations. Fleet buyers accounted for about 65 percent of the 75,761 Chevettes sold last year, industry analysts say.

If Chevette sales miss the 100,000-mark in the coming year, it is likely that GM will proceed with plans to discontinue production of that model next spring, he said.

"We tend to think in modules of 100,000 units to justify gearing up a plant for production," Kramer said. "We obviously are well below that capacity with the Chevette."

Source: Warren Brown, "Chevette Sales Ploy: Cut Prices," *The Washington Post*, October 15, 1986, F1. © 1986 The Washington Post, reprinted with permission.

Questions

1. Using the data provided in the article, estimate the price elasticity of demand for Chrysler's Omni/Horizon. (Throughout this problem, assume that the changes in sales volume indicate movements along demand curves resulting from the change in price.)

2. If Chevette sales were to increase to 100,000 units in the year following the price cut, what would be the price elasticity of demand for the car?

3. Suppose that demand for the Chevette is elastic, so that the firm's revenues will increase if the price is cut. Does that automatically mean that the firm's profit will increase?

Suggestions for Further Reading

Browning, Edgar K., and Jacqueline M. Browning. *Public Finance and the Price System.* 3d ed. New York: Macmillan, 1986.

Public finance is the branch of economics that studies taxation and government expenditures from both a micro- and a macroeconomic point of view. This or any other public finance text will provide additional details on tax incidence.

Gardner, Bruce. *The Governing of Agriculture.* Lawrence: Regents Press of Kansas, 1981.

An excellent overview of farm policy.

Varian, Hal. *Intermediate Microeconomics.* Hinsdale, Ill.: Dryden Press, 1987, Chapter 5.

This or any other intermediate microeconomics text will give further details on the definition of elasticity and practical problems associated with measuring elasticity of demand.

PART TWO

Introduction to Macroeconomics

4

In Search of Stability and Prosperity

**Before reading this chapter,
make sure you know the meaning of:**

Positive and normative economics (Chapter 1)

Production possibility frontiers (Chapter 1)

After reading this chapter, you will understand:

The meaning of unemployment and its importance
for economic policy.

The meaning of inflation and its impact on the
economy.

Trends in economic growth in the United States.

The nature of the business cycle.

Jobless Rate Steady for Record Ninth Straight Month

The number of workers on industry payrolls surged in January and again in February, the Labor Department said yesterday in a report that provided new evidence that the American economy is not about to drop into a recession.

The civilian unemployment rate remained at 5.3 percent on a seasonally adjusted basis for an unprecedented ninth month in a row. The number of workers without jobs but seeking work rose slightly to 6.6 million.

Part of the large 372,000 gain in payroll jobs last month was because of special factors, including the return to work of about 90,000 automobile workers who had been laid off in January. Warm weather also probably increased the number of constuction workers on the job, the department said.

Nevertheless, analysts said most of the new jobs were created to meet the continuing strong demand by Americans for services of all types and therefore were a sign of the economy's underlying strength. The gains last month were the largest in health care, retail trade and business services, while manufacturing jobs lagged.

At the White House, Michael Boskin, chairman of the Council of Economic Advisers, declared, "This is good news on the jobs front. We believe the economy, after a period of pretty slow growth, is likely to show progress in 1990."

Photo source: Reuters/Bettmann Newsphotos.

Source: John M. Berry, "Jobless Rate Unchanged in February," *The Washington Post*, March 10, 1990, C1. © 1990 The Washington Post, reprinted with permission.

The latest data on unemployment are always headline news—and justly so. Together with the rate of inflation and the growth of real output, the level of unemployment is one of the key indicators of success in the search for economic stability and prosperity.

In a general sense, stability and prosperity have been among the primary goals of government policy for centuries. Following the birth of modern macroeconomics during the Great Depression of the 1930s, the government's commitment to these goals was given a legal framework in the Employment Act of 1946. The act declared it to be the responsibility of the federal government to use all practical means consistent with free competitive enterprise to create conditions under which those able, willing, and seeking to work will be afforded useful employment opportunities. Later, Congress amended the 1946 legislation with the Full Employment and Balanced Growth Act of 1978, which established numerical goals for unemployment and inflation. Although the specific goals of the 1978 act were not achieved during the 1980s, the economy's performance did improve substantially compared with the troubled 1970s.

This chapter reviews the experience of the U.S. economy since World War II in terms of the three key goals of high employment, price stability, and economic growth. The concepts introduced here will serve as background for the development of a variety of macroeconomic theories and models in the following chapters.

4.1   High Employment

Employed
A term used to refer to a person working at least 1 hour a week for pay or at least 15 hours per week as an unpaid worker in a family business.

Unemployed
A term used to refer to a person who is not employed but is actively looking for work.

As the Employment Act of 1946 indicates, achieving a high level of employment is a key goal of macroeconomic policy. A person is considered to be **employed** if he or she works at least 1 hour per week for pay or at least 15 hours per week as an unpaid worker in a family business. A person who is not currently employed but is actively looking for work is said to be **unemployed.** A high level of employment is an important goal for both positive and normative reasons.

Costs of Unemployment

In terms of positive economics, more jobs mean more output and more material satisfaction. An economy that fails to make use of labor resources that are voluntarily supplied to the market is operating inside its production possibility frontier. The lost output resulting from unemployment can at times amount to hundreds of billions of dollars.

In the minds of many people, however, billions of dollars of lost output are secondary compared with the normative costs of unemployment—the costs in terms of human lives and values. Many people's sense of self-worth is closely tied to the work they do. To find that no employer wants their contribution is psychologically damaging. The damage can be seen statistically in the tendency for rates of divorce, family violence, murder, heart disease, and a number of other social and medical disorders to rise during periods of high unemployment. Many people also link the disintegration of families and neighborhood structures in poor inner-city areas to the high rates of unemployment that prevail there, especially among teenagers and members of minority groups.

All things considered, then, it is small wonder that policymakers keep a close eye on the unemployment reports. Because of their importance, it is worth seeing where those numbers come from.

Measuring Unemployment

The Bureau of Labor Statistics, in conjunction with the Bureau of the Census, obtains the data used in calculating unemployment from a monthly sample of about 50,000 randomly selected households. Field agents go to those households and ask a series of questions about the job status of each member of the household. The questions include such things as: Did anyone work last week? Did anyone look for work? How long has the person been looking for work? How did the person go about looking?

On the basis of their answers to these questions, people are counted as employed or unemployed according to the definitions given earlier. The employed plus the unemployed—that is, those who are either working or looking for work—constitute the **labor force.** The **unemployment rate** is simply the percentage of the labor force that is unemployed.

If people are neither employed nor actively looking for work, they are not counted as members of the labor force. This group includes many people who could work but choose not to for one reason or another. (They may be full-time students or retired, or they may work full time but not for pay as homemakers.) Two groups are automatically considered to be outside the labor force: children under 16 years of age and people who are confined to prisons and certain other institutions.

Members of the armed forces are a special category. The *total labor force* includes members of the armed forces on active duty; the *civilian labor force* excludes those individuals. This distinction has an effect on the calculation of the unemployment rate. The *civilian unemployment rate* is the percentage of the *civilian* labor force that is unemployed, whereas the *total unemployment rate* is the percentage of the *total* labor force that is unemployed. Because all members of the armed forces on active duty are by definition employed, the total unemployment rate is lower than the civilian rate, usually by about a tenth of a percentage point. The civilian unemployment rate is the one that is more widely reported.

In this book, as in most other sources, the terms *unemployment rate* and *labor force* refer to the civilian labor force. However, some argue that the total unemployment rate gives a better picture of labor market conditions, considering that membership in the armed forces is, for economic purposes, much like any other job.

Exhibit 4.1 presents unemployment data for the United States since 1950. The shaded band labeled "low to moderate unemployment" reflects a range of views about reasonable economic performance. During the 1950s and 1960s, the unemployment rate generally stayed within this range. Rates higher than the upper end of the range occurred in only a couple of years. In the 1970s and early 1980s, the unemployment rate took a turn for the worse. It jumped to 8.3 percent in 1975 and fell into the moderate range in only 2 of the next 12 years. Not until 1989 did it again reach the levels achieved in the early 1970s.

Gray Areas in the Measurement of Unemployment

There are many gray areas in the measurement of unemployment. The official unemployment rate can be criticized for both understating and overstating the "true" number of unemployed. One way to understand these gray areas better is to compare the official definition of unemployment with two commonsense definitions, namely, "not working" and "can't find a job."

Labor force
The sum of all individuals who are employed and all individuals who are unemployed.

Unemployment rate
The percentage of the labor force that is unemployed.

Exhibit 4.1   Unemployment in the United States Since 1950

There is no one unemployment rate that is universally accepted as best for the economy. Some unemployment is always present as people change jobs and enter the labor force in a normally functioning economy. In this figure, a range of 4 to 6.5 percent unemployment is characterized as "low to moderate." Until 1975, unemployment stayed within that range, for the most part. The mid-1970s and early 1980s saw much higher rates, however.

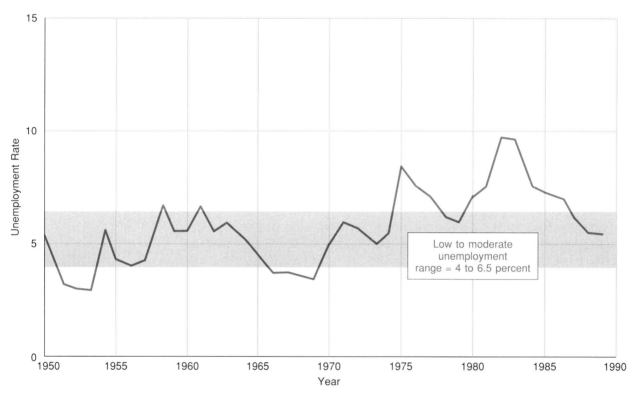

Source: President's Council of Economic Advisers, *Economic Report of the President* (Washington, D.C.: Government Printing Office, 1990), Table C-39.

"Unemployed" versus "not working."   The official definitions of employment and unemployment differ greatly from the simple definitions of "working" and "not working." On the one hand, there are many people who work but are not officially employed. By far the largest such group consists of people who work full time at housekeeping and child care. These occupations are counted as employment if they are performed for pay, but the bulk of such work is done without pay. There are also a certain number of children under 16 who work for pay but are not counted as employed. Children under 16 working without pay for a family farm or business also are not counted as employed.

On the other hand, not everyone who does not work is counted as unemployed. There are millions of people who are not looking for work and therefore are not counted in the labor force. There are also those who are absent from their jobs because of illness, bad weather, or labor disputes. All of these are counted as employed. Finally, there are those who work part time and are counted as employed but are actively seeking full-time employment. People in this last situation are sometimes referred to as *underemployed*.

"Unemployed" versus "can't find a job."   The second commonsense definition of unemployment, "can't find a job," also only loosely fits the official definition. In some ways, the official definition overstates the number of people who cannot find jobs. Some people who are counted as unemployed are on layoffs from jobs to which they expect to be recalled or have found jobs that they expect to start within 30 days. Other people who are counted as unemployed could easily find a job of some kind but prefer to take their time and find just the kind of job they want. (People who are not the sole income earners in their households, for example, may be in a position to look longer and be more selective than people in households with no other income.) Still other people register as unemployed to meet the requirements of income transfer programs even though they may not be qualified for any available work and only go through the motions of looking for a job. Finally, there is some doubt as to whether the description "can't find a job" fits people who could have stayed on at their last job but quit to look for a better one.

In other ways, however, the official definition of unemployment understates the number of people who cannot find jobs. For example, it does not include **discouraged workers,** people who are not looking for work because they believe no suitable jobs are available. The Bureau of Labor Statistics officially counts as a discouraged worker anyone who has looked for work within the last six months but is no longer actively looking. The description "can't find a job" could also be applied to the underemployed—those who have part-time jobs but would take full-time jobs if they could find them.

Discouraged worker
A person who would work if a suitable job were available but has given up looking for such a job.

The Employment-Population Ratio

Although the unemployment rate is the most widely publicized measure of the state of the labor market, it is not necessarily the best one. In addition to the problems of definition just discussed, there are other reasons why changes in total employment are not always reflected in changes of the unemployment rate.

The problem is illustrated by the news item at the beginning of the chapter, which noted that the unemployment rate remained steady in February 1990 even though the economy generated 372,000 new jobs. Part of the reason for the apparent disparity is that there are two different sources of employment data. The figure of 372,000 new jobs quoted in the article comes from a survey of payroll reports filed by employers. In the same month, the survey of households on the basis of which the unemployment rate is calculated showed an increase of just 172,000 employed people. The discrepancy between the two data sources arises in part from the fact that some people hold more than one job.

Even with the smaller number of newly employed workers recorded in the household survey, the unemployment rate would have fallen but for the fact that there was an equal increase in the size of the labor force as a whole. This continued a long-established tendency of the U.S. labor force to increase more rapidly than the population. The growth of the labor force offset the increase in jobs so that the unemployment rate remained unchanged even though the percentage of the population that was employed increased.

Employment-population ratio
The percentage of the noninstitutional adult population that is employed.

Because of this property of the unemployment rate, some economists consider another statistic, the **employment-population ratio,** to be a more revealing indicator of the health of the economy. This ratio is the percentage of the noninstitutional adult population that is employed. The denominator of the employment-population ratio, which is governed by demographic factors such as birthrates and death rates, changes slowly and predictably. Hence, this ratio is less likely than the unemployment rate to stand still while the economy moves ahead or to give other misleading signals.

The employment-population ratio not only gives a better picture of the short-term state of the economy than the unemployment rate does, but it also presents a quite different picture of long-term trends. When viewed in terms of the unemployment rate, as is done in Exhibit 4.1, the U.S. economy has not performed very consistently over the past two decades. However, employment figures show that throughout this period the U.S. economy was a remarkable job-creating machine. In 1969 jobs were available for only 59 percent of the noninstitutional adult population; by 1989 the proportion was 63 percent, an all-time record. In absolute terms, the number of people holding jobs rose from 78 million to 117 million.

The image of the United States as a job-creating machine is further enhanced by some international comparisons. Between 1959 and 1988, the U.S. economy added some 50 million new jobs, a 75 percent increase. Over the same period, the United Kingdom added fewer than 3 million jobs, a 13 percent increase, and West Germany added fewer than 2 million, an 8 percent gain. The employment-population ratio in the United States rose during this period from 56 percent to more than 62 percent; in Germany the employment-population ratio fell from 59 percent to 52 percent and in the United Kingdom, from 60 percent to 58 percent. Job growth in the United States over the period included manufacturing as well as the service sector, although the latter grew more rapidly. From 1960 to 1988, the United States added some 4 million manufacturing jobs, almost as many as were created in the Japanese economy. Over the same thirty-year period, Germany and the United Kingdom both lost manufacturing jobs.

Despite this remarkable performance, the U.S. economy still faces some problems. Manufacturing jobs reached a peak in 1979; they have declined by about 1 million jobs since that time, although the total number of jobs has grown strongly. Some critics characterize the nonmanufacturing jobs as "junk jobs." They say that the United States is changing from an economy of steel- and autoworkers into one of hamburger flippers and parking lot attendants. ***Applying Economic Ideas 4.1*** addresses this issue. A more serious concern is that unemployment is concentrated in certain subgroups of the population—workers displaced by plant closings, workers with few skills and little education, and members of some minority groups. Exhibit 4.2 shows the uneven distribution of unemployment among various population groups. The next section looks at three different types of unemployment, some of which are a greater cause for concern than others.

Types of Unemployment

A change in the unemployment rate reflects a change in the flows of workers into and out of the pool of unemployed workers. Given a labor force of constant size, the unemployment rate rises when the rate of inflow into the pool of unemployed

Applying Economic Ideas 4.1
A "Junk Job" Explosion?

The U.S. economy has a remarkable record of job creation, but even this record has had its critics. In a study released in late 1986 by the Joint Economic Committee of Congress, economists Barry Bluestone of the University of Massachusetts and Bennett Harrison of the Massachusetts Institute of Technology voiced their concern over an "alarming trend toward low-pay jobs." In particular, Bluestone and Harrison found that in the 1979 to 1984 period, 58 percent of new jobs paid less than half of the median wage, or $7,102 a year in constant 1984 dollars, up from 37.5 percent in the mid-1970s. In the same period there was a loss of 5.5 percent in jobs paying more than twice the median versus the 11.2 percent gain of the mid-1970s.

These data were cited in support of several programs aimed at protecting high-pay jobs (for example, by blocking imports or restricting factory closings) and reducing low-pay jobs (such as by raising the federal minimum wage to half of the median wage).

Bluestone and Harrison's conclusions have been sharply disputed by other analysts. The accompanying table shows that if the data are put in a broader context, the trend is not so clear. When the data are arranged in terms of presidential budget cycles, the job-creating performance of the economy in the Reagan years appears to be better, not worse, than the previous record. (This arrangement of years takes into account the fact that in the first year of each president's term, the government operates under a budget tailored by the preceding president.)

As Janet Norwood, the nonpartisan commissioner of labor statistics, has said, "The findings are extremely sensitive to the particular set of data used and the years chosen for analysis." The Bluestone-Harrison study focused on the worst possible case by including the double-digit inflation of 1979 and 1980 and the back-to-back recessions of 1980 and 1981 to 1982. These episodes were especially tough on high-pay jobs. Since then, high-pay jobs have rebounded.

Source: Based on Joint Economic Committee and Warren T. Brookes, "Low-Pay Jobs: The Big Lie," *The Wall Street Journal*, March 25, 1987, 30.

Net New Jobs (Thousands)

	Low (Under $7,012)		Middle ($7,012-$28,048)		High ($28,048 and over)	
	Number	Share	Number	Share	Number	Share
Nixon-Ford 1973–1977	2,550	37.5%	3,490	51.3%	758	11.2%
Carter 1977–1981	3,837	41.7	6,277	68.2	−912	−9.9
Reagan 1981–1985	412	6.0	3,180	46.2	3,169	46.1
Bluestone-Harrison 1979–1984	4,687	58.0	3,837	47.5	−442	−5.5

Note: Salaries in 1984 constant dollars.

Source: Joint Economic Committee.

workers exceeds the rate of outflow; the unemployment rate falls when the rate of outflow from the pool exceeds the rate of inflow. The difference between the rate of inflow and the rate of outflow determines how long the average person remains unemployed. During the past 20 years, the average duration of unemployment has ranged from a low of 7.8 weeks in 1969 to a high of 20.0 weeks in 1983.

The duration of unemployment varies not only from year to year but also from one unemployed worker to another. As Exhibit 4.3 shows, depending on the state of the economy between one-third and three-fifths of all unemployed people are out of work for less than five weeks. At the other end of the scale, 5 to 25 percent of unemployed people are out of work for six months or more.

Exhibit 4.2   Unemployment by Population Groups, June 1989

This table shows unemployment rates and, where applicable, employment-population ratios for various population subgroups. The relatively low rates for married men and women with spouse present are probably close to the frictional level needed to match jobs with job seekers. At the other extreme, the 33.1 percent unemployment rate for black teenagers clearly contains a large structural component.

	Unemployment Rate	Employment-Population Ratio
Civilian population	5.2	63.0
Men, 20 years and older	4.3	74.6
Married men, spouse present	2.9	
Women, 20 years and older	5.0	55.0
Married women, spouse present	3.8	
Women who maintain families	8.0	
Both sexes, 16 to 19 years	14.7	47.1
White	4.6	66.8
Men, 20 years and older	3.8	75.5
Women, 20 years and older	4.3	55.0
Both sexes, 16 to 19 years	13.4	50.5
Black	10.9	57.4
Men, 20 years and older	9.3	67.2
Women, 20 years and older	9.9	54.9
Both sexes, 16 to 19 years	33.1	31.9
Hispanic origin	9.0	62.2

Source: U.S. Department of Labor, Bureau of Labor Statistics, *Employment Situation: July 1989.*

Variations in the duration of unemployment serve as a basis for distinguishing among *frictional, structural,* and *cyclical unemployment.*

Frictional unemployment
The portion of unemployment that is accounted for by the short periods of unemployment needed for matching jobs with job seekers.

Frictional unemployment.   The term **frictional unemployment** refers to the short periods of unemployment that are needed to match jobs and workers. Much of this short-term unemployment is voluntary. It represents people who quit old jobs to look for new ones, people who take a week or so to move or go on vacation before starting a newly found job, and people who enter occupations, such as construction work, in which temporary layoffs are frequent but year-round earnings are good. Economists view a certain level of frictional unemployment as necessary in a labor market in which information is incomplete and the costs of job search are often high.

Structural unemployment
The portion of unemployment that is accounted for by people who are out of work for long periods because their skills do not match those required for available jobs.

Structural unemployment.   The term **structural unemployment** refers to a situation in which people spend long periods out of work, often with little prospect of finding adequate jobs. This prolonged joblessness occurs partly because the shifting structure of the economy has made their skills obsolete. This category of workers also includes people with few skills and little work experience. Teenagers and some minority groups are particularly affected by this type of unemployment.

Exhibit 4.3   Unemployment by Duration

As this chart shows, there is considerable variation in the length of time people are unemployed. Depending on the state of the economy, about one-third to three-fifths of all unemployed workers spend less than five weeks out of work. On the other hand, 5 to 25 percent are out of work for six months or more.

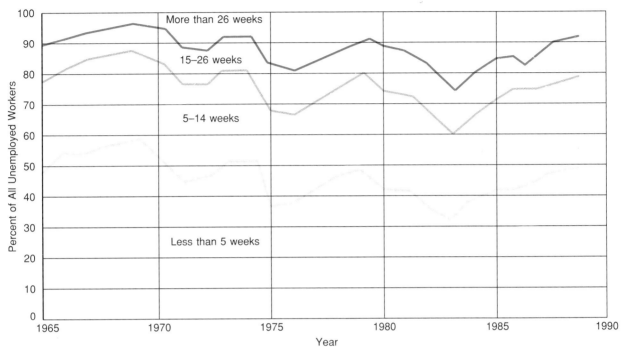

Source: President's Council of Economic Advisers, *Economic Report of the President* (Washington, D.C.: Government Printing Office, 1990), Table C-41.

For these people, structural unemployment is not merely a problem of lack of jobs. Certain types of jobs—hospital orderly jobs, fast-food work, and car washing, for example—are almost always available and require few specific skills. But structurally unemployed workers who do take such jobs often work at them only for short periods before quitting to look for something better. Working for brief periods at dead-end jobs tends to build up a pattern of poor work habits and absenteeism that makes many structurally unemployed workers unattractive to potential employers.

The natural rate of unemployment.   Frictional and structural unemployment are present in good as well as bad years. The sum of frictional and structural unemployment is often referred to as the **natural rate of unemployment.** This term can be thought of as the rate of unemployment that persists during a period of macroeconomic stability. Later in the book we will see that the natural rate can be defined more precisely as the rate that prevails when the rate of inflation is neither accelerating nor decelerating. As of the late 1980s, the natural rate of unemployment was thought to lie in the 5.5 to 6.0 percent range.

Natural rate of unemployment
The sum of frictional and structural unemployment; the rate of unemployment that persists when the economy is experiencing neither accelerating nor decelerating inflation.

Some economists object to using the term *natural* to refer to unemployment that is partly structural, because it seems to imply that the human suffering that accompanies structural unemployment is acceptable in some normative sense. They have tried to replace it with a more neutral term such as *nonaccelerating-inflation rate of unemployment (NAIRU)*. Whatever the merits of the issue, however, the simple term natural seems to have caught on.

Cyclical unemployment.   In practice, unemployment is not always at its "natural" benchmark. As we will see later in the chapter, over time the economy undergoes cycles of expansion and contraction. As it does so, the unemployment rate changes. As a result of vigorous economic expansion, unemployment may drop below its natural rate. In such a period, the job market may be so strong that the duration of unemployment falls below normal, reducing the number of people who are usually unemployed for frictional reasons. Even many of the hard-core structurally unemployed find jobs. On the other hand, in periods of business contraction, the unemployment rate rises above its natural rate. At such times even workers with strong job attachment and excellent skills may find themselves temporarily laid off. The average duration of unemployment rises above normal frictional levels.

The difference between the actual unemployment rate at a given time and the natural rate is known as **cyclical unemployment.** When the economy slows down, cyclical unemployment is added to frictional and structural unemployment. At the peak of an expansionary period, cyclical unemployment is negative. The cyclical behavior of the unemployment rate will be examined more closely later in the chapter, but first, we must explore some of the basic concepts of inflation and economic growth.

Cyclical unemployment
The difference between the observed rate of unemployment at a given point in the business cycle and the natural rate of unemployment.

4.2   Price Stability

Inflation means a sustained increase in the average level of prices of all goods and services. **Price stability**—a situation in which the rate of inflation is low enough so that it is not a significant factor in business and individual decision making—can be considered the second major goal of macroeconomic policy.

Exhibit 4.4 shows the trend of inflation in the U.S. economy since 1950 as measured by the annual rate of change in the **consumer price index,** a widely reported average of prices of goods and services purchased by a typical urban household.[1] As the exhibit shows, the inflation rate generally stayed within the low to moderate range of 0 to 3 percent throughout the 1950s and early 1960s. In fact, for the entire century from the Civil War to the mid-1960s, the peacetime inflation rate averaged only about 2 percent per year. Beginning in 1968, however, inflation rose above the 3 percent rate and became highly variable. In the ensuing two decades the rate dropped below 3 percent only once, in 1986. The struggle against inflation was a dominant theme in economic policy throughout the 1980s.

Inflation
A sustained increase in the average price level of all goods and services.

Price stability
A situation in which the rate of inflation is low enough that it is not a significant factor in business and individual decision making.

Consumer price index
An average of the prices of goods and services purchased by a typical urban household.

[1]The consumer price index and other measures of the average price level will be discussed in detail in Chapter 6 and in the appendix to that chapter.

Exhibit 4.4   Inflation in the United States Since 1950

Price stability is a situation in which the rate of inflation is low enough that it is
not a significant factor in business decision making. Many economists believe that
a measured inflation rate of 1 percent or less would qualify as price stability by
that definition. Here, the range of 0 to 3 percent is labeled "low to moderate
inflation." Inflation stayed in that range throughout much of the 1950s and 1960s.
However, the rate has dropped below 3 percent in only one year since 1967.

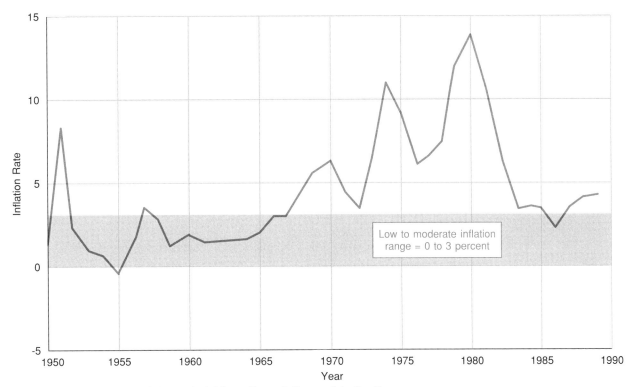

Source: President's Council of Economic Advisers, *Economic Report of the President*
(Washington, D.C.: Government Printing Office, 1990), Table C-61. The data given are year-to-
year percentage changes in the consumer price index.

The Costs of Inflation

As in the case of unemployment, the costs of inflation are distributed unevenly
across the population. The effects of inflation depend on one's position with
regard to source of income, debtor or creditor status, and wealth, among other
factors. All discussions of inflation must distinguish between effects measured in
real terms and effects measured in *nominal* terms. Economists use the term **real**
to refer to data that have been adjusted to take inflation into account; they use
the term **nominal** to refer to data that are presented in the ordinary way, without
adjustment for inflation.

Effects on wage and salary income.   Most people receive the bulk of their
income in the form of wages and salaries. Wage and salary earners often feel that
they are badly hurt by inflation. They compare what their paychecks can buy

Real
In economics, a term that
refers to data that have been
adjusted for the effects of
inflation.

Nominal
In economics, a term that
refers to data that have not
been adjusted for the effects
of inflation.

each month at ever-higher prices with what they would be able to buy with the same paychecks if prices remained stable. However, a closer look shows that the effects of inflation on real wage and salary income are less than they are often perceived to be.

During a period of general inflation all prices tend to rise together, including wages and salaries, which are the prices that firms pay for labor. Consider the inflationary 1970s, for example. From 1970 to 1979 the consumer price index rose by 87 percent. This means that by the end of the decade it would have taken $187 to buy the same basket of goods that could have been bought for $100 at the beginning of the decade. But wages also rose during that period. In 1970, the average hourly wage in the private nonfarm sector of the economy was $3.23; by 1979, it had risen to $6.16, that is, by 91 percent. When the 91 percent increase in the nominal wage is compared with the 87 percent increase in consumer prices, it can be seen that the real value of the average hourly wage was actually slightly greater in 1979 than it had been in 1970.

Not all workers are as well protected from inflation as others, of course. In some industries workers are protected by "escalator clauses" that automatically raise nominal wages when the consumer price index rises. Economists use the term **indexation** to refer to such devices. Complete indexation of wages is not widespread in the United States, however. Thus, even though wages tend to rise in step with inflation on the average, there may be individual winners and losers during any given period.

Indexation
A policy of automatically adjusting a value or payment in proportion to changes in the average price level.

Transfer payments
Payments to individuals that are not made in return for work they currently perform.

Transfer payments.   Many people receive income in the form of private pensions and government benefits that are not made in return for work they currently perform. These are called **transfer payments.** At one time the recipients of transfer payments, especially retired people living on pensions that were fixed in nominal terms, were seriously hurt by inflation. Today this is less true than it once was, largely because social security, the biggest single transfer program, is fully indexed. Nominal social security benefits now rise automatically in step with consumer prices, thereby preserving their real value. Some private pensions and some forms of personal saving are not indexed, however, so inflation is still damaging to some elderly people. Transfer payments received by the nonelderly poor, such as food stamps and welfare payments, are sometimes, but not always, indexed to protect the recipients against inflation.

Interest income—debtors versus creditors.   We turn next to the effects of inflation on the real income of creditors, who receive interest income from mortgage loans, corporate bonds, and the like, and on the real income of debtors, who pay that interest. The effects of inflation in this case are somewhat more complex than is true for wage income and transfer payments, but they are worth considering in some detail.

The traditional view is that inflation injures creditors and aids debtors. Suppose, for example, that I borrow $100 from you today, promising to repay the $100 of principal plus $5 interest, or $105 in all, at the end of a year. If there is no inflation during the year, I get the use of the funds for the year and you get $5 of real income in the form of the interest on the loan. But suppose that during the year the price level goes up by 10 percent. In that case I get the use of the funds for the year, and what is more, I pay you back in depreciated dollars. The $105 I give you at the end of the year will buy only about as much then as $95 will buy today. Your real income is negative, because the real value of $105 a year from now is less than the real value today of the $100 that I borrow. I, the debtor, benefit from inflation, and you, the creditor, are hurt.

However, the traditional view of the effects of inflation is incomplete in that it does not distinguish between *unexpected* and *expected* inflation. The example just given implicitly assumes that neither I, the borrower, nor you, the lender, expected any inflation at the time the loan was made. Suppose instead that we both had expected a 10 percent increase in the price level between the time the loan was made and the time it was repaid. In that case you would not have loaned me the $100 in return for a promise to repay just $105 at the end of the year. Instead, you would have insisted on a repayment of $115—the $100 principal, plus $10 to compensate you for the decline in purchasing power of the principal plus $5 of real interest income. I, in turn, would have agreed to those terms, knowing that the $115 payment under conditions of 10 percent inflation would be no more burdensome than the $105 payment I would have agreed to if no inflation had been expected.

This example shows that we need to distinguish between two interest concepts: the **nominal interest rate,** which is the interest rate expressed in the ordinary way, in current dollars, and the **real interest rate,** which is the nominal rate minus the rate of inflation. In the example, a 15 percent nominal interest rate, given a 10 percent rate of inflation, corresponds to a 5 percent real interest rate.

The distinction between real and nominal interest rates can be used to state the impact of expected and unexpected inflation on debtors and creditors. *Expected* inflation, it turns out, is neutral between debtors and creditors because the parties will adjust the nominal interest rate, taking the expected inflation into account. If they would agree to a 5 percent nominal interest rate given no expected inflation, they would agree to a 15 percent nominal rate given 10 percent expected inflation, a 20 percent nominal rate given 15 percent expected inflation, and so on. All correspond to a 5 percent real rate. *Unexpected* inflation is not neutral, however. Unexpected inflation harms creditors and benefits debtors. If you lend me $100 at a 5 percent nominal rate of interest and the price level unexpectedly rises by 10 percent over the year before I repay the loan, the real rate of interest that you realize is *minus* 5 percent.

The effects of expected and unexpected inflation can be clearly seen in the market for home mortgage loans. During the 1950s and 1960s, when little or no inflation was expected, millions of homeowners took out mortgage loans from banks and savings and loan associations at nominal interest rates of 4 to 6 percent. By the end of the 1970s, the rate of inflation had risen to more than 10 percent per year. The market value of the homes rose in step with inflation, benefiting homeowners, whereas the payments on their mortgages, which were fixed in nominal terms, did not change. Homeowners thus received a windfall at the expense of the banks. By the 1980s, however, inflation was no longer unexpected. Banks were no longer willing to make fixed-interest mortgage loans unless they included a hefty inflation premium. Mortgages with nominal interest rates of 12 or even 14 percent became commonplace. Today fixed-rate home mortgages continue to include an inflation premium, although not as high a premium as was common a decade ago. To avoid the uncertainties associated with inflation, borrowers and lenders often agree to variable-rate loans. Under the terms of these loans, nominal interest payments tend to rise during periods when higher inflation is expected and fall during periods when lower inflation is expected.

Nominal interest rate
The interest rate expressed in the usual way: in terms of current dollars without adjustment for inflation.

Real interest rate
The nominal interest rate minus the rate of inflation.

Other effects of inflation.   So far our discussion of inflation has concentrated on the distributional effects of inflation. It implies that although there are losers, there are also winners; although inflation imposes costs on some people, it benefits others. The discussion would be incomplete, however, without pointing out that inflation has some costs that are not distributional in nature, costs that place a burden on the economy as a whole without producing offsetting benefits.

One set of costs has to do with the way inflation upsets economic calculations. In an inflationary environment, households and firms have a hard time distinguishing changes in relative prices of goods and services from changes in the general price level. Partly for this reason, in an economy in which the rate of inflation is high and variable, as it was in the United States in the 1970s and early 1980s, business planning becomes difficult. The outcome of investment projects that require firms to incur costs now in the hope of making profits later come to depend less on manufacturing and marketing skills than on the ups and downs of wages, interest rates, and the prices of key raw materials. As the investment environment becomes riskier, firms may avoid projects with long-term payoffs in terms of future productivity gains and gamble instead on strategies that promise short-term financial gains. Similarly, households, facing more uncertainty about future price trends, may reduce their long-term saving in favor of increased current consumption. These effects are hard to measure, but many economists think that they are substantial. We will return to this issue in Chapter 17, which examines the topics of productivity and saving in detail.

Another set of costs arise from the effort to rid the economy of inflation once it has become established. The experiences of many countries in many periods suggest that it is rarely possible to bring inflation under control without serious economic disruption during a transition period. The slowdown of inflation in the United States from 1980 to 1983 is a case in point. A comparison of Exhibit 4.4 and Exhibit 4.1 shows that the drop in inflation during those years coincided with a surge in the unemployment rate, which reached a post–World War II peak of 10 percent in the summer of 1982. The increase in unemployment, in turn, represented a major loss of potential output of goods and services. The linkages among inflation, unemployment, and real output will be a major theme of Chapters 7 through 16.

The distributional effects of inflation—its erosion of seemingly fixed paychecks, its impact on interest rates—are probably the dominant reason that inflation ranks highly as an economic evil in the public mind. Most economists, however, see inflation's effects on economic calculation, business planning, and productivity as its greatest threat.

4.3   Economic Growth

Economic growth is the third major goal of economic policy. Some economic growth is necessary just to provide jobs for new workers entering the labor force and thus prevent a rise in unemployment. Economic growth faster than population growth is needed to provide a rising standard of living.

Measuring Economic Growth

Gross national product (GNP)
A measure of the economy's total output of goods and services.

Economic growth is most frequently expressed in terms of **gross national product (GNP),** a measure of the economy's total output of goods and services. If GNP is to provide a meaningful measure of growth over time, it, like other economic quantities, must be expressed in real terms; that is, it must be adjusted for the effects of inflation. For example, from 1982 to 1989 nominal GNP grew from $3,166 billion to $5,233 billion. However, about half the increase in nominal GNP can be attributed to the substantial rise in the average price level during the period. Adjusted for inflation and expressed in constant 1982 dollars, 1989 real GNP was only $4,143 billion.[2] The term **real output** is frequently used as a synonym for real gross national product.

Real output
A synonym for real gross national product.

From 1950 through the late 1980s, the rate of growth of real GNP in the United States averaged about 3 percent per year, a rate that most economists consider satisfactory. However, as Exhibit 4.5 shows, GNP did not follow a

---

[2]Chapter 6 will explain in detail the methods by which real and nominal GNP are measured.

Exhibit 4.5   Economic Growth in the United States Since 1950

This chart shows the growth of the U.S. economy since 1950. Real gross national product is shown for each year, along with a trend line averaging about 3 percent growth of real GNP per year over the entire period. A growth rate of 3 percent or more is generally considered healthy.

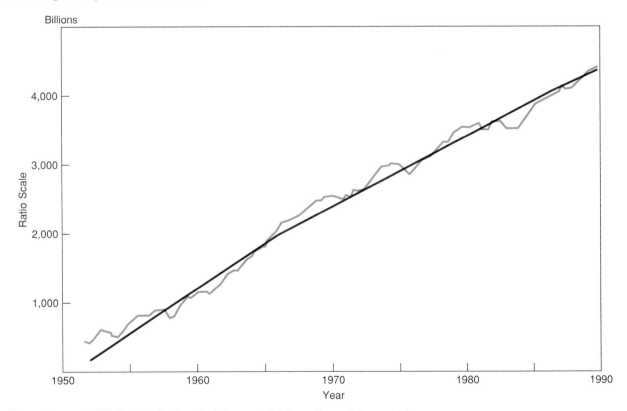

Source: For real GNP, President's Council of Economic Advisers, *Economic Report of the President* (Washington, D.C.: Government Printing Office, 1990), Table B-2. Trend line based on estimate of natural real output by staff of the Board of Governors of the Federal Reserve System.

smooth upward trend. In some years, output fell below the trend; in others, it rose above the trend. The early 1980s—which, as we have already seen, was a time of high inflation and high unemployment—was characterized by a major shortfall of real GNP from its trend.

The Benefits and Costs of Economic Growth

The benefits of economic growth are numerous. The most obvious is that growth provides consumers with a higher standard of living in the form of more goods and services. Growth also provides people with greater opportunities to choose between work and leisure. If more people choose to work, as has recently been the case in the United States, economic growth makes possible the capital investment needed to create jobs for them. Over a longer span of U.S. history, however, people have opted for more leisure. As the economy grew during the nineteenth and early twentieth centuries, it was possible to shorten the average workweek at the same time that material living standards were rising. Finally, economic growth is often credited with reducing poverty and economic injustice; a rising tide, it is said, lifts all boats.

However, economic growth has had its critics. More than a century ago the English economist John Stuart Mill worried that growth might cause the loss of "a great portion of the earth's pleasantries" (see **Who Said It? Who Did It? 4.1**). This sentiment is shared in our own time by environmentalists, who worry that economic growth is bringing increased pollution, destruction of wilderness areas, and the possibility of a global climatic disaster.

Criticisms of economic growth have their merits; we have only to look around us to see that the economic growth we have experienced has brought costs as well as benefits. However, the critics can be faulted for often failing to distinguish between two issues: the rate of economic growth and its direction.

Exhibit 4.6 Environmental Quality and Economic Growth

This exhibit shows a production possibility frontier for "cars," symbolizing material production, and "clean air," symbolizing environmental quality. In any single year, there is a trade-off between cars and clean air. More cars make the air dirtier, whereas fewer cars make cleaner air possible. Over time, improvements in technology and availability of additional productive resources shift the production possibility frontier outward. A choice can be made between two growth paths as the frontier expands. The path from A to B shows an increase in the output of cars and a decrease in air quality. The path from A to C shows a smaller increase in the number of cars and cleaner air. The move from A to C results in more cars *and* cleaner air.

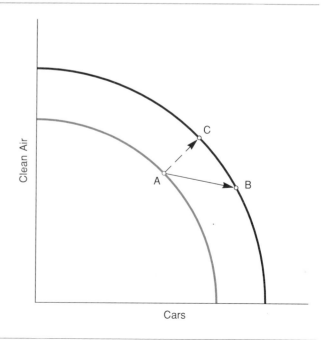

Who Said It? Who Did It?   4.1
John Stuart Mill on the Stationary State

Economic growth was a major concern of the classical economists of the nineteenth century. Then as now, most of the leading economists were inclined to view growth as a good thing. However, some of them feared that the pressure of population on limited natural resources would sooner or later bring growth to a halt. Economists portrayed the "stationary state" toward which society was moving as one of poverty and overpopulation, causing one critic to dub economics the "dismal science."

John Stuart Mill, whose work marked a high point of classical economics, thought otherwise. Mill was one of the most remarkable figures of the nineteenth century. Eldest son of the prominent economist James Mill, John Stuart Mill began studying Greek at age 3, was tutoring the younger members of his family in Latin at age 8, and first read Smith's *Wealth of Nations* at age 13. His *Principles of Political Economy*, published in 1848, was the standard text on the subject until Alfred Marshall transformed "political economy" into "economics" at the end of the century.

Mill agreed with earlier classical economists that the economy would sooner or later reach a stationary state, but he did not view the prospect as entirely gloomy:

I cannot . . . regard the stationary state of capital and wealth with the unaffected aversion so generally manifested towards it by political economists of the old school. I am inclined to believe that it would be, on the whole, a very considerable improvement on our present condition. I confess I am not charmed with the ideal of life held out by those who think that the normal state of human beings is that of struggling to get on; that the trampling, crushing, elbowing, and treading on each other's heels, which form the existing type of social life, are the most desirable lot of human kind, or anything but the disagreeable symptoms of one of the phases of our industrial progress. . . .

If the earth must lose that great portion of its pleasantries which it owes to things that the unlimited increase

of wealth and population would extricate from it, for the mere purpose of enabling it to support a larger, but not a better or happier population, I sincerely hope, for the sake of posterity, that they will be content to be stationary long before necessity compels them to.

Today Mill's sentiments have been echoed by writers who are concerned about problems of population, pollution, and resource depletion. E. F. Schumacher's *Small Is Beautiful* expressed this line of thought;[a] so did another best-selling book of the 1970s, *The Limits to Growth*, which advocated a policy of stabilizing both world population and the world capital stock by the end of the twentieth century.[b] Its proposals, set forth in the form of computer-generated charts rather than the elegant prose of a John Stuart Mill, were roundly denounced by "orthodox" economists. However, the wide audience that the book attracted indicates that growth is still not universally accepted as a good thing.

---

[a]E. F. Schumacher, *Small Is Beautiful* (New York: Harper & Row, 1973).
[b]Donnella H. Meadows, Dennis L. Meadows, Jorgen Randers, and William W. Behrens III, *The Limits to Growth* (New York: Signet, 1972).

In Exhibit 4.6 a production possibility frontier is used to help separate the two issues. The diagram shows an economy in which two goods, clean air and cars, are produced. For an economy operating efficiently on its production possibility frontier, there is a trade-off between the two goods. More cars will make the air dirtier; fewer cars will allow cleaner air.

As technology is improved and more resources become available, the production possibility frontier shifts outward. If the economy follows a growth path from point A to point B, people will complain that growth has led to a deterioration of environmental quality. It is not the mere fact of growth that is to blame, however. Instead, the problem lies in the *direction* of growth, that is, the combination of outputs that has been chosen. The same expansion of the production possibility frontier could have made possible a growth path from point A to point C. That growth path would be possible if more effort and expense were devoted to building cars that run more cleanly. Comparing point A with point C, we see that growth can bring both more cars and cleaner air (or in general, both more material output and improved environmental quality) *if people choose to go that way.* As is often the case, our problems turn out to arise not from inescapable economic laws but from the choices we make.

4.4   The Business Cycle

Business cycle
A pattern of irregular but repeated expansion and contraction of aggregate economic activity.

As Exhibit 4.5 showed, the U.S. economy has grown substantially during the post–World War II period, but the pace of growth has not been steady. Real GNP has moved sometimes above, sometimes below the long-term trend line. In some years real GNP has not just grown more slowly but actually fallen. This pattern of irregular but repeated expansion and contraction of aggregate economic activity is known as the **business cycle.**

Phases of the Business Cycle

An idealized business cycle is shown in Exhibit 4.7. The cycle can be divided into four phases as the economy fluctuates around the long-term growth trend. The *peak* of the cycle is the point at which real output reaches a maximum. The period during which real output falls is known as the *contraction* phase. At the end of the contraction, real output reaches a minimum known as the *trough* of the cycle. After the trough, real output begins to grow again and the economy enters an *expansion* that lasts until a new peak is reached.

Recession
A cyclical economic contraction that lasts six months or more.

A contraction lasting six months or more is termed a **recession.** (Several recessions, of which the most recent ended in 1982, can be identified in

---

Exhibit 4.7   An Idealized Business Cycle

This exhibit shows an idealized business cycle. The cycle begins from a peak, then enters a contraction. A contraction lasting six months or more is called a recession. The low point of the cycle is known as its trough. Following the trough, the economy enters an expansion until a new peak is reached. Because real GNP varies about an upward trend, each cyclical peak tends to carry the economy to a higher level of real GNP than the previous one.

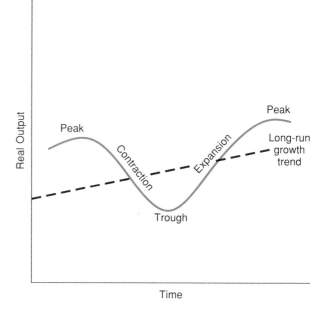

Exhibit 4.5.) The nineteenth and early twentieth centuries saw a number of cyclical contractions that were much more severe than any of the post–World War II recessions. These were called *depressions*. The most spectacular of these was the Great Depression of the 1930s, which actually consisted of two contractionary periods separated by an incomplete recovery. During this episode real output fell by one-third, the price level fell by one-quarter, and the unemployment rate climbed to 24 percent of the labor force. Because no succeeding contraction has come close to it in severity, the term *depression* has passed out of use in all but historical contexts.

Unemployment and Output over the Business Cycle

The preceding section portrayed the business cycle in terms of real national product, but changes in real output are linked to changes in employment. The trend line around which the idealized business cycle fluctuates represents a situation in which the economy expands at a rate that is consistent with its long-run growth potential. Under such conditions the economy is said to be at its **natural level of real output** or, alternatively, its *natural level of real national product*. The natural real output is the level that is consistent with the natural rate of unemployment.

> **Natural level of real output**
> The level of real output that is consistent with the natural rate of unemployment.

When an expansion carries real output above its natural level, unemployment tends to fall below its natural rate. The underlying reason is simple: More workers are needed to produce the additional output. Likewise, when contraction takes real output below the natural level, unemployment rises above its natural rate because fewer workers are required.

However, the linkage between changes in real output and unemployment is not a simple one-to-one relationship as is implied by the assumption that "more output requires more workers." Instead, according to a widely used rule of thumb, for each 2 percent by which real output rises above its natural level, the unemployment rate tends to fall by one percentage point, and for each 2 percent by which real output falls below its natural level, the unemployment rate tends to rise by one percentage point. This rule of thumb is known as **Okun's law.** It is named after Arthur Okun, who was a member of President Kennedy's Council of Economic Advisers at the time he formulated it (see ***Who Said It? Who Did It? 4.2***).[3]

> **Okun's law**
> A rule of thumb according to which each 2 percent by which real output rises above (or falls below) its natural level results in an unemployment rate one percentage point below (or above) the natural rate.

Suppose, for example, that the natural level of real output is $1 trillion and the natural rate of unemployment is 6 percent. In that case, a 4 percent decrease in real output, to $960 billion, would tend to raise the unemployment rate to 8 percent. Likewise, a 2 percent increase in real output from $1 trillion to $1.02 trillion would push unemployment one percentage point below its natural rate, to 5 percent.[4]

Why is there a 2-to-1 ratio between changes in real output relative to its natural level and changes in the unemployment rate relative to its natural rate?

---

[3]Okun's original study was based on data for the U.S. economy through the early 1960s. These data suggested a 3-to-1 ratio for his rule of thumb. Studies based on more recent data indicate that the relevant ratio is now 2-to-1, which is the ratio used in this text.

[4]We use the phrase "percentage point" because the unemployment rate itself is already expressed in percentage terms. It would be misleading to say "a 1 percent drop in the unemployment rate," which might be taken to mean a drop in the unemployment rate from 6.0 to 5.94 percent (5.94 being 99 percent of 6.0). A "one percentage point" drop in the unemployment rate clearly means a drop from 6.0 percent to 5.0 percent.

Who Said It? Who Did It?   4.2
Arthur Okun: Policy Economist

Arthur Okun was one of the best known of a generation of "new economists" who dominated economic policymaking during the Kennedy and Johnson administrations of the 1960s. In 1961, the young associate professor left Yale to join the "New Frontier" as a staff economist on the President's Council of Economic Advisers. In 1964, he became a full member of the council, and in 1968 and 1969 he served as its chairman. When Johnson left office, Okun stayed in Washington as a senior fellow of the Brookings Institution, a position that permitted him to combine research with active involvement in public affairs.

Okun's name first became well known in connection with research that related changes in unemployment to changes in real national product. In a paper written for the American Statistical Association in 1962, he tried to answer the question of how much output the economy could produce under conditions of full employment. Because of his concern about "the enormous social cost of idle resources," he found this question crucial to economic policy.

During Okun's service on the Council of Economic Advisers, economists' enthusiasm for economic growth was at its height. Okun saw rapid economic growth as es-

sential to avoiding the waste and extravagance of unemployment. "The economy loses ground if it stands still," he wrote. He added:

> *Unless the growth of total output keeps pace with our ever-expanding potential, the unemployment rate tends to rise. The nation needs continually to set new records in production and sales. Its economy needs to grow bigger and better than ever before — because its labor force, capital stock, technology, and managerial and organizational resources are always getting bigger and better.*

Okun's work at the Brookings Institution reflected the change from the optimistic, growth-oriented 1960s to the problem-ridden, inflationary 1970s. Okun contributed to our understanding of chronic inflation and proposed a variety of initiatives for combating it, including reduction of sales and payroll taxes and provision of tax rewards for wage-price restraints. In 1979 Okun was awarded the Seidman Foundation prize for his impact on public policy.

Photo source: Courtesy of The Brookings Institution.

Why doesn't adding 1 percent to real output cut unemployment by a full percentage point? There seem to be two basic reasons.

First, hiring and laying off workers is a costly process. Firms that hire new workers must bear the costs of advertising for applicants and screening them when they arrive. Also, new workers may not be fully productive until they have gone through a period of on-the-job training. Firms that lay off workers also bear costs. Some contracts call for severance payments. Some skilled workers may get other jobs after being laid off. Employers that have made many layoffs may be required by law to make higher payments to state and federal unemployment insurance funds. Because of these costs, firms tend to "hoard" labor during business downturns by cutting back their workers' hours or finding make-work projects for them instead of laying them off. Moreover, during upturns they may find it cheaper to put workers on overtime, even at time-and-a-half wages, rather than go to the trouble of finding new ones.

But labor hoarding does not fully explain the 2-to-1 ratio of Okun's law. A second explanation of the ratio lies in the way the unemployment rate itself is calculated. As we saw earlier in the chapter, the unemployment rate is the ratio of unemployed workers to the civilian labor force. During a business upturn, when firms are creating new jobs at a rapid rate, some previously unemployed workers find jobs. At the same time, however, the improved job market attracts workers who previously had not even looked for work. Not all the new entrants find work right away; some join the ranks of the unemployed instead. The upshot is that when output expands, the increase in the number of employed is accompanied by some growth of the labor force. As a result, a 1 percent increase in the number of jobs tends to be linked with a drop in the unemployment rate of less than one percentage point.

Inflation and the Business Cycle

The rate of inflation also tends to vary over the course of the business cycle. As the economy approaches the trough of a cycle, with real output falling below its natural level, the rate of inflation tends to slow. Historically, severe business downturns like the Great Depression produced not just a slowdown in the rate of inflation but also an actual drop in the price level (that is, a negative rate of inflation), although there have been no such episodes since World War II. On the other side of the cycle, the rate of inflation tends to accelerate as real output moves above its natural level and the economy approaches a cyclical peak.

The reasons for variations in inflation over the business cycle are complex. At one time it was common to explain the relationship in terms of constraints in the economy's production capacity and labor force. In this view, as the economy expands to a cyclical peak, firms run out of capacity and have difficulty recruiting new workers. Strong demand combined with limited supply then lead to a general rise in prices and wages. Thus rising real output is seen as the cause of rising prices.

Today this view is considered to be oversimplified. As we will see in coming chapters, economists now recognize that causation can run in the other direction as well. Under certain circumstances an increase in the rate of inflation can cause unemployment to fall and real output to rise. Chapters 7 through 16 will develop a macroeconomic model that incorporates this view of the relationship between inflation and real output as well. The model will also account for the fact that during the early stages of economic contractions the rate of inflation can continue to rise after real output and employment have already begun to fall. Similarly, in the early stages of an expansion, inflation can continue to slow even after real output and employment have begun to rise. A rough idea of these relationships can be gained by comparing Exhibits 4.1, 4.4, and 4.5. The relationships will be examined in much greater detail in later chapters.

Summary

1. **What is unemployment and why is it important for economic policy?** A person who works at least 1 hour a week for pay or 15 hours per week as an unpaid worker in a family business is considered to be *employed*. A person who is not currently employed but is actively looking for work is *unemployed*. The *unemployment rate* is the percentage of the *labor force* that is not employed. Unemployment has economic costs in terms of lost output and psychological damage. It may be classified as *frictional*, *structural*, or *cyclical*, depending on its cause. Structural plus frictional unemployment is known as the *natural rate of unemployment*. The *employment-population ratio*, which is the percent-

age of the adult noninstitutional population that is employed, is an alternative measure of the economy's success in meeting the goal of high employment.

2. **What is inflation and what impact does it have on the economy?** *Inflation* is a sustained increase in the average level of prices of all goods and services. *Price stability*, a situation in which the rate of inflation is low enough so that it is not a significant factor in business and individual decision making, is a second major goal of economic policy. Inflation is frequently measured in terms of the rate of change in the *consumer price index*. In measuring economic quantities, a dis-

tinction must be made between *real* values, or values adjusted for inflation, and *nominal* values, or values expressed in the ordinary way, in current dollars. Applying these concepts to interest rates, we can say that the *real interest rate* is equal to the *nominal interest rate* minus the rate of inflation. Inflation disrupts the economy in two ways. First, it harms or benefits individuals according to their source of income; second, it disrupts economic calculation, thereby discouraging saving and investment. In addition, the effort to stop inflation once it has begun often entails substantial costs.

3. **What trends has economic growth followed in the United States?** Economic growth is most commonly expressed in terms of the rate of growth of *gross national product*, a measure of the economy's total output of goods and services. To avoid distortions caused by inflation, gross national product is expressed in real terms. Real gross national product has grown at an average rate of about 3 percent since 1950, although that growth has not been steady. Economic growth is widely seen as beneficial, in that it makes possible higher living standards, jobs for those who want them, and more leisure for those who want it. Some people criticize growth as damaging to the environment. In evaluating such damage, the composition of real national product as it grows must be considered as well as its rate of growth.

4. **What is the nature of the business cycle?** Over time, the economy undergoes a pattern of irregular but repeated expansion and contraction of aggregate economic activity that is known as the *business cycle*. The point at which output reaches a maximum is known as the peak of the cycle. This is followed by a contraction, a trough, an expansion, and a new peak. A contraction lasting six months or more is known as a *recession*. Over the course of the business cycle, the economy sometimes rises above and sometimes falls below its *natural level of real output*. The natural level of real output is the level that is consistent with the economy's long-run growth potential and the natural rate of unemployment. According to *Okun's law*, for each 2 percent by which real output changes relative to its natural level, the unemployment rate changes by one percentage point in the opposite direction. The rate of inflation also varies over the business cycle. It tends to rise during times when real output is above its natural level and to fall when real output is below its natural level.

Terms for Review

· employed
· unemployed
· labor force
· unemployment rate
· discouraged worker
· employment-population ratio
· frictional unemployment
· structural unemployment
· natural rate of unemployment
· cyclical unemployment
· inflation
· price stability
· consumer price index
· real
· nominal
· indexation
· transfer payments
· nominal interest rate
· real interest rate
· gross national product (GNP)
· real output
· business cycle
· recession
· natural level of real output
· Okun's law

Questions for Review

1. What criteria are used to determine whether a person is employed? Unemployed? In the labor force? A discouraged worker?

2. What are the positive and normative costs of unemployment?

3. How does the concept of unemployment differ from "not working" and from "can't find a job"?

4. Explain why it is possible for the employment-population ratio to increase while the unemployment rate remains unchanged or rises. Describe the trends in these two statistics over the past 20 years.

5. What is meant by the natural rate of unemployment? How does the officially reported unemployment rate relate to the natural rate at various points in the business cycle?

6. Why is price stability considered to be an important goal of economic policy?

7. If the nominal rate of interest is 8 percent and the rate of inflation is 5 percent, what is the real rate of interest?

8. List some benefits and costs of economic growth. Under what conditions, if any, can economic growth take place with less damage to the environment?

9. Distinguish among the terms *contraction*, *recession*, and *depression*. How are they related? How do they differ?

10. If the unemployment rate is initially 5 percent and real GNP then declines by 5 percent, what will happen to the unemployment rate?

11. What tends to happen to the rate of inflation over the course of the business cycle?

Problems and Topics for Discussion

1. **Examining the lead-off case.** Using the information given in the case at the beginning of the chapter, calculate the size of the civilian labor force and the number of civilians who were employed. Why did the large increase in the number of workers employed not lead to a decrease in the unemployment rate?

2. **Your personal labor force status.** What is your current labor force status? Are you a member of the labor force? Are you employed? Unemployed? Explain the basis for your answers. When was the last time your labor force status changed? Do you expect it to change soon? Give details.

3. **Employment hardship.** It has been suggested that the unemployment rate should be replaced with an "employment hardship index" that tries to measure the percentage of people who suffer hardship because of their labor force status. What kinds of people who are not now counted as unemployed might fit into the hardship category? What kinds of people who are now counted as unemployed would not suffer hardship? Discuss.

4. **Real and nominal interest rates.** Check with your local bank to find out what interest rates currently apply to (a) one-year savings certificates and (b) three-year automobile loans. Compare these nominal interest rates with the current rate of inflation as measured by the most recently announced rate of change in the consumer price index. (That number is announced in the middle of each month for the previous month; check business periodicals for the latest data.) If the current rate of inflation were to continue unchanged, what real rate of interest would you earn on the saving certificate? What real rate of interest would you pay on the loan?

5. **Economic growth and the environment.** The pace of economic growth varies from one area of the United States to another. Some regions are growing rapidly, with people moving in, much new construction, rising incomes, and so on. Other areas are stagnant or declining, with little new construction and people moving away. Which type of area do you live in? Can you identify any environmental problems in your area that seem to be caused by economic growth? Can you identify any environmental problems that seem to be caused by economic decline? What policies could you suggest that would permit growth in your area to take place with less environmental disruption?

6. **The current state of the business cycle.** Unemployment and inflation data are announced monthly, and data on economic growth are announced on a quarterly basis. Watch your local newspaper, *The Wall Street Journal*, or business magazines such as *Business Week* for discussions of the most recent data. What changes have there been? What is happening to the employment rate? Are the employment and unemployment rates moving in the same direction or in opposite directions? What is the current rate of inflation? Is it increasing, decreasing, or staying the same? Judging from available data, in which phase of the business cycle does the economy appear to be at the moment?

Case for Discussion

"No Matter Where I'd Go, I'd Be One of the First Laid Off"

After five jobs in seven years, 49-year-old Al Kaczor saw a pattern he didn't like. "I had seen my parents laid off and all the relatives laid off from factories," he says. "No matter where I'd go, I'd be one of the first laid off."

Instead, Kaczor is dropping out of the work force this fall to complete his bachelor's degree. He also will disappear from the unemployment statistics, becoming what economists call a discouraged worker, someone who wants a job but has given up looking. Economists estimate that if discouraged workers were included in unemployment figures, unemployment rates would be much higher than they are now.

For Kaczor, the decision came slowly. In April, he lost his $2,300-a-month job as a safety engineer at InteCom Inc. in a 200-worker cutback. During the next three months, he applied to 50 companies, certain that a job would come along.

"I'd been unemployed once before for eight months. Things came through then," he says. That was in 1981, when his contract as a maintenance engineer at a nuclear power plant expired. Eventually he got a lower-paying job as a technical writer. And jobs worked out before that. A high-school dropout, he found a career in the Air Force. When he left the Air Force 22 years later, in 1978, he worked at two minimum-wage jobs before landing the nuclear plant job.

This time, however, many nearby manufacturing concerns, like InteCom, fell victim to the current electronics slump, and Kaczor didn't get a single interview. "I could find work, I'm sure, although I may have to work at McDonald's," he says. But it hit home that a college degree might be the only way to a more secure job, or at least to help him start his own business.

Source: Karen Blumenthal, "Low Unemployment in Boston and Dallas Isn't a Job Guarantee," *The Wall Street Journal*, August 26, 1985, 1. Reprinted by permission of *The Wall Street Journal*, © Dow Jones & Company, Inc., 1985. All Rights Reserved Worldwide.

Questions

1. Identify Kaczor's labor market status at the points in his career at which he was (a) in the Air Force; (b) working for InteCom; (c) applying to 50 jobs in three months after leaving InteCom; (d) working at a McDonald's (if he did so) while waiting for college to start in the fall; (e) in college; (f) out of college, looking for a new job but not yet having found one; (g) working in his own business.

2. Discuss Kaczor's position at various times in terms of the concept "can't find a job."

3. Would you classify Kaczor's unemployment spells as frictional, structural, or cyclical? Are there elements of each type of unemployment at various points in his career? Explain.

Suggestions for Further Reading

Kaufman, Bruce E. *The Economics of Labor Markets and Labor Relations*. Hinsdale, Ill.: Dryden Press, 1986.

Chapter 13 deals with the measurement of unemployment and the distinction among various types of unemployment.

Meadows, Donnella H., et al. *The Limits to Growth*. New York: Signet, 1972.

A classic statement of the case against economic growth.

President's Council of Economic Advisers. *Economic Report of the President*. Washington, D.C.: Government Printing Office, annual.

Discusses the latest trends in unemployment, inflation, and economic growth, among other subjects; includes an appendix with extensive data on these and other macroeconomic variables.

Reich, Robert B. *The Next American Frontier*. New York: Times Books, 1983.

The author makes a case for promoting economic growth and suggests ways of doing so.

CHAPTER

5

The Circular Flow of Income and Product

**Before reading this chapter,
make sure you know the meaning of:**

Theories and models (Chapter 1)

Investment (Chapter 1)

Equilibrium (Chapter 2)

Inventories (Chapter 2)

Gross national product (Chapter 4)

Real and nominal values (Chapter 4)

Transfer payments (Chapter 4)

After reading this chapter, you will understand:

How households and firms are linked by incomes
and expenditures.

How income is related to money.

How the concepts of supply and demand can be
applied to the economy as a whole.

How the various pieces of the economy—
households, firms, government, and financial
markets—fit together.

How the U.S. economy is linked to the rest of the
world.

124

Be Prepared

Interest rates will head up this year, not down, as investors and government officials recognize a quickening of inflation. A recession can't be ruled out completely, but optimists have the better case. Total hours worked increased in February, the second monthly rise in a row after two months of decline. Industrial production climbed, mainly because Detroit speeded assemblies after dealers got inventories down to healthy levels. Car sales, the prime weakness in consumer spending, have averaged a 9.8 million annual rate this year including imports, up from the dismal 8.7 million pace in the autumn.

The Commerce Department's revisions of fourth-quarter GNP data also provide encouragement. Inventory accumulation was revised down several billion dollars from the first estimate, indicating that businesses won't have to cut back as much as it appeared they would to reach sustainable levels. And exports climbed significantly faster than imports, contrary to the first report, showing that trade was still providing a lift.

Where does that leave prospects for interest rates? Total borrowing will amount to some $700 billion, about the same as in 1989. Consumer borrowing will not change much. Business demands for credit may even slip a bit despite greater capital spending needs. The odds are looking better for serious federal budget cutting.

That leaves most economists fairly sanguine about interest rates, but our higher inflation outlook, starting with strong growth of nominal GNP leaves us more bearish. Rates won't rise enough to trigger a recession before midyear at least. But they will make a cliffhanger of whether, in October 1991, this expansion will enter the record books as the longest in history.

Photo source: Tim Brown/Tony Stone Worldwide.

Source: Todd May, Jr., "Be Prepared: Interest Rates Will Head Up This Year, Not Down," *Fortune*, April 9, 1990, 25–27.

The preceding chapter looked at inflation, unemployment and real output—three key macroeconomic indicators. But as this forecast from *Fortune* magazine shows, there are many more pieces to the puzzle than these three. Interest rates, inventories, consumer spending, imports, exports, the federal budget deficit—how can they all possibly fit together? How do the actions of millions of individual firms and households, each making decisions independently, interact to produce recessions, recoveries, slowdowns, and booms? This chapter identifies the major pieces of the puzzle and their relationships to one another. In so doing, it lays the foundation for all of the macroeconomic models that follow.

5.1   The Circular Flow in a Simple Economy

Circular flow of income and product
The flow of goods and services between households and firms, balanced by the flow of payments made in exchange for goods and services.

The model around which this chapter is built is the **circular flow of income and product**—that is, the flow of goods and services between households and firms, balanced by the flow of payments made in exchange for them.

To see the circular flow in its simplest form, we will begin with an economy in which there is no government, no financial markets, and no imports or exports. To make things even simpler, imagine that the households in this economy live entirely from hand to mouth, spending all their income on consumer goods as soon as they receive it, and that the firms sell all their output directly to consumers as soon as they produce it.

The Basic Circular Flow

Exhibit 5.1 shows the circular flow of income and product for this ultrasimple economy. Real goods and services are shown flowing clockwise. Two sets of markets link households and firms. *Product markets*, which appear at the top of the diagram, are those in which households buy the goods and services that firms produce. *Factor markets*, which appear at the bottom, are those in which firms obtain the factors of production they need—labor services, capital, and natural resources—from households.

The clockwise flows of goods and services through these markets are balanced by counterclockwise flows of payments. Households make payments for the things they buy in product markets. Firms make *factor payments*—wages, interest payments, rents, royalties, and so on—in exchange for the labor services and other resources they buy.

By convention, when firms use factors of production that they themselves own, they are counted as "buying" them from the households that are the ultimate owners of the firms. All production costs therefore can be viewed as payments for factors of production purchased from households. If a firm has something left over after meeting all its costs, it earns a profit. Profits too are counted as flowing directly to the households that own the firms, even though a firm may retain some profit to increase its owners' equity rather than paying it out as dividends. For the purposes of the circular flow, then, profit is lumped together with factor payments.

Stocks and Flows

Flow
A process that occurs continuously through time, measured in units per time period.

We refer to all the amounts shown as arrows in Exhibit 5.1 as **flows** because they are continuously occurring processes. Flows are measured in units per time period—dollars per year, gallons per minute, or tons per month. Measurements of flows are measurements of rates at which things are happening.

Exhibit 5.1   The Basic Circular Flow

In this simple economy, households spend all their income on consumer goods as soon as they receive it and firms sell all their output to households as soon as they produce it. Goods and services flow clockwise, and the corresponding payments flow counterclockwise.

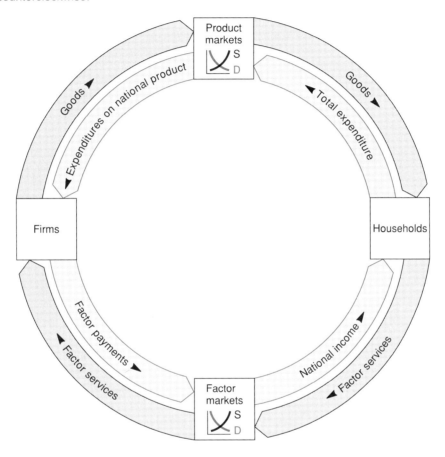

Flows must be distinguished from stocks. **Stocks** are quantities that exist at a given point in time. Stocks are measured in terms of dollars, gallons, tons, and so on at a given point in time. The amusement park ride described in ***Applying Economic Ideas 5.1*** provides a simple illustration of the relationship between stocks and flows.

Stock
A quantity that exists at a given point in time, measured in terms of units only.

Money in the Circular Flow

The fluid that keeps the economy's plumbing system working is money. *Money* is what we use as a means of payment for buying goods and services. (A formal definition of money will be given in Chapter 11.) The forms of money that are most familiar to consumers are coins, paper currency, and bank account balances. Just as there is a certain stock of water in the White Water Canyon ride on any given day, there is a given stock of money in the economy at any point in time—so many dimes, so many $20 bills, and so on. For example, in the week

Applying Economic Ideas   5.1
White Water Canyon

King's Dominion is a huge amusement park near Richmond, Virginia. The summer weather is hot there, which helps explain why one of the most popular rides in the park is one called White Water Canyon.

In White Water Canyon, riders are seated in a round rubber raft. After they are buckled in, the raft is swept down a twisting concrete chute through a series of wild rapids. Riders are guaranteed to get soaked to the skin in cool water as they hit waves and shoot under waterfalls. Then they get back in line, hoping to reach the boarding point again before they dry off.

The chute down which the rafts ride looks much like a real river, but it is artificial. An electric pump circulates the water from a pond at the bottom of the chute back up to the top. The speed of the ride is controlled by the speed of the motor. When the motor runs faster, more water is pumped through the chute and the rafts are carried along at a higher speed. If the speed of the pump is reduced, the rafts slow down until they hit bottom and cease to move at all.

The system is connected to a pipeline that can be used to add water to replace water lost through splashing and evaporation. However, adding water does not in itself control the speed of the ride. If the pump's speed remains constant, extra water added to the system simply collects in the pond at the bottom of the chute.

This amusement park ride provides a simple illustration of the concepts of stocks and flows. The *stock* of water used in the ride is the number of gallons the system contains at any given time. When the pumps are turned off for the night, the stock of water in the system stays the same; all those gallons just trickle down into the pond at the bottom of the chute. When the pumps are turned on in the morning, the same stock of water is set in motion again.

The *flow* of water through the ride is the number of gallons per minute passing a given point in the system— say, the point at which riders board the rafts. The faster the pumps run, the faster the flow. When the pumps are turned off, the flow falls to zero even though the stock of water remains constant.

ending November 24, 1989, the U.S. money stock was $3.2 trillion, according to a widely used measure. Unless the government or private banks do something to change the stock of money (such as printing more $20 bills and putting them into circulation), that $3.2 trillion is what the economy has to work with, just as the stock of water in the ride is what its operators have to work with (unless they change it by opening the drain or inlet valve).

The economy's money stock, like the water in the ride, does not just lie there. To do any useful work, it must be constantly circulated through the plumbing. Economic flows, such as income and expenditures, are measures of the speed with which money is moving through the system. These economic flows are measured in dollars per year in the same way that the flow of water in the ride is measured in gallons per minute. National income—in dollars per year—is greater than the stock of money because each unit of money can be spent more than once each year: workers spend their pay at supermarkets; supermarkets spend their revenues to meet their payrolls; checkout clerks spend their paychecks at gas stations; and so on. For example, in 1989 national income was flowing at a rate of well over $5 trillion per year even though the stock of money was just $3.2 trillion.

In both the White Water Canyon ride and the U.S. economy, stocks and flows are related and changes in one are often associated with changes in the other. Yet stocks and flows can also vary independently:

- In the case of the ride, turning on the inlet valve will increase the stock of water. However, as long as the pumps continue to run at the same speed, the added water will just sit at the bottom and the rate of flow through the chute will not change. On the other hand, the flow can be increased by speeding up the pump even while the drain and inlet valves remain closed and the stock of water in the system stays fixed.

- In the case of the economy, adding more money—in the form of $20 bills, bank balances, or whatever—will not speed up the flow of income if the money just sits in people's pockets and bank accounts. On the other hand, the flow of income can be speeded up even if the stock of money remains fixed if people increase the rate at which they pass the money from hand to hand.

The relationship between the stock of money in the economy and the flow of income is one of the crucial keys to understanding macroeconomics. We will return to this relationship repeatedly in later chapters.

National Income and Product

Look again at Exhibit 5.1. Two of the flows shown there deserve special attention. The first is labeled "national income." **National income** is the total value of all wages, rents, interest payments, and profits earned by households. The second is labeled "expenditures on national product." **National product** is the total value of all goods and services produced. Expenditures on national product are the dollar flow to firms that balances the flow of products themselves from firms to product markets, for example, the payments for clothing that manufacturers receive in return for the shirts and blouses that consumers receive. National income is the dollar flow from firms to households in return for labor and other factors of production, for example, the paychecks that apparel workers receive for sewing shirts and blouses. National income and national product are, by definition, equal in this simple economy.[1] This can be verified in two ways.

First, consider household expenditures as a link between national income and national product. Households are assumed to spend all their income on consumer goods as soon as they receive it, and firms are assumed to sell all their output directly to households. The payments made by buyers must equal the payments received by sellers; thus, viewed from this side of the circular flow, national product must equal national income.

Second, consider payments for labor and other factors as a link between national income and national product. When firms receive money for the goods and services they sell, they use part of it to pay workers, owners of natural resources, and suppliers of capital. Anything left over is profit. Thus, factor payments, including profits, account for all the money earned by households, and total factor payments are equal to national income. From this it follows that national income and national product are equal when viewed from this side of the circular flow, too.

National income
The total income earned by households, including wages, rents, interest payments, and profits.

National product
The total value of all goods and services produced in the economy.

---

[1]As we will see in the next chapter, establishing the equality of national income and product as measured in the official national income accounts requires a bit more detail than is shown here. Among other things, we will have to distinguish between *gross* and *net* national product, which are two ways of measuring this part of the circular flow. However, these details of national income accounting are not critical to the discussion of macroeconomic theory in this and later chapters.

Exhibit 5.2   The Circular Flow with Saving and Investment

When saving and investment are added to the circular flow, there are two paths
by which funds can travel on their way from households to product markets. One
path is direct, via consumption expenditures. The other is indirect, via saving,
financial markets, and investment. The clockwise flows of goods and services
have been omitted from this diagram; only flows of funds are shown.

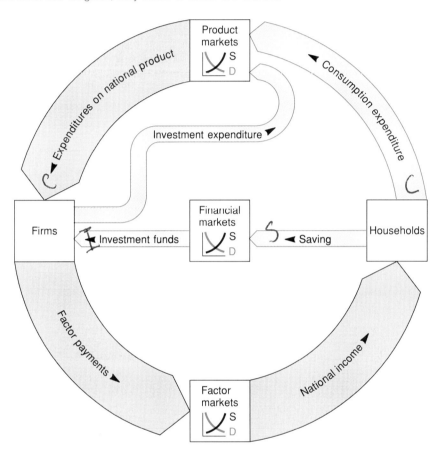

Saving, Investment, and Financial Markets

The circular flow shown in Exhibit 5.1 is only a first step in laying out the
linkages between households and firms. The next step is to add a second set of
linkages that involve saving, investment, and financial markets. These linkages
are shown in Exhibit 5.2. To simplify this and the following circular flow diagrams, the clockwise flows of goods and services are omitted.

Saving.   On the average, households spend less each year than they receive in
income. The portion of household income that is not used to buy goods and
services or to pay taxes is termed **saving.** (There are no taxes in this economy
yet, but they will soon be added.)

The most familiar form of saving is the use of part of a household's income
to make deposits in bank accounts or to buy stocks, bonds, or other financial

Saving
The part of household
income that is not used to
buy goods and services or to
pay taxes.

instruments, rather than to buy goods and services. However, economists take a broader view of saving. They also consider households to be saving when they repay debts. Debt repayments are a form of saving because they, too, are income that is not devoted to consumption or taxes.

Investment.   Whereas households, on the average, spend less each year than they receive in income, business firms, on the average, spend more each year than they receive from the sale of their products. They do so because, in addition to paying for the productive resources they need to carry out production at its current level, they desire to undertake *investment*. As we saw in Chapter 1, investment includes all spending that is directed toward increasing the economy's stock of capital.

If we examine this topic more closely, we can distinguish between two categories of investment. The first, **fixed investment,** means the purchase of newly produced capital goods, such as production machinery, office equipment, and newly built structures. The second is **inventory investment**—the accumulation of stocks of raw materials prior to use or of finished products prior to sale. Inventories held by businesses are counted as part of the economy's stock of capital; they are just as necessary to the production process as capital in the form of machinery or buildings. Inventory investment can be less than zero in periods when firms are reducing their stocks of raw materials and finished products. The term *investment* used alone refers to the sum of fixed investment and inventory investment.

Investment is defined somewhat more narrowly in economics than in everyday usage. In common terms, investment means the purchase of almost any kind of asset; thus, a person or firm might be said to "invest" in corporate stocks, a previously built house, or secondhand oil tankers. However, none of these purchases is an investment in the economic sense because it adds nothing to the economy's total stock of capital goods or total inventories.

Suppose, for example, that Exxon buys a brand-new, custom-built oil tanker. That would be an investment, because the tanker is a new addition to the economy's stock of capital. A few years later Exxon decides to sell the tanker to Mobil. For carrying oil, a used tanker is just as good as a new one. Yet the purchase is not an investment in the economic sense; it is not an addition to the economy's stock of capital in the year in which it changes hands. Likewise, purchases of other used capital goods, real estate (other than new structures), mineral deposits, forests, and so on are not investments in the economic sense. They are simply transfers of assets from the balance sheet of one household or firm to that of another.

Financial markets.   As we have seen, households tend to spend less each year than they receive in income, whereas firms tend to spend more than they receive from the sale of their products. The economy contains a special set of institutions whose function is to channel the flow of funds from households, as savers, to firms, as borrowers.[2] These are known as **financial markets.** Financial markets are pictured in the center of the circular-flow diagram in Exhibit 5.2.

Fixed investment
Purchases by firms of newly produced capital goods, such as production machinery, office equipment, and newly built structures.

Inventory investment
Changes in the stocks of finished products and raw materials that firms keep on hand; the figure is positive if such stocks are increasing and negative if they are decreasing.

Financial markets
A set of market institutions whose function is to channel the flow of funds from net savers to net borrowers.

[2]The version of the circular flow presented in Exhibit 5.2 shows households as the only source of saving and firms as the only borrowers. Reality is somewhat more complex. Later in the chapter we will see that federal, state, and local governments, as well as foreign firms and governments, participate in financial markets as savers or borrowers. In addition, it should be kept in mind that although households on the average are savers and firms on the average are borrowers, some households are borrowers and some firms are savers.

Financial intermediaries
A group of firms, including banks, insurance companies, pension funds, and mutual funds, that gather funds from net savers and lends them to net borrowers.

Common stock
A certificate of shared ownership in a corporation that gives the owner a vote in the selection of the firm's management and the right to a share in its profits.

Bond
A certificate that represents a promise, in return for borrowed funds, to repay the loan over a period of years, with interest, according to an agreed-upon schedule.

Securities
A collective term for common stocks, bonds, and other financial instruments.

Aggregate supply
The value of all goods and services produced in the economy; a synonym for national product.

Aggregate demand
The value of all planned expenditures.

Banks are among the most familiar and important institutions found in financial markets. Banks, together with insurance companies, pension funds, mutual funds, and certain other institutions, are termed **financial intermediaries** because their role is to gather funds from savers and channel them to borrowers in the form of loans.

More than half of all saving flows through financial intermediaries. The remainder is obtained directly from households through the sale of stocks, bonds, and other securities. **Common stocks** are certificates of shared ownership in a corporation that give the owner a vote in the selection of the firm's management and the right to a share in its profits. (The word *stock* used as a shorthand for *common stock* has nothing to do with the concept of stocks as distinguished from flows, defined earlier.) **Bonds** are certificates that represent a promise, in return for borrowed funds, to repay the loan over a period of years, with interest, according to an agreed-upon schedule. Bonds, stocks, and certain other financial instruments are collectively referred to as **securities.** A variety of markets exist in which securities are bought, sold, and resold among households, firms, and financial intermediaries. The New York Stock Exchange, located on Wall Street in New York City, is the best known of the securities markets.

5.2   Aggregate Supply and Demand

Adding saving and investment to the circular flow raises a new issue. There are now two pathways along which funds flow from households to product markets: a direct path, through consumption expenditures, and an indirect path, through saving and financial markets to investment expenditures. Corresponding to these two paths are two separate sets of decision makers: households, which make consumption decisions, and businesses, which make investment decisions. How can we be sure that when the two types of expenditures are added together they will match the amount of available goods and services? In other words, how can we be certain that national income will still equal national product?

These questions can be answered using the familiar concepts of supply and demand in a new way. First, we define **aggregate supply** as the value of all goods and services produced in the economy. We already have another term for the same thing: *national product.* Next, we define **aggregate demand** as the value of all the purchases of newly produced goods and services that buyers plan to make. Thus, we can compare aggregate supply and aggregate demand to see whether, for the economy as a whole, buyers' plans mesh with sellers' plans in the same way that we compare supply and demand in the case of a single market.

Equilibrium in the Circular Flow

To see how aggregate supply can be compared with aggregate demand, imagine an economy in which only three goods are produced: apples, radios, and milling machines. The firms in this economy plan to produce apples at a rate of $30,000 per year, radios at a rate of $30,000 per year, and milling machines at a rate of $40,000 per year. As they carry out their plans, output flows at a rate of $100,000 per year. This flow, which can be called either national product or aggregate supply, is shown in lines 1 through 4 of Exhibit 5.3.

Exhibit 5.3   Example of a Simple Economy in Equilibrium

This exhibit shows a simple economy in which aggregate supply is exactly equal to aggregate demand. The plans of buyers and sellers match when they are tested in the marketplace, and no unplanned inventory changes take place. National product and total planned expenditures are equal.

Output Resulting from Producers' Plans		
1 Total national product (aggregate supply)		$100,000
2 Apples	$30,000	
3 Radios	30,000	
4 Milling machines	40,000	

Expenditures Resulting from Buyers' Plans			
5 Total consumption expenditures		$60,000	
6 Apples	$30,000		
7 Radios	30,000		
8 Total planned investment		40,000	
9 Fixed investment (milling machines)	40,000		
10 Planned inventory investment	0		
11 Total planned expenditure (aggregate demand)			$100,000

While producers are busy carrying out their plans, buyers are making their own plans. Consumers plan to buy apples at a rate of $30,000 per year and radios at a rate of $30,000 per year. The firms that make radios plan to buy milling machines at a rate of $40,000 per year to increase their radio-producing capacity. No one plans to increase or decrease the stocks of finished products held in inventory; therefore, planned inventory investment is zero. All of these buying plans are expressed in lines 5 through 11 of Exhibit 5.3. The value of all planned expenditures (consumption plus fixed investment plus planned inventory investment) is shown in line 11 as aggregate demand.

Comparing line 1 with line 11, we see that in this example buyers' and sellers' plans match perfectly. Aggregate supply and aggregate demand are equal. When the plans of buyers and sellers mesh in this way, we say that the circular flow as a whole is in *equilibrium*, just as we say that a market is in equilibrium when the plans of buyers and sellers in that market mesh.

Disequilibrium

In practice, the plans of buyers and sellers almost never fit together as neatly as they do in Exhibit 5.3. In fact, it would be surprising if they did. After all, buyers and sellers do not always consult one another before production takes place. Each firm bases its production plans on the information available to it. Buyers base their plans on market prices and expectations about the future. Because production plans are often set before buyers' plans have been formed, there is no way to be sure the two sets of plans will mesh.

Exhibit 5.4 shows what happens when buyers' and sellers' plans do not mesh. Here the situation is the same as in Exhibit 5.3, except that now consumers plan to buy only $25,000 worth of apples and firms plan to buy only $35,000 worth of investment goods (milling machines). Thus, aggregate demand (line 11) is only $90,000, even though aggregate supply (line 1) is still $100,000.

Exhibit 5.4 Example of a Simple Economy in Disequilibrium

In this example, planned purchases of apples and milling machines fall short of the amounts of those goods produced. When plans are tested in the marketplace, producers of apples and milling machines experience an unplanned increase in inventories. Total planned expenditure (aggregate demand) falls short of national product (aggregate supply). However, total realized expenditures, including both planned expenditures and unplanned inventory investment, equal national product.

Output Resulting from Producers' Plans				
1	Total national product (aggregate supply)			$100,000
2	Apples	$30,000		
3	Radios	30,000		
4	Milling machines	40,000		
Expenditures Resulting from Buyers' Plans				
5	Total consumption expenditures		$55,000	
6	Apples	$25,000		
7	Radios	30,000		
8	Total planned investment		35,000	
9	Fixed investment (milling machines)	35,000		
10	Planned inventory investment	0		
11	Total planned expenditure (aggregate demand)			$ 90,000
Other Expenditures				
12	Total unplanned inventory investment			10,000
13	Unsold apples	5,000		
14	Unsold milling machines	5,000		
Summary				
15	Total national product			$100,000
16	Total realized expenditure			100,000
17	Planned	$90,000		
18	Unplanned	10,000		

When these plans are tested in the marketplace, there will be some disappointment: All the radios will be sold, but $5,000 worth of apples and $5,000 worth of milling machines will be left over. What will happen to these unsold goods? Once they have been produced, they will not vanish into thin air; instead, they will pile up as inventories in the warehouses of apple farmers and machine tool companies. Those producers did not *plan* to make any inventory investments, but they nonetheless find themselves doing so. The $5,000 of unsold apples and the $5,000 of unsold milling machines are therefore listed in lines 12 through 14 of Exhibit 5.4 as *unplanned* inventory investments. Because buyers' and sellers' plans do not mesh, the circular flow is said to be in *disequilibrium*.

Reactions to Disequilibrium

In Exhibit 5.4 aggregate supply exceeds aggregate demand. Because buyers' and sellers' plans do not mesh, there is an unplanned buildup of inventories. Because firms would not want this inventory buildup to continue, they would limit or reverse it by doing one or both of two things. First, they might cut their prices to stimulate sales. If they did this, the volume of the circular flow measured in nominal terms (that is, in terms of dollars' worth of goods and services at current prices) would shrink. Second, they might cut their rate of output. If they did this, the circular flow would shrink both in real terms (that is, in terms of output of goods and services adjusted for changes in prices) and in nominal terms.

At another time, aggregate demand might exceed aggregate supply. Suppose, for example, that instead of the planned expenditures shown in Exhibit 5.4 consumers plan to buy $35,000 worth of apples and firms $45,000 worth of milling machines. When these plans are tested in the marketplace, sales will exceed current output. The result will be unplanned depletion of inventories as stocks of apples and milling machines are used to meet the strong demand. Firms will react in a way that is opposite to their reaction to an unplanned inventory buildup. If they try to stop the inventory depletion by raising their prices, the circular flow will grow in nominal terms. If they also increase output, the circular flow will grow in both real and nominal terms.

Equality of National Income and Product

As Exhibits 5.3 and 5.4 show, national product (aggregate supply) equals planned expenditure (aggregate demand) only when the economy is in equilibrium. However, whether or not the economy is in equilibrium, national product always equals **realized expenditure,** that is, the total of planned and unplanned expenditures. This is so because unplanned inventory investment acts as a balancing item. When planned expenditure falls short of aggregate supply, inventories pile up. In that case, adding unplanned inventory investment to planned expenditure makes total realized expenditure equal to aggregate supply. On the other hand, if planned expenditure exceeds aggregate supply, inventories are run down. In that case, adding the negative unplanned inventory investment to planned consumption and investment makes total realized expenditure equal to aggregate supply. In equation form:

Realized expenditure
The sum of all planned and unplanned expenditures.

$$\begin{array}{c}\text{National} \\ \text{product}\end{array} = \begin{array}{c}\text{Total} \\ \text{planned} \\ \text{expenditure}\end{array} + \begin{array}{c}\text{Unplanned} \\ \text{inventory} \\ \text{investment}\end{array} = \begin{array}{c}\text{Total} \\ \text{realized} \\ \text{expenditure}\end{array}$$

Another way of writing the same thing is:

$$\begin{array}{c}\text{Aggregate} \\ \text{supply}\end{array} = \begin{array}{c}\text{Aggregate} \\ \text{demand}\end{array} + \begin{array}{c}\text{Unplanned} \\ \text{inventory} \\ \text{investment}\end{array}$$

Having shown that national product equals total realized expenditure in this economy, we can also show that national product equals national income. As in the ultrasimple economy of Exhibit 5.1, the equality of national income and product can be shown in one of two ways.

First, we can take advantage of the fact that payments for factor services and profits provide a link between national income and national product. In Exhibits 5.3 and 5.4 firms are shown as producing $100,000 worth of goods each year, all of which is either sold to investors and consumers or added to inventory. In the course of producing this quantity of goods, firms incur costs, which enter the national income stream as wages, interest payments, rents, and so on. Anything left over after all costs have been paid is profit for the firms—and this, too, is counted as going into the national income stream. The total of factor payments plus profits thus account for the entire $100,000 of national product (sales to final users plus inventory change).

Second, the equality of national income and product can be shown using expenditures as a link. In Exhibit 5.3 households plan to spend $60,000 on consumer goods (radios and apples). The other $40,000 leaves the circular flow as saving. Firms plan to invest $40,000 in milling machines, so the $40,000 is injected back into the economy as investment spending. Total expenditures (consumption plus investment) thus equal national income (saving plus consumption). Also, total expenditures, as shown earlier, equal national product.

In Exhibit 5.4 the plans of households and firms do not mesh so neatly, but total realized expenditures still provide a link between national income and national product. Households plan to spend just $55,000 and save $45,000; firms plan to invest only $35,000. Saving thus exceeds planned investment by $10,000. However, as we saw before, the $10,000 of goods that firms produce but that no one plans to buy do not vanish into thin air; instead, they pile up in inventory, where they are counted as unplanned inventory investment. When this is taken into account, total **realized investment** ($35,000 planned plus $10,000 unplanned) equals saving. Again, therefore, national income (saving plus consumption) equals total realized expenditure (consumption plus realized investment) and, as always, total realized expenditure equals national product.

Realized investment
The sum of planned and unplanned investment.

5.3   Adding Government to the Circular Flow

The next step in our analysis of the circular flow is to add the public sector. Government is linked to the rest of the economy in three ways: through taxes, expenditures, and government borrowing. These three links are added to the circular flow in Exhibit 5.5.

First, consider taxes. For purposes of macroeconomic theory, we need to measure the flow of funds withdrawn from the household sector by government. Clearly, taxes—including income, payroll, and property taxes—are withdrawals. However, this flow of funds from the household sector is partly offset by a flow of funds returned to households in the form of transfer payments, such as social security benefits and unemployment compensation. Therefore, to get a proper measure of the net flow of funds from households to government, we must subtract transfer payments from total taxes. The difference between taxes and transfers is called **net taxes** and is indicated in Exhibit 5.5 by the arrow linking households and government.

Net taxes
Taxes paid to government minus transfer payments made by government.

Next, consider the link between government and product markets. We have already accounted for transfers in calculating net taxes. The remainder of government spending consists of purchases of goods and services, including those bought from private firms and the wages and salaries of government employees. For purposes of the circular flow, government employees' wages and salaries are treated as if they passed through product markets on their way to households.

Finally, consider the link between government and financial markets. Governments do not always balance their budgets. The public sector as a whole, taking federal, state, and local governments together, tends to spend more than it takes in as taxes. (The federal government almost always runs a deficit. State and local governments often have surpluses, but—at least in recent years— these have not been large enough to offset the federal deficit.) For example, in

Exhibit 5.5   The Circular Flow with Government Included

This circular-flow diagram shows three links between government and the rest of the economy. The first is net taxes (taxes minus transfer payments), which flow from households to government. The second is government purchases, which flow from government to product markets. If government purchases exceed net taxes (a budget deficit), the government must borrow from financial markets. The deficit case is shown here. If net taxes exceed government purchases, government repayments of past borrowing will exceed new government borrowing, resulting in a net flow of funds from government to financial markets. This case is not shown here.

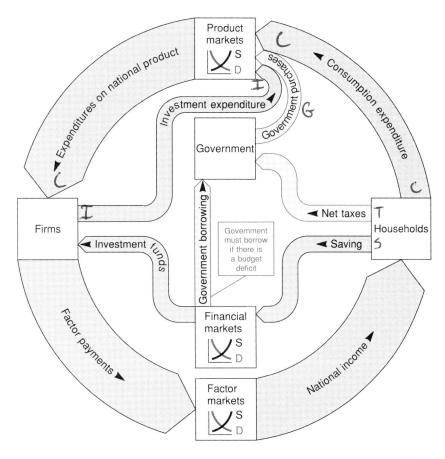

1989 the federal government had a budget deficit of $149 billion and state and local governments had a surplus of $45 billion, for a combined deficit of $104 billion.

The government deficit must be financed by borrowing in financial markets. Usually this borrowing takes the form of sales of government bonds and other securities to the public or to financial intermediaries. In Exhibit 5.5 the arrow from financial markets to government represents government borrowing. Over the years, repeated government borrowing adds to the national debt. The *debt* is a stock that reflects the accumulation of annual *deficits*, which are flows.

In years when the public sector as a whole runs a budget surplus (that is, when net taxes exceed government purchases), the direction of the arrow is reversed. Governments pay off old borrowing at a faster rate than that at which new borrowing occurs, thereby creating a net flow of funds into financial markets. In the United States the combined government sector last showed a budget surplus in 1979.

Leakages and Injections

Take a moment to compare the circular flow shown in Exhibit 5.5 with the simpler version shown in Exhibit 5.1. In Exhibit 5.1 all of national income flows directly from households to product markets in the form of consumption spending. Nothing is withdrawn from the stream of income and consumption spending, and nothing is added to it. In Exhibit 5.5, however, additional flows have been added.

First, there are two uses for income that do not result directly in purchases of goods and services. These are net taxes, which flow to government rather than to product markets, and saving, which flows to financial markets rather than to product markets. These two uses of funds are termed **leakages** from the circular flow. Because saving is defined as whatever income is left over after households buy goods and services and pay net taxes, consumption plus the two leakages always add up to national income.

Second, there are two kinds of expenditures, namely investment and government purchases, that do not come directly from households. These are termed **injections** into the circular flow. Because investment includes unplanned inventory investment, total realized expenditures—consumption plus injections—always equal national income.

Equality of National Income and Product

Adding government to the circular flow does not disturb the equality of national income and national product. Exhibit 5.6 shows an economy in equilibrium with the government sector added. Line 1 indicates that national product is $100,000. Lines 2 through 6 show the spending plans of households, firms, and government. Households plan to buy $70,000 worth of consumer goods and services; firms plan to buy $15,000 worth of investment goods; and the government plans to buy $15,000 worth of goods and services. Total planned expenditures come to exactly $100,000, and there are no unplanned inventory changes. When planned expenditures (aggregate demand) just equal national product (aggregate supply), we know that the economy is in equilibrium.

Production of $100,000 worth of goods and services generates a national income, consisting of wages, interest, profits, and so on, of $100,000 (line 8). Lines 9 through 11 show how this national income is used: $70,000 goes for consumption (as we saw before); $20,000 is saved; and $10,000 is taken in as taxes. These three uses account for the entire national income of $100,000.

The relationships shown in Exhibit 5.6 can be summarized in the following equation:

National product = Consumption + Investment + Government purchases
= Consumption + Saving + Net taxes
= National income

Leakages
The parts of national income that are not used by households to buy domestic consumer goods; included are saving, net taxes, and purchases of imports.

Injections
Flows of funds into domestic product markets that do not begin with the consumption expenditures of domestic households; included are investment, government purchases, and exports.

Exhibit 5.6   Example of Equilibrium with Government Included

This exhibit shows the equality of national income and product for an economy with government purchases and taxes included. The total of consumption plus investment plus government purchases equals the total of consumption plus saving plus net taxes. As shown here, the economy is in equilibrium and there is no unplanned inventory investment. However, the equality would hold even if total realized investment included some unplanned inventory investment.

1	National product		$100,000
	Expenditures		
2	Consumption		$70,000
3	Investment		15,000
4	Planned	$15,000	
5	Unplanned	0	
6	Government purchases		15,000
7	Total expenditures		$100,000
8	National income		$100,000
	Uses of National Income		
9	Consumption		$70,000
10	Saving		20,000
11	Net taxes		10,000
12	Total uses		$100,000

These equations hold even if the economy is not in equilibrium. In that case, realized investment includes some unplanned inventory investment along with planned investment. But national product, including planned plus unplanned investment, equals national income whether or not the economy is in equilibrium.

Government Influence on the Circular Flow: A Preview

A close look at Exhibit 5.5 suggests that the government is able to regulate the size of the overall circular flow through its control over some of the flow components. Much of the discussion in later chapters will be devoted to describing this power and how it is used. Here we will simply give a preview.

One way in which government can affect the circular flow is through its purchases of goods and services. Starting from a state of equilibrium, a reduction in government purchases would lead to unplanned inventory buildup by the firms that made the products that the government unexpectedly stopped buying. As unwanted inventories piled up, firms would react by cutting back output, reducing prices, or some of both. As they did so, the volume of the circular flow would fall in both real and nominal terms. If, on the other hand, the government increased its purchases of goods and services—again starting from equilibrium—there would be unplanned inventory depletion. Firms would react by increasing output, raising prices, or some of both. This would cause the volume of the circular flow to rise in both real and nominal terms. We see, then, that by adding to aggregate demand through increased purchases or reducing aggregate demand through lowered purchases, government can cause the level of national product to rise or fall.

Taxes give the government a second means of controlling the circular flow. If tax rates are increased, households will have less after-tax income to spend on consumer goods. This will reduce aggregate demand and cause an unplanned inventory buildup. In response, firms will reduce output, prices, or both, thereby reducing the volume of the circular flow. If tax rates are lowered, the process will work in reverse. With more after-tax income, consumer spending will increase. The additional aggregate demand will cause an unplanned inventory depletion, to which firms will react by increasing output, prices, or both. In this case the volume of the circular flow and national product will rise. The effects of changes in taxes and government purchases, which together are known as *fiscal policy*, will be discussed in Chapter 10.

The government has a third, indirect means of regulating the volume of the circular flow, namely, its influence over the money stock. The Federal Reserve System, an independent unit of the federal government, can take actions that affect the stock of money in the economy. As we saw earlier in the chapter, increasing the stock of money would not necessarily cause the rate of flow of income and product to increase if the new money lay idle in people's pockets and bank accounts. However, as we will see in coming chapters, the actions through which the Federal Reserve injects new money into the economy have many indirect effects, including effects on interest rates and financial markets. If monetary policy eases the availability of loans and lowers interest rates, firms will be encouraged to step up their rate of investment spending. This, in turn, will cause the circular flow to expand. On the other hand, if monetary policy actions cause the interest rate to rise, firms will be discouraged from making investments and the circular flow will tend to shrink. These matters will be discussed in detail in Chapters 12 through 15.

5.4   Adding the Foreign Sector to the Circular Flow

Closed economy
An economy that has no links to the rest of the world.

Open economy
An economy that is linked to the outside world by imports, exports, and financial transactions.

Up to this point we have developed the circular-flow model only for a **closed economy,** that is, one that has no links to the rest of the world. The U.S. economy is not closed to the rest of the world, however; it is an **open economy**— and increasingly so. Goods and services with a value equal to some 25 percent of national product cross the nation's borders in the form of either imports or exports, not to mention the hundreds of billions of dollars' worth of international financial transactions that take place each year. This section extends the circular-flow model to an open economy by adding a foreign sector to the household, firm, and government sectors already included.

Exhibit 5.7 shows that the foreign sector, like the government, is linked to the rest of the economy in three ways. Imports of goods and services provide the first link. Recall that all the components of the circular flow represent flows of money payments, not flows of goods. Payments for imports are shown by an arrow leading away from the economy to the rest of the world. Households, firms, and government all buy some imported goods and services. To keep Exhibit 5.7 manageable, however, only imports by consumers, which form part of total consumption expenditure, are shown.

Exports provide the second link between the domestic economy and the rest of the world. Funds received in payment for goods and services sold abroad flow into product markets, where they join funds received from sales of goods and

Exhibit 5.7 Circular Flow with Foreign Sector Included

This circular-flow diagram shows three links between the domestic economy and the rest of the world. Imports are the first link. Payments for imports are shown as an arrow from households to foreign economies. Exports are the second link. Payments by foreign buyers of exports are shown as an arrow leading to domestic product markets. If too few goods and services are exported to pay for all the imports, the remaining imports must be paid for by borrowing from foreign sources or by selling real or financial assets to foreign buyers. Such transactions, known as *net capital inflows,* are shown as a flow into domestic financial markets. Exports might also exceed imports, in which case the arrow would be reversed to show *net capital outflows.*

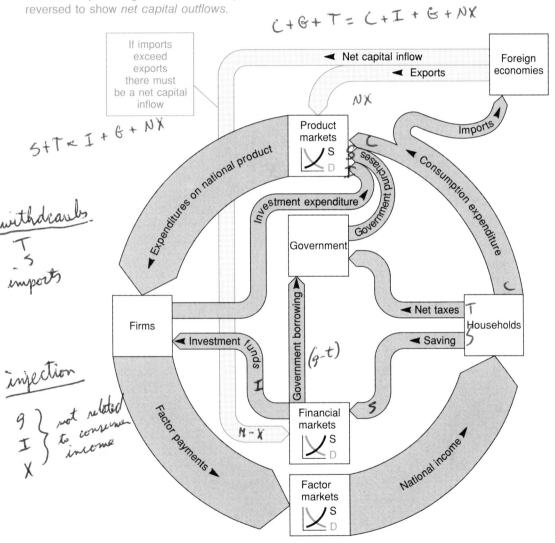

$$C + G + T = C + I + G + NX$$

$$S + T < I + G + NX$$

withdrawls.
T
- S
imports

injection
G
I } not related to consumer income
X

Net exports
Exports minus imports.

services to domestic households, government, and firms. Receipts from the sale of exports are shown as an arrow leading into product markets. The value of exports minus the value of imports is referred to as **net exports.** If the value of imports exceeds that of exports, we can say that there are *negative net exports* or, more simply, that there are *net imports.*

The third link between the domestic economy and the rest of the world consists of international financial transactions. These include international borrowing and lending and international purchases and sales of assets. Like imports and exports of goods and services, international financial transactions give rise to flows of dollar payments into or out of the U.S. economy. Suppose, for example, that a Japanese pension fund buys a bond issued by the U.S. government. It pays for the bond with dollars; as a result, dollars flow into the U.S. economy just as they do when a Japanese firm buys a U.S.-built computer. Much the same thing happens when a U.S. chemical company borrows $1 million from a London bank. The bank is given a promissory note and in return turns over $1 million to the U.S. firm. In both cases, there is an inflow of dollars from abroad to the U.S. economy as a result of the financial transaction.

Capital inflows
Net borrowing from foreign financial intermediaries and net funds received from sales of real or financial assets to foreign buyers.

Flows of dollars into the economy that result from net purchases of assets by foreign buyers and net borrowing from foreign financial intermediaries are known as **capital inflows.**[3] Strictly speaking, it might be better to call them *financial inflows*, because we are talking about the direction of dollar flows, not flows of capital equipment. However, the term *capital inflows* is well established.

Capital outflows
Net lending to foreign borrowers and net funds used to purchase real or financial assets from foreign sellers.

Capital inflows have their mirror images. If a U.S. pension fund buys stock in a Swedish paper company or a U.S. bank makes a loan to a Jamaican mining concern, funds flow out of the U.S. economy. Net purchases of foreign assets and net loans to foreign borrowers by U.S. financial intermediaries are known as **capital outflows.**

There is a link between the flows of payments that arise from imports and exports of goods and services and those that arise from financial flows. The logic of this connection can be seen in a highly simplified example. Suppose you are the only person in the United States doing business with France. You want to buy French wine and, at the same time, are willing to sell U.S.-made maple syrup to the French. You place an order for $1,000 worth of wine, but you can find French buyers for only $600 worth of syrup. Does your failure to export as much as you want to import mean that you will have to cancel part of your wine order? No, because there are other ways to settle your accounts with the French: You can either borrow the $400 you need from a French bank or sell a French buyer $400 worth of common stock in your syrup company. To put it another way, you can pay for your imports via either exports or capital inflows in any combination you desire. If the tables were turned and the French wanted to buy syrup worth more than the wine you wanted to import, they would have to borrow from a U.S. financial intermediary or sell assets to a U.S. buyer. In that case there would be a capital outflow from the U.S. economy.

Chapter 6 will add details, but the principle is clear from this simple example. A country can import more than it exports if it experiences net capital

---

[3]By *net* borrowing we mean new borrowing minus repayments of old loans. Similarly, we say *net* sales of U.S. assets to foreign buyers to allow for the possibility that foreign parties holding previously purchased U.S. assets will resell them to U.S. buyers. For example, suppose that Japanese pension fund A buys $100 million of U.S. bonds while Japanese pension fund B sells $10 million in previously purchased U.S. government bonds to a U.S. insurance company. In this case there is a *net* increase of $90 million in foreign holdings of U.S. government bonds.

inflows, that is, capital inflows that exceed capital outflows. This happens when the country borrows more from abroad than foreigners borrow from it, or when it sells more assets to foreigners than it buys from them. This is the case shown in Exhibit 5.7, and it corresponds to the experience of the United States since the early 1980s.

By the same token, a country can export more than it imports if it experiences a net capital outflow, that is, if its capital outflows are greater than its capital inflows. This happens when a country makes more loans to foreigners than it borrows from them or buys more assets from foreigners than it sells to them. Thus, a country with net exports must also experience a net capital outflow. In that case the arrow between the foreign sector and financial markets in Exhibit 5.7 would be reversed and labeled "net capital outflow." This would represent U.S. experience in earlier post–World War II decades.

All of our discussions of open-economy macroeconomics in the following chapters will be based on the interplay of imports, exports, and capital flows. When reading these sections it may be helpful to turn back occasionally to Exhibit 5.7

Equality of National Income and Product with the Foreign Sector

Adding the foreign sector to the circular flow still leaves all of the basic equalities intact, as we will now see. In Exhibit 5.8 the economy is once again shown with a national product of $100,000 (line 1). Lines 2 through 12 list expenditures. Line 2 shows that households plan to spend $70,000 on consumer goods during the year. Of this, they will spend $10,000 on imports, which means that only $60,000 of their total spending will flow into domestic product markets. An adjustment for this fact is shown farther down in the table, as we will see in a moment.

Lines 5 through 7 show that firms plan to invest $10,000, and line 8 shows planned government purchases of $15,000. Lines 9 through 11 show the contribution of the foreign sector. Foreign buyers plan to purchase $15,000 of domestically produced goods and services (line 10). These purchases represent a flow of expenditures into domestic product markets. However, $10,000 of this flow is offset by the planned purchases of imported goods by domestic consumers. This item, first shown in line 3, is repeated in line 11 with a negative sign. The net contribution of foreign trade to expenditures on domestic goods and services thus is $15,000 minus $10,000, or $5,000. The difference between exports and imports (net exports) is shown in line 9. Adding total consumption (consumption of domestic goods plus consumption of imports), planned investment, government purchases, and net exports gives total expenditures on domestic goods and services of $100,000 (line 12).

Lines 13 through 16 of Exhibit 5.8 show the uses of national income. Consumption expenditures account for $70,000 (of which $10,000 is consumption of imports). Another $10,000 goes to the government as net taxes. The remaining $20,000 is saving. These uses of funds thus account for the entire $100,000 of national income, which in turn equals total expenditures on domestic goods and also equals national product.

In Exhibit 5.8 the plans of buyers and sellers mesh, putting the circular flow in equilibrium. If those plans did not mesh, however, national income and product would still be equal. Suppose, for example, that firms planned to invest

Exhibit 5.8   National Income and Product in the Complete Circular Flow

This example shows the equality of national income and product for the complete circular flow. In the case shown here, there are net exports of $5,000. The corresponding capital outflow is not shown directly in the table, but it can be computed as follows. First, $20,000 flows into financial markets in the form of saving. Of this, $5,000 is used by government to cover its budget deficit. (Government purchases exceed net taxes by $5,000.) Another $10,000 is borrowed by domestic firms to finance their planned investment expenditures. The remaining $5,000 of saving is loaned to foreigners or used to buy foreign real and financial assets to enable foreign countries to purchase $15,000 worth of U.S. goods while selling only $10,000 worth of goods to the United States.

1	National product		$100,000
	Expenditures on Domestic Goods and Services		
2	Consumption (including imports)		$70,000
3	Imports	$10,000	
4	Consumption of domestic goods	60,000	
5	Investment		10,000
6	Planned	10,000	
7	Unplanned	0	
8	Government purchases		15,000
9	Net exports		5,000
10	Exports	15,000	
11	Imports	−10,000	
12	Total expenditures on domestic goods		$100,000
	Uses of National Income		
13	Consumption		$ 70,000
14	Saving		20,000
15	Net taxes		10,000
16	Total uses of national income		$100,000

a little less, or foreign buyers planned to purchase fewer exports, or government planned to spend less on goods and services, or consumers planned to buy more imports in place of domestic goods. If any or all of these things were to happen, total planned expenditures on domestic goods would fall short of national product. Some sellers would be disappointed and would find themselves holding inventories of unsold goods. These would be entered in Exhibit 5.8 as unplanned investment, just making up the shortfall in planned expenditures. Total realized expenditures, including planned and unplanned expenditures, would, as always, equal national product and, in turn, national income.

Then again, the combined spending plans of households, firms, government, and foreign buyers might add up to more than national product. If this were the case, producers would find themselves selling goods faster than they could produce them. As a result, their inventories would fall below planned levels. The inventory change would show up as a negative number on the unplanned investment line, just balancing the excess aggregate demand. The basic equality of national income and product would, as always, hold.

As before, these rules can be expressed in the form of a four-part equation, as follows:

$$\frac{\text{National}}{\text{product}} = \text{Consumption} + \text{Investment} + \frac{\text{Government}}{\text{purchases}} + \text{Exports} - \text{Imports}$$

$$= \text{Consumption} + \text{Saving} + \text{Net taxes}$$

$$= \text{National income}$$

The Equality of Leakages and Injections

In this four-part set of equations, consumption appears twice: First as one of the categories of expenditures on national product, and then again as one of the uses of national income. If we subtract consumption from both total expenditures and total income, and then shift imports to the left-hand side, we get another useful equation:

$$\text{Investment} + \text{Government purchases} + \text{Exports} = \text{Saving} + \text{Net taxes} + \text{Imports}$$

This equation says that total injections equal total leakages. It is only the totals of leakages and injections that need to add up. The individual components do not have to match: saving need not equal investment, net taxes need not equal government purchases, and imports need not equal exports. The example in Exhibit 5.8 is a case in point. Total injections are $40,000, exactly equal to total leakages. However, exports ($15,000) exceed imports ($10,000), meaning that the country has net exports of $5,000. Government purchases ($15,000) exceed net taxes ($10,000), meaning that there is a government budget deficit of $5,000. The financial needs of the foreign sector (to pay for net exports) and the government (to cover the budget deficit) can be met because households supply more to financial markets in saving ($20,000) than firms withdraw from financial markets for investment ($10,000).

In later chapters the relationship between total leakages and total injections will prove useful in understanding the domestic and international macroeconomic experience of the United States over the past decade.

Looking Ahead

The circular-flow model presented in this chapter provides a good overview of the macroeconomy, but it leaves many questions unanswered. One of those questions is how actual measurements can be taken of national product, national income, and the other quantities in the circular flow. We will deal with this matter in Chapter 6. Other unanswered questions concern the government's control over the volume of the circular flow via spending, taxes, and monetary policy. Just how are these policy tools used, how large are the effects of a given policy tool, and how do the various tools interact? These questions will be answered in Chapters 10 through 14.

Still another set of questions concerns the connections among changes in nominal national product, real national product, and the average price level. We have seen that when aggregate demand rises, firms tend to respond by increasing real output, raising prices, or some of both. Under what conditions are they likely to do each? The answer is crucial for the macroeconomic goals of high employment, price stability, and real economic growth. This set of questions will be previewed in Chapter 7 and examined more fully in Chapters 15 through 18. Chapter 19 will round out the discussion of macroeconomic theory and policy with an in-depth look at international issues.

Summary

1. **How are households and firms linked by incomes and expenditures?** The *circular flow of income and product* is the flow of goods and services between households and firms, balanced by the flow of payments made in exchange for goods and services. In the simplest case, households spend all their money on consumer goods produced by firms and firms use all the proceeds of the sales to pay wages, rent, interest, and profits to households. *National product* is the value of all goods and services produced in the economy. *National income* is the total income earned by households, including wages, rents, interest payments, and profits. The two are always equal, because for every dollar that firms receive from the sale of their products, they pay one dollar in factor payments and profits.

2. **How is income related to money?** In economics, the term *flow* refers to any process that occurs continuously through time, while a *stock* is the total amount of something that exists at a given point in time. The distinction between stocks and flows is useful for understanding the role of money. The *stock* of money consists of the coins, paper currency, and bank account balances used for transactions and saving. As money is spent it moves through the economy, creating various *flows*, such as income, saving, investment, and government purchases.

3. **How can the concepts of supply and demand be applied to the economy as a whole?** *Aggregate supply* is the value of all goods and services produced in the economy; it means the same thing as national product. *Aggregate demand* is the value of all planned expenditures in the economy. The circular flow is said to be in equilibrium when aggregate supply and aggregate demand are equal. In that case, there are no unplanned changes in inventories. If aggregate demand exceeds aggregate supply, there will be unplanned decreases in inventory (negative inventory investment). Firms will tend to react by increasing output, raising prices, or some of both. The circular flow will then expand. If aggregate supply exceeds aggregate demand, there will be unplanned increases in inventories. Firms' reactions will cause the circular flow to shrink.

4. **How do the various pieces of the economy—households, firms, government, and financial markets—fit together?** Firms are linked to households through product markets (expenditures on national product) and factor markets (national income). Both are linked to *financial markets*, through which household saving flows to firms, which use the funds to make investments. The government sector is connected to the circular flow in three ways. First, households pay *net taxes* (taxes minus transfer payments) to the government. Second, the government buys goods and services in product markets. Third, the government borrows from financial markets to finance a deficit, or supplies funds to financial markets when it runs a surplus.

5. **How is the U.S. economy linked to the rest of the world?** The foreign sector, like the government sector, is connected to the circular flow in three ways: First, households pay foreign sellers for imported goods. Second, foreign buyers make payments to domestic firms for exported goods. Third, the foreign sector supplies funds to U.S. financial markets if the United States has negative net exports. The funds thus supplied are called *net capital inflows*. Positive net exports by the United States must be offset by *net capital outflows* to foreign financial markets.

Terms for Review

- circular flow of income and product
- flow
- stock
- national income
- national product
- saving
- fixed investment
- inventory investment
- financial markets
- financial intermediaries
- common stock
- bond
- securities
- aggregate supply
- aggregate demand
- realized expenditure
- realized investment
- net taxes
- leakages
- injections
- closed economy
- open economy
- net exports
- capital inflows
- capital outflows

Questions for Review

1. Sketch the circular flow of income and product for an economy made up of only households and firms. Show both flows of payments and flows of goods and services. Give examples of payments that flow from households to firms and of payments that flow from firms to households.

2. Give several examples of stocks and related flows other than those used in the chapter.

3. What is the link between aggregate supply and national product? Between aggregate demand and national product? What does it mean to say that the circular flow of income and product is in equilibrium?

4. What role do financial markets play in the economy? What are financial intermediaries and what role do they play? Do all funds passing through financial markets involve financial intermediaries?

5. Sketch a circular flow for an economy in which there are households, firms, financial markets, and government. Show the three connections between the government sector and the rest of the economy.

6. Sketch a circular flow for an economy in which the foreign sector is added. How is the foreign sector linked to households, product markets, and financial markets?

7. List the principal leakages and injections for a closed economy and an open economy. How are leakages and injections related in each case?

Problems and Topics for Discussion

1. **Examining the lead-off case.** Show the position in the circular-flow diagram (Exhibit 5.7) of as many of the terms used in the case as you can.

2. **Your personal money stock.** How much money do you own at this moment in the form of coins, paper currency, and the balance in your checking or savings account, if you have one? What was your flow of income in the past month? How would a change in your income affect your stock of money?

3. **Banks as financial intermediaries.** Many local banks provide leaflets advertising their services. Ask for information of this kind at a local bank. What services are provided to borrowers? To depositors? How are the two kinds of services related to the bank's activities as a financial intermediary?

4. **Planned inventory changes.** Not all changes in inventories are unplanned. Why would a firm plan to in-

crease or decrease its inventories? How would you plan your inventories over the course of the year if you were a seller of children's toys? Of air conditioners? How would you plan your inventories of parts if you were the manager of an auto parts store in a town with a growing population? In one with a shrinking population?

5. **Disequilibrium with excess aggregate demand.** Rework the table in Exhibit 5.4 for the case of excess aggregate demand. (Let consumption of apples be $35,000, consumption of radios $30,000, and planned investment in milling machines $40,000.) How would producers tend to adjust to these changes? Now assume that radio dealers plan to add $5,000 to their inventories. What does this do to total aggregate demand? Will the dealers be able to carry out their plans?

6. **Reactions to disequilibrium in the circular flow.** Starting from a state of equilibrium, trace the effects of each of the following through the circular flow. What happens to inventories? How do firms tend to react? What happens to the size of the circular flow as measured in nominal terms?

    a. Business managers suddenly decide to increase investment in order to expand their firms' productive capacity.

    b. The federal government reduces income tax rates.

    c. Good harvests throughout the world reduce the demand for exports of U.S. farm products.

7. **Real and nominal output changes.** In response to an increase in demand, the nation's hay farmers increase production of hay from 1 billion to 1.2 billion bales per year. At the same time, as the market moves up its supply curve, the price rises from $2 to $2.50 a bale. What happens to the output of hay measured in real terms (that is, in terms of the value of output at unchanged prices)? In nominal terms (that is, in terms of the value of output with respect to the prices at which the output was sold)?

Case for Discussion
Summer Doldrums

Summer doldrums beset the largest sector of the economy in 1984 as consumers retrenched sharply. After a 6 percent annual rate of increase in real terms during the first 18 months of the recovery from the 1981–1982 recession, personal consumption expenditures fell back in July and August of 1984 to a level barely above the second-quarter average. A 5 percent decline in third-quarter auto sales contributed to the weakness, no doubt partly due to shortages of popular models. But consumers stayed away from lots of other goods.

Business outlays for capital goods also slowed dramatically during the third quarter, judging by monthly data available for shipments of machinery and equipment as well as for business construction. After rising at a 20 percent annual rate in real terms for a year, the pace probably slowed to around 10 percent. But although increases are likely to be smaller in the months ahead, construction contracts and orders for new equipment indicate continued expansion.

The most worrisome signal regarding third-quarter activity is from a sector that speeded up—inventory accumulation. Businesses replenishing empty shelves and showrooms added a powerful push to the economy right from the start of the recovery. Now a few hints are appearing that they have enough stocks on hand. *Fortune* estimates that the ratio of inventory to final sales increased 2 percent in the third quarter, bringing it above what business wants for the first time since early 1983. To the extent that the third-quarter bulge in inventory was unplanned and unwanted, the effect will be felt quickly. Industrial production, which hardly grew in August, could level off for a few more months.

Source: "Growth Will Slow—But Not Too Much," *FORTUNE*, October 15, 1984, 48–49.
© 1984 The Time Inc. Magazine Company. All rights reserved. Reprinted with permission.

Questions

1. Circle each word in this news item that you can identify as part of the circular flow as depicted in Exhibit 5.5.

2. Explain why a decrease in consumer spending on automobiles would tend to (a) slow the rate of expansion of the circular flow or (b) cause it to increase.

3. Do you think that the growth of inventories during 1984 represented planned inventory investment, unplanned inventory investment, or some of both? Is there anything in the news item that gives you a clue? Discuss.

Measuring National Income and Product

GNP Was Flat in Fourth Quarter, Preliminary Data Show

WASHINGTON, D.C.—Will it or won't it?

The government's first estimate of overall economic growth for the fourth quarter shows it was at a near standstill by the end of 1989, leading some analysts to conclude that the economy is slouching toward recession. Others contend it will skirt a downturn and scramble back to slow but solid growth.

For now the numbers clearly show the economy is very weak.

The real gross national product—the total value of the nation's goods and services, adjusted for inflation—expanded at an annual rate of 0.5 percent in the fourth quarter after growing at a 3.0 rate in the third period, the Commerce Department reported.

Moreover, what little growth there was last quarter was undesirable, economists said. Stocks of unsold goods built up at a far faster clip than in the previous quarter, while consumer spending and business investment declined. If those goods aren't sold, businesses will cut back on orders and factories on production, setting off a chain that can lead to layoffs and ultimately shove the economy into a recession.

Another new report, however, showed a strong rise in orders for big-ticket manufactured products, unusual for a severely ailing economy. Orders for durable goods, items expected to last at least three years, shot up 2.5 percent in December on top of a 4.9 percent jump in November, the Commerce Department reported.

Even though the rise was concentrated in the aircraft industry, Norman Robertson, chief economist at the Mellon Bank in Pittsburgh, said the orders nevertheless "weren't consistent with the economy falling into a recession."

Photo source: Courtesy of Beech Aircraft Corporation.

Source: Hilary Stout, "GNP Was Flat in 4th Quarter, New Data Show," *The Wall Street Journal*, January 29, 1990, A2. Reprinted by permission of *The Wall Street Journal*, © Dow Jones & Company, Inc., 1990. All Rights Reserved Worldwide.

Government reports of the latest data for national product and the price level are regularly featured in the financial press. This report clearly demonstrates that the concepts introduced in Chapter 5—national product, national income, investment, inventories, and so on—can be put to work by decision makers in business and government only if they are *measured*, that is, only if numbers are fitted to the various stocks and flows.

The government statisticians whose job it is to make these measurements for the U.S. economy are widely held to be the best such team in the world. Yet, as this chapter will show, they face many problems. There are technical problems posed by sampling errors and survey methods. There are conceptual problems that arise when real-world institutions do not match the theoretical categories of economic models. Finally, there are problems of timeliness. Because of budgetary priorities, government decision makers must sometimes work with preliminary data. For example, the news item just given was based on the first report on economic activity for the fourth quarter of 1989. This report, made in late January, just four weeks after the end of the quarter, made it appear that the economy might be very close to a recession. But eight weeks later, in March of 1990, a revised report on 1989 fourth-quarter real GNP showed a somewhat stronger growth rate of 1.1 percent. Although still weak, this was considered much less likely to portend an actual recession.

This chapter examines the problems of measuring national income, national product, and the price level. We begin with a look at the methods used to measure the economy in nominal terms. Following a short discussion on measuring international linkages, we turn to methods of measuring real income and the price level. Finally, we examine the question of how well the nation's national income accountants are doing their job.

6.1 Measuring National Income and Product

We begin with the measurement of national income and product in nominal terms, that is, in terms of the prices at which goods and services are actually sold. However, nominal measures do not tell the whole story. For example, if we read that the value of output of the U.S. automobile industry was $45 billion in 1980 and $90 billion in 1990, we know that we must interpret these numbers with care. The doubling of nominal output does not mean that the number of cars produced doubled, because the price of cars also went up. Suppose that total 1980 output was 9 million units at an average price of $5,000 per unit. Was total 1990 output 9 million units at $10,000 per unit, 10 million units at $9,000 per unit, or 6 million units at $15,000 per unit? With no information on prices, data on nominal quantities tell only part of the story.

Nevertheless, nominal measurements provide a starting point. Data are collected in nominal form, and only after a set of nominal accounts have been assembled can the process of adjusting for price changes begin.

Gross National Product

Gross national product (GNP)
The dollar value at current market prices of all final goods and services produced annually by a nation's factors of production.

The most comprehensive nominal measure of total production is gross national product. We first mentioned this concept in Chapter 4. Now we will define it precisely: **Gross national product (GNP)** is the dollar value at current market prices (that is, the nominal value) of all final goods and services produced annually by a nation's factors of production.

The term **final goods and services** is a key part of the definition of gross national product. GNP attempts to measure the sum of the economic contributions of each firm and industry without missing anything or counting anything twice. To do this, care must be taken to count only goods sold to *final users*—parties that will use them for domestic consumption, government purchases, investment, or export. *Intermediate goods*—those that are purchased for use as inputs in producing other goods or services—are excluded.

Exhibit 6.1 shows why counting both final and intermediate goods would overstate total production. The exhibit traces the process of producing a kitchen table with a retail price of $100. The final stage of production takes place in the furniture plant, but the manufacturer does not do $100 worth of work. Instead, the manufacturer takes $40 worth of lumber, turns it into a table, and gets $60 in exchange for the labor, capital, and other factors of production used in the process of running the furniture plant. The $40 worth of lumber is an intermediate good; the $60 contribution made by the manufacturer is the **value added** to the product at its final stage. (In practice, other intermediate goods, such as paint and fuel for heating the plant, are used in making the table. To simplify the example we assume that the table is made solely from lumber plus the manufacturer's effort.)

The second section of Exhibit 6.1 shows the next-to-last stage of production: making the lumber. The lumber mill buys $15 worth of logs, saws them into lumber that sells for $40, and gets $25 in exchange for the mill's work. The value added at the sawmill stage is $25.

Going still further back, we come to the stage at which the logs were produced. To produce $15 worth of logs, a forest products company bought $5 worth of fuel, equipment, and so on and kept $10 in exchange for the effort

Final goods and services
Goods and services that are sold to or ready for sale to parties that will use them for consumption, investment, government purchases, or export.

Value added
The dollar value of an industry's sales less the value of intermediate goods purchased for use in production.

Exhibit 6.1 Value Added and the Use of Final Products in GNP

This table shows why GNP must include only the value of final goods and services if it is to measure total production without double counting. The value of sales at each stage of production can be divided into the value added at that stage and the value of purchased inputs. The selling price of the final product (a $100 table, in this case) equals the sum of the values added at all stages of production.

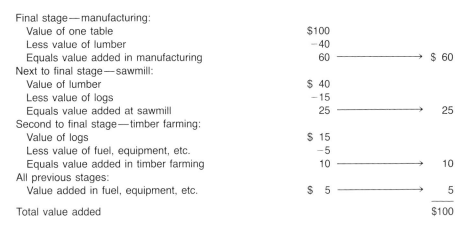

Final stage—manufacturing:		
Value of one table	$100	
Less value of lumber	−40	
Equals value added in manufacturing	60 ⟶	$ 60
Next to final stage—sawmill:		
Value of lumber	$ 40	
Less value of logs	−15	
Equals value added at sawmill	25 ⟶	25
Second to final stage—timber farming:		
Value of logs	$ 15	
Less value of fuel, equipment, etc.	−5	
Equals value added in timber farming	10 ⟶	10
All previous stages:		
Value added in fuel, equipment, etc.	$ 5 ⟶	5
Total value added		$100

involved in tending the trees and harvesting the logs. That is an additional $10 of value added.

Clearly, the process of making the table could be traced back indefinitely. The last section of the exhibit sums up the value added at all stages of production prior to timber farming—the fuel and equipment suppliers, their own suppliers, and so on. If production were traced back far enough, every penny could be attributed to the value added to the final product somewhere in the chain of production.

Now compare the first and last lines of the exhibit. Lo and behold, the value of the final good—the table—turns out to be a precise measure of the sum of the values added at each stage of production. This is why only final goods are counted in GNP. Adding together the $100 value of the table, the $40 value of the lumber, the $15 value of the timber, and so on would far overstate the true rate of productive activity (the true total value added) in the economy.

The Expenditure Approach to Measuring GNP

In principle, GNP could be measured by adding together the value of each final good or service sold or by adding up the value added at each stage of production, as shown in Exhibit 6.1. To simplify the process, however, national income accountants make use of the equality of national product and total expenditure. It is easier to gather data on the total expenditures of households, investors, governments, and buyers of exports on final goods produced in the domestic economy than it is to stand at factory gates and count goods as they roll off assembly lines. This method of measuring GNP is known as the *expenditure approach*. Exhibit 6.2 shows how it works, using 1989 data for the U.S. economy.

Consumption. The first line of Exhibit 6.2 gives total household consumption of both domestically produced and imported goods and services. The national income accounts divide consumption into three categories: durable goods, nondurable goods, and services. In principle, goods that do not wear out within a year, such as cars, furniture, and appliances, are durable, whereas goods that are used up in less than a year, such as soap, food, and gasoline, are nondurable. In practice, however, these categories are somewhat arbitrary. For example, all clothing is considered nondurable, whether the item is a pair of stockings that may last only a few weeks or a wool coat that may last ten years. The remaining category—services—includes everything that is not in the form of a physical object when sold. Examples include haircuts, legal advice, financial services, and education.

All three components of consumption contain some items that bypass the marketplace on their way to consumers. One such item is an estimate of the quantity of food produced and consumed on farms; another is an estimate of the rental value of owner-occupied homes. However, by no means are all nonmarket goods and services captured in the national income accounts.

Investment. The item termed *gross private domestic investment* is the sum of all purchases of newly produced capital goods (fixed investment) plus changes in business inventories (inventory investment). The fixed-investment component includes both business fixed investment—all new equipment and structures bought by firms—and the value of newly constructed residential housing. In the

Exhibit 6.2   Nominal Gross National Product by
Type of Expenditure, 1989 (Dollars in Billions)

Gross national product is estimated using the expenditure approach. This involves adding together the values of expenditures on newly produced final goods and services made by all economic units to get a measure of aggregate economic activity. Net national product is derived from gross national product by excluding the value of expenditures made to replace worn-out or obsolete capital equipment.

Personal consumption expenditure		$3,470.3
Durable goods	$ 473.6	
Nondurable goods	1,122.6	
Services	1,874.1	
Plus gross private domestic investment		777.1
Fixed investment	747.7	
Change in business inventories	29.4	
Plus government purchases of goods and services		1,036.6
Federal	404.1	
State and local	632.5	
Plus net exports of goods and services		−50.8
Exports	624.4	
Less imports	−675.2	
Equals gross national product (GNP)		$5,233.2
Less capital consumption allowance		−552.2
Equals net national product (NNP)		$4,681.0

Source: President's Council of Economic Advisers, *Economic Report of the President* (Washington, D.C.: Government Printing Office, 1990), Tables C-1 and C-22.

national income accounts, then, a homeowning household is treated like a small firm. When the house is bought, it is counted as an investment. Then, as we saw earlier, the firm's "product"—the rental value of its shelter services—is considered as part of consumption each year.

Government purchases. Government's contribution to GNP at the federal, state, and local levels is treated much like consumption. The goods and factor services bought by government are considered to be "used up" as soon as they are purchased. Government purchases are valued at cost in the national income accounts. No attempt is made to measure the value added by government, because most government outputs—primary and secondary education, defense services, and police protection, to name a few—are provided free rather than sold to the public. Transfer payments are not included in the expenditure approach to GNP, because they do not represent purchases of newly produced final goods and services.

Net exports. The last item in the GNP account is *net exports*—exports minus imports. In calculating GNP, imports must be subtracted from exports to avoid double counting. Some of the goods bought by consumers, investors, and government and included in their expenditures are not produced in the domestic economy. For example, a consumer might buy a Japanese television set, an insurance company might buy Italian typewriters for use in its offices, and a city government might buy a Swedish-built police car. The figures for consumption, investment, and government purchases therefore overstate the final use of domestically produced goods and services to the extent that some of those goods and services were produced abroad. To correct for the overstatement in earlier lines in Exhibit 6.2, imports are subtracted from exports at the bottom. Adding total consumption plus total investment plus total government purchases plus exports less imports yields the same sum as would be obtained by adding domestic consumption of domestically produced goods, domestic purchases of domestically produced capital goods, domestic government purchases of domestically produced goods, and total exports.

Gross versus Net National Product

What makes gross national product "gross" is the fact that gross private domestic investment measures total additions to the nation's capital stock without adjusting for losses through wear and tear or obsolescence. Gross private domestic investment minus an allowance for depreciation and obsolescence yields *net private domestic investment*, a measure of the actual net addition to the nation's capital stock each year. Only net investment adds to the capital stock, thereby helping to expand the economy's production possibility frontier. The part of gross investment that covers depreciation and obsolescence is needed just to keep the frontier from shrinking inward. Although depreciation and obsolescence are hard to measure accurately, national income accountants use an approximate measure called the *capital consumption allowance*. Gross national product minus the capital consumption allowance yields **net national product (NNP)**.

Net national product (NNP)
Gross national product minus an allowance (called the *capital consumption allowance*) that represents the value of capital equipment used up in the production process.

National Income

In Chapter 5, we looked at the economy in terms of a circular flow of income and product. The official national income accounts cut into the circular flow at two points: that at which they measure GNP by the expenditure approach and that at which they measure national income by the income approach. As the term implies, the *income approach* measures economic activity by adding together all the different kinds of income earned by households. The national income accounts break down total income into the set of categories shown in Exhibit 6.3.

Compensation of employees consists of wages and salaries plus certain supplements. The first is employer contributions to social insurance (social security). As the social security tax law is written, employees are legally required to pay only half of the tax; employers must pay the other half. Because both halves contribute to employees' retirement benefits, however, both are counted as part of employee compensation. The *supplements* line of the national income accounts also includes fringe benefits other than social insurance that employers pay for, such as health insurance and private pension plans.

Rental income of persons consists of all income in the form of rent and royalties received by property owners. *Net interest* includes interest income received by households less consumer interest payments.

Corporate profits encompass all income earned by the stockholders of corporations, regardless of whether they actually receive that income. Dividends are the part of corporate income that stockholders actually receive. Another part of corporate profits goes to pay corporate profits taxes. A third part—undistributed corporate profits—is kept by corporations for use in making invest-

Exhibit 6.3   Nominal National Income, 1989 (Dollars in Billions)

National income is measured using the income approach. This involves adding together the values of all forms of income earned by households. Some items of income, such as the portion of corporate profits that goes to pay corporate profits taxes, are counted as "earned" by households even though households never receive the income.

Compensation of employees		$3,145.4
Wages and salaries	$2,632.0	
Supplements	513.4	
Plus rental income of persons		8.0
Plus net interest		461.1
Plus corporate profits		298.2
Dividends	122.1	
Corporate profits taxes	129.0	
Undistributed corporate profits	36.2	
Inventory and capital consumption adjustments	10.9	
Plus proprietors' income		352.2
Equals national income		4,265.0

Source: President's Council of Economic Advisers, *Economic Report of the President* (Washington, D.C.: Government Printing Office, 1990), Table C-24.

ments. In measuring national income, corporate profits must be adjusted for changes in inventory values and for capital consumption (depreciation). The final component of national income, *proprietors' income*, lumps together all forms of income earned by self-employed professionals and owners of unincorporated businesses.

Reconciling the Income and Expenditure Approaches

In the simplified circular flows presented in Chapter 5, national income and national product are always equal. In the official national income accounts, however, the two sums fit together less neatly. Some adjustments must be made to match GNP, measured by the expenditure approach, with national income, measured by the income approach. Exhibit 6.4 shows these adjustments.

First, the capital consumption allowance must be subtracted from gross national product to yield net national product. In a sense, gross national product overstates the volume of the circular flow because it includes investments that are made solely to replace worn-out or obsolete equipment. Such expenditures are counted as costs by the firms that make them, and hence they do not show up as proprietors' or stockholders' income.

Next, an adjustment must be made for the fact that part of the revenue that firms receive for their products never reaches the suppliers of factor services or the firms' owners. Instead, it is taken by government in the form of so-called *indirect business taxes*, which include sales taxes, excise taxes, and business property taxes. These taxes are treated differently than the corporate profits tax, which is viewed as being earned by owners and then taken from them by the tax collector. Indirect taxes are included in the prices at which goods and services are sold; therefore, they are part of national product but are not counted as earned in national income.

Exhibit 6.4 National Income Related to
Gross National Product, 1989 (Dollars in Billions)

In economic theory, national income and national product are equal by definition. In the official accounts, however, some adjustments must be made to get the two to fit because they are measured in different ways. First, the capital consumption allowance is subtracted from GNP to get net national product. Then indirect business taxes and the statistical discrepancy are subtracted from NNP to get national income.

Gross national product	$5,233.2
Less capital consumption allowance	−552.2
Equals net national product	4,681.0
Less indirect business taxes[a]	−439.4
Less statistical discrepancy	23.4
Equals national income	4,265.0

[a]Includes minor adjustments for business transfer payments and subsidies to government enterprises.

Source: President's Council of Economic Advisers, *Economic Report of the President* (Washington, D.C.: Government Printing Office, 1990), Table C-22.

In principle, subtracting the capital consumption allowance and indirect business taxes from GNP should yield national income, but in practice there is a further problem: GNP is measured by the expenditure approach using one set of data, and national income is measured by the income approach using a different set of data. No matter how carefully the work is done, there will be some errors and omissions, and therefore the two sets of figures will not quite fit together. The difference between NNP minus indirect business taxes on the one hand, and national income, on the other, is called the *statistical discrepancy*. Most of the time this error is well below 1 percent of GNP.

Personal Income

National income, as we have repeatedly seen, is a measure of income earned by households regardless of whether those households ever actually get their hands on it. For example, it includes income that is earned by capital and natural resources owned by corporations but is retained by them rather than distributed as dividends. For some purposes, it is more useful to measure what households actually receive than what they earn. The total income received by households is called **personal income.**

Exhibit 6.5 shows the steps required to go from national to personal income. First, three items that are earned but not received by households are subtracted: contributions for social insurance (both employer and employee), taxes on corporate profits, and undistributed corporate profits. Next, transfer payments—payments received by households but not earned by them—are added. The result is personal income.

One further income measure is shown at the bottom of Exhibit 6.5; it is **disposable personal income,** or simply **disposable income.** This is the personal income that is left over after households have paid personal taxes (particularly income taxes) to federal, state, and local governments.

Personal income
The total income received by households, including earned income and transfer payments.

Disposable personal income (disposable income)
Personal income less personal taxes (particularly income taxes).

Exhibit 6.5   National Income and Personal
Income, 1989 (Dollars in Billions)

National income is a measure of all income earned by households; personal
income is a measure of the income that households actually receive. To go from
national income to personal income, subtract payroll taxes, corporate profits
taxes, and undistributed corporate profits; then add transfer payments. If personal
taxes are subtracted from this figure, the result is disposable personal income.

National income	$4,265.0
Less contributions for social insurance	−479.3
Less corporate profits taxes and undistributed profits	−165.2
Plus transfer payments[a]	808.2
Equals personal income	4,428.7
Less personal taxes	−648.7
Equals disposable personal income	3,780.0

[a]Includes business and personal transfer payments, plus adjustments for interest payments.

Source: President's Council of Economic Advisers, *Economic Report of the President*
(Washington, D.C.: Government Printing Office, 1990), Tables C-23, C-26.

   This completes our discussion of the domestic national income accounts.
The next section looks at the linkages between the domestic economy and the
economies of other nations. After that we will turn to the problem of adjusting
nominal income and product measures for changing price levels.

6.2   Measuring International Linkages

The item "net exports" in the national income accounts gives a glimpse of the
linkage between the domestic economy and the rest of the world. These ties have
grown much stronger in recent years. In 1960, U.S. exports amounted to only 6
percent of GNP and imports less than 5 percent. By 1989, exports had grown to
12 percent of a much larger GNP. Imports grew even more rapidly over the same
period, reaching 13 percent of GNP. In view of the growing importance of the
foreign sector, then, it is worth taking a closer look at the international ties of the
U.S. economy.
   Any discussion of an economy's balance of international payments is complicated by the fact that thousands of different kinds of international payments
are made every day. Payments for the goods and services that are exported and
imported come to mind first, but there are many others. Equally important are
the long- and short-term loans made to finance imports and exports and the
payments made in international markets in connection with purchases or sales of
assets such as securities or real estate. In addition, governments and private
individuals make many kinds of transfer payments to residents of other countries, including outright gifts, pension payments, and official foreign aid. Finally, the U.S. Federal Reserve System and foreign central banks engage in
many kinds of official transactions. Exhibit 6.6 shows a simplified version of the
accounts used to keep track of these international transactions for the United
States.

Exhibit 6.6   U.S. International Accounts for 1989 (Dollars in Billions)

This table gives details of U.S. international transactions for 1989. The first section shows current account transactions, consisting of imports and exports of goods and services, together with international transfer payments. The second section shows capital account transactions, consisting of international borrowing and lending, international sales of assets, and official reserve transactions of central banks. If all amounts were measured completely and accurately, the current account and capital account balances would be equal and opposite in sign. In practice, there is a statistical discrepancy indicating errors and omissions in measurement.

Current Account		
Merchandise balance		−127.2
Exports	319.3	
Imports	−446.5	
Plus Services, net		15.2
Investment income	2.2	
Other services	13.0	
Plus Transfers, net		− 14.6
Equals Current account balance		−126.6
Capital Account		
Plus Capital account balance		137.3
Capital outflows (net)	−78.6	
Capital inflows (net)	180.4	
Net official reserve transactions	35.3	
Plus Statistical discrepancy		− 10.7
Equals Total of all items, including statistical discrepancy		0.0

Source: U.S. Commerce Department News Release, March 13, 1990.

The Current Account

The first section of the international accounts shown in Exhibit 6.6 contains what are called **current account** transactions. These include imports and exports of goods and services and international transfer payments. The current account, in turn, is broken down into several components.

Current account
The section of a country's international accounts that consists of imports and exports of goods and services and unilateral transfers.

Merchandise imports and exports.   Imports and exports of merchandise (goods) are the most widely publicized items in the international accounts. During much of the nineteenth century the United States was a net importer of merchandise. From 1894 to 1970 it was a net exporter. Since 1970 it has again become largely a net importer. Exhibit 6.6 shows a negative **merchandise balance**. The negative number indicates net merchandise imports. (News reports often refer to the merchandise balance as the *balance of trade*.)

Merchandise balance
The value of a country's merchandise exports minus the value of its merchandise imports.

Services.   In addition to trade in merchandise, the United States and other countries carry on a very large trade in services. Among these are transportation, tourism, insurance, and other financial services. Net earnings on foreign investment, including interest on financial assets, are also treated as an export of services. Adding net exports of services to the merchandise balance gives *net exports of goods and services*.

Transfers.   The final item on the current account balance consists of net transfer receipts. This typically is a negative item in the U.S. international accounts, because transfers to other countries exceed transfers received from them. This item takes into account both government transfers, such as foreign aid and social security payments to retired workers living abroad, and private transfers, such as private famine relief and church missions.

Current account balance.   When merchandise trade, net trade in services, and net transfers are combined, the result is the country's **current account balance.** (News accounts that refer to the *balance of payments* usually mean the current account balance.) Exhibit 6.6 shows a current account deficit for the United States. The last year in which the country experienced a current account surplus was 1981.

The Capital Account

Current account transactions are not the only ones that take place among residents of different countries. The international lending and borrowing and international sales and purchases of assets mentioned in Chapter 5 also account for an enormous volume of daily transactions. A U.S. company, for example, might obtain a short-term loan from a London bank to finance the purchase of a shipload of beer for import to the United States. The Brazilian government might get a long-term loan from Citibank of New York to help finance a hydroelectric project. A U.S. millionaire might open an account in a Swiss bank. A Japanese automaker might buy a piece of land in Tennessee on which to build a new plant. All of these transactions are recorded in the **capital account** section of Exhibit 6.6.

As explained in Chapter 5, purchases of U.S. assets by foreigners and borrowing from foreign financial intermediaries by U.S. firms and individuals create flows of funds into the United States that are termed *capital inflows.* Purchases of foreign assets by U.S. residents or loans by U.S. financial intermediaries to foreigners create flows of funds out of the United States that are termed *capital outflows.*

The capital inflows and outflows listed in Exhibit 6.6 are made for commercial purposes by households, private firms, and in some cases government agencies. In addition to these transactions, the central banks of various countries—the Federal Reserve System in the United States, the Bank of England in the United Kingdom, and so on—engage in sometimes large transactions for purposes of international financial policy. These *official reserve transactions* involve the purchase and sale of government securities; in concept, they are similar to purchase and sale of securities by private parties. They are listed separately because, as will be explained in later chapters, they serve a special purpose in regulating international economic linkages.

Relationship of the Accounts

As we saw in Chapter 5, capital account transactions are logically related to the current account surplus or deficit. If the United States runs a current account deficit, its earnings from the sales of exports will not be enough to pay for all of its imports. Additional funds for financing imports can be obtained through net capital inflows, that is, through U.S. borrowing from abroad that exceeds U.S.

Current account balance
The value of a country's exports of goods and services minus the value of its imports of goods and services plus its net transfer receipts from foreign sources.

Capital account
The section of a country's international accounts that consists of purchases and sales of assets and international borrowing and lending.

lending to foreigners or through sales of U.S. assets to foreigners that exceed purchases of assets abroad. This is the case for the U.S. international transactions shown in Exhibit 6.6. On the other hand, a country with a current account surplus can use its extra import earnings to make net loans to foreign borrowers or net purchases of foreign assets. This would result in a negative balance on the capital account.

In principle, the balances of the current and capital accounts should be equal and opposite in sign. If there is a current account surplus of $100 billion (entered with a plus sign in the accounts), there should be a net capital outflow of $100 billion (entered with a minus sign in the accounts). The reason for this symmetry is that the two account components taken together include all the sources and uses of the funds that change hands in international transactions. Every dollar used in international transactions must have a source; thus, when the sources (+) and the uses (−) are added together, the sum should be zero.

In practice, however, government statisticians always miss some items when they tally up imports, exports, and capital flows. As a result, the numbers do not quite add up. In the official accounts, this measurement problem is reflected in an item labeled *statistical discrepancy* (formerly called *errors and omissions*). Much of the discrepancy is believed to reflect unrecorded capital flows.

6.3   Measuring Real Income and the Price Level

Between 1979 and 1989, the U.S. gross national product, measured in nominal terms, rose from $2,508 billion to $5,233 billion. To anyone living through those years, however, it is clear that even though nominal GNP more than doubled, the real output of goods and services did not. Much of the increase in the dollar value of GNP reflected an increase in the prices at which goods and services were sold. To understand what really happened to output in those years, then, we must adjust the growth of nominal GNP to account for inflation.

Real Gross National Product and the Deflator

To adjust nominal GNP for the effects of inflation, we need a measure of the change in the average prices of goods and services. The most broadly based measure of price changes for the U.S. economy is the GNP deflator. The appendix to this chapter explains how it is calculated. For now, we will simply define the **GNP deflator** as a weighted average of the prices of all the final goods and services that make up GNP.

Choosing a base year.   When we speak of price changes, the first question that comes to mind is: change beginning from what? We can answer this question by choosing a convenient **base year** as a benchmark against which to measure change. Since 1986, U.S. national income accountants have used 1982 as a base year for calculating the GNP deflator. The base year is changed from time to time; before 1986 the base year was 1972.

The base year can be used in one of two ways in stating a weighted average of prices. One way is to let the base year value equal 1.0. A statement of average prices relative to a base year value of 1.0 is called a statement of the **price level;** for example, the 1989 price level, relative to the 1982 base year, was 1.263. The other way is to let the base year value equal 100. A statement of average prices

GNP deflator
A weighted average of the prices of all final goods and services produced in the economy.

Base year
The year that is chosen as a basis for comparison in calculating a price index or price level.

Price level
A weighted average of the prices of goods and services expressed in relation to a base year value of 1.0.

relative to a base year value of 100 is known as a **price index.** Thus, using 1982 as a base year we could say that the 1989 price index was 126.3. The price level and price index are two different ways of stating the same information. In news reports the index form is used most frequently, whereas in building economic models the price level form is more convenient.

Price index
A weighted average of the prices of goods and services expressed in relation to a base year value of 100.

Using the GNP deflator.   Exhibit 6.7 shows nominal GNP, real GNP, and the GNP deflator (stated in price level form) for the United States in each year since 1960. To convert nominal GNP for any year to real GNP stated in constant 1982

Exhibit 6.7   Nominal GNP, Real GNP, and the GNP Deflator, 1960–1989 (Dollars in Billions)

This table shows nominal and real GNP and the GNP deflator for the U.S. economy for the years 1960 to 1989. The base year for the GNP deflator is 1982. To calculate real GNP in constant 1982 dollars for any current year, divide current-year nominal GNP by the GNP deflator. Your answer may differ slightly from the real GNP given in the table because of rounding.

	Nominal GNP	Real GNP	GNP Deflator
1960	515.3	1,665.3	.309
1961	533.8	1,708.7	.312
1962	574.6	1,799.4	.319
1963	606.9	1,873.3	.324
1964	649.8	1,973.3	.329
1965	705.1	2,087.6	.338
1966	772.0	2,208.3	.350
1967	816.4	2,271.4	.359
1968	892.7	2,365.6	.377
1969	963.9	2,423.3	.398
1970	1,015.5	2,416.2	.420
1971	1,102.7	2,484.8	.444
1972	1,212.8	2,608.5	.465
1973	1,359.3	2,744.1	.495
1974	1,472.8	2,729.3	.540
1975	1,598.4	2,695.0	.593
1976	1,782.8	2,826.7	.631
1977	1,990.5	2,958.6	.673
1978	2,249.7	3,115.2	.722
1979	2,508.2	3,192.4	.786
1980	2,732.0	3,187.1	.857
1981	3,052.6	3,248.8	.940
1982	3,166.0	3,166.0	1.000
1983	3,405.7	3,279.1	1.039
1984	3,772.2	3,501.4	1.077
1985	4,014.9	3,618.7	1.109
1986	4,231.6	3,717.9	1.138
1987	4,524.3	3,853.7	1.174
1988	4,880.6	4,024.4	1.213
1989	5,233.2	4,142.6	1.263

Source: President's Council of Economic Advisers, *Economic Report of the President* (Washington, D.C.: Government Printing Office, 1990), Tables C-1, C-2, C-3.

dollars, we simply divide nominal GNP by the price level for that year. For convenience, we can refer to the year for which we are making the adjustment as the *current year*. In equation form, then, the rule for adjustment can be stated as follows:

$$\text{Current-year real GNP} = \frac{\text{Current-year nominal GNP}}{\text{Current-year price level}}$$

As Exhibit 6.7 shows, applying this formula to current years after 1982 yields real-GNP values measured in constant dollars of the 1982 base year that are below current-year nominal GNP. Applying the formula to current years before 1982, when the GNP deflator had values of less than 1.0, yields real-GNP values in 1982 dollars that exceed nominal GNP for those years.

For example, dividing the 1979 nominal GNP of $2,508.2 billion by the 1979 price level of .786 yields a 1979 real GNP of $3,191 billion. (This figure does not quite agree with the one in Exhibit 6.7 because of rounding.) Likewise, dividing the 1989 nominal GNP of $5,233.2 billion by the 1989 price level of 1.263 yields a 1989 real GNP of $4,143 billion. Comparing the 1989 real GNP with the 1979 real GNP shows that real GNP increased about 27 percent over the period. The remainder of the increase in nominal GNP can be attributed to the 61 percent increase in the price level between 1979 and 1989. (The 1989 price level of 1.263 is approximately 61 percent higher than the 1979 price level of .786.)

The consumer price index.   Although the GNP deflator is the most broadly based price index for the U.S. economy, it is not the best-known one. That honor belongs to the consumer price index. Rather than taking into account the prices of all final goods and services produced in the economy, as the GNP deflator does, the **consumer price index (CPI)** considers only the goods and services that make up the "market basket" purchased by a typical urban household.

Consumer price index (CPI)
A price index based on the market basket of goods and services purchased by a typical urban household.

Exhibit 6.8 presents values for the CPI (stated in index form) from 1960 to 1989. The CPI uses the period 1982–1984 rather than a single year as its base year. The appendix to this chapter explains how the CPI is calculated.

The CPI plays a key role in the economy partly because it is widely used to index wages, government transfers, and many other payments. As explained in Chapter 4, indexation of a payment means automatically adjusting it on a regular schedule for changes in the price index involved. Take, for example, the indexing of social security payments. From 1988 to 1989 the CPI rose from 118.3 to 124.0, an increase of 4.8 percent. As a result, social security payments were automatically increased by the same percentage. Millions of workers whose contracts include *cost-of-living-adjustment (COLA)* clauses also receive automatic raises as a result of increases in the CPI.

Producer Price Indexes

Producer price index (PPI)
A price index based on a sample of goods and services bought by business firms.

Another widely publicized set of price indexes consists of **producer price indexes.** These are price averages for three classes of goods that are traded among business firms. Exhibit 6.8 shows the producer price index for *finished goods*— investment goods plus other goods that are ready for final use but have not yet been sold to consumers. Other producer price indexes cover intermediate goods and crude materials ready for further processing. The producer price indexes

Exhibit 6.8   Consumer and Producer Price Indexes, 1960–1989

This table shows two commonly used price indexes that are more narrowly based than the GNP deflator. The first is the consumer price index, which is based on a market basket of goods purchased by a typical urban household. The second is the producer price index for finished goods, which is based on a sample of finished goods traded among business firms.

Year	CPI	PPI (finished goods)
1960	29.6	33.4
1961	29.9	33.4
1962	30.2	33.5
1963	30.6	33.4
1964	31.0	33.5
1965	31.5	34.1
1966	32.4	35.2
1967	33.4	35.6
1968	34.8	36.6
1969	36.7	38.0
1970	38.8	39.3
1971	40.5	40.5
1972	41.8	41.8
1973	44.4	45.6
1974	49.3	52.6
1975	53.8	58.2
1976	56.9	60.8
1977	60.6	64.7
1978	65.2	69.8
1979	72.6	77.6
1980	82.4	88.0
1981	90.9	96.1
1982	96.5	100.0
1983	99.6	101.6
1984	103.9	103.7
1985	107.6	104.7
1986	109.6	103.2
1987	113.6	105.4
1988	118.3	108.0
1989	124.0	113.5

Source: President's Council of Economic Advisers, *Economic Report of the President* (Washington, D.C.: Government Printing Office, 1990), Tables C-58, C-63.

use a base year of 1982. Because producer price indexes measure prices at early stages in the production process, they are often studied for hints of trends in consumer prices. They are also frequently used to index payments that firms agree to make to one another.

The GNP deflator, CPI, and producer price indexes by no means exhaust the possible ways of measuring changes in the price level. There are many other indexes, including regional price indexes and special-purpose indexes that give higher or lower weights to various items. There is even a "nuisance index"—a weighted average of the prices of small, frequently purchased items (see ***Economics in the News 6.1***). Each of these indexes can shed light on some aspect of the general question of how prices are changing.

Economics in the News   6.1
Nuisance Index Signals Inflation

Linda Barbanel is still fuming. To get a silk blouse dry-cleaned, the New Yorker recently paid $6, up 33 percent from the $4.50 she paid less than a year ago. "You can buy the blouse in China for what they now want to clean it," she complains.

Although economists are just beginning to worry that inflation is reawakening after a five-year slumber, consumers such as Barbanel say they noticed its early stirrings months ago.

That's because prices of commonly used goods and services that shape consumers' perceptions about inflation — things such as toothpaste, coffee, haircuts and taxi rides — are soaring even though the overall rise in the cost of living continues moderate.

"Consumers have a gnawing suspicion that there is more inflation out there than is captured in official government statistics — and the skepticism is justified," says Irwin Kellner, the chief economist at Manufacturers Hanover Trust Co.

In a recent survey, the New York bank found that prices of these so-called nuisance items are rising three to four times faster than the government's consumer price index. The bank's nuisance index, which consists of three dozen goods and services commonly purchased during a month's time, rose at an average rate of 15 percent a year in 1985 and 1986.

The government, in a first-quarter report yesterday on the economy, said prices as gauged by a measure known as the deflator rose at a 3.5 percent annual rate in the first quarter of 1987 after increasing at a 0.7 percent pace in the fourth period of 1986.

Meanwhile, the government's closely watched CPI — which gives more weight to expensive items such as houses and cars — rose only 3.8 percent in 1985 and a scant 1.1 percent in 1986.

Some economists contend that the nuisance index may provide a truer picture of how inflation is depleting consumers' pocketbooks. Raymond DeVoe calls it the "piranha" factor. A jump in a hairdresser's or housekeeper's bill "won't devour your budget at once the way an auto-price increase will, but those small bites are sharp and can be just as painful," the economist at Legg Mason Wood Walker Inc. says.

Two Measures of Consumer Price Changes

The Nuisance Index[a]

Item	January 1985	January 1987	Percent Change
Ground coffee (1 lb.)	$ 1.79	$ 3.19	78.2%
Toothpaste (5 oz.)	.99	1.39	40.4
Taxi (2-mile ride)	3.10	4.25	37.1
Pack of gum	.45	.60	33.3
Dry cleaning of a suit	6.00	6.75	12.5
Woman's haircut	20.00	25.00	25.0
Shoe shine	1.25	1.50	20.0

The Consumer Price Index[b]

(Percent Change on Selected Items from February 1985 to February 1987)

New car	7.6%
Refrigerators	−2.7
Rent	11.5
Television	−11.5
Furniture	4.5

Notes: [a]Based on New York retail prices.
[b]Changes are calculated using unadjusted figures and represent percent changes in the index for urban consumers.

Source: Manufacturers Hanover Trust Company.

Source: Constance Mitchell, "Prices of Small Items, Services Rise Rapidly, Hint of New Inflation," *The Wall Street Journal*, April 24, 1987, 1. Reprinted by permission of *The Wall Street Journal*, © Dow Jones & Company, Inc., 1987. All Rights Reserved Worldwide.

How Good Are the National Income Accounts?

This chapter began by stressing the importance of the national income accounts to economics and warning that they are less than perfect. Now that we have surveyed the main components of the nominal and real national income accounts, it is time to try to answer the question of how good those accounts are.

We will focus on four possible problem areas: the accuracy and timeliness of the data, the underground sector of the economy, price index biases, and the non-material aspects of the standard of living.

Accuracy and timeliness.   Government decision makers pay close attention to national income accounting data to get an indication of unfolding economic trends. Unfortunately, however, there is a trade-off between the timeliness and the accuracy of GNP data. A case in point was the "flash" estimate of real GNP that until 1986 was published two weeks before the end of each calendar quarter. For example, the flash index for the fourth quarter, which includes the months October through December, was published in mid-December. The flash estimate was given widespread publicity, but it was not a reliable number; it was subject to revisions averaging some 2.5 percentage points in either direction. (A 2.5 percentage point revision in the upward direction would mean revising a 4.0 percent growth rate estimate to 6.5 percent; in a downward direction, it would mean revising a 4.0 percent estimate to 1.5 percent.) In 1986 the Department of Commerce stopped trying to arrive at such early estimates of GNP growth, but even the preliminary estimates that are now released 15 and 45 days after the end of the quarter are subject to substantial revision. For example, as mentioned at the beginning of the chapter, the estimated real-GNP growth rate of 0.5 percent for the fourth quarter of 1989, announced in mid-January 1990, was revised upward in mid-March 1990 to 1.1 percent. Moreover, as reported in ***Economics in the News 6.2,*** some observers think that budget cuts, combined with demands to speed the release of data are making the problems of accuracy and timeliness worse. In later chapters we will see that lags in the availability of accurate data on GNP, inflation, and other economic quantities have major implications for policymakers' ability to tune economic policy to fit events as they unfold.

The underground economy.   The economic activity that is measured in the national income accounts constitutes the observed sector of the economy. But a vast amount of production, consumption, and investment is never officially measured. This unobserved sector includes activities ranging from teenage baby-sitting to multimillion-dollar drug and gambling rings to the multibillion-dollar value of cooking, cleaning, and child care performed in the home. The national income accounts attempt to consider this unobserved sector when they include estimates of the rental value of owner-occupied housing and the value of food produced and consumed on farms. Those items are only the tip of the iceberg, however. The bulk of the unobserved sector is missing from the official accounts. Although no one knows exactly how big this sector is, some parts of it are known to be enormous.

Some have estimated that organized crime produces some $150 billion a year in illegal goods and services in the form of drugs, gambling, pornography, and so on. If this estimate is correct, it makes organized crime the second-largest industry in the United States after the oil industry. However, organized crime is probably not the largest sector of the so-called underground economy. The unreported income of businesses and self-employed people may add as much as $250 billion. This includes cash income that goes unreported for tax purposes (for example, a plumber fixing leaky faucets for cash on her day off) and barter transactions that involve no cash at all (for example, the plumber gets her teeth straightened in exchange for installing a new bathroom in the orthodontist's home).

Economics in the News   6.2
U.S. Statistics— Are They Getting Worse?

WASHINGTON, D.C.—Tomorrow the government will release its anxiously awaited statistics on employment in August.

Beware.

This year, the Labor Department has repeatedly issued reports on the sluggish growth of the nation's employment—only to say "never mind" within a month.

While Wall Street bet billions, while the Federal Reserve set policy and while corporate boards examined their buying and borrowing plans, the government revised so many statistics so significantly that the forecasts of many economists flipped in only a few weeks.

All of this confusion culminated in a recent report on the bottom-line performance of the economy, the nation's total output of goods and services. The annual rate of growth in gross national product for the second quarter of 1989 was revised upward to 2.7 percent from 1.7 percent. The makeover spelled the difference between an economy on the brink of recession and one showing rosy growth.

Many government officials and private economists see the foundation of economic policy and business planning at stake. "The quality of statistics as a whole is a serious problem," says Michael Boskin, President Bush's chief economic adviser. "We make everything from budget policy to trade policy to monetary policy based on these numbers."

Why the big revisions? Private economists and some government officials offer some theories.

Source: Hilary Stout, "U.S. Statistics Mills Grind Out More Data That Are Then Revised," *The Wall Street Journal*, August 31, 1989, 1. Reprinted by permission of *The Wall Street Journal*, © Dow Jones & Company, Inc., 1989. All Rights Reserved Worldwide.

Consider the plight of one analyst who helps compile statistics at the Census Bureau, which puts out many of the government's monthly economic reports. Dozens of the nation's large companies have stopped completing the monthly surveys that the department uses for vital information on orders and sales. Many of the companies were taken over, and their new managers are obsessed with cutting costs. "One of the first things they do is stop filling out our reports because they're voluntary," the Census official says. "What that does is make our statistics less reliable."

And of course, statistical agencies, like virtually every office in the government, have been squeezed in the federal budget crunch. Some officials complain that the widening gap between government and private salaries has made it difficult to attract top-notch Ph.D. economists to analyze the data—and every statistic involves some degree of judgment and analysis.

The hunger for instant, down-to-the-decimal numbers is another factor that helps set the stage for sizable revisions. "There is a need and a desire to have estimates as soon as possible, both for business's own planning and government policymaking," says Robert Ortner, who was undersecretary of commerce during the Reagan administration. "There are trade-offs between accuracy and timeliness."

In the interest of accuracy, Ortner, while at the Commerce Department, proposed abolishing the monthly report on factory orders for durable goods because another report, issued just over a week later, contained the same information—and it was based on more complete data.

He took his idea to Federal Reserve Board Chairman Alan Greenspan. Ortner says Greenspan, a well-known number junkie, shot it down. "He was willing to live with some of the problems in the data just to have information as early as possible," Ortner says. "But for most purposes and most people, I think we would have been better served to make that change."

But even if the U.S. underground economy amounts to as much as 10 percent of officially measured GNP, that proportion is moderate by world standards. The French underground economy is thought to equal one-third of that country's GNP; in Italy, the figure may be 40 percent; and in many third world countries, the official GNP data bear only the haziest relationship to what is actually going on in the economy.

Price index biases. A third problem with the official national income accounts is that of price index biases. The accuracy with which changes in price levels are measured became a matter of growing concern as inflation increased in the late 1970s and indexing and automatic cost-of-living adjustments became more widespread. If the official price indexes are found to understate inflation, we may want to make a greater effort than usual to restore price stability. On the other hand, if price indexes overstate inflation, contracts that provide automatic adjustments for inflation may be too generous.

The problem of price index biases has been closely studied, and the results are far from reassuring. The consumer price index has been criticized for two built-in biases that have caused it to overstate inflation: substitution bias and quality bias.

Substitution bias. The first reason that the consumer price index tends to overstate the true rate of increase in the cost of living is the so-called substitution bias. As the appendix to this chapter explains, the CPI is a weighted average of the prices of goods that are typically purchased by urban consumers. Because the weights used to calculate the index remain constant, they always reflect patterns of consumption at some point in the past. (They now reflect consumption patterns in the 1982 to 1984 base period.) However, because patterns change over time, the weights typically are not those of the most recent year being observed.

If changes in buying patterns were random, an obsolete set of weights would cause only random errors, not an upward bias, in the CPI. The bias results from the fact that consumer demand is influenced by changes in relative prices. As time passes, consumers tend to buy less of the goods whose prices have risen most and more of those whose prices have lagged behind the average or have actually fallen. Thus, the CPI tends to overstate the increase in the cost of living because it assigns unrealistically large weights to products whose prices have increased but that are consumed in relatively smaller amounts than formerly.

Quality bias. A second source of bias in the consumer price index is the failure to adjust product prices for changes in quality. It would be highly misleading, for example, to say that a 1990 model car costs three times as much as a 1970 model without considering the fact that the 1990 model gets better gas mileage, can be driven longer between tune-ups, and is much safer than the 1970 model. In terms of dollars per unit of transportation service, the newer model clearly would be less than three times as expensive.

For automobiles, computers, and a few other major goods, the Bureau of Labor Statistics does try to make quality adjustments. The importance of the effort can be seen in the case of electronic equipment ranging from calculators to mainframe computers. As recently as the late 1960s, it cost over $1,000 to buy a desk-size electromechanical calculator that would add, subtract, multiply, and divide. Today the same sum will buy a basic personal computer, and a calculator equivalent to the 1960 model can be purchased for $5. A study of changes in computer quality led to large adjustments in price indexes during the 1980s. However, national income accountants do not have the resources to make such detailed studies of all items that enter into GNP.

Nonmaterial sources of welfare. The final problem with gross national product is that it measures only material sources of welfare (which, after all, is all it tries to do). Sometimes per capita GNP is used as an indication of living standards, but when one is comparing living standards over time and across countries, nonmaterial sources of welfare are important, too.

One key nonmaterial component of the standard of living is the quality of the environment. This not only varies widely from one place to another but has changed greatly over time. Today's problems of acid rain, toxic wastes, and nuclear radiation are "bads" that, in principle, should be subtracted from GNP just as "goods" are added to it. In the same spirit, Robert Repetto of the World Resources Institute in Washington, D.C., recommends that depletion of such natural resources as oil fields and tropical forests should be subtracted along with the capital consumption allowance in calculating net national product. For countries such as Indonesia and Brazil, which have undergone resource-intensive growth, the effect of this adjustment could cut measured rates of economic growth nearly in half.

A second nonmaterial source of welfare is the state of human health. By broad measures, especially life expectancy, standards of health in the United States appear to be improving. For example, since World War II the life expectancy of a typical 45-year-old American has increased from 72 years to 77, and a 65-year-old American can now expect to live to the age of 81. This increase clearly improves human welfare even for people who add nothing to measured GNP after they retire from their jobs. If the improvement in health could be measured, it would add to the growth of U.S. GNP. On the other hand, such an adjustment would reduce the already faltering growth rate of the Soviet Union, one of the few developed countries where health indicators such as life expectancy and infant mortality have gotten worse in recent years.

The list of nonmaterial sources of welfare is endless. How important are satisfying work, friendship, social justice, economic equality, and freedom? Everyone knows of people who have been willing to give up income and wealth in pursuit of these things. Yet they must remain unmeasured.

For all of these reasons, then, GNP cannot be used as a measure of the true level of human welfare and can be used only with the greatest caution even for comparisons of material welfare over time and place.

Summary

1. **How is gross national product officially defined and measured?** Two national product concepts are featured in the official accounts of the United States. *Gross national product (GNP)* is defined as the dollar value at current market prices of all *final goods and services* produced in a given year. *Net national product* is derived from GNP by subtracting a capital consumption allowance that reflects the value of capital goods worn out during the year. National product is measured by adding together consumption, investment, government purchases, and net exports.

2. **How does the measurement of national income differ from that of gross national product?** National income is measured by adding together the total of wages and supplements, rental income of persons, corporate profits, and proprietors' income. Gross national product and national income differ by the amount of the capital consumption allowance, indirect business taxes, and the statistical discrepancy. *Personal income* is the total income that households receive; national income is the total income that they

earn. Personal income includes transfer payments, which households receive but do not earn, and excludes contributions to social insurance, taxes on corporate profits, and undistributed corporate profits, which households earn but do not receive. Personal income less personal taxes equals *disposable personal income*.

3. **What are the major types of international transactions?** Many types of transactions appear in the nation's international accounts. Exports less imports of goods constitute the *merchandise balance*. Adding net exports of services yields net exports of goods and services. Adding net international transfers (normally a negative number for the United States) yields the most widely publicized balance-of-payments measure, the *current account balance*. In addition, the international accounts record the capital inflows and outflows resulting from private financial transactions and official reserve transactions by the Federal Reserve and foreign central banks.

4. **How are changes in the price level measured?** The *GNP deflator* is the most broadly based measure of the *price level*. It can be viewed as a weighted average of the prices of all final goods and services that go into GNP. The *consumer price index (CPI)* includes only the market basket of goods purchased by a typical urban household. The *producer price index (PPI)* is based on goods that are typically bought and sold by business firms.

5. **What are the limitations of official economic statistics?** The national income statistics of the United States are considered to be among the best in the world. However, they have some limitations. Potential problem areas include timeliness of data, the unobserved sector of the economy, price index biases, and nonmaterial aspects of the standard of living.

Terms for Review

- gross national product (GNP)
- final goods and services
- value added
- net national product (NNP)
- personal income
- disposable personal income (disposable income)
- current account
- merchandise balance
- current account balance
- capital account
- GNP deflator
- base year
- price level
- price index
- consumer price index (CPI)
- producer price index (PPI)

Questions for Review

1. What is the difference between *gross* and *net* national product?

2. What three items are subtracted from gross national product to arrive at national income? How does personal income differ from national income? How does disposable personal income differ from personal income?

3. List examples of transactions that are recorded in the current account and those in the capital account. What is the relationship between the accounts?

4. How can the GNP deflator be used to calculate real income for a given current year in terms of the prices of a chosen base year? What are the differences among the GNP deflator, the consumer price index, and the producer price index?

5. What are four potential problem areas concerning the accuracy and completeness of the U.S. national income accounts?

Problems and Topics for Discussion

1. **Examining the lead-off case.** How are the data reported in the article measured? What does the article and subsequent revisions to data reported there suggest regarding the trade-off between the timeliness and the accuracy of economic data? Why was the accumulation of inventories during the fourth quarter of 1989 viewed as a worrisome sign?

2. **Updating the national income accounts.** Using the *Economic Report of the President* or another suitable data source, update the national income and product accounts in this chapter to the most recent year. Note that in some ways the official accounts are more detailed than those given in the text.

3. **Inventory in the GNP accounts.** A firm sells $10,000 worth of shoes that it has held in inventory for several years. What happens to GNP as a result? Which of its components are affected, and how?

4. **Payroll taxes in the GNP accounts.** The government raises employers' share of the social security payroll tax from 6 to 10 percent of wages. What happens to GNP, national income, and personal income?

5. **International accounts.** Following the pattern of the table given in Exhibit 6.6, show how the international accounts might look for a year in which there was a $50 billion surplus on current account, no official reserve transactions, and no statistical discrepancy. What would the capital account balance have to be?

6. **The current account deficit.** "A current account deficit is a very healthy thing. If we can get foreigners to give us real goods and services and talk them into taking pieces of paper in return, why should we want anything different?" Do you agree or disagree with this statement? Discuss.

7. **Real and nominal quantities.** In 1982 to 1984, the base period used for the consumer price index, the average earnings of construction workers were $442.74 per week. By 1989 the earnings of construction workers had reached $506.72 per week but the consumer price index had risen to 124.0. What were construction workers' real earnings in 1989 stated in 1982–1984 dollars?

8. **Changes in prices and qualities.** Try to find a mail-order catalog that is at least ten years old and a recent catalog. Compare the ads for various items. By how much has the price of each item gone up? What changes in quality have occurred? Assuming that you could buy at list price from either the new or the old catalog, which items would you buy from the old one and which from the new one?

Case for Discussion

Laid-Off Steelworkers Join the Underground Economy

HOMESTEAD, PA. A half-dozen men lounge on metal folding chairs outside a storefront on Ann Street, sweating in the muggy afternoon air and talking baseball. A pay phone rings inside, and a young man runs to answer it. Moments later, he speeds off in a long, beat-up sedan.

The man is about to cheat the government. He and the other men drive people around town for a fee, but they don't pay any taxes on the fares they receive. What's more, they don't see why they should.

Most of the men used to work at the sprawling Homestead Works a half block away. Now that the steel mill has closed, their car service allows them to make a living. "It ain't bothering anyone. It ain't stealing," says Earl Jones, who was laid off last December after 36 years at the mill. How much does he make? "Ain't saying," he replies with a smile.

The men are part of a vast underground economy made up of people who work "off the books" for cash. From the tired mill towns of the Midwest to the oil patches dotting the Southwest, the underground thrives. In communities that have suddenly lost a major employer, it helps those who were laid off make ends meet, and it helps keep towns like Homestead alive.

The number of Homestead residents with off-the-books livelihoods began to increase in the early 1980s when USX Corp.'s Homestead Works, which employed about 15,000 at its peak, started to lay off workers in droves. The mill's few remaining workers lost their jobs early in 1986. For most residents here, where only half the people have their high-school diplomas, the mill was all there was.

After they were laid off, many older workers retired and some of the younger ones withdrew their savings and migrated south, chasing dreams of work in more prosperous states. But many others stayed, bound by their unmarketable homes, their families or a strong sense of community. Unable to find legitimate jobs, they have parlayed their handyman skills underground.

One former mill worker says that half the people he knows are working off the books. For the most part, they are intensely proud people who hang the American flag from their neat front porches on holidays and respect the law, believing strongly in right and wrong. They definitely don't like the underground's seamy side—thefts and drugs. But their changed circumstances have altered the way many of them think.

"You tell me. Your kids go to bed crying at night because they're hungry. Is 'off the books' going to bother you?" asks a former steelworker.

Source: Clare Ansberry, "Laid-Off Steelworkers Find That Tax Evasion Helps Make Ends Meet," *The Wall Street Journal*, October 1, 1986, 1. Reprinted by permission of *The Wall Street Journal*, © Dow Jones & Company, Inc., 1986. All Rights Reserved Worldwide.

Questions

1. What are the advantages of work "off the books" from the viewpoint of the people involved?

2. How might the failure to measure off-the-books activity affect economic policy decisions?

3. How might off-the-books work affect the statistical discrepancy in the national income accounts?

Suggestions for Further Reading

Feige, Edgar L. *The Underground Economies: Tax Evasion and Information Distortion.* New York: Cambridge University Press, 1989.

This book contains a number of articles bearing on the question of the size and growth of the underground sector of the U.S. economy.

President's Council of Economic Advisers. *Economic Report of the President.* Washington, D.C.: Government Printing Office, published annually.

A readily available source of national income statistics and other useful data.

U.S. Department of Commerce. *The National Income and Product Accounts of the United States, 1929–74.* Washington, D.C.: Government Printing Office, 1976.

Provides historical data on all items in the national income accounts.

U.S. Department of Commerce. *Survey of Current Business.* Washington, D.C.: Government Printing Office, published monthly.

Contains the most recent data on national income.

U.S. General Accounting Office. *A Primer on Gross National Product Concepts and Issues.* Washington, D.C.: U.S. General Accounting Office, 1981.

Details the definitions and methods behind the national income accounts.

Appendix to Chapter 6
Computation of Price Indexes

This appendix provides further information on the GNP deflator and consumer price index. Knowing these details will make it easier to see the differences between the two indexes and to understand the source of the substitution bias, which affects each one differently.

The GNP Deflator for a Simple Economy

A much simpler economy than that of the United States will serve to illustrate the computation of price indexes. Exhibit 6A.1 shows price and quantity data for two years for an economy in which only three goods are produced: movies, apples, and shirts. The exhibit shows that nominal GNP grew from $400 in 1982

Exhibit 6A.1 Nominal GNP for a Simple Economy

In this simple economy in which only three goods are produced, nominal national product grew from $400 in 1982 to $1,000 in 1990. Prices also went up during that time, however; thus, people did not really have 2.5 times as many goods in 1990 as they did in 1982.

1982	Quantity	Price	Value
Movies	50	$ 2.00	$ 100
Apples	1,000	.20	200
Shirts	10	10.00	100
1982 nominal GNP			$ 400

1990	Quantity	Price	Value
Movies	100	$ 4.00	$ 400
Apples	500	.60	300
Shirts	20	15.00	300
1990 nominal GNP			$1,000

to $1,000 in 1990. But what do these figures indicate? Do they mean that people really had more of the things they wanted in 1990 than in 1982? More precisely, do they mean that people had 2.5 times as much? These questions cannot be easily answered by looking at the exhibit in its present form.

A line-by-line comparison of the two years shows that the figures on nominal product do not tell the whole story. Clearly, prices went up sharply between 1982 and 1990. Movies cost twice what they used to, apples three times as much, and shirts half again as much. The amounts of goods produced also have changed. Twice as many movies and shirts were produced in 1990 as in 1982 but only half as many apples.

If we wish to know how much better off people were in 1990 than in 1982, we need a way to separate the quantity changes that have taken place from the price changes. One way to do this is to ask how much the total value of output would have changed from 1982 to 1990 if prices had not changed. This approach gives the results shown in Exhibit 6A.2. There we see that the 1990 output of 100 movies, 500 apples, and 20 shirts, which had a value of $1,000 in terms of the prices at which the goods were actually sold, would have had a value of only $500 in terms of the prices that prevailed in 1982. The $500 thus is a measure of real GNP for 1990. It is this measure that we should compare with the 1982 GNP of $400 if we want to know what really happened to output between the two years. Instead of having 250 percent as much output in 1990 as in 1982, as indicated by the change in nominal GNP from $400 to $1,000, the people in this simple economy really had only about 125 percent as much, as indicated by the change in real GNP from $400 to $500.

Now we know how to compute real and nominal GNP for 1990 directly from price and quantity data without using a price index to convert nominal values into real values. But although we have not explicitly used a price index, we have created one implicitly. This implicit index, or implicit GNP deflator, is the ratio of current-year nominal GNP to current-year real GNP times 100, as expressed in index form by the following formula:

Exhibit 6A.2   Nominal and Real GNP for a Simple Economy

This table shows how the figures from Exhibit 6A.1 can be adjusted to take changing prices into account. The 1990 quantities are multiplied by 1982 prices to get the value of 1990 GNP that would have existed had prices not changed. The total of 1990 quantities valued at 1982 prices is a measure of real GNP for 1990 stated in constant 1982 dollars. The implicit GNP deflator for 1990, calculated as the ratio of 1990 nominal GNP to 1990 real GNP, has a value of 200.

	1990 Quantity	1990 Price	Value at 1990 Price	1982 Price	Value of 1990 Output at 1982 Price
Movies	100	$ 4.00	$ 400	$ 2.00	$200
Apples	500	.60	300	.20	100
Shirts	20	15.00	300	10.00	200
Totals		1990 nominal GNP = $1,000		1990 real GNP = $500	

$$\text{GNP deflator} = \frac{\text{Current-year output valued at current-year prices}}{\text{Current-year output valued at base-year prices}} \times 100$$

Applying the formula to the data in Exhibits 6A.1 and 6A.2 gives a value of 200 for the deflator.

The Consumer Price Index for a Simple Economy

The consumer price index differs from the GNP deflator in two ways. First, as mentioned in Chapter 6, it takes into account only the prices of goods and services consumed by a typical urban household. Second, it is calculated according to a formula that uses base-year rather than current-year quantities. The first difference does not matter for this simple economy in which all goods are consumer goods, but the second does, as Exhibit 6A.3 shows.

To calculate the CPI for this economy, instead of asking how much current-year output would have cost at base-year prices, we begin by asking how much base-year output would have cost at current-year prices. We then calculate the index as the ratio of the two different valuations of base-year quantities:

$$\text{Consumer price index} = \frac{\begin{array}{c}\text{Base-year market basket valued}\\ \text{at current-year prices}\end{array}}{\begin{array}{c}\text{Base-year market basket valued}\\ \text{at base-year prices}\end{array}} \times 100$$

The CPI is calculated using base-year quantities partly because current price data are easier to collect than current output data. This index, therefore, can be announced each month with little delay.

Exhibit 6A.3   A Consumer Price Index for a Simple Economy

The consumer price index can be calculated as the base-year market basket of goods valued at current-year prices divided by the base-year market basket valued at base-year prices multiplied by 100. This table shows how such an index can be calculated for a simple economy. The 1982 output cost $400 at the prices at which it was actually sold. Had it been sold at 1990 prices, it would have cost $950. Thus, the CPI for 1990 is 237.5.

Good	1982 Quantity	1982 Price	Value of 1982 Quantity at 1982 Price	1990 Price	Value of 1982 Quantity at 1990 Price
Movies	50	$ 2.00	$100	$ 4.00	$200
Apples	1,000	.20	200	.60	600
Shirts	10	10.00	100	15.00	150
Totals			$400		$950

$$\text{CPI} = \frac{\$950}{\$400} \times 100 = 237.5$$

Comparing the CPI and the GNP Deflator

As Exhibit 6A.3 shows, the CPI for 1990 in our simple economy had a value of 237.5, whereas the GNP deflator for 1990 was only 200. Both indexes were calculated using the same data, and both used 1982 as a base year. Which, if either, is the true measure of the change in prices between the two years?

The answer is that neither the CPI nor the GNP deflator is the only correct measure of change in the price level; instead, each answers a different question. The GNP deflator answers the question "How much more did the 1990 output cost at the prices at which it was actually sold than it would have cost had it been sold at 1982 prices?" The CPI, in contrast, answers the question "How much more would the 1982 output have cost had it been sold at 1990 instead of 1982 prices?"

A close look at the data shows why the answers to the two questions differ. In 1982, lots of apples and few shirts were produced compared with 1990. Yet between the two years, the price of apples increased 200 percent, whereas the price of shirts increased only 50 percent. Because the CPI uses base-year quantities, it gives a heavy weight to apples, which showed the greatest relative price increase, and a lower weight to shirts, which showed only a modest price increase. In contrast, the GNP deflator uses current-year quantities, thereby decreasing the importance of apples and increasing that of shirts.

We can now see why the CPI tends to have an upward substitution bias relative to the GNP deflator. However, that does not make the GNP deflator a true measure of change in the cost of living. It could just as easily be said that the GNP deflator has a downward substitution bias relative to the CPI or that each has an opposite bias from some "true" price index. As yet there is no foolproof way to calculate the true cost-of-living index, although some interesting attempts have been made. A discussion of these more complex types of price indexes would take us far beyond the scope of this book. However, the basic types of price indexes covered here are the ones most commonly used for policymaking purposes.

PART THREE

Models of National Income Determination

CHAPTER

7

The Aggregate Supply and Demand Model

Before reading this chapter, make sure you know the meaning of:

Supply and demand (Chapter 2)

Elasticity (Chapter 3)

Real and nominal values (Chapter 4)

Natural level of real output (Chapter 4)

Money (Chapter 5)

Aggregate supply and demand (Chapter 5)

Final goods (Chapter 6)

Price level (Chapter 6)

After reading this chapter, you will understand:

The conditions that determine the slope of the aggregate demand curve.

The sources of shifts in the aggregate demand curve.

The conditions that determine the slopes of short- and long-run aggregate supply curves.

The sources of shifts in the aggregate supply curves.

How prices, real output, and unemployment behave as the economy responds to an increase in aggregate demand.

Industrial, Retail Sectors Lag, Inflation Threat Wanes

WASHINGTON—The economy's industrial and retail sectors weakened sharply last month, according to government reports.

Production at the nation's factories, mines, and utilities tumbled 0.7 percent, hobbled partly by the earthquake in California and a strike at Boeing Co., the Federal Reserve said.

At the same time, retail sales, a major force in the economy's growth in the third quarter, sank 1 percent in October, their steepest decline since January 1987. Sales were crippled by a 5.1 percent plunge in auto sales, which remained at dismally low levels during the first ten days of November. Excluding car dealers, retailers posted a 0.2 percent increase in sales last month.

Analysts said last month's decline in industry operating rates is one solid sign that inflationary threats are waning. At the start of this year, the country's factories, mines, and utilities were using so much of their production facilities that economists were concerned they wouldn't be able to increase production fast enough to meet rising demand, and that prices would start rising as a result.

After reviewing yesterday's report, Gary Chiminero, chief economist at Fleet/Norstar Financial Group in Providence, Rhode Island, said: "Worries that capacity constraint was engineering rapid inflation should be a lot less than earlier this year."

Photo source: © Pierre Kopp/Westlight.

Source: Hilary Stout, "Industrial, Retail Sectors Weaken," *The Wall Street Journal*, November 15, 1989, A2. Reprinted by permission of *The Wall Street Journal*, © Dow Jones & Company, Inc., 1989. All Rights Reserved Worldwide.

The preceding news item highlights the relationship between changes in real output and changes in the price level. In this case decreasing the output of goods and services is expected to slow the rate of increase in prices. The relationship between the price level and real output was discussed in a general way in Chapter 5. There we noted that expansion of the circular flow of income and product tends to be accompanied by rising prices, whereas contraction is accompanied by falling prices. This chapter looks more closely at the relationship between prices and output, using a model of aggregate supply and demand that will serve as a basic tool of analysis in coming chapters.

7.1   The Aggregate Demand Curve

Aggregate demand curve
A graph showing the relationship between real planned expenditures on final goods and the average price level of final goods.

Chapter 5 defined aggregate demand as total planned expenditure. Using a concept introduced in Chapter 6, we can say more precisely that aggregate demand means total planned expenditure on *final goods*. In this section, we will examine the relationship between total planned expenditure on final goods and services measured in real terms—real aggregate demand—and the average price level for final goods and services. Represented graphically, this relationship is known as the **aggregate demand curve.** Exhibit 7.1 shows a typical aggregate demand curve.

Aggregate and Market Demand Curves

An analogy can be drawn between the aggregate demand curve for the economy as a whole and the demand curves for individual markets that were introduced in Chapter 2. Both kinds of curves represent inverse relationships between price and quantity variables. Both summarize the market choices made by many indi-

Exhibit 7.1   An Aggregate Demand Curve

The aggregate demand curve shows the relationship between total real planned expenditure on final goods and the average price level of final goods. The curve has a negative slope because each of the major components of real aggregate demand—consumption, planned investment, government purchases, and net exports—varies inversely with the price level of final goods. Aggregate demand is relatively inelastic with respect to changes in the price level. As a result, nominal aggregate demand (real aggregate demand times the price level) increases as one moves up along the curve. For example, nominal aggregate demand is $1,000 billion at point A and $1,500 billion at point B.

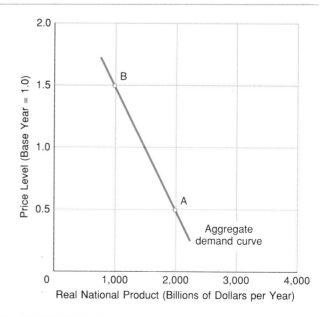

vidual buyers. And, as we will show, both kinds of curves interact with other curves representing supply to determine equilibrium conditions. However, there are also important differences between the aggregate demand curve and market demand curves. Two of the most important differences concern the "other things being equal" conditions that lie behind them.

1.   The market demand curve for a good such as corn is drawn on the assumption that the prices of all other goods remain constant as the price of corn varies. No comparable assumption is made for the aggregate demand curve. As the economy moves along the aggregate demand curve, the prices of any or all goods and services produced by the economy may change as the average level changes.

2.   A market demand curve is drawn on the assumption that consumers' nominal incomes remain constant at all points along the demand curve. The same is not true of nominal national income in relation to the aggregate demand curve. As Chapter 5 showed, changes in aggregate demand associated with changes in the price level cause the circular flow of income and product to expand or contract. Thus, as the economy moves along the aggregate demand curve in response to changes in the price level, nominal national income does not necessarily remain constant.

These points should be kept in mind as we address the question of the slope of the aggregate demand curve. To reason that the aggregate demand curve must have a negative slope simply because the individual demand curves for all the goods entering into aggregate demand have negative slopes is tempting. But because the two kinds of demand curves involve different "other things being equal" assumptions, such a line of reasoning is invalid. A different approach must be taken instead.

The Slope of the Aggregate Demand Curve

The best approach to understanding the slope of the aggregate demand curve is to break down aggregate demand into its principal components: consumption, investment, government purchases, and net exports. By looking at how decisions regarding the real levels of each of these components are affected by changes in the price level, we can understand why the aggregate demand curve as a whole has a negative slope.

Consumption.   We begin by considering how the real demand for consumer goods is affected by an increase in the average price level. When the price level rises, firms' earnings from sales of goods and services also rise by the same proportion. As those earnings are passed along to households in the form of factor payments and profits, consumers' nominal incomes also rise proportionately. This shields them, in part, from the effects of inflation.

However, even if the gain in nominal income keeps up with the increase in the price level, consumers are not fully protected from the effects of inflation. The money that they hold in currency and balances in various kinds of bank accounts has a fixed nominal value. As the price level increases, the real purchasing power of these nominal money balances falls. For example, $100 in $20 bills might initially be enough to buy a week's worth of groceries; but if a person holds onto those five twenties for a year while the average price level rises 15 percent by the end of the year, the bills will buy enough groceries to last about six days. Because of the falling real value of nominal money balances, then, consumers feel less wealthy in terms of real purchasing power and will tend to buy less real output than they would have if the price level had not risen.

Similar reasoning would apply to a period during which the average price level fell. Although it has been many years since the United States has experienced a sustained drop in the price level, the effect of such a drop would be to increase the real value of consumers' nominal holdings of money. As the purchasing power of each dollar in circulation increased, real wealth would rise, real consumption would be stimulated, and real aggregate demand would increase. Taking both increases and decreases in the price level into account, then, we conclude that the real consumption component of aggregate demand varies inversely with the price level.

Investment.   Real investment will also be affected by changes in the price level, but for a different reason. As will be explained more fully in coming chapters, an increase in the price level tends to push interest rates higher. Higher interest rates raise the cost of borrowing and hence discourage firms from undertaking fixed investment. Higher interest rates also raise the costs of carrying inventories of finished products and raw materials; thus, firms may react by reducing their inventories. Therefore, an increase in the price level, via its effect on interest rates, causes the real planned investment component of aggregate demand to decrease. By similar reasoning, a decrease in the price level would cause interest rates to fall; as a result, real planned investment would tend to increase.

Government purchases.   The effect of a change in the price level on real government purchases is not the same for all budget items or for all levels of government. Some government purchase decisions are made in real terms. For example, Congress might decide to authorize the Pentagon to buy 100 jet fighters. If the price per plane goes up, more dollars will be spent to purchase the authorized number of planes. However, other government purchase decisions are made in nominal terms. For example, the Virginia Department of Transportation may be given a budget of $50 million for road improvements. If the price of asphalt goes up, the department, constrained by its $50 million budget, will be unable to pave as many miles of roads as it had planned. Perhaps it will be able to persuade the legislature to increase its budget next year, but in the meantime the price increase results in less spending in real terms.

Generalizing from this example, we conclude that to the extent that some elements of government budgets (federal, state, and local) are set in nominal terms, the government purchases component of aggregate demand will tend to fall in real terms as the price level rises, at least in the short run.

Net exports.   Prices can rise in one country and remain the same in others. Suppose, for example, that the United States experiences higher prices while domestic prices in Japan stay the same. With a given exchange rate between the dollar and the Japanese yen, U.S. goods will become more expensive for Japanese buyers and Japanese goods will become relatively cheaper for U.S. buyers. As U.S. buyers switch from domestic goods to imports and U.S. exports become harder to sell abroad, the real net export component of aggregate demand falls.

A complete analysis of the effects of price-level changes on real net exports requires that one take into account changes in exchange rates and interest rates. These issues will be discussed in Chapter 19. Meanwhile, we will assume an inverse relationship between the price level and the net export component of aggregate demand.

As the price level changes, the changes in the real values of each of the components of aggregate demand interact with one another. In particular, changes in planned investment, government purchases, and net exports will affect the real incomes of households who work to produce the goods and services that enter into those components of aggregate demand. An increase in the price level, which reduces the real demand for goods purchased for investment, use by government, and export, will cause real household income to decrease. In response to the decrease in real income, households will tend to decrease their real purchases of consumer goods. This provides an additional reason why real consumption expenditure decreases as the price level increases, beyond the impact on the real value of money balances that was mentioned earlier. These interactions among the components of aggregate demand will be explored in more detail in coming chapters.

The Elasticity of Aggregate Demand

The examination of real values of consumption, investment, government purchases, and net exports indicates that each component of real aggregate demand varies inversely with the price level. We conclude, then, that the aggregate demand curve as a whole must have a negative slope, as shown in Exhibit 7.1.

As we learned in Chapter 3, it is sometimes useful to know the elasticity of a demand curve as well as whether its slope is positive or negative. For reasons that will be explained more completely in coming chapters, we will draw aggregate demand curves that are relatively inelastic with respect to changes in the average price level. This means that a given percentage change in the price level will cause a smaller percentage change in the level of real planned expenditure.

In Chapter 3 we saw that the price elasticity of demand for a single good determines what happens to revenues from sale of the good as its price changes. When the demand for a good is relatively elastic, an increase in its price will cause revenue to decrease, because a given percentage increase in the price will not increase the amount of revenue per unit enough to offset the larger percentage reduction in units sold. When demand is relatively inelastic, an increase in price will cause revenue to increase, because a given price increase will have a relatively small effect on the number of units sold.

Using similar reasoning, we can show that the elasticity of the aggregate demand curve determines how nominal aggregate demand is affected by a change in the average price level. Nominal aggregate demand means total demand for all final goods and services stated in terms of the prices at which the goods are actually sold. Nominal aggregate demand is equal to real aggregate demand times the price level. If aggregate demand is relatively inelastic, a given percentage increase in the price level will cause a smaller percentage decrease in real aggregate demand. As a result, nominal aggregate demand tends to increase as we move upward along a relatively inelastic aggregate demand curve.

Consider, for example, the aggregate demand curve in Exhibit 7.1. This curve is relatively inelastic along the segment from point A to point B.[1] At point

---

[1]Chapter 3 showed that elasticity varies from one point to another along a straight-line demand curve. Any straight-line demand curve becomes relatively elastic as it approaches its intersection with the vertical axis. Strictly speaking, it would be better to draw aggregate demand curves whose slope increases toward the top of the diagram. Such curves could be drawn with a constant elasticity that is less than unity throughout their length. We use straight-line aggregate demand curves in this book because they simplify the diagrams. This will cause no difficulty as long as we focus on changes occurring along the relatively inelastic part of the curve.

A the price level is 0.5 and the quantity of real national product demanded is $2,000 billion. Nominal aggregate demand at point A thus is 0.5 × $2,000 billion, or $1,000 billion. As we move along the curve to point B, the price level rises from 0.5 to 1.5 and the quantity of real national product demanded falls from $2,000 billion to $1,000 billion. As a result, nominal aggregate demand at point B is $1,500 billion. Nominal aggregate demand thus is higher at point B than at point A, as would be expected for a relatively inelastic aggregate demand curve.

Shifts in the Aggregate Demand Curve

As in the case of individual demand curves, a change in market conditions other than the price level will cause the aggregate demand curve to shift to the left or right. However, because of differences in the "other things being equal" assumptions underlying the two kinds of demand curves, the sources of the shifts are different. Among the sources of shifts in aggregate demand curves are expectations, changes in government policy, and changes in the world economy. (Each of these will be discussed in detail in coming chapters.)

Expectations. Expectations are one of the conditions that are held constant in drawing an aggregate demand curve. If consumers become more optimistic about the future, they may increase their real planned expenditures at any given price level. Similarly, an increase in firms' optimism about future profit opportunities may increase real planned investment at any given price level. In either case, the aggregate demand curve shifts to the right, as illustrated by the shift from AD_1 to AD_2 in Exhibit 7.2. A swing toward pessimistic expectations by consumers or firms will shift the aggregate demand curve to the left.

Exhibit 7.2 Shifts in the Aggregate Demand Curve

A change in economic conditions can cause the quantity of real planned expenditure associated with a given price level to change. In that case the aggregate demand curve will shift, as shown in this diagram. Among the sources of shifts are changes in consumer or business expectations; changes in policies regarding government purchases, taxes, or money; and changes in the world economy.

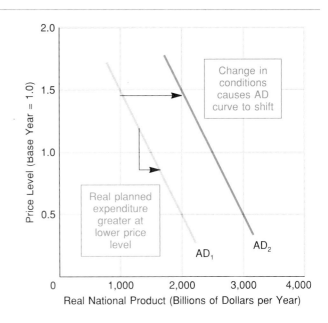

Changes in government policy.   In Chapter 5 we pointed out that several kinds of changes in government policy can affect aggregate demand. An increase in the government purchases component of real planned expenditure, other things being equal, tends to shift the aggregate demand curve to the right. On the other hand, an increase in taxes, which cuts into consumers' disposable incomes, tends to depress the consumption component and shift the aggregate demand curve to the left. Finally, as we will see in Chapters 11 through 14, Federal Reserve policies that increase the economy's stock of money tend to shift the aggregate demand curve to the right, whereas policies that restrict the stock of money tend to shift it to the left. Policies dealing with government purchases, taxes, and the money stock are held constant in drawing a single aggregate demand curve.

Changes in the world economy.   Events in foreign countries have an impact on aggregate demand in the United States via the net exports component of planned expenditure. For example, suppose that the rate of real economic growth increases in the economy of a major trading partner—say, Canada. When this happens, Canadian firms and consumers will tend to buy more imported goods, thereby boosting the real net exports component of U.S. aggregate demand. Also, changes in price levels in foreign countries will affect U.S. net exports by changing the relative prices of imported and exported goods. The effects of price-level changes may be felt, in part, through changes in the relative values of U.S. and Canadian currencies in foreign-exchange markets. The whole set of variables related to events in the world economy is held equal in drawing the aggregate demand curve.

7.2   The Aggregate Supply Curve

We turn now to the supply side of our aggregate model. In Chapter 5 we introduced the term *aggregate supply* as a synonym for the economy's total real output, or real national product. Thus, an **aggregate supply curve** shows the quantity of real national product supplied by the economy at various price levels. As with aggregate demand, we cannot move directly from individual market demand curves to aggregate curves, because we must rethink the assumptions that lie behind the curves.

When thinking about the aggregate supply curve, one must give careful attention to the distinction between the prices of final goods and those of productive inputs. The price level of final goods is stated in terms of a measure, such as the GNP deflator, that is a weighted average of the prices of the final goods that enter into GNP. An index of input prices, on the other hand, shows the average price level of the basic factors of production (labor, capital, and natural resources) and intermediate goods (energy, manufactured inputs such as steel and paper, and so on) that are used to produce GNP.

The producer price indexes mentioned in Chapter 6 are partial indexes of input prices, but the level of input prices discussed here is a broader concept because it covers labor as well as nonlabor inputs. Labor is by far the most important input, accounting for about three-quarters of all input costs for a typical firm. Thus, wages and salaries are particularly important elements of the average level of input prices.

Aggregate supply curve
A graph showing the relationship between real output (real national product) and the average price level of final goods.

Fully Flexible Input Prices

The most important assumption underlying the aggregate supply curve concerns what firms expect to happen to the average level of input prices when there is a change in the average level of prices of final goods. One possibility is that when there is a change in the price level of final goods, input prices will change in the same proportion. There are two reasons why firms might expect this to happen.

One reason stems from the impact of changes in output prices on wages and salaries. When the average price level of final goods rises, workers' costs of living also increase. If nominal wages and salaries remain the same, real wages will fall; for example, when the price level of final goods doubles, a wage of $5 per hour will buy only half the groceries or pay half the rent that it did previously. Workers will ask for raises to maintain their standard of living, and firms — which are, after all, getting twice as much sales revenue as before for their outputs — will be able to grant the raises. If some employers try to hold the line against wage increases, they will lose their most skilled and mobile workers to other employers that are willing to protect workers' real earnings against the effects of inflation.

The other reason is that many goods serve both as final goods and as inputs. Oil, electric power, natural gas, and other forms of energy are examples. If the forces of supply and demand raise the prices paid for these products in markets where they are sold as final goods, their prices will also rise in markets where they are sold to firms for use as productive inputs.

Suppose, then, that firms expect the prices of all inputs to rise proportionately whenever the price level for final goods rises. What will happen to total real output, that is, real national product, as the price level changes? The conclusion must be that the quantity of real national product supplied will remain constant. After all, profit-seeking firms decide how much to produce by balancing the prices they can get for their goods against the prices they must pay for the inputs they use. If both output and input prices rise by the same percentage, profit margins will be unchanged in real terms. There is therefore no reason to produce either more or less than before.

We conclude, then, that the assumption that producers expect input prices to be fully flexible implies a vertical aggregate supply curve such as the one shown in part (a) of Exhibit 7.3. This curve is located at the economy's natural level of real output, for reasons that will become clear as the full aggregate supply and demand model is developed. Part (a) of Exhibit 7.3 represents the economy's *long-run aggregate supply curve* because, in the opinion of most economists, input prices do tend to move in proportion to the prices of final goods in the long run.

Gradual Adjustment of Input Prices

There are, however, strong reasons to expect that the adjustment of input prices to changes in the prices of final goods is not instantaneous. Instead, when rising demand forces up the prices of final goods, firms may react as though they expect input prices to adjust only gradually. There are several reasons for them to expect less than complete adjustment of input prices in the short run.

1. *Long-term contracts.* The prices of some inputs are fixed by long-term contracts. Union labor contracts are one example. Some firms may also rent buildings, buy fuel, or hire transportation services under long-term con-

Exhibit 7.3   Agggregate Supply Curves

An aggregate supply curve shows the relationship between the level of final goods prices and the level of real output (real national product). The slope of the aggregate supply curve depends on the way input prices are assumed to adjust to changes in the prices of final goods. In the long run, input prices are expected to adjust flexibly to changes in the prices of final goods. The long-run aggregate supply curve therefore is a vertical line drawn at the economy's natural level of real output, as shown in part (a). In the short run, input prices are assumed to adjust only gradually to changes in the prices of final goods. Thus, the short-run aggregate supply curve has a positive slope, as shown in part (b).

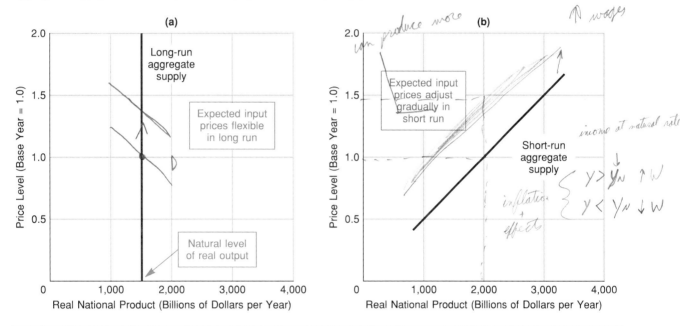

tracts. When the price level of final goods rises, the prices of these inputs cannot rise until it is time to renegotiate the contracts.

2. *Inventories.* Inventories tend to have a cushioning effect on input prices. To illustrate, suppose that a bakery experiences an increase in demand for its bread. At first it will gladly bake and sell more bread, running down its inventories of flour in the process. If prices have been rising throughout the economy, the bakery may have to pay more for the next batch of flour it orders. This change in input prices will cause it to revise its output and pricing plans, but by then a certain amount of time will have passed.

3. *Incomplete knowledge.* Firms may mistake broad changes in demand for local changes affecting only their own market. For example, the bakery might think that the increased demand for bread is limited to the city it serves. Such a local change in demand would not be expected to have a perceptible effect on the price of flour, which is determined in a nationwide market. Only later will the bakery find out that the increase in demand for its bread is part of a broad increase in aggregate demand—but again, some time will have passed by then.

If firms expect input prices to adjust only partially in the short run, they will perceive improved profit opportunities when the demand for their products increases. They may take advantage of the favorable demand conditions by raising their prices, by increasing their output, or very likely by doing some of both.[2] It follows, then, that when firms expect gradual adjustment of input prices, the aggregate supply curve will, in the short run, have a positive slope, as in part (b) of Exhibit 7.3. The positively sloped aggregate supply curve in part (b) is termed a *short-run aggregate supply curve* because it represents the reaction of firms to a change in circumstances before input prices have had a chance to adjust fully.

Just how short is this short run, and how gradual is the gradual adjustment of prices? Although there is no simple answer, in practice, the rate at which input prices adjust will depend on a variety of circumstances and will vary from one input to another. In working with the supply-and-demand model, it is often useful to make a simplifying assumption: When final goods prices change, firms expect that the prices of all inputs will remain unchanged for a certain period—say one year—and then move up or down all at once in accordance with the preceding change in the prices of final goods. This stepwise adjustment of input prices is, of course, only a convenient approximation to the more complex adjustment process that takes place in the real world.

Shifts in the Short-Run Aggregate Supply Curve

The distinction between the price levels for final goods and inputs and the distinction between long-run and short-run adjustments provide a basis for understanding shifts in the aggregate supply curves. We begin with shifts in the short-run curve.

When the economy is in long-run equilibrium at its natural level of real output, markets for individual goods, services, and factors of production also are in equilibrium. In that situation the prices of final goods and services that firms sell and the prices of the inputs they use must be related in certain consistent ways:

1. In equilibrium, the prices of final goods must be at levels that will bring in sufficient revenue for firms to cover the costs of all inputs, given the prices of those inputs, and obtain a normal profit.

2. In equilibrium, the prices of labor inputs must be sufficient to balance supply and demand in labor markets. This means that, given the cost of living as determined by the prices of consumer goods, wages and salaries must be high enough to make it worthwhile for workers to acquire the skills they need for each kind of job and to show up for work each day.

Suppose that we choose as a base year one in which the economy is in long-run equilibrium. In that year the prices of inputs and final goods will be related in the ways just described. We can assign a value of 1.0 to both the average level of input prices and the average level of prices of final goods for that year. We can then measure changes relative to those base year levels.

In graphical terms, the situation in such a base year is represented by point A in Exhibit 7.4. Real output is equal to its natural level, which is also its

---

[2]Readers who have studied microeconomics can verify, using standard profit maximization models, that a rightward shift in the market demand curve for a good will, in the short run, cause an increase in both price and quantity of output under a variety of market structures.

Exhibit 7.4   A Shift in the Short-Run
Aggregate Supply Curve

The short-run aggregate supply curve is drawn so
that it intersects the long-run aggregate supply curve
at the expected level of input prices. Here, the short-
run aggregate supply curve AS$_1$, which intersects the
long-run aggregate supply curve at point A, is based
on an expected input price level of 1.0. If the
expected level of input prices later increases to 2.0,
the aggregate supply curve will shift upward to the
position AS$_2$.

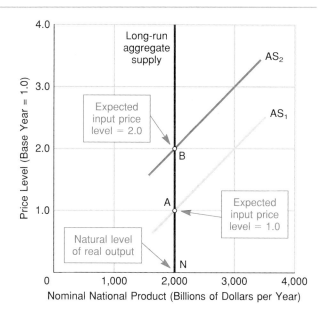

long-run equilibrium level. Point A thus is on the long-run aggregate supply
curve, which is a vertical line at the natural level of real output. The short-run
aggregate supply curve AS$_1$ that passes through point A shows the way firms will
react to changes in aggregate demand, given the prevailing level of input prices,
1.0. From point A, the economy is poised to move up or down along its short-
run aggregate supply curve over a short-run time horizon for which input prices
are expected to remain unchanged, and up or down along its long-run aggregate
supply curve over a long-run time horizon for which input prices are expected to
adjust in proportion to changes in the prices of final goods.

Over time, as economic conditions change, the economy may move to a new
equilibrium. Suppose that after a number of years, the average price level of
final goods has risen to 2.0 and input prices have had time to adjust fully, so that
they too have risen to an average level of 2.0. Such a situation is shown as point B
in Exhibit 7.4. In that situation input prices and the prices of final goods will
once again be in an equilibrium relationship. Firms will be selling their outputs
for twice as much, enabling them to pay for their inputs, which also cost twice as
much. Workers will be earning double the nominal wages and salaries they
earned previously, which is just enough to allow them to maintain their original
standard of living, given the doubled level of price level of consumer goods.

Given this new equilibrium situation, a new short-run aggregate supply
curve AS$_2$ can be drawn through point B. This new aggregate supply curve
shows how firms will react to changes in aggregate demand if they expect input
prices to remain at the new level of 2.0 for the short run. The short-run aggregate supply has shifted upward because the level of input prices that firms expect
to prevail when they make short-run production plans has increased.

To summarize:

1. The short-run aggregate supply curve intersects the long-run aggregate supply curve at a height corresponding to the level of input prices that firms
   expect to prevail in the short run. The expected level of input prices thus is

the key "other things being equal" assumption underlying the short-run aggregate supply curve.

2. A change in the expected level of input prices will cause the short-run aggregate supply curve to shift upward or downward to a new intersection with the long-run aggregate supply curve.

Shifts in the Long-Run Aggregate Supply Curve

The key "other things being equal" assumption that underlies the long-run aggregate supply curve and determines its position is the economy's natural level of real output—the level of real output that can be produced with given technology and productive resources when unemployment is at its natural rate. Over time, as explained in Chapter 1, the economy can expand its production potential through development of new technologies, growth of the labor force, investment in new capital, and development of new natural resources. In Chapter 1 that kind of long-run growth was represented as an outward expansion of the economy's production possibility frontier. Using the model presented in this chapter, the same kind of expansion can be represented by an increase in the natural level of real output and a consequent rightward shift in the long-run aggregate supply curve.

For the next several chapters we will be focusing on shifts in the aggregate demand curve and the short-run aggregate supply curve. To simplify matters in discussing these shifts, we will assume that the economy's long-run aggregate supply curve will remain fixed. We will return to the topic of changes in natural real output and shifts in the long-run aggregate supply in Chapter 17, which is devoted to economic growth and productivity.

7.3   The Interaction of Aggregate Supply and Demand

Now that we have reviewed the conditions that determine the slopes of the aggregate supply and demand curves and shifts in those curves, we can put the curves together to form a complete aggregate supply and demand model. This model will be applied to many issues of theory and policy in coming chapters. In this section we illustrate its basic principles by showing how the economy responds to an increase in aggregate demand, beginning from a position of long-run equilibrium.

Characteristics of Short- and Long-Run Equilibrium

The story begins at point E_0 in Exhibit 7.5, where the economy is in a position of both short- and long-run equilibrium. This situation is characterized by the intersection of three curves: the aggregate demand curve AD_1, the short-run aggregate supply curve AS_1, and the long-run aggregate supply curve. The significance of each of the intersections is as follows:

1. Input prices and prices of final goods are in their long-run equilibrium relationship at the intersection of the short-run aggregate supply curve AS_1 with the long-run aggregate supply curve. *The height of the intersection of the long- and short-run aggregate supply curves indicates the expected level of input prices.*

Exhibit 7.5   Short- and Long-Run Equilibrium

The economy is in short-run equilibrium at the point where the aggregate demand curve intersects the short-run aggregate supply curve. It can be in long-run equilibrium only at a point where the aggregate demand curve intersects the long-run aggregate supply curve. In this diagram, point E_0 is a point of both long- and short-run equilibrium, assuming that the aggregate demand curve is in the position AD_1. If the aggregate demand curve shifts to the position AD_2, the short-run equilibrium point moves to E_1. E_1 is not a point of long-run equilibrium because it is not on the long-run aggregate supply curve.

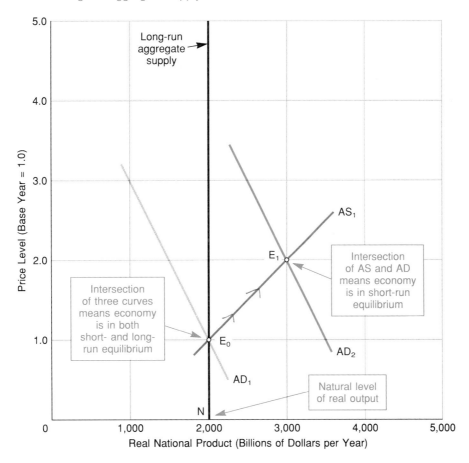

2. The intersection of AS_1 with AD_1 indicates the level of final goods prices and real national product for which aggregate supply equals aggregate demand, given the expected level of input prices used in drawing AS_1. *The intersection of the short-run aggregate supply curve with the aggregate demand curve is always the economy's point of short-run equilibrium.*

3. The intersection of AD_1 with the long-run aggregate supply curve indicates the price level at which total real planned expenditures are equal to the economy's natural level of real output. *The economy can be in long-run equilibrium only at a point where the aggregate demand curve intersects the long-run aggregate supply curve.*

4. The intersection of all three curves at E_0 indicates a price level and real national product that meet *both* the short-run and the long-run equilibrium conditions.

These four characteristics of short- and long-run equilibrium are essential to understanding the aggregate supply and demand model. Along with an understanding of the sources of shifts in each of the curves, they provide a set of basic working rules that can be applied to solve any problem that falls within the scope of the model.

Short-Run Effects of an Increase in Aggregate Demand

Now suppose that, beginning from point E_0 in Exhibit 7.6, something causes an increase in total real planned expenditure so that the aggregate demand curve shifts to the right from AD_1 to AD_2. For the moment it does not matter just what causes the shift. It could be a change in government policy, a spontaneous increase in real consumption spending, an increase in real planned investment resulting from greater business confidence, a boom in demand for U.S. real exports, or some combination of these factors.

Whatever the cause, the immediate effect of the increase in real aggregate demand will be an unplanned decline in inventories. Seeing that their products are being bought up faster than they can be produced, firms will alter their plans accordingly. As explained earlier, their short-run reactions to the change in demand will be based on the assumption that input prices will not immediately adjust to the change in demand for final goods. Given that assumption, firms will react to the increase in demand partly by increasing output and partly by raising prices. In graphical terms, these reactions are shown by a movement up and to the right along the short-run aggregate supply curve AS_1, which is drawn on the assumption that input prices are expected to remain at their initial level of 1.0.

When the economy reaches point E_1, where AS_1 and AD_2 intersect, planned expenditure and national product will be back in balance and the unplanned inventory depletion will cease. This is a new position of short-run equilibrium for the economy that is applicable as long as the aggregate demand and short-run aggregate supply curves remain in the positions shown.

Transition to a New Long-Run Equilibrium

The point where curves AS_1 and AD_2 intersect is a point of short-run equilibrium for the economy, but it is not a point of long-run equilibrium. The reason is that the price level of final goods is not equal to the expected level of input prices at that point. Expected input prices are still at level 1.0, shown by the intersection of AS_1 with the long-run aggregate supply curve. Prices of final goods, however, have risen to a level of 2.0 at E_1. This situation cannot be maintained indefinitely. Over time, input prices will gradually adjust to the change that has taken place in final goods prices.

Exhibit 7.6 shows what happens as this adjustment takes place. Suppose that after a certain period (say, one year), input prices increase to a level of 2.0, catching up with the increase in prices of final goods that took place as the economy moved from E_0 to E_1. This new level of input prices will become the basis for business expectations in the subsequent year. Graphically, the increase

Exhibit 7.6   Short-Run and Long-Run Adjustment to
an Increase in Aggregate Demand

Beginning from an initial long-run equilibrium at E_0, a shift in the aggregate
demand curve to AD_2 will cause the economy to move to a new short-run
equilibrium at E_1. As it does so, real output will rise above its natural level, the
price level of final goods will rise, and unemployment will fall below its natural
rate. After a time, the expected level of input prices will begin to move upward in
response to the increase that has taken place in the prices of final goods. As this
happens, the short-run aggregate supply curve will shift upward, and the economy
will move up and to the left along AD_2. Eventually it will reach a new equilibrium
at E_3. As the economy moves from E_1 to E_3, the price level of final goods will
continue to rise, real output will fall back to its natural level, and unemployment
will rise back to its natural rate.

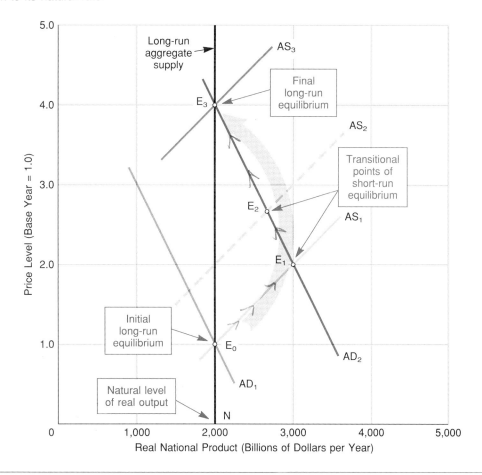

in the expected level of input prices is shown as an upward shift in the short-run
aggregate supply curve, from AS_1 to AS_2. AS_2 now intersects the long-run aggregate supply curve at the new expected level of input prices, 2.0.

   Assuming that no further change takes place in planned expenditures, the
aggregate demand curve will remain at AD_2. Given an unchanged level of aggregate demand, firms will react to the new, higher expected level of input prices by

raising their prices and reducing their output. As they do so, the economy will move along the aggregate demand curve from E_1 to E_2, where AS_2 and AD_2 intersect.

However, like E_1, E_2 is not a point of long-run equilibrium. In the process of moving to E_2, the prices of final goods have increased again, reaching a level of about 2.7. They are again out of balance with the expected level of input prices, which is now 2.0. Whenever the price level of final goods is above the expected level of input prices, input prices will tend to increase. Input prices thus will continue their gradual upward adjustment. As they do so, the short-run aggregate supply curve will continue to shift upward.

A succession of further intermediate positions could be shown as the aggregate supply curve shifts up along the aggregate demand curve. To make a long story short, however, we will jump ahead to the point at which it has shifted all the way up to the position AS_3. When it reaches that position, its intersection with the aggregate demand curve AD_2 is at point E_3, which is also where AD_2 intersects the long-run aggregate supply curve. At E_3, then, all three curves intersect at a common point. The economy is once again in both short-run and long-run equilibrium. The gradual process through which expected input prices catch up to the prices of final goods is complete. Both input prices and output prices have reached the level of 4.0 and are in a consistent relationship to one another. If there is no further shift in aggregate demand, the economy can remain at E_3 indefinitely.

The Adjustment Process in Summary

So that the adjustment of the economy to an increase in aggregate demand is not lost in a forest of detail, let's summarize the process, still using Exhibit 7.6. The process began at E_0 with the economy in equilibrium at its natural level of real output. There was then an increase in aggregate demand. Firms at first reacted by increasing real output and raising final goods prices, so that the economy moved up and to the right along its initial short-run aggregate supply curve. Then, as actual and expected input prices began to adjust to the increase in final goods prices, firms revised their plans by cutting back output and making further price increases. In this phase, the short-run aggregate supply curve shifted upward and the economy moved up and to the left along the aggregate demand curve. The process continued until real output had returned to its natural level at E_3. At that point, the only lasting effect of the increase in demand was an increase in the price level (for both inputs and final goods) from 1.0 to 4.0. The entire adjustment process follows the broad shaded arrow in the exhibit.

Although the two-dimensional diagram shows only price and output variables directly, the effects on the unemployment rate can be inferred from it. As explained in Chapter 4, an increase in real national product above its natural level will pull unemployment below its natural rate. As the economy moves from E_0 to E_1, then, the unemployment rate will fall. As it subsequently moves from E_1 to E_2, the unemployment rate will rise again to its natural rate. Taking into account all three of the key macroeconomic variables, the adjustment of the economy to an increase in aggregate demand can be summarized as follows:

1. The short-run reaction to an increase in aggregate demand, beginning from long-run equilibrium, is an increase in the level of real output, an increase in the level of final goods prices, and a decrease in the unemployment rate.

2. As actual and expected input prices begin gradually to adjust, the economy will experience a further increase in final goods prices accompanied by a decrease in real output and a rise in the unemployment rate.

3. The only lasting effect of the increase in aggregate demand in the new, long-run equilibrium will be a higher price level (for both inputs and final goods). Real output will return to its natural level and unemployment will return to its natural rate.

Looking Ahead

This chapter has introduced the aggregate supply and demand model and used it to analyze the effects of an increase in aggregate demand. In later chapters, we will apply it to numerous other problems.

Chapter 8 will consider the economy's reaction to a decrease in aggregate demand. The results include a drop in real output, a rise in unemployment, and a drop in the price level—a recession, or in extreme cases, a depression. After an optional digression in Chapter 9 to consider an alternative macroeconomic model, Chapters 10 through 14 will look in detail at the way the policies regarding government purchases, taxes, and money produce shifts in the aggregate demand curve.

Chapter 15 applies the aggregate supply and demand model to inflation. Several scenarios are considered beyond the simple case of a one-time shift in aggregate demand that we have laid out in this chapter. Chapter 16, another optional digression, develops an alternative model of inflation.

Economic growth and shifts in the long-run aggregate supply curve are covered in Chapter 17. The final two chapters of the macroeconomics course contain advanced applications of macroeconomic models to problems of domestic and international economic policy.

A thorough grasp of the principles of aggregate supply and demand, as set forth in this chapter, is essential to all of the subsequent discussion of macroeconomic theory and policy.

Summary

1. **What are the conditions that determine the slope of the aggregate demand curve?** The *aggregate demand curve* shows the relationship between real planned expenditure on final goods and the average price level of final goods. The curve has a negative slope because each of the components of real aggregate demand—consumption, planned investment, government purchases, and net exports—varies inversely with the price level. The aggregate demand curve is relatively inelastic. As a result, the nominal value of planned expenditure (real planned expenditure times the price level) increases as one moves up and to the left along the curve.

2. **What are some sources of shifts in the aggregate demand curve?** Movements along the aggregate demand curve are associated with changes in the price level for final goods. Changes in other conditions can cause shifts in the curve. Among the sources of shifts are changes in consumer or business expectations; changes in policy regarding government purchases, taxes, and money; and changes in the world economy.

3. **What are the conditions that determine the slopes of the short- and long-run aggregate supply curves?** An *aggregate supply curve* shows the relationship between the quantity of real output supplied (that is, real national product) and the average price level for final goods. The slope of the curve depends on what assumption is made about the way firms expect input prices to be affected by changes in the prices of final goods. In the long run, input prices tend to adjust proportionately to changes in the prices of final goods. In that case, firms have no incentive to increase or decrease output, so the long-run aggregate supply curve is a vertical line drawn at the economy's natural

level of real output. In the short run, input prices adjust only gradually to changes in the prices of final goods. Thus, in the short run firms find it worthwhile to increase both output and prices in response to an increase in demand.

4. **What are the sources of shifts in the aggregate supply curves?** At the intersection of the long- and short-run aggregate supply curves, the price level of final goods and the expected level of input prices are equal. An increase (or decrease) in the expected level of input prices thus will cause the short-run aggregate supply curve to shift up (or down) along the long-run aggregate supply curve. The location of the long-run aggregate supply curve is determined by the natural level of real output. An increase in natural real output resulting from improved technology or greater availability of productive resources will cause a rightward shift in the long-run aggregate supply curve.

5. **How do prices, real output, and unemployment behave as the economy responds to an increase in aggregate demand?** Beginning from a state of long-run equilibrium, an increase in real aggregate demand will, in the short run, cause the economy to move up and to the right along its short-run aggregate supply curve. As it does so, the prices of final goods will rise, real output will rise above its natural level, and unemployment will fall below its natural rate. After a time, the expected level of input prices will begin to rise as a result of the increases that have taken place in the prices of final goods. As that happens, the economy will move up and to the left along the aggregate demand curve, assuming no further shift in that curve. The price level of final goods will continue to rise, real output will fall back toward its natural level, and unemployment will rise back toward its natural rate. When the economy reaches a new long-run equilibrium, the only lasting effect of the shift in demand will be an increase in the price level. Real output will have returned to its natural level and unemployment will be back at its natural rate.

Terms for Review

- aggregate demand curve
- aggregate supply curve

Questions for Review

1. What are two major differences between the "other things being equal" assumptions underlying the aggregate demand curve and those underlying demand curves for individual goods?

2. Explain how each of the following real spending categories changes in response to an increase in the price

level: consumption, planned investment, government purchases, and net exports.

3. Characterize the aggregate demand curve in terms of *slope* and *elasticity*.

4. What might cause the aggregate demand curve to shift to the right? Give at least three examples.

5. In drawing aggregate supply curves, certain assumptions are made about the way firms expect input prices to change in response to a change in the prices of final goods. How do those assumptions differ for the short-run and long-run aggregate supply curves?

6. At what point does the long-run aggregate supply curve intersect the horizontal axis? What can cause a shift in the long-run aggregate supply curve? At what point does the short-run aggregate supply curve intersect the long-run aggregate supply curve? What can cause a shift in the short-run aggregate supply curve?

7. How does one identify the economy's point of short-run equilibrium on an aggregate supply and demand diagram? What condition is necessary for long-run equilibrium to exist? Under what conditions can a point on an aggregate supply and demand diagram represent both short- and long-run equilibrium?

8. Beginning from a state of long-run equilibrium, explain how each of the following changes in the short run as the economy responds to an increase in real aggregate demand: real output, the price level of final goods, the unemployment rate, and the expected level of input prices. What further changes in each of these variables occurs as the economy moves to a new long-run equilibrium, assuming no further increase in aggregate demand?

Problems and Topics for Discussion

1. **Examining the lead-off case.** According to the news item at the beginning of the chapter, real output of at least some sectors of the economy fell during October. A subsequent report by the Department of Commerce showed that the rate of growth of real GNP slowed in the fourth quarter of 1989 (October through December) compared with its rate of growth earlier in the year. The economy was experiencing inflation (that is, prices of final goods were rising), but observers expected the rate of inflation to slow in the future. The rate of unemployment (not mentioned in the article) was 5.3 percent, compared with a natural rate of unemployment of 5.5 to 6 percent. On the basis of this information, at about what point would you place the economy relative to an adjustment process such as that shown in Exhibit 7.6? Near the initial long-run equilibrium, E_0? At some point along AS_1 between E_0 and E_1? At E_1? At some point along AD_2 between E_1 and

E_3? At the final long-run equilibrium, E_3? Explain your reasoning.

2. **Elasticity of aggregate demand.** Turn to the aggregate demand curve AD_2 in Exhibit 7.2. Along that curve, as the price level rises from 0.5 to 1.5, the quantity of real output demanded declines from $3,000 billion to $2,000 billion. What happens to the aggregate quantity demanded in *nominal* terms over this interval? Using the formula for price elasticity of demand given in Chapter 3, what is the elasticity of aggregate demand over this interval?

3. **Long- and short-run aggregate supply curves.** On a piece of graph paper draw a set of axes such as those in Exhibit 7.4, but do not draw the supply curves shown there. Instead, draw a long-run aggregate supply curve based on the assumption that the natural level of real output is $3,000 billion. What is the slope of the curve? At what point does it intersect the horizontal axis? Next draw a short-run aggregate supply curve based on the assumption that the expected level of input prices is 1.5. Where does this short-run aggregate supply curve intersect the long-run aggregate supply curve that you drew?

4. **Final goods prices and expected input prices.** Given an aggregate demand curve and a short-run aggregate supply curve, how can you determine the short-run equilibrium price level of final goods? Given a long-run aggregate supply curve and a short-run aggregate supply curve, how can you determine the expected level of input prices? Turn to Exhibit 7.6. Give the short-run equilibrium price level of final goods and the expected level of input prices for each of the points E_0, E_1, E_2, and E_3.

5. **Long- and short-run equilibriums.** On a piece of graph paper draw a set of axes identical to those in Exhibit 7.6. Draw a long-run aggregate supply curve based on the assumption that a natural level of real output is $2,500 billion. Draw a short-run aggregate supply curve that passes through the points (2,500, 1.0) and (3,500, 2.0). Label it AS_1. What is the expected level of input prices indicated by this supply curve? Draw an aggregate demand curve that passes through the points (2,000, 2.0) and (2,500, 1.0). Label it AD_1. Given these three curves, where is the economy's point of short-run equilibrium? Where is its point of long-run equilibrium? Now draw another aggregate demand curve that passes through the points (2,500, 4.0) and (4,000, 1.0). Label it AD_2. Given AD_2 and the aggregate supply curves on your diagram, where is the economy's point of short-run equilibrium? What is the relationship between the short-run equilibrium price level of final goods and the expected level of input prices? Is there a possible point of long-run equilibrium for the economy, given AD_2 and the long-run aggregate supply curve? If so, explain how the economy can reach that point starting from the short-run equilibrium just described.

Case for Discussion
Setting Menu Prices at Jose Muldoon's

George Hanna used to wince when his customers ordered the guacamole.

"We had already introduced our menu—and then the price of avocados suddenly tripled," he recalls. "That meant that the price we were charging for the guacamole didn't cover our cost. We'd expected the price to go up because of the season, but we didn't expect it to triple. We got burned on that one."

Hanna manages Jose Muldoon's, a successful Colorado restaurant featuring Southwestern and Mexican dishes. Like other restaurant managers, Hanna must set prices in his menus well in advance.

"We generally run a menu at least six to eight months," he says. "Sometimes we'll keep the same menu close to a year."

While a restaurant could change its price for a certain dish whenever its costs changed, such a tactic might irritate customers. To give customers predictable prices—and to save on printing costs—menus are not changed frequently.

That leaves Hanna with the problem of making price decisions he must stick with for a long time. If his costs of labor, food, or other inputs go up in the meantime, his profits suffer.

"I look at what costs have been over the last year, and pretty much base my cost estimates on that. My costs have been fairly stable lately, so looking at the last year works pretty well. Our restaurant also has a long track record of experience that we can draw from in estimating costs."

Source: Timothy Tregarthen, "Prices: Figuring Out What to Expect," *The Margin* (September/October 1988): 20. Reprinted with permission.

Questions

1. Why does Hanna base his pricing decisions on the *expected* prices of his inputs rather than adjusting his prices every day in response to what actually happens to input prices?

2. Once Hanna has printed a menu that includes a fixed price for guacamole based on an expected price for avocados, what effect will an increase in demand for guacamole have on the quantity of guacamole sold?

3. At first Hanna was surprised when the price of avocados tripled. But he now expects the price of avocados to remain high. How will that expectation affect the price of guacamole on the next menu he publishes? Assuming that there is no change in the demand for guacamole, what effect will an increase in the price of guacamole have on the quantity of guacamole sold?

4. Picture the following sequence of events: Beginning from a state of equilibrium, there is a nationwide increase in the demand for guacamole. The increased demand, in turn, causes an increase in demand for the avocados used in making it. As the avocado market adjusts to these increases, the price of avocados rises. Later, restaurant owners change their menu prices to reflect the change in avocado prices. What happens to the price and quantity sold of guacamole in the short run in response to the increase in demand? What happens to the price and quantity sold in the long run?

5. In what way does the microeconomic adjustment of the guacamole market to a change in demand for guacamole resemble the macroeconomic adjustment of the economy as a whole to a change in aggregate demand? In what ways do the two processes differ?

8

Classical and Keynesian Theories of Income Determination

After reading this chapter, you will understand:

Why the classical economists thought that flexible prices would prevent lasting depressions.

How planned investment and saving respond to changes in the interest rate.

Why the theories of John Maynard Keynes were received so favorably by economists in the 1930s.

Why Keynes thought that small changes in planned expenditures could cause large disturbances in the economy.

The implications of Keynes's theories for economic policy.

We Weren't Talking Revolution; We Were Talking Jobs

Ed Paulsen's family was from South Dakota. He finished high school in 1930, as the country was sliding toward the depths of the Great Depression. He went west to pick apples in Washington State and then worked on road gangs. In 1931 he ended up in San Francisco. These are his words:

I tried to get a job on the docks. I was a big husky athlete, but there just wasn't any work. Already by that time, if you were looking for a job at a Standard Oil service station, you had to have a college degree. It was that kind of market. . . .

I'd get up at five in the morning and head for the waterfront. Outside the Spreckles Sugar Refinery, outside the gates, there would be a thousand men. You know dang well there's only three or four jobs. The guy would come out with two little Pinkerton cops: "I need two guys for the bull gang. Two guys to go into the hole." A thousand men would fight like a pack of Alaskan dogs to get through there. Only four of us would get through. I was too young a punk. . . .

These were fathers, 80 percent of them. They had held jobs and didn't want to kick society to pieces. They just wanted to go to work and they just couldn't understand. There was a mysterious thing. You watched the papers, you listened to rumors, you'd get word somebody's going to build a building.

So the next morning you get up at five o'clock and you dash over there. You got a big tip. There's three thousand men there, carpenters, cement men, guys who knew machinery and everything else. These fellas always had faith that the job was going to mature somehow. More and more men were after fewer and fewer jobs. . . .

We weren't greatly agitated in terms of society. Ours was a bewilderment, not an anger. Not a sense of being particularly put upon. We weren't talking revolution; we were talking jobs.

Photo source: George W. Ackerman, 1929. Records of the Federal Extension Service.

Source: Excerpts from Studs Terkel, *Hard Times: An Oral History of the Great Depression* (New York: Pantheon Books, 1970), 29–31.

The Great Depression of the 1930s, when hundreds of men would fight over a day's work as a common laborer, brought many changes to law, politics, and social consciousness. It also created a revolution in economic thought.

Before the Great Depression, economists had stressed the economy's ability to adapt to changing conditions and absorb shocks. Of course, they recognized that business cycles interrupted the nation's prosperity from time to time, but they saw such episodes as temporary and believed that recovery from them was automatic. Then, following the spectacular stock market crash of 1929, the economy slid into a depression from which there seemed no hope of rebounding. Prices fell. Wages fell. Real output fell. Unemployment soared until nearly one-quarter of the labor force was out of work. These conditions lasted not months but years. Although the economy hit rock bottom in 1933, it did not return to its 1929 level of real output for a full decade. What went wrong?

The most influential attempt to answer this question proved to be that of the British economist John Maynard Keynes. Keynes denied the adequacy—indeed, the very existence—of the economy's shock-absorbing mechanisms. He envisioned an expanded role for government in stabilizing the economy and preventing repetition of the 1930s disaster. Although not all the details of Keynes's work have withstood the test of time, his general approach has left its mark to this day. A review of Keynes's theory and the context in which it emerged is therefore an essential part of the study of macroeconomics.

8.1   The Classical Self-Regulating Economy

A fundamental tenet of pre-Keynesian economics—"classical" economics, to use Keynes's term—was the notion that the economy would gravitate toward a natural level of real output.[1] The natural level was viewed as being determined by resources, technology, and willingness to work—that is, by the conditions that determine the economy's production possibility frontier. At the peak of the business cycle, the economy might temporarily move a bit beyond the frontier as the result of overtime work and negative cyclical unemployment. Conversely, during a slump it might fall below the natural level, but this too would be temporary. In this section we look briefly at the mechanisms that, in the classical view, direct the economy toward the natural level of real output.

Price Flexibility

One of the mechanisms that drives the economy toward the natural level of real output is the flexibility of prices and wages. Chapter 7 explained how upward flexibility of prices of final goods and productive inputs causes the economy to return to a new equilibrium at the natural level of real output following an increase in aggregate demand. This chapter is concerned primarily with the

---

[1]The term *classical economics* has a confusing variety of meanings. In the mid-nineteenth century, Karl Marx used it to refer to his predecessors, Adam Smith and David Ricardo. Later the term was broadened to include both Marx himself and his more orthodox contemporary, John Stuart Mill. Used in this sense, the term distinguishes economics from the time of Smith to that of Mill from the neoclassical tradition founded by Alfred Marshall at the end of the nineteenth century. Keynes, however, used the term *classical* in referring to Marshall and Marshall's successor at Cambridge, A. C. Pigou. Today the term *classical economics* is generally used in the Keynesian sense in macroeconomic contexts and in the pre-Marshallian sense in microeconomic contexts.

opposite case—the behavior of the economy during a recession caused by a decrease in real aggregate demand. Exhibit 8.1 uses the aggregate supply and demand model to illustrate this case, which is in most respects the mirror image of that discussed in the preceding chapter.

Initially the economy is in equilibrium at point E_0. There the price level for both final goods and inputs is 1.0, real output is at its natural level, and total planned expenditures, shown by aggregate demand curve AD_1, are sufficient to absorb all of the national product. Now something happens to decrease the real planned expenditure that will be undertaken at any given price level. The demand curve shifts leftward to AD_2. At a price level of 1.0 there is insufficient aggregate demand to absorb the national product being produced, and as a result inventories accumulate. The classical economists would have referred to this inventory buildup as a "glut" of commodities.

The classical economists were prepared to admit that a glut might temporarily depress output as well as prices. In our modern aggregate supply and demand model, this would be shown as a movement along the short-run aggregate supply curve AS_1 to point E_1. But this situation will not last long. As the economy moves into recession, the unemployment rate rises. At E_1 some workers who are willing to work will not find jobs; they will compete with those who still have jobs, thereby driving down wages. Owners of other productive resources that are temporarily idled by the glut may offer their services at a discount as well.

As input prices fall in response to the drop in demand, firms will begin to revise their expectations of input prices downward, and the aggregate supply curve will begin to shift downward. As it does so, assuming no further change in aggregate demand, the economy will move down aggregate demand curve AD_2 to a new equilibrium at point E_2. There real output will have returned to its natural level. Input prices and prices of final goods will have declined in proportion to the amount by which the new equilibrium level of nominal aggregate

Exhibit 8.1 Recovery from Recession in the Classical Model

This exhibit illustrates recovery from recession through the classical mechanism of flexible prices. Beginning from equilibrium at point E_0, where real output is at its natural level, the aggregate demand curve shifts leftward from AD_1 to AD_2. As it does, prices, output, and employment all decline. The economy moves along short-run aggregate supply curve AS_1 to point E_1. Soon, however, competition among unemployed workers and owners of other idle resources begins to push input prices down. As the input prices expected by firms fall, the short-run aggregate supply curve shifts downward and the economy moves down along the aggregate demand curve to a new equilibrium at the natural level of real output. At point E_2, real output returns to its natural level, unemployment reverts to its natural rate, and only the prices of inputs and final goods are affected permanently.

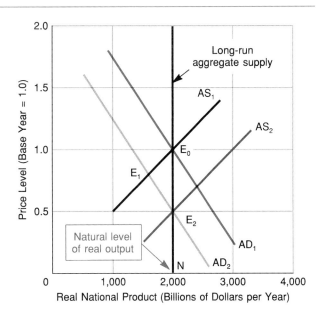

demand has decreased. The new short-run aggregate supply curve, AS_2, will intersect both AD_2 and the economy's long-run aggregate supply curve at the new long-run equilibrium point. Real output will have returned to its natural level and unemployment to its natural rate. The only lasting impact of the shift in demand will be a lower level of prices.

The classical economists outlined this mechanism most clearly for the case in which the shift in demand originated with a disturbance in the stock of money. In the nineteenth century and earlier, "money" meant, in large part, gold and silver. An increase in the stock of gold and silver would cause a rightward shift in the aggregate demand curve, whereas a decrease in the stock of gold and silver would cause a leftward shift. In later chapters we will see that the aggregate supply and demand mechanism works much the same way in a modern economy whether the source of the demand disturbance is monetary or nonmonetary.

The Classical Theory of Saving and Investment

In addition to flexible prices and wages, according to the classical economists, there is a second shock-absorbing mechanism: flexible interest rates. Flexible interest rates have the effect of adjusting planned investment to the level of saving that takes place when the economy is producing at its natural level of national product. This mechanism can be explained most easily in terms of a simple economy with no government or foreign sector, such as the one illustrated in the circular flow diagram in Exhibit 5.2 (page 130). In such an economy, there is only one leakage from the circular flow—saving—and only one injection—planned investment.

Given this situation, total real planned expenditures will not add up to real national product unless firms plan to undertake an amount of investment that is equal to household saving. If firms plan too little investment, aggregate demand will fall short of aggregate supply. Goods that have already been produced cannot vanish into thin air, so they will pile up as unplanned inventory investment. Firms will react by cutting their output and prices, and real output will fall below its natural level.

If the economy was to remain in equilibrium at the natural level of output, then, the classical economists needed to identify a mechanism that would guarantee that planned investment would automatically absorb whatever portion of national income households decided to save. The mechanism they came up with was based on the concept of the interest rate as a link between saving and investment. We will begin by looking at the effect of the interest rate on planned investment, which plays a role not only in classical theory but also in Keynesian and post-Keynesian theory.

The opportunity cost of investment. Business firms constantly plan to make both fixed and inventory investments. To do so, they must somehow acquire the funds needed to finance the investments. Many firms are fortunate enough to have steady flows of profits, some of which can be used for investment before the rest is paid out to owners. Others obtain funds by borrowing, either directly from the public or through financial intermediaries.

Whatever the source of a firm's investment funds, acquiring new fixed capital or inventory always involves an opportunity cost. The opportunity cost of investment is the interest rate that must be paid for funds that are obtained from outside the firm or that could be earned by investing the firm's own funds elsewhere. There is no free source of funds. A firm that spends its own profits on new office equipment could have earned interest on those funds by depositing them in a bank, buying government securities, or lending them to another firm. A firm that borrows in order to buy capital goods must pay the interest rate charged by lenders.[2]

At any given time, there may be dozens or hundreds of investment opportunities available to a firm. A regional sales office could be built in a distant city. Production equipment could be modernized. Larger supplies of raw materials could be kept on hand to guard against supply disruptions. Somehow the firm's managers must decide which projects to undertake and how far to carry each one. In doing so, they must balance the potential benefits, in terms of increased profits, against the opportunity cost of obtaining the investment funds.

Suppose, for example, that a firm decides to improve the insulation in the roof of its warehouse. A consultant estimates that 6 inches of insulation will reduce the firm's fuel costs by $2,000 per year. Doubling the added insulation to 12 inches will save another $1,000 per year, bringing the total yearly savings to $3,000. Each six inches of insulation costs $10,000. How much insulation should be used—12 inches, 6 inches, or none?

The correct choice can be made by comparing the return on investment, stated as a percentage of the cost of the investment, to the opportunity cost of capital, that is, the rate of interest. In this case the return on investment takes the form of a reduction in fuel costs. The first 6 inches of insulation brings a reduction of $2,000 per year, or 20 percent of its cost. Installing it therefore will be worthwhile so long as the interest rate is less than 20 percent. The second 6 inches will reduce fuel costs by another $1,000 per year, or 10 percent of its cost. Adding it will be worthwhile only if the interest rate is less than 10 percent. Thus, we see that the firm will install 12 inches of insulation if the interest rate is below 10 percent, 6 inches if it is 10 percent or more but less than 20 percent, and none if it is 20 percent or more.

The planned-investment schedule. As simple as it is, this example illustrates a basic principle: Other things being equal, the lower the opportunity cost of investment, the higher a firm's rate of planned investment. Generalizing from this principle, we can draw a **planned-investment schedule** for a firm and, by extension, for the economy as a whole. Such a schedule shows the amount of planned investment associated with each interest rate.

Part (a) of Exhibit 8.2 shows the planned-investment schedule for our hypothetical firm based on the example just given. At an interest rate of 20 percent or more, it will not be worthwhile to do any insulating. As soon as the interest rate drops below 20 percent, the first $10,000 of insulation becomes worthwhile. The second 6 inches of insulation begins to pay for itself when the interest rate falls below 10 percent. Given the 15 percent rate shown in the diagram, investment is cut off at $10,000.

Part (b) of Exhibit 8.2 shows an investment schedule for the economy as a whole. With tens of thousands of firms and millions of potential investment

Planned-investment schedule
A graph showing the relationship between the total quantity of real planned-investment expenditure and the interest rate.

---

[2]In the real world the opportunity cost of investment may vary according to the source of funds. The job of the firm's financial managers is to choose carefully among the sources of funds so as to keep the firm's total cost of investment to a minimum. This is not a course on managerial finance, so we will ignore such details; as far as we are concerned, the firm will face the same opportunity cost or interest rate regardless of its source of funds.

Exhibit 8.2   Planned-Investment Schedules for a
Hypothetical Firm and for the Economy as a Whole

Part (a) shows planned investment for a hypothetical firm; part (b) shows a
planned-investment schedule for the economy as a whole. At a 15 percent
interest rate, the hypothetical firm will invest at a real rate of $10,000 per year,
and real planned investment for the economy as a whole will be $225 billion per
year. Both for the firm and for the economy, the amount of real planned
investment rises as the interest rate falls, other things being equal.

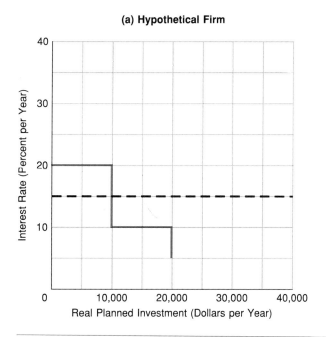

(a) Hypothetical Firm

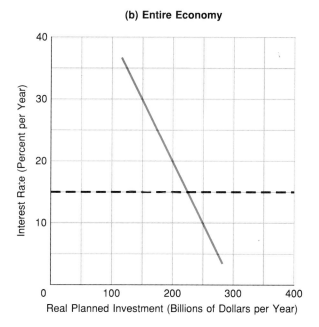

(b) Entire Economy

projects, the stairsteps of the single-firm, single-project investment schedule are
smoothed out. In this schedule, a 15 percent interest rate is associated with $225
billion of real planned-investment spending per year for the economy as a whole.

Any change in the interest rate, other things being equal, will produce a
movement along the planned-investment schedule. In part (b) of Exhibit 8.2, for
example, a decrease in the interest rate to 10 percent will increase planned
investment to $250 billion. Likewise, an increase in the interest rate to 20 per-
cent will reduce total planned investment to $200 billion.

Of course, the interest rate is not the only factor that affects investment
decisions. Anything else that affects the expected profitability of an investment—
forecasts of product demand, expected changes in technology, trends in labor
supply—will also cause the amount of investment to change. Increased optimism about profit opportunities thus will cause the planned-investment schedule to shift to the right, and increased pessimism will cause it to shift to the left.

Saving and the interest rate.   The classical economists thought that saving
would also be affected by the interest rate. Interest may be paid to a saver by a
firm that borrows investment funds directly from a household, for example, by
selling corporate bonds. Or it may be paid by a financial intermediary such as a

bank, which accepts savings or other deposits and lends the proceeds to firms seeking investment funds. In either case interest payments represent the reward for saving. The greater the reward, thought the classical economists, the greater the saving that would be forthcoming. This implies a positively sloped real **saving schedule,** such as the schedule SS shown in part (a) of Exhibit 8.3.

Another circumstance that affects real saving is income. Other things being equal, an increase in the incomes of households will cause them to save more at any given interest rate. Thus, an increase in real national income will cause the real saving schedule to shift to the right, and a decrease in real national income will cause it to shift to the left.

The saving-investment equilibrium.   Exhibit 8.3 shows how the planned-investment (PI) and saving schedules (SS) together determine an equilibrium in

Saving schedule
A graph showing the relationship between the total quantity of real saving and the interest rate.

Exhibit 8.3   The Classical Investment/Saving Stabilization Mechanism

In classical economic theory the planned-investment schedule, PI, is negatively sloped because the interest rate is the opportunity cost of investment; the saving schedule, SS, is positively sloped because the interest rate is the reward for saving. Part (a) shows that in this case real saving and investment are equal at the natural level of real output, given a 4 percent interest rate. If a change in business expectations shifts the planned-investment schedule leftward, as in part (b), the interest rate will fall by enough to maintain the equality of saving and planned investment with real national product remaining at the natural level. The decrease in saving as households move down and to the left along their saving schedule is equivalent to an increase in consumption in a simple economy in which the government and foreign sectors are omitted. There is no shift in the saving schedule because there is no change in real national income or product as the economy makes the necessary adjustments.

$Y = C + S$
$AD = C + I$
$AD = Y$

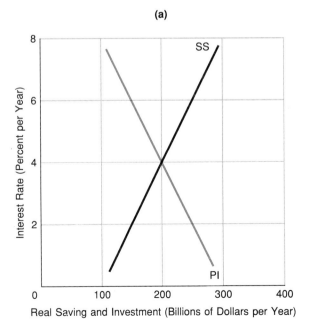

(a)

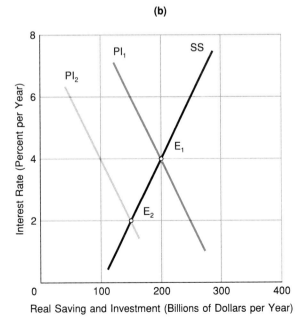

(b)

which real saving and real planned investment are equal. Both schedules are drawn as they would appear when real national income and product are at their natural levels. In part (a) the two schedules intersect at an equilibrium interest rate of 4 percent. At any lower interest rate—say, 2 percent—the quantity of saving would fall short of planned investment. Investors competing among one another for the available funds would bid the interest rate up. As the interest rate rose, the quantity of saving would increase and planned investment would decrease as both savers and investors moved along their respective schedules. When the interest rate reached 4 percent, real saving and investment would again be equal.

If the interest rate were higher than 4 percent, savers would not find takers for all of their savings. Given the surplus of savings, investors would realize that they could pay a lower rate and still get all the funds they need. As the interest rate fell toward 4 percent, equilibrium would be restored under conditions consistent with production of the natural level of real output.

Response to a shift in investment.   In the classical view, a flexible interest rate would keep aggregate demand equal to aggregate supply at the natural rate of real output despite changing market conditions. This is illustrated in part (b) of Exhibit 8.3. Initially real output is at its natural level, the interest rate is 4 percent, and saving and investment are equal at $200 billion per year. Then some change in conditions—say, the end of a railroad-building boom—causes firms to scale back their investment plans. The planned-investment schedule shifts from PI_1 to PI_2. If the interest rate stayed at 4 percent, planned investment would drop by $100 billion. Unless this investment is replaced by some other category of expenditure, inventories will accumulate, the circular flow will begin to contract, and national income and product will fall in both real and nominal terms.

Before this happens, according to the classical view, the interest rate will begin to fall. By the time it reaches 2 percent, firms will modify their investment plans and real planned investment will rise to $150 billion. (This increase in investment in response to the lower interest rate corresponds to a downward movement along PI_2.) At the same time, households, faced with a smaller reward for thrift, will cut back their real saving by $50 billion. (The decrease in saving in response to the lower interest rate corresponds to a downward movement along SS.) Because saving is the part of income that is not consumed, this is the same as saying that households will increase their real consumption by $50 billion. When the economy reaches E_2, where SS and PI_2 intersect, equilibrium will be restored. In the new equilibrium, investment will be $50 billion less than it was to begin with, but this will have been offset by the $50 billion increase in consumption. The level of real aggregate demand thus will remain sufficient to absorb all of the natural level of real output. The adjustment of saving to the change in planned investment, via a change in the interest rate, occurs without a change in the level of real national income and product, so no shift in the saving schedule takes place.

Say's Law

In short, the classical economists were convinced that there could not be a persistent deficiency of real aggregate demand that would depress real output below its natural level. The view that demand would always be sufficient to absorb all of the output that firms and workers were willing to produce using given technology and resources came to be known as **Say's law,** after the French economist Jean Baptiste Say. Say himself, an early follower of Adam Smith, did not elaborate the flexible-price and flexible-interest-rate mechanisms, but other nineteenth-century economists did. Economic heretics, including Karl Marx, challenged the prevailing doctrine from time to time. Marx was convinced that gluts and general depressions not only were possible but would grow so severe that they would bring down the capitalist system. By and large, however, the classicists' faith in the self-adjusting economy remained intact until the Great Depression of the 1930s.

Say's law
The proposition that real aggregate demand will automatically be sufficient to absorb all of the output that firms and workers are willing to produce using given technology and resources.

8.2 Keynes's Challenge to the Classicists

The length and severity of the Great Depression cast doubt on the adequacy of the classical self-correcting mechanisms. However, such facts alone are not enough to bring about abandonment of a long-established theory. A new theory is needed—one that offers a superior interpretation of the facts. Economists of the 1930s found the theory they were looking for in Keynes's 1936 work, *The General Theory of Employment, Interest, and Money* (see **Who Said It? Who Did It? 8.1**). In this section we look first at Keynes's critique of classical theory and then at the new theory he proposed to replace it.

Unresponsive Saving and Investment

Keynes had little faith in the ability of interest rate changes to bring saving and investment into equilibrium, as the classical theory maintained they would. In his view, neither the saving nor planned investment schedule was very sensitive to changes in interest rates.

Keynes thought that the dominant influence on real saving is the level of real disposable income, with the interest rate playing only a minor role. "There are not many people," he wrote, "who will alter their way of living because the rate of interest has fallen from 5 to 4 percent."[3] Therefore, little can be expected from the saving side to bring saving and investment into line.

On the investment side, Keynes acknowledged that, other things being equal, a drop in the interest rate would increase the quantity of planned investment. However, other things did not remain equal for long. Changes in expectations could shift the planned-investment schedule, and in Keynes's view expectations were quite volatile. Psychological and speculative impulses were more important than economic calculations in determining whether or not a business would undertake a particular project. As Keynes put it,

> It is characteristic of human nature that a large proportion of our positive activities depend on spontaneous optimism rather than on a mathematical expectation. . . . Most, probably, of our decisions . . . can only be taken as a result of animal spirits—of a spontaneous urge to action rather than inaction, and not as the outcome of a weighted average of quantitative benefits multiplied by quantitative probabilities.[4]

---

[3]John Maynard Keynes, *The General Theory of Employment, Interest, and Money* (New York: Harcourt, Brace, and World, 1936), 94.
[4]Ibid., 161.

Who Said It? Who Did It?   8.1
John Maynard Keynes and
The General Theory

John Maynard Keynes was born into economics. His father, John Neville Keynes, was a lecturer in economics and logic at Cambridge University. John Maynard Keynes began his own studies at Cambridge in mathematics and philosophy. However, his abilities so impressed Alfred Marshall that the distinguished teacher urged him to concentrate on economics. In 1908, after Keynes had finished his studies and done a brief stint in the civil service, Marshall offered him a lectureship in economics at Cambridge; Keynes accepted.

Keynes is best remembered for his 1936 work, *The General Theory of Employment, Interest, and Money*, in which he departed from classical and neoclassical economic theory. Although this was by no means Keynes's first major work, it was the foundation for his reputation as the outstanding economist of his generation. Its major features are a bold theory based on broad macroeconomic aggregates and a strong argument for activist and interventionist policies.

Keynes was interested in more than economics. He was an honored member not only of Britain's academic upper class but also of the nation's highest financial, political, diplomatic, administrative, and even artistic circles. He had close ties to the colorful "Bloomsbury set" of London's literary world. He was a friend of Virginia Woolf, E. M. Forster, and Lytton Strachey, and, in 1925, he married the ballerina Lydia Lopokovia. He was a dazzling success at whatever he turned his hand to, from mountain climbing to financial speculation. As a speculator, he made a huge fortune for himself; as bursar of Kings College, he built an endowment of 30,000 pounds into one of over 380,000 pounds.

In *The General Theory*, Keynes wrote:

The ideas of economists and political philosophers, both when they are right and when they are wrong, are more powerful than is commonly understood. Indeed the world is ruled by little else. Practical men, who believe themselves to be quite exempt from any intellectual influences, are usually the slaves of some defunct economist. Madmen in authority, who hear voices in the air, are distilling their frenzy from some academic scribbler of a few years back. . . . There are not many who are influenced by new theories after they are twenty-five or thirty years of age, so that the ideas which civil servants and politicians and even agitators apply to current events are not likely to be the newest.

Was Keynes issuing a warning here? Whether or not he had any such thing in mind, his words are ironic because he himself has become one of the historical economists whose ideas remain influential long after they were first articulated.

In graphical terms, then, the Keynesian version of the relationship of real saving and investment to the interest rate would look like Exhibit 8.4. There the planned investment schedule is shown as much less elastic with respect to the interest rate than in the classical case depicted in Exhibit 8.3, and the saving schedule is shown as perfectly inelastic. Suppose that when real output is at its natural level, the saving schedule is in the position SS_1. If the planned-investment schedule is initially in the position PI_1, an equilibrium will be reached at point E_1, where the rate of interest is 4 percent.

Now suppose that a pessimistic turn in the "animal spirits" of entrepreneurs shifts the planned-investment schedule leftward to PI_2. The interest rate falls, but the change in the interest rate does not affect saving because the saving schedule is perfectly inelastic. As long as the saving schedule is in the position

Exhibit 8.4   Keynes's Critique of the Investment/Saving Mechanism

Keynes believed saving was unresponsive to changes in the interest rate, making the saving schedule perfectly inelastic. He also believed that investment is less elastic with respect to changes in the interest rate than the classical economists thought it was, although he did not view it as perfectly inelastic. In this exhibit real planned investment and real saving are equal at E_1, given PI_1 and SS_1. If the planned-investment schedule shifts leftward to PI_2, as it might during a depression, there will be no interest rate that is low enough to bring planned investment and saving back into line while real national income and product remain at the natural level. Equilibrium can be restored at a positive rate of interest only through a decline in national income and product, which would shift the saving schedule leftward to a position such as SS_2.

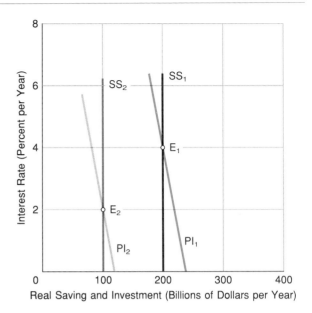

SS_1, planned investment and saving cannot be brought into equality even if the interest rate drops to zero.

Some other way to restore equilibrium must be found. Because planned investment is less than saving, aggregate demand will fall short of aggregate supply, inventories will accumulate, and the circular flow will begin to contract. As real national income and product fall below their natural level, the saving schedule will shift to the left until it intersects with PI_2 at a positive rate of interest. From the diagram alone, it might seem that the saving schedule would have to shift only far enough to meet the planned investment schedule at a zero rate of interest. However, in Keynes's view certain technicalities of the operation of money markets prevent interest rates from falling all the way to zero. In keeping with this view, the new equilibrium position of the saving schedule is SS_2. The interest rate in the new equilibrium is lower than it was initially, but greater than zero. And, of course, the new equilibrium real output is below the natural level.

Critique of the Flexible-Price Mechanism

Having cast doubt on the effectiveness of the interest rate mechanism, Keynes turned his attention to the issue of price flexibility. Up to a point, Keynes concurred with the classical economists regarding the effects of a decrease in aggregate demand. He agreed that a drop in aggregate demand would carry the economy down and to the left along a positively sloped aggregate supply curve, with prices, real output, and employment all falling.[5] However, Keynes sharply disagreed with the classical belief that a continued fall in the price levels of inputs

---

[5]For example, at the end of Chapter 20 of *The General Theory*, Keynes notes that "a deflation of effective demand below the level required for full employment [the natural level, in modern terminology] will diminish employment as well as prices" (page 291).

and final goods would bring real output back to its natural level. He used two arguments to make his point: rigid wages and the slope of the aggregate demand curve.

Rigid wages.   In Chapter 7 we saw that the short-run aggregate supply curve shows how firms would react to a change in aggregate demand if they expected input prices not to change, at least for the time being. But we noted that input prices would eventually adjust to the changed conditions. At that point the original short-run aggregate supply curve would shift downward and output would return to its natural level.

Keynes's first criticism of this mechanism was that wages — the most important class of input prices — are not very flexible in the downward direction. To be sure, workers sometimes accept cuts in their nominal wages, and many did so in the 1930s. However, these cuts met with widespread resistance in the form of strikes and protests. The resistance was strong enough, Keynes thought, to indicate that as a working approximation one would do better to assume that wages are completely rigid in a downward direction than to suppose that they are completely flexible. And because wages account for such a large share of total input prices, input prices in general could be considered inflexible in the downward direction.

Even with inflexible input prices, Keynes thought, the average level of prices of final goods would still fall when aggregate demand fell. In reaching this conclusion, Keynes relied on accepted microeconomic theory, again agreeing with the classical economists. Briefly, as explained in Chapter 2, each individual firm is thought to have an upward sloping supply curve in the short run because costs per unit of output tend to increase as output is increased within a plant of fixed size. (In microeconomics this is termed the principle of diminishing returns.) As the economy enters a recession, then, firms' costs per unit of output fall because their output falls below their plant capacity. Reduced unit costs plus the pressure of competition causes firms to cut their prices as demand contracts.

The conclusion, then, is that with rigid wages the economy's long-run aggregate supply curve will coincide with its short-run aggregate supply curve. When aggregate demand falls, the economy will move down along the aggregate supply curve to a point below the natural level of real output and will stay there. As long as wages and other input prices do not fall, the aggregate supply will not shift downward and the economy will not return to its natural level of real output.

The elasticity of aggregate demand.   In making this argument Keynes was not straying very far from the classical view. In the 1930s some of the classical economists themselves had pointed to rigid wages as tending to prolong the depression. They favored government policies actively promoting wage cuts as a way of bringing real output back to the natural level.

But at this point Keynes advanced his second argument: Even if all input and final goods prices are fully flexible in the downward direction, the aggregate quantity of goods demanded will be affected only slightly, if at all. If nominal wages fall, Keynes argued, the nominal spending power of the working population will fall by the same amount. Even if firms cut their prices to match the fall in wages, workers will not be able to buy more goods, in real terms, than they could before. If firms temporarily step up their output in the hope of selling more goods at the lower prices, they will be disappointed. The extra goods they produce will pile up in inventory, and they will have to retrench again. "There is, therefore," Keynes wrote, "no ground for the belief that a flexible wage policy is capable of maintaining a state of continuous full employment. . . . The economic system cannot be made self-adjusting along these lines."[6]

In terms of the model we have been using, this argument amounted to saying that the aggregate demand curve was perfectly inelastic, or close to it. The aggregate demand curve thus should not be represented as negatively sloped, as we have been drawing it, but instead, as vertical.

But what about the four factors listed in Chapter 7 that, according to economists today, give the aggregate demand curve a negative slope? Two of them—the impact of prices on consumption via changes in the real value of nominal money balances and the impact of prices on the government budget—were not considered by Keynes. The third factor—the favorable impact of lower prices on net exports—was considered as possibly important for Britain but not for the United States. (At that time the sum of imports and exports came to just 8 percent of U.S. GNP compared with 25 percent today.) The fourth factor—the impact of falling prices on investment via a reduction in interest rates—was admitted as a theoretical possibility. However, because Keynes thought that planned investment is inelastic with respect to the interest rate and also that there are technical limits on how low interest rates can fall, he believed that this effect would be quite weak.

The Keynesian version of aggregate supply and demand.   Although Keynes discussed the concepts of aggregate supply and demand at length in his *General Theory*, he did not draw aggregate supply and demand curves of the sort used today. Nevertheless, the modern model can be adapted to contrast Keynes's views with that of the classical economists. This is done in Exhibit 8.5, in which part (a) shows the world according to Keynes and part (b) represents the classical theory.

In both parts of the exhibit, the story begins at E_0, with real output at its natural level. Now a disturbance takes place—say, a reduction in real planned investment that is not offset by an increase in consumption. This shifts the aggregate demand curve leftward to AD_2. In both the Keynesian and classical cases, real output, employment, and the price level decline and the economy moves along the short-run aggregate supply curve to E_1.

At this point the two theories part ways. If Keynes's rigid wage argument is accepted, the economy simply comes to rest at E_1. Prices do not fall any further, and the economy remains parked in an underemployment equilibrium until something happens to revive aggregate demand.

For the sake of argument, however, Keynes was willing to consider the case in which wages and prices are perfectly flexible over time. When the prices of inputs and final goods are flexible in the long run, as in the classical theory, the aggregate supply curve will shift downward over time. A new equilibrium will be reached when the aggregate supply curve falls low enough to intersect the aggregate demand curve at the natural level of real output. This occurs at E_2 in part (b) of Exhibit 8.5.

In contrast, in the Keynesian version, even if wages and other input prices fall, permitting the aggregate supply curve to shift downward, the economy will not return to its natural level of real output because the aggregate demand curve

---

[6]Keynes, *General Theory*, 167.

Exhibit 8.5   Adjustment to Falling Aggregate Demand:
The Keynesian and Classical Views

This exhibit contrasts the Keynesian and classical views regarding the economy's adjustment to a leftward shift in the aggregate demand curve. In both cases the leftward shift initially causes a movement down and to the left along the short-run aggregate supply curve, from E_0 to E_1. In part (b) (the classical case), the level of input prices that firms expect then falls, causing the aggregate supply curve to shift downward until a new equilibrium, E_2, is reached at the natural level of real output. Keynes argued that the resistance of nominal wages to downward movement would prevent the aggregate supply curve from shifting downward. The economy therefore would remain at E_1 rather than moving on down the aggregate demand curve. Moreover, he thought that even if nominal wages and other input prices did fall, the aggregate demand curve would be too inelastic to permit a new equilibrium at the natural level of real output. Thus, even if the prices of final goods and input prices fell continuously, the economy could remain in a state of depressed output and high unemployment for a prolonged period.

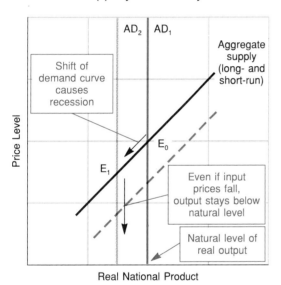

(a) Keynesian Theory

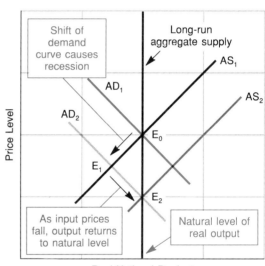

(b) Classical Theory

is inelastic. As shown in part (a) of Exhibit 8.5, the economy goes into a free fall downward along the vertical aggregate demand curve AD_2. There is no mechanism to bring real output back to its natural level.

Given the abysmal performance of the U.S. economy and other economies at the time that Keynes was writing, the Keynesian scenario seemed to fit the facts much more closely than the classical story of self-adjustment.

The Multiplier Effect

We now have a clear contrast between the classical view of the self-stabilizing economy and the Keynesian version of an economy that is at the mercy of investors' "animal spirits." In the classical view, a shift in the planned-investment schedule will not disturb aggregate demand for long because a flexible interest rate will quickly bring real saving and real planned investment back into line at the natural level of real output. Even if this defense fails and there is a drop in aggregate demand, flexible prices of inputs and final goods will return the economy to its natural level of real output. In the Keynesian view, flexible interest rates will not prevent a drop in planned investment from affecting aggregate demand. Further, rigid wages and the insensitivity of aggregate demand to changes in the price level will prevent a return to the natural level of real output.

But this is not the whole story. In *The General Theory*, Keynes argued that shifts in real planned investment (or in other components of aggregate demand) pose an even greater threat to economic stability than we have yet seen. From what we have said so far, it might seem that a given drop in planned investment—say, $100 million—would shift the aggregate demand curve to the left by just that amount. But Keynes maintained that the shift would actually be a *multiple* of $100 million—$400 million, $500 million, or even more. This phenomenon is called the **multiplier effect.** Let's see how it comes about.

Marginal propensity to consume. The origin of the multiplier effect lies in the relationship between disposable income and consumption. Keynes argued that for each $1 change in real disposable income, households change their real consumption in the same direction by a fraction of a dollar. He called this fraction the **marginal propensity to consume.** For example, suppose that households tend to spend $.75 of every $1 of additional disposable income on consumer goods and save the rest. In this case, the marginal propensity to consume is .75. Given this marginal propensity to consume, a $100 million increase in disposable income for the economy as a whole will cause total consumption expenditure to rise by $75 million. Likewise, a $100 million drop in disposable income will cause consumption to fall by $75 million.

Tracing the effects of a drop in planned investment. Given a marginal propensity to consume of .75, let's trace the effects of a $100 million drop in planned investment. Specifically, we will assume that this decline takes the form of a slowdown in the construction of new factories. This drop in planned investment reduces aggregate demand by $100 million. It is recorded as the "first-round" effect in Exhibit 8.6.

The $100 million reduction in factory construction means that many construction workers, subcontractors, and materials suppliers will face a loss of income of $100 million. According to the assumed marginal propensity to consume, they will then cut their consumption expenditures by $75 million. This $75 million is recorded in Exhibit 8.6 as the "second-round" effect of the slowdown in factory construction.

The repercussions of the slowdown do not end here. The $75 million drop in consumption expenditures by unemployed construction workers means that a lot of grocers, barbers, and so on will have their real incomes reduced by $75 million. For each dollar of lost income, they too will cut consumption expenditures by $.75. The resulting $56,250,000 cutback in their real consumption is the "third-round" effect of the original cutback in factory construction.

Next, the grocers' and barbers' tailors and bartenders will feel the pinch; then the tailors' and bartenders' accountants and coal dealers will be hit; and the process will continue for round after round, as shown in Exhibit 8.6. Nevertheless, there is a limit to the *total* reduction in real planned expenditures, because

Multiplier effect
The tendency for a given shift in real planned investment (or another component of real aggregate demand) to cause a larger shift in total real aggregate demand.

Marginal propensity to consume
The proportion of each added dollar of real disposable income that households devote to real consumption.

Exhibit 8.6 The Multiplier Effect

Keynes observed that households tend to devote a fraction of each dollar of added real disposable income to consumption and to reduce real consumption by the same amount when disposable income falls. The fraction, assumed to be .75 in this case, is called the *marginal propensity to consume*. This behavior tends to amplify the effect of any change in planned investment. Here real planned investment drops by $100 million in the first round. This causes a loss of $100 million in income for construction workers, who cut back their consumption expenditures by $75 million in the second round. In turn, the people who supplied the workers with consumer goods lose $75 million in income as a result and cut back their own consumption by $56,250,000. By the time the whole process has run an infinite number of rounds, total planned expenditure (planned investment plus consumption) will have fallen by four times the initial change in planned investment.

Round	Decrease in Real Income	Decrease in Real Expenditure
1		$100,000,000 (Planned investment)
2	$100,000,000	75,000,000 (Consumption)
3	75,000,000	56,250,000 (Consumption)
4	56,250,000	42,187,500 (Consumption)
5	42,187,500	31,640,625 (Consumption)
.		
.		
.		
Sum for infinite number of rounds	$400,000,000	$400,000,000 (Total planned expenditure)

with each round the reduction gets smaller. If the series given in the exhibit is added up over an infinite number of rounds, the total comes to $400 million, including $100 million of planned investment in the first round and a total of $300 million in consumption in all successive rounds. We can conclude that a $100 million drop in planned expenditures will decrease aggregate demand by $400 million rather than by just $100 million.

The ratio of the total change in planned expenditure at the original level of prices to the initial change in planned investment expenditure is known as the **expenditure multiplier.** The size of the multiplier depends on the marginal propensity to consume. A larger marginal propensity to consume will make the cutback in consumption at each round larger and hence raise the multiplier; a smaller marginal propensity to consume will make the cutback at each round smaller and hence lower the multiplier. The value of the expenditure multiplier for any given marginal propensity to consume (mpc) can be calculated using the following formula:[7]

$$\text{Expenditure multiplier} = 1/(1 - \text{mpc})$$

Expenditure multiplier
The ratio of the resultant shift in real aggregate demand to an initial shift in real planned investment (or other expenditure).

[7]The multiplier can be derived algebraically as follows:
Let ΔE be the total impulse to planned expenditure resulting from a $1 increase in autonomous

Thus, a marginal propensity to consume of .75 implies a multiplier of 4; an mpc of .9 implies a multiplier of 10; an mpc of .5 implies a multiplier of 2; and so on.

Policy Implications of the Keynesian Theory

The multiplier effect, combined with other elements of Keynesian theory, has strong implications for economic policy. The economy is seen as inherently unstable. A small change in real planned investment (or in other elements of real planned expenditure) will be amplified by the multiplier effect and hence will cause a large shift in the aggregate demand curve. Moreover, when the aggregate demand curve shifts, no reliable automatic mechanism exists for bringing the economy back to its natural level of real output. Once a depression sets in, then, it can go on for years, as happened in the 1930s.

However, at the same time that Keynesian theory suggests that the private economy is unstable, it also implies that the government has powerful policy tools with which to remedy the instability. The chief tool of Keynesian policy is the federal budget. Government purchases, like planned investment, are subject to the multiplier effect. Thus, if workers who have been laid off from factory construction can be put to work building highways and dams for the government, not only they but their grocers, barbers, tailors, bartenders, and so on can be kept working. To a lesser extent, tax cuts can be used to boost disposable income and thereby give a multiple boost to consumption expenditures. Policies regarding government purchases and net taxes—which, when taken together, are known as *fiscal policy*—are the subject of Chapter 10. Readers who are interested in a detailed graphical exposition of the Keynesian multiplier model may, if they wish, read the optional chapter which follows before proceeding to Chapter 10.

Looking Ahead

Much of the remainder of the macroeconomics course consists of a closer examination of themes that have been introduced in this chapter. One major task will be to examine in greater detail the financial sector of the economy, particularly the role of money and monetary policy. Another will be to scrutinize the behavior of the economy under conditions of inflation. As we move through this material, we will find that some elements of the Keynesian view have stood the test of time and are widely accepted today. On the whole, however, modern economists are neither as pessimistic about the stability of the private economy

---

expenditure, and let **b** be the marginal propensity to consume. The "round by round" analysis of the multiplier shows that:

$$\Delta E = 1 + \mathbf{b} + \mathbf{b}^2 + \mathbf{b}^3 + \cdots$$

Now multiply both sides of the equation by **b** to give a new equation:

$$\mathbf{b}\,\Delta E = \mathbf{b} + \mathbf{b}^2 + \mathbf{b}^3 + \cdots$$

Subtract this new equation from the original one, giving:

$$\Delta E - \mathbf{b}\,\Delta E = 1$$

Simplified, we get:

$$\Delta E = 1/(1 - \mathbf{b}),$$

which is the multiplier formula given in the text.

as Keynes was nor as optimistic about the government's ability to remedy economic problems. As we will see, many elements of the classical view have been rehabilitated, and today's Keynesians state their views more cautiously than their predecessors did.

Summary

1. **Why did the classical economists think that flexible prices would prevent lasting depressions?** In the classical view, a leftward shift in the aggregate demand curve would at first carry the economy down and to the left along a short-run aggregate supply curve. As this happened, the price level of final goods, real output, and employment would fall. However, competition among unemployed workers and owners of other idle inputs would soon depress input prices. As input prices fell, firms' expectations regarding input prices would decline, and the short-run aggregate supply curve would shift downward and move to a new equilibrium point at which it would intersect the aggregate demand curve at the natural level of real output.

2. **How do planned investment and saving respond to changes in the interest rate?** The interest rate is the opportunity cost of investment. In deciding whether to undertake an investment, a firm must balance the opportunity cost against the investment's expected returns. Other things being equal, the lower the interest rate, the greater the amount of real planned investment that will be undertaken. The classical economists thought that real saving would also respond positively to changes in the interest rate, because the interest rate is the reward for saving. Taking these two effects together, the classical economists thought that a flexible interest rate would maintain equality of real saving and real planned investment at the natural level of real output.

3. **Why were the theories of John Maynard Keynes received so favorably by economists in the 1930s?** During the Great Depression, economists lost faith in the classical model of a self-stabilizing economy. Keynes's work offered an explanation for the economy's failure to maintain equilibrium at the natural level of real output. He placed most of the blame on three factors: the lack of responsiveness of saving and investment to changes in interest rates; a rigidity of nominal wage rates in the face of downward pressure; and the lack of responsiveness of aggregate demand to changes in the price level. Keynes's theory can be represented in terms of a positively sloped long-run aggregate supply curve and a vertical or nearly vertical aggregate demand curve.

4. **Why did Keynes think that small changes in planned expenditures could cause large disturb-**

ances in the economy? Keynes thought that a given disturbance to one category of real planned expenditure—say, planned investment—causes aggregate demand to change by a multiple of the initial disturbance. The cause of this *multiplier effect* is the tendency of households to reduce real consumption by a fraction of each dollar by which real disposable income decreases (the *marginal propensity to consume*). Thus, a drop in planned investment will put some people out of work; the unemployed workers will reduce their consumption, thereby lowering the income of merchants from whom they buy goods and services; the merchants and their suppliers, in turn, will have to cut back on consumption; and so on. The ratio of the change in real aggregate demand to the initial change in real planned expenditure is called the *expenditure multiplier*. Its value is given by the formula $1/(1 - mpc)$, where mpc is the marginal propensity to consume.

5. **What were the implications of Keynes's theories for economic policy?** Keynes's multiplier theory implied that the economy would contract sharply in response to a relatively small drop in planned investment. His critique of the classical theory implied that the contraction would not easily correct itself. However, the multiplier effect would also apply to changes in government purchases. By increasing government purchases to offset any drop in private planned investment, the government could keep the economy at full employment.

Terms for Review

- planned-investment schedule
- saving schedule
- Say's law
- multiplier effect
- marginal propensity to consume
- expenditure multiplier

Questions for Review

1. According to the classical theory, how do prices of final goods, input prices, real output, and employment respond to a drop in aggregate demand in the short run? In the long run?

2. Explain why the interest rate represents the opportunity cost of investment even when a firm is able to finance an investment project from its own profits.

3. Explain why the planned-investment schedule has a negative slope and the saving schedule has a positive slope. Identify sources of shifts in each schedule.

4. Use a planned-investment schedule and a saving schedule to show how, according to classical theory, a flexible interest rate would keep real saving equal to real planned investment at the natural level of real output.

5. How did Keynes compare the relative importance of expectations and the interest rate as factors affecting the level of planned investment? What were his views regarding elasticity of the planned-investment and saving schedules?

6. Why would workers' resistance to cuts in nominal wages prevent a return to the natural level of real output following a drop in aggregate demand?

7. Why did Keynes think the aggregate demand curve would be perfectly inelastic or nearly so?

Problems and Topics for Discussion

1. **Examining the lead-off case.** Why is a decline in real output during a recession or depression accompanied by an increase in the unemployment rate? Why, in Keynes's view, does unemployment sometimes persist for years rather than disappearing as workers compete with one another for available jobs?

2. **Aggregate supply and demand in periods of expansion and contraction.** Compare the classical version of the economy's response to a drop in aggregate demand with the economy's response to an increase in aggregate demand as outlined in Chapter 7. What are the similarities and differences?

3. **The classical investment/saving model.** Use a classical planned-investment schedule and saving schedule to show how the economy would respond to (a) an increase in planned investment caused by a general trend toward optimism in business expectations and (b) a decision by households to increase the proportion of any given real income level that they would save at any given interest rate. For each case, show which schedule shifts and explain the responses of firms, households, and financial markets in both written and graphical form.

4. **An investment decision.** Your college football stadium is sold out for ten games each year. Tickets cost $20. The school is thinking of adding a new section to the stands that would hold 1,000 more people. Its construction would cost $1 million. The school can borrow the money at an interest rate of 14 percent. Should it do so? If it keeps adding seats, at some point it will become impossible to fill all seats for every game. At what point would it no longer be worthwhile to add more seats?

5. **Say's law.** Say's law is sometimes explained in terms such as the following: "Nobody will supply labor or any other factor of production unless they have a use in mind for the income they will earn by doing so. The use must be either to spend the income on consumption goods or make an investment. Therefore, the act of supplying factors of production guarantees that there will always be enough demand for all the goods supplied. There can never be a general glut of goods, because supply creates its own demand." Do you think this explanation is adequate? How does it compare with the classical investment/saving and flexible-price mechanisms?

6. **The classical model.** Suppose that the classical investment/saving mechanism works quickly and smoothly in the manner shown in Exhibit 8.3. Show that in this case a change in planned investment will not cause a recession even if the Keynesian assumptions about rigid wages and the slope of the aggregate demand curve hold true.

7. **The multiplier effect.** Rework Exhibit 8.6 for the following cases:
    a. A $100 million reduction in real planned investment assuming a marginal propensity to consume of .9
    b. A $100 million increase in real government purchases devoted to highway construction

    For part b, tell a "story" to go with your table, as is done in the text for the case of a drop in planned investment.

Case for Discussion

President Struggles with Congress over Highway Bill

MARCH 28, 1987. The president yesterday vetoed a popular $87.5 billion transportation bill that contained funds for highway construction in every state. He called the bill a "budget buster" and "pork barrel politics." He was especially critical of "demonstration projects" in the bill that demonstrated such things as construction of parking lots in the districts of key members of Congress.

In place of the vetoed bill the administration offered an $82 billion alternative that cut most of the demonstration projects.

Democrats in Congress vowed that they would vote to overturn the veto. (A two-thirds majority of both houses of Congress is required to overturn a veto.) They claimed that the bill would create hundreds of thousands of jobs in the construction industry and elsewhere in the economy. The administration's alternative bill could not be passed by Congress in time for the short construction season in northern states, supporters said.

Supporters of the vetoed measure pointed to the slowdown in economic growth in the fourth quarter of 1986. In that quarter, the economy was estimated to have grown by just 1.1 percent—almost a standstill. The slowdown was attributed in large part to a decline in business fixed investment. Without the highway spending, supporters claimed, the economy might slow further or even slide into a recession.

Questions

1. Use aggregate supply and demand curves to show how a reduction in business fixed investment might have caused a recession if investment had continued to drop in 1987.

2. Speaking from a Keynesian point of view, justify an increase in federal highway construction spending to offset declining private investment. Include the multiplier effect in your argument.

3. Speaking from a classical point of view, argue against passage of the highway bill. Explain why the drop in private investment observed in the fourth quarter of 1986 would probably be only temporary and why any recession— if one were to occur—would be short.

Suggestions for Further Reading

Breit, William, and Roger L. Ransom. *The Academic Scribblers*, rev. ed. Hinsdale, Ill.: Dryden Press, 1983.

The title of this book is taken from Keynes's remark that policymakers are the slaves to past economists. Chapter 7 covers Keynes, and Chapters 8 and 9 discuss two of his important followers in the United States.

Hansen, Alvin H. *A Guide to Keynes*. New York: McGraw-Hill, 1953.

This book by an early follower of Keynes is an aid to reading The General Theory.

Keynes, John M. *The General Theory of Employment, Interest, and Money*. New York: Harcourt, Brace, and World, 1936.

Although much of this book is hard going even for professional economists, some passages are quite accessible to the general reader.

The Income-Expenditure Model

**Before reading this chapter,
make sure you know the meaning of:**

Transfer payments (Chapter 4)

Government purchases (Chapter 5)

Net taxes (Chapter 5)

Planned versus unplanned investment (Chapter 5)

Marginal propensity to consume (Chapter 8)

Expenditure multiplier (Chapter 8)

After reading this chapter, you will understand:

More about how consumption is related to disposable income.

How consumption is affected by various kinds of taxes.

How the equilibrium level of national income is determined in the income-expenditure model.

How the income-expenditure model can be used to demonstrate the multiplier effect.

How the income-expenditure model can be reconciled with the aggregate supply and demand model.

Teenage Mutant Ninja Turtles and the Economy

It's shaping up as a healthy Christmas season for turtles and bargain hunters. But retailers are feeling a bit queasy.

Midway through the Christmas shopping season, Teenage Mutant Ninja Turtles have emerged as the season's hot action-figure in what industry experts say is a pretty cold toy market. Big-ticket items such as personal computers seem to be lagging, and quick-delivery promotions have boosted catalog sales.

Overall, most retailers say they have posted sales increases over the prior year, albeit modest ones. But although they have been discounting early and often since the Thanksgiving kickoff of America's annual shopping spree, traffic remains light in many locales and gawkers have frequently outnumbered buyers.

Some consumers, concerned about the economy or rising personal debt, say they are cutting back their Christmas spending. Marilyn McFarland, a 28-year-old airline customer service supervisor from Lansing, Michigan, shopping on Chicago's retail-rich Michigan Avenue, said she has spent about $10 less per person on gifts and did it without the help of credit cards.

At the eight Pittsburgh-area Benetton stores, a spokeswoman said, the average sale is $40 to $60, off 40 percent from a year ago.

Photo source: © Craig Aurness/Westlight.

Source: "Retailers Counting on Late Sales Surge," *The Wall Street Journal*, December 12, 1989, p. B1. Reprinted by permission of *The Wall Street Journal*, © Dow Jones & Company, Inc., 1989. All Rights Reserved Worldwide.

The Marilyn McFarlands of the world—that is, consumers—have enormous power over the economy. They control some two-thirds of the spending flows that pour into total national product. Multiplied by hundreds of millions, their decisions to spend $10 more or less on Teenage Mutant Ninja Turtles for their nieces and nephews can change the direction of the economy. In this chapter we will see that Keynes's model of the determination of real national income focuses on the factors that influence how much consumers spend and may cause them to change their spending plans. We will see how consumer pessimism can make a bad recession worse and how a return to optimism—as occurred at the beginning of 1983—can fuel a recovery. Chapter 8 introduced some of the basic concepts of the Keynesian income-expenditure model, including the marginal propensity to consume and the multiplier effect. This chapter provides greater detail and presents a graphical version of the model.

In this chapter we will make a number of simplifying assumptions. At first we will assume that the price level in the economy is fixed. This is not a true Keynesian assumption—in fact, prices fluctuated dramatically during the period in which Keynes was writing. Keynes recognized this fact and discussed it in his *General Theory*. However, Keynes's followers generally make an initial presentation of his income-expenditure model in a fixed-price context to simplify the analysis.

In addition, we will make three assumptions that eliminate certain differences between the circular flow models of Chapter 5 and the official national income accounts of Chapter 6. First, we will drop the distinction between gross and net national product by assuming the capital consumption allowance to be zero. Second, we will eliminate the difference between net national income, as measured by the income approach, and national product, as measured by the expenditure approach, by assuming that indirect business taxes and the statistical discrepancy are zero. Finally, we will assume undistributed corporate profits to be zero so that disposable personal income equals national income minus net taxes. These assumptions can be expressed in equation form as follows:

$$\frac{\text{Disposable}}{\text{income}} + \frac{\text{Net}}{\text{taxes}} = \frac{\text{National}}{\text{income}} = \frac{\text{National}}{\text{product}}$$

9.1 The Consumption Schedule

Consumption schedule (consumption function) A graph that shows how real consumption expenditure varies as real disposable income changes, other things being equal.

As we saw in Chapter 8, Keynes regarded the division of real disposable income between consumption and saving as a key to regulating the circular flow. Starting from the observation that consumers consistently spend part—but not all—of each additional dollar of income, he proposed a relationship between real disposable income and real consumption expenditure that resembled the one shown in Exhibit 9.1. This relationship is known as the **consumption schedule** or **consumption function.**

Autonomous Consumption

The consumption schedule shown in part (b) of Exhibit 9.1 does not pass through the origin; rather, it intersects the vertical axis somewhere above zero. This indicates that a certain part of real consumption expenditure is not associated with any particular level of real disposable income. The component of real

Exhibit 9.1   The Consumption Schedule

Parts (a) and (b) both present a simple example of the connection between real
disposable income and real consumption. The $100 billion level of real
autonomous consumption is shown in part (b) by the height of the intersection of
the consumption schedule with the vertical axis. The slope of the consumption
schedule equals the marginal propensity to consume.

(a)

Disposable Income (1)	Consumption Expenditure (2)	Change in Income (3)	Change in Consumption (4)	Marginal Propensity to Consume (5)	Average Propensity to Consume (6)
$ 0	$ 100				—
100	175	$100	$75	0.75	1.75
200	250	100	75	0.75	1.25
300	325	100	75	0.75	1.08
400	400	100	75	0.75	1.00
500	475	100	75	0.75	0.95
600	550	100	75	0.75	0.91
700	625	100	75	0.75	0.89
800	700	100	75	0.75	0.88
900	775	100	75	0.75	0.86
1,000	850	100	75	0.75	0.85
1,100	925	100	75	0.75	0.84
1,200	1,000	100	75	0.75	0.83

Note: All amounts are in billions of dollars per year.

(b)

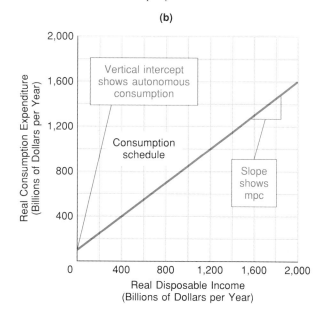

consumption that is equal to the vertical intercept of the consumption schedule
is called **autonomous consumption.** In the context of the Keynesian model, the
term **autonomous** applies to any expenditure category that does not depend on
the income level.

Autonomous consumption
The part of total real consumption expenditure that is independent of the level of real disposable income; for any given consumption schedule, real autonomous consumption equals the level of real consumption associated with zero real disposable income.

Autonomous
In the context of the Keynesian income-expenditure model, refers to an expenditure that is independent of the level of real national income.

Average propensity to consume
Total consumption for any income level divided by total disposable income.

The $100 billion level of autonomous consumption suggests that total consumption expenditure is $100 billion even if total disposable income is zero. In practice, disposable income never falls to zero for the economy as a whole. However, individual households sometimes have zero income. When they do, they do not cut consumption to zero. Instead, they draw on past savings or borrow against future income to maintain some minimal consumption level. In this sense the concept of autonomous consumption is rooted in actual consumer behavior.

Marginal Propensity to Consume

Columns 1 through 4 in part (a) of Exhibit 9.1 show that whenever disposable income rises, some of the additional income is spent on consumption above and beyond autonomous consumption. As we saw in Chapter 8, the fraction of each added dollar of real disposable income that goes to added consumption is called the *marginal propensity to consume (mpc)*. For example, a $100 billion increase in disposable income—from $500 billion to $600 billion—raises consumption by $75 billion—from $475 billion to $550 billion. Likewise, a $100 billion decrease in disposable income—from $500 billion to $400 billion—causes consumption to fall by $75 billion—from $475 billion to $400 billion. Thus, the value of the marginal propensity to consume in this example is .75 ($75/$100).

In geometric terms, the marginal propensity to consume equals the slope of the consumption schedule. In part (b) of Exhibit 9.1, a horizontal movement of $100 billion in disposable income corresponds to a vertical movement of $75 billion in planned consumption. The slope of the consumption schedule, then, is $75/$100 = .75, the same as the marginal propensity to consume.

Marginal versus average propensity to consume.   It is helpful to contrast the marginal propensity to consume with the average propensity to consume. The **average propensity to consume** for any real income level equals total real consumption divided by real disposable income. It is shown in column 6 of Exhibit 9.1. For income levels below $400 billion, consumption exceeds disposable income, so the average propensity to consume is greater than 1. As disposable income increases, the average propensity to consume falls. However, because total consumption always includes a constant level of autonomous consumption—at least in the short run—the average propensity to consume is always greater than the marginal propensity to consume.[1]

Short run versus long run.   In practice, the actual values of both the average and marginal propensities to consume depend on the time horizon. In the United States consumption spending has tended to rise over long periods by about $.90 for every $1 increase in disposable income, which implies a long-run marginal propensity to consume of about .9. (Since 1970, however, the implied long-run marginal propensity to consume has been higher than the historical average.) Also, the long-run level of autonomous consumption, as implied by

---

[1]The relationship between average and marginal propensity to consume can also be expressed in algebraic terms. Let C represent consumption, Y disposable income, a autonomous consumption, and b marginal propensity to consume. The consumption schedule can then be written as $C = a + bY$ and the average propensity to consume as $C/Y = (a + bY)/Y = a/Y + b$. The latter expression clearly shows that the average propensity to consume exceeds the marginal propensity to consume as long as autonomous consumption is greater than zero.

Exhibit 9.2   Consumption Schedules for Various
Marginal Propensities to Consume

The slope of the consumption schedule equals the
marginal propensity to consume. Here consumption
schedules are shown for marginal propensities to
consume of .9, .66, and .5. Autonomous consumption
of $100 billion is assumed for all the curves.

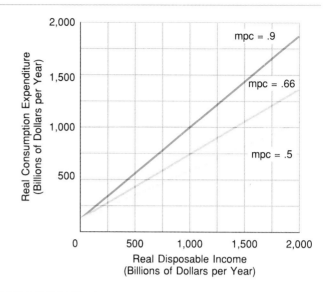

historical data, approaches zero. As a result, the average and marginal propensities to consume are equal in the long run.

In the short run (a year or less), people tend to change their consumption by less than $.90 for every $1 change in income. Also, autonomous consumption is positive in the short run; thus, the marginal propensity to consume is less than the average propensity to consume.

One reason for this is that year-to-year changes in disposable income are not always permanent. People tend to make smaller changes in their consumption in response to temporary changes in income than they do in response to permanent ones. For example, a household that is used to an annual income of $30,000 would no doubt cut back somewhat on its consumption in a year when its income temporarily dropped to $28,000. However, as long as it expected better times to return, it would probably reduce its consumption by less than it would if it expected the lower income level to be permanent. Therefore, as long as the drop in income was seen as temporary, the household would offset it to some degree by reducing its rate of saving, by dipping into past savings, or by borrowing.

Even permanent changes in income are not always perceived as permanent in the short run. Thus, a household that experiences a permanent income increase of $2,000 per year might at first treat part of the added income as temporary and consume less of it than it otherwise would. Over a longer period, as it becomes clear that the higher income level is permanent, more of the increase is likely to be consumed.

Because this book focuses mainly on short-run economic stabilization policy, the examples in this chapter use a marginal propensity to consume of .75, somewhat lower than the observed long-run mpc for the United States. However, there is nothing sacred about the value .75; under different short-run conditions, a higher or lower value might be appropriate. Exhibit 9.2, for example, shows the consumption schedule for marginal propensities to consume of .9, .66, and .5. A $100 billion level of real autonomous consumption is assumed for each schedule; thus, they differ only in their slopes. The higher the marginal propensity to consume, the steeper the consumption schedule.

Shifts in the Consumption Schedule

The consumption schedules that we have drawn so far show the link between real disposable income and real consumption spending. A movement along the consumption schedule shows how real consumption spending changes along with real disposable income, other things being equal. In this section, we will see what is covered by the "other things being equal" clause in this case. This will generate a list of factors that can shift the consumption schedule.

Wealth.   One consideration that is assumed to remain constant as we move along the consumption schedule is real wealth. A household's *wealth* is the total value of everything it owns—money, securities, real estate, consumer durables, and so on—minus the debts it owes. Wealth is a stock concept; it is measured in dollars at a point in time. Income, in contrast, is a flow; it is measured in dollars per unit of time. Of two households with equal income, we expect the one with greater wealth to spend more freely on consumer goods than the one with less wealth. Thus, anything that happens to increase the total real wealth of all households will cause an upward shift in the consumption schedule. This effect shows up as a change in autonomous consumption; the marginal propensity to consume and, hence, the slope of the consumption schedule remain unchanged.

Consider the following example: Many people hold some of their wealth in the form of corporate stocks. A rise in the average price of all corporate stocks thus could produce an upward shift in the consumption schedule. Similarly, a drop in total wealth could cause consumption to fall. Some people think that the stock market crash of 1929 caused a downward shift in the consumption schedule that helped trigger the Great Depression. Today economists still watch the stock market for possible effects on consumer behavior (see ***Applying Economic Ideas 9.1***).

Although for now we are holding the price level constant, a change in the price level can affect real wealth via a change in the real purchasing power of nominal money balances. A rise in the price level means that a $20 bill or $100 in a checking account will buy less than before; a fall in the price level means that it will buy more. Thus, a rise in the price level tends to cut real autonomous consumption and shift the consumption schedule downward, whereas a fall produces an upward shift. In Chapter 7 this effect was listed among the factors that give the aggregate demand curve a negative slope.

Expectations.   People's spending decisions depend not only on their current real income and wealth but also on their expected future real income and wealth. Any change in their expectations can cause a shift in the consumption schedule. This chapter opened with an example of a person who was holding down her level of spending because she was pessimistic about the state of the economy. When all consumers become pessimistic—as they tend to do during a recession—the consumption schedule can shift downward; when they become more optimistic, it can shift upward again.

Net taxes.   Up to this point we have graphed the consumption schedule using real disposable income on the horizontal axis. For many purposes, however, it is more useful to substitute real national income. In a world with no taxes or transfer payments, such a change would not affect the consumption schedule at all, because without taxes national income and disposable income would be

Applying Economic Ideas 9.1
The Stock Market and the Economy

The prosperity of the Roaring Twenties was marked by a soaring stock market. Then, on October 28, 1929, the market crashed. The widely watched Dow Jones average of industrial stock prices fell 38 points to close at 261, a 12.8 percent drop, and dove another 31 points the next day. Those two days of panic came to be known as the Great Crash. Wall Street saw nothing like them again until the Dow fell 508 points, or 22.6 percent, on October 19, 1987.

The Great Crash of 1929 came to be viewed as the beginning of the decade-long Great Depression. But was it merely a symbol, or was it actually a factor that helped to cause the downturn? This question, which has been much debated over the years, took on a new relevance in the light of the market turmoil of 1987.

Evidence that the 1929 crash was merely symbolic is found in the fact that the peak of the 1920s expansion had been reached in August 1929. From then to October, production fell at an annual rate of 20 percent and personal income at an annual rate of 5 percent. This suggests that the crash reflected a decline that had already begun. In contrast, the economic news in the July-to-September quarter of 1987 was dominated by an increased rate of GNP growth and the lowest unemployment rate since the start of the 1980s.

But there are two plausible arguments in support of the idea that the stock market crash of 1929 helped cause, or at least deepened, the Great Depression. Many economists believe that they apply to the 1980s as well.

One argument notes that a drop in stock prices is a reduction in real personal wealth. Since wealth can affect consumption independently of changes in income, a drop in stock prices will tend to shift the consumption function downward. A rule of thumb that was used by some forecasters in the 1980s links each $1 drop in stock market wealth to a $.05 drop in consumption. That would translate into a $50 billion loss of consumption for the trillion-dollar loss of wealth in the bear market of August-to-October 1987. The 1929 numbers were smaller, but they were of comparable significance in the much smaller economy of that time.

A second argument emphasizes the psychological impact of falling stock prices. One needs to consider not only the confidence of consumers but also that of business managers who make investment decisions. Both the consumption function and the planned-investment curve are sensitive to changes in expectations. Therefore, a big drop in stock prices can shift these curves via an expectations effect as well as via a wealth effect.

Changes in expectations are easier to capture in words than in numbers. The significance of the 1929 crash to contemporaries was expressed by Fred Allen in his book *Only Yesterday*: "There was hardly a man or woman in the country whose attitude toward life had not been affected by it [the bull market of the 1920s] in some degree and was not now affected by the sudden and brutal shattering of hope."

The crash of October 1987, which was comparable in percentage terms to that of 1929, awakened memories of the earlier era. In the first days following the 1987 crash, many people worried that it would touch off, if not a major depression, at least a recession. As it turned out, however, the effect of the 1987 crash on consumption, although measurable, was small. Other areas of spending, including investment and net exports, showed enough strength to offset the slight decline in the average propensity to consume. Although a few sectors, notably luxury cars, did suffer reduced sales, the expansion of the economy as a whole that had begun in 1982 continued right through the end of the decade.

Sources: Milton Friedman and Anna J. Schwartz, *A Monetary History of the United States* (Princeton, N.J.: Princeton University Press, 1963), Chapter 7; Peter Temin, *Did Monetary Forces Cause the Great Depression?* (New York: Norton, 1976), Chapter 3.

---

equal. Once we introduce net taxes, however, the level of disposable income on which consumption decisions depend will differ from the level of national income. As a result, changes in net taxes become another source of shifts in the consumption schedule.[2] The type of shift produced varies, depending on how the taxes are related to income.

---

[2]We continue to assume that there are no indirect business taxes. Only corporate profits taxes, payroll taxes, and personal taxes, such as personal income taxes and personal property taxes, are taken into account. Thus, it continues to be true that national income minus net taxes equals disposable income.

Exhibit 9.3   National Income and Consumption
with Autonomous Net Taxes

Autonomous net taxes do not change when the level of real national income
changes. This exhibit shows how introducing an autonomous net tax of $100
billion shifts the consumption schedule downward when the schedule is drawn
with national income on the horizontal axis. The amount of the shift is equal to
the level of autonomous net taxes times the marginal propensity to consume.

(a)

National Income (1)	Consumption with No Tax (2)	Autonomous Net Tax (3)	Disposable Income (4)	Consumption with Tax (5)
$ 0	$ 100	$100	$−100	$ 25
100	175	100	0	100
200	250	100	100	175
300	325	100	200	250
400	400	100	300	325
500	475	100	400	400
600	550	100	500	475
700	625	100	600	550
800	700	100	700	625
900	775	100	800	700
1,000	850	100	900	775
1,100	925	100	1,000	850
1,200	1,000	100	1,100	925

Note: All amounts are in billions of dollars per year.

(b)

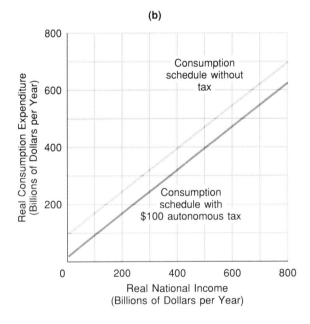

Autonomous net taxes
Taxes or transfer payments
that do not vary with the
level of national income.

Autonomous net taxes.   Taxes and transfer payments that do not vary with
national income are called **autonomous net taxes.** Personal property taxes are a
major example on the revenue side of the net tax picture. On the transfer side,

items ranging from interest on the national debt to government pensions are not directly linked to changes in income.

Exhibit 9.3 shows how the consumption schedule is affected by introducing autonomous net taxes of $100 billion into an economy that had no taxes before. The first two columns of part (a), which are the same as those in Exhibit 9.1, show national income and the resulting level of consumption that would take place if there were no taxes. The consumption schedule assumes autonomous consumption of $100 billion and a marginal propensity to consume of .75. Columns 3 and 4 show that the $100 billion autonomous net tax reduces disposable income to a level $100 billion below that of national income. As column 5 shows, this $100 billion reduction cuts $75 billion from consumption at each income level in accordance with the .75 marginal propensity to consume. The remaining $25 billion of the tax is accounted for by a reduction in saving. As before, consumption is at the autonomous level of $100 billion when disposable income is zero. However, zero disposable income now corresponds to $100 billion of national income, as line 2 of the table shows. At a national income of zero, consumption is $25 billion.

Part (b) of Exhibit 9.3 shows the effect of the autonomous net tax in graphical terms. Introducing the tax produces a downward shift in the consumption schedule as it is drawn here, with real national income on the horizontal axis. The new schedule is parallel to the old one but is shifted downward by an amount equal to the marginal propensity to consume times the level of autonomous net taxes—in this case, $75 billion. The vertical intercept of the new schedule equals autonomous consumption minus the marginal propensity to consume times the level of autonomous net taxes, or $25 billion in this case.

Income taxes.   Autonomous taxes are an important source of revenue for state and local governments, and autonomous transfers are an important item on the expenditure side of the federal budget. The largest sources of federal revenue, however, are the social security payroll tax and the personal income tax. These income-linked taxes have a somewhat different effect on the consumption schedule, as Exhibit 9.4 shows.

Part (a) of Exhibit 9.4 assumes a 20 percent **marginal tax rate** on income from all sources; it also assumes autonomous net taxes of zero. As columns 3 and 4 show, this means that the tax takes $.20 of each added dollar of national income. Disposable income thus increases by $.80 for each added dollar of national income. As columns 4 and 5 show, the marginal propensity to consume of .75 applies to this $.80 of added disposable income. All told, then, of each added dollar of real national income $.20 goes for real taxes and $.60 of the remaining $.80 goes for real consumption.

Part (b) of Exhibit 9.4 shows the effect of an income tax in graphical terms. Instead of causing a downward shift that leaves the new schedule parallel to the old one, the income tax reduces the slope of the consumption schedule. With no income tax in effect, the slope of the schedule equals the marginal propensity to consume (in this case, .75). With a 20 percent proportional income tax in effect, the slope is reduced to .6. The formula for the slope of the consumption schedule with an income tax in effect is:

$$\text{Slope of consumption schedule} = \text{mpc}(1 - t),$$

where t stands for the marginal tax rate.

Marginal tax rate
The percentage of each added dollar of real national income that must be paid in taxes.

Exhibit 9.4   The Consumption Schedule with an Income Tax Added

When the consumption schedule is drawn with national income on the horizontal axis, introducing an income tax reduces its slope. This example assumes a marginal propensity to consume of .75 and a marginal tax rate of .20. The slope of the consumption schedule with the income tax in effect equals mpc(1 − t), where t is the marginal tax rate.

(a)

National Income (1)	Consumption with No Tax (2)	20% Income Tax (3)	Disposable Income (4)	Consumption with Tax (5)
$ 0	$ 100	$ 0	$ 0	$100
100	175	20	80	160
200	250	40	160	220
300	325	60	240	280
400	400	80	320	340
500	475	100	400	400
600	550	120	480	460
700	625	140	560	520
800	700	160	640	580
900	775	180	720	640
1,000	850	200	800	700
1,100	925	220	880	760
1,200	1,000	240	960	820

Note: All amounts are in billions of dollars per year.

(b)

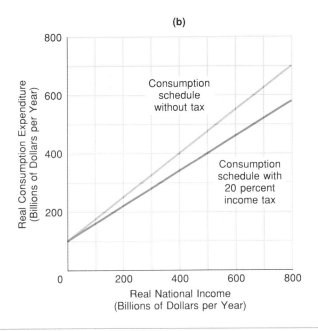

9.2 Graphing the Income-Expenditure Model

In Chapter 5 we saw that the circular flow can be in equilibrium only when planned expenditure (aggregate demand) equals national product (aggregate supply). If planned expenditure exceeded national product, buyers' attempts to purchase more than was being produced would lead to unplanned decreases in business inventories. Firms would react to those decreases by increasing their output, thereby causing the level of the circular flow to rise. Except in the present case, where the price level is held constant by assumption, the expansion of the circular flow would also tend to be accompanied by a rise in the price level. Similarly, if planned expenditure fell short of national product, business inventories would build up more rapidly than planned. Firms would react by cutting their output and—except in the present special case—lowering their prices.

These principles are central to Keynes's theory of equilibrium national income. In this section we will use them to develop a graphical model of that theory. Because Keynes saw planned expenditure primarily as a function of income rather than of prices, the model presented here is called the **income-expenditure model.**

The Planned-Expenditure Schedule

The first step is to construct a **planned-expenditure schedule** for the economy. This is a graph that shows the total real planned purchases of goods and services corresponding to each level of real national income. This curve differs from the aggregate demand curve introduced in Chapter 7 in that it relates the level of real planned expenditure to the level of real national income rather than to the price level. In constructing the planned-expenditure schedule, we will deal with each component of expenditure in turn as we did in the case of the aggregate demand curve.

Consumption. We have already discussed the relationship between real consumption and real national income. The consumption schedule serves as the foundation of the planned-expenditure schedule. The vertical intercept of the consumption schedule equals the level of autonomous consumption, adjusted, if necessary, for autonomous net taxes. Its slope equals the marginal propensity to consume, adjusted, if need be, for the marginal income tax rate. In this initial version of the planned-expenditure schedule, we will assume that there is no income tax and that autonomous net taxes are fixed by law at $100 billion, as was the case in Exhibit 9.3.

Investment. The second component of planned expenditure is planned investment. As explained in Chapter 5, this includes fixed investment plus planned changes in inventories; unplanned inventory changes are not counted.

As we saw in Chapter 8, the level of real planned investment depends on interest rates and business expectations. In the simple version of the income-expenditure model developed here, neither the interest rate nor expectations will be assumed to vary systematically with the income level. This means that we can treat investment as a type of autonomous expenditure along with autonomous consumption.

Income-expenditure model
The Keynesian model in which the equilibrium level of real national income is determined by treating real planned expenditure and real national product as functions of the level of real national income.

Planned-expenditure schedule
A graph showing the level of total real planned expenditure associated with each level of real national income.

Exhibit 9.5   The C, I, and G Components
of the Planned-Expenditure Schedule

This exhibit shows the consumption, planned investment, and government
purchases components of the planned-expenditure schedule. In the simple case
represented here, consumption is the only element that varies directly with real
national income. The slope of the C + I + G schedule thus equals the marginal
propensity to consume of .75.

(a)

National Income (1)	Consumption Expenditure (2)	Planned Investment (3)	Government Purchases (4)	C + I + G (5)
$ 0	$ 25	$125	$150	$ 300
100	100	125	150	375
200	175	125	150	450
300	250	125	150	525
400	325	125	150	600
500	400	125	150	675
600	475	125	150	750
700	550	125	150	825
800	625	125	150	900
900	700	125	150	975
1,000	775	125	150	1,050
1,100	850	125	150	1,125
1,200	925	125	150	1,200
1,300	1,000	125	150	1,275
1,400	1,075	125	150	1,350
1,500	1,150	125	150	1,425
1,600	1,225	125	150	1,500

Note: All amounts are in billions of dollars per year.

(b)

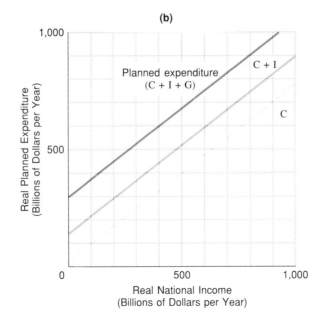

Once we know the level of planned investment for a given year, we can add it to planned consumption spending as a second component of planned expenditure, as shown in Exhibit 9.5. The C + I schedule in part (b) of the exhibit is the sum of the consumption and planned investment shown in columns 2 and 3 of part (a).

Government purchases.   The third component of planned expenditure is government purchases. Under the federal government's current budget procedures, the president proposes a level of expenditures for each year as part of the administration's budget message. Congress takes the proposed budget into account, together with the views of its own members, in setting a spending limit for the coming year. The congressional budget resolution is supposed to serve as a ceiling on expenditures for the year, including both government purchases and transfer payments. Similar budget procedures are used at the state and local levels. Chapter 10 explains the federal government's budget procedures in detail.

In practice, political and economic conditions often disrupt these budget procedures, necessitating adjustments during the course of the year. For our purposes in this chapter, however, we will proceed as if government purchases for each year were fixed by law in real terms. This will allow us to treat government purchases as a category of autonomous expenditure.

Exhibit 9.5 shows how government purchases can be added to consumption and planned investment as a third component of planned expenditure. The C + I + G schedule in part (b) corresponds to the sum of columns 2 through 4 of part (a). Regardless of the national income level, government purchases are assumed to be limited to $150 billion.

The Net Exports Component of Planned Expenditure

The final component of planned expenditure is real net exports, that is, real exports minus real imports. Exports can be considered autonomous from the standpoint of the domestic economy; they are determined by economic conditions in foreign countries. Imports, however, do depend on the level of domestic national income. Because some of the goods that households consume are imported, imports increase when consumption expenditures rise. To calculate total planned expenditure including net exports, these imports, which are already included in the consumption component of planned expenditure, must now be subtracted.

For example, suppose that, as in Exhibit 9.3, the marginal propensity to consume is .75 and autonomous consumption and autonomous net taxes are $100 billion. Suppose too that one-fifth of each added dollar of consumption expenditures is devoted to imported goods. This means that for each $1 increase in disposable income, consumption will rise by $.75 and imports will rise by one-fifth of that, or $.15. In economic terminology, there is a **marginal propensity to import** of .15. (The marginal propensity to import is expressed as a fraction of real disposable income, rather than as a fraction of consumption.)

Part (a) of Exhibit 9.6 shows how imports, exports, and net exports are related to national income. Consider imports first. As in Exhibit 9.3, consumption is $25 billion when national income is zero. One-fifth of this is spent on imported consumer goods; thus, imports are $5 billion when national income is zero. For each added $100 billion of national income, imports increase by

Marginal propensity to import
The percentage of each added dollar of real disposable income that is devoted to real consumption of imported goods and services.

Exhibit 9.6   Adding Net Exports to the
Planned-Expenditure Schedule

Part (a) shows how imports, exports, and net exports behave as real national income changes. Real national income in the domestic economy does not affect exports; hence, exports are represented by a horizontal line at an assumed level of $185 billion. When national income is zero, consumption is $25 billion; thus, imports are $5 billion. With a marginal propensity to import of .15, imports increase by $15 billion for each $100 billion increase in real national income. The net export line shows exports minus imports. Net exports are equal to zero at $1,200 billion. Part (b) of the exhibit shows how net exports can be added to consumption, government purchases, and planned investment to give the complete planned-expenditure schedule.

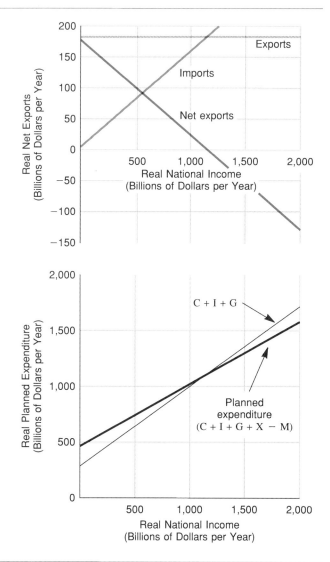

$15 billion in accordance with the marginal propensity to import of .15. Therefore, when national income is $100 billion, imports are $20 billion, when national income is $1,000 billion, imports are $155 billion, and so on. The slope of the import schedule is .15.

Next, consider exports. These depend on the income level and the marginal propensity to import in foreign countries. In this case, we assume that foreign buyers purchase $185 billion of exports. This quantity does not depend on the level of domestic national income; hence, the export schedule in part (a) of Exhibit 9.6 is a horizontal line. Subtracting imports from exports yields the net export schedule. Like the import schedule, this has a slope equal (in absolute value) to the marginal propensity to import. When national income is zero, net exports equal $180 billion ($185 billion of exports minus $5 billion of imports). Net exports remain positive up to a national income of $1,200 billion; at $1,200 billion net exports are zero; and at national income levels above $1,200 billion, they become negative.

Part (b) of Exhibit 9.6 adds the net export schedule to consumption, planned investment, and government purchases to yield the complete planned-expenditure schedule. The autonomous component of this schedule (shown by its vertical intercept at $480 billion) is the sum of autonomous consumption adjusted for autonomous net taxes ($25 billion), planned investment ($125 billion), government purchases ($150 billion), and net exports ($180 billion). The slope of the schedule (in this case, .6) equals the marginal propensity to consume minus the marginal propensity to import.

In this example it is assumed that there is no income tax. If there were, the calculation of the slope of the planned-expenditure schedule would have to take this into account. Using mpc for the marginal propensity to consume, mpm for the marginal propensity to import out of disposable income, and t for the marginal tax rate, the formula for the slope of the planned-expenditure schedule becomes (mpc − mpm) (1 − t).

In this treatment, real net exports depend only on real disposable income in the domestic economy. In practice, they also depend on real national income in foreign countries, which determines the level of real exports, and also on the exchange rate of the dollar relative to foreign currencies, which affects both imports and exports. We will explore these aspects of the foreign sector in more detail in later chapters.

Determining the Equilibrium Level of National Income

The planned-expenditure schedule shows how aggregate demand varies as national income changes, with the price level held constant. To find the equilibrium level of national income, all we need to do now is find the income level at which aggregate demand (that is, planned expenditure) equals aggregate supply (that is, national product). Exhibit 9.7 shows how this is done. The example is simplified by assuming a closed economy, that is, zero net exports.

The income-product line.   The first step is to add a line showing the relationship between national income and national product. Under our simplifying assumptions, national income and product are equal. Using the horizontal axis to represent real national income and the vertical axis to represent real national product, then, the relationship between the two can be shown as a straight line with a slope of 1 passing through the origin. We will refer to this line as the **income-product line.** It is simply a graphical representation of the equality of national income and product. (In Chapter 5, we saw that this equality is a fundamental property of the circular flow.)

Income-product line
A graph showing the level of real national product (aggregate supply) associated with each level of real national income.

Planned expenditure and national product.   When the income-product and planned-expenditure lines are drawn on the same diagram, as they are in Exhibit 9.7, it is a simple matter to find the income level for which real planned expenditure and real national product are equal. This equality occurs at the intersection of the two lines—$1,200 billion in Exhibit 9.7. Because *planned expenditure* is simply another term for *aggregate demand*, and *national product* is a synonym for *aggregate supply*, this intersection point is a point of equilibrium for the circular flow.

At no other level of national income can the circular flow be in equilibrium. If national income is lower than the equilibrium level—say, $1,000 billion— planned expenditure (aggregate demand) will exceed national product (aggre-

Exhibit 9.7 Using the Income-Expenditure Model to Find the Equilibrium Level of Real National Income

The income-expenditure model is formed by the planned-expenditure schedule and the income-product line. This exhibit shows a simple way to determine the equilibrium level of real national income given the underlying conditions that determine the position of the planned-expenditure schedule. Any national income higher than the equilibrium level will cause unplanned inventory buildup and downward pressure on real output. Any level of national income below equilibrium will cause unplanned inventory depletion and upward pressure on real output. The example is simplified by assuming a closed economy, so that net exports are zero at all levels of real national income.

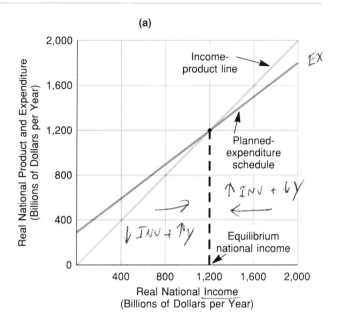

(a)

(b)

Real National Income (1)	Real Planned Expenditure (2)	Real National Product (3)	Unplanned Inventory Change (4)	Tendency of Change in National Income (5)
$ 0	$ 300	$ 0	−$300	Increase
100	375	100	−275	Increase
200	450	200	−250	Increase
300	525	300	−225	Increase
400	600	400	−200	Increase
500	675	500	−175	Increase
600	750	600	−150	Increase
700	825	700	−125	Increase
800	900	800	−100	Increase
900	975	900	−75	Increase
1,000	1,050	1,000	−50	Increase
1,100	1,125	1,100	−25	Increase
1,200	1,200	1,200	0	No change
1,300	1,275	1,300	25	Decrease
1,400	1,350	1,400	50	Decrease
1,500	1,425	1,500	75	Decrease
1,600	1,500	1,600	100	Decrease

Note: All amounts are in billions of dollars per year.

gate supply). There will be an unplanned drop in inventories equal to the vertical distance between the planned-expenditure schedule and the income-product line. In trying to restore inventories to their planned levels firms will increase their output, thereby causing national income to rise. As income rises, planned expenditure increases, but only by a fraction of the amount by which national product increases. The gap thus narrows until equilibrium is restored.

If, on the other hand, national income is higher than the equilibrium level—say, $1,500 billion—planned expenditure will fall short of output. The unsold goods will become unplanned inventory investment equal to the gap between the planned-expenditure and income-product lines at the $1,500 billion income level. Firms will react to the unplanned inventory buildup by cutting production. Their actions will cause real national income and product to fall to the equilibrium level.

In Exhibit 9.7 the same story is told twice—graphically in part (a) and numerically in part (b). Both approaches confirm that $1,200 billion is the only possible equilibrium level for national income, given the underlying assumptions on which the planned-expenditure schedule is based.

The Multiplier Effect

The level of real planned expenditure for the economy depends on many factors. First and foremost, planned spending varies as real national income changes. In the graphs used in this chapter, such changes are shown as movements upward or downward along the planned-expenditure schedule. Other factors that affect planned expenditure—changes in expectations, consumer wealth, interest rates, taxes, government purchases, or foreign markets—cause upward or downward shifts in the planned-expenditure schedule. In the preceding section we saw how, under given conditions, the level of real national income tends to move upward or downward as planned expenditure varies along the planned-expenditure schedule to the point of equilibrium. Now we turn to the effects of shifts in the planned-expenditure schedule on the equilibrium level of national income.

Exhibit 9.8 shows the effects of a $100 billion annual increase in planned expenditure at each possible national income level. For the moment, it does not matter whether the shift begins in the household, investment, or government sector; the effect in any case is to shift the planned-expenditure schedule upward by $100 billion, from PE_1 to PE_2.

What happens to the equilibrium level of real national income when the planned-expenditure schedule shifts upward by $100 billion? The immediate effect is that planned expenditure exceeds national product. As a result, inventories start to fall at a rate of $100 billion per year. Firms react to this unplanned inventory depletion by increasing their output. (In a model with flexible prices, they would tend to increase both real output and prices.) As a result, the circular flow expands. National income continues to rise until the gap between planned expenditure and national product—that is, between aggregate demand and aggregate supply—disappears. This occurs at an income level of $1,600 billion.

We see, then, that a $100 billion upward shift in the planned-expenditure schedule has caused a $400 billion increase in equilibrium real national income. This ability of a given vertical shift in planned expenditure to cause a greater increase in the equilibrium level of national income is the multiplier effect. At this point it may be helpful to compare the graphical demonstration of the multi-

Exhibit 9.8   Multiplier Effect in the
Income-Expenditure Model

A given vertical shift in the planned-expenditure
schedule produces a greater increase in the
equilibrium level of real national income. This
constitutes a graphical representation of the multiplier
effect. Here a $100 billion upward shift in the planned-
expenditure schedule causes a $400 billion increase
in equilibrium real national income. The ratio of the
change in equilibrium income to the initial shift in
demand, which is the expenditure multiplier, has a
value of 4 in this example. In this simplified example,
the marginal tax rate and the marginal propensity to
import are assumed to be zero.

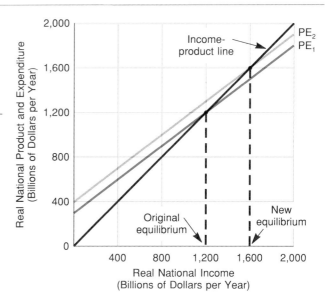

plier effect in Exhibit 9.8 with the numerical example given in Exhibit 8.6 (page
216).

Modifications in the Multiplier Formula

In Chapter 8 the formula for the expenditure multiplier was presented as $1/(1 -$
mpc). The marginal propensity to consume (mpc) is the slope of the planned-
expenditure schedule in a closed economy without income taxes. In this chapter
we have added some details to the model that require that we modify the formula. The modifications can be derived from this general form for the multiplier:

$$\text{Expenditure multiplier} = \frac{1}{1 - \text{Slope of planned-expenditure schedule}}.$$

The formula given in Chapter 8 is the simplest case. Starting from there, anything that affects the slope of the planned-expenditure schedule will affect the
multiplier, as we will now show.

The effect of an income tax in a closed economy.   Earlier in this chapter we
saw that the addition of an income tax changes the slope of the consumption
schedule from mpc to mpc$(1 - t)$, where t is the marginal tax rate. The formula
for the multiplier in a closed economy with a proportional income tax imposed at
a marginal tax rate of t thus is

$$\text{Expenditure multiplier with income tax added} = \frac{1}{1 - \text{mpc}(1 - t)}.$$

This formula shows that the imposition of an income tax reduces the value of the
multiplier. For example, a closed economy with a marginal propensity to con-

sume of .8 will have an expenditure multiplier of 5 if there is no income tax. With an income tax at a 25 percent marginal rate, the denominator of the multiplier formula will be .4, and the multiplier therefore will fall to 2.5. In general, the higher the marginal tax rate, the smaller the effect of a disturbance in planned expenditure on the equilibrium level of real national income.

The effect of net exports.   Including the foreign sector also changes the slope of the planned-expenditure schedule and, therefore, the multiplier. In addition to t, the marginal tax rate, we now add the term *mpm*, representing the marginal propensity to import. The mpm shows the share of each dollar of added disposable income that goes to imports. The slope of the planned-expenditure schedule is now (mpc − mpm)(1 − t), so the formula for the expenditure multiplier becomes

$$\text{Expenditure multiplier} = \frac{1}{1 - (\text{mpc} - \text{mpm})(1 - t)}.$$

For example, suppose that the marginal propensity to consume is .9, the marginal propensity to import is .15, and the marginal tax rate is .33. With no income tax or imports, the multiplier for an economy with an mpc of .9 will be 10. Adding imports will reduce the slope of the planned-expenditure schedule to .75 and, hence, reduce the multiplier to 4. Adding a marginal tax rate of .33 will further reduce the slope of the planned-expenditure schedule to .5, thereby reducing the expenditure multiplier to 2.

In Chapter 8 we noted that in his *General Theory* Keynes emphasized the economy's sensitivity to even small changes in planned investment. Since that time, however, both imports and income taxes have become much more important in relation to the size of the economy. By reducing the multiplier, the increased importance of imports and income taxes is thought to have reduced the economy's sensitivity to small disturbances in autonomous aggregate demand.

9.3   The Relationship between the Income Determination Models

We now have two models for determining the equilibrium level of real national income and product: the aggregate supply and demand model, which treats real planned expenditure and real national product as functions of the price level, and the income-expenditure model, which treats them as functions of the level of real national income. This section briefly outlines how these two models can be reconciled; a fully rigorous reconciliation is a subject for a more advanced course.

In this section we drop our assumption of a fixed price level.

The Two Models in the Short Run

Exhibit 9.9 illustrates the relationship between the two models in the short run. Initially the economy is in equilibrium with real national product at its natural level and the price level at 1.0. This equilibrium is shown as E_1 in the aggregate supply and demand model of part (a) and as e_1 in the income-expenditure model of part (b). Now suppose that something happens to increase real autonomous

Exhibit 9.9   Reconciling the Income-Expenditure and Aggregate Supply and Demand Models

Both the income-expenditure and aggregate supply and demand models determine the equilibrium level of real national income and product. This exhibit shows how they can be reconciled when the effect of a change in the price level on planned expenditure is taken into account. The economy begins at E_1 in part (a) and e_1 in part (b). Autonomous expenditure then increases by $500 billion. The aggregate demand curve shifts from AD_1 to AD_2. With no price change, the economy would end up at E_2 and e_2. However, the price level increases as the economy moves up along the aggregate supply curve to E_3. This causes the planned-expenditure schedule to halt its upward movement at PE_3. Thus, the short-run equilibrium as shown in the income-expenditure model is e_3, which occurs at the same level of national product shown by E_3 in part (a).

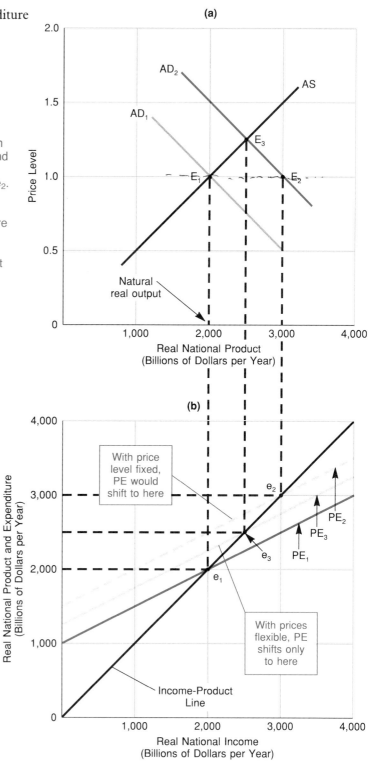

Note: All amounts are in billions of constant dollars per year.

expenditure by $500 billion; for our present purposes it does not matter whether the increase comes from autonomous consumption, planned investment, government purchases, or net exports. The increase in autonomous expenditure shifts the planned-expenditure schedule upward. This causes unplanned depletion of inventories, and the economy begins to expand.

Short-run equilibrium with flexible prices.   If there were no change in the price level, a $500 billion increase in autonomous expenditure would move the planned-expenditure schedule to PE_2, and real output would find a new equilibrium at $3,000 billion.[3] In part (b), this equilibrium would occur at e_2. In part (a), a $1,000 billion increase in national product with no price change would put the economy at E_2 in accordance with the multiplier effect.

However, we are no longer dealing with a fixed-price economy. In a world of flexible prices, an increase in aggregate demand causes the price level to increase as well as the level of real output. This is shown in part (a) of Exhibit 9.9 as a movement up and to the right along the economy's short-run aggregate supply curve, AS. As soon as the economy begins to move up along the aggregate supply curve, things start to happen in the income-expenditure model in part (b). As discussed in Chapter 7, the rising price level reduces real autonomous consumption via its effect on the real value of nominal money balances; it reduces real planned investment via an increase in the interest rate; it may lower real government purchases if government budgets are set partly in nominal terms; and it cuts real net exports by increasing the prices of domestic goods relative to foreign goods. These effects partially offset those of the original increase in autonomous expenditure. The planned-expenditure schedule does not move all the way to PE_2; instead, the rise in the price level allows it to shift only as far as PE_3.

Because the planned-expenditure schedule shifts only to PE_3, equilibrium real output rises only to $2,500 billion, rather than to $3,000 billion as it would if prices remained fixed. The new short-run equilibrium in the income-expenditure model is e_3. This corresponds to point E_3 in the aggregate supply and demand model—a point on the aggregate supply curve that is above and to the right of the initial equilibrium, E_1.

Effect on the aggregate demand curve.   Our analysis of the movement to the new equilibrium helps us to understand some important features of the aggregate demand curve. The initial equilibrium, E_1, lies on aggregate demand curve AD_1 at the point at which it intersects the aggregate supply curve, AS. What about points E_2 and E_3? E_2 shows what would have happened to the equilibrium level of aggregate demand if the price level had remained at 1.0. E_3 shows what happens to it when the economy instead moves up along the aggregate supply curve. Points E_2 and E_3 both lie on a new aggregate demand curve, AD_2. The various points along that curve show the level of aggregate demand at different possible price levels, given the original shift in autonomous expenditure that moved the economy away from its old equilibrium.

---

[3]In Chapter 14, we will see that expansion of the economy even without a change in the price level can cause the interest rate to rise, thus depressing planned investment. Here we assume, in effect, that the underlying change in real autonomous expenditure is strong enough to increase real autonomous expenditure by $500 billion and thus to shift the planned-expenditure curve upward by that amount even after this interest rate effect is taken into account.

Our example thus confirms two points about the aggregate demand curve that were made in Chapters 7 and 8. First, we see that the negative slope of the aggregate demand curve arises from the effects of a change in the price level on real planned expenditure. These are the same forces that limit the shift in the planned-expenditure schedule to PE$_3$. Second, we see that an initial increase in autonomous expenditure, whether in the form of a change in autonomous consumption, planned investment, government purchases, or net exports, causes a horizontal shift in the aggregate demand curve. This shift (the distance between E$_1$ and E$_2$ in part (a) of Exhibit 9.9) equals the expenditure multiplier times the initial increase in autonomous expenditure.[4] However, the actual increase in equilibrium aggregate demand is less than the horizontal shift in the aggregate demand curve, because the price level increases as the economy moves up and to the right along its short-run aggregate supply curve.

The Two Models in the Long Run

So far our reconciliation of the income-expenditure model with the aggregate supply and demand model has dealt only with short-run effects. The effect of long-run adjustments in the two models is demonstrated in Exhibit 9.10. This exhibit begins where Exhibit 9.9 left off—with the economy in short-run equilibrium at E$_3$ in part (a) and at e$_3$ in part (b). The schedule PE$_2$ and the corresponding points e$_2$ and E$_2$ have been deleted to simplify the diagrams.

As we have seen in earlier chapters, the economy can remain in short-run equilibrium at E$_3$ only as long as firms expect input prices to remain constant. Of course, this will not continue forever. In the long run, firms' expectations regarding input prices will adjust to the changes in prices of final goods that have already taken place, and the short-run aggregate supply curve will begin to shift upward. Input prices will return to a consistent equilibrium relationship with final goods prices only when the short-run aggregate supply has shifted up all the way from AS$_1$ to AS$_2$. The economy will then reach a new long-run equilibrium at point E$_4$ in part (a) of Exhibit 9.10. That is the point at which aggregate demand curve AD$_2$ intersects the long-run as well as the short-run aggregate supply curve.

The move from E$_3$ to E$_4$ involves a further increase in the level of final goods prices. As prices rise beyond the level of 1.25, real planned expenditure begins to decrease. In part (a) of Exhibit 9.10, this is indicated by a movement upward and to the left along the aggregate demand curve AD$_2$. The decrease in real planned expenditure reflects a drop in consumption as real income falls and rising prices erode the real value of money, declines in real planned investment and government purchases, and falling net exports. If we look at these events in terms of the income-expenditure model in part (b) of the exhibit, we see that they take the form of a downward shift of the planned-expenditure schedule; it drops below PE$_3$ and does not stop until it is all the way back to PE$_1$. At that point the depressing effects of rising prices on real planned expenditure fully offset the initial increase in autonomous expenditure. The long-run equilibrium in the income-expenditure model is thus e$_4$, which is exactly the same as the initial equilibrium, e$_1$. This result is a more elaborate restatement of one that we originally noted in Chapter 7: given that prices for both inputs and final goods are fully flexible in the long run, a shift in aggregate demand has no lasting effect

---

[4]The qualification regarding the interest rate that was given in footnote 3 applies here as well.

Exhibit 9.10   Long-Run Effects of Expansion
in the Two Models

This exhibit picks up where Exhibit 9.9 left off.
The short-run equilibrium following an increase in
autonomous expenditure is E_3 in part (a) and e_3
in part (b). Over time, as the input prices
expected by firms adjust, the short-run aggregate
supply curve shifts up from AS_1 to AS_2, and the
economy moves to a new long-run equilibrium at
E_4. As it does, prices rise further and the planned-
expenditure schedule in part (b) shifts all the way
back down to its original position at PE_1. The
final equilibrium in part (b) is e_4, which is identical
to the initial equilibrium, e_1. Thus, we see that in
a fully flexible-price model, a shift in the
aggregate demand curve has no permanent
effect on the equilibrium level of real national
income and product.

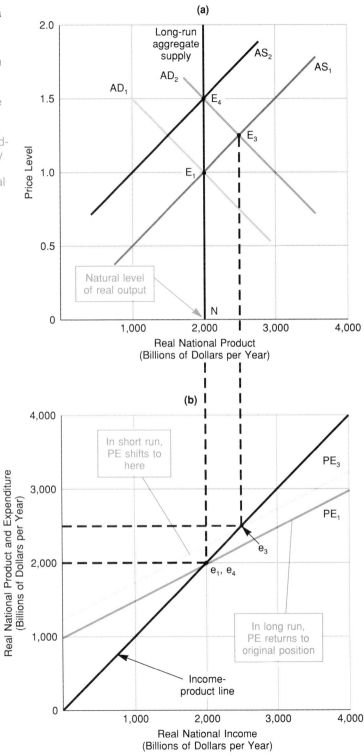

Note: All amounts are in billions of constant dollars per year.

on the equilibrium level of real national income and product. The only lasting effect is on the levels of final goods and input prices. We will return to the implications of this proposition at several points in later chapters.

Summary

1. **How is consumption related to disposable income?** The relationship between real consumption and real disposable income can be represented by a graph known as the *consumption function*. The vertical intercept of the consumption function, which represents the part of real consumption expenditure not associated with a particular real income level, is known as *autonomous consumption*. The slope of the consumption function equals the marginal propensity to consume. Changes in real wealth, the average price level, or expectations can shift the consumption function.

2. **How is consumption affected by various kinds of taxes?** The basic form of the consumption function relates real consumption expenditure to real disposable income. The consumption function can be redrawn with national rather than disposable income on the horizontal axis, provided that an appropriate adjustment is made for the effect of taxes. An *autonomous net tax* shifts the consumption function downward by an amount equal to the tax times the marginal propensity to consume. Such a tax does not change the slope of the consumption function. An income tax does change the slope, however. With an income tax, the slope of the consumption function is mpc$(1 - t)$, where t is the *marginal tax rate*.

3. **How is the equilibrium level of national income determined in the income-expenditure model?** The income-expenditure model consists of the *planned-expenditure schedule* and the *income-product line*. The point at which they intersect shows the level of real national income corresponding to equilibrium in the circular flow, that is, the level of national income at which planned expenditure (aggregate demand) equals national product (aggregate supply). At any higher level of national income, there will be unplanned inventory accumulation, which is shown by the vertical gap between the two schedules. At any lower level of national income, there will be unplanned inventory depletion.

4. **How can the income-expenditure model be used to demonstrate the multiplier effect?** Any shift in the position of the planned-expenditure schedule will change the real income level at which it intersects the income-product line. The greater the slope of the planned-expenditure schedule, the greater the change in equilibrium real national income that will result from a given change in autonomous expenditure. This is the multiplier effect.

5. **How can the income-expenditure model be reconciled with the aggregate supply and demand model?** The income-expenditure model relates real planned expenditure to the level of real national income, whereas the aggregate supply and demand model relates real planned expenditure to the price level. The two can be reconciled if the effects of changes in the price level on real planned expenditure are taken into account. In general, an increase in the price level causes the planned-expenditure schedule to shift downward and a decrease causes it to shift upward. An initial increase in autonomous planned expenditure shifts the aggregate demand curve to the right by an amount that depends on the size of the expenditure multiplier. In the short run, there is an increase in both real output and the price level as the economy moves up and to the right along the aggregate supply curve. In the long run, a shift in real aggregate demand has no lasting effect on the equilibrium level of real national income once both input and final goods prices have changed by enough to bring real national product back to its natural level.

Terms for Review

- consumption schedule (consumption function)
- autonomous consumption
- autonomous
- average propensity to consume
- autonomous net taxes
- marginal tax rate
- income-expenditure model
- planned-expenditure schedule
- marginal propensity to import
- income-product line

Questions for Review

1. What assumptions are needed to establish the condition that disposable income plus net taxes equals national product and the condition that gross and net national product are equal?

2. What considerations determine the slope and intercept of the consumption function?

3. How is the consumption function affected by (a) an increase in real wealth, (b) an increase in the price level while the nominal quantity of money balances remains constant, and (c) a shift in expectations?

4. When the consumption function is graphed with national income on the horizontal axis, how are its slope and intercept affected by autonomous taxes? By income taxes?

5. What is the relationship between the planned-expenditure schedule and the consumption function? Between the planned-expenditure schedule and the aggregate demand curve?

6. Why does the income-product line always pass through the origin and have a slope of 1?

7. How is the value of the expenditure multiplier related to the slope of the planned-expenditure schedule?

8. How is the planned-expenditure schedule affected by an increase in autonomous expenditure? By a decrease in autonomous expenditure?

Problems and Topics for Discussion

1. **Examining the lead-off case.** Use the income-expenditure model to show what happens to the equilibrium level of real national income when a large proportion of consumers cut back on their autonomous spending the way Marilyn McFarland did. Show too what happens when they become optimistic again and begin buying all the toys, clothing, and perfumes they want to put under the Christmas tree. In each case assume that the change in mood is not initially caused by a change in real disposable income. Once the mood change is established, however, will it cause a change in total real disposable income? Why or why not?

2. **Permanent and transitory changes in income.** Suppose that you won $1,000 in a lottery. How much would you spend and how much would you save? (Remember that debt repayment counts as saving.) Would you save more or less of this $1,000 windfall than of the first $1,000 of a pay increase that you expected to be permanent? Would it surprise you to learn that some surveys have found that the marginal propensity to consume from windfall income is smaller than the marginal propensity to consume from permanent income changes? Explain.

3. **Graphing the consumption schedule.** On a sheet of graph paper, draw consumption schedules for the following values of real autonomous consumption (a) and the marginal propensity to consume (mpc): a = 1,000, mpc = .5; a = 1,200, mpc = .6; a = 500, mpc = .9.

4. **Taxes and the consumption schedule.** On a sheet of graph paper, draw a consumption schedule based on the following assumptions: no taxes at all, autonomous consumption of $100 billion, and a marginal propensity to consume of .8. Label the horizontal axis "real national income." Now modify this schedule for the following tax assumptions:
   a. Real autonomous net taxes of $50 billion
   b. An income tax with a marginal tax rate of 25 percent
   c. Both (a) and (b)
   Bonus question: Calculate the value of the expenditure multiplier for each of the preceding cases.

5. **Effects of a decrease in autonomous expenditure.** Rework Exhibit 9.8 for a $100 billion decrease in real autonomous planned expenditure. Explain step by step what will happen on the way to the new equilibrium.

6. **Income-expenditure model with special Keynesian assumptions.** In his *General Theory*, Keynes argued that a change in the price level would have little or no effect on real planned expenditure. Rework Exhibit 9.9 using these Keynesian assumptions. Your aggregate supply and demand diagram should resemble part (a) of Exhibit 8.5 (page 214).

7. **Effects of a decrease in autonomous expenditure with flexible prices.** Rework Exhibits 9.9 and 9.10 for a $250 billion decrease in real autonomous planned expenditure. Explain what happens at each step in the transition to a new short- and long-run equilibrium.

Case for Discussion
The Urge for New Equipment Will Keep Investment Growing

DECEMBER 1989—American businesses may well fixate too shortsightedly on the quarter in front of them, but you wouldn't guess that from their views about capital spending. Investment in plant and equipment will increase next year—modestly, to be sure, with most of the strength in equipment—despite a slower-growing economy and rotten 1989 profits. What's on the minds of those executives? Brighter prospects for the next year and, yes, the next decade. The possibilities for growth around the world in the long term look better now than they did even a few months ago.

In *Fortune's* recent survey of the business mood, executives said they are more confident about the economy and more aggressive in their spending plans than they have been in two years. That confidence surprised some analysts, partly because of the weakness in capacity use during the past few months. Putting that softness in historical context lessens the mystery. For business as a whole, utilization has barely inched down and is still near its high for the 1980s. Capital stock has been expanding better than 3 percent a year for most of this decade, but no excess capacity appears to be building up.

The real action in 1990 will be in computers. "Talk about capital spending and you are talking information processing," says Adrian Dillon, chief economist of Eaton Corp. Computers account for nearly half of equipment purchases, and after two volatile years, Dillon is expecting a substantial increase in spending.

Questions

1. How does an increase in capital spending by businesses affect the economy? Explain in terms of the circular flow model discussed in Chapter 5, the aggregate supply and demand model discussed in Chapters 7 and 8, and the income-expenditure model presented in this chapter. Compare and contrast the three approaches.

2. To what does *Fortune* attribute the strong prospects for business investment in 1990? Putting it in terms of the planned-investment schedule introduced in Chapter 8, would you characterize the developments discussed in this article as a shift in the schedule or a movement along it? Why?

3. At the end of the second quarter of 1989, total spending on producers' durable equipment in the U.S. economy was about $400 billion. Assuming that the planned-expenditure schedule has a slope of .75, by how much will the equilibrium level of nominal national income increase as a result of a 5 percent increase in capital spending, assuming a constant price level? How will the effects differ if a flexible price level is assumed?

**Before reading this chapter,
make sure you know the meaning of:**

Indexation (Chapter 4)

Real and nominal interest rates (Chapter 4)

Transfer payments (Chapter 4)

Government purchases (Chapter 5)

Net taxes (Chapter 5)

Expenditure multiplier (Chapter 8)

After reading this chapter, you will understand:

How fiscal policy—that is, changes in government purchases and net taxes—can be used to fight recession and inflation.

How government receipts and expenditures are affected by changing economic conditions.

How the federal budgetary system works and the limitations of that system.

The priorities that guided federal tax and spending decisions in the 1980s.

How the federal budget deficit is measured and why it has grown.

Whether large federal deficits are a threat to economic stability.

Fighting Breaks Out Over "Peace Dividend"

WASHINGTON—With the unveiling of the Bush administration's proposed 1991 budget, the "peace dividend" seems like it should be close at hand. The peace dividend consists of the anticipated multibillion-dollar cuts in the nation's defense budget that some expect the end of the cold war to make possible.

The National Urban League sees the peace dividend as a $50 billion panacea for poverty. Physicists dream of a voyage to Mars, physicians of a cure for AIDS. "If they can tear down the iron curtain," says Marian Wright Edelman of the Children's Defense Fund, "we ought to be able to have a revolution at home about helping our needy."

Or perhaps the money should be spent instead to unburden the taxpayer. Democratic Senator Daniel Moynihan of New York has proposed a huge $55 billion cut in the social security payroll tax. Republican Senator Phil Gramm of Texas fancies deep, 1981-style income tax cuts.

There's just one hitch: There isn't any peace dividend to speak of—not yet, at least.

That has become more starkly apparent than ever with the Bush administration's proposed total 1991 outlays of $1.23 trillion. As for the peace dividend, the administration is actually calling for a 1.9 percent *increase* in Defense Department outlays from 1990, according to budget documents, although that's less than needed to make up for inflation.

Moreover, to reach the requirements of the Gramm-Rudman deficit reduction law, Congress has had to reduce the federal deficit by $35 billion. Congress will undoubtedly opt to cut Pentagon spending, but most of the $35 billion in savings will still have to come out of new revenues and cuts in social spending programs.

Photo source: Reuters/Bettmann Newsphotos.

Source: Alan Murray, "Post-Cold War Budget Is Here, so Where Is the Peace Dividend?" *The Wall Street Journal*, January 29, 1990, 1.

In the meantime, the peace dividend debate may worsen the nation's fiscal problems. While struggling over a pot of money that doesn't exist, people here are already displaying much less willingness to make the compromises necessary to restore the nation's fiscal balance. Who wants to cut Medicare or raise taxes when a windfall may be at hand?

Seldom have expectations here been raised so high with so little likelihood of being fulfilled. "People who are thinking that the peace dividend from reductions in defense spending will free up a cornucopia of new resources for the many investments we hope to be making are going to be sorely disappointed," says Stuart Eizenstat, a lobbyist who served as President Carter's domestic policy adviser. "The vast majority of that money will go for deficit reduction, and that which doesn't will have been grabbed so many times that there will be crumbs left."

Fiscal policy
Policy that is concerned with government purchases, taxes, and transfer payments.

Welcome to the world of **fiscal policy**—the area of economic policy that is concerned with government purchases, taxes, and transfer payments. In this chapter, we use the models developed earlier to explore the economics of fiscal policy, including such topics as the peace dividend, the federal budget deficit, and the Gramm-Rudman-Hollings deficit reduction law. We will discuss both the short-run effects on prices and real output of changes in government purchases and net taxes and the long-run implications of fiscal policy for the way we use the $5 trillion of gross national product produced annually by the U.S. economy.

10.1 The Theory of Fiscal Policy

Economists of all schools agree that fiscal policy has important effects on the economy. In the policy debates of the past half-century, however, the view of fiscal policy as a constructive tool for furthering the goals of full employment, price stability, and growth has been most closely associated with Keynes and his followers. It is fitting, then, to begin our discussion of fiscal policy where Chapter 8 left off—with the use of fiscal policy as a tool for combating economic contractions.

Using Government Purchases to Combat a Contraction

Exhibit 10.1 begins from a situation described in Chapter 8. The economy has fallen into recession at point E_1, where the aggregate supply curve, AS_1, meets aggregate demand curve AD_1. There real national product is $500 billion below its natural level of $2,000 billion, and unemployment is above its natural rate. According to the classical economic theory, the expected and actual levels of input prices would gradually adjust to this level of demand in the long run. Real output would eventually return to its natural level as the aggregate supply curve shifted downward and the economy slid down and to the right along AD_1. But as Keynes once said, "in the long run, we are all dead."

The president and Congress do not want to wait for the long run. They want to do something about the recession now, before the next election. The problem is insufficient aggregate demand. Given the position of the aggregate supply curve, the aggregate demand curve needs to be shifted from AD_1 to AD_2 in order to bring real output back to its natural level at E_2. How can this be done?

Exhibit 10.1   Using Fiscal Policy to
Combat an Economic Contraction

In this figure, the economy has fallen into recession at
E_1. To reach the natural level of real output at E_2
without waiting for a downward shift of the aggregate
supply curve, the aggregate demand curve must be
shifted to the right by $1,000 billion, from AD_1 to AD_2.
This can be done by increasing real government
purchases and taking advantage of the multiplier
effect. Given an expenditure multiplier of 4, a $250
billion increase in government purchases will bring
about the required $1,000 billion shift in the aggregate
demand curve. However, because the price level
rises, equilibrium real national product does not
increase by the full $1,000 billion by which the
aggregate demand curve shifts. The same shift can
be accomplished with a cut in net taxes, but the
multiplier effect of a tax cut will be smaller than that
of an increase in government purchases.

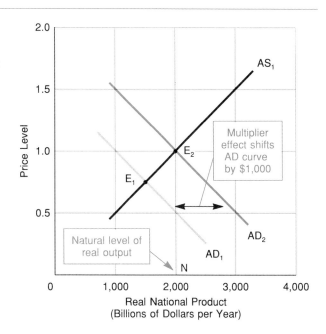

Identifying the spending gap.   Although real national product is only $500
billion below its natural level, the horizontal gap between AD_1 and AD_2 is
$1,000 billion, as shown by the arrow in Exhibit 10.1. This means that the
equilibrium level of real planned expenditure at any given price level falls short
of what is needed by $1,000 billion. If policymakers can find a way to fill that
gap, they can shift the aggregate demand curve to the position AD_2 and bring
national product to its natural level.

In principle, any increase in expenditure can serve this purpose. Exports
might pick up; business managers might become more optimistic and increase
planned investment; a rise in consumer confidence might spur consumption.
But these things are not certain to happen. Instead of waiting and hoping, therefore, policymakers turn to the element of planned expenditure that is most directly under their control: government purchases. There is always a backlog of
projects that members of Congress would gladly see undertaken using federal
resources. A new postal sorting station here, a stretch of interstate highway
there, new vehicles for park rangers somewhere else — it is easy to list the things
that the government might buy. But just how much spending for new government purchases is needed?

Using the multiplier effect.   To move the aggregate demand curve to the right
by $1,000 billion, it is not necessary to increase government purchases by that
amount. The reason, as explained in Chapter 8, is that each dollar of new government purchases is amplified by the multiplier effect. Spending $1 on a federal
highway project boosts the income of construction workers, who then spend
more on, say, groceries, clothing, and cars. Their spending raises the incomes of
grocers, textile workers, and autoworkers, who in turn consume more. As the
multiplier effect cascades through the economy, each $1 of new government
purchases stimulates more than $1 of total planned expenditure.

Let us assume, as we did in Chapter 8, that the marginal propensity to consume is .75. Using the formula for the expenditure multiplier, $1/(1 - \text{mpc})$, we find that the value of the expenditure is 4. This means that \$1 of government purchases will raise the equilibrium level of planned expenditure at a given price level by \$4. (This calculation takes into account both the initial increase in government purchases and the induced increases in consumption expenditure.) Given an expenditure multiplier of 4, then, it will take \$250 billion of additional government purchases to shift the aggregate demand curve to the right by \$1,000 billion.[1]

Changing prices and aggregate demand.   As the aggregate demand curve shifts from AD_1 to AD_2, the economy moves up and to the right along the aggregate supply curve. As it does so, the increase in prices affects real planned expenditure in ways that partially offset the multiplier effect of the original increase in government purchases. Chapter 7 presented four reasons why a change in the price level will affect real planned expenditure, all of which are at work in the present situation:

1. Real consumption is restrained by the fact that the real value of nominal money balances falls as the price level rises.

2. Real planned investment is moderated by the higher interest rates associated with a higher price level.

3. The parts of government budgets that are set in nominal terms will command fewer real goods and services as the price level rises.

4. Real net exports will fall because domestic prices will rise relative to prices abroad.

These effects of a change in the price level on aggregate demand are built into the slope of the aggregate demand curve. They do not cause the aggregate demand curve to shift away from its new position at AD_2. Instead, they cause the economy to end up at a point on AD_2 at which the equilibrium level of real planned expenditure increases by less than the full \$1,000 billion horizontal shift in the aggregate demand curve. In Exhibit 10.1 the new equilibrium is at point E_2. There equilibrium planned expenditure is \$2,000 billion, which is only \$500 billion greater than at E_1, despite the fact that the aggregate demand curve has shifted to the right by \$1,000 billion.

In short, because a rise in the price level tends to lower every type of planned expenditure, the equilibrium level of real national product rises by less than the expenditure multiplier times the initial change in real government purchases.

Using a Change in Taxes or Transfer Payments to Combat a Contraction

Government purchases are only one side of the fiscal policy equation. The other side consists of net taxes. As explained in Chapter 5, the term *net taxes* means tax

---

[1]This is an approximation. It assumes both that there are no income taxes and that net exports and net investment are unaffected by a change in real national product at a given price level. In a more elaborate model that allowed for these factors, the general principles discussed in this section would still hold. However, in that model, each \$1 in additional government purchases would shift the aggregate demand curve to the right by more than \$1 but less than the \$4 predicted by the simple expenditure multiplier calculated using a marginal propensity to consume of .75.

revenues collected by government minus transfer payments made by government to individuals. A tax cut or an increase in transfer payments operates on the economy via its effect on consumption.

Let us return to point E₁ in Exhibit 10.1 and see how a change in net taxes can be used to combat the contraction. As before, the problem is to shift the aggregate demand curve to the right by $1,000 billion. Suppose that to stimulate the economy Congress votes a $100 billion increase in real social security benefits while leaving taxes unchanged. This is a $100 billion cut in real net taxes. How does it affect aggregate demand?

To begin with, the action raises the real disposable incomes of social security recipients by $100 billion. In response—once again assuming a marginal propensity to consume of .75—they raise their real consumption by $75 billion. As in the earlier case, the increase in consumer spending for groceries, cars, and the like boosts the incomes of grocers, autoworkers, and others by $75 billion; they, in turn, increase their consumption expenditures by $56,250,000,000; and so on.

In short, a cut in net taxes touches off a multiplier process similar to that resulting from an increase in government purchases. This is true whether the reduction in net taxes takes the form of a cut in taxes paid to government or an increase in transfer payments made by government.

Multiplier effects of a change in net taxes. The multiplier effects of a change in net taxes are shown in Exhibit 10.2, which compares the effects of the $100 billion net tax cut to those of a $100 billion increase in government purchases.

Exhibit 10.2   The Net Tax Multiplier

This exhibit compares the multiplier effects of a $100 billion cut in real net taxes with those of an equal increase in real government purchases. Both result in $300 billion of induced real consumption expenditure over an infinite number of rounds. However, the increase in government purchases itself adds $100 billion to aggregate demand; thus, the total effect, combining direct and induced planned expenditure, is greater for the increase in government purchases. In general, the net tax multiplier equals the expenditure multiplier minus 1.

		Increase in Real Expenditure for a $100 Billion:		
Round	Increase in Real Income	Increase in Government Purchases	Cut in Net Taxes	
1		$100,000,000		(Direct)
2	$100,000,000	75,000,000	$ 75,000,000	(Induced)
3	75,000,000	56,250,000	56,250,000	(Induced)
4	56,250,000	42,187,500	42,187,500	(Induced)
5	42,187,500	31,640,625	31,640,625	(Induced)
.				
.				
.				
All rounds		$400,000,000	$300,000,000	(Total)

Net tax multiplier
The ratio of an induced
change in real aggregate
demand to a given change in
real net taxes.

The difference between the two lies in the first round of the process. A $100 billion increase in government purchases is itself a $100 billion *direct* addition to aggregate demand. The multiplier chain goes on from there with additional *induced* increases in consumption expenditures totaling $300 billion. Thus, the total change in planned expenditure is $400 billion. However, a $100 billion tax cut or increase in transfer payments is not in itself a direct addition to aggregate demand, because it does not represent a decision by government to buy any newly produced goods and services. Therefore, the only effect of the cut in net taxes is the induced increases in consumption expenditures. These total just $300 billion.

Generalizing from this example, we see that a cut in net taxes has a multiplier effect that is smaller than that of an equal increase in planned expenditure. The ratio of an induced shift in aggregate demand to a given change in real net taxes is known as the **net tax multiplier.** Mathematically, the absolute value of the net tax multiplier is given by the formula

$$\text{Net tax multiplier} = \text{Expenditure multiplier} - 1.$$

Substituting $1/(1 - mpc)$ for the expenditure multiplier and simplifying, we can also write this as follows:

$$\text{Net tax multiplier} = mpc/(1 - mpc).$$

Applying the net tax multiplier. We can now return to Exhibit 10.1 and see how much of a cut in real net taxes is needed to bring the economy out of its recession. The required shift in the aggregate demand curve is $1,000 billion. Using the formula just given, a marginal propensity to consume of .75 yields a net tax multiplier of 3. Thus, $333 billion in tax cuts or transfer payment increases are needed to shift the aggregate demand curve to the right by $1,000 billion. In response to this shift, real output rises by $500 billion, taking into account the effects of a rising price level on the various components of real planned expenditure.

Qualifications. This analysis suggests that, on a dollar-for-dollar basis, changes in net taxes are only slightly less effective than changes in government purchases in influencing the level of aggregate demand. However, we have made a number of simplifying assumptions. The most important of these is the idea that households will spend the same fraction of an additional dollar received through tax cuts as they will of an additional dollar in earned income. As **Applying Economic Ideas 10.1** indicates, some economists think that this may not be the case. If they are correct, tax changes would be a much less effective fiscal policy tool than our simple model suggests.

Fiscal Policy and Inflation

In previous sections we have seen how fiscal policy can be used to speed up recovery from a contraction caused by, say, a drop in planned investment. Keynesian economics, born of the Great Depression, emphasizes this role of fiscal policy. However, fiscal policy can also play a part in fighting inflation or, for that matter, causing inflation if used irresponsibly.

Applying Economic Ideas 10.1
Do Tax Changes Really Affect Aggregate Demand?

The net tax multiplier correctly predicts the effect of tax changes on equilibrium aggregate demand only if people treat a dollar of added disposable income received through a tax cut the same way they treat a dollar received from any other source: dividing it between saving and consumption according to the marginal propensity to consume. However, recent U.S. experience suggests that in practice saving is more strongly and consumption less strongly affected by tax changes than by other changes in disposable income.

The accompanying chart shows personal saving and total personal tax payments at all levels of government as a percentage of personal income since 1960. Tax cuts, such as the tax rebate of 1975, appear to produce an offsetting jump in saving; as a result, they add little to consumption. Likewise, tax increases, such as the tax surcharge of 1968 and the one-time increase in tax payments in April 1987, produce a jump in tax payments but an offsetting drop in

saving. This implies a smaller net tax multiplier than that given by the usual formula. If a tax change were fully offset by a change in saving, it would have no multiplier effect at all. In practice, econometric studies indicate that tax changes are partly but not wholly offset by changes in saving.

Economists differ in the reasons they give for the relatively small impact of tax cuts on consumption. One far-reaching hypothesis has been put forth by Robert J. Barro of Harvard University. Barro points out that today's tax cut has implications for tomorrow's fiscal policy. If the government cuts taxes today and does not cut spending, it will have to increase its borrowing in order to cover the resulting deficit. In the future, then, taxes will have to be raised to repay this borrowing, or at least to pay interest on it. If households think ahead, Barro says, they will react to a tax cut today by increasing their saving. Income from assets that they buy with the added savings will allow them to afford the higher future taxes needed to cover today's government borrowing. To protect themselves fully against the higher future taxes, they must save 100 percent of today's tax cut. Attributing the idea to the nineteenth-

(continued)

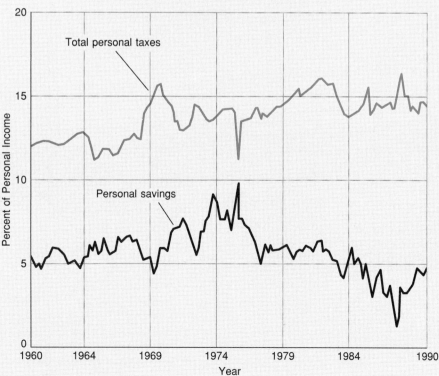

Total Personal Taxes and Personal Savings
(Percent of Personal Income)

century British economist David Ricardo, Barrow refers to it as the "Ricardian" view of taxation.

Other economists are skeptical of the Ricardian view. They doubt that consumers are so farsighted as to adjust their saving to offset the future effects of today's tax cuts in full. They see a simpler explanation for the tendency of tax changes to be offset by changes in saving: the fact that consumers tend to save a higher percentage of temporary changes in income than of permanent changes. Some tax changes have been explicitly labeled as temporary, such as the income tax surcharge of 1968 and the tax rebate of

1975. There was also a temporary bulge in tax revenues in the second quarter of 1987. This reflected heavy realization of capital gains in late 1986 in anticipation of higher capital gains tax rates, which were scheduled to go into effect in 1987. As the chart shows, these tax changes were almost fully offset by changes in saving, at least in the short run. Even tax changes that are said to be permanent may at first be treated as if they were temporary. Only after enough time has passed for consumers to adjust to the tax changes will these changes affect consumption in proportion to the full long-run marginal propensity to consume.

Counteracting projected inflation. Consider the situation shown in Exhibit 10.3. The economy has been in equilibrium for some time at E_1, where real output is at its natural level. As the federal budget for the coming year is being prepared, forecasters warn of the possibility of inflation. The threat stems from a projected growth in the private components of aggregate demand—a surge in export demand, a boom in consumer spending, or an increase in planned investment. If something is not done, the forecasters say, the aggregate demand curve for the coming year will shift rightward to AD_2. That will drive the economy up and to the right along aggregate supply curve AS_1, to E_2.

The result will be an increase in the price level from P_1 to P_2. But inflation will not stop there. The rise in the prices of final goods will, in time, cause firms to raise their expectations regarding wages and other input prices. As a result, the short-run aggregate supply curve will shift upward to AS_2. As real output

Exhibit 10.3   Fiscal Policy and Inflation

Initially the economy is at E_1. Forecasts show that if no policy changes are made, increases in real private planned expenditure will shift the aggregate demand curve from AD_1 to AD_2, causing the price level to rise as the economy moves to a short-run equilibrium at E_2. In the long run, assuming nothing is done about aggregate demand, the price level would rise still more as the aggregate supply curve shifted upward and the economy moved toward a new long-run equilibrium at E_3. To prevent an increase in the price level, government purchases can be cut or net taxes increased to offset the projected change in private planned expenditure, thus restoring the aggregate demand curve to position AD_1.

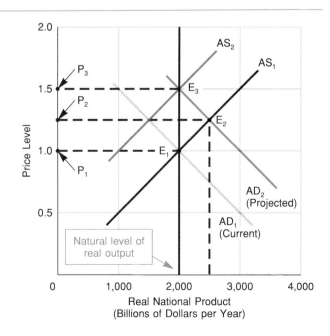

falls back to its natural level, the price level will continue to rise until it reaches a new long-run equilibrium at P_3.

Restrictive fiscal policy is one way of warding off the inflation threat. The federal budget for the coming year can be written in such a way as to combine cuts in government purchases and increases in net taxes that will offset the projected increases in private aggregate demand. Suppose that the marginal propensity to consume is .75, as in our earlier examples. For each $100 by which aggregate demand is projected to shift beyond the level needed to reach the natural level of real output, government purchases can be cut by $25 or net taxes increased by $33. The right combination of cuts in government purchases, cuts in transfer payments, and increases in taxes will hold the aggregate demand curve in the desired position at AD_1.

Expansionary fiscal policy as a source of inflation.   In the preceding example, federal policymakers are the "good guys," crafting a sensible budget designed to restrain inflation. That is the role we would hope for them to play. However, the same diagram could be used to tell a different story.

In this scenario the economy is in equilibrium at E_1 and forecasters expect it to stay there. However, there is an election coming up. Members of Congress would like to please the voters by boosting federal benefits, cutting taxes, and initiating public works projects. The president, who is also up for reelection, would like to conduct the coming campaign in an atmosphere of rising real output and falling unemployment. Seeing their common interests, Congress and the president craft a strongly expansionary budget for the upcoming election year. As the expansionary budget first goes into effect, the economy moves from E_1 to E_2 in Exhibit 10.3. As hoped, real output expands and unemployment falls, with only a moderate increase in the price level. Voters are pleased, and everyone is reelected.

The next year, however, wages and other input prices begin to rise. As firms adjust their expectations to the new circumstances, not only does inflation of final goods prices continue but real output falls and the unemployment rate rises. The hangover from the election party sets in. This contrast between the relatively benign initial effects of expansionary policy and its less desirable long-run effects is a theme to which we will return several times in later chapters.

Automatic Fiscal Policy

The type of fiscal policy discussed so far—changes in the laws regarding government purchases, taxes, and transfer payments designed to increase or decrease aggregate demand—is known as **discretionary fiscal policy.** In practice, however, the levels of government purchases and net taxes can change even if no discretionary changes are made in the laws governing them. The reason is that many tax and spending laws are written in such a way that the levels of fiscal policy variables change automatically as economic conditions vary. Such changes in government purchases or net taxes, which are known as **automatic fiscal policy,** are most closely associated with changes in real output, the price level, and interest rates.

Changes in real output.   The level of real output is important because it affects both tax revenues and outlays. An increase in real output increases real revenues from all major tax sources, including income taxes, social security payroll taxes, taxes on corporate profits, and sales taxes. At the same time, an increase in real output cuts real government outlays for transfer payments. This occurs largely

Discretionary fiscal policy
Changes in the laws regarding government purchases and net taxes.

Automatic fiscal policy
Changes in government purchases or net taxes that are caused by changes in economic conditions given unchanged tax and spending laws.

because increases in real output are associated with decreases in the unemployment rate. Taking both effects together, an increase in real national product tends to reduce the federal budget deficit in both real and nominal terms.

Changes in the price level.   An increase in the price level affects both sides of the federal budget. With real output held constant, an increase in the price level tends to increase federal tax receipts in nominal terms. Where tax rates are not indexed—that is, not adjusted automatically to reflect inflation—inflation can also cause real tax receipts to rise. (This used to be the case with the federal income tax. However, income taxes are now indexed so that inflation does not push taxpayers into higher tax brackets.) At the same time, an increase in the price level tends to increase nominal expenditures. This is partly because most major transfer programs are now indexed so that they can be adjusted for changes in the cost of living and partly because inflation raises the prices of the goods and services that government buys. However, as pointed out before, some elements of government expenditures are fixed in nominal terms. This means that the increase in nominal expenditures will tend to be less than proportional to the increase in the price level, so that real expenditures will fall.

If all elements of the budget were indexed, an increase in the price level would have no effect on the real deficit. In practice, the budget is not perfectly indexed, so that nominal taxes rise more both absolutely and in percentage terms than nominal expenditures. Thus, an increase in the price level, other things being equal, reduces the deficit in nominal terms and causes a proportionately greater reduction in the real deficit.

Changes in interest rates.   An increase in nominal interest rates raises the nominal cost of financing the national debt. This is only slightly offset by increases in nominal government interest income. Therefore, on balance, an increase in nominal interest rates shifts the budget toward deficit in both nominal and real terms.

Automatic stabilization.   We have seen that when the economy expands real output rises, the price level rises, and unemployment falls. Each of these effects tends to move the government budget toward surplus in real terms, that is, to increase receipts, depress outlays, or both. Whichever side of the budget we look at, then, automatic fiscal policy operates so as to restrain aggregate demand during an expansion. By the same token, when the economy slows down, the growth rate of real output drops and unemployment rises. The inflation rate slows even if the contraction is not severe enough to cause the price level actually to fall. Thus, during a contraction the real budget swings toward deficit.

Automatic stabilizers
Those elements of automatic fiscal policy that move the federal budget toward deficit during an economic contraction and toward surplus during an expansion.

Because automatic fiscal policy operates to offset changes in other elements of planned expenditure, budget components such as income taxes and unemployment benefits are known as **automatic stabilizers.** These mechanisms serve to moderate the economy's response to changes in consumption, private planned investment, and net exports.

10.2   Fiscal Policy in the Income-Expenditure Model[2]

The income-expenditure model developed in Chapter 9 provides an alternate way of looking at the effects of fiscal policy. This model has the advantage of focusing more directly on the multiplier effect. However, it can be misleading if

[2]If Chapter 9 was omitted, omit this section also and turn to page 263.

it is not used cautiously, because it tends to lose sight of the effects of changes in the price level.

Fiscal Stimulus

Part (a) of Exhibit 10.4 uses the fixed-price version of the income-expenditure model to show how fiscal policy can be used to avoid a recession. The figure is drawn assuming no income or payroll taxes, no net exports, and a marginal propensity to consume of .75. In this case we suppose that policymakers wish to keep the economy at its natural level of real output of $2,000 billion. However, as they prepare a budget for the coming year, their forecasters say that, given current tax and spending laws, planned expenditure will be insufficient and the planned-expenditure schedule will slip to PE_1, putting equilibrium national income at only $1,000 billion.

To keep income at the natural level, the planned-expenditure schedule must be at PE_2 rather than PE_1. If nothing is done, the shortfall of autonomous

---

Exhibit 10.4 Fiscal Policy in the Income-Expenditure Model

This exhibit illustrates fiscal policy in terms of the fixed-price income-expenditure model introduced in Chapter 9. In part (a), forecasters project an equilibrium real national income for the coming year that is $1,000 billion below the natural level. The low equilibrium value for real national income is caused by a $250 billion shortfall of real autonomous planned expenditure. A $250 billion increase in government purchases or a $333 billion cut in autonomous net taxes will restore autonomous expenditures to the desired level, shifting the planned-expenditure curve from PE_1 to PE_2. In part (b), the situation is reversed. A projected excess of autonomous expenditure will put the planned-expenditure curve at PE_3 unless something is done. The prescription for this situation is a $250 billion cut in government purchases or a $333 billion increase in autonomous net taxes.

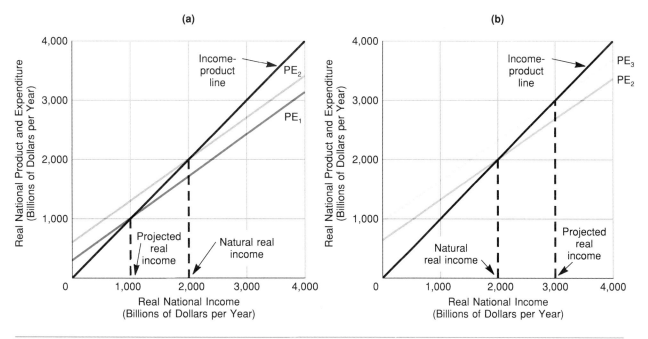

expenditure will cause a recession. The autonomous-expenditure shortfall is shown by the vertical gap between the two planned-expenditure curves. In our example the shortfall is $250 billion.

To avoid the recession, tax and spending laws must be changed so as to plug the gap. A $250 billion increase in government purchases would be one way to do this. Another would be to stimulate autonomous consumption by reducing autonomous net taxes. However, a $250 billion cut in autonomous net taxes will not be enough to fill the gap, because households will spend only $.75 of each $1 of added disposable income that the tax cut (or increase in transfers) provides. A $250 billion upward shift of the planned-expenditure curve thus will require a $333 billion cut in autonomous net taxes.

Note that the $1,000 billion gap between the projected level of national income and the natural level equals the expenditure multiplier of 4 times the shortfall of autonomous expenditure. It also equals the required cut in autonomous net taxes times the net tax multiplier of 3.

Fiscal Restraint

Part (b) of Exhibit 10.4 shows how fiscal restraint can be used to stem an excess of aggregate demand that would cause real output to rise above its natural level—an occurrence that would cause inflation in a world with flexible prices. In this case we suppose that forecasts for the coming year show that under current tax and spending laws the planned-expenditure curve will be at the position PE_3. This will cause equilibrium national income to rise to $3,000 billion, which is $1,000 billion above the natural level. Unless something is done, the economy will overheat.

The excess of real national income is produced by a projected excess of autonomous expenditure, which is represented by the vertical gap between PE_2 and PE_3 in part (b) of Exhibit 10.4. Fiscal policy can be used to close this gap, as in the case of recession, but the direction of the policy change must be reversed: government purchases must be cut by $250 billion or autonomous net taxes increased by $333 billion, or the two approaches must be combined in some way.

A Change in the Income Tax Rate

The preceding examples illustrate the effects of changes in government purchases and autonomous net taxes. The income-expenditure model can also be used to show the effects of a change in the marginal tax rate.

In Exhibit 10.5 the natural level of real income is again assumed to be $2,000 billion. Forecasts show that if no changes are made in tax or spending laws in the coming year, the planned-expenditure schedule will be at the position PE_1, which is based on a marginal propensity to consume of .75 and a 33 percent marginal tax rate. As we saw in Chapter 9, the slope of the planned-expenditure schedule under these conditions is mpc $(1 - t)$ or, in this case, .5; this means that the expenditure multiplier is 2. Total autonomous expenditure is $800 billion, as can be seen from the vertical intercept of the planned-expenditure schedule. The projected level of national income ($1,600 billion) equals total autonomous expenditure ($800 billion) times the expenditure multiplier (2).

Exhibit 10.5   Using a Change in the Marginal Tax Rate to Boost Planned Expenditure

This exhibit shows how a change in the marginal tax rate of an income or payroll tax can be used to boost planned expenditure. Initially forecasts show a projected equilibrium real national income of $1,600 billion, $400 billion short of the natural level. This projection assumes $800 billion in autonomous planned expenditures, a marginal propensity to consume of .75, and a marginal tax rate of .33; the slope of planned-expenditure schedule PE$_1$ is, consequently, .5. By cutting the marginal tax rate to .20 with no change in autonomous planned expenditure, the slope of the planned-expenditure schedule is increased to .6. This puts the planned-expenditure schedule at PE$_2$, which restores equilibrium real national income to its natural level.

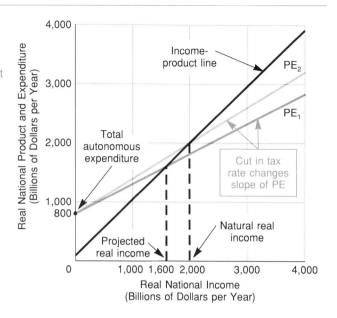

The equilibrium level of national income can be increased to $2,000 billion without changing the level of autonomous expenditure if the planned-expenditure schedule is shifted to PE$_2$. This can be done by cutting the marginal tax rate from .33 to .20. The slope of the planned-expenditure schedule will then increase from .5 to .6. The expenditure multiplier for the new schedule will be 2.5. Applying that multiplier to the same $800 billion of autonomous expenditure will yield the required $2,000 billion equilibrium level of national income.

A Word of Caution

Exhibits 10.4 and 10.5 are based on the fixed-price version of the income-expenditure model. Thus, they exaggerate the impact of a given change in government purchases, taxes, or transfer payments on the equilibrium level of real national income. In a world with flexible prices, as we saw in Chapter 9, price changes would cause additional shifts in the planned-expenditure schedule that would partially offset the impact of the fiscal policies considered here even in the short run and would fully offset them in the long run. Hence, when the price level is subject to change—as it is in the real world—the aggregate supply and demand model gives a better picture of the effects of fiscal policy than the fixed-price version of the income-expenditure model.

10.3   Problems of Fiscal Policy for the 1990s

The discussion of fiscal policy in the preceding section is couched in terms of what ought to be done to stabilize the economy at its natural level of real output. Our discussion would be incomplete, however, without at least a brief look at the important question of how federal officials actually go about making tax and spending decisions and the relationship of those decisions to the theoretical model of discretionary fiscal policy.

In practice, the actual decision-making process for fiscal policy often has little or nothing to do with the theory of discretionary policy that we have just discussed. The large federal budget deficits that have made headlines since the mid-1980s have not resulted from systematic decisions to stimulate the economy through fiscal policy. They are better understood as the residual outcome of a certain set of spending decisions and another set of tax decisions, neither of which have focused consistently on macroeconomic goals.

We will begin our discussion of problems facing U.S. fiscal policy with a discussion of the budget-making process and its limitations. We will then turn to budget priorities. Finally, we will examine the federal deficit and the national debt that have resulted from past tax and spending decisions.

The Federal Budgetary System

Economists view fiscal policy as the management of aggregate demand through manipulation of taxes, transfers, and government purchases. However, the federal budgetary process is more complex than this definition suggests. For one thing, no single agency is responsible for fiscal policy; budgetary authority is divided between the president and Congress. Also, budgetary policy must serve many goals, ranging from national security and social equity to simple political ambition, as well as price stability, full employment, and economic growth.

Outline of the budgetary system. A brief look at the federal budgetary process will indicate where the formal authority for fiscal policy lies. The U.S. government operates on a **fiscal year** that runs from October through September; for example, fiscal 1992 runs from October 1, 1991, through September 30, 1992. About 18 months before the beginning of a fiscal year, the executive branch begins preparing the budget. The Office of Management and Budget (OMB) takes the lead in this process. It receives advice from the Council of Economic Advisers (CEA) and the Department of the Treasury. After an outline of the budget has been drawn up, it is sent to the various departments and agencies. Within the executive branch, a period of bargaining ensues in which the Pentagon argues for more defense spending, the Department of Transportation for more highway funds, and so on. During this process the OMB is supposed to act as a restraining force, keeping macroeconomic goals in mind.

By January—nine months before the fiscal year starts—the president must submit the budget to Congress; the news item at the beginning of the chapter refers to President Bush's budget for fiscal year 1991, which was submitted in January 1990. After the budget has been submitted, Congress assumes the lead in the budgetary process. Its committees and subcommittees look at the president's proposals for the programs and agencies under their jurisdiction. The Congressional Budget Office (CBO) employs a staff of professionals who advise the committees on economic matters, in somewhat the same way that the OMB and CEA advise the president. In May the House and Senate are expected to pass a first budget resolution that sets forth overall spending targets and revenue goals.

Bargaining among committees, between the House and the Senate, and between Congress and the executive branch continues throughout the summer. During this period committees prepare specific spending and tax laws; these are supposed to be guided by the May resolution. Finally, in September, Congress is supposed to pass a second budget resolution that sets binding limits on spend-

Fiscal year
The federal government's budgetary year, which starts on October 1 of the preceding calendar year.

ing and taxes for the fiscal year beginning October 1. Any bills passed earlier that do not fit within these guidelines are expected to be changed accordingly.

Limitations of the budgetary process.   In practice, many things can—and do—go wrong with this process.

The first and most basic problem is that macroeconomic goals—full employment, price stability, and economic growth—carry little weight in the actual budgetary process. Tax and spending decisions are made in dozens of subcommittees, where they are dominated by interest group pressures, vote trading, and the desire of each member of Congress to help the folks at home.

A second problem is that Congress has proved unwilling to follow its own rules. The required budget resolutions often are not passed on time; if they are passed, they are not treated as binding. Often the fiscal year starts without a budget. Then agencies must operate on the basis of "continuing resolutions," meaning that they can go on doing whatever they were doing the year before. In 1986, in one of its worst performances, Congress failed to pass a single one of the appropriations bills that were supposed to set spending for various government areas for the fiscal 1987 budget. That year, in a last-minute rush, Congress had to pass a massive continuing resolution that rolled all government spending decisions for the entire year into a single vote. In some years even the continuing resolutions for some agencies have not been passed on time, and federal government employees have been sent home until there were funds to pay them.

Finally, there is the problem of so-called uncontrollable costs. These include **entitlements,** which are transfer programs governed by long-term laws that are not subject to annual budget review. Examples include social security, military retirement pay, and Medicare. Another major expense that is uncontrollable—for a different reason—is interest on the national debt. Given the debt's size, its interest costs are determined by market interest rates, which, in turn, are influenced by many factors that are beyond the control of fiscal policy. Today well over half of the federal budget is in the "uncontrollable" category. Congress could control most of these costs by passing new laws to replace the current ones, but doing so is not part of the normal budgetary process.

Entitlements
Transfer payments governed by long-term laws that are not subject to annual budget review.

The Gramm-Rudman-Hollings Experiment

By the mid-1980s the budgetary process had fallen into such disarray that Herbert Stein, a former chairman of the Council of Economic Advisers, wrote, "We have no long-run budget policy—no policy for the size of deficits and for the rate of growth of the public debt over a period of years." Each year, Stein said, the president and Congress make short-term budgetary decisions that are wholly inconsistent with their declared long-run goals, hoping "that something will happen or be done before the long-run arises, but not yet."[3]

In 1985, responding to this and similar criticisms, Congress made a heroic attempt to reform the budgetary system. The focus of its effort was on reducing the federal deficit as a symbol of concern for the macroeconomic impact of the federal budget. The result was the Gramm-Rudman-Hollings law, which was passed in December 1985. In that year (that is, fiscal year 1986), the federal budget deficit was a record $221 billion. The law established a declining set of deficit targets, beginning with $144 billion for fiscal 1987, $108 billion for fiscal

---

[3]Herbert Stein, "After the Ball," *AEI Economist* (December 1984): 2.

1988, and so on until the deficit would be eliminated in 1991. An exception was written into the law allowing the deficit ceiling to be waived in the event of a projected recession, or in the event of two consecutive quarters in which real GNP grows at an annual rate of 1 percent or less.

The feature that was supposed to give Gramm-Rudman-Hollings some real teeth was a provision for making mandatory spending cuts if Congress and the administration failed to come up with a budget that would come within $10 billion of the law's targets. Suppose, for example, that Congress passed (and the president signed) laws that would result in a $158 billion deficit for fiscal 1988 despite a set deficit limit of $108 billion. In that case spending would automatically have to be cut by $50 billion. However, programs comprising over half the budget were shielded from the Gramm-Rudman-Hollings ax. The protected programs included social security, Medicare, the major antipoverty programs, and interest on the national debt. Each of the remaining budget areas—national defense and unprotected domestic programs—was to bear about half of any automatic reductions. The bill's sponsors hoped that the mandatory cuts would not be necessary and that instead the threat of such cuts would force Congress to make rational decisions on budget priorities.

The Gramm-Rudman-Hollings experiment has been at best a mixed success, as is shown by Exhibit 10.6. With some modifications, the law survived a Supreme Court challenge to the constitutionality of its key provision, the mandatory budget cuts. The 1987 budget was projected to meet the $144 billion target

Exhibit 10.6   Federal Deficits and Targets
under the Gramm-Rudman-Hollings Act

The Gramm-Rudman-Hollings Act was passed in late 1985 in an attempt to curb the growth of the federal deficit. The act originally specified a set of declining budget targets that would have led to balance in 1991. These targets were modified in 1987, delaying the balanced budget date to 1993. The original and revised targets are shown in the first two columns of this table. The third column shows the actual deficit for each year, which in every year was higher than the target. Nevertheless, despite the missed targets, some observers consider the act at least a partial success, inasmuch as deficits did decline as a percentage of GNP in each year after 1986.

	[Billions of dollars]			
Fiscal Year	**1985 Target**	**1987 Target**	**Actual Deficit**	**Actual as Percent of GNP**
1986 · · · · · · · · · ·	171.9	171.9	221.2	5.3
1987 · · · · · · · · · ·	144.0	144.0	149.7	3.4
1988 · · · · · · · · · ·	108.0	144.0	155.1	3.2
1989 · · · · · · · · · ·	72.0	136.0	152.0	2.9
1990 · · · · · · · · · ·	36.0	100.0	NA	NA
1991 · · · · · · · · · ·	.0	64.0	NA	NA
1992 · · · · · · · · · ·	.0	28.0	NA	NA
1993 · · · · · · · · · ·	.0	.0	NA	NA

Source: President's Council of Economic Advisers, *Economic Report of the President*, (Washington, D.C.: Government Printing Office, 1990), Table 3–1.

for that year, and in fact it came close, missing by less than $6 billion. That year's deficit was reduced by $71 billion from the fiscal 1986 deficit. The 1988 deficit target proved harder to meet, however. Failing to come up with a plan that could meet the original target of $108 for that year, Congress raised the target to $144 billion and postponed the date for a balanced budget to 1993. The actual fiscal 1988 deficit came in at $155 billion, higher than the 1987 figure. In 1989, the deficit started edging downward again, but again it missed its target. At the time of writing, preliminary data indicate that there will be another huge miss in fiscal 1990. Anyone taking bets on the matter would have had to be skeptical that President Bush's fiscal 1991 budget proposal, which dutifully promised to meet the $64 billion deficit target for that year, would actually do so.

The Gramm-Rudman-Hollings Act has many detractors. Some point to its focus on budget projections rather than on results. The mandatory cuts go into effect only if Congress fails to come up with a budget by October 15 that is projected to meet that year's deficit target. Once October 15 has passed, there is no penalty if the actual deficit fails to match the projection.

Others object that the law has encouraged Congress to meet the target with accounting tricks rather than with actual spending cuts and revenue increases. For example, in 1989 Congress moved a Pentagon payday from October 1, the first day of fiscal 1990, to September 29, which was still in fiscal 1989. This made it possible to lower the 1990 deficit projection by $4 billion, although it caused the 1989 deficit to rise further above its projected level by exactly the same amount. Another trick has been "off budget" treatment for the Post Office operating deficit.

Alice Rivlin, a former director of the Congressional Budget Office, characterizes Gramm-Rudman-Hollings as a "well-intentioned experiment that failed."[4] But others still give it at least faint praise. "As near as I can see, it is the only element of discipline left in the system," says Minnesota Representative Bill Frenzel, the senior Republican member of the House Budget Committee. "It may not be a very good one, but I certainly would be reluctant to make changes in it."[5]

Setting Budget Priorities

Many people both inside and outside government castigate Congress and the White House for inability to set priorities. In one sense the failure to adhere to an orderly budgetary process and the tendency to lump everything into "continuing resolutions" bear this out. But in another sense, it can be said that priorities have been set—that is, the priorities that are implicit in the decisions that have actually been made. Let's see what those priorities have been over the past two decades.

Taxes, spending, and the deficit.   Exhibit 10.7 presents data on federal tax revenues and total federal outlays (government purchases of goods and services plus transfer payments) for the 1970s and 1980s. Column 1 shows that despite a decade of rhetoric to the contrary under Presidents Reagan and Bush, cutting the overall tax burden was not given high priority. True, the 1980s saw a major

[4]Quoted in John E. Yang, "Ever-Growing Deficits Establish the Failure of Gramm-Rudman," *The Wall Street Journal*, October 3, 1989, A1.
[5]Ibid., A14.

Exhibit 10.7 Federal Revenues, Outlays, and Deficit as a Percentage of GNP

This exhibit shows trends in federal revenues, outlays, and deficits as a percentage of GNP during the 1970s and 1980s. Column 1 shows that despite the cuts in personal income tax rates that resulted from the 1981 tax law, federal revenues rose as a share of GNP in the 1980s. Federal outlays, on the other hand, grew to record levels in the early 1980s and decreased only slightly in the later 1980s, as shown in column 2. The conclusion is that the increase in the federal deficit, shown in column 7, stems from spending increases rather than tax cuts. Within specific categories of expenditures, defense, transfer payments, and interest increased as a share of GNP during the 1980s. The big losers in the federal budget were nondefense purchases of goods and services and grants-in-aid to state and local governments. These and some smaller categories are included in column 6.

Calendar Years	(1)	(2)	(3)	(4)	(5)	(6)	(7)
	Receipts	Expenditures					Deficit
		Total	Defense	Transfers to Persons	Interest	Other	
1971–75	18.7	20.6	5.8	7.4	1.3	6.1	1.9
1976–80	19.7	21.5	5.0	8.5	1.6	6.4	1.8
1981–85	19.8	24.1	6.1	9.5	2.8	5.7	4.3
1986–89	19.9	23.4	6.2	8.8	3.2	5.2	3.5

Source: President's Council of Economic Advisers, *Economic Report of the President*, (Washington, D.C.: Government Printing Office, 1990), Table C-81.

restructuring of tax rates, featuring reduced marginal tax rates on income, which affected primarily upper-income taxpayers, and higher social security payroll taxes, which mainly affected low- and middle-income taxpayers. Nevertheless, the share of federal taxes in GNP continued to creep upward in the 1980's although less rapidly than in the previous decade.

Cutting government spending was given an even lower priority. Column 2 shows that outlays rose to an unprecedented share of GNP in the first half of the 1980s and fell back only slightly as GNP grew strongly in the later 1980s. The combined effect of trends in expenditures and revenues was a sharp increase in the budget deficit, as shown in column 7. Despite the pledges of two Republican administrations to cut taxes, hold the line on spending, and balance the budget, the story told by the numbers is that the deficit increase was caused not by tax cuts but by spending increases.

Priorities among programs. The remaining columns of Exhibit 10.7 show what happened to the composition of federal spending by type of program. Column 3 shows that with respect to national defense, the announced priorities of the Reagan and Bush administrations were carried out. The share of GNP going to defense did rise significantly in the 1980s compared with the 1970s. To put the 1980s defense buildup in perspective, however, it should be noted that the 1970s were a low point for defense expenditures in the post–World War II years. In the 1960s defense expenditures had averaged almost 9 percent of GNP. The level of Pentagon spending in the 1980s never came close to that level.

If the numbers are allowed to speak for themselves, transfer payments to persons were another spending priority of the 1980s, as shown in column 4 of Exhibit 10.7. Whatever their other disagreements with Congress, the Reagan and Bush administrations agreed with Congress that most transfer programs were untouchable. This can be seen, for example, in the Gramm-Rudman-Hollings bill, which exempted the largest transfer programs, but not defense, from automatic budget cuts. Two very costly programs for the elderly, social security and Medicare, accounted for about two-thirds of total transfer payments in the 1980s.

Column 5 of Exhibit 10.7 shows the increasing share of GNP taken by interest on the national debt. This reflects higher interest rates as well as the growth of the debt itself relative to GNP. Once the debt has been incurred, there is no way to control this category of spending. However, the reason the debt grew so rapidly is that balancing the budget ranked lower on the list of priorities than entitlements and defense.

Finally, column 6 of the exhibit shows the big budgetary loser in the 1980s—other items that include most discretionary nondefense spending. Within this category, nondefense purchases of goods and services—a category that includes everything from the federal judiciary to national parks—fell from 10 percent of federal expenditures in 1980 to 8 percent in 1989. Grants-in-aid to state and local governments fell even more sharply, from 14 percent of expenditures to 10 percent over the same period. If the Reagan and Bush administrations' budget-cutting intentions have had any impact, it has been here. But these programs are such a small fraction of the total budget that cuts in them were not even enough to offset the rise in interest payments on the national debt.

Consumption versus investment. In the eyes of many observers, there is another priority hidden in the federal budgets of the 1980s: Consumption was given priority over investment. One way to think of this is in terms of the circular flow of income and product. Setting aside the foreign sector for a moment, as in Exhibit 5.5 (page 137), there is one flow of saving into financial markets, namely, net private domestic saving. This must finance two outflows: private investment and the combined budget deficit of federal, state, and local governments. What is used for one purpose cannot be used for another. In the 1960s, net private domestic saving amounted to 8.1 percent of GNP. The combined government deficit took .3 percent, leaving 7.8 percent potentially available for private investment. In the 1970s, saving held steady at 8.1 percent of GNP but the deficit grew to .9 percent, leaving 7.2 percent for private investment. In the 1980s, saving fell to 6.2 percent of GNP while the combined government deficit grew to 2.6 percent, leaving just 3.6 percent for private investment.

Taking the foreign sector into account gives domestic private investment a little more breathing room than these figures suggest. In the 1960s and 1970s, part of U.S. domestic savings was invested abroad. In the 1980s, the direction of international capital flows was reversed, and funds from foreign sources allowed U.S. private investment to stay one GNP percentage point or more higher than it otherwise would be. Thus, the actual drop in net private domestic investment was from 6.9 percent of GNP in the 1970s to 4.6 percent in the 1980s—still a major shift.

There are other indications of priority being given to consumption rather than investment. These include reductions in federal spending on civilian research and development and support for education; a shift in federal capital spending away from civilian infrastructure projects, such as highways and sewers, toward defense goods, such as aircraft carriers; and, with the 1986 tax reform, a shift away from taxes on households toward taxes on business.

On balance, then, fiscal priorities of the 1980s can be characterized as follows:

- A priority on holding the line on the overall tax burden but not for actually cutting it; low priority on restricting total spending and the federal deficit.

- High priority on increasing defense spending; a slightly lower priority on increasing transfer payments, especially to the elderly; and a moderate priority on reducing discretionary nondefense spending.

- A priority on encouraging consumption at the expense of investment.

10.4   The Debate Over the Deficit and the National Debt

Federal budget deficits are not a new phenomenon. What distinguishes the deficits of recent years is their size. Between 1950 and 1980, the cumulative deficit was $388 billion, slightly offset by a cumulative $17 billion surplus. In the 1980s, as much was added to the cumulative deficit every two years as in the previous thirty, and there were no offsetting federal surpluses. In this section we look at some economic principles that will shed some light on the origins of the deficit and its effects.

Structural versus Cyclical Deficit

In part, the federal budget deficit is a result of discretionary policy decisions. However, policymakers do not determine precise levels of government receipts and expenditures. Instead, they pass general laws setting tax rates, benefit formulas for transfer payments, and goals for purchases of goods and services. Given these laws, the actual levels of receipts and expenditures are strongly affected by the stage of the business cycle. As we saw earlier in the chapter, the budget shifts toward deficit when the economy contracts, as tax collections fall and transfer payments rise. During expansions the budget shifts toward surplus.

One way to separate the effects of discretionary policy changes from those of the business cycle is to calculate what the federal surplus or deficit would be at the natural rate of unemployment. An unemployment rate of 6 percent, which is currently thought to be close to the natural rate, is commonly used as a benchmark.

The budget surplus or deficit that the federal government would run, given the 6 percent benchmark unemployment rate, is called the **structural deficit.** Changes in the structural deficit are interpreted as representing discretionary fiscal policy. The difference between the actual and structural deficits is called the **cyclical deficit.** When unemployment rises above the 6 percent benchmark level, the cyclical deficit becomes positive because the actual deficit exceeds the structural deficit. When unemployment falls below the benchmark, the actual

Structural deficit
The budget surplus or deficit that the federal government would incur given current tax and spending laws and a 6 percent unemployment rate.

Cyclical deficit
The difference between the actual federal deficit and the structural deficit.

deficit is less than the structural deficit. At such times the cyclical deficit is negative—or, to express it a different way, there is a cyclical surplus. Changes in the cyclical deficit reflect changes in taxes and spending that occur automatically as real output, unemployment, and inflation change over the course of the business cycle.

Exhibit 10.8 shows actual and structural federal budget deficits for the U.S. economy in relation to GNP in recent years. The cyclical deficit appears on the chart as the difference between the two. A noteworthy feature of the chart is the dramatic growth in the structural deficit after 1982. For a time the increase of the structural deficit was accompanied by growth in the actual deficit, but after 1983 the actual deficit was stabilized and then began to fall. After 1983 continued growth of the structural deficit was offset first by a narrowing of the cyclical deficit and then, after 1988, by the appearance of a cyclical surplus.

Exhibit 10.8   Actual, Cyclical, and Structural Federal Deficits, 1970–1989

This chart breaks down the actual federal deficit stated as a percentage of GNP into actual, cyclical, and structural components. The structural component is the estimated deficit that would be produced given current tax and spending laws and a 6 percent unemployment rate. The cyclical component is the difference between the actual deficit and the structural component. The structural deficit increased, on balance, after 1981. This growth is largely attributable to increased defense and entitlements spending.

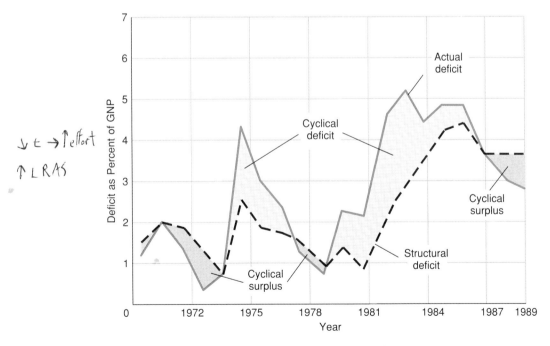

Source: President's Council of Economic Advisers, *Economic Report of the President,* (Washington, D.C.: Government Printing Office, 1990), Table C-79, and *Survey of Current Business,* February 1990, 25. The actual deficit is given on a calendar year national income accounts basis. The structural deficit is the Department of Commerce's cyclically adjusted calendar-year deficit as it would be if GNP followed a trend reflecting 6 percent unemployment.

The Deficit as a Policy Issue

As far back as the 1930s, when Keynesian theories of discretionary fiscal policy were first gaining popularity, fiscal conservatives became worried about the asymmetry of fiscal policy. They warned that if the government allows larger and more frequent deficits than surpluses, it will run up an endlessly growing national debt that could lead to financial ruin. They also raised some important questions: Can the government go on spending beyond its means forever? Should the government be required to balance its budget each year, financing all programs on a pay-as-you-go basis, in order to avoid bankruptcy? Even if debts are paid on time, does financing today's spending programs with borrowed money create distortions in the economy and place an unfair burden on future generations?

Exhibit 10.9   Federal Debt Held by Private Investors as a Percentage of Gross National Product, 1940–1989*

As this chart shows, the federal debt held privately reached a record high of 102 percent of GNP at the end of World War II. From that time through 1974, the debt grew less rapidly than GNP. Then, in 1974, the debt began growing again in relation to GNP. Since 1986, however, the rate of increase of the debt relative to GNP has slowed markedly, reflecting a decline in the size of the federal budget deficit expressed as a share of GNP.

*Excludes debt held by the Federal Reserve.
Source: Office of Management and Budget, *Budget of the United States Government, Fiscal Year 1991* (Washington, D.C.: Government Printing Office, 1990), A-304.

Almost half a century after Keynes, these questions are still being asked. They were given new prominence by the unprecedented size of federal deficits in the mid-1980s. In addition, the size of the national debt—the accumulated result of past deficits—began to grow as a percentage of GNP after reaching a post-World War II low in 1974, although since 1986, as the deficit has fallen, the growth of the debt relative to GNP has slowed markedly (see Exhibit 10.9).

Even so, many economists—and noneconomists as well—look with foreboding at the current size of the federal deficit relative to GNP. We will discuss their reasons for worrying about this situation shortly. But first, we will look briefly at the thinking of a minority of economists who believe that it is not necessary to be so concerned about the current level of the federal deficit.

Reasons Not to Worry about the Deficit

Economists who argue that the federal deficit is nothing to worry about begin by making a series of numerical adjustments. These adjustments, they say, show that the federal deficit is not really as large as it seems, either in absolute terms or compared with figures for past years. We will look at four of these adjustments here.

Adjusting for the state and local surplus.   The first adjustment is based on the notion that it is not the federal deficit that matters but the combined deficit or surplus of federal, state, and local governments. Although the federal government has been running record-breaking deficits, state and local governments have been running substantial surpluses. The state and local surpluses represent a flow of saving into financial markets that can be used to finance private investment and the federal deficit.

Adjusting for the cyclical component.   When one assesses the impact of fiscal policy on the economy, one should also adjust the federal deficit to remove its cyclical component. The reason is that the cyclical component reflects the state of the economy rather than discretionary policy decisions. For example, in 1983, when the unemployment rate averaged 9.6 percent, this adjustment would have taken some $82 billion off the deficit. By 1989, however, when the unemployment rate had dropped below 6 percent, this adjustment began to cut the other way. A cyclical surplus appeared, and the structural deficit became larger than the unadjusted actual deficit.

Adjusting for capital expenditures.   Households and private firms routinely make a distinction between borrowing for purposes of capital investment and borrowing to cover current expenses. Suppose, for example, that you borrow $1,000 to take a vacation. You enjoy the vacation, but you acquire nothing tangible to offset the burden of paying off the loan in the months ahead. On the other hand, suppose that you borrow $60,000 to buy a townhouse. Doing so allows you to move out of your rented apartment. In this case you acquire a tangible asset to offset the debt, and your saving in rent offsets your monthly mortgage payments.

The federal government makes no such distinction between capital and current expenses in figuring its surplus or deficit, but many economists think that it should. After all, suppose that the government builds a new office building to replace rented office space. The funds borrowed to finance the construction will be no burden on taxpayers, because interest payments on the borrowing will be offset by reduced rent payments. The federal government's net capital spending is hard to calculate precisely, but estimates made in the mid-1980s suggest that the adjustment should now be on the order of $30 billion per year.[6]

Adjusting for inflation.   A final adjustment is needed to take the effects of inflation into account. Each year inflation erodes the real value of the federal debt held by the public. To maintain the real value of federal securities they hold, private investors must reinvest a portion of the federal interest payments they receive. For example, in 1983 the nominal value of federal debt in the hands of private investors was nearly $1 trillion and the inflation rate was almost 4 percent. Thus, private investors would be willing to absorb almost $40 billion in new nominal debt just to keep the real value of the total debt constant. This part of the deficit, it is argued, puts no burden on the rest of the economy. Some economists claim that the deficit should be adjusted for the expected inflation rate rather than for the actual rate. Through most of the 1980s, the expected rate was evidently higher than the actual rate, which would make for a larger adjustment. However, by the end of the 1980s, survey results suggest that the expected and actual rates were about equal.

Exhibit 10.10 summarizes these four adjustments to the federal deficit for 1983, 1986, and 1989. When allowances are made for state and local surpluses, the cyclical component of the deficit, capital spending by government, and inflation, the 1983 deficit of $176 billion, which was considered shocking at the time, actually turns into a $12 billion surplus. In 1986 and 1989 the combined federal, state, and local government budgets show deficits when the adjustments are made, but the deficits are much smaller than the unadjusted federal deficit taken by itself.

The deficit and private saving.   Some economists offer another, rather different reason not to worry about the deficit. This is based on Robert Barro's argument, mentioned in *Applying Economic Ideas 10.1,* that changes in taxes tend to be fully offset by changes in private saving. If this is true, it means that the burden the federal budget puts on the rest of the economy depends only on the level of government purchases, not on how they are financed. According to Barro, the public would respond to a tax cut by increasing saving by just the amount needed to buy the extra securities the Treasury would have to sell in order to finance the added deficit. Likewise, a tax increase made to reduce the deficit would decrease saving by the same amount, leaving no additional resources with which to finance private investment.

To be sure, most economists doubt that changes in taxes are fully offset by changes in saving. But even if there is only a partial adjustment of saving, the burden of the deficit will be eased and the case for raising taxes to cut the deficit weakened.

Reasons to Worry about the Deficit

Despite the arguments just given, many economists—probably the majority—still worry about current and projected federal budget deficits. Let's look at some of their concerns.

[6]Robert Eisner has estimated federal net investment at $20 billion for 1982. See "Which Budget Deficit?" *American Economic Review* 74 (May 1984): 138–143. Using a different methodology, Michael J. Boskin, Marc S. Robinson, and John M. Roberts have estimated federal net investment at $23 billion for 1983 and $19 billion for 1984. See "New Estimates of Federal Government Tangible Capital and Net Investment" (Working Paper No. 1774, National Bureau of Economic Research, December 1985).

Exhibit 10.10   Adjustments to the Federal Deficit
(Selected Years, Billions of Dollars)

In nominal terms, the federal deficit rose to record levels in the mid-1980s. Many people found the deficit numbers alarming, but some economists think they overstate the deficit's impact on the economy. To assess the true impact, they say, the deficit should be adjusted to take into account state and local government surpluses, the cyclical component of the federal deficit, capital spending by the federal government, and the effects of inflation. This exhibit shows the results of these adjustments. They suggest that the nominal deficits that are usually cited overstate the true macroeconomic impact of the deficit.

	1983	1986	1989
Actual federal deficit	$176	$207	$149
Less:			
State and local surplus	48	63	45
Cyclical component	82	19	−39[a]
Federal capital spending	20	25	31
Inflation adjustment	38	40	74
Equals: Adjusted deficit	−12[a]	60	38

[a]Negative number denotes surplus.

Source: Author's calculations based on official data from various sources. The actual federal deficit and the state and local surpluses are stated on a calendar year GNP basis. The cyclical component is based on the Department of Commerce's 6 percent unemployment benchmark. Federal capital spending is estimated at $20 billion for 1983 and is assumed to remain at a constant percent of GNP in succeeding years. The inflation adjustment is calculated as the annual change in the GNP deflator times privately held federal debt.

Effects on investment.   Earlier in the chapter we saw that when the Treasury borrows to finance a deficit, it adds to total demand for the limited funds made available by private domestic saving, thereby pushing up interest rates. Private borrowers are then crowded out of financial markets. The reduction in private investment is a burden on the economy that slows economic growth and reduces the living standards of future generations. Thus, the drop in the share of net private investment in GNP from 6.9 percent in the 1970s to 4.6 percent in the 1980s is identified as one of the most harmful effects of deficits.

Borrowing from abroad.   In defense of deficits it is sometimes said that the national debt is something "we owe to ourselves." In other words, taxes collected to repay the debt come out of the pockets of some U.S. citizens but go back into the pockets of others, leaving the country as a whole no poorer. However, it is argued, federal budget deficits push up interest rates in the United States relative to those in the rest of the world. Attracted by the high rates, foreign buyers purchase many of the securities that the Treasury sells to finance the deficit. In addition, because high interest rates on government securities push up the rates on competing private securities, many private U.S. securities also move into foreign hands.[7] In future years repaying the part of public and

[7]These effects can also be expressed in terms of the concepts introduced in the sections of Chapters 5 and 6 that dealt with international economic relations: An increase in the federal deficit, other things being equal, tends to move the capital account in the direction of a net capital inflow. This must be offset by a movement of the current account toward deficit. Thus, in an open economy, a federal deficit crowds out net exports as well as domestic investment.

private debt owed to foreign investors will place a real burden on the U.S. economy. The argument that we owe it to ourselves does not apply in this case.

The enlarged structural deficit.   It is widely acknowledged that any cyclical component of a federal deficit is less of a problem than the structural component. What worries many economists is the way the structural component grew during the 1980s as the cyclical component moved into surplus. In 1983, just as the economy began its recovery from recession, the cyclical deficit came to $82 billion out of a total deficit of $176 billion. By 1987, the cyclical component had disappeared, to be replaced, after 1988, by a cyclical surplus. If the structural component had remained constant at its 1983 level, the actual deficit would have fallen to $55 billion instead of remaining at nearly $150 billion. With the other adjustments shown in Exhibit 10.10, the budget would have been in surplus as far as its macroeconomic impact is concerned. Instead of shrinking, however, the structural deficit grew. By 1989, it had risen to $187 billion, more than double its 1983 level.

In short, the increase in tax receipts that came from economic expansion after the recessions of the early 1980s was used not to reduce the structural deficit but to finance an increase in government expenditures. A recession in the early 1990s could easily raise the cyclical deficit to $75 billion. In that event, the total deficit could approach $250 billion. Yet tax increases or spending cuts would be difficult to undertake because their multiplier effects would deepen the recession.

The danger of an "exploding" deficit.   The growth of the structural deficit calls attention to another worry: the increase in the part of the deficit associated with interest payments on the debt. As mentioned earlier, this part of the deficit has already doubled as a percentage of the budget since 1974. Some economists think that under certain circumstances interest payments can experience "explosive" growth.

In the explosive-growth scenario, the amount of borrowing needed just to make interest payments on the debt is so great that the debt grows faster than national income even if the rest of the budget remains in balance. As the government borrows more and more each year to make interest payments, it adds to the demand for loanable funds in credit markets. This pushes interest rates higher, making it necessary to borrow even more to make the interest payments. Eventually the deficit "explodes" and threatens to swallow the entire national income.[8]

As the point of explosive growth approaches, the government is left with only one way out. It begins to "monetize" the deficit, which in effect means that it finances the deficit by creating new money rather than by borrowing. But financing deficits with newly created money is the classic formula for inflation — too much money chasing too few goods. Thus, monetization of the deficit converts an explosive deficit into explosive inflation.

---

[8]The issue of the exploding deficit was raised in Thomas J. Sargent and Neil Wallace, "Some Unpleasant Monetarist Arithmetic," *Federal Reserve Bank of Minneapolis Quarterly Review* (Fall 1981): 1–17. Michael R. Darby refines the argument by showing that the deficit will explode if the real rate of interest (that is, the nominal market rate minus the inflation rate), adjusted for the average tax rate on federal interest payments, exceeds the long-term rate of growth of real GNP. See "Some Pleasant Monetarist Arithmetic," *Federal Reserve Bank of Minneapolis Quarterly Review* (Spring 1984).

Is this scenario too farfetched to be a real threat? Not at all. Creating new money to cover the government deficit is the source of the runaway inflations (at annual rates of 1,000 percent per year and more) that devastated such countries as Bolivia, Argentina, Brazil, and Israel in the early 1980s. Today inflation is not running out of control in the United States; in fact, it has slowed dramatically from the double-digit rates of a decade ago. Nevertheless, many economists think that continuing large federal deficits are a potential danger that cannot be ignored. In the next four chapters, we will gain a better understanding of this danger as we look at the mechanisms that are used to create and control money in the U.S. economy.

Summary

1. **How can fiscal policy be used to fight recession and inflation?** *Fiscal policy* means policy that is related to government purchases and net taxes. If a decrease in private planned expenditure threatens to send the economy into a recession, an increase in government purchases or a cut in net taxes can be used to shift the aggregate demand curve to the right, restoring the economy to its natural level of real output. (In the income-expenditure model, such expansionary fiscal policy will shift the planned-expenditure schedule upward.) If an excess of private planned expenditure threatens the economy with inflation, a cut in government purchases or an increase in net taxes can shift the aggregate demand curve to the left, restoring stability. (In the income-expenditure model, restrictive fiscal policy will shift the planned-expenditure schedule downward.)

2. **How are government receipts and expenditures affected by changing economic conditions?** Some changes in government receipts and expenditures reflect *discretionary* changes in the laws that govern fiscal policy. However, changes in the levels of these items can also result *automatically* from changes in economic conditions, including real output, unemployment, and the price level. In general, economic expansion tends to raise receipts and restrain expenditures, thereby moving the budget toward surplus. Contraction tends to lower receipts and raise expenditures, thereby moving the budget toward deficit. These automatic changes in receipts and expenditures damp the economy's response to shifts in private planned expenditure and, hence, are known as *automatic stabilizers*.

3. **How does the federal budgetary system work, and what are the limitations of that system?** In the United States authority for fiscal policy is divided between the president and Congress. Each year the president submits a budget plan, which Congress modifies and enacts into law by the beginning of the *fiscal year* on October 1. In practice, macroeconomic goals play a

secondary role to political considerations in setting budget priorities. Also, in recent years Congress has found it difficult to follow its own budgetary rules and to pass required legislation in a timely manner.

4. **What priorities guided federal tax and spending decisions in the 1980s?** If budget numbers are allowed to speak for themselves, they tell a different story than that presented by the rhetoric of tax cuts and spending restrictions. In practice, total taxes were not cut but held steady as a share of GNP. The large deficits of the 1980s appear to have been caused not by tax cuts but by increased spending. Defense and *entitlements* accounted for the greatest spending increases. Cuts in other nondefense programs—which now account for less than one-fifth of the budget—have not been enough to offset the growth in interest payments on the national debt. A final implicit fiscal priority has been to favor consumption at the expense of saving and investment.

5. **How is the federal deficit measured, and why has it grown?** The federal deficit can be divided into a cyclical component and a structural component. The *structural deficit* is the estimated level of the deficit, given current tax and spending laws and a benchmark unemployment rate of 6 percent. The *cyclical deficit* is the difference between the actual and structural deficits. The cyclical deficit tends to increase during a recession and to decrease during an expansion. If unemployment drops below 6 percent at the peak of an expansion, the cyclical deficit can be negative (that is, there will be a cyclical surplus). During the expansion that followed the 1981 to 1982 recession, the cyclical component of the deficit first declined and then moved into surplus while the structural component grew dramatically.

6. **Are large federal deficits a threat to economic stability?** The extent of the threat posed by federal deficits is a matter of dispute. Some economists argue that if the federal deficit is adjusted for state and local gov-

ernment surpluses, the cyclical component of the deficit, capital expenditures, and the effects of inflation, it looks somewhat less threatening. Others claim that the deficit crowds out private investment. They are also concerned about borrowing from abroad to finance the deficit and the possibility that explosive growth of the deficit could ultimately cause severe inflation.

Terms for Review

- fiscal policy
- net tax multiplier
- discretionary fiscal policy
- automatic fiscal policy
- automatic stabilizers
- fiscal year
- entitlements
- structural deficit
- cyclical deficit

Questions for Review

1. How does each of the following affect the aggregate demand curve: (a) an increase in government purchases; (b) an increase in taxes; and (c) an increase in transfer payments? (In the income-expenditure model, how does each of these affect the planned-expenditure schedule?)

2. Why is the net tax multiplier less in absolute value than the government purchases multiplier?

3. How could fiscal policy cause an increase in the price level?

4. Why does the government budget tend to move toward surplus during an expansion and toward deficit during a contraction?

5. What are the responsibilities of the president and Congress in preparing the federal budget? What agencies provide economic advice to each?

6. In what respects has the federal budgetary process encountered difficulties in recent years? What was the intent of the Gramm-Rudman-Hollings experiment? Did it succeed?

7. What were the budgetary priorities of the 1980s as revealed in actual tax and spending figures?

8. How did the actual, cyclical, and structural federal budget deficits behave during the 1980s?

9. List four adjustments to the federal budget deficit that appear to reduce its impact.

10. Why do many economists think that high budget deficits, such as those of the 1980s, are a threat to economic stability?

Problems and Topics for Discussion

1. **Examining the lead-off case.** Suppose that the political events of the early 1990s were to result in a "peace dividend" of $50 billion, that is, a $50 billion cut in the defense budget. Assuming no other changes in government policy and an expenditure multiplier of 4, how would a defense spending cut of that magnitude affect the economy? How do you think such a peace dividend should be used? To increase spending in other programs? If so, which other programs? To reduce the federal budget deficit? What arguments would you advance in favor of your proposed use of the peace dividend?

2. **Unemployment and fiscal policy.** At point E_1 in Exhibit 10.1, real output is $1,500 billion compared with a natural level of real output of $2,000 billion. Apply Okun's law to estimate the unemployment rate at E_1 assuming a natural unemployment rate of 6 percent.

3. **Applying the multipliers.** Suppose that real output is at its natural level in the current year but forecasts show that if no action is taken, the aggregate demand curve will shift to the left by $500 billion in the coming year. Assuming an expenditure multiplier of 2.5, what change in real government purchases will be needed to keep real output at the natural level? If a change in real net taxes is used instead, what change will be required?

4. **Impact of government purchases financed by increased taxes.** Assume that real output is currently at its natural level. For the coming year, Congress passes a budget that includes $100 million in added real government purchases to be paid for by a $100 million increase in real net taxes. What effect will this have on the aggregate demand curve? On the equilibrium level of real output? Does your answer depend on the value of the expenditure multiplier? Why or why not?

5. **A balanced budget amendment.** From time to time it has been proposed that a law or constitutional amendment be passed that will force the federal government to balance its budget every year. Do you think it would be possible to keep the actual budget deficit at zero each year, or should such an amendment aim only to keep the structural deficit at zero? Discuss.

Fiscal Policy at the State Level

In February 1982, when the U.S. economy was deep in recession, the Chicago Tribune *published the following item discussing the tax and spending problems of the Illinois state government:*

Warning that state revenues are lagging behind expectations, Governor James R. Thompson announced Tuesday that he has halted most new state construction work for the next six months.

Referring to "disturbing news on the economic front," the governor also announced that:

- He is reworking his proposed state budget to include additional spending cuts.

- He has ordered state agencies under his control to cut $30 million from their budgets.

- He repeated his call for a new state liquor tax to raise an additional $50 million a year.

To save an estimated $20 million in interest payments, the amount of money to be raised by State of Illinois bond issues during the next five months will be cut almost in half, from $380 million to $200 million.

"Interest rates are too high," the governor told a press conference in the Westin Hotel here.

Later, in a speech to the Illinois Board of Higher Education, Thompson said that in January state income tax revenues were $10 million lower than projected while sales tax revenues were $25 million less than projected.

"Right now, we don't know if it's an aberration or a trend. I suspect it's a trend," Thompson said.

He warned that if the revenue shortfalls continue for a full year, the loss in state revenue could total $420 million.

Thompson also had other bad news for the educators.

Speaking of the financial problems facing the state, he said, "There will be some pain for higher education and for elementary and secondary education."

He described the upcoming budget as "the tightest of the six budgets I have presented to the General Assembly."

Questions

1. Do Governor Thompson's policy actions count as fiscal policy even though they take place at the state level? Assuming an expenditure multiplier of 2.5 for the economy as a whole, what would his $30 million in spending cuts do to the U.S. aggregate demand curve? To equilibrium real national income?

2. Why do you think income tax revenues were $10 million and sales tax revenues $25 million lower than had been projected?

3. Suppose that all state governors were to follow Thompson's lead and try to cut spending and raise taxes when state budget deficits increased during a

recession. Will this make it easier or harder for the economy to recover from a recession? What would happen if the federal government followed policies similar to Thompson's when the economy entered a recession?

Suggestions for Further Reading

Barro, Robert J. "The Ricardian Approach to Budget Deficits." *Journal of Economic Perspectives* (Spring 1989): 37–54.

A short exposition of Barro's reasons for thinking that budget deficits do not matter.

Eisner, Robert. "Budget Deficits: Rhetoric and Reality." *Journal of Economic Perspectives* (Spring 1989): 73–94.

A discussion of adjustments to the budget deficit and other reasons for thinking that deficits are not threatening to the economy.

President's Council of Economic Advisers. *Economic Report of the President.* Washington, D.C.: Government Printing Office, annually.

Discusses current fiscal policy issues each year. Use the table of contents to find the relevant sections.

Rivlin, Alice M. "Economics and the Political Process." *American Economic Review* (March 1987): 1–10.

Reflections on ways to improve the federal budget process by a former director of the Congressional Budget Office.

Rauch, Jonathan. "The Fiscal Ice Age." *National Journal*, January 10, 1987, 58–64, and "The Politics of Joy." *National Journal*, January 17, 1987, 125–130.

This pair of articles discusses fiscal priorities in the 1980s and the current federal budgetary process.

Schultz, Charles L., and Thomas E. Mann. "Getting Rid of the Budget Deficit." In *Critical Choices*, Barry P. Bosworth et al., Washington, D.C.: Brookings, 1989.

An essay explaining why the federal budget deficit should be reduced and how it could be done.

PART FOUR

Monetary Economics

11

Money and the Banking System

**Before reading this chapter,
make sure you know the meaning of:**

Financial intermediaries (Chapter 5)

The role of money in the circular flow (Chapter 5)

After reading this chapter, you will understand:

What money is and what it does.

How the stock of money in the economy is measured.

The structure of the U.S. banking system.

How the safety and stability of the banking system are maintained.

Where Life Is Easy and the Currency Is Hard

On the tiny South Pacific island of Yap, life is easy and the currency is hard.

Elsewhere, the world's troubled monetary system creaks along; floating exchange rates wreak havoc in currency markets, and devaluations are commonplace. But on Yap the currency is as solid as a rock. In fact, it is rock. Limestone, to be precise.

For nearly 2,000 years the Yapese have used large stone wheels to pay for major purchases, such as land, canoes, and permission to marry. Yap is a U.S. trust territory, and the dollar is used in grocery stores and gas stations. But reliance on stone money, like the island's ancient caste system and the traditional dress of loincloths and grass skirts, continues.

Stone wheels don't make good pocket money, so for small transactions Yapese use other forms of currency, such as beer. Beer is proffered as payment for all sorts of odd jobs, including construction. Besides stone wheels and beer, the Yapese sometimes spend "gaw," consisting of necklaces of stone beads strung together around a whale's tooth. They also can buy things with "yar," a currency made from large seashells. But these are small change.

The people of Yap have been using stone money ever since a Yapese warrior named Anagumang first brought the huge stones over from limestone caverns on neighboring Palau, some 1,500 to 2,000 years ago. Inspired by the moon, he fashioned the stone into large circles. The rest is history.

By custom, the stones are worthless when broken. Rather than risk a broken stone—or back—Yapese tend to leave the larger stones where they are and make a mental accounting that the ownership has been transferred—much as gold bars used in international transactions change hands without leaving the vault of the New York Federal Reserve Bank.

Photo source: © Susan Pierres/Peter Arnold, Inc.

Source: Art Pine, "Fixed Assets, or: Why a Loan in Yap Is Hard to Roll Over," *The Wall Street Journal*, March 29, 1984, 1. Reprinted by permission of *The Wall Street Journal*, © Dow Jones & Company, Inc., 1984. All Rights Reserved Worldwide.

Just three decades ago, Yap was little changed from the way it had been for centuries. But now things are changing. To help preserve the tradition of stone money, Andrew Ken, a Yapese monetary thinker, is trying to persuade the Yap government to start a stone money exchange. This would allow the Yapese to trade their boulders for dollars, or buy them back, whenever they wish. "We're losing because we can't liquidate," Ken complains.

As we saw in Chapter 5, money is the fluid that moves in the circular flow of income and product. Money can take many forms: giant stones on the Pacific island of Yap; gold coins throughout much of the world in earlier centuries; and electronic entries in banks' computers in the United States today.

Although we have mentioned money often, in this and the following three chapters we give it center stage. We will begin with a formal definition of money and a brief discussion of the complicated matter of measuring how much of it exists in the economy. Next we will explore the banking system. In Chapter 12 we will look at the ways in which the Federal Reserve, a government agency, controls the stock of money. In Chapter 13 we will turn to a discussion of the demand for money and how that demand interacts with supply in financial markets. Finally, in Chapter 14 we will see that changes in the money stock can have a strong impact on the decisions of households, firms, and government units. Thus, creating the conditions that permit a stable monetary system is an important part of national economic policy.

11.1   Money: What it Is and What it Does

Money
An asset that serves as a means of payment, a store of purchasing power, and a unit of account.

Money is best defined in terms of what it does: It serves as a means of payment, a store of purchasing power, and a unit of account. Money serves these functions regardless of its name or form—U.S. dollars, Japanese yen, or Yapese stone wheels can all function in all three ways.

The Functions of Money

As a means of payment, money reduces the costs of carrying out transactions. Using money avoids the complexities of barter. This can be seen by imagining a market in which farmers meet to trade produce of various kinds. Apples will get you peppers, cauliflower will get you beets, and turnips will get you garlic. But what if you want garlic and have only potatoes? What you need is a universal means of exchange—one that all sellers will accept because they know that others will also accept it; one that is in limited supply so that you know its exchange value will remain constant; and one that is easily recognized and hard to counterfeit. The Yapese find that stone wheels work well for large transactions, and they use "yar" or "gaw" for small ones. In the United States, coins and paper currency serve as pocket money and bank deposits, transferable by check or computer networks, are used for bigger business deals.

As a store of purchasing power, money makes it possible to arrange economic activities in a convenient manner over time. Income-producing activities and spending decisions need not occur simultaneously. Instead, we can accept payment for our productive efforts in money and keep the money handy until we decide how to spend it. The U.S. dollar is a fairly good store of purchasing power, although as we saw in Chapter 6, its purchasing power has been hurt by inflation in recent decades. Yapese stone wheels evidently work even better—they have held their value for centuries.

Finally, as a unit of account money makes it possible to measure and record economic stocks and flows. A household's needs for food, shelter, and clothing can be expressed in dollar terms. The nation's output of movies, apples, and airplanes can be added together in dollar terms. Without money as a unit of account, private and public economic planning would be virtually impossible.

Money as a Liquid Asset

Any asset that a household, firm, or government unit owns is a store of purchasing power in that it can be sold and the proceeds can be used to buy something else. Money, however, has two important traits that no other asset has, at least not to the same extent. One is that money itself can be used as a means of payment without first having to be exchanged for something else. A house, a corporate bond, or a blast furnace may have great value, but it can rarely be traded without first being exchanged for an equivalent amount of money. The other trait is that money can neither gain nor lose in nominal value; this is necessarily so, because money is the unit of account in which nominal values are stated. Thus, a house, a bond, or a blast furnace may be worth more or fewer dollars next year than this year, but the nominal value of a dollar is always a dollar—no more and no less.

An asset that can be used as or readily converted into a means of payment and is protected against gain or loss in nominal value is said to have **liquidity.** No other asset is as liquid as money. In fact, a comparison of the definitions of money and liquidity suggests that any perfectly liquid asset is, by definition, a form of money.

Liquidity
An asset's ability to be used directly as a means of payment, or to be readily converted into one, and to retain a fixed nominal value.

Measuring the Stock of Money

For purposes of economic analysis and policy, we need to know not only what money is but also how it can be measured. In all modern economies the stock of money is controlled by government. As we will see, if government fails to supply enough money, real output and employment will decrease, at least temporarily. Indeed, some economists believe that the Great Depression was caused or at least aggravated by such a failure. On the other hand, flooding the economy with too much money causes inflation.

Although since World War II the U.S. economy has been free of major depressions and extreme inflation, in recent decades it has not performed as well as many economists and other observers believe it could. If the economy is to perform well in the future, a sound monetary policy will be needed. Because the money stock cannot be controlled if it cannot be measured, the problem of measurement is an important one.

Currency and transaction deposits. We begin with a once common but rather restrictive definition that views money as consisting of just two highly liquid types of assets: currency and transaction deposits. **Currency** includes coins and paper money. **Transaction deposits**—popularly known as *checking accounts*—are deposits from which money can be withdrawn by check or electronic transfer without advance notice for making payments to third parties. (*Third parties,* in

Currency
Coins and paper money.

Transaction deposit
A deposit from which funds can be freely withdrawn by check or electronic transfer to make payments to third parties.

this sense, are parties other than the depositor or the institution that houses the account.)

In the United States, currency consists of the familiar Federal Reserve notes, which are issued in denominations of $1, $2, $5, $10, $50, and $100 and of coins minted by the Treasury. Coins and paper money were formerly backed by precious metals. Until 1934 the U.S. government issued both gold coins and paper currency that could be exchanged for gold on demand; silver coins and silver-backed paper money survived until the mid-1960s. Today coins and paper money are simply tokens whose value is based on the public's faith in their usefulness as means of paying for goods and services. In this regard, the use of dollars in the United States is no different from the use of stone wheels on the island of Yap.

Exhibit 11.1 shows that the currency in the hands of the public in the United States totaled $232 billion as of January 1990. A small quantity of traveler's checks is included in this total.

Transaction deposits are available in a number of forms. One major type of transaction deposit is the *demand deposit*. By law, demand deposits cannot pay interest, but banks provide demand-deposit customers with various other services below cost. Until the mid-1970s demand deposits were the only kind of transaction deposit available in the United States and were offered only by **commercial banks.** They have since been joined by a variety of interest-bearing checkable deposits, notably negotiable order of withdrawal or NOW accounts. These are available to consumers through commercial banks and **thrift institutions (thrifts)**—savings and loan associations, savings banks, and credit unions. Banks and thrifts are referred to collectively as **depository institutions.** (We will look in more detail at these institutions later in the chapter.)

Commercial banks
Financial intermediaries that provide a broad range of banking services, including accepting demand deposits and making commercial loans.

Thrift institutions (thrifts)
A group of financial intermediaries that operate much like commercial banks; they include savings and loan associations, savings banks, and credit unions.

Depository institutions
Financial intermediaries, including commercial banks and thrift institutions, that accept deposits from the public.

Exhibit 11.1   Components of the U.S. Money Stock, January 1990
(Billions of Dollars, Seasonally Adjusted)

This table breaks down the U.S. money supply into its components as of January 1990. It gives two of the most commonly used money supply measures. M1 is the total of currency and transaction deposits; M2 includes M1 plus other highly liquid assets.

Currency[a]		$ 232.1
Plus transaction deposits		562.6
Demand deposits	$277.3	
Other checkable deposits	285.3	
Equals M1		794.7
Plus money market deposit accounts		484.9
Plus money market mutual fund shares		318.0
Plus savings deposits		410.2
Plus small-denomination time deposits		1,142.5
Plus overnight repurchase agreements[b]		63.9
Plus selected other liquid assets[b]		16.9
Equals M2		$3,229.1

[a]Includes traveler's checks.
[b]Not seasonally adjusted. Components do not add to total because of incomplete seasonal adjustment of these components.

Source: Federal Reserve H-6 Statistical Release, April 19, 1990.

Applying Economic Ideas 11.1
"Plastic Money"

Many people wonder how "plastic money"—the Master-Cards, Visa cards, and other bank cards that so many people carry these days—fits into the "Ms." Just what role do these cards play in the payments system?

Credit cards, the most common type of plastic money, are not really a form of money at all. What sets credit cards apart from currency, bank deposits, and other forms of money is the fact that they are not a store of value. Instead, they are documents that make it easy for their holders to obtain a loan.

When you go into a store, present your credit card, and walk out with a can of tennis balls, you have not yet paid for your purchase. What you have done is borrow

from the bank that issued the card. At the same time, you have instructed the bank to turn over the proceeds of the loan to the store. Later the bank will send money to the store (either in the form of a check or by crediting the amount to the store's account). This will pay for the tennis balls. Still later you will send money to the bank to pay off the balance on your credit card account.

A less common form of plastic money, but one that is becoming more widespread, is the *debit card*. A debit card looks just like a credit card, but it does not work the same way. When you present your debit card to a merchant, you instruct your bank to transfer money directly from your bank account to the store's account. If the store is linked to the bank by a special computer hookup, the transfer may be made instantly. If you have no money in your account, you cannot use your debit card.

As Exhibit 11.1 shows, in early 1990 demand deposits made up somewhat less than half of the total transaction deposits and all other checkable deposits accounted for somewhat more than half. Currency plus all forms of transaction deposits totaled nearly $795 billion as of January 1990. The sum of currency and transaction deposits is known as **M1.**

Some readers may find it odd that "plastic money"—credit cards—does not appear in Exhibit 11.1 along with transaction deposits. After all, from the consumer's point of view paying for a purchase with a credit card is a close substitute for paying by cash or check. ***Applying Economic Ideas 11.1*** discusses the nature of credit cards and explains why they do not figure in the measurement of the nation's money stock.

M1
A measure of the money supply that includes currency and transaction deposits.

The broadly defined money stock. The rationale behind the narrow definition of the money stock, M1, is that almost all transactions are made with either currency or transaction deposits. However, if one chooses to focus on the function of money as a store of value rather than as a means of payment, there are a number of other assets that are almost as liquid as the components of M1 and serve as close substitutes for them.

Shares in money market mutual funds are one example. A *money market mutual fund* is a financial intermediary that sells shares to the public. The proceeds of these sales are used to buy short-term, fixed-interest securities such as Treasury bills. Almost all the interest earned on securities bought by the fund is passed along to shareholders. (The fund charges a small fee for its services.) Shareholders can redeem their shares in a number of ways—by writing checks on the fund (usually in amounts above a minimum of $500), by telephone transfer, or by transfer to another fund.[1] Because the proceeds from sales of shares are

[1]Money market mutual funds, which compete with banks and thrifts for household savings, make every effort to make their services as convenient as those of their competitors. They provide statements, checkbooks, deposit slips, and so on that closely resemble those used by banks and thrifts. Technically, however, their liabilities are shares in the fund's portfolio of assets, not deposits. Therefore, money market mutual funds are not considered to be depository institutions.

invested in very safe short-term assets, a money market mutual fund is able to promise its shareholders a fixed nominal value of $1 per share, although the interest paid on the shares varies with market rates. Except for the minimum-amount requirement on checks, then, money market mutual fund balances are almost as liquid as those of ordinary transaction accounts. Money market funds grew rapidly in the late 1970s and early 1980s, when market interest rates rose while rates paid by banks and thrifts were limited by federal regulations.

In late 1982 banks and thrifts were allowed to compete with money market mutual funds by offering so-called *money market deposit accounts (MMDAs)*. These accounts may have only limited checking privileges, but they offer higher interest rates than the transaction accounts included in M1. MMDAs therefore are fairly liquid. Their volume grew very rapidly after their introduction. In 1990, as Exhibit 11.1 shows, MMDA deposits had reached a total of nearly $485 billion.

Banks and thrifts also offer a number of other accounts that serve as reasonably liquid stores of purchasing power. **Savings deposits** are a familiar example. Although checks cannot be written on these deposits, they are fully protected against loss in nominal value and can be redeemed at any time. Banks and thrifts also offer **time deposits.** In the case of small-denomination time deposits (up to $100,000), funds must be left on deposit for a fixed period, ranging from less than a month to many years, in order to earn the full interest rate, and they normally cannot be transferred to another person before maturity. This feature makes them less liquid than savings deposits or MMDAs, but in return they usually pay a higher interest rate. They, too, are protected against loss of nominal value. Interest rate regulations on savings and time deposits were phased out during the 1980s, the last restrictions being lifted in April 1986.

Another liquid asset that deserves mention is the **repurchase agreement (RP),** which is an arrangement in which firms (and occasionally consumers) buy securities from a financial institution subject to an agreement to sell them back —often on the next business day—at a slightly higher price. The difference between the buying and selling prices amounts to an interest payment for the institution's use of the funds. Repurchase agreements are popular because they allow firms to put large sums of cash to work earning interest for short periods. (Business firms are not allowed to use interest-bearing transaction deposits.) As Exhibit 11.1 shows, overnight repurchase agreements totaled almost $64 billion as of January 1990.

Money market mutual fund shares, MMDAs, savings deposits, small-denomination time deposits, and overnight repurchase agreements, along with small amounts of other liquid assets, are added to M1 to create a measure of the money supply known as **M2.** As Exhibit 11.1 shows, M2 amounted to $3,229 billion in January 1990.

Besides M1 and M2, there are other, still broader measures. M3 includes such items as large-denomination time deposits ($100,000 and up) and repurchase agreements with longer terms, and a measure called L includes short-term Treasury securities, among other assets.

Why Money Matters

In presenting alternative measures of the money stock, we might seem to have wandered rather far afield from our main macroeconomic themes of price stabil-

---

Savings deposit
A deposit at a bank or thrift institution from which funds can be withdrawn at any time without payment of a penalty.

Time deposit
A deposit at a bank or thrift institution from which funds can be withdrawn without payment of a penalty only at the end of an agreed-upon period.

Repurchase agreement (RP)
A short-term liquid asset that consists of an agreement by a firm or person to buy securities from a financial institution for resale at an agreed-upon price at a later date (often the next business day).

M2
A measure of the money supply that includes M1 plus money market mutual fund shares, money market deposit accounts, savings deposits, small-denomination time deposits, overnight repurchase agreements, and certain other liquid assets.

ity, real output, and employment. In fact, however, these key variables are closely related to money. Much of the next three chapters will be devoted to showing why this is so, but a preliminary overview can be given here.

The equation of exchange.   The relationship between money and other key variables can be stated in the form of the following equation, which is termed the **equation of exchange:**

$$MV = Py,$$

where M stands for a measure of the money stock, P for a measure of the price level, and y for real national product. The remaining variable, V, stands for **velocity** or, more fully, the **income velocity of money.** Velocity can be thought of as the average number of times each dollar of the money stock is spent each year for income-producing transactions. It can also be thought of as the ratio of nominal national product to the money stock.[2]

The equation of exchange shows that any change in the money stock must affect the price level, real output, velocity, or some combination of these variables. To the extent that at least some of the effect of a change in the money stock is felt by real output, the unemployment rate will also be affected. Thus, control over the money stock gives the government another policy instrument, in addition to fiscal policy, with which to influence key macroeconomic variables. Chapters 12 through 14 will show in detail the means by which policymakers can influence the money stock. They will also discuss the effects of changes in the money stock on other variables.

Which M is best?   As we have seen, there are various measures of the money stock. All of these measures are determined by establishing a cutoff point along a range of financial assets with varying degrees of liquidity, from currency at one end to long-term securities at the other. No hard-and-fast answer can be given to the question of which M is "best" without also asking, "Best for what?"

As mentioned earlier, the basic idea of M1 is to measure the money stock available for use as a means of payment. However, it does not do this perfectly. On the one hand, some consumers use interest-bearing transaction accounts, such as NOW accounts, primarily as a store of purchasing power. This savings motive is reflected in the fact that some of these accounts have a low *turnover rate;* that is, the ratio of the volume of transactions per year to the average balance is low. On the other hand, as we have seen, money market mutual funds and MMDAs have limited checking features that allow them to serve as means of payment. These assets are not included in M1 partly because they have even lower turnover rates, but they are still used for some transactions. Thus, M1 is far from perfect as a measure of means-of-payment money.

Similar problems plague M2, which is intended to measure the stock of money as a short-term, highly liquid store of purchasing power. M2 includes items such as savings and small-denomination time deposits, which have fixed nominal values despite their low turnover rates. But the cutoff line between M2 and M3—for example, the $100,000 cutoff for time deposits—is arbitrary.

Equation of exchange
An equation that shows the relationship among the money stock (M), the income velocity of money (V), the price level (P), and real national product (y); written as MV = Py.

Velocity (income velocity of money)
The ratio of nominal national income to the money stock; a measure of the average number of times each dollar of the money stock is used each year for income-producing purposes.

---

[2]This can be demonstrated as follows: First, the right-hand side of the equation, the price level times real national product, can be replaced by Y, standing for nominal national product. Next, both sides of the equation can be divided by M to give V = Y/M.

There have been experiments to devise still other measures of the money stock. One such approach is to compute a weighted average of currency, transaction deposits, savings deposits, and so on with the weights related to the assets' turnover rates. These new measures of the money stock show some promise, but they are by no means free from problems.

For purposes of macroeconomic modeling and policy, the best money stock measure would be the one with the most stable velocity and, hence, the most predictable relationship to the variables lying on the right-hand side of the equation of exchange, that is, real output and the price level. For many years economists were confident that M1, whatever its imperfections, was the best available measure in this regard. In the 1980s, as banking institutions and ways of doing business changed, many economists began to emphasize M2. That trend is reflected in this book. Unless we specify otherwise, in later chapters the term *money* can be understood to refer to M2.

11.2   The Banking System

As Exhibit 11.1 shows, less than 20 percent of M2 consists of currency issued by the federal government and money market mutual funds. The other components of M2 consist of transaction deposits, savings deposits, small-denomination time deposits, RPs, and other financial instruments issued by commercial banks and thrifts. For this reason, an understanding of monetary theory and policy requires a knowledge of the structure and operations of depository institutions. This section develops certain basic principles that will be applied in following chapters.

Types of Depository Institutions

There are four principal types of depository institutions in the United States. They differ in the types of loans and deposits in which they specialize, although their operations increasingly overlap.

The largest group of depository institutions is *commercial banks.* These usually include the word *bank* in their names. One of their specialties is making commercial loans—that is, loans to businesses, frequently short term. They also make consumer loans and home mortgage loans. Until the 1970s commercial banks were the only institutions that could offer checkable transaction accounts, and they still hold the bulk of demand and other checkable deposits. They also raise funds by offering savings and time deposits, RPs, and other financial instruments. Large commercial banks provide many services, such as wire transfers and international banking facilities, to business customers.

Savings and loan associations (also known as *savings and loans* or *S&Ls*) specialize in home mortgage lending, although they also make other real estate loans, consumer loans, and a limited number of commercial loans. Household savings and time deposits have traditionally been their main source of funds, but today they also offer fully checkable deposits as well as MMDAs with limited checking privileges. Although they may not use the word *bank* in their names, some savings and loan associations shape their operations to resemble those of commercial banks as closely as regulations permit. Many savings and loans are "mutuals"; that is, they are owned by their depositors rather than by a group of stockholders.

Savings banks are a type of depository institution that emerged in the nineteenth century to serve the needs of working-class households needing a depository for their small amounts of savings. Some still have names that reflect these origins, such as "Dime Savings Bank." They originally were organized as benevolent institutions with mutual ownership, but this characteristic of their operations has faded. Savings banks offer the same range of deposits as savings and loan associations, but they tend to offer more diversified types of loans.

Credit unions are small financial intermediaries organized as cooperative enterprises by employee groups, union members, or certain other groups with shared work or community ties. They specialize in small consumer loans, although a few also make mortgage loans. They offer both transaction and savings deposits.

Since the mid-1970s the traditional distinctions among these four types of institution have eroded. Today, both from the viewpoint of the consumer and in macroeconomic terms, there is no real difference between a transaction deposit in a commercial bank and one in a thrift institution. Therefore, we will use the terms *bank* and *banking system* to refer to all depository institutions except when there is a particular reason to single out one type of institution.

The Banking Balance Sheet

The operations of a commercial bank can best be understood by reference to its balance sheet. A firm's or household's **balance sheet** is a financial statement showing what it owns and what it owes, or, to use more technical language, its *assets*, *liabilities*, and *net worth*. **Assets,** which are listed on the left-hand side of the balance sheet, are all the things that the firm or household owns or to which it holds a legal claim. **Liabilities,** which are listed on the right-hand side of the balance sheet, are all the legal claims against a firm by nonowners or against a household by nonmembers. **Net worth,** also listed on the right-hand side of the balance sheet, is equal to the firm's or household's assets minus its liabilities. In a business firm, net worth represents the owners' claims against the business. *Equity* is another term that is often used to refer to net worth. In banking circles net worth is often referred to as *capital*.

The balance sheet gets its name from the fact that the totals of the two sides always balance. This follows from the definition of net worth. Because net worth is defined as assets minus liabilities, liabilities plus net worth must equal assets. In equation form, this basic rule of accounting reads as follows:

$$\text{Assets} = \text{liabilities} + \text{net worth}.$$

Exhibit 11.2 shows a total balance sheet for U.S. commercial banks. Balance sheet items for thrift institutions would differ in size, but the concepts involved would be the same.

Assets.   On the assets side of the balance sheet, the first line lists non-interest-bearing deposits that banks maintain with the Federal Reserve System (which we will look at in more detail shortly). The next line, vault cash, consists of currency that banks keep in their own vaults. Deposits at the Federal Reserve plus vault cash constitute a bank's **reserves.** Historically, banks held reserves of cash or deposits that could be quickly converted into cash because at any moment some depositors might want to withdraw their funds. They could do this

Balance sheet A financial statement showing what a firm or household owns and what it owes.

Assets All the things that the firm or household owns or to which it holds a legal claim.

Liabilities All the legal claims against a firm by nonowners or against a household by nonmembers.

Net worth The firm's or household's assets minus its liabilities.

Reserves Cash in bank vaults and non-interest-bearing deposits of banks with the Federal Reserve System.

Exhibit 11.2   Total Balance Sheet for U.S. Commercial Banks
January 31, 1990 (Billions of Dollars)

This table shows the total balance sheet for all U.S. commercial banks as of
January 31, 1990. Assets of banks include non-interest-bearing reserves and
interest-bearing loans and securities. Liabilities include deposits of all kinds and
other borrowings. Net worth equals assets minus liabilities. The balance sheets of
thrift institutions would show the same basic categories but would differ in details.

Assets		Liabilities and Net Worth	
Reserve deposits with		Transaction deposits	$ 613.7
Federal Reserve banks	$ 24.5	MMDAs and savings deposits	542.7
Cash in vaults	28.1	Time deposits	1,085.5
Other cash assets	170.6	Borrowings	551.7
Loans	2,186.5	Miscellaneous liabilities	222.1
Securities	594.8	Total liabilities	$3,015.7
Miscellaneous assets	214.0	Net worth	202.8
		Total liabilities and	
Total assets	$3,218.5	net worth	$3,218.5

Source: *Federal Reserve Bulletin*, April 1990, Table 1.25.

either by writing a check to someone who would deposit it in another bank or by walking up to the teller's window and asking for currency. Today the minimum level of reserves is not left to the judgment of banks; rather, federal regulations require banks to hold reserves equal to a certain percentage of certain categories of deposits. As we will see in Chapter 12, the Federal Reserve's power to regulate the level of reserves in the banking system is a major tool of monetary policy. Other cash assets, shown in line 3 of the balance sheet and sometimes known as *secondary reserves*, give banks the liquidity to meet unexpected needs.

The next two items on the assets side of the balance sheet show the banks' main income-earning assets. The largest item is loans made to firms and households. In addition, commercial banks hold a substantial quantity of securities, including securities issued by federal, state, and local governments. The final item on this side includes some smaller income-earning items plus the value of the banks' buildings and equipment.

Liabilities.   The first three items on the liabilities side of the banks' balance sheet are various kinds of deposits. They are liabilities because they represent funds to which depositors hold a legal claim.

Funds that banks have borrowed are also liabilities. A small portion of these are borrowed from the Federal Reserve and the rest from private sources. Because the banks' total liabilities are less than their assets, they have a positive net worth. This sum represents the claim of the banks' owners against the banks' assets.

The Federal Reserve System

We have already mentioned the Federal Reserve System, or the *Fed*, as it is known in financial circles. The Fed is the central banking system of the United States. It operates a check-clearing system, runs a system for wire transfers of funds, and provides other banking services to private banks and thrifts as well as to the federal government. It is one of the chief regulators and supervisors of the banking system. Its responsibility for monetary policy makes it a major partner with Congress and the executive branch in macroeconomic policymaking.

The Fed was established in 1913 as an independent agency of the federal government and therefore is not under the direction of the executive branch. It is subordinate to Congress, but Congress does not intervene in its day-to-day decision making. The reason for making the Fed independent was to prevent the Department of the Treasury from using monetary policy for political purposes. In practice, however, the Fed's monetary actions are coordinated with the Treasury's fiscal actions. The chair of the Fed's Board of Governors is in frequent contact with the secretary of the Treasury, the chair of the President's Council of Economic Advisers, and the director of the Office of Management and Budget. By law, the Fed also presents a formal report to Congress twice a year. It also explains how its monetary policy objectives are related to economic conditions and to the economic goals set by the administration and Congress.

Federal Reserve banks. The structure of the Federal Reserve System is shown in Exhibit 11.3. At the heart of the system are the 12 Federal Reserve banks. These district banks have 25 branches. The district boundaries and the banks' locations are shown in panel (b) of the exhibit.

Each Federal Reserve bank is a separate unit chartered by the federal government. Its stockholders are commercial banks that are members of the Federal Reserve System. Although Federal Reserve banks issue stock to their members, they are not typical private firms in that they are neither operated for profit nor ultimately controlled by their stockholders. The Federal Reserve banks earn income from their holdings of federal securities and, since 1981, from charges for services provided to banks and thrift institutions. Each year the Reserve banks return all their income, minus operating costs, to the Treasury.

Each bank is managed by a nine-member board. Six of those members are selected by the member banks; the other three are appointed by the Fed's Board of Governors. Each board sets the policies of its own bank under the supervision of the Board of Governors. The Board of Governors also approves the appointments of each Reserve bank's top officers.

The Federal Reserve banks perform a number of important functions in the banking system; these include clearing checks, handling reserve deposits, and making loans to depository institutions. They also issue paper currency in the form of Federal Reserve notes and supply Treasury coins. Finally, they provide banking services to the Treasury.

The Board of Governors. The highest policymaking body of the Federal Reserve System is its Board of Governors. The Board, which supervises the 12 Federal Reserve banks, has seven members who are appointed by the president and confirmed by the Senate. Each governor serves a single 14-year term, with one term expiring every other year. The president appoints one of the board members to serve as chair for a four-year term.

The Board of Governors has the power to approve changes in the interest rate on loans made to banks and thrifts by the Reserve banks. It also sets, within limits determined by law, the minimum level of reserves that banks and thrifts are required to hold relative to certain deposits. The Board supervises and regulates many types of banking institutions, including state-chartered member

Exhibit 11.3   Structure of the Federal Reserve System

Panel (a) of this exhibit shows the structure of the Federal Reserve System. The highest policymaking body of the Fed is the Board of Governors. The map in panel (b) gives the locations of the 12 Federal Reserve banks.

(a)

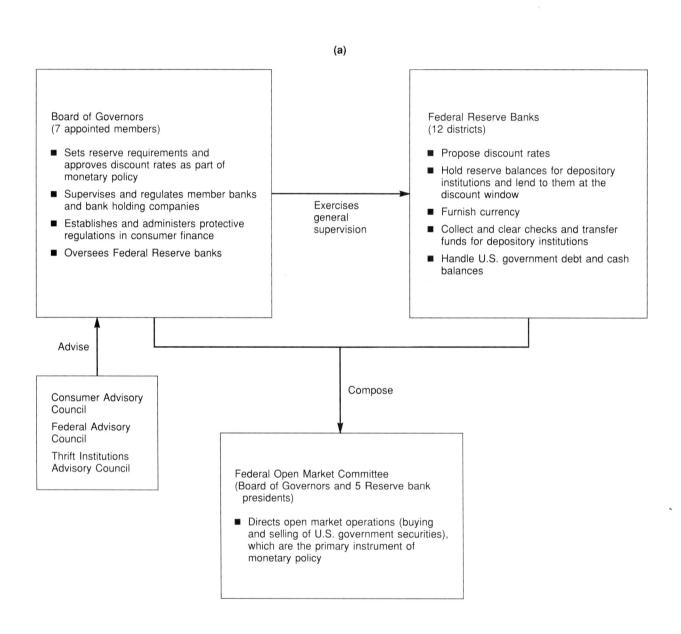

Source: Board of Governors, Federal Reserve System, *The Federal Reserve System: Purposes and Functions*, 7th ed. (Washington, D.C.: Federal Reserve System, 1984), 5, 8.

(b)

Seattle
Portland
Helena
⑨
Minneapolis ◉
⑦
Detroit
Buffalo
①
Boston ◉
②
New York
Philadelphia ◉
③
Pittsburgh
Chicago
Cleveland
Omaha
Cincinnati
④
Baltimore
WASHINGTON
⑫
Culpeper
Richmond ◉
San Francisco ◉
Salt Lake City
⑩
Kansas City ◉
St. Louis ◉
⑧
Louisville
⑤
Denver
Charlotte
Nashville
Los Angeles
Oklahoma City
Little Rock
Memphis
Birmingham
Atlanta ◉
⑥
Dallas ◉
El Paso
⑪
Jacksonville
Houston
New Orleans
San Antonio
Miami

HAWAII
⑫

ALASKA
⑫

———— Boundaries of Federal Reserve districts

———— Boundaries of Federal Reserve branch territories

◉ Board of Governors of the Federal Reserve System

◉ Federal Reserve bank cities

● Federal Reserve branch cities

■ Federal Reserve bank facility

banks, bank holding companies, and U.S. offices of foreign banks. It also approves bank mergers and implements consumer credit regulations.

The Federal Open Market Committee.   Authority over purchases and sales of government securities held by the Fed—its most important monetary policy tool—rests with the Federal Open Market Committee (FOMC). The FOMC is made up of the seven members of the Board of Governors plus five district bank presidents. The president of the Federal Reserve Bank of New York is a permanent member; the remaining four seats rotate among the other 11 district banks. The committee meets about eight times a year (and also confers by telephone) to set a general strategy for monetary policy. Committee decisions regarding changes in the Fed's holdings of securities are carried out through the open market trading desk of the Federal Reserve Bank of New York.

Member and nonmember banks.   As of the end of 1989, 5,204 of the country's 12,706 commercial banks, including most large banks, were members of the Federal Reserve System. National banks—those that are chartered by the federal government—are required to be members; state-chartered banks may or may not be members. Until 1980 member banks enjoyed certain privileges and received free services from the Fed, but in return they were subject to generally stricter regulation than nonmember banks, especially with regard to minimum reserve levels. The reserve requirements were felt to be burdensome, and as a result many banks decided to leave the Federal Reserve System. This made it more difficult to conduct monetary policy.

In 1980 Congress passed the Depository Institutions Deregulation and Monetary Control Act, which did away with many of the distinctions between member and nonmember banks and between commercial banks and thrift institutions. As a result, since 1980 member banks, nonmember commercial banks, savings and loans, savings banks, and credit unions have all been subject to more uniform reserve requirements. In return, thrift institutions won the right to compete more directly with commercial banks in making certain types of loans and offering transaction accounts. Nonmember institutions achieved access to Fed services such as check clearing, wire transfers, and loans on the same terms as member banks. In 1982 small depository institutions were exempted from reserve requirements. As a result of the Monetary Control Act, the distinction between banks and thrift institutions became less important.

The Fed's balance sheet.   Exhibit 11.4 shows a balance sheet for the Federal Reserve System. Government securities are by far the Fed's largest asset. As we will see in Chapter 12, these security holdings play a key role in the Fed's control of the money stock. Loans to banks and thrifts are small compared with other assets, but they are listed separately because they are important for policy purposes. Normally these loans are made to depository institutions on a short-term basis to enable them to meet their reserve requirements. However, in special circumstances longer-term loans are made to banks and thrifts that are experiencing a seasonal need for funds or financial difficulties. Other assets include those denominated in foreign currencies; these are important in carrying out the Fed's functions in the international monetary system.

Federal Reserve notes, which account for almost all of the nation's stock of currency, are the Fed's largest liability. These are followed by the reserves deposited with the Fed by banks and thrifts. Other liabilities include deposits of

Exhibit 11.4 Consolidated Balance Sheet of the Federal Reserve Banks
January 31, 1990 (Billions of Dollars)

The Federal Reserve banks have liabilities to the general public in the form of
Federal Reserve notes and to banks and thrifts in the form of reserve deposits.
The Fed's main assets are government securities. Loans to banks with which to
meet reserve requirements are small, but they are a key aspect of banking and
monetary policy.

Assets		Liabilities and Net Worth	
Securities	$224.9	Federal reserve notes	$234.5
Loans to banks and thrifts	0.7	Reserves on deposit	29.5
Other assets	66.4	Other liabilities and net worth	28.0
Total	$292.0	Total	$292.0

Source: *Federal Reserve Bulletin*, April 1990, Table 1.18.

the Treasury and of foreign central banks. Because the Fed's assets exceed its
liabilities, it has a positive net worth.

11.3 Ensuring the Safety and Stability of the Banking System

Banks play a vital role in our economy, yet we often take them for granted until
they experience problems. Unfortunately, parts of the banking system have experienced serious problems in recent years. Headlines about bank and thrift
failures and financial wrongdoing have become all too common. This section
looks at the sources of these failures and also at the policies used by government
to ensure that the problems of individual institutions do not threaten the safety
and stability of the banking system as a whole.

Risks of Banking

Banks earn a profit by lending the deposits they receive or by using them to buy
securities at interest rates higher than those they pay to depositors. Banks have
been earning profits in this way for hundreds of years, but there are some well-
known risks involved.

One is the risk of loan losses. What happens if a bank makes a loan to a
customer who is unable to repay it? When a loan goes bad, the bank's net worth
is reduced by an equal amount. (In balance sheet terms, writing off the bad loan
is a reduction in assets. Liabilities—that is, deposits and borrowing—do not
change. Therefore, net worth, which equals assets minus liabilities, must fall.) If
loan losses are too great, the bank's net worth may fall below zero. At that point
the bank will no longer have enough assets to pay off all of its depositors and
other creditors. A bank whose liabilities exceed its assets is said to be *insolvent*
and usually must cease doing business.

A second risk that banks face is *illiquidity*, that is, having insufficient liquid assets to cover withdrawals. When a depositor withdraws funds from a bank, the bank pays partly by drawing down the reserves it holds on deposit with the Fed and partly by drawing down other liquid assets that it holds for this purpose. Under normal conditions new deposits approximately offset withdrawals, and the bank does not need to draw on its less liquid assets, such as loans and long-term securities, to cover withdrawals. If an unexpected wave of withdrawals occurs, however, the bank may use up all of its liquid assets. It will then have to convert some of its less liquid assets into cash. This may not be easy, especially if the wave of withdrawals takes place when business conditions are unfavorable, requiring the bank to sell the assets at less than the value at which they are entered on the bank's books. For example, a bank might have paid $1,000,000 for bonds issued by a state government agency at the time the bonds were issued. Later it might have to sell them, under unfavorable market conditions, for just $800,000. Sales of assets at less than book value have an effect on the balance sheet similar to that of loan losses: in accordance with the basic equation of accounting, the reduction in the value of assets causes an equal reduction of the bank's net worth. If net worth falls below zero, the bank becomes insolvent.

Whether the bank's troubles begin with loan losses or with illiquidity, there is a danger that they may trigger a run on the bank. A *run* is a situation in which depositors begin to withdraw their funds because they fear that the bank may become insolvent. Afraid that the bank may be able to pay only the first in line, depositors compete for first place. Thus, their fears become self-fulfilling and the bank fails.

In the worst possible case, the whole banking system, not just one bank, could get into trouble. If many banks faced loan losses or runs at the same time, they could not help one another with temporary loans of reserves. If large banks failed, smaller banks, which keep deposits in the large ones or make other loans to them, might be brought down, too. If many banks simultaneously tried to meet deposit outflows by selling their holdings of securities, the market price of the securities might fall, adding to their losses. A general bank *panic*, in which the stability of the whole system would be threatened, could ensue.

Policies to Ensure Safety and Soundness

During the nineteenth century a number of bank panics were touched off by recessions. Both state and federal governments experimented with policies designed to ensure the safety and soundness of the banking system. Out of these efforts has evolved a system that is based on three basic tools: bank supervision and regulation, loans to troubled banks, and deposit insurance.

Supervision and regulation.   Bank inspections were the first tool devised to ensure the banking system's safety and soundness. These inspections, conducted by state or federal officials, were intended to ensure that banks did not make unduly risky loans, that they valued their assets honestly, and that they maintained an adequate level of net worth. Honest bookkeeping, prudent lending, and adequate net worth, it was hoped, would enable banks to survive business downturns without becoming insolvent. Today a variety of federal and state agencies, including the Federal Reserve and the Comptroller of the Currency (part of the Treasury) share responsibility for supervision and regulation. Bank inspections are conducted as part of the process of enforcing a battery of banking regulations designed to ensure the safety and soundness of the system. Among the most important of these are *capital requirements*, under which net worth must be kept at or above a minimum fraction of all assets.

At the end of 1990, all banking regulatory agencies are to begin phasing in so-called risk-based capital standards. Under these regulations, relatively risky assets will require proportionately more capital as backing. This regulation has been introduced in compliance with an international agreement known as the Basle Accord.

Loans to illiquid banks.   Despite inspections, banking panics continued to occur. In 1907 an especially severe panic took place, eventually leading to the establishment of the Federal Reserve System in 1913. Among other duties, the Fed was given the power to aid the banking system in times of trouble by acting as a lender of last resort. This function remains important today. For example, when the stock market experienced a record 22.6 percent loss on October 19, 1987, the Fed quickly announced that it stood ready to lend extra funds to any banks that needed additional cash because of customers' stock market losses.

Deposit insurance.   Even with these powers, the Fed failed to prevent a major bank panic in 1933, during the Great Depression. At that time business conditions were so bad that even loans that had appeared prudent when they were made during the 1920s were not paid off. The Fed's power to lend reserves to troubled banks was not enough to maintain public confidence in the banking system. Panicky depositors converted hundreds of millions of dollars of deposits into currency, and bank failures became widespread.

In response to the collapse of the banking system, Congress established the Federal Deposit Insurance Corporation (FDIC) in 1934. A similar fund, the Federal Savings and Loan Insurance Corporation (FSLIC), was later set up to insure deposits at savings and loan associations. Since the Monetary Control Act of 1980, all deposits are insured up to $100,000 per customer per institution and even more in special cases. In 1989, for reasons to be discussed shortly, the insurance funds were reorganized and the FSLIC was dissolved.

The idea of deposit insurance is to short-circuit runs on banks. If deposits are insured, depositors need not run to the bank to withdraw their funds; even if the bank fails, the government will pay them their money or arrange for the transfer of their deposits to a solvent bank. Also, if runs can be avoided, the problems of one or a few banks will not touch off a panic that threatens the whole system. Depository institutions are supposed to bear the cost of deposit insurance through premiums charged by the insurance funds. However, in recent years, premiums have fallen short of costs and taxpayers have had to cover the insurance funds' losses.

The Banking System in the 1990s: Problems and Prospects

For the past half-century the U.S. banking system has avoided a repeat of the general collapse that led to nationwide bank closures and contributed to mass unemployment during the Great Depression. However, it has not been all calm waters and smooth sailing. During the 1980s failures of banks and thrifts reached their highest rates in the post-World War II period. And some economists see fundamental flaws in the policies used by the federal government to ensure the safety and soundness of the banking system.

The savings and loan crisis.   The most publicized problems have involved the collapse of high-flying savings and loan associations. For decades, the savings and loan industry was a quiet and conservative side street in the financial marketplace. Most savings and loan associations were small, and all were required under federal regulations to channel the bulk of their lending to home mortgages. In compensation for tight restrictions on lending practices, S&Ls were allowed to pay depositors a slightly higher interest rate than that paid by commercial banks.

Reforms of financial regulations in the early 1980s lifted many of the restrictions on the operations of S&Ls. They were allowed to enter markets for riskier commercial real estate loans and to buy a broader variety of securities. At the same time, all restrictions on interest paid to depositors were removed, and S&Ls and banks were left free to compete for depositors' loyalty. Some prudently managed S&Ls grew into strong competitors of commercial banks in the new, less strictly regulated environment. Unfortunately, however, the industry was invaded by many less prudent operators who turned sleepy small-town S&Ls into financial giants overnight by means of high-risk, high-reward lending practices. By the end of the 1980s dozens of these financial empires had collapsed amidst charges of fraud and mismanagement. *Economics in the News 11.1* provides a sampler of S&L horror stories.

The savings and loan crisis reveals weaknesses in all three major aspects of the federal government's policies for ensuring the safety and stability of the banking system.

- Supervision and regulation did not ensure sound banking practices. Inspections did not spot bad loans; often inspectors were deceived by fraudulent practices of S&L operators. Capital requirements were either watered down by Congress or not enforced by regulators; many institutions were allowed to operate without an adequate cushion of net worth.

- Loans by the Fed to troubled institutions are useful primarily as a device to help fundamentally sound and solvent banks during temporary periods of illiquidity. They cannot solve the problems of banks and thrifts that have fallen into insolvency because of imprudent management practices leading to massive loan losses.

- Deposit insurance can help prevent bank runs; however, in the 1980s S&L losses were so large that the FSLIC itself was forced into insolvency. Deposit insurance also encouraged S&Ls to take undue risks with their depositors' money; the depositors did not object, knowing that the federal government would bail them out if the institution failed.

Coping with the crisis.   In 1989 Congress passed the Financial Institutions Reform, Recovery, and Enforcement Act of 1989 (FIRREA) in an attempt to resolve the crisis in the troubled savings and loan industry. The act has a number of provisions.

One set of provisions completely reorganizes deposit insurance. The FSLIC was dissolved and separate Bank Insurance Funds (BIF) and Savings Association Insurance Funds (SAIF) were established under administrative authority of the FDIC. Thrifts insured by the SAIF were required to meet regulatory standards that are no less stringent as those to which commercial banks are subject. Thrifts were also required to invest a higher minimum percentage of their assets

Economics in the News   11.1
The Savings and Loan Crisis

In recent years the U.S. financial system has faced a serious crisis: the failure of hundreds of savings and loan institutions. As of January 1, 1990, roughly one-third of the nation's 2,941 S&Ls were in trouble. Federal authorities had taken control of 393 institutions; 157 were insolvent but still operating; and 400 more, which were operating with inadequate capital, were considered to be threatened by insolvency. Behind these numbers lay some spectacular tales of imprudent risk taking and outright fraud by the industry's high rollers. Some examples:

- In 1983 David Paul took over the virtually insolvent Dade Savings and Loan Association of Miami, Florida. In five years he built it into the largest thrift institution in the southeastern United States, with $8.2 billion in assets. The skyscraper that he built as headquarters for his financial empire, renamed CenTrust, dominated the skyline in the opening shot of the "Miami Vice" television series. Money flowed freely: In one promotional extravaganza, Paul flew in six chefs from France to star in a dinner party that cost $122,726.20. To generate the income needed to pay for such activities, he loaded the asset side of the institution's balance sheet with high-yield, poorly secured "junk bonds." When the market for junk bonds collapsed, CenTrust crashed with it. Federal officials seized the "unsafe and unsound" institution in February 1990.

- Citizen's Savings and Loan of Grand Prairie, Texas, had modest assets of $40.5 million when Thomas M. Gaubert bought it in 1983. He renamed it Independent American Savings Association and launched it on a growth trajectory that peaked at $1.86 billion in assets. Gaubert invested heavily in the booming Texas real estate market of the mid-1980s. In that market it was common for bankers to make loans that exceeded the purchase price of a property and to rely for income on huge loan origination fees rather than on interest payments.

Sources: Based on Myra MacPherson, "The Banker's Toppled Tower," *The Washington Post*, March 19, 1990, C1; Leonard M. Apcar, "Texas S&L Disasters Are Blamed, in Part, on Freewheeling Style," *The Wall Street Journal*, July 13, 1987, 1; Brooks Jackson, "How Regulatory Error Led to the Disaster at Lincoln Savings," *The Wall Street Journal*, November 20, 1989, A1.

In the hope of holding federal regulators at bay, Gaubert and others in the Texas thrift industry gave generously to the campaign funds of Democratic congressional candidates. Today the Texas thrift industry lies in ruins, brought down by the collapse of the oil market and a plunge in real estate values. Dallas alone has vacant office space equivalent to 17 Empire State Buildings. Gaubert no longer runs Independent American; the insolvent institution now operates under federal supervision.

- In 1984, less than five years after the Securities and Exchange Commission had charged Charles Keating, Jr., with fraud in an Ohio loan scam, regulators decided to let him buy Lincoln Savings and Loan in California. Within days Keating began firing Lincoln's conservative loan officers and auditors and plunging into high-risk but often profitable speculation in currency futures, junk bonds, hotels, and land in the Arizona desert. Regulators in California became alarmed at Lincoln's operations. In 1987 they sent a recommendation to Washington asking the FSLIC to take over the institution and asking the FBI to look into possible criminal charges. The Washington regulators moved slowly, however. It was later alleged that five U.S. senators, for whom Keating had arranged $1.4 million in campaign donations, had used their influence to delay regulatory action. By the time the regulators finally acted, Lincoln's losses had soared. It is estimated that cleaning up the mess at Lincoln will ultimately cost U.S. taxpayers as much as $2.5 billion, making it the most expensive S&L failure of all.

Paul, Gaubert, Keating, and many other former officers of failed thrifts deny that they have engaged in any wrongdoing. They portray themselves as aggressive but law-abiding entrepreneurs who are victims of "rules changed in midstream." They say that they were encouraged by federal regulatory changes to enter admittedly risky but potentially highly profitable lines of business. When circumstances changed, they complain, regulators cut them off at the knees.

Whoever is to blame, freewheeling entrepreneurs or erratic government regulators, taxpayers will be the ones to pick up the tab. The cost of having the government take over failed thrifts, dispose of their assets at prices far below book value, and pay off their insured depositors will total as much as $200 billion, according to some estimates.

in long-term housing loans and to divest themselves of certain categories of risky assets.

Other parts of FIRREA provide a mechanism for raising the funds needed to close failed institutions or to merge them with sound banks or thrifts on favorable terms. This process is expected to cost federal taxpayers $200 billion or more over the course of the 1990s above and beyond what can be recovered by selling the marketable assets of insolvent thrifts taken over by the federal government, but much of the cost will ultimately be borne by the taxpayer.

The future of deposit insurance.   Many critics of federal banking policy have focused on deposit insurance as a key element in the current crisis. For decades, deposit insurance has been viewed as crucial to maintaining the safety and stability of the banking system. However, an increasing number of observers have come to view it as a destabilizing element instead. In their view, it makes it too easy for poorly managed banks to attract deposits.

Suppose there were no insurance, the argument goes, so that people knew they would lose everything if a bank where they held deposits were to fail. In such a case depositors would carefully check the soundness of the bank before they did business with it. They would look at the quality of the bank's assets: Are its loans backed by adequate collateral? Are the securities it invests in of the highest quality? They would also look for banks with a strong net worth. Adequate net worth provides a cushion against loan losses, and it also shows that the bank's owners are willing to put their own funds at risk alongside those of depositors.

If deposits were uninsured, then, banks with low-quality assets or low net worth would be unable to attract deposits or would be able to do so only by offering a much higher interest rate on deposits than that paid by their sounder competitors. On the other hand, if deposits are insured, depositors have little reason to care whether a bank is sound or not. If it pays even a fraction of a percent more interest on its deposits, they will be willing to move funds from sound banks into the weak one, knowing that the federal government will make good on the deposits if the bank fails.

Several possible reforms of deposit insurance have been suggested. All aim to retain the benefits of deposit insurance while minimizing the dangers noted by its critics:

- The $100,000 limit on insured deposits could be strictly enforced or even lowered. The idea behind such a move is that firms and individuals with hundreds of thousands or millions of dollars on deposit are those with the greatest ability and motivation to check the quality of the institutions in which they maintain deposits.
- A deductible clause could be inserted in federal deposit insurance so that, say, the first $5,000 of deposits would be uninsured. That would encourage small depositors to be careful where they put their money, just as deductible clauses in automobile insurance encourage people to drive more carefully.
- The premiums that banks pay for deposit insurance could be restructured to reflect the soundness of the bank's operations. Currently all banks pay the same low premium, and all thrifts pay a premium that is only slightly higher. Instead, institutions that made risky loans or carried inadequate net worth could be charged much higher premiums,

much as people who smoke are charged higher premiums for life insurance than nonsmokers.

To date, none of these reforms has been adopted, but they are receiving increasing attention among academic economists and policymakers.

Free banking.   Recent threats to the stability of the banking system have stimulated interest in more radical proposals than simply modifying current regulations. Of these, perhaps the most radical is *free banking*, or complete deregulation of banking. This would mean not only abolishing bank inspections, deposit insurance, reserve requirements, and the like, but also eliminating any government role in the nation's monetary system. Even the issuance of coins and paper currency would be taken over by private banks.

Free banking is not a new idea. Many countries, including Scotland, Canada, China, Australia, and South Africa, have had free banking systems at one time or another, although all have central banks now. The United States never had an entirely free banking system, but some elements of such a system, including issuance of paper currency by private commercial banks, were in operation during much of the nineteenth century.

Proponents of free banking count on competition rather than regulation to ensure the safety and soundness of the banking system. They argue that bankers would have enough incentive to maintain adequate reserves and net worth and to make only prudent loans if they were forced to compete for deposits in a world without federal deposit insurance. History does provide at least some examples of banking systems that remained stable for sustained periods under the discipline of market competition.

A majority of economists remain skeptical, however. They argue that during bank panics failing banks can pull down sound institutions. They also argue that a strong central bank is needed to maintain control of the overall size of the money stock and thereby control inflation. Free bankers counter that central banking did not prevent bank panics in the 1930s, nor did it prevent inflation in the 1970s.

The immediate future is far more likely to see continued tinkering with existing regulations than more radical reforms. However, if the kinds of problems encountered by the savings and loan industry in the 1980s spread to commercial banks in the 1990s, radical proposals might attract increasing interest.

Summary

1. **What is money, and what does it do?** *Money* is an asset that serves as a means of payment, a store of purchasing power, and a unit of account. To serve as money an asset must be generally accepted and limited in supply. Because money can be used as a means of payment and has a fixed nominal value, it is said to be *liquid*.

2. **How is the stock of money in the economy measured?** A narrowly defined measure of the money stock, known as *M1*, includes the most commonly used means of payment: *currency* (coins and paper money) plus *transaction deposits* (deposits on which

checks can be freely written). A broader measure, *M2*, which is favored by many economists for purposes of model building, includes the components of M1 plus a number of assets that serve as a liquid store of purchasing power but have limited usefulness in making transactions. These include money market mutual fund shares, money market deposit accounts, *savings deposits*, small-denomination *time deposits*, overnight *repurchase agreements*, and certain other liquid assets. The relationship between money and other economic variables can be stated as the *equation of exchange:* $MV = Py$, in which M stands for the money stock, V for *velocity*, P for the price level, and y for real national product.

3. **What is the structure of the U.S. banking system?** The U.S. banking system consists of four types of *depository institutions*. The most important are *commercial banks*, which specialize in commercial loans and transaction deposits. In addition, there are three types of *thrift institution:* savings and loan associations, savings banks, and credit unions. These can also offer transaction deposits, but they make a relatively limited number of commercial loans. The Federal Reserve System is the nation's central bank. It provides services to depository institutions, holds much of their required *reserves*, and, together with other federal agencies, regulates the banking system.

4. **How are the safety and stability of the banking system maintained?** Banks fail if they become insolvent, that is, if their assets fall below the level of their liabilities. This may happen because of loan losses or because deposit withdrawals have exhausted liquid assets. The government has three principal tools for ensuring the safety and soundness of the banking system: supervision and regulation; loans to banks and thrifts experiencing liquidity problems; and deposit insurance.

Terms for Review

- money
- liquidity
- currency
- transaction deposit
- commercial banks
- thrift institutions (thrifts)
- depository institutions
- M1
- savings deposit
- time deposit
- repurchase agreement (RP)
- M2
- equation of exchange
- velocity (income velocity of money)
- balance sheet
- assets
- liabilities
- net worth
- reserves

Questions for Review

1. What properties make an asset suitable for use as money? What are some examples of assets that serve as money in the U.S. economy today? In other economies, past or present?

2. List some assets that you own, ranging from the most to the least liquid.

3. What assets most frequently serve as means of payment? List some assets that serve as a liquid store of purchasing power but rarely, if ever, are used as a means of payment.

4. State the equation of exchange. What is the meaning of the term *velocity* as used in the equation of exchange?

5. What characteristics distinguish commercial banks, savings and loan associations, savings banks, and credit unions from one another? What distinguishes them from other financial intermediaries?

6. What is the role of the Federal Reserve System? The Federal Reserve banks? The Board of Governors of the Federal Reserve? The Federal Open Market Committee?

7. What does it mean to say that a bank is *insolvent?* To say that it is *illiquid?* What circumstances can cause these conditions?

8. What are the policy tools used to ensure the safety and soundness of the U.S. banking system? How well have these tools worked in recent years?

Problems and Topics for Discussion

1. **Examining the lead-off case.** What characteristics of stone wheels make it possible for them to serve as money in the Yap economy? Why are other forms of money used for some transactions? Discuss.

2. **The functions of money.** Money serves three functions: as a means of payment, a store of purchasing power, and a unit of account. How does inflation undermine each of these functions?

3. **Barter in the modern economy.** For most purposes money lowers the cost of making transactions relative to barter — the direct exchange of one good or service for another. However, barter has not disappeared, even in an advanced economy such as that of the United States. Can you give an example of the use of barter in the U.S. economy today? Why is barter used instead of money in this case?

4. **Plastic money.** Do you use any credit cards? Does their use reduce the amount of money you need? Which forms of money do you need less of because you have a credit card?

5. **The banking balance sheet.** Go to a commercial bank or thrift institution in your area and ask for a copy of a summary balance sheet (these are readily available at most banks). How does this balance sheet compare with that of all commercial banks as given in Exhibit 11.2? (*Bonus question:* Obtain and compare the balance sheets of a bank and a thrift.)

6. **Current monetary data.** Every Thursday the Federal Reserve reports certain key data on money and the banking system. These are published in the Friday edition of *The Wall Street Journal* and other major financial newspapers. Find the Federal Reserve report from *The Wall Street Journal* for the most recent Friday and use it to answer the following questions:

   a. What items are included in M2 that are not included in M1? What was the total of such items in the most recent month for which data are reported? M3 is a money supply measure that includes large-denomination certificates of deposit and long-term repurchase agreements. What is the total of these items? Which of these money measures grew most quickly in the most recent month for which data are reported?

   b. The tables report key assets and liabilities of the ten leading New York banks. Demand and other transaction deposits at these banks account for about what percentage of M1?

7. **Recent bank failures.** Look in *The Wall Street Journal* or another business publication for news of a recent failure of a bank or thrift institution. Why did the institution fail? How did federal authorities respond to the failure?

Case for Discussion

Makeshift Money in the French Colonial Period

The following letter was written by de Meulle, governor of the French province of Quebec, in September 1685:

My Lord—

I have found myself this year in great straits with regard to the subsistence of the soldiers. You did not provide for funds, My Lord, until January last. I have, notwithstanding, kept them in provisions until September, which makes eight full months. I have drawn from my own funds and from those of my friends, all I have been able to get, but at last finding them without means to render me further assistance, and not knowing to what saint to pay my vows, money being extremely scarce, having distributed considerable sums on every side for the pay of the soldiers, it occurred to me to issue, instead of money, notes on [playing] cards, which I have had cut in quarters. I send you My Lord, the three kinds, one is for four francs, another for forty sols, and the third for fifteen sols, because with these three kinds, I was able to make their exact pay for one month. I have issued an ordinance by which I have obliged all the inhabitants to receive this money in payments, and to give it circulation, at the same time pledging myself, in my own name, to redeem the said notes. No person has refused them, and so good has been the effect that by this means the troops have lived as usual. There were some merchants who, privately, had offered me money at the local rate on condition that I would repay them in money at the rate in France, to which I could not consent as the King would have lost a third; that is, for 10,000 he would have paid 40,000 livres; thus personally, by my credit and by my management, I have saved His Majesty 13,000 livres.
[Signed] de Meulle
Quebec, 24th September, 1685

Source: From *Canadian Currency, Exchange and Finance During the French Period*, vol. 1, ed. Adam Shortt (New York: Burt Franklin, Research Source Works Series no. 235, 1968).

Questions

1. What indication do you find that the playing-card notes issued by the governor served as a means of payment? Why were they accepted as such?

2. What indicates that the notes served as a store of value? What made them acceptable as such?

3. Did the invention of playing-card money change the unit of account in the local economy?

Suggestions for Further Reading

Board of Governors, Federal Reserve System. *The Federal Reserve System: Purposes and Functions,* 7th ed. Washington, D.C.: Federal Reserve System, 1984.

This useful booklet provides many details on topics covered in this and the following chapters. A copy can be obtained free from Publications Services, Division of Support Services, Board of Governors of the Federal Reserve System, Washington, DC 20551.

Federal Reserve Bank of New York. *The Story of Money; The Story of Checks and Electronic Payments; The Story of Consumer Credit; The Story of Banks; The Story of Inflation.*

These comic-book-style publications of the Federal Reserve Bank of New York look almost silly, but they pack in a lot of information that textbooks leave out. They are available from the bank's Public Information Department, 33 Liberty Street, New York, NY 10045.

Federal Reserve Bulletin, monthly.

Each issue contains the most recent monetary data, which can be used to update the exhibits in this chapter.

Selgin, George A. *The Theory of Free Banking.* Washington, D.C.: Cato Institute, 1988.

A comprehensive study of the theory of an entirely unregulated banking system.

12

Central Banking and Money Creation

Before reading this chapter, make sure you know the meaning of:

M1, M2 (Chapter 11)

Balance sheets (Chapter 11)

Federal Reserve System (Chapter 11)

Federal Open Market Committee (Chapter 11)

Bank reserves (Chapter 11)

After reading this chapter, you will understand:

How banks create money.

Why the size of the money stock is limited by the quantity of bank reserves.

The instruments available to the Fed for controlling the money stock.

How closely the money stock can be controlled.

The activities that the Fed undertakes in the international sphere.

Inside the Fed

As powerfully as the moon affects the tides, the Federal Reserve System influences American finance and business. Like the moon, the Fed is mysterious, unseen most of the time, and only partly illuminated the rest. Here H. Robert Heller, who served on the Fed's Board of Governors under Chairmen Paul Volcker and Alan Greenspan, tells what it was like to be a member of this august group.

One of the most breathtaking moments of my life was the first time I walked into a meeting of the Federal Open Market Committee. Volcker had administered the oath of office to me at 8:55 a.m. on August 19, 1986. Then the door to the boardroom, which adjoins his office, opened, and we walked into an FOMC meeting, which began at nine o'clock. Everybody was already seated at the table, and they all rose. It was sort of like being inducted into the College of Cardinals.

Then the discussion started. I was trying to keep track of the various positions. There was a broad range of views, with some advocating a little easier monetary policy, and some a little tighter. And I thought, "My God, what if I'm the swing vote?" Cold sweat started running down my back. Finally, when it came to the roll call, to my enormous surprise almost everybody agreed to ease monetary policy slightly.

I began to realize that the FOMC is an enormous consensus builder. That makes it very different from the Supreme Court. Five-to-four decisions are the rule there. What we tend to see here is either 12-0 or 11-1 decisions. Though people walk into the meeting with somewhat divergent views, the sharp edges are worn off in discussion. Eventually a consensus emerges and is formulated by the chairman. Following further discussion and possible modification of the chairman's proposal, it is put to a vote. You think: Can I associate myself sufficiently with the consensus to vote yes, or am I so opposed that I must say, "This policy would be unacceptable." I never dissented, and I'm proud of that, because I believe I helped to build that consensus.

Photo source: UPI/Bettmann Newsphotos.

Writing a check, getting an auto loan, getting cash from an automatic teller machine — these are the kinds of interactions most people have with the banking system. We do these things without much thought. Yet, as this chapter will show, each of these actions sends tiny ripples through the financial system. Each depositor's and each borrower's actions ultimately influence and are influenced by decision makers throughout the financial system, including those who sit on the Federal Open Market Committee. Understanding the linkages among banks, their customers, and government agencies is critical to understanding how the banking system works and how the stock of money is determined.

This chapter draws on the description of the banking system presented in Chapter 11. We begin by examining how banks create money in a simplified system. Then we discuss the tools that the Federal Reserve uses to control the money stock within the country. Finally we look briefly at the Fed's role in international financial markets.

12.1   The Creation of Money

As we saw in Chapter 11, the bulk of the U.S. money supply consists of the liabilities of banks and thrift institutions. In this section we will see how these institutions create money on the basis of reserves supplied by the Federal Reserve System.

A Simplified Banking System

As we have done in building models of other parts of the economy, we begin with a simplified situation; details will be added later. Initially we will deal with the following simplified banking system:

1. The system consists of ten identical banks.
2. The banks' only assets are loans and reserve deposits at the Fed; there is no vault cash.
3. The banks' only liabilities are demand deposits; their net worth is zero.
4. Demand deposits are the only form of money in the banking system.
5. The system is regulated by a simplified Federal Reserve System that has the power to set uniform reserve requirements on all deposits.
6. The Fed's only assets are government securities, and its only liabilities are the reserve deposits of member banks. Banks do not borrow reserves from the Fed.

Simplified as it is, this ten-bank system can show us a great deal about the mechanics of money creation in the U.S. banking system.

Required reserves
The minimum amount of reserves that the Fed requires depository institutions to hold.

Required-reserve ratio
Required reserves stated as a percentage of the deposits to which reserve requirements apply.

Excess reserves
Total reserves minus required reserves.

Reserves: required and excess.   The Federal Reserve System sets a minimum percentage of certain categories of deposits that each bank or thrift must hold as reserve deposits with the Fed or as vault cash. These are called **required reserves.** The ratio of required reserves to these deposits is the **required-reserve ratio.** If the bank holds more than the minimum amount of required reserves, the balance is known as **excess reserves.** In equation form, the relationships among required reserves, excess reserves, deposits, and the required-reserve ratio can be stated as follows:

$$\text{Required reserves} = \text{Deposits} \times \text{Required-reserve ratio}$$

and

$$\text{Excess reserves} = \text{Total reserves} - \text{Required reserves.}$$

For our simplified banking system, we will assume a required-reserve ratio of 10 percent on all deposits. This is somewhat below the maximum required-reserve ratio of 12 percent for transaction deposits in the U.S. banking system.

Balance sheet equilibrium.   As profit-seeking firms, banks want to earn all the interest they can; thus, they normally use up almost all their excess reserves by making loans or buying securities. In recent years U.S. banks' excess reserves have tended to be around 2 percent of their total reserves.

Ignoring the small amount of excess reserves that banks hold voluntarily, the situation in which required reserves equal total reserves represents a state of equilibrium. Although banks cannot maintain reserves exactly at their equilibrium level at all times, in our simplified banking system we will assume that banks soon bring their excess reserves back to zero if they temporarily rise above or fall below the desired level.

Mechanics of Money Creation

Now we are ready to examine the mechanics of money creation in our simplified banking system. As the following example will show, money creation is governed by the required-reserve ratio, the amount of reserves supplied, and banks' efforts to maximize their profits.

Initial balance sheets.   Assume that each bank in the system starts out with a balance sheet that looks like this:

Initial Balance Sheet of a Representative Bank

Assets			Liabilities	
Reserves		$ 10,000	Demand deposits	$100,000
Required	$10,000			
Excess	0			
Loans		90,000		
Total assets		$100,000	Total liabilities	$100,000

Also assume that the Fed's initial balance sheet looks like this:

The Fed

Assets		Liabilities	
U.S. government securities	$100,000	Reserve deposits	$100,000

Starting from this point, we will look at the effects of an injection of reserves into the banking system. Each bank receives new reserves every time a customer deposits funds that were withdrawn from another bank. However, this does not increase the reserves in the banking system as a whole. For total reserves to be increased, new reserves must come from outside the system. The chief source of new reserves is the Fed.

Open market operation
A purchase (sale) by the Fed
of government securities
from (to) the public.

Suppose that the Fed decides to increase the amount of reserves available to the banking system by $10,000. It usually does this by adding to its holdings of government securities, buying such securities from a securities dealer. Such an action is called an **open market operation** (in this case, an open market purchase) because the Fed, acting through the Federal Reserve Bank of New York, goes to the securities market and bids against other buyers to purchase the securities. Thus, the Fed buys $10,000 in securities from a dealer and pays for them through a wire transfer to the dealer's bank, which we will call Albany National Bank. The *wire transfer* is an electronic instruction made through the Fed's computer network that credits Albany National Bank's reserve account at the Fed with $10,000 and simultaneously directs the bank to credit the same amount to the dealer's demand-deposit account.

At this point the Fed's initial goal of injecting $10,000 of new reserves into the system has been achieved. The balance sheets of the Fed and Albany National Bank now look like this (changes from the previous balance sheet are shown in parentheses):

The Fed

Assets		Liabilities	
U.S. government securities	$110,000 (+10,000)	Reserve deposits	$110,000 (+10,000)

Albany National Bank

Assets			Liabilities	
Reserves		$ 20,000 (+10,000)	Demand deposits	$110,000 (+10,000)
Required	$11,000 (+1,000)			
Excess	9,000 (+9,000)			
Loans		90,000		
Total assets		$110,000 (+10,000)	Total liabilities	$110,000 (+10,000)

Lending out the excess reserves.   Note how the $10,000 in new reserves at Albany National Bank is divided between required and excess reserves. Deposits have gone up by $10,000, meaning that the bank must hold $1,000 more in required reserves. The other $9,000 in new reserves need not be held against deposits and hence is listed as excess reserves. Albany National Bank is no longer in equilibrium; it can increase its profits by lending out the excess reserves.

Of course, in order to make a loan the bank must find a borrower. Suppose that on the morning on which Albany gets its new reserves James Anderson walks in and applies for a $9,000 auto loan. The loan is granted and the $9,000 is credited to Anderson's checking account balance. (If Anderson had no checking account at Albany, he could instead ask the bank to pay him the proceeds of the loan in the form of a check or even currency. In that case some of the intermediate steps in the following process would differ, but the end result would be the same.) At the moment at which the loan is completed—but before Anderson pays for the car—Albany National Bank's balance sheet looks like this:

Albany National Bank

Assets			Liabilities	
Reserves		$ 20,000	Demand deposits	$119,000
Required	$11,900			
	(+900)			
Excess	8,100			
	(−900)			
Loans		99,000		
		(+9,000)		
Total assets		$119,000	Total liabilities	$119,000
		(+9,000)		(+9,000)

Checking away the loan proceeds. In crediting Anderson's account with
$9,000, Albany National Bank has created a new $9,000 asset (the loan) matched
by a new $9,000 liability (the deposit). Because of the new deposit, its required
reserves have risen by $900. At this point Albany still has $8,100 in excess
reserves. Why, then, does it not use those reserves to make yet another loan?

The reason the bank cannot safely make new loans greater than the original
amount added to its excess reserves is that it knows Anderson will not leave the
$9,000 sitting in his account; instead, he will write a check to pay for his new
car. Let's see what happens when he does so.

We will call the dealer who sells the car Joyce Barnard and assume that she
keeps her checking account at Bethel National Bank. When Barnard deposits
Anderson's Albany National Bank check in her Bethel account, Bethel sends it
to the Fed for clearance. *Clearing the check* simply means that the Fed credits
$9,000 to Bethel's reserve account and subtracts $9,000 from Albany's reserve
account. The Fed then puts the check in the mail so that Albany can forward it
to Anderson for his records. When all these transactions have taken place, the
two banks' balance sheets look like this:

Albany National Bank

Assets			Liabilities	
Reserves		$ 11,000	Demand deposits	$110,000
		(−9,000)		(−9,000)
Required	$11,000			
	(−900)			
Excess	0			
	(−8,100)			
Loans		99,000		
Total assets		$110,000	Total liabilities	$110,000
		(−9,000)		(−9,000)

Bethel National Bank

Assets			Liabilities	
Reserves		$ 19,000	Demand deposits	$109,000
		(+9,000)		(+9,000)
Required	$10,900			
	(+900)			
Excess	8,100			
	(+8,100)			
Loans		90,000		
Total assets		$109,000	Total liabilities	$109,000
		(+9,000)		(+9,000)

A careful look at these balance sheets reveals two important things. First, we clearly see why Albany National Bank could not safely lend out more than its initial $9,000 of excess reserves. It knew that the $9,000 deposit it created by writing the loan to Anderson would not stay on its books for long. As soon as the check cleared, $9,000 of deposits and reserves would be lost (unless the car dealer also kept an account at Albany). The $9,000 loss in deposits lowered its required reserves by only $900 (10 percent of the change in deposits); it needed the $8,100 of excess reserves to make up the difference.

Second, we see that Albany's loss is Bethel's gain. Albany lost $9,000 in reserves ($900 required and $8,100 excess) when the check was written and cleared, and Bethel gained exactly the same amounts. The check-clearing process thus has left the banking system's total reserves unchanged.

Keeping the expansion going with another loan.   The clearing of Anderson's check put Albany National Bank back in equilibrium, with $10,000 more in total assets and $10,000 more in liabilities than it started with. But now Bethel is out of equilibrium, with $8,100 in excess reserves. The logical thing for Bethel to do is to make a loan of its own using its excess reserves. (We now know that the proceeds of this loan will be checked away quickly, so we will skip the intermediate balance sheet.) After Bethel's borrower has written a check for $8,100, which is deposited in, say, Cooperstown National Bank, Bethel's and Cooperstown's balance sheets looks like this:

Bethel National Bank

Assets			Liabilities	
Reserves		$ 10,900 (−8,100)	Demand deposits	$109,000
Required	$10,900 (unchanged)			
Excess	0 (−8,100)			
Loans		98,100 (+8,100)		
Total assets		$109,000	Total liabilities	$109,000

Cooperstown National Bank

Assets			Liabilities	
Reserves		$ 18,100 (+8,100)	Demand deposits	$108,100 (+8,100)
Required	$10,810 (+810)			
Excess	7,290 (+7,290)			
Loans		90,000		
Total assets		$108,100 (+8,100)	Total liabilities	$108,100 (+8,100)

Further rounds in the expansion of deposits.   We need not go through all the rounds of the expansion process in detail, because a clear pattern has emerged. The initial open market purchase of securities by the Fed injected $10,000 of new reserves into the system. The first bank to receive the funds kept $1,000 (10 percent) as required reserves and lent out the remaining $9,000. When the loan proceeds were checked away, they became $9,000 in new deposits and reserves for a second bank, which kept $900 (10 percent) and lent out the remaining $8,100. The next bank, in turn, would be able to lend out $7,290, the next one $6,561, and so on round after round. The loans create new deposits at each round; therefore, the money supply, made up entirely of deposits, expands by $10,000 + $9,000 + $8,100 + $7,290 + $6,561, and so on. In the end, the whole process creates $100,000 in new deposits.

To summarize the process of deposit expansion, let's compare the beginning and final balance sheets for the ten-bank system as a whole. Initially the balance sheet looked like this:

Initial Balance Sheet for the Ten-Bank System

Assets			Liabilities	
Reserves		$100,000	Demand deposits	$1,000,000
Required	$100,000			
Excess	0			
Loans		900,000		
Total assets		$1,000,000	Total liabilities	$1,000,000

After the injection of $10,000 in new reserves, the combined balance sheet for the ten banks looks like this:

Final Balance Sheet for the Ten-Bank System

Assets			Liabilities	
Reserves		$ 110,000	Demand deposits	$1,100,000
		(+10,000)		(+100,000)
Required	$110,000			
	(+10,000)			
Excess	0			
Loans		990,000		
		(+90,000)		
Total assets		$1,100,000	Total liabilities	$1,100,000
		(+100,000)		(+100,000)

We see, then, that the expansion of deposits continues until excess reserves have disappeared. By the time the new reserves have become fully absorbed, total demand deposits will have expanded by $100,000. On the assets side of the balance sheet, this $100,000 of new liabilities will be offset by $10,000 in new required reserves and $90,000 in new loans.

Contraction of the Money Supply

When the Fed withdraws reserves from the banking system, the whole process works in reverse. For example, assume that all the banks are back in the initial position in the last example and that the Fed decides to withdraw, say, $1,000 in reserves. It can do this by making an open market sale of $1,000 of securities from its portfolio.[1] Now suppose that the securities are bought by a dealer who pays for them with a wire transfer from an account at Denver National Bank. To complete the transfer, the Fed deducts $1,000 from Denver's reserve account.

---

[1]About half of all primary security dealers are banks; the remainder are independent institutions. For clarity, we assume in this discussion that the Fed does business only with nonbank dealers.

At that point Denver's balance sheet looks like this:

Denver National Bank

Assets			Liabilities	
Reserves		$ 9,000	Demand deposits	$99,000
		(−1,000)		(−1,000)
Required	$9,900			
	(−100)			
Excess	−900			
	(−900)			
Loans		90,000		
Total assets		$99,000	Total liabilities	$99,000
		(−1,000)		(−1,000)

The loss of $1,000 in deposits when the dealer bought the security reduced required reserves by only $100, whereas Denver's total reserves fell by $1,000 when the Fed completed the transaction. This leaves the bank with negative excess reserves—that is, a $900 reserve deficiency—that it must attempt to correct. In our simplified banking system, Denver must make up the deficiency by reducing its loans. It therefore leaves the next $900 it receives in loan payments in its reserve account. (We assume that if the bank did not have the reserve deficiency, it would make new loans as old ones were paid off, keeping its total loan holdings steady.) In the real world, a bank with a reserve deficiency has a number of other options. One is to sell other assets, such as government securities. Another is to borrow reserves from a bank that has excess reserves. Still another is to borrow from the Fed itself. We will return to these options later.

When Denver National Bank reduces its loan holdings to make up its reserve deficiency, it drains reserves from some other bank in the system. For example, suppose that Maria Espinosa writes a check on Englewood National Bank to pay off $900 that she borrowed from Denver. At the moment when the wire transfer is complete, the balance sheets of the Denver and Englewood banks will look like this:

Denver National Bank

Assets			Liabilities	
Reserves		$ 9,900	Demand deposits	$99,000
		(+900)		
Required	$9,900			
	(unchanged)			
Excess	0			
	(+900)			
Loans		89,100		
		(−900)		
Total assets		$99,000	Total liabilities	$99,000

Englewood National Bank

Assets			Liabilities	
Reserves		$ 9,100	Demand deposits	$99,100
		(−900)		(−900)
Required	$9,910			
	(−90)			
Excess	−810			
	(−810)			
Loans		90,000		
Total assets		$99,100	Total liabilities	$99,100
		(−900)		(−900)

At this point, then, Denver has made up its reserve deficiency, but $810 of it has been passed along to Englewood. Now it is Englewood's turn to reduce its loan holdings. Using an $810 loan repayment that it has received from some other bank, Englewood will build up its reserves by the required amount, but a $729 deficiency will appear somewhere else. The contraction process will continue until deposits in the banking system as a whole have been reduced by $10,000—ten times the loss of reserves that resulted from the Fed's open market security sale.

The Money Multiplier for the Simplified Banking System

As these examples have shown, the total amount of demand deposits that the banking system can hold depends on the total amount of reserves supplied by the Fed and on the required-reserve ratio. In equation form, with rr standing for the required-reserve ratio, the relationship is as follows:

$$\text{Total demand deposits} = (1/rr) \times \text{Total reserves.}$$

Thus, when total reserves were $100,000, the total money stock (consisting entirely of demand deposits in our example) was $1 million. When the Fed injected $10,000 of new reserves into the system, bringing total reserves to $110,000, the money stock rose by $100,000, to $1.1 million. When the Fed withdrew $1,000 of reserves through an open market sale, reducing total reserves to $99,000, the money stock fell by $10,000, to $990,000.

The term $1/rr$ in the above equation is called the **money multiplier** and is the ratio of the equilibrium money stock to total reserves. In our simplified banking system, in which the required-reserve ratio was 10 percent, the value of the money multiplier was 10. Each injection or withdrawal of reserves by the Fed thus increases or decreases the money stock by ten times the change in reserves.

Money multiplier
The ratio of the equilibrium money stock to the banking system's total reserves.

12.2 The Tools of Monetary Policy

In Chapter 11, we discussed the Fed's role in providing services to the banking system and in ensuring the system's safety and stability. Our discussion of money creation here shows that the Fed has another power, namely, the power to control the money stock. Now that we know how money is created, we can examine the policy tools that give the Fed this power.

Open Market Operations

The preceding section illustrated the most important of the policy tools that the Fed uses to control the money stock: open market operations. If the Fed wants to expand the money stock, it instructs the open market trading desk at the Federal Reserve Bank of New York to buy government securities. This is known as an *open market purchase*. **Economics in the News 12.1** presents an eyewitness account of an open market purchase of securities by the Fed.

Sometimes, as in the news item, the Fed makes an outright purchase of securities, but more frequently it buys the securities subject to a repurchase agreement. In such an arrangement the dealer selling the securities to the Fed agrees to buy them back at a later date. Open market operations involving repurchase agreements have only a temporary effect on bank reserves; reserves return to their initial level as soon as the "repurchase" part of the agreement is carried

Economics in the News   12.1
"The Fed's In!"

Scene: Morning. The trading desk at Aubrey Lanston & Co., a major New York bond dealer. There is the usual pandemonium associated with financial trading. Dealers are on the phone, sometimes on many phones at once. They are all shouting.

Suddenly, the Fed light flashes on. The room goes quiet. Bond dealer Richard Kelly grabs the direct line to the Fed. The message is quick, guarded:

"We're taking offerings of bills. Regular delivery."
Click.

"The Fed's in!" Kelly shouts. The pandemonium resumes. On a scale of one to deafening, it's gone from a 6.0 to a 9.8.

Lanston is one of 44 primary bond dealers in New York that got the same call. Traders working the eighth-floor open market desk at the New York Federal Reserve Bank would have reached all of them with the same message in the space of a minute.

The message means that the Fed is buying short-term securities—Treasury bills—in the open market. "Regular delivery" means the Fed will take them the next day. Traders from the Fed will call the firms back in a few minutes to

let the dealers know how much time they have to get their offers together. It won't be much; the Fed will have finished its dealing, buying more than a billion dollars worth of bills, by that afternoon.

"As soon as we hear from the Fed, we'll call our customers who might have bills they want to sell, and we'll also evaluate our own holdings to see whether we want to make an offer. Then, at the appointed time, we'll call back and make our offers to sell."

When Kelly calls back with an offer of securities already held by Lanston or from Lanston's customers, he'll list specific amounts of bills and the "discounts"—percentage reductions from the face values of the bills—at which Lanston or its customers are willing to offer them. The discount determines the price at which the bill is offered—the higher the discount, the lower the price of the bill.

Once the Fed has received offers from Lanston and the other primary dealers, staffers at the stately old New York Federal Reserve Bank will compare offers. They'll take the best—those that offer the highest discounts—for the total quantity the Fed is buying that day.

If the Fed chooses to take any of the bills offered by Lanston, it will place funds directly in Lanston's account. Those funds will constitute new reserves of the banking system. Because some of the purchases will be from Lanston's customers, Lanston will transfer those funds to its customers' banks all over the country.

Source: Timothy Tregarthen, "Making Money at the Fed," *The Margin* (November/December 1988): 6.

out. Such actions are used to make relatively small day-to-day adjustments in bank reserves.

Whichever form the purchase takes, the Fed pays for the securities by means of a wire transfer that adds funds to the reserves of the seller's bank. Because these are newly created reserves and not just a transfer of reserves from one bank to another, they add to the banking system's total reserves. Further, each dollar of reserves added to the banking system permits the volume of deposits subject to reserves to expand by several dollars. The amount of the expansion—the number of dollars added to the money stock per dollar of added reserves—is determined by the money multiplier. In the real world, however, the factors determining the value of the money multiplier are more complex than in the simplified system discussed in the preceding section.

If the Fed wants to decrease the money stock, it reverses this process: It instructs the trading desk to carry out an open market sale of securities, either outright or subject to a repurchase agreement. When a dealer buys securities from the Fed and pays for them with a wire transfer of funds from its deposit at a commercial bank, reserves will be drained from the banking system. The money supply will contract by an amount equal to the money multiplier times the size of the open market sale.

Although open market operations are the most frequently used tool for controlling the money stock, they are not the only one. If we remove some of the simplifying assumptions used so far in this chapter, we can see how these other tools work.

The Discount Rate

In our simplified banking system, banks can acquire new reserves only by attracting additional deposits. In practice, however, banks and thrifts that want additional reserves either to meet the Fed's requirements or to expand their loans have another option: borrowing reserves.

One possibility is to borrow the reserves from another bank. The market in which banks make short-term loans of reserves to other banks is known as the **federal funds market.** The interest rate charged on such loans is called the **federal funds rate.** Transactions in this market, in which the usual loan term is 24 hours, total billions of dollars per day.

Banks can also borrow reserves from the Fed through the so-called **discount window.** (This facility is a department of the district Reserve banks and not, of course, an actual window.) Banks borrow from the Fed in two kinds of situations. Most often they borrow for short periods to adjust their reserves when unexpected withdrawals have left them with less than the required amount of reserves. Such *adjustment borrowing,* as it is called, is subject to administrative constraints. Banks are discouraged from borrowing too often or too much, and the more frequently an institution borrows at the discount window, the greater the administrative pressure to reduce borrowing. In cases in which banks want to expand their reserves simply because they see profitable loan opportunities, they are encouraged to seek other sources of funds, such as new deposits.

In addition to making short-term adjustment loans through the discount window, the Fed sometimes makes longer-term loans under special conditions. Sometimes, for example, loans are made to small banks to help them meet seasonal needs. Also, loans are sometimes made to troubled banks to give them time to get their affairs in order.

The interest rate that the Fed charges on loans made through the discount window—known as the **discount rate**—is a second policy tool for controlling the money supply. If the Fed wants to encourage more discount borrowing, it lowers the discount rate. As the discount rate falls relative to the federal funds rate, the explicit cost of discount borrowing falls relative to the cost of borrowing from other banks and the volume of discount borrowing expands. However, there is a limit to how much discount borrowing banks will want to undertake even when the discount rate falls well below the federal funds rate. Instead, as discount borrowing expands, at some point the implicit cost of the administrative pressures that the Fed uses to discourage too much discount borrowing becomes great enough to offset the interest rate advantage of the discount window. Banks thus go to the discount window only to the point where the full cost of an added dollar of discount window borrowing, including both the explicit cost of the discount rate and the implicit cost of administrative pressure, is brought into equality with the federal funds rate. It takes only a relatively small change in discount borrowing to reach this point when the discount rate changes relative to the federal funds rate.

If the Fed wants to reduce borrowing from the discount window, it raises the discount rate. As the discount rate rises relative to the federal funds rate, the discount window becomes less attractive as a source of funds.

Federal funds market
A market in which banks lend reserves to one another for periods as short as 24 hours.

Federal funds rate
The interest rate on overnight loans of reserves from one bank to another.

Discount window
The department through which the Federal Reserve lends reserves to banks.

Discount rate
The interest rate charged by the Fed on loans of reserves to banks.

Funds that banks borrow from one another through the federal funds market have no effect on total bank reserves; this type of borrowing just moves reserves around from one bank to another. However, funds borrowed through the discount window are net additions to reserves. They form a basis for multiple expansion of deposits in the same way as reserves injected through open market purchases. Because this form of borrowing affects the volume of reserves, then, changes in the discount rate give the Fed another tool for controlling the money stock. Raising the discount rate cuts borrowed reserves and hence tends to lower the money stock; lowering it boosts borrowed reserves, which allows the money stock to increase.

Changes in Required-Reserve Ratios

Changes in required-reserve ratios are a third policy tool that the Fed can use to control the money supply. Earlier in the chapter we showed that the total volume of demand deposits in a simplified banking system is determined by the formula

$$\text{Total demand deposits} = (1/\text{rr}) \times \text{Total reserves},$$

where rr stands for the required-reserve ratio. Similar but somewhat more complex formulas apply to the relationship between required-reserve ratios and all of the elements of M1 and M2 in the actual U.S. banking system. Thus, reduction in required-reserve ratios will increase the money stock that a given quantity of reserves can support, and an increase in the ratios will decrease the money stock for a given quantity of reserves.

Although changes in required-reserve ratios were never used for day-to-day control over the money supply, in the past the Fed sometimes changed the ratios when it wanted to make a strong move toward expansion or contraction of the money supply. For example, during the severe recession of 1974 to 1975 the Fed lowered reserve requirements three times.

The Monetary Control Act of 1980 broadened the coverage of the Fed's required-reserve ratios. Before the act was passed, the Fed could set such ratios only for member commercial banks. Now it can set reserve requirements on transaction deposits at all but the smallest depository institutions. By law the Fed can adjust the required-reserve ratio within a range of 8 to 14 percent for institutions whose total transaction deposits are above a certain amount. It can also impose supplemental reserve requirements on transaction deposits under some conditions. In addition it can impose a required-reserve ratio of 0 to 9 percent on nonpersonal time deposits and certain other liabilities at institutions above a certain size.

In practice, however, technicalities connected with the phased implementation of reserve requirements under the Monetary Control Act made it less attractive for the Fed to use changes in required-reserve ratios as a policy tool. Thus, this tool, though legally still available, has been shelved since 1980. Whether it will be used in the future is not known at this time.

Actual Multipliers for M1 and M2

In a simplified banking system such as the one in our example, the Fed's control over the money stock is direct and complete. In the real world, things are far less simple, as Exhibit 12.1 shows. Both the quantity of reserves and the money

Exhibit 12.1   Variations in the Money Multiplier

Part (a) of this exhibit shows the M1 money multiplier, that is, the ratio of M1 to total reserves. Part (b) shows the M2 multiplier measured as the ratio of M2 to total reserves. As can be seen, both multipliers are subject to variations from month to month. The variations in the M2 multiplier are greater, however, because not all M2 components are subject to uniform required-reserve ratios, as are demand deposits, the principal component of M1. As a result, it is more difficult for the Fed to maintain precise control over the quantity of M2 by means of controlling total reserves.

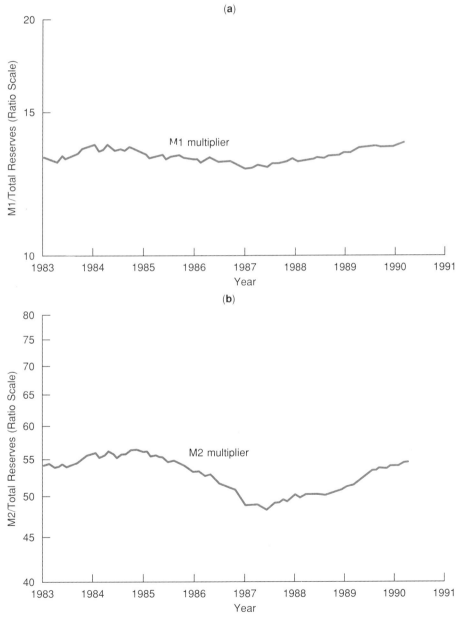

Source: Federal Reserve Board of Governors.

multiplier can change for reasons that are not directly under the Fed's control. A decline in either reserves or the money multiplier will tend to cause the money stock to drop. This effect can be prevented with an open market purchase. Similarly, the effects of an increase either in reserves or in the money multiplier, which tend to cause the money stock to rise, can be offset with an open market sale. Let's look at some situations that may result in a need for defensive open market operations.

In our simplified banking system, the money multiplier equals 1 divided by the required-reserve ratio. In the real world, however, the money multiplier can vary from month to month even if no changes are made in required-reserve ratios. The exhibit shows changes in money multipliers in recent years. Part (a) shows the M1 multiplier, that is, the ratio of M1 to total reserves. Part (b) shows the M2 multiplier, that is, the ratio of M2 to total reserves. The scales are adjusted so that equal percentage variations are represented by equal vertical movements in the two charts.

Movements in the M2 multiplier are larger and less predictable than movements in the M1 multiplier. The reason has to do with the structure of reserve requirements under the Monetary Control Act. Transaction deposits, the principal component of M1, are subject to virtually uniform reserve requirements. In contrast, the bulk of M2 consists of nontransaction balances that are not subject to reserve requirements. Thus, shifts of funds within M2 between its transactions and nontransactions components cause relatively large changes in the M2 multiplier. That makes it more difficult for the Fed to maintain precise control over the quantity of M2 by maintaining a certain target level of total reserves.

Other factors affecting the money multiplier and reserves.   Certain other factors can also affect the value of the money multipliers or the quantity of reserves. For example, in our simplified example we assumed that banks wanted to keep the level of excess reserves at zero. In practice, banks purposely hold small quantities of excess reserves as a precaution against unexpected outflows of reserves. Funds held voluntarily as excess reserves do not contribute to the multiple expansion of deposits. Therefore, the higher the desired level of excess reserves, the lower the money multiplier. In addition, decisions by the public to convert deposits to currency can affect both total reserves and the money multipliers.

Today the Fed routinely monitors various measures of the money stock and tries to adjust them appropriately in the face of changing economic conditions. This was not always the case, however. *Applying Economic Ideas 12.1* tells the story of monetary policy during the Great Depression, when the Fed failed to use open market operations to offset currency drains and the accumulation of excess reserves. Its failure in this regard is considered to have made the Depression longer and more severe than it needed to be.

12.3   The Federal Reserve in the International Economy

Earlier in the chapter we saw that the Fed is an active trader in markets for U.S. securities. Its sales and purchases in these markets are its principal means for controlling the stock of money. However, the Fed is also an occasional participant in the **foreign-exchange markets,** in which the dollar is exchanged for Japanese yen, West German marks, British pounds, and the currencies of other countries. As the U.S. economy has become increasingly open to international influences, the Fed's activities in the foreign-exchange markets have made the financial headlines nearly as often as its domestic open market operations. In this section, we take a preliminary look at the mechanics of the Fed's activities in the foreign-exchange markets and the relationship between those activities and domestic monetary policy. Succeeding chapters add details relating exchange rates to the balance of payments, interest rates, inflation, and economic growth.

Foreign-exchange market
A market in which the currency of one country is traded for that of another.

The Structure of Foreign-Exchange Markets

As a traveler you may have had occasion to exchange U.S. dollars for Canadian dollars, Mexican pesos, or the currency of some other country. This trading in paper currencies is a small corner of the largest set of markets in the world—the foreign-exchange markets, in which hundreds of billions of dollars are traded each day. Such trading reflects the fact that virtually every international transaction in goods, services, or financial assets is preceded by the exchange of one currency for another.

Suppose, for example, that a U.S. department store chain wants to buy a shipload of Japanese video recorders and pay for it in dollars. However, to meet its payroll, pay its suppliers, and so on, the Japanese firm needs yen, not dollars. The solution: The U.S. importer goes to the foreign-exchange market and uses its dollars to buy the yen that the Japanese firm wants as payment.

Obviously, large transactions in the foreign-exchange market are not carried out with paper currency; like large domestic transactions, they are conducted with transaction deposits in commercial banks. The central players in the foreign-exchange markets are large banks in the world's money centers—London, Zurich, Tokyo, and other cities—which are known as *trading banks*. Unlike the typical small-town savings and loan, these banks have branches all over the world and accept deposits denominated in many different currencies. U.S. banks act as trading banks primarily through their foreign branches.

Suppose that Macy's department store in New York is the one that needs to buy yen to purchase Japanese goods. It can ask Chase Manhattan Bank to debit its dollar-denominated account and credit a deposit of equal value to an account in Tokyo denominated in yen that it can use to pay a Japanese supplier. Similarly, if a Japanese pension fund wants to buy U.S. Treasury bills, it can exchange a deposit denominated in yen at a Japanese or U.S. trading bank for a deposit denominated in dollars and then use those dollars to buy the bills. The trading banks make a profit on these transactions by charging an *asked* price for the currency they sell that is slightly higher than the *bid* price they pay for the currency they buy.

Supply and Demand in Foreign-Exchange Markets

What determines the number of yen that a customer gets in exchange for its dollars? Why, on a given day, is the exchange rate 150 yen per dollar rather than 125 or 200? The answer is that the rate depends on supply and demand. Here, we will consider a simplified illustration of the foreign-exchange market in which dollars are exchanged for yen. (Chapter 19 explores supply and demand in the foreign-exchange markets in detail.)

Applying Economic Ideas   12.1
Monetary Policy during the Great Depression

Although economists have debated the causes of the Great Depression for nearly 60 years, they still do not completely understand why what began as a fairly ordinary business contraction in the summer of 1929 led to a four-year downward spiral in which real output fell by one-third and unemployment rose to one-quarter of the labor force. But it is widely believed that the collapse of the banking system and a precipitous decline in the money stock, as shown in the accompanying chart, played a major role.

The question is: Why did the money stock fall? In *A Monetary History of the United States*, Milton Friedman and Anna J. Schwartz examine the decline in detail. In the initial phase of the contraction, which lasted from August 1929 to October 1930, the money supply fell because reserve borrowing at the Fed's discount window declined. The Fed could have kept total reserves from declining either by lowering the discount rate enough to keep it in line with falling short-term market rates or through open market purchases of securities. However, it did neither. The discount rate was lowered, but not as quickly as market rates fell, and little use was made of open market operations. Nevertheless, the decline in the money stock was modest during this period.

Then, in October 1930, the character of the contraction changed dramatically. A crop of bank failures, particularly in farm states such as Missouri, Indiana, Illinois, Iowa, Arkansas, and North Carolina, spread fear among depositors throughout the nation. Since there was no federal deposit insurance in those days, a bank failure could completely wipe out a depositor's savings. All over the country bank runs began as people tried to convert their deposits into currency. The runs brought down hundreds of banks; 256 banks failed in November and 352 in December. Many of them were small rural banks, but the December failures included the collapse of the giant Bank

of the United States in New York. Although this was in fact an ordinary commercial bank, its official-sounding name made its failure a tremendous blow to confidence in the system.

The bank runs show up clearly in the accompanying chart in the form of a sharp decline in the ratio of deposits to currency. The rush to convert deposits into currency continued through a second banking crisis in 1931 and a final one in 1933. To cope with the last crisis, newly elected President Franklin Roosevelt declared a banking holiday, closing all banks in the country for more than a week while matters were sorted out.

The conversion of deposits into currency drained reserves from the banking system and accelerated the decline in the money stock. Matters were worsened by banks' reactions to the crisis. Knowing that a run of depositors was an ever present danger, banks that had not yet failed increased their liquidity by building up excess reserves. This precaution caused a decrease in the ratio of deposits to total reserves, as shown in the chart. Banks' reluctance to lend out their excess reserves also lowered the overall money multiplier. In a period in which reserves were already falling, the decline in the money multiplier made the money stock fall even more rapidly.

What did the Fed do? It could have used open market operations to pump new reserves into the system, replacing those lost to currency and offsetting the declining deposit-to-reserve ratio. But the Fed did not act vigorously enough. It allowed some increase in what Friedman and Schwartz call "high-powered money," meaning the total of reserves plus currency. However, the increase in high-powered money was not nearly enough to offset the decline in reserves and in the money multiplier and, hence, in the money stock itself.

Friedman and Schwartz sum up their analysis of the period as follows:

> *Prevention or moderation of the decline in the stock of money . . . would have reduced the contraction's severity and almost as certainly its duration. The contraction might still have been relatively severe. But it is hardly conceivable that money income could have declined by over one-half and prices by over one-third in the course of four years if there had been no decline in the stock of money.*

Source: Milton Friedman and Anna Jacobson Schwartz, *A Monetary History of the United States, 1867–1960*, Chapter 7. Copyright © 1963 by NBER. Published by Princeton University Press. Graph reprinted with permission of Princeton University Press.

We saw in Chapter 6 that *current account transactions* include imports and exports of goods and services and international transfer payments, and *capital account transactions* involve international purchases and sales of assets and international borrowing and lending. Both play a role in determining the supply and demand for dollars in foreign-exchange markets.

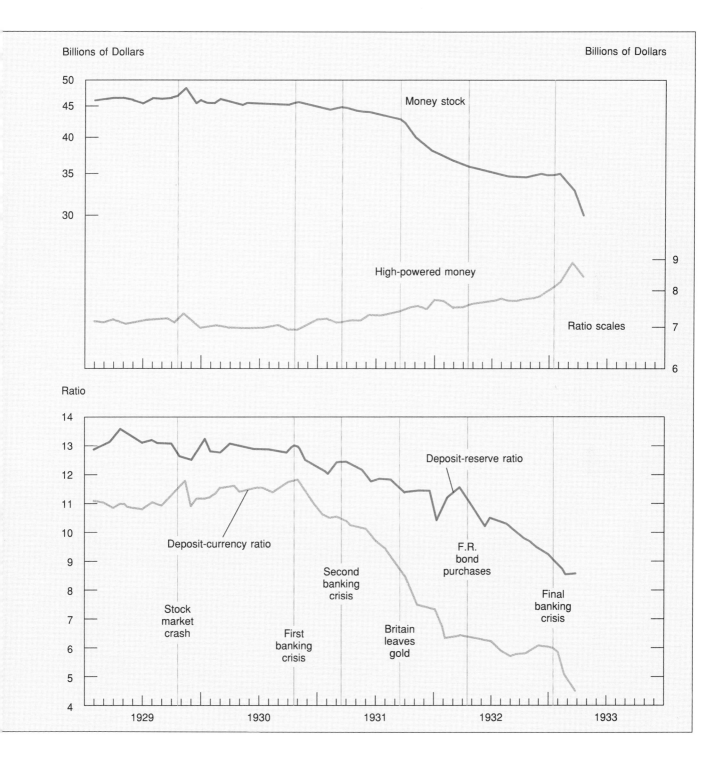

In the example given earlier, a U.S. department store wanted to buy Japanese video recorders. To buy the recorders, it must first buy yen. An importer of goods or services to the United States enters the foreign-exchange market as a *supplier* of dollars. The supply curve for dollars shown in Exhibit 12.2 combines the transactions of all importers. In this diagram the supply curve has a positive

Exhibit 12.2   The Foreign-Exchange Market
for Dollars and Yen

This diagram represents the foreign-exchange market
in which U.S. dollars are exchanged for Japanese yen
and yen are exchanged for dollars. The exchange
rate is expressed as the number of yen required to
purchase one U.S. dollar. The supply curve of dollars
reflects the activities of U.S. importers of Japanese
goods and services. They sell dollars to obtain the
yen they need in order to buy Toyotas, Sony
television sets, and so on. The demand curve for
dollars reflects the activities of Japanese buyers of
exports from the United States. They use yen to buy
the dollars they need to buy Boeing aircraft, Sunkist
oranges, and so on. The demand curve also includes
the effects of net capital inflows to the United States.
For example, a Japanese pension fund that wants to
buy U.S. government bonds first needs to exchange
yen for dollars to use in purchasing the bonds.

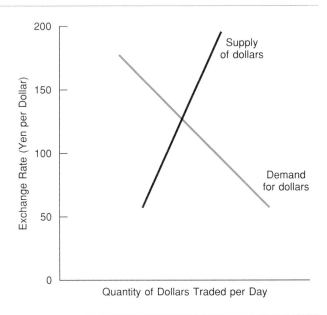

slope, indicating that an increase in the exchange rate of the dollar relative to the
yen (meaning that more yen can be bought per dollar) will increase the number
of dollars supplied.[2]

On the other side of the market, a Japanese grocery chain that wishes to buy
oranges exported from the United States must buy U.S. dollars to carry out the
transaction. A buyer of U.S. exports enters the foreign-exchange market as a
demander of dollars. The demand curve shown in Exhibit 12.2 includes the
demand for dollars of all Japanese buyers of U.S. exports.

In addition to current account transactions, U.S. and Japanese firms and
individuals carry out numerous capital account transactions. For example, a
Japanese pension fund that wishes to buy U.S. Treasury bills must first buy
dollars to use in paying for those securities. A *capital inflow* to the United States
thus is associated with a demand for dollars above and beyond the demand
arising from current account transactions. What about a *capital outflow*, such as
a purchase of foreign securities by a U.S. buyer? Such a transaction could be
counted as a source of dollars supplied to the foreign-exchange market, but to
simplify the diagram, a different approach is taken in Exhibit 12.2. There, capital outflows are first subtracted from capital inflows to arrive at a figure for *net
capital inflows*. Only these net capital inflows (the excess of inflows over outflows) are added to the current account demand for dollars in drawing the dollar
demand curve. As discussed in earlier chapters, the United States has experienced a net capital inflow each year for more than a decade. Still another source
of demand for dollars, net purchases by central banks on the official reserve
account, will be discussed in the next section and in Chapter 19.

---

[2]As Chapter 19 will explain, the slope of the current account supply curve for dollars depends
on the price elasticity of demand for Japanese goods imported into the United States. The preliminary conclusions drawn in this section will be restated to apply to a broader variety of circumstances in that chapter.

Exhibit 12.3   Foreign-Exchange Rates

In foreign-exchange markets the dollar is traded for the currencies of other countries. Exchange rates vary from day to day according to supply and demand conditions. This exhibit shows the foreign-exchange quotations from *The Wall Street Journal* for March 12, 1990. Exchange rates are quoted in both U.S. dollars per unit of the foreign currency (such as $.17370 per French franc) and units of the foreign currency per dollar (5.7570 francs per dollar). Forward rates are given for some major currencies. *Forward exchange contracts* are agreements to buy or sell a currency at a future date at a price that is agreed on today.

EXCHANGE RATES

Friday, March 9, 1990

The New York foreign exchange selling rates below apply to trading among banks in amounts of $1 million and more, as quoted at 3 p.m. Eastern time by Bankers Trust Co. Retail transactions provide fewer units of foreign currency per dollar.

Country	U.S. $ equiv. Fri.	U.S. $ equiv. Thurs.	Currency per U.S. $ Fri.	Currency per U.S. $ Thurs.
Argentina (Austral) ...	.0001852	.0001852	5399.86	5399.86
Australia (Dollar)	.7599	.7615	1.3160	1.3132
Austria (Schilling)	.08342	.08361	11.99	11.96
Bahrain (Dinar)	2.6522	2.6522	.3771	.3771
Belgium (Franc)				
Commercial rate ...	.02823	.02833	35.43	35.30
Brazil (Cruzado)	.02754	.02904	36.31	34.43
Britain (Pound)	1.6150	1.6420	.6192	.6090
30-Day Forward	1.6048	1.6329	.6232	.6124
90-Day Forward	1.5883	1.6154	.6296	.6190
180-Day Forward	1.5623	1.5898	.6401	.6290
Canada (Dollar)	.8471	.8485	1.1805	1.1785
30-Day Forward	.8437	.8452	1.1853	1.1832
90-Day Forward	.8374	.8385	1.1942	1.1926
180-Day Forward	.8292	.8301	1.2060	1.2047
Chile (Official rate) ...	.003523	.003523	283.87	283.87
China (Yuan)	.211752	.211752	4.7225	4.7225
Colombia (Peso)	.002188	.002188	457.00	457.00
Denmark (Krone)	.1531	.1534	6.5330	6.5200
Ecuador (Sucre)				
Floating rate	.001433	.001433	698.00	698.00
Finland (Markka)	.24919	.24956	4.0130	4.0070
France (Franc)	.17370	.17391	5.7570	5.7502
30-Day Forward	.17338	.17361	5.7677	5.7599
90-Day Forward	.17271	.17294	5.7900	5.7825
180-Day Forward	.17173	.17204	5.8230	5.8126
Greece (Drachma)	.006188	.006211	161.60	161.00
Hong Kong (Dollar) ...	.12801	.12802	7.8120	7.8115
India (Rupee)	.05889	.05889	16.98	16.98
Indonesia (Rupiah)	.0005543	.0005543	1803.98	1803.98
Ireland (Punt)	1.5600	1.5667	.6410	.6383
Israel (Shekel)	.4988	.4988	2.0049	2.0049
Italy (Lira)	.0007949	.0007981	1257.99	1252.99
Japan (Yen)	.006612	.006623	151.25	151.00
30-Day Forward	.006617	.006628	151.12	150.87
90-Day Forward	.006628	.006639	150.88	150.63
180-Day Forward	.006643	.006653	150.54	150.30
Jordan (Dinar)	1.5076	1.5076	.6633	.6633
Kuwait (Dinar)	3.4360	3.4360	.2910	.2910
Lebanon (Pound)	.001803	.001803	554.50	554.50
Malaysia (Ringgit)	.3698	.3696	2.7040	2.7055
Malta (Lira)	2.9985	2.9985	.3335	.3335
Mexico (Peso)				
Floating rate	.0003639	.0003639	2747.93	2747.93
Netherland (Guilder) .	.5214	.5229	1.9180	1.9125
New Zealand (Dollar) .	.5910	.5885	1.6920	1.6992
Norway (Krone)	.1521	.1522	6.5725	6.5700
Pakistan (Rupee)	.0471	.0471	21.25	21.25
Peru (Inti)	.00007810	.00007810	12804.10	12804.10
Philippines (Peso)	.04556	.04556	21.95	21.95
Portugal (Escudo)	.006682	.006682	149.65	149.65
Saudi Arabia (Riyal) ..	.26681	.26681	3.7480	3.7480
Singapore (Dollar)	.5343	.5338	1.8715	1.8735
South Africa (Rand)				
Commercial rate	.3859	.3862	2.5913	2.5893
Financial rate	.2601	.2608	3.8447	3.8344
South Korea (Won)	.0014390	.0014390	694.95	694.95
Spain (Peseta)	.009137	.009162	109.45	109.15
Sweden (Krona)	.1622	.1624	6.1650	6.1585
Switzerland (Franc) ..	.6627	.6640	1.5090	1.5060
30-Day Forward	.6623	.6638	1.5099	1.5065
90-Day Forward	.6616	.6633	1.5116	1.5076
180-Day Forward	.6605	.6627	1.5140	1.5090
Taiwan (Dollar)	.038022	.038491	26.30	25.98
Thailand (Baht)	.03887	.03887	25.73	25.73
Turkey (Lira)	.0004153	.0004153	2407.96	2407.96
United Arab (Dirham) .	.2722	.2722	3.6735	3.6735
Uruguay (New Peso)				
Financial	.001243	.001243	804.50	804.50
Venezuela (Bolivar)				
Floating rate	.02299	.02299	43.50	43.50
W. Germany (Mark) ...	.5874	.5882	1.7025	1.7000
30-Day Forward	.5875	.5884	1.7021	1.6995
90-Day Forward	.5874	.5885	1.7023	1.6993
180-Day Forward	.5864	.5876	1.7052	1.7018
SDR	1.30509	1.30788	.76623	.76460
ECU	1.19823	1.20061	....	....

Special Drawing Rights (SDR) are based on exchange rates for the U.S., West German, British, French and Japanese curren-cies. Source: International Monetary Fund.

European Currency Unit (ECU) is based on a basket of community currencies. Source: European Community Commission.

Source: *The Wall Street Journal*, March 12, 1990, C10.

Prices in foreign-exchange markets.   Foreign-exchange rates—the prices of currencies in terms of other currencies, as determined by supply and demand— are published daily in financial newspapers. Exhibit 12.3 shows the foreign-exchange rate quotations from *The Wall Street Journal* for a typical day. Each currency is quoted in two equivalent ways. For example, the exchange rate between the yen and the dollar can be quoted in terms of yen per dollar, as was done in labeling the vertical axis in Exhibit 12.2. On the other hand, the price can be quoted in terms of dollars per yen. Most currencies are quoted on a *spot* basis, that is, for immediate delivery. Some of the major currencies are also traded on a *forward* basis, meaning that the currencies will be exchanged at an agreed-upon future date at a price that is set today.

As supply and demand conditions change from day to day, exchange rates also change, as shown by the difference between the rates for Thursday and Friday in Exhibit 12.3. A number of factors can contribute to such changes. For example:

- Expansion of the U.S. economy would increase the demand for all sorts of goods, including goods imported from Japan. Sales of dollars by U.S. importers acquiring the yen needed to purchase those goods would cause the supply curve for dollars to shift to the right. A recession in the U.S. economy would decrease the demand for goods imported from Japan and, hence, cause the supply curve to shift to the left.

- Expansion of the Japanese economy would increase the demand for goods exported from the United States. Purchases by Japanese importers of the dollars needed to buy those goods would cause the demand curve for dollars to shift to the right. A recession in the Japanese economy would cause the demand curve for dollars to shift to the left.

- An increase in any condition making U.S. assets more attractive to Japanese buyers would increase net capital inflows to the United States and produce a rightward shift in the demand curve for dollars. Examples might include an increase in the profit potential of U.S. corporations, which would make their stocks more attractive, or an increase in interest rates on U.S. government securities. Similarly, any condition making Japanese assets more attractive to U.S. buyers, such as an increase in Japanese interest rates relative to U.S. interest rates, would reduce net capital inflows and, hence, would shift the dollar demand curve to the left.

These are only a few of the factors that can affect supply and demand in foreign-exchange markets. More detail is provided in Chapter 19.

Intervention in the Foreign-Exchange Markets

Exchange rates are not mere numbers; they have major impacts on the economy. For example, if the dollar rises in price relative to the yen, as it did during the first half of the 1980s, more yen can be bought for a dollar. Japanese goods thus become inexpensive for U.S. consumers. Imports from Japan increase, and U.S. firms competing with those imports face possibly devastating competition. At the same time, U.S. goods and services become more expensive to Japanese buyers, not because the price in dollars has gone up, but because it now takes more yen to buy those dollars. U.S. exporters thus feel a decline in demand for their products when the value of the dollar rises against the yen.

When the dollar falls in value relative to the yen, as it did after February 1985, these effects are reversed. More dollars must be spent to import a given quantity of Japanese goods. The price that U.S. consumers pay for imports rises, and U.S. firms face less competition than before. U.S. exporters benefit from a fall in the value of the dollar, because Japanese buyers now find it easier to buy their products.

Because exchange rates affect the welfare of consumers and firms, their level is a matter of concern for policymakers. Consequently, from time to time central banks in the United States and other countries intervene in foreign-exchange markets in an attempt to stabilize exchange rates by offsetting market pressures that tend to raise or lower the exchange values of their currencies. In the United

States, foreign-currency operations are directed by the Treasury, which has overall responsibility for the management of international financial policy, in close cooperation with the Federal Open Market Committee. They are carried out by the Fed through its foreign trading desk in New York.

Suppose, for example, that equilibrium has been established at an exchange rate of 125 yen to the dollar, as shown by point E_1 in Exhibit 12.4. Firms and consumers have adjusted to this exchange rate, and the Treasury would like to avoid a sudden change. However, the U.S. economy now begins to expand strongly, shifting the dollar supply curve to the right, from S_1 to S_2. If no action is taken, a new equilibrium will be established at an exchange rate of 100 yen to the dollar—point E_2 in the exhibit. What can the Fed do to stabilize the exchange rate at 125 yen?

Mechanics of intervention.   To support the price of the dollar relative to the yen, the Treasury instructs the Fed to intervene in a way that increases the quantity of dollars demanded. The mechanics of this action are similar to those of an open market operation. What makes intervention possible is the fact that on the assets side of its balance sheet the Fed holds foreign securities along with its holdings of U.S. government securities; these include yen-denominated securities issued by the Japanese government.

To resist downward pressure on the exchange rate, the Fed first sells some yen-denominated securities to a securities dealer in Tokyo. It receives payment in the form of a yen-denominated transaction deposit at the Bank of Japan, that country's central bank. The Bank of Japan acts as the Fed's agent in this transaction. To acquire dollars the Fed sells the yen-denominated deposit to a Tokyo branch of one of the New York trading banks. The bank pays for the yen deposit by drawing on the reserves of dollars it has on deposit with the Fed in the United States. The end result of this series of transactions is a purchase of dollars by the Fed whose effect is to increase the demand for dollars. This shifts the demand

Exhibit 12.4   Effects of Intervention in the Foreign-Exchange Market

The Federal Reserve can intervene in foreign-exchange markets to resist changes in currency values. In this case the exchange rate is initially in equilibrium at a rate of 125 yen per dollar. Expansion of the U.S. economy increases U.S. demand for imports from Japan, thus increasing the supply of dollars and shifting the supply curve to the right, from S_1 to S_2. By itself, this shift would lower the equilibrium exchange rate to 100 yen per dollar. However, the Fed intervenes by purchasing dollars in exchange for yen. This has the effect of shifting the demand curve for dollars to the right, preventing a decrease in the exchange rate.

curve to the right, from D_1 to D_2. A new equilibrium is established at E_3, where the exchange rate is unchanged because supply and demand have increased equally. In the international accounts described in Chapter 6, the Fed's purchase of dollars appears as a positive net official reserve transaction in the capital account section.

If at another time the Fed wants to counter upward pressure on the value of the dollar, it must reverse these transactions. In that case it buys a yen-denominated deposit from the New York trading bank and pays for it with a wire transfer crediting the appropriate number of dollars to the bank's reserve account at the Fed. The Fed then uses the yen deposit to buy Japanese government securities for its portfolio. This set of trades tends to nudge down the value of the dollar in the foreign-exchange markets. This transaction is entered as a negative net official reserve transaction on the capital account.

Effects on the domestic money stock.   As the preceding description of exchange market intervention makes clear, these transactions affect the U.S. banking system's reserves at the same time that they influence the dollar's exchange value. When the Fed buys foreign currencies to push down the value of the dollar, it increases the U.S. banking system's reserves in exactly the same way that it does when it buys securities on the open market. When it sells foreign currencies to support the value of the dollar, bank reserves are depleted just as they are when the Fed conducts an open market sale of securities. Thus, the Fed's actions in the exchange markets potentially affect bank reserves and domestic monetary policy.

Sterilization
The Fed's use of open market operations to offset the effects of exchange market intervention on domestic reserves and on the money stock.

To offset the effects of its foreign-exchange activities on domestic bank reserves, the Fed routinely engages in a special type of open market operation known as **sterilization.** To sterilize a sale of foreign currencies, which tends to decrease U.S. bank reserves, the Fed simultaneously makes an equal open market purchase of U.S. government securities. The open market purchase restores total reserves to their previous value. To sterilize a purchase of foreign currencies, which tends to increase bank reserves, the Fed carries out an offsetting domestic open market sale.

Stated in these terms, sterilization sounds simple: One set of transactions offsets the other. However, in practice, sterilization does not achieve a complete separation of domestic monetary policy from exchange rate developments. To be sure, domestic monetary policy, which is under control of the Fed, is separate from exchange market intervention policy, which is under the control of the Treasury and only carried out by the Fed. Even so, the Fed's decisions about domestic monetary policy that affect domestic interest rates, real output, and the price level also influence the value of the dollar via their effects on supply and demand in the foreign-exchange markets. Because movements in exchange rates have such far-reaching effects on the domestic economy, the Fed must take developments in the foreign-exchange market into account in determining domestic monetary policy. For these reasons one rarely reads a newspaper article related to domestic monetary policy that does not also discuss effects on the international value of the dollar or a story on the value of the dollar that does not end by discussing U.S. monetary policy and interest rates.

Summary

1. **How do banks create money?** Banks can make loans whenever their *reserves* exceed the minimum amount of *required reserves* set by the Fed. When a bank makes a loan, it credits the proceeds to the borrower's transaction account. When the borrower spends this newly created money, the recipient deposits it in another

bank, which in turn can use its excess reserves to make another loan. In this way, each dollar of new reserves that the banking system receives becomes the basis for a multiple expansion of deposits.

2. **Why is the size of the money stock limited by the quantity of bank reserves?** Although banks can create money, they can do so only to the extent that they have *excess reserves*. This means that the total quantity of deposits that the banking system can create is limited by the total quantity of reserves available and the *required-reserve ratio*. In a simplified banking system the number of dollars of deposits that can be created for each dollar of reserves equals 1/rr, where rr is the required-reserve ratio. The ratio 1/rr is the *money multiplier* for the simplified banking system. Although the formula for the money multiplier in the actual U.S. banking system is more complex, required-reserve ratios still play a central role in the formula.

3. **What instruments are available to the Fed for controlling the money stock?** *Open market operations*, in which the Fed affects the banking system's reserves through purchases or sales of government securities, are the Fed's principal instrument of monetary control. An open market purchase injects reserves and allows the money stock to expand; an open market sale drains reserves and causes the money stock to contract. Changes in the *discount rate* charged by the Fed on loans of reserves to banks and thrifts are a second instrument of monetary control. An increase in the discount rate reduces the quantity of reserves borrowed. This absorbs excess reserves and thus tends to cause the money stock to contract. Lowering the discount rate encourages borrowing of reserves and thus tends to allow the money stock to expand. Changes in required-reserve ratios are a third means of controlling the money stock, but this mechanism has not been used since the 1970s. A decrease in the required-reserve ratio creates excess reserves and allows the money stock to expand; an increase in the ratio causes the money stock to contract.

4. **How well can the money stock be controlled?** The Fed is able to control the money stock reasonably closely through the use of open market operations and changes in the discount rate. However, its control is not perfect; unpredicted variations in the money multiplier or in total reserves can cause unexpected changes in the money stock. To the extent that these events can be predicted, as in the case of seasonal variations in currency demand, they can be offset with open market operations.

5. **What activities does the Fed undertake in the international sphere?** Each day billions of dollars are traded for currencies of other countries in the *foreign-exchange market*. Because the exchange rate of the dollar relative to other currencies affects U.S. importers and exporters, the Fed sometimes intervenes in for-

eign-exchange markets to counteract upward or downward pressure on the dollar's value relative to other currencies. It can lower the exchange value of the dollar by selling dollars and buying foreign currencies; and it can raise the value of the dollar by buying dollars and selling foreign currencies. Intervention in the foreign-exchange markets can potentially affect the U.S. banking system's reserves and, hence, the domestic money stock. These effects on the domestic money stock are routinely avoided because the Fed offsets the reserve impact of its interventions through domestic open market operations—a practice known as *sterilization*. However, sterilization by no means breaks the linkage between domestic and international monetary and financial developments.

Terms for Review

-   required reserves
-   required-reserve ratio
-   excess reserves
-   open market operation
-   money multiplier
-   federal funds market
-   federal funds rate
-   discount window
-   discount rate
-   foreign-exchange market
-   sterilization

Questions for Review

1. Why is it unsafe for a bank to make loans in amounts greater than its excess reserves?

2. What does the Fed buy or sell in an open market operation? If the Fed wants to increase bank reserves, should it conduct an open market sale or an open market purchase?

3. If a withdrawal leaves a bank with reserves that are below the required level, what can the bank do to correct the situation?

4. What are the Fed's three main instruments for controlling the money stock? Which does it use most frequently? Least frequently?

5. What is the federal funds market? Why does the level of the discount rate relative to the federal funds rate affect the level of bank reserves?

6. What actions does the Fed take when it wants to intervene in foreign-exchange markets to raise the dollar's exchange value relative to, say, the British pound? What actions does it take when it wants to lower the dollar's value? Why do these actions affect the domestic money stock unless they are offset through sterilization?

Problems and Topics for Discussion

1. **Examining the lead-off case.** What are the duties of the Federal Open Market Committee? Who are the committee's voting members? Why is it considered such a powerful body? A vote to ease monetary policy means a vote to increase the growth of the money stock compared with the growth that would otherwise be experienced. What methods for implementing such a decision are available to the Fed?

2. **Multiple expansion of deposits.** Rework the deposit expansion examples in this chapter on the basis of the following assumptions:
   a. An injection of $5,000 in reserves via an open market purchase
   b. An injection of $20,000 in reserves with a 20 rather than 10 percent required-reserve ratio
   c. Withdrawal of $500 in reserves via an open market sale

3. **Currency and the money stock.** Use a balance sheet approach to trace the effects of a withdrawal of $1,000 in currency from a bank. Assume that reserves are initially held half in the form of vault cash and half in the form of reserves on deposit with the Fed. Also assume that after the initial currency withdrawal there are no further changes in currency holdings by the public.

4. **The federal funds rate and the discount rate.** The *Federal Reserve Bulletin*, published monthly by the Fed, gives the values of the discount and federal funds rates and data for total and borrowed reserves. What has happened to the difference between these rates recently? Has the discount rate been changed? What has happened to the volume of borrowed reserves? Have they moved in the direction you would expect given the behavior of interest rates?

5. **Foreign-exchange markets.** In *The Wall Street Journal* or the financial pages of another newspaper, find the most recent foreign-exchange quotations. How has the value of the dollar changed relative to other major currencies compared with the data given in Exhibit 12.3?

Case for Discussion
Intervention Fails to Revive the Slumping Yen

NEW YORK—Another round of token intervention failed to revive the Japanese yen and convinced many traders that the Group of Seven industrial nations is unwilling to throw any weight behind its recent statements.

A handful of European central banks, led by the West German central bank, moved to blunt the dollar's advance against the yen as the U.S. currency climbed well above 158 yen.

But currency dealers said yesterday's intervention, like Monday's central-bank performance, was little more than a symbolic effort.

To some dealers, the conspicuous absence of the Federal Reserve from yesterday's dollar sales offered further proof that the United States is reluctant to prop up the Japanese currency while Japan refrains from raising interest rates.

On Saturday, the G-7 ministers—representatives from the U.S., Japan, Britain, West Germany, France, Italy, and Canada—met in Paris. They said the yen's decline against the dollar would have "undesirable consequences."

Talk has crept into the market that Japan might move to raise interest rates this weekend. But, according to Scott Greene, chief dealer at Bank Julius Baer & Co., while a rate boost might temporarily strengthen the yen, any recovery would be short-lived.

Japan last raised its discount rate in early March, lifting it a full percentage point to 5.25 percent. The discount rate is the central bank's base rate on loans to commercial banks.

Source: Caitlin Randall, "Another Round of Bank Intervention Is Unable to Revive the Slumping Yen," *The Wall Street Journal*, April 12, 1990, C13. Reprinted by permission of *The Wall Street Journal*, © Dow Jones & Company, Inc., 1990. All Rights Reserved Worldwide.

Questions

1. Using a foreign-exchange market diagram, explain why sales of dollars in exchange for yen by central banks would tend to lower the exchange rate of the dollar relative to the yen or to resist a tendency for the exchange rate to increase if it would otherwise be increasing.

2. Suppose that you, an American consumer, are considering the purchase of a new car: either a Japanese-built Infiniti or a German-built Mercedes. How will your decision be affected by an increase in the value of the dollar relative to the yen, while at the same time the value of the dollar is unchanged relative to the German mark? Would action by the central bank of Japan to prevent a rise in the dollar's value relative to the yen help or hurt German exporters?

3. An increase in the Bank of Japan's discount rate would tend to push up interest rates on all types of Japanese securities. Suppose that you were the manager of a Japanese pension fund and were considering the purchase of either U.S. government bonds or bonds issued by the Japanese government. How would your decision be affected if the interest rate on Japanese bonds rose while that on U.S. government bonds remained the same? Use a foreign-exchange market diagram to explain why an increase in Japanese interest rates would tend to lower the exchange value of the dollar relative to the yen.

CHAPTER

13

The Supply and Demand for Money

**Before reading this chapter,
make sure you know the meaning of:**

Elasticity (Chapter 3)

Real and nominal interest rates (Chapter 4)

Stocks and flows (Chapter 5)

M2 (Chapter 11)

Liquidity (Chapter 11)

Equation of exchange (Chapter 11)

Velocity (Chapter 11)

Federal funds market (Chapter 12)

After reading this chapter, you will understand:

How income and interest rates affect the demand for money.

The characteristics of the money demand curve.

How the equilibrium interest rate is affected by a change in the money supply.

How the equilibrium interest rate is affected by a change in nominal national income.

The targets the Fed has used as guides for its open market operations.

"Mr. Chairman. . . ."

The Chairman of the Federal Reserve Board is required by law to report to Congress twice each year on issues of monetary policy. The following are excerpts from the testimony of Fed Chairman Alan Greenspan before the Senate Committee on Banking, Housing and Urban Affairs, February 22, 1990.

Mr. Chairman and Members of the Committee, I appreciate the opportunity to testify today.

Last year marked the seventh year of the longest peacetime expansion of the U.S. economy on record. Some 2 1/2 million jobs were created, and the civilian unemployment rate held steady at 5 1/4 percent. Inflation was held to a rate no faster than that in recent years, but unfortunately no progress was made in 1989 toward price stability. Thus, while we can look back with satisfaction at the economic progress made last year, there is still important work to be done.

About a year ago, Federal Reserve policy was in the final phase of a period of gradual tightening, designed to inhibit a buildup of inflation pressures. Interest rates moved higher through the winter, but started down when signs of more restrained aggregate demand and of reduced potential for higher inflation began to appear. As midyear approached, a marked strengthening of the dollar on foreign-exchange markets further diminished the threat of accelerating inflation. New economic data suggested that the balance of risks had shifted toward the possibility of an undue weakening in economic activity. The Federal Reserve in June embarked on a series of measured easing steps that continued through late last year. Interest rates declined further to levels about 1 1/2 percentage points

Photo source: UPI/Bettmann Newsphotos.

Source: Testimony by Alan Greenspan, Chairman, Board of Governors of the Federal Reserve System before the Committee on Banking, Housing and Urban Affairs of the United States Senate, February 22, 1990.

below March peaks. Reductions in inflation expectations and reports of a softer economy evidently contributed to the drop in rates in longer-term markets.

So far this year, the federal funds rate has remained around 8 1/4 percent, but rates on Treasury securities and longer-term private instruments have reversed some of their earlier declines. Investors have reacted to stronger-than-expected economic data, a runup in energy prices, and increasingly attractive investment opportunities abroad, especially in Europe.

We now know what money is, how it is measured, and how it is related to reserves, but Greenspan's testimony underscores an important relationship to which we have so far paid little attention: that between monetary policy and interest rates. In this chapter we will use the tools of supply and demand to analyze this relationship. This will set the stage for Chapter 14, in which we will take up the broader relationships between monetary policy and inflation, unemployment, and economic growth.

13.1   The Demand for Money

The concept of demand is by now a familiar tool of analysis. Chapters 2 and 3 discussed demand for individual goods and services. Chapters 5 and 7 introduced aggregate demand curves. Now we apply the concept of demand in still another context. The theory of demand for money applies familiar ideas in new ways. As we did when we introduced aggregate demand, we can begin by calling attention to key differences between the new application and previous ones.

A key difference between the demand for money and previous applications is that money is a *stock*, not a *flow*. When we discuss the demand for chicken, we do so in terms of pounds of chicken demanded *per year*. When we discuss aggregate demand, we speak in terms of constant dollars of total planned expenditure *per year*. But when we speak of the demand for money, we are talking about the quantity of an asset that people want to hold *at a point in time*. Money is the stock of liquid assets used as means of payment, store of purchasing power, and unit of account. To be more technical, money, as used in this book, generally means the total of the assets that enter into *M2*, that is, currency, transaction deposits, MMDAs, savings and small-denomination time deposits, money market mutual funds, repurchase agreements, and certain other items. When we occasionally refer to M1, we will make the distinction clear.

Nominal Income and Money Demand

Unfortunately, it is easy to forget that money, as the term is used in economics, refers to a stock of liquid assets. The confusion arises from our habit of using "money" as a careless synonym for "income" in everyday conversation. "I'm going to get a part time job so I can make some money," we say, when the correct economic terminology would be, "I'm going to get a part time job so that I can earn some income." From the careless use of "money" to mean "income," it is a short step to the idea that the "demand for money" is unlimited—because other things being equal, everyone would always want more income rather than less.

Once we focus on the notion that money means a stock of certain liquid assets, we can see that the demand for money is a question of how much money people want to hold *given* the income they earn and other economic conditions. Centuries of experience have demonstrated that other things being equal (we will get to those "other things" shortly), people want to hold a stock of money that varies in proportion to their income. Thus, in a feudal society, the peasant living on a subsistence income has a few copper coins in a jar in the cupboard, whereas the lord of the manor, with a princely income, keeps bags of gold coins in his strong room. In modern times, the average college student's stock of money may consist of a few Federal Reserve notes in her purse, whereas her parents, who earn higher income from full-time jobs, hold substantial balances in their liquid accounts. Looking at matters from the viewpoint of the economy as a whole, the total stock of money held by all households and firms varies in proportion to the level of nominal national income, other things being equal.

The desire to hold a stock of money related to income arises in part from the nature of money as a means of payment that can be used to carry out transactions ranging from the purchase of a candy bar to the purchase of a house. Because the nominal volume of transactions made in the economy varies in proportion to nominal national income, other things being equal, so does the demand for money used by households and firms as a means of payment. The demand for money also reflects its nature as a readily accessible liquid store of value. As the incomes of households and firms rises, so does their wealth, and they will want to hold part of that wealth in liquid nontransactions balances, such as savings deposits, that are also included in M2.

The proportionality of money demand to income can be expressed as the desired ratio of money to nominal national income, or equivalently, as the desired ratio of nominal national income to money. As we saw in Chapter 11, the ratio of nominal national income to money is termed the *income velocity of money*. Thus, to say that people want to hold a stock of liquid assets that varies in proportion to nominal national income, other things being equal, is equivalent to saying that they desire to maintain a certain constant income velocity of money as nominal national income varies. In this and later chapters, we will frequently employ the term *velocity* in connection with the demand for money.

The Opportunity Cost of Holding Money

Useful though money is for carrying out transactions and as a store of value, its usefulness comes with an opportunity cost. The opportunity cost arises from the fact that funds held in the form of money could instead be held in the form of some less liquid asset, and as a general rule, relatively less liquid assets earn a higher return for their owners than relatively more liquid assets.

Consider the various components of M2. Currency and traditional demand deposits earn no interest at all. NOW accounts, MMDAs, savings and small-denomination time deposits, and money market mutual funds do earn some interest, as do repurchase agreements and other M2 components held by business firms. But the interest rates earned by these assets are lower, on average, than the interest rates on less liquid assets such as government securities, corporate stocks, or home mortgages.

The opportunity cost of money, then, can be specified as the difference between the interest rate on a representative nonmonetary asset and the weighted average interest rate on the components of M2. Usually the nonmonetary asset chosen for comparison is one that is fairly liquid but not liquid enough to count as part of M2. A nonmonetary interest rate we will use in measuring the opportunity cost of money is the rate on three-month Treasury bills. In recent years the opportunity cost of M2 measured in comparison to the Treasury bill rate has varied in the range of 1 to 3 percentage points.

Opportunity Cost and Money Demand

Let us turn back now to our earlier assertion that the quantity of money demanded varies in proportion to nominal national income, other things being equal. The key item covered by the "other things being equal" clause in this statement is the opportunity cost of holding money. If we hold opportunity cost constant, the quantity of money demanded is very closely proportional to nominal national income. However, if the opportunity cost of money increases, the quantity of money demanded at a *given* level of nominal national income will decrease. It will do so because firms and households will forgo some of the convenience of money's liquidity to earn the higher interest rate available on nonmonetary assets.

Consider a household that holds funds for day-to-day transactions in a checking account and a reserve of liquid funds in a money market mutual fund. If interest rates on less liquid assets rise relative to the rate paid by the money market fund, the household may be tempted to convert part of the liquid reserve to a less liquid mutual fund that invests in corporate stocks or bonds. Or consider a firm that holds funds with a bank in demand deposits and repurchase agreements. If interest rates on less liquid assets rise relative to the RP rate, it may consider converting part of those funds to, say, large certificates of deposit, which do not count as part of M2.

When the household or firm makes the decision to switch from an M2 component to a less liquid asset, it earns more interest income, but there is a trade-off. First, the less liquid asset cannot be used as a means of payment. If the household or firm later decides to spend those funds, it will first have to sell the less liquid asset, which may involve a delay and the payment of a broker's fee. Second, there is some risk of loss because the less liquid asset does not have a fixed nominal value. There is no guarantee that it can be sold for the same price as was paid for it. Because of this trade-off, if the interest rate on nonmonetary assets falls again, households and firms will retreat to the convenience and safety of money for an additional part of their assets.

The same tendencies can also be expressed in terms of velocity. Velocity is the ratio of nominal national income to the stock of money. If people reduce the quantity of money they hold per dollar of nominal national income, velocity will rise; if they increase the quantity of money they hold per dollar of national income, velocity will fall. We expect, then, that M2 velocity will vary directly with the opportunity cost of M2. And that is just what happens, as shown by the data presented in Exhibit 13.1.

The Opportunity Cost of M2 and Market Interest Rates

At this point a question arises: Why does the opportunity cost of M2 ever vary? The answer is not obvious. Suppose, for example, that all money was held in NOW accounts (interest-bearing checking accounts). To cover costs of processing checks and earn the returns expected by their shareholders, banks either charge fees to depositors or pay a lower rate of interest on NOW accounts than they earn on the assets they hold, such as federal funds, securities, and loans. But suppose that a spread of 2 percentage points is the minimum needed to cover

Exhibit 13.1 M2 Velocity and M2 Opportunity Cost

Velocity is the ratio of nominal national income to the stock of money. If people reduce the quantity of money they hold per dollar of nominal national income, velocity will rise; if they increase the quantity of money they hold per dollar of national income, velocity will fall. This chart shows that M2 velocity varies closely with the opportunity cost of holding M2, which is represented here by the difference between the three-month Treasury bill rate and the weighted average interest rate offered on the components of M2.

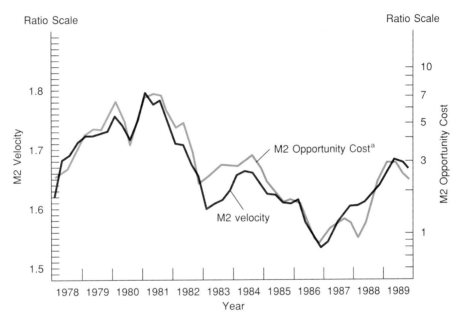

[a]Three-month Treasury bill rate minus average offering rate on M2 components, two-quarter moving average.

Source: Federal Reserve Board of Governors.

the banks' costs and the return to their shareholders. Why wouldn't competition among banks cause them to adjust the rate offered on NOW accounts point-for-point every time market rates changed? In other words, why wouldn't they pay 4 percent on NOW accounts when the federal funds rate was 6 percent, 8 percent on NOW accounts when the federal funds rate was 10 percent, and so on? If interest rates on NOW accounts and other M2 components behaved this way, the opportunity cost of holding M2 would never change, velocity would never change, and a graph such as that in Exhibit 13.1 would be a straight, horizontal line.

The world does not work that way for a number of reasons. Interest rates on money market mutual funds and personal small-denomination time deposits do tend to adjust point-for-point to changes in market rates, although not instantaneously. For other M2 components, though, the adjustment to changes in market rates is incomplete. In particular:

- Currency and demand deposits pay no interest at all. Thus, when market rates rise, the opportunity cost of these M2 components rises by the same amount.

• NOW accounts are subject to reserve requirements at a ratio of up to 12 percent. Certain *nonpersonal* nontransactions accounts—that is, MMDAs, savings deposits and small-denomination time deposits not owned by individual households—are subject to a 3 percent reserve requirement. Banks earn no interest on the vault cash or deposits with the Fed that they hold as reserves against these deposits. Therefore, banks' opportunity cost of holding reserves reduces the interest rates they can profitably offer on these types of accounts and prevents their full adjustment to changes in market rates.

Exhibit 13.2   Market Interest Rates and Opportunity Cost of M2

The opportunity cost of holding M2 is equal to the difference between the market rate on a typical nonmonetary asset, in this case, the three-month Treasury bill rate and the average interest rate on the components of M2. If a 1 percentage point change in the market interest rate were always immediately matched by an equal change in the weighted average interest rate on M2 components, the difference between the two rates would not change. However, as this chart shows, a 1 percentage point increase in the market rate causes the M2 interest rate to change, but by less than 1 full percentage point in the short run. As a result, the opportunity cost of M2, shown here as the gap between the two interest rates, tends to increase when the market interest rate rises and to decrease when the market interest rate falls.

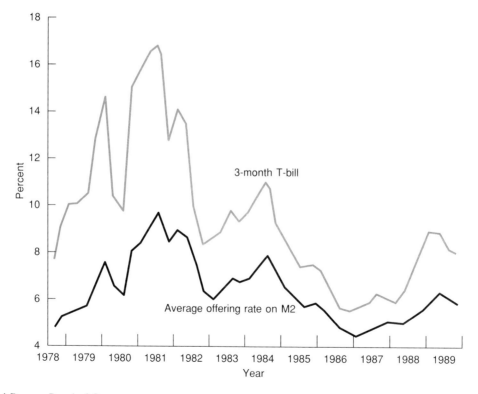

Source: Federal Reserve Board of Governors.

- Personal MMDAs and savings deposits are not subject to reserve requirements. In principle, banks could adjust their offering rates in step with market rates. In practice, however, they do so only very sluggishly. As a matter of marketing practice, banks seem to have chosen to compete for the funds of interest-sensitive customers ("hot money," in bank jargon) by adjusting rates on small-denomination time deposits and to compete for other household accounts on the basis of convenience and service rather than interest.

Putting all these considerations together, we find that the weighted average of interest rates on all M2 components does not adjust point-for-point with short-run changes in market interest rates. This is shown clearly in Exhibit 13.2, which compares the average rate of interest offered on M2 components (the M2 offering rate) with the three-month Treasury bill rate. The M2 rate rises when the T-bill rate rises, but not by a full percentage point for every percentage-point change in the T-bill rate. The same applies to decreases in the T-bill rate. Thus, the opportunity cost of M2 varies directly with variations in market interest rates.

The Money Demand Curve

The general ideas expressed in our discussion of portfolio balance can be used to construct a money demand curve for the economy as a whole. Such a curve shows the total quantity of money that all firms and households want to hold under given conditions.

In drawing a money demand curve, we place the quantity of money (M2) on the horizontal axis. On the vertical axis, we place the nominal interest rate on a typical nonmonetary asset. Logically, it might seem more straightforward to place the opportunity cost of M2 on the vertical axis. However, as we will see in the next two chapters, it is easier to relate money demand to events in other parts of the economy if we draw the money demand curve in terms of the interest rate. It is justifiable to do so because, as we have seen, market interest rates and M2 opportunity cost move closely together.

Part (a) of Exhibit 13.3 shows two money demand curves. Each money demand curve has a negative slope. The negative slope of the money demand curve reflects the fact that other things being equal, people want to hold less money and instead, more nonmonetary assets, as market interest rates rise. As market interest rates fall, they tend to reduce their holdings of nonmonetary assets in order to gain the liquidity benefits of holding more money.

Shifts in the money demand curve.   Money demand curves, like other demand curves, are drawn on the basis of "other things being equal." In the money demand curve, the most important condition that is held equal for a given demand curve is the level of nominal national income. As we have explained, the quantity of money people desire to hold at any given interest rate tends to vary in proportion to nominal national income. Thus, if there is a change in nominal national income, the money demand curve will shift.

Suppose, for example, that nominal national income doubles, because real incomes double while the price level is unchanged, because prices double while real income is unchanged, or as a result of a combination of both kinds of change. Whatever the cause of the doubling of nominal national income, every

Exhibit 13.3   A Money Demand Schedule for a Simple Economy

This exhibit shows how the amount of money demanded varies in a simple economy as the interest rate on a representative nonmonetary asset and the level of nominal national income vary. The entries in part (b) show the amount of money demanded at the interest rate corresponding to each row and the nominal national income corresponding to each column. Each column can be graphed to get a money demand curve for a given level of nominal national income. MD_1 corresponds to the fourth column ($600 billion) and MD_2 to the last column ($1,200 billion).

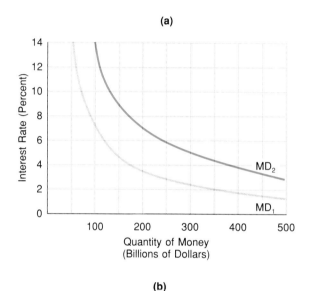

(a)

(b)

Interest Rate (Percent)	Nominal National Income (Billions of Dollars)					
	$200	$400	$600	$800	$1,000	$1,200
2	$120	$240	$360	$480	$600	$720
3	80	160	240	320	400	480
4	60	120	180	240	300	360
6	40	80	120	160	200	240
8	30	60	90	120	150	180
10	24	48	72	96	120	144
12	20	40	60	80	100	120
14	17	34	51	68	85	102
16	15	30	45	60	75	90

household and firm will, on the average, undertake twice the nominal volume of transactions as before. Other things being equal (that is, at any given level of the interest rate), they would want to hold twice as much money to facilitate these transactions. They would also tend to double their nontransactions balances used as a liquid store of purchasing power. Therefore, as shown in part (a) of Exhibit 13.3, a doubling of nominal national income will cause the money demand curve to shift to the right, from MD_1 to MD_2.

Money demand in numerical form.   To further clarify the relationships among the interest rate, nominal national income, and the quantity of money demanded, part (b) of Exhibit 13.3 presents these relationships in numerical form. Each column of the table represents a single money demand curve. The columns show what happens to the quantity of money demanded as the interest rate changes while nominal national income remains the same. Each row of the table, on the other hand, shows how money demand responds to a change in nominal national income at a given interest rate. The general principle is that when the interest rate is held constant, the quantity of money demanded is proportional to nominal national income.

Money demand and velocity.   The data in part (b) of Exhibit 13.3 imply that at any given nominal interest rate there will be a certain ratio of nominal national income to the quantity of money demanded. For example, consider the row of the table corresponding to an interest rate of 12 percent. Reading along that row, we see that when nominal national income is $200 billion, the quantity of money demanded is $20 billion; when nominal national income is $400 billion, the quantity of money demanded is $40 billion; and so on. For an interest rate of 12 percent, then, the ratio of nominal national income to the quantity of money demanded—that is, the income velocity of money—is 10:1 for all levels of nominal national income. Looking at other rows in the table, we see that velocity is 5:1 when the interest rate is 6 percent, 2.5:1 when the interest rate is 3 percent, and so on.

Expressing the money demand relationship in terms of velocity provides a convenient way of comparing the theoretical relationship of Exhibit 13.3 with actual data from the U.S. economy. That is done in Exhibit 13.4. The data presented there are consistent with such a relationship. In Exhibit 13.4, the left-hand vertical scale shows M2 velocity, that is, the ratio of nominal GNP to M2. The right-hand vertical scale shows the three-month Treasury bill rate. The graphs of M2 velocity and the nominal interest rate fit closely over the 12-year period represented in the exhibit. This is what is to be expected, because we have already shown a strong relationship between velocity and M2 opportunity cost (Exhibit 13.1) and between M2 opportunity cost and the nominal interest rate on our typical nonmonetary asset (Exhibit 13.2).

13.2   Supply, Demand, and the Money Market

Having looked in some detail at the demand for money, we are ready to put demand together with supply. The result is a graph such as that shown in Exhibit 13.5. The horizontal axis shows the money stock, measured in dollars; the vertical axis shows the interest rate as a percentage per year. Changes in the interest rate, as we have seen, are associated with changes in the opportunity cost of holding part of a portfolio of assets in the form of M2 rather than in the form of a representative nonmonetary interest-bearing asset.

The money demand curve in Exhibit 13.5 shows the amount of money that people want to hold at each given interest rate assuming nominal national income of $1,200 billion. An increase in nominal national income will shift the money demand curve to the right, and a decrease will shift it to the left.

Exhibit 13.4   M2 Velocity and the Nominal Interest Rate

The money demand relationship of Exhibit 13.3 implies that M2 velocity—the
ratio of nominal national income to money—will be constant for all levels of
nominal national income for a given nominal interest rate and will vary directly
with variations in the interest rate. The relationship shown here between the
nominal interest rate on three-month Treasury bills and M2 velocity is consistent
with a such a relationship. Over time, nominal national income has increased
steadily, but the ratio of nominal national income to M2 has closely followed
variations in the nominal interest rate.

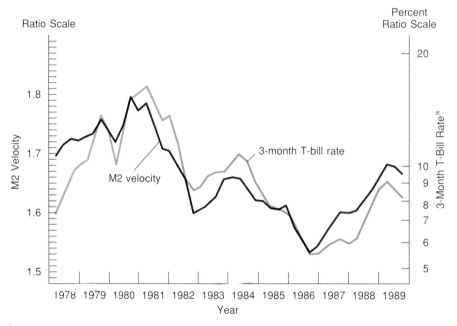

[a]Two-quarter moving average.

Source: Federal Reserve Board of Governors.

As discussed in Chapter 12, the money supply is under the control of the
Federal Reserve. The exact shape of the money supply curve depends on how
the Fed chooses to use its tools of monetary control. The supply curve in Exhibit 13.5 assumes that the Fed sets a target for the money stock ($180 billion in
this case) and uses open market operations to stabilize reserves so as to keep the
money stock on target regardless of what happens to the interest rate. This
assumption results in a vertical money supply curve. The final section of this
chapter discusses other possible money supply curves.

We will refer to the supply and demand situation shown in Exhibit 13.5 as
the "money market," but this is not a market in the usual sense. We typically
think of a market as a place where people buy and sell things, that is, exchange
things for money. People do not "buy" and "sell" money in this sense. Also, the
vertical axis in this market does not show the price of money relative to the price
of something else; rather, it shows the interest rate on a representative nonmone-

Exhibit 13.5   Equilibrium in the Money Market

The money demand curve shown here is based on the data given in part (b) of Exhibit 13.3, assuming a nominal national income of $1,200 billion. The money supply curve assumes that the Fed sets a money supply target of $180 billion and adjusts total reserves to maintain this quantity of money regardless of what happens to interest rates. Under these conditions, the equilibrium interest rate is 8 percent.

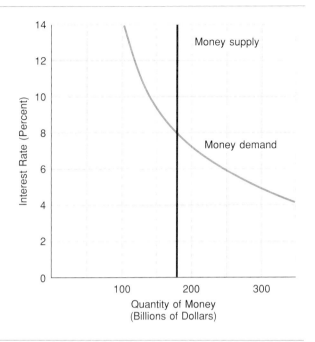

tary asset, which, as we have shown, is linked to the opportunity cost of holding money. Despite these unusual features, however, supply and demand interact in the so-called money market to produce an equilibrium much as they do in more familiar kinds of markets.

Equilibrium in the Money Market

The supply and demand curves in Exhibit 13.5 intersect at an interest rate of 8 percent. At that rate, the amount of money supplied by the banking system (which is determined, in turn, by the amount of reserves the Fed supplies to the banking system) just equals the amount people want to hold. There is neither upward nor downward pressure on interest rates.

No other interest rate would permit such an equilibrium. Suppose, for example, that the interest rate were just 4 percent. With such a low implied opportunity cost of money, people would want to hold more of it. They would try to obtain more money by borrowing from banks, but as long as the total quantity of bank reserves is constant, the banking system as a whole cannot increase the total quantity of deposits.[1] However, any one bank can acquire the added reserves it would need to expand loans and deposits by borrowing those reserves from other banks in the federal funds market. Competition among banks in the federal funds market would drive up the federal funds rate. Other short- and long-term market interest rates tend to adjust quickly to changes in the federal

---

[1]To be precise, we should say that they cannot increase the total quantity of deposits subject to reserves. To simplify matters, we will assume that all deposits are subject to a uniform required-reserve ratio.

funds rate, so that the whole family of interest rates would rise to the level corresponding to 8 percent on the vertical axis of Exhibit 13.5. The money market would then be back in equilibrium.

In Exhibit 13.5, a rising interest rate brings the market back into equilibrium by reducing the amount of money demanded rather than by increasing the amount of money supplied. As long as the Fed provides no more reserves to the banking system, banks cannot supply any more money. Even though any one person can add money to his or her portfolio by borrowing or by selling some other asset, this will not affect the amount of money in the banking system as a whole.

The same story can be told in reverse for the case in which the interest rate is higher than its equilibrium value. In that event people would not be willing to hold all the money that banks want to supply. Banks cannot force people to hold deposits. They can, however, attempt to put excess reserves to work by lending them in the federal funds market. Under such circumstances, competition among banks will drive the federal funds rate down, and other interest rates will fall as a consequence. As the interest rate falls, the public becomes willing to hold the quantity of money that banks would like to supply, given the amount of reserves available to the system.

Effects of a Change in the Money Supply

Our description of the money market is useful for a number of purposes. Let us begin by using it to analyze the effects of shifts in the money supply curve.

Exhibit 13.6 shows the money market in equilibrium at E_1 with a money supply of $180 billion and an interest rate of 8 percent. Starting from this point, the Fed decides to increase the money supply to $360 billion. Assuming a money multiplier of 10, it can do this by injecting $18 billion of new reserves into the banking system by means of open market purchases.

The immediate impact of the open market operation is to boost banks' excess reserves. To restore their balance sheets to equilibrium, banks set out to convert the excess reserves into earning assets. The quickest way to do so is to

Exhibit 13.6 Effects of an Increase in the Money Supply

The money stock starts out at $180 billion, putting the money supply curve in the position MS_1. An open market purchase by the Fed injects new reserves into the banking system. Banks' competitive efforts to put the new reserves to work drive rates down, first in the federal funds market and then in other markets. As the money supply expands, the economy moves toward a new equilibrium, E_2, where the interest rate has fallen by enough to make people willing to hold the larger quantity of money.

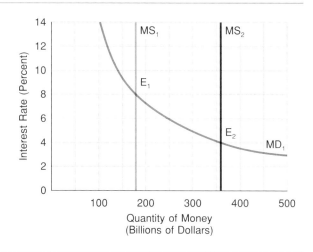

lend the excess reserves in the federal funds market. Their attempts to do so will drive down the federal funds rate. Soon the decline in interest rates will spread to other markets, including the markets for consumer and business loans.

As the volume of borrowing expands, the quantity of deposits supplied to the public increases, as explained in Chapter 12. In Exhibit 13.6 this is shown as a shift in the money supply curve from MS_1 to MS_2. At point E_1 people were content to hold the old quantity of money, $180 billion, in their portfolios. Now falling interest rates reduce the opportunity cost of holding money and make people willing to absorb the increased quantity supplied by banks. Thus, as the injection of reserves shifts the money supply curve to the right, falling interest rates cause people to move downward and to the right along their money demand curve. In time a new equilibrium is reached at point E_2, where the money stock is greater and the interest rate lower than before.

If the Fed withdraws reserves from the banking system through an open market sale, the same process operates in reverse. Banks find themselves with less than the required quantity of reserves. At first, they will try to obtain the reserves they need in the federal funds market. However, with total reserves fixed, their attempts to do so will only drive up the federal funds rate. As that happens, banks may decide to restore their balance sheets to equilibrium by reducing their holdings of securities or loans. To do so, they sell securities or they accept payments on old loans without making new loans to replace them. New loans thus become harder for borrowers to obtain. Competition among borrowers soon drives interest rates on loans upward. As interest rates in general rise, people become willing to hold a smaller quantity of money in their portfolios. A new equilibrium is reached in which the money supply is smaller and the interest rate higher than before.

Effects of an Increase in Income

In discussing the effects of a change in the money supply, we have assumed that the level of nominal national income remained constant. Let us reverse that assumption and see what happens to the money market when nominal national income changes while the money supply curve stays put.

Exhibit 13.7 sets the stage. It shows the market in equilibrium at E_1 with an interest rate of 4 percent and a money supply of $180 billion. Nominal national income is assumed to be $600 billion, which puts the money demand curve in the position MD_1.

Now assume that nominal national income rises to a level of $1,200 billion. As we saw earlier in the chapter, an increase in nominal national income, other things being equal, shifts the money demand curve to the right. The new position of the money demand curve is MD_2.

At the new, higher income level, other things being equal, people will want more money with which to carry out transactions and to hold as a liquid store of value. They will attempt to obtain the additional money partly by borrowing from banks. Banks, in turn, will try to get the reserves they need to support the added loans and deposits by borrowing in the federal funds market. But the federal funds market only moves reserves around from one bank to another. The banking system as a whole cannot increase its total deposits given the total reserves supplied by the Fed. Competition among borrowers thus will not increase the money stock as a whole, but will instead drive up interest rates. The higher interest rates will make people willing to get along with the limited money stock

Exhibit 13.7   Effects of an Increase
in Nominal National Income

A nominal national income of $600 billion puts the
money demand curve at MD₁. The equilibrium interest
rate is 4 percent given this income and the money
supply of $180 billion. If an increase in nominal
income to $1,200 billion shifts the money demand
curve to MD₂, there will be an excess demand for
money at the initial interest rate. People will try to
increase the quantity of money they hold, in part by
borrowing from banks. As a result of competition
among banks for reserves to meet the increased loan
demand, interest rates will rise, first in the federal
funds market, and then in the loan market and other
markets.

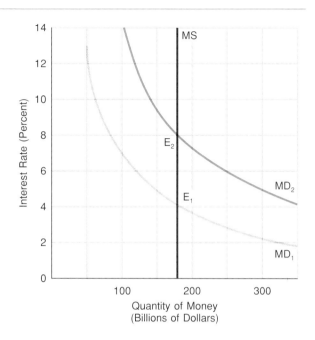

available despite their higher incomes. Thus, the economy will move to a new
equilibrium at E_2. There nominal national income and the interest rate are
higher than before and the money stock has not changed.

If nominal national income falls, the same process will occur in reverse.
With lower incomes, people will require less money. If the interest rate does not
change, they will reduce their demand for deposits, in the process tending to pay
off old loans without taking out an equal volume of new ones. Banks will attempt
to lend the resulting excess reserves in the federal funds market, but because
many banks are doing so at once, their efforts will cause the federal funds rate to
fall. Other rates, including, eventually, loan rates, will be pushed down as well.
When interest rates fall enough to make people content to hold the existing
money stock even at a lower level of nominal national income, the money market
will be back in equilibrium. The interest rate will be lower than before; nominal
national income will be lower; and the money stock will not have changed.

The Money Market, Interest Rates, and
the Aggregate Demand Curve

In the preceding section we saw that an increase in nominal national income
tends to raise the equilibrium interest rate, because it shifts the money demand
curve to the right. This is true regardless of the form of the increase in nominal
national income.

One possibility is an increase in real income with no change in the price
level. In this case people will want to hold a greater quantity of money in part to
make the transactions connected with the production and sale of a larger volume
of real output, and in part to add to savings-type balances. The money supply

curve will shift to the right, as shown in Exhibit 13.6, and the interest rate will rise.

On the other hand, the increase in nominal income may take the form of a higher price level with no change in the real income level. In that case the physical volume of transactions will not change, but more money will be needed to carry out the transactions because goods and services will have higher prices. Also, with a higher price level, more nominal savings balances will be needed to maintain the real value of those balances. Thus, an increase in the price level is also capable of shifting the money demand curve to the right and driving up the equilibrium interest rate.

In practice, changes in nominal national income usually reflect some combination of changes in the price level and changes in real income. However, separating the two effects helps us understand the nature of the economy's aggregate demand curve. The reasons for the negative slope of the aggregate demand curve presented in Chapter 7 included a statement that, other things being equal, a rise in the price level tends to increase the interest rate, thereby depressing the level of planned investment expenditure. We now see why this is so. A higher price level pushes up the interest rate because it shifts the money demand curve. A given money stock can be considered one of the "other things being equal" conditions that lies behind the economy's aggregate demand curve.

We can also see why the aggregate demand curve is relatively inelastic with respect to the price level. As the price level increases, the interest rate rises. As we saw earlier in the chapter, an increase in the interest rate causes velocity to rise. According to the equation of exchange, if velocity rises while the quantity of money remains constant (as it does at all points on a given aggregate demand curve), nominal national product must rise. For nominal output to rise as we move upward along the negatively sloped aggregate demand curve, the percentage decrease in real output must be less than the percentage increase in price. And a percentage change in quantity demanded that is smaller than the associated percentage change in price is the definition of relatively inelastic demand.

13.3   Operating Targets, Interest Rates, and the Money Supply

The examples given in the preceding section used a vertical money supply curve, indicating that the Fed set a target value for the money stock and undertook open market operations as necessary to keep it at that value. The key variable used by the Fed to guide its open market operations—in this case, a fixed value for the money stock—is known as the Fed's **operating target.** As we will see in this section, other operating targets are possible, and the target chosen will affect the money supply curve.

As we look at the various operating targets that the Fed might use—or has used at one time or another—we will find that the role played by interest rates in guiding the Fed's operations is a matter of controversy. Some economists believe that the Fed's job is to keep the money supply under control; once it has done so, it should let interest rates go wherever the market sends them. Other economists, along with many businesspeople, think that part of the Fed's job should be to prevent sharp ups and downs in interest rates. Large swings in interest rates, they say, can disrupt business planning, thereby hurting employment and productivity.

Operating target
A financial variable for which the Fed sets a short-term target, which it then uses as a guide in the day-to-day conduct of open market operations.

Three Operating Targets

Exhibit 13.8 shows three possible operating targets, each represented by a different money supply curve. Part (a) shows a money stock target as assumed in the preceding section. Here the Fed selects a target for the money stock and adjusts the level of bank reserves to maintain the money stock at that level regardless of what happens to interest rates. This procedure results in the vertical money supply curve MS_1. With the money demand curve in the position MD_1, a money supply of $180 billion would, as shown, result in an equilibrium interest rate of 8 percent for a representative short-term security.

The second operating target, shown in part (b) of the exhibit, focuses on the interest rate. In this case the Fed begins by deciding what the interest rate should be. It then uses open market operations to adjust the money supply so as to bring the equilibrium interest rate to the target level. This strategy is represented by a horizontal money supply curve. If the interest rate target is 8 percent, the money supply curve will be in the position MS_2. Given the money demand curve MD_1, the Fed would have to allow the money stock to settle at $180 billion in order to hit the 8 percent target. If the money demand curve were to shift to the right or left, the Fed would use open market purchases or sales to adjust the money stock along the path MS_2.

The third possibility is represented by MS_3 in part (c) of the exhibit. In this case the Fed targets neither the money supply nor the interest rate. Instead, it allows the money supply to expand whenever the interest rate rises, but not by enough to completely offset the rise in the interest rate.

Responses to Changes in the Demand for Money

As we have seen, the economy's money demand curve is subject to occasional shifts. Changes in nominal income are one major source of such shifts. Institutional changes, such as the introduction of new types of transaction deposits, are another. Short-term shifts that are hard to predict or explain also occur. Exhibit 13.8 can be used to show how the money market responds to shifts in money demand under various operating targets.

The first case—that of a money stock target—has already been discussed. When the money demand curve shifts from MD_1 to MD_2, there is an excess demand for money at the initial interest rate of 8 percent. People try to obtain more money by borrowing; banks' attempts to serve their needs drive up the federal funds rates and other interest rates, but as long as the Fed does not supply more reserves to the banking system, the money supply as a whole cannot increase. A new equilibrium is reached at E_1 with an interest rate of 12 percent.

Next consider the effects of a shift in the money demand curve when the Fed is following an interest rate target, as in part (b) of Exhibit 13.8. This target produces the money supply curve MS_2. Again assume that the money demand curve shifts from MD_1 to MD_2. As before, the initial effect is an excess demand for money, which puts upward pressure on interest rates. Now, however, the Fed's reaction is different. Suppose that the manager of the Fed's open market desk in New York has been instructed to keep an eye on the federal funds rate.

As soon as the excess demand for money starts to push up the federal funds rate, the open market desk begins buying securities. As explained in Chapter 13, this increases the banking system's total reserves. The increase in reserves relieves the upward pressure on interest rates. As banks expand deposits on the

Exhibit 13.8   Operating Targets and the Money Supply Curve

The slope of the money supply curve depends on the Fed's operating target. The Fed can set a target for the money supply and stick to it regardless of what happens to interest rates. In this case, the money supply curve will be vertical, as shown by MS_1 in part (a). Instead, the Fed can set a target for the interest rate and use open market operations to stabilize it (at least in the short run) regardless of what happens to the money stock. In this instance, the money supply curve is horizontal, as shown by MS_2 in part (b). Finally, the Fed can allow the money supply to expand as the interest rate rises. This results in a positively sloped money supply curve, as shown by MS_3 in part (c). A given shift in money demand, such as from M_1 to M_2, will have different effects on the money stock and interest rate depending on the shape of the money supply curve.

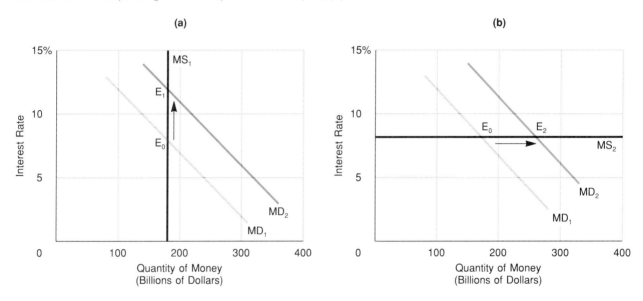

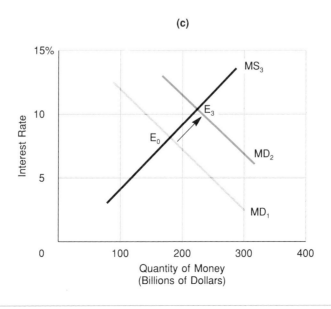

basis of the new reserves, the money stock grows. The result of this process is a rightward movement along the money supply curve MS_2 to a new equilibrium at E_2. In the new equilibrium the money supply has increased to $260 billion and the interest rate is unchanged at 8 percent.

Finally, consider the third possibility, represented by money supply curve MS_3 in part (c) of the exhibit. Here, as in part (b), the Fed reacts to an upward movement in the federal funds rate by injecting new reserves into the banking system. Now, however, it makes only a limited volume of open market purchases. Enough reserves are supplied to let the money supply expand somewhat, but the amount supplied is not enough to keep the interest rate from rising. The result is a new equilibrium at E_3. The interest rate rises less than with a money stock target but more than with an interest rate target; the money stock expands more than with a money stock target but less than with an interest rate target.

Evolution of the Fed's Operating Strategy

Over the years the Fed's strategy for conducting its operations has changed. At one time or another it has included elements of each of the three approaches just described.

Interest rate targeting and its problems. During World War II, the Fed set strict interest rate targets. These were very low by today's standards: 2 1/2 percent on government bonds with maturities longer than 10 years, 7/8 percent on 1-year government securities, and just 3/8 percent on 90-day Treasury bills. The purpose of these low ceilings was to reduce the cost to the Treasury of financing the huge federal budget deficit caused by the war. Also, because the interest rate ceilings would stabilize bond prices, they would prevent wartime speculation in government bonds.

The interest rate ceilings were kept in force for several years after the war. They were abandoned in 1951, but interest rates remained the chief focus of the Fed's policy. Although interest rates were allowed to rise and fall to some extent, the Fed still tended to respond to increases in money demand by supplying new reserves.

As inflation began to accelerate in the late 1960s and early 1970s, economists became critical of the Fed's emphasis on stable interest rates. The problem as they saw it was that targeting interest rates gave monetary policy either an inflationary or a deflationary bias, depending on underlying macroeconomic conditions. For example, they feared that if interest rates were pegged at too low a level, monetary policy would serve as part of a feedback process that worked like this:

1. Expansion of nominal national income increases money demand, putting upward pressure on interest rates.

2. The Fed responds by increasing bank reserves.

3. Increased reserves lead to an expansion of the money stock and to more borrowing and spending by firms and households.

4. More borrowing and spending add to aggregate demand; prices and real output rise as the economy moves up along its aggregate supply curve.

5. The increase in prices and real output means that nominal national income rises, resulting in a further increase in the demand for money.

Where does the process stop if the Fed responds to each increase in money demand with actions that create conditions for a further increase? According to the critics, as long as the Fed keeps supplying new money to feed the growth of nominal income, there is nothing to halt the process short of runaway inflation.

Under other circumstances, the opposite could occur. Suppose that the interest rate is pegged too high and the economy begins to contract. As it does, there will be a tendency for interest rates to fall below the Fed's target level. If the Fed reacts by cutting back on bank reserves to support interest rates, the result will be a deepening contraction.

The Mid- to Late 1970s

By the mid-1970s the Fed was heeding its critics. It continued to use a federal funds rate target as its guide for day-to-day open market operations, but it also set longer-term targets for the growth rates of M1 and M2. Those targets were set at a level that the Fed believed would keep inflation in check. If the money supply grew faster than the targets over a period of weeks or months, and if inflationary pressure seemed to be intensifying, the Fed took this as a sign that its federal funds rate target was too low. To slow the rate of growth of the money supply, it would set a new, higher federal funds rate target to guide its day-to-day operations.

Unfortunately, this strategy did not work very well. The Fed's reactions to faster-than-intended money supply growth in a context of rising inflation were too little too late. Inflation and interest rates continued to drift upward. By 1979 both the inflation rate and the short-term interest rates were in the teens, and there were widespread demands that something be done about the situation.

The Late 1970s to the Early 1980s

In October 1979 the Fed announced a dramatic shift in its monetary control strategy: It would stop using the federal funds rate as a guide for day-to-day policy and instead focus on bank reserves. At each meeting of the Federal Open Market Committee, a target would be set for *nonborrowed* reserves of the banking system. By "nonborrowed reserves" the Fed meant all bank reserves except those that it lends to banks through its discount window. By maintaining tight control over nonborrowed reserves, the Fed would restrain excess money supply growth and inflation. During this period, the Fed's primary focus was on long-run control of M1.

This strategy did not amount to strict targeting of the money stock. Total reserves and the total money stock could still fluctuate to the extent that banks' borrowings from the discount window varied. Thus, the nonborrowed-reserves strategy produced a positively sloped money supply curve. Banks could respond to increased demand for money by borrowing more reserves from the Fed. But because the Fed does not allow unlimited or continual borrowing from its discount window, increases in the demand for money still put upward pressure on interest rates.

The Fed stuck to this strategy for three turbulent years—from October 1979 to October 1982. The results were dramatic. On the plus side, the chain reaction from money growth to inflation to more money growth and more inflation was broken. On the negative side, however, interest rates as well as real output went on a roller coaster ride. As we would expect when the money supply curve has a positive slope, in periods when demand for money strengthened, the money stock was pulled above its target level and interest rates rose. When the demand for money moderated, the money stock fell below its target range and interest rates declined.

The Early to Mid-1980s

In late 1982 the Fed changed its strategy again. It was pleased with the progress that had been made in fighting inflation, but it was concerned about possible adverse effects of its policy. For one thing, experience had shown that targeting nonborrowed reserves could result in huge swings in interest rates during periods of unstable money demand. The Fed wanted to avoid such extreme fluctuations. It felt that another such episode would severely damage the depressed U.S. economy as well as the economies of third world countries that owed billions of dollars to U.S. banks. In addition, the Fed was unsure of the impact of changes in banking regulations that were under way, including the relaxation of interest rate ceilings on certain kinds of deposits and the introduction of super-NOW accounts and MMDAs.

Also during this period, the Fed had increasing doubts about the wisdom of continuing to focus on M1. The growth of highly liquid assets not included in M1 and of savings-type balances in the NOW component of M1 was viewed as a sign that the links between M1 and broader economic activity might be less predictable than in the past. The Fed began to deemphasize M1. In 1987, it stopped announcing a policy target for M1 altogether.

By late 1982 the Fed had decided that its monetary policy should not be guided by hard-and-fast rules for the time being; instead, it should take into account a broad range of factors—growth of broader measures of money and credit, growth of real national income, price-level changes, interest rates, and foreign-exchange rates—in guiding open market operations and changes in the discount rate. As a practical matter, at that time it began using a borrowed-reserves operating target rather than a nonborrowed-reserves target to guide its day-to-day operations. This change eliminated the automatic feedback from a surge in money demand and the money stock to higher required and borrowed reserves to a higher federal funds rate. Instead, the Fed reacted to a tendency for borrowed reserves to increase by using open market purchases to supply the desired reserves through nonborrowed channels. To be sure, the target level of borrowed reserves was adjusted frequently, as was the discount rate, in response to economic developments. Nonetheless, unless there was a deliberate decision to make such a change, there was a constraint on the movement of the federal funds rate.

The Current Period

The degree of constraint on movements of the federal funds rate has been narrowed even further since the stock market crash of October 1987. Initially the Fed wanted to limit volatility of the federal funds rate to avoid destabilizing financial markets. However, it gradually became apparent that banks' borrowing behavior at the discount window had become less predictable and less closely tied to the spread between the discount rate and the federal funds rate. Among other things, as problems of the thrift industry worsened, depository institutions of all kinds became more reluctant to be seen at the discount window for fear that doubts would be raised about their solvency.

Under these conditions, the Fed began to fear that use of a borrowed-reserves operating target would lead to excessively wide swings in the federal funds rate. Accordingly, the FOMC has directed a "flexible" approach to the borrowed-reserves objective with an eye to maintaining a fairly stable federal funds rate. Although operating policy has not returned all the way to the day-to-day funds rate target of the 1970s, it has retreated to a position close to that outcome in practice.

Under Chairman Greenspan, frequent adjustments have been made to the FOMC's target area for the federal funds rate in response to incoming data on economic and financial trends. However, each adjustment has been small—typically in quarter-percentage-point steps. Strings of consecutive funds rate increases have been followed by strings of moves in the opposite direction. Thus a policy of measured gradualism in operating policy adjustments seems to have emerged.

In view of the frequent deliberate changes in the intended trading area for the federal funds rate in response to variations in money growth and other variables, it is difficult to present the Fed's current policy in graphic form. It is safe to say, though, that current policy lies somewhere between the extremes of strict money supply targeting and strict interest rate targeting. The Fed often seems willing to allow shifts in money demand to affect both interest rates and the money stock. In this sense, the Fed appears to be operating along an upward-sloping money supply curve. However, the curve remains much flatter than during the period from October 1979 to October 1982. It is also more subject to discretionary shifts in reaction to new information about a variety of monetary and nonmonetary indicators.

Looking Ahead

This chapter has filled out our picture of the banking system and the money market by showing how the Fed's actions affect interest rates. In addition, it has described the evolution of the Fed's monetary policies. The next chapter develops linkages between monetary policy and the rest of the economy and explores the interaction between monetary and fiscal policy.

Summary

1. **How do income and interest rates affect the demand for money?** According to the theory of money demand, people hold part of their assets in the form of money in order to gain the benefits of liquidity. Other things being equal, the quantity of money people desire to hold varies in proportion to nominal national income. Because the components of M2 pay a lower interest rate on average than a typical nonmonetary asset, such as three-month Treasury bills, an opportunity cost is associated with holding money rather than less liquid assets. This cost varies directly with market interest rates. For a given nominal national income, the quantity of money demanded varies inversely with market interest rates. Another way to express the same thing is to say that velocity—the ratio of nomi-

nal national income to money—varies directly with market interest rates.

2. **What are the characteristics of the money demand curve?** The demand for money can be represented by a downward-sloping curve on a graph in which the horizontal axis measures the quantity of money and the vertical axis measures the interest rate. At any given interest rate, there will be a certain ratio between the quantity of money demanded and nominal national income. Thus, an increase in nominal national income shifts the money demand curve to the right, and a decrease shifts it to the left.

3. **How is the equilibrium interest rate affected by a change in the money stock?** An expansion of bank

reserves increases the quantity of money that banks are willing and able to supply, shifting the money supply curve to the right. As banks seek to convert their excess reserves into income-earning assets, competition among banks drives interest rates down, first in the federal funds market and then in other markets. The decrease in interest rates increases the quantity of money that the public is willing to hold. The economy thus moves down along the money demand curve to a new equilibrium in which the interest rate is lower. A decrease in bank reserves causes a reversal of this sequence of events. The money supply curve shifts to the left, and the interest rate rises.

4. **How is the equilibrium interest rate affected by a change in nominal national income?** An increase in nominal national income increases the quantity of money that people would like to hold at any given interest rate. This is represented by a rightward shift of the money demand curve. People attempt to obtain more money by borrowing more from banks, causing banks to compete in the federal funds market for the limited available supply of reserves. This competition drives interest rates up until a new equilibrium is reached at which people are satisfied to hold the existing quantity of money at the new level of nominal national income. Similarly, a decrease in nominal national income shifts the money demand curve to the left, causing a decrease in the equilibrium interest rate.

5. **What targets has the Fed used as guides for its open market operations?** The slope of the money supply curve is determined by the Fed's *operating target*. If the Fed chooses a money stock target, the money supply curve will be vertical. If it sets an interest rate target, the money supply curve will be horizontal. In cases in which the interest rate is allowed to vary but an increase in the interest rate resulting from an increase in money demand is partly offset by a rise in the money stock, the money supply curve has a positive slope. During and after World War II, the Fed set targets for interest rates on government securities. Later interest rates were allowed to move somewhat, but they remained the focal point of the Fed's policies. During the 1970s, the Fed began to place more emphasis on the money supply. From 1979 through 1982, it pursued a strategy of targeting nonborrowed reserves. This resulted in a much steeper—though not vertical—money supply curve. After 1982, the Fed for a time placed more emphasis on a borrowed-reserves target. Since 1987, Federal Reserve policy has evolved in the direction of a federal funds rate target with frequent discretionary adjustment.

Term for Review

- operating target

Questions for Review

1. How is the quantity of money that people want to hold affected by nominal national income, other things being equal?

2. What determines the opportunity cost of holding money? How does the opportunity cost of money affect the quantity of money demanded? How is the opportunity cost of holding money related to market interest rates?

3. How is velocity affected by an increase in the nominal interest rate? By a decrease in the nominal interest rate?

4. Are the effects of an increase in nominal national income more properly shown by a movement along the money demand curve or a shift in the curve? In which way are the effects of a change in the interest rate best shown?

5. Are the effects of an open market purchase by the Federal Reserve best shown by a rightward shift in a vertical money supply curve, by a leftward shift in the curve, or by a movement along the curve? How does the interest rate change in response to an open market purchase, other things being equal?

6. With no change in the money supply, are the effects of an increase in nominal national income best shown by a rightward shift in the money demand curve, a leftward shift in the curve, or a movement along the curve? What happens to interest rates as a result of an increase in nominal national income?

7. What is the shape of the money supply curve when the Fed pursues a money stock operating target? When it pursues an interest rate target? What conditions result in a positively sloped money supply curve?

8. If the demand for money increases, what happens to the amount of money supplied and the interest rate assuming that the Fed follows (a) a money stock target, (b) an interest rate target, or (c) a nonborrowed-reserves target?

9. How has the Fed's monetary control strategy changed over time? How can the evolution of its strategy be represented in terms of the money supply curve?

Problems and Topics for Discussion

1. **Examining the lead-off case.** In the excerpt at the beginning of the chapter, Fed Chairman Greenspan notes that in early 1989 the economy was expanding in real terms and the price level was rising. Under these circumstances, would the Fed need to reduce bank reserves to "tighten" monetary policy, that is, to cause interest rates to increase? Or would it be enough just to slow or stop the growth of reserves? Explain in terms of money supply and demand curves. Later in

the year the growth of nominal GNP slowed, although it did not stop. Under those circumstances, what would the Fed have to do to cause interest rates to fall?

2. **Velocity.** Using the *Economic Report of the President*, the *Federal Reserve Bulletin*, or another source, find the values of M2, nominal GNP, and the three-month Treasury bill rate for the two most recent years reported. Calculate velocity for the two years. If the T-bill rate changed from one year to the next, did velocity change in the same direction, as expected? If the Treasury bill rate was unchanged, did velocity also remain unchanged?

3. **Money demand and the price level.** Some economists draw a different type of money demand curve from the one used in this book. They begin with a diagram that shows the quantity of money demanded on the horizontal axis and the price level on the vertical axis. Sketch these axes on a sheet of graph paper. Number the vertical axis from 0 to 10 and the horizon-

tal axis from 0 to $500 billion. Assume a constant real national income of $200 billion and a constant nominal interest rate of 4 percent. Using part (b) of Exhibit 13.3 as a guide, draw a curve showing how the quantity of money demanded varies as the price level changes. (Remember that nominal national income equals real national income times the price level.) How does this version of the money demand curve shift if the interest rate rises from 4 to 6 percent?

4. **Effects of a decrease in the money supply.** Rework the example given in Exhibit 13.6 for the case of a decrease in the money supply from $180 billion to $120 billion.

5. **Effects of a decrease in nominal national income.** Rework the example given in Exhibit 13.7 for the case of a decrease in nominal national income from $600 billion to $400 billion. (Use part (b) of Exhibit 13.3 to draw the demand curve for a nominal national income of $400 billion.)

Case for Discussion
Bond Prices Tumble on Inflation Fears

NEW YORK—Bond prices tumbled for the second day in a row on U.S. inflation fears and more selling by Japanese investors.

Treasury bond prices fell the hardest. Some actively traded bonds dropped 1-1/8 points, or $11.25 for each $1,000 in face amount. Their yield jumped to 8.83 percent, the highest in nearly a year, and most short-term interest rates also rose.

Investors are still reeling from Tuesday morning's news that U.S. consumer prices surged 0.5 percent last month. The increase was more than twice as large as economists had expected, bringing the first quarter's annualized inflation rate to a sizzling 8.5 percent.

That news quickly extinguished hopes for a credit-easing move by the Federal Reserve any time soon. Many analysts now say that the Fed's next step probably will be to push interest rates higher. That speculation has intensified lately because of indications that the economy is perking up.

Source: Tom Herman and Susan Scherreik, "Bond Prices Tumble on Inflation Fears," *The Wall Street Journal*, April 19, 1990, C21. Reprinted by permission of *The Wall Street Journal*, © Dow Jones & Company, Inc., 1990. All Rights Reserved Worldwide.

Questions

1. Bonds are sold in units with a face value of $1,000. Each unit pays the bondholder a *coupon interest rate* that is fixed in nominal terms (say, $100 per year) over the life of the bond (say, 20 years). At the end of that period, the bond matures and the original $1,000 face value is paid to the bondholder along with the final coupon interest payment. Why would the news of an expected increase in the rate of inflation cause a reduction in the price investors would willingly pay for such a bond?

2. The coupon interest rate on a bond is stated as a percentage of its $1,000 face value. For example, a bond that pays $100 in interest annually is said to have a 10 percent coupon interest rate. A bond's *yield*, on the other hand, refers to the bond's annual nominal interest payment expressed as a percentage of the current market price of the bond. What would happen to the yield on a bond with a 10 percent coupon rate if its market price fell to $500, that is, to half the bond's face value? What would happen to the bond's yield if its market price rose to $2,000? Following this reasoning, explain why the news item states that as bond prices "tumbled," yields on the same bonds "jumped."

3. Assuming no change in the rate of growth of real national income, what effect would an increase in the rate of inflation have on the rate of growth of nominal national income? What effect would the increase have on the money demand curve? If the Fed did not change its money supply target, what effect would the increase have on interest rates?

4. In financial jargon, a "credit-easing move" by the Fed means an action that tends to reduce interest rates. Under conditions in which nominal national income is expanding more rapidly than expected, what would the Fed have to do for interest rates to fall? Why might the Fed be reluctant to undertake such a move if the increase in the rate of growth of nominal national income is caused by an unexpected increase in the rate of inflation?

Suggestions for Further Reading

Bryant, Ralph C. *Controlling Money: The Federal Reserve and Its Critics.* Washington, D.C.: Brookings Institution, 1983.

Discusses alternative operating targets and other issues raised in this chapter.

Campbell, Colin D., Rosemary G. Campbell, and Edwin G. Dolan. *Money, Banking, and Monetary Policy.* Hinsdale, Ill.: Dryden Press, 1988.

Chapters 15 through 17 cover the subject of this chapter in greater detail.

Darby, Michael R., William Poole, David E. Lindsey, Milton Friedman, and Michael J. Bazdarich. "Recent Behavior of the Velocity of Money." *Contemporary Policy Issues* (January 1987): 1–33.

A roundtable discussion among noted experts that focuses on the behavior of money demand during 1985 and 1986.

Small, David H., and Richard D. Porter. "Understanding the Behavior of M2 and V2." *Federal Reserve Bulletin* (April 1989): 244–254.

Discusses the relationships among M2, the velocity of M2, market interest rates, and the opportunity cost of M2.

CHAPTER

14

An Integrated View of Monetary and Fiscal Policy

Balancing Fiscal and Monetary Policy

The Administration's primary economic policy goal is to promote further growth. Containing and eventually reducing inflation is key to achieving this goal. It is not sufficient merely to avoid a recession. Administration policies seek to remove impediments to more rapid growth. Faster growth carries with it expanded employment opportunities, an improved atmosphere for the creation of new business, and the means for society both to meet its obligations in the present and to provide for future generations.

Economic growth will continue to raise Federal receipts and lower the budget deficit. However, it is essential that continued restraint on the growth of Federal spending permit the deficit to decline, leading to a balanced budget in fiscal 1993 and to a reduction in the national debt thereafter. . . . A credible commitment to reduced Federal borrowing will hasten the reduction in interest rates and the increase in investment.

The outlook for the economy depends in part on recent and projected monetary policy. Over the second half of 1989, the Federal Reserve eased the stance of monetary policy in view of signs of slower economic growth and reduced inflationary pressures. The lower interest rates that resulted from this easing should help to cushion the slowing in spending that became evident in 1989. . . .

In any event, the Administration anticipates that monetary policy will continue to support economic growth with progress toward reduced inflation. The Administration's program to reduce deficits and raise government saving will complement the Federal Reserve's efforts by fostering lower real interest rates, which will help maintain economic growth while progress is made toward price stability.

Photo source: © Fukuhara Photography, Inc./Westlight.

Source: President's Council of Economic Advisers, *Economic Report of the President* (Washington, D.C.: Government Printing Office, 1990), 51–54.

In the preceding three chapters, we have looked at the monetary sector of the economy in isolation. We have seen how the banking system operates, how the Fed controls the money stock, and how monetary policy affects interest rates. In this chapter we return to the broader themes of inflation, real output, and employment and see how these are shaped by developments in the monetary sector. We will combine what we have learned about the monetary sector with what we previously learned about fiscal policy and the determination of real output, employment, and the price level.

The passages just quoted from the 1990 *Economic Report of the President* emphasize the interaction between monetary and fiscal policy. The long-term goals of high employment, price stability, and economic growth require the president, Congress, and the Federal Reserve to work together. By combining the money market model of Chapter 13 with the aggregate supply and demand model developed earlier, we will gain a better understanding of the need for such coordination and its potential benefits.

14.1   Money and Aggregate Demand

In earlier chapters we saw that a change in any of the components of aggregate demand affects prices, real output, and employment. An increase in aggregate demand pushes the economy up along the aggregate supply curve in the short run; as this happens, prices and real output rise and the unemployment rate falls. A decrease in aggregate demand has the opposite effect: In the short run prices and real output fall and the unemployment rate rises. In Chapter 10 we saw that fiscal policy is capable of affecting output, prices, and employment via its effect on aggregate demand. We will begin this chapter by showing that monetary policy also acts on the economy by way of its effects on aggregate demand.

Short-Run Effects of Monetary Policy

Transmission mechanism
The set of channels through which monetary policy affects real output and the price level.

The set of channels through which money affects the economy is known as the **transmission mechanism.** In this section we will focus on an important aspect of the transmission mechanism, which runs from money to interest rates to the planned-investment component of aggregate demand. Exhibit 14.1 shows how this transmission mechanism works when the economy is exposed to a one-time change in the money stock.

Initially the money market is in equilibrium at point E_1 in part (a) of the exhibit. The money supply curve is in the position MS_1, and the money demand curve is at MD_1; thus, the equilibrium nominal interest rate is R_1. According to the planned-investment schedule in part (b), interest rate R_1 will result in a level of real planned investment indicated by I_1. This level of planned investment is built into aggregate demand curve AD_1 in part (c) along with given conditions regarding consumption, government purchases, and net exports. The initial equilibrium point in part (c) thus is e_1, at the intersection of AD_1 and the aggregate supply curve, AS. Equilibrium real output is y_1, and the price level is P_1.

Effects of expansionary monetary policy.   Now we assume that the Fed raises its target value for the money stock. This is shown in part (a) of Exhibit 14.1 as a rightward shift of the money supply curve to the position MS_2. The shift is

Exhibit 14.1   Short-Run Effects of Expansionary Monetary Policy

A one-time increase in the money stock shifts the money supply curve from MS$_1$ to MS$_2$. The interest rate begins to fall. Real planned investment begins to increase as the economy moves down and to the right along the planned-investment schedule. The increase in planned investment shifts the aggregate demand curve from AD$_1$ to AD$_2$, raising real output and the price level. The resulting rise in nominal national income shifts the money demand curve to the right from MD$_1$ to MD$_2$. This shift is enough to limit the drop in the interest rate but not sufficient to prevent it altogether. In the new short-run equilibrium, the interest rate is lower and real investment, real output, and the price level are all higher than they were initially.

$$\uparrow M_s \rightarrow \downarrow r \rightarrow \uparrow I \rightarrow \uparrow y$$

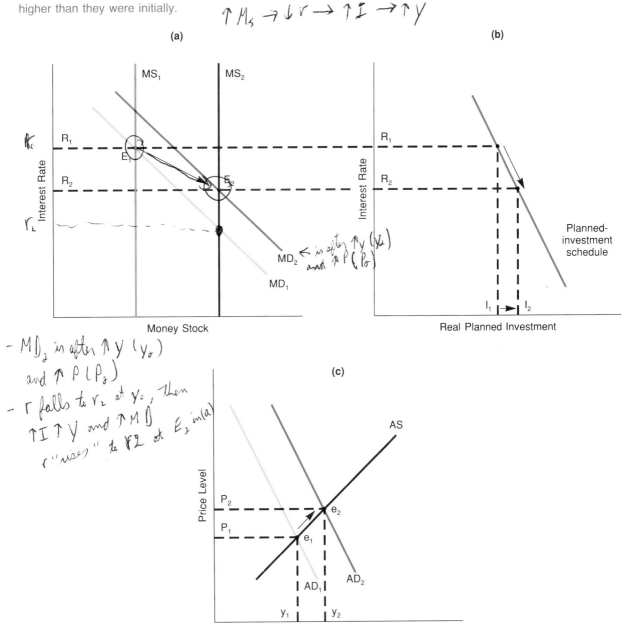

- MD$_2$ is after ↑ y (y$_\sigma$) and ↑ P (P$_2$)
- r falls to r$_2$ at y$_\sigma$, then ↑I ↑Y and ↑MD r "rises" to r$_2$ at E$_2$ in (a)

accomplished by means of an injection of new reserves into the banking system via open market purchases.

As banks compete to put their new reserves to work, the interest rate falls. The falling interest rate lowers the opportunity cost of investment; thus, firms move downward and to the right along the planned-investment schedule shown in part (b). The increase in real planned investment, in turn, causes the aggregate demand curve to shift to the right, as shown in part (c). In response to the boost in demand, real output and the price level both increase and the economy moves upward and to the right along its short-run aggregate supply curve.

As the economy expands, the increase in prices and real output causes nominal national income to rise. Bringing the story full circle, the rise in nominal national income causes the money demand curve to shift to the right, from MD_1 to MD_2. This limits the fall in the interest rate, but the curve does not shift enough to prevent the interest rate from falling somewhat. The money market comes into equilibrium at point E_2, where the new money supply and demand curves intersect. At the new equilibrium interest rate, R_2, real planned investment is I_2. This level of planned investment, together with the same underlying conditions as before regarding real consumption, government purchases, and net exports, puts the aggregate demand curve in the position AD_2. The new short-run equilibrium for the economy thus is e_2 in part (c), where real national product is y_2 and the price level is P_2.

To summarize, expansionary monetary policy has the following effects in the short run:

1. A reduction in the interest rate

2. An increase in the level of real output

3. An increase in the price level

Short-Run Effects of Contractionary Monetary Policy

Exhibit 14.1 can also be used to illustrate the short-run effects of contractionary policy. Starting at E_2 in the money market, the Fed lowers its money stock target, shifting the money supply curve to the left. All the arrows are now reversed. A rising interest rate causes a reduction in planned investment. Falling planned investment shifts the aggregate demand curve to the left, causing prices and real output to fall. This, in turn, means that nominal income declines, causing the money demand curve to shift to the left as well, but not enough to prevent some increase in the interest rate. In the new short-run equilibrium, the money market returns to E_1 and the economy as a whole returns to e_1.

To summarize, contractionary monetary policy has the following effects in the short run:

1. An increase in the interest rate

2. A decrease in the level of real output

3. A decrease in the price level

Long-Run Effects and the Neutrality of Money

In Chapter 7 we explained the distinction between the positively sloped short-run aggregate supply curve and the vertical long-run aggregate supply curve. Movements along the short-run curve are based on firms' expectation that input prices will not change immediately in response to a change in aggregate demand. However, a change in the prices of the final goods that go into national product will eventually affect the level of input prices. As the actual and expected values of input prices adjust to changes in the prices of final goods, the short-run aggregate supply curve shifts upward until the economy returns to equilibrium at the natural level of real output.

Long-run effects of expansionary monetary policy. The economy will undergo such a long-run process of adjustment when the money stock changes and then remains at its new level. This process of long-run adjustment is shown in Exhibit 14.2.

Part (a) of Exhibit 14.2 shows what goes on in the money market as the economy fully adjusts to a once-and-for-all expansion of the money supply. Beginning from E_1, the Fed uses open market purchases to shift the money

Exhibit 14.2   The Neutrality of Money

A one-time increase in the money stock will not cause real output to remain indefinitely above its natural level as at e_2 in part (b) of this exhibit. As expected input prices begin to adjust upward, the aggregate supply curve will shift from AS_1 to AS_2. The economy will move along aggregate demand curve AD_2 until it reaches a new long-run equilibrium at e_3. As it does so, nominal national income will continue to rise, shifting the money demand curve further to the right. The new long-run equilibrium in the money market, shown as E_3 in part (a), will take place at the same interest rate as the original equilibrium. Thus, in the long run, a one-time increase in the money stock will only induce a proportional increase in the price level and leave real output and the interest rate unchanged. This result is known as the *neutrality of money*.

$y > y^*,\ \uparrow w$ SRAS
moves left.
$\uparrow P \rightarrow \uparrow MD$ to MD_3

(a)

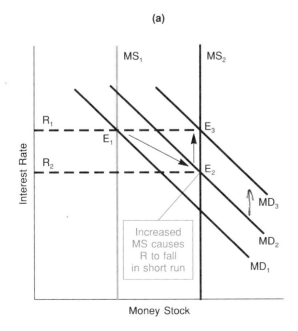

(b)

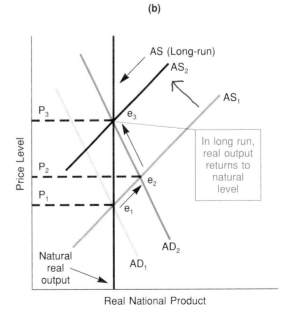

supply curve to MS$_2$. As before, this causes the interest rate to fall and real planned investment (not shown here) to increase. The aggregate demand curve shifts rightward, from AD$_1$ to AD$_2$, and the economy moves to a new short-run equilibrium at e$_2$ in part (b). The increase in nominal national income as the economy moves from e$_1$ to e$_2$ causes the money demand curve to shift from MD$_1$ to MD$_2$. This is where we left off in Exhibit 14.1. Now let us see what happens next.

As the economy moves from e$_1$ to e$_2$, the price level of final goods increases. After a time, this causes input prices to increase as well. As we saw in Chapter 7, this happens partly because some goods serve as both inputs and final goods, and partly because the rise in the price level raises the cost of living, putting upward pressure on wage rates. Once this process begins to affect firms' expectations regarding input prices, the assumption underlying the initial short-run aggregate supply curve AS$_1$ no longer holds. The price level rises above the level that it reached at e$_2$. The short-run aggregate supply curve shifts upward to AS$_2$. As it does so, the economy moves up and to the left along aggregate demand curve AD$_2$ until it returns to the natural level of real output at e$_3$. At that point both final goods prices and input prices have adjusted upward in proportion to the initial increase in the money stock. For example, if the money stock increases by 10 percent, both final goods prices and input prices will also increase by 10 percent.

For reasons discussed in the preceding chapter, the aggregate demand curve is relatively inelastic. Therefore, as the economy moves up and to the left along the curve, the percentage increase in price is greater than the percentage decrease in real output. As a result, nominal national income and product increase. In the money market, the increase in nominal national income shifts the money demand curve farther to the right. This causes the interest rate to rise again as the money market moves straight up along MS$_2$ toward E$_3$. Real planned investment, which had increased while interest rates were reduced, decreases again as interest rates rise. By the time the interest rate returns to R$_1$, real planned investment is back where it started.

The transition from short-run to long-run equilibrium in Exhibit 14.2 can also be described in terms of the equation of exchange, $MV = Py$. Both the aggregate demand curve AD$_2$ and the vertical money supply curve MS$_2$ are drawn on the assumption of a constant money stock. With the money stock, M, unchanged, nominal national income, Py, can increase only if velocity, V, increases. As we saw in the preceding chapter, velocity varies directly with the nominal interest rate. This indicates that as the economy moves from e$_2$ to a new long-run equilibrium at e$_3$, the interest rate must increase at the same time that nominal national income increases—and that is exactly what happens.

The neutrality of money. The preceding analysis shows that a one-time increase in the money stock has the following long-run effects:

Neutrality of money
The proposition that in the long run a one-time change in the money stock affects only the price level and not real output, employment, interest rates, or real planned investment.

1. An increase in the equilibrium levels of both final goods and input prices in proportion to the change in the money stock
2. No change in the equilibrium level of real output
3. No change in the equilibrium interest rate

This set of conclusions is often referred to as the principle of the **neutrality of money.** Money is neutral in the sense that one-time changes in its level do not

Who Said It? Who Did It?   14.1
David Hume on the Neutrality of Money

David Hume was an early member of the classical school of economics as well as a noted historian and philosopher. Born in 1711, he was a colleague of Adam Smith at Edinburgh University. He much admired Smith's *Wealth of Nations*, which was published in 1776, the year Hume died. Although today Smith's contributions to economics overshadow Hume's, many of Hume's writings are regarded as insightful for his time.

Eighteenth-century economists widely agreed that an increase in the money stock—chiefly gold and silver coins at the time—would raise the price level. Price increases had been observed, for example, when the Spanish began bringing gold back to Europe from the New World. A less settled question was whether an increase in the money stock would also "stimulate industry," that is, cause real output to increase. Today we would say that the issue concerned whether or not money is "neutral."

On that subject Hume says that although an increase in the price of goods is a "necessary consequence" of an

increase in the stock of gold and silver, "it follows not immediately." The change in the money stock does not affect all markets at once: "At first, no alteration is perceived; by degrees the price rises, first of one commodity, then of another; till the whole at last reaches a just proportion with the new quantity of [money]." Agreeing with the modern theory that the stimulus to real output during this phase is only temporary, Hume continues: "In my opinion, it is only in this interval or intermediate situation, between the acquisition of money and the rise of prices, that the increasing quantity of gold and silver is favorable to industry." In Hume's view, there is no long-run effect on real output. In the long run, unlike the short run, money is neutral. A one-time change in the quantity of money has a lasting proportional effect on the price level but on nothing else.

Source: David Hume, "Of Money," in his *Writings on Economics*, ed. Eugene Rotwein (Madison: University of Wisconsin Press, 1955). Quotations from Hume are taken from Thomas M. Humphrey, "The Early History of the Phillips Curve," *Economic Review* (September/October 1985).

affect the long-run equilibrium values of *real* variables such as real output, real planned investment, or employment. In the long run, a one-time change in the money stock affects only price levels.

The principle of the neutrality of money has a long history in economics. It was stated clearly by Adam Smith's friend David Hume (see ***Who Said It? Who Did It? 14.1***). It can also be stated in terms of the equation of exchange. If the terms are rearranged, the equation of exchange can be written in the form $P = MV/y$. As we know, the value of velocity depends on the interest rate. Because the long-run equilibrium value of the interest rate is not affected by a one-time change in the money stock, velocity, too, will be unaffected by such a change. Thus, the above equation tells us that if y is held constant at its natural level and V is unchanged, a one-time change in the money stock will produce a proportional change in the price level. For example, in Exhibit 14.2 a doubling of the money stock from MS_1 to MS_2 has the long-run effect of doubling the price level from P_1 to P_3.

Effects of lasting changes in the money growth rate.   Up to this point we have considered only the effects of one-time changes in the money stock. In practice, changes in the money stock typically do not occur in sudden spurts; rather, the money stock grows gradually as the economy grows. A change in monetary policy is usually reflected in a change in the growth rate of the money stock that persists for some time, rather than a sudden, once-and-for-all jump in the stock itself.

Much of our discussion of the effects of one-time changes requires only minor translation to fit the case of a lasting change in the rate of growth of the money stock. For example, a lasting increase in the rate of money growth tends to increase the level of real output in the short run, but in the long run it is neutral with respect to real output. The long-run effect of an increase in the rate of money growth is a rise in the inflation rate for both final goods and input prices, with real output returning to its natural level. However, the effects of lasting changes in the rate of money growth on interest rates require some additional explanation. These effects depend on the distinction between real and nominal interest rates.

Taking this distinction into account, we must modify our earlier statements about the effects of expansionary monetary policy and the neutrality of money as they apply to interest rates. The most important new conclusion is that a lasting increase in the growth rate of the money stock will tend to raise the nominal interest rate even though it may be neutral with respect to the real interest rate.

First, although there is no practical limit to the rate at which monetary policy can cause nominal national income to expand, there is a limit to how rapidly real national income can grow. This limit is established by the trends in technology, capital accumulation, and the labor force that determine the growth rate of natural real output over time. During the 1970s and 1980s, the trend rate of growth of real GNP in the United States was in the neighborhood of 2 1/2 to 3 percent per year. In the long run, then, if expansionary monetary policy forces the growth rate of nominal GNP above 2 1/2 to 3 percent, the excess growth must take the form of inflation.

Next, consider how lenders and borrowers react to inflation. As explained in Chapter 4, lenders and borrowers will focus on the real rate of interest that they expect will prevail over the period of the loan, that is, the nominal interest rate minus the expected inflation rate. For any given nominal interest rate, an increase in the expected inflation rate will drive the expected real interest rate down. To compensate for this effect, lenders will demand an "inflation premium" in the form of a higher nominal interest rate. Borrowers, realizing that they will repay the loan in future dollars whose real value will be reduced by inflation, willingly pay the premium. Thus, an increase in the expected rate of inflation will push up the whole family of nominal interest rates.

What happens to real interest rates as a result of a lasting increase in the rate of money growth depends on the time horizon being considered. In the short run real interest rates will tend to fall if lenders and borrowers do not immediately and fully adjust their inflation expectations to the change in monetary policy. As they adjust to the new circumstances, however, an inflation premium equal to the excess of the money growth rate over the rate of growth of real output will be included in all financial contracts. At that point if the nominal interest rate increases point-for-point with the increase in the rate of inflation, the real interest rate will be left where it started.

For example, suppose that initially the rate of money growth is 3 percent, just matching the growth rate of natural real output. There is no inflation, and the real and nominal interest rates are equal at 5 percent. The rate of money growth then increases by seven percentage points, to 10 percent, bringing on a steady 7-percent-per-year inflation. The inflation pushes up the nominal interest rate by seven percentage points—from 5 to 12 percent—but the real rate remains at 5 percent.

The proposition that a lasting change in the rate of money growth will, in the long run, not only leave real output unchanged but also leave the real interest rate unchanged is sometimes known as the *superneutrality* of money. Superneutrality is generally accepted as a good first approximation to the effects of changes in money growth on real interest rates, even though certain considerations, such as tax deductibility of some interest payments and effects of inflation on real wealth and saving, raise doubts about whether superneutrality holds exactly.

Money and Fiscal Policy

In Chapter 10 we looked at the effects of fiscal policy in terms of the aggregate supply and demand model. An increase in real government purchases or a cut in real net taxes was shown to shift the aggregate demand curve to the right, thereby raising real output and the price level in the short run and lowering unemployment; a decrease in government purchases or an increase in net taxes was shown to have opposite short-run effects. In this section we return to the topic of fiscal policy to see effects that reach beyond prices and real output to interest rates and investment.

The crowding-out effect.   Exhibit 14.3 presents the expanded analysis of the effects of fiscal policy. Initially the economy is in equilibrium at point e_1 in part (c). Real output is at its natural level, y_1; the price level is at P_1 and stable. The money market, shown in part (a), is in equilibrium at E_1 with an interest rate of R_1; because the price level is stable, the real and nominal interest rates are equal. This interest rate results in real planned investment at the level I_1, as shown in part (b). Such a planned-investment level is one of the elements that determines the position of aggregate demand curve AD_1; other elements are conditions governing real consumption, government purchases, and net exports.

Now the government undertakes expansionary fiscal policy in the form of, say, an increase in real government purchases. (A cut in taxes or an increase in transfer payments would have essentially the same effects.) As shown in Chapter 10, the result is a rightward shift of the aggregate demand curve. The economy begins to expand. The price level and real output both increase as the economy moves up and to the right along the short-run aggregate supply curve.

Now consider the effects on the money market, shown in part (a) of Exhibit 14.3. Because both prices and real output are increasing, nominal national income must also be rising. The money demand curve therefore shifts to the right. With the money supply curve unchanged, the real and nominal interest rates rise. As they do so, firms move up and to the left along the planned-investment schedule shown in part (b). The level of real planned investment begins to fall.

This tendency for an increase in government purchases to cause a decrease in real private planned investment is known as the **crowding-out effect.** The crowding out of real investment spending limits the expansion of real output. In Exhibit 14.3 the economy reaches a new short-run equilibrium at point e_2 in part (c), where real output is at y_2 and the price level at P_2. This point corresponds to point E_2 in the money market diagram in part (a).

Crowding-out effect
The tendency of expansionary fiscal policy to raise the interest rate and thereby cause a decrease in real planned investment.

Exhibit 14.3   The Crowding-Out Effect

Expansionary fiscal policy shifts the aggregate demand curve to the right from
AD_1 to AD_2, as shown in part (c). The resulting increase in nominal national
income shifts the money demand curve to the right from MD_1 to MD_2, as shown
in part (a). As the real and nominal interest rates rise, real planned investment
will decrease and the economy will move to the left along the planned-investment
schedule shown in part (b). The tendency of expansionary fiscal policy to reduce
private planned investment is known as the *crowding-out effect*.

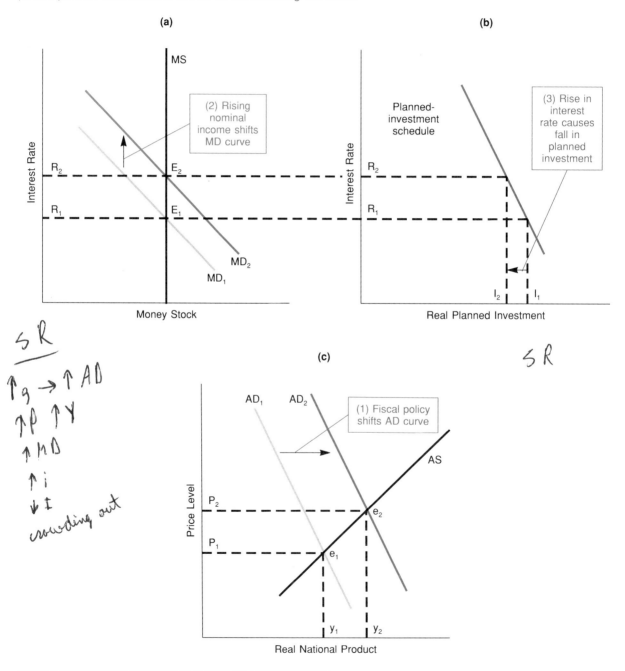

Chapter 10 discussed the effects of fiscal policy in terms of the multiplier effect. Now we see that because of crowding out, a given increase in government purchases shifts the aggregate demand curve by less than the expenditure multiplier would imply. Suppose, for example, that the expenditure multiplier is 4 and the change in government purchases is $100 billion. Multiplying these two numbers would lead one to expect a $400 billion shift. But in practice the shift is less because the expansionary effect of the increase in government purchases is partially offset by a decrease in private planned investment.[1] What is more, the price increases caused by the aggregate demand shift push interest rates up still higher and further reduce planned investment.

Extensions of the crowding effect.   The version of the crowding-out effect discussed in the preceding section concerns the tendency of an increase in government purchases to reduce private planned investment. This idea can be extended in several ways.

First, it can be extended to all types of fiscal policy. As Chapter 10 showed, expansionary fiscal policy can also take the form of a cut in taxes or an increase in transfer payments. Because these types of expansionary policy also cause nominal national income to rise, they increase the demand for money, push up interest rates, and cut into real planned investment.

Second, the concept can be extended to incorporate components of aggregate demand other than planned investment. Chapter 7 showed that all components of aggregate demand are potentially subject to crowding out when expansionary fiscal policy (or any other factor) raises the price level. Consumption may fall because an increase in the price level reduces the real purchasing power of given nominal money balances and because other components of real income tend to decline as the price level rises, which also affects consumption. Net exports may fall because a higher price level makes domestic goods more costly for foreign buyers while making foreign goods relatively less expensive for domestic buyers. Further, an increase in federal government purchases may, by raising the price level, crowd out some state and local government expenditures (and even some federal expenditures on programs that have not been increased) to the extent that some portions of government budgets are set by law in nominal terms.

Finally, all forms of the crowding-out effect are reversible. A decrease in government purchases or an increase in net taxes causes nominal national income to fall. This shifts money demand to the left and causes interest rates to fall. Real planned investment increases, partly offsetting the contractionary

[1] In Chapter 10 we assumed, as a working approximation, that the change in government purchases times the expenditure multiplier would equal the horizontal shift in the aggregate demand curve. Now we can see why this was only an approximation: There would be some crowding out even if the economy moved horizontally to the right on the aggregate supply and demand diagram with the price level unchanged. Even with no change in the price level, there would be some increase in nominal national income as a result of the increase in real national product. That alone would be enough to shift the money demand curve to the right, although not as far as the shift to MD_2 shown in Exhibit 14.3. Thus, the interest rate would rise somewhat, and there would be some crowding out of private investment. This fixed-price portion of the crowding-out effect keeps the aggregate demand curve from shifting to the right by the full amount of the change in government purchases times the multiplier. However, the amount of the shift can still be thought of as equal to the change in autonomous expenditure times the expenditure multiplier, provided that the change in autonomous expenditure is interpreted as the increase in government purchases minus the change in planned investment resulting from the fixed-price component of crowding out.

effect of the assumed fiscal policy. The tendency of contractionary fiscal policy to increase planned investment might thus be called "crowding in."

The long run and nonneutrality of fiscal policy. Fiscal policy is no more able than monetary policy to permanently raise real national product above its natural level. Exhibit 14.4 picks up where 14.3 left off; it shows the long-run effects of expansionary fiscal policy.

Expansionary policy has shifted the aggregate demand curve in part (c) from AD_1 to AD_2, moving the economy to a short-run equilibrium at e_2. Compared with the situation in the initial equilibrium, e_1, real output is above the natural level and the level of final goods prices has increased. Over time, as the rise in the prices of final goods begins to affect the expected level of input prices, the short-run aggregate supply curve shifts upward. As the economy moves up and to the left along the aggregate demand curve AD_2, prices continue to rise, but real output falls back toward the natural level. A new long-run equilibrium is reached at e_3.

Because the aggregate demand curve is relatively inelastic, nominal national income increases in the course of the move from e_2 to e_3. As nominal national income rises, the money demand curve must shift farther to the right, from MD_2 to MD_3 in part (a) of Exhibit 14.4. This causes further crowding out of private planned investment. A continued increase in the interest rate pushes firms farther up and to the left along the planned-investment schedule, as shown in part (b). A new long-run equilibrium is not reached until the expansionary effects of the original fiscal policy action are completely crowded out. The aggregate demand curve remains in its new position, AD_2, but the economy's movement upward and to the left along this curve brings real national product all the way back to its natural level.

In one respect, the long-run effects of fiscal policy are similar to those of monetary policy: In both cases there is a higher price level in the new long-run equilibrium but no permanent change in real output. However, there is one important difference. Monetary policy is said to be "neutral" because a one-time increase in the money stock (and perhaps even a lasting change in the rate of money growth) has no long-run effects on any real variables—real output, planned investment, or real interest rates. But fiscal policy is not "neutral" in this sense. Even though expansionary fiscal policy does not change the long-run equilibrium level of real output, it does change the long-run equilibrium values of the real and nominal interest rates and real planned investment.

Compare Exhibit 14.4 with Exhibit 14.2 in this regard. In Exhibit 14.2 expansionary monetary policy moves the money market to a long-run equilibrium at E_3, where the real and nominal interest rates are at the level from which they started. But in Exhibit 14.4 expansionary fiscal policy moves the money market to a long-run equilibrium at E_3, where the real and nominal rates are higher. Consequently, the long-run level of private planned investment is lowered by expansionary fiscal policy but not by expansionary monetary policy.

The importance of the fiscal-monetary policy mix. Chapter 10 mentioned the crowding-out effect in connection with the debate over the federal budget deficit. As we saw there, the budget deficits of the Reagan era resulted partly from increased government purchases and partly from increased transfer payments while tax revenues remained roughly constant as a share of GNP. To contain inflationary pressure, the Fed was forced to maintain a relatively tight monetary

Exhibit 14.4   Crowding Out in the Long Run

Point e_2 in part (c) of this exhibit is only a short-run equilibrium. As the aggregate supply curve shifts upward and the economy moves to a new long-run equilibrium at e_3, nominal national income continues to rise. The money demand curve shifts further to the right from MD_2 to MD_3, as shown in part (a). As it does, the economy moves further to the left along the planned-investment schedule, as shown in part (b). Thus, the crowding-out effect intensifies in the long run as real output returns to its natural level.

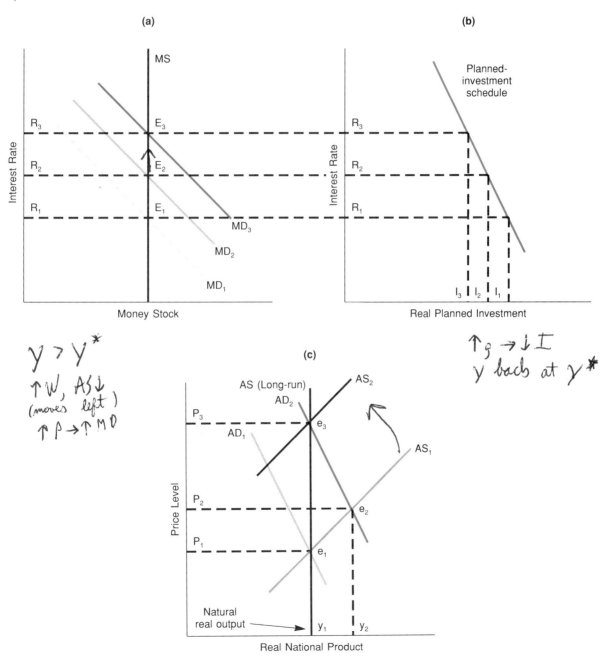

(a)

(b)

(c)

$y > y^*$

$\uparrow w,\ AS\downarrow$
(moves left)

$\uparrow P \rightarrow \uparrow MD$

$\uparrow g \rightarrow \downarrow I$
$y\ back\ at\ y^*$

policy during the 1980s. The resulting policy mix—expansionary fiscal policy combined with restrictive monetary policy—pushed up interest rates, thereby tending to crowd out private investment. On balance, net domestic investment fell from an average rate of 6.7 percent of NNP in the 1970s to less than 5 percent of NNP in the 1980s. As a result, the critics say, future generations will be left with a smaller stock of capital—buildings, equipment, scientific achievements, and so on—than they would have if the federal budget had been balanced in the 1980s.

The Bush administration's team of economic advisers has been very sensitive to this criticism. As noted in the excerpt from the 1990 economic report at the beginning of the chapter, the administration places a high priority on growth of real output. As part of its strategy for promoting growth, the administration proposes to eliminate the federal budget deficit. By itself, elimination of the deficit would have a contractionary effect in the short run, possibly leading to a recession. However, this danger can, at least in theory, be avoided if the Fed pursues a somewhat more expansionary monetary policy. The new mix of more conservative fiscal policy combined with more expansionary monetary policy will tend to reverse the crowding-out effect. If that goal is achieved, it may prove possible to reduce real interest rates, increase investment, and increase long-run economic growth while still making progress toward price stability. That, at least, is the hope.

14.2   Fiscal Policy in an Open Economy

In Chapter 12 we saw that monetary policy affects imports, exports, capital flows, and the foreign-exchange value of the dollar. It does so partly via effects on national income, which in turn affect the level of imports, and partly via effects on interest rates, which in turn affect capital flows. In this chapter we have shown that fiscal policy also affects both national income and interest rates. This being the case, we would expect fiscal policy also to have international implications—and so it does.

Leakages and Injections

The international implications of fiscal policy can be understood in terms of the concepts of leakages and injections from the circular flow. In Chapter 5 we stated the basic relationship between leakages and injections in equation form as follows:

$$S + T + M = I + G + X,$$

where S stands for saving, T for net taxes, M for imports, I for investment, G for government purchases, and X for exports. For our present purposes, it is useful to rearrange the terms of the equation in the following form:

$$I + (G - T) = S + (M - X).$$

The terms of this equation can be interpreted as follows: I and S, as before, stand for investment and saving. The term $(G - T)$ represents the government budget deficit. The term $(M - X)$ can be interpreted in two ways. First, it represents the economy's *current account deficit*—the amount by which imports of goods and services exceeds exports. Second, it represents *net capital inflows* into the economy. As explained in Chapters 5 and 6, an excess of imports over exports must be financed by a net capital inflow, that is, by net borrowing from abroad or plus net sales of assets to foreign buyers, so that the value of the current account deficit and the value of capital inflows must be equal.[2]

The modified leakages-injections equation also has a simple interpretation in terms of the circular flow diagram in Exhibit 14.5. The terms on the right-hand side of the equation, domestic saving and net capital inflows, represent *sources* of funds to financial markets; they are shown in the diagram by the two arrows pointing into financial markets. The terms on the left-hand side of the equation, investment and the government budget deficit, represent *uses* of funds drawn from financial markets; they are shown in the diagram by the two arrows pointed out from financial markets.

The Twin Deficits

The leakages-injections equation shows that the economy can compensate for an increase in the government budget deficit in one of three ways:

1. Investment can decrease.
2. Saving can increase.
3. The current account deficit (and, at the same time, net capital inflows) can increase.

In which of these ways did the U.S. economy respond to the increase in the government budget deficit during the 1980s? An examination of the evidence suggests that the largest burden of adjustment was borne by the current account deficit. This gave rise to the phenomenon of the "twin deficits"—the record deficits of the federal budget *and* the balance of payments on current account that were both recorded in the mid-1980s.

Exhibit 14.6 presents some data. Part (a) shows the path of the two deficits over time. Until the 1970s, the federal budget and the current account were both close to balance. In the early 1970s, and then more decisively in the early 1980s, the federal budget moved sharply into deficit, followed shortly by a move toward deficit in the current account. The mechanisms giving rise to the lagged association between the federal budget deficit and the current account deficit can be summarized as follows:

1. The move toward fiscal stimulus raised U.S. interest rates.
2. Higher U.S. interest rates encouraged a net capital inflow, which, in turn, increased the demand for dollars in the foreign-exchange market and raised the foreign-exchange value of the dollar.
3. The higher value of the dollar encouraged imports and discouraged exports, thereby, with a lag, widening the U.S. current account deficit.

As part (b) of Exhibit 14.6 shows, there were other changes in leakages and injections as well. Saving and investment both declined in the 1980s compared

---

[2]The concepts of current and capital account balances were introduced in Chapter 6. This discussion simplifies matters somewhat by assuming that international transfer payments and the statistical discrepancy are both zero. It also ignores some technical differences in accounting conventions between the national income and product accounts and the balance of payments statistics.

Exhibit 14.5 Leakages, Injections, and the Twin Deficits in the Circular Flow

In this diagram, saving and net capital inflows are shown as sources of funds to financial markets, and investment and the government budget deficit are shown as uses of funds from financial markets. To maintain an equality of leakages and injections in the circular flow, domestic investment plus the government budget deficit must be equal to private saving plus net capital inflows. Net capital inflows, in turn, are equal to the current account deficit (imports minus exports). In particular, if the government budget deficit increases, as it did during the 1980s, investment must fall, saving must rise, or net capital inflows (and with them, the current account deficit) must rise. As things worked out during the 1980s, the increase in the government budget deficit was accompanied by an increase in the current account deficit—a phenomenon known as the "twin deficits."

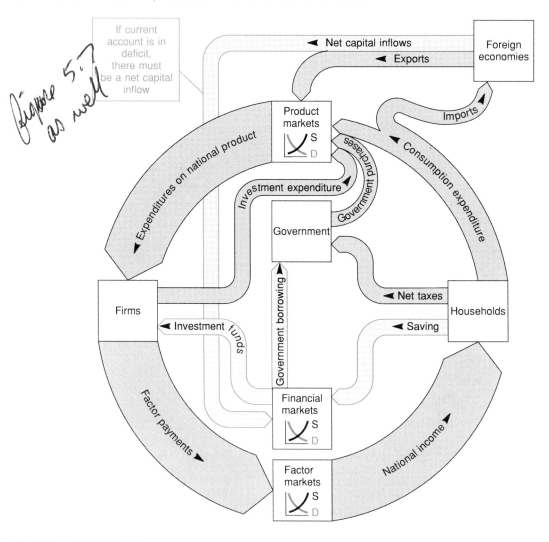

Exhibit 14.6   Data on the ~~Twin Deficits~~

Part (a) shows that until the 1970s, the U.S. government budget and current account were close to balance on average. Beginning in the 1970s and then more strongly in the 1980s, the government budget swung toward deficit. The current account balance, although lagging somewhat behind, moved in the same direction, giving rise to the twin deficits. Part (b) provides data on all elements of the leakages-injections equation. Comparing the 1970s with the early 1980s, it can be seen that the federal deficit at first increased by more than the swing toward net inflow on the capital account. By the latter 1980s, the federal budget deficit began to decline as a percentage of GNP while net capital inflows continued to increase. Throughout the period, net domestic saving fell. To maintain a balance of leakages and injections under these circumstances, net domestic investment fell sharply in the early 1980s. In the latter 1980s, the combination of a lower federal budget deficit and greater net capital inflows allowed net domestic investment to recover somewhat despite a further decline in net domestic saving.

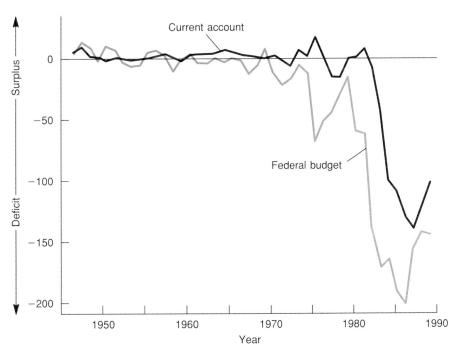

(a) Nominal Current Account and Federal Budget Deficits

(b) Government Deficit, Net Capital Flows
(Saving and Investment as Share
of Net National Product, 1971–1989)

	1971–1980	1981–1985	1986–1989
Net domestic investment	6.7	4.4	4.8
Federal budget deficit	1.8	4.3	3.6
Net private saving	8.8	7.5	5.7
Net capital inflow[a]	−0.3	1.2	2.7

[a]Negative number indicates net capital outflow.

Source: Federal Reserve Board of Governors.

with the 1970s, although not at the same rates; if saving and investment had changed exactly in step with each other, the current account deficit would have tracked the budget deficit more closely. By the latter 1980s, the increase in net capital inflow was enough to finance the federal budget deficit with something left over to moderate the impact on domestic investment of the decline in domestic saving.

The twin deficits have provided additional ammunition for critics of the budget priorities of the 1980s. Those priorities—increased outlays for entitlements and defense with no increase in the share of GNP going to taxes—were described in Chapter 10. Critics charge that the resulting fiscal policy has left the nation burdened with debts owed to foreign lenders and has caused export industries to lose market share in an increasingly competitive world economy as well as starving domestic firms of investment capital via the crowding-out effect.

14.3   The Keynesian-Monetarist Debate over the Role of Money

This chapter has presented a view of the role of money in the economy that is now widely accepted. This was not always so, however; in particular, John Maynard Keynes and his followers saw a much smaller role for money in the economy, especially during depressions. In Chapter 8 we looked briefly at the debate between Keynes and his predecessors, the classical economists, concerning the economy's ability to rebound from a contraction. In this section we will return to that debate in the light of what we have learned about the monetary sector. We will then introduce the *monetarists*, a school of economists who have been highly influential during the post-World War II period.

The Keynesian View of Money in the Depression

The model presented earlier in this chapter emphasizes a transmission mechanism for monetary policy that runs from money to interest rates to investment. Keynes recognized the existence of this mechanism in *The General Theory*. However, he thought that it was relatively weak, at least under conditions of depression.

Keynes's reasoning was outlined briefly in Chapter 8. First, Keynes thought that investment is relatively insensitive to changes in interest rates—in other words, that the planned-investment schedule is relatively inelastic. He also believed that in a depression interest rates might reach a floor below which they could drop no further. This amounted to saying that the money demand curve would become highly elastic—nearly horizontal, in fact—at low interest rates. Such behavior was called a "liquidity trap" because people's inclination to accumulate liquid assets (money) would keep interest rates from falling, thus trapping the economy in a state of low planned investment.

The set of circumstances that Keynes hypothesized is represented in part (a) of Exhibit 14.7. There the money demand curve is shown as having a horizontal "tail" at a low interest rate, and the planned-investment schedule is nearly vertical. The weakness of the transmission mechanism under these circumstances has two implications for policy.

First, it means that a fall in the price level will have little effect on aggregate demand. A drop in the price level with real national income constant means a drop in nominal national income. As shown in part (b) of the exhibit, such a

Exhibit 14.7   The Keynesian View of Money in the Depression

Keynes and his early followers thought that the monetary sector played an insignificant role in the economy under depression conditions. There were two reasons for this, as shown in part (a) of this exhibit. One reason was that they thought the money demand curve becomes highly elastic at low interest rates. The other is that they believed the planned-investment schedule is almost perfectly inelastic. Part (b) shows that given these elasticities for the curves, a fall in the price level will shift the money demand curve to the left but have little or no effect on interest rates or planned investment. This was one of Keynes's reasons for thinking that the economy's aggregate demand curve would be nearly vertical. As a result, the economy could not recover from a depression by itself. In addition, part (c) shows that under the Keynesian assumptions expansionary monetary policy has little effect on interest rates or real planned investment. This means that such a policy would do little to lift the economy out of a depression. That left expansionary fiscal policy as the only reliable route to recovery in the Keynesian view.

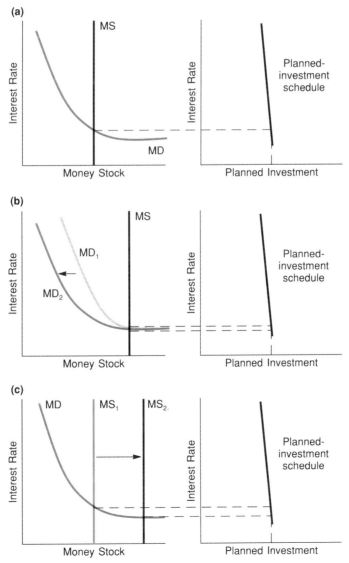

drop in nominal national income will shift the money demand curve leftward from MD_1 to MD_2. However, because of the curve's shape, the interest rate will hardly be affected. Given the inelastic planned-investment schedule, there will be only a very small increase in real planned investment, if any. If a drop in the price level does not affect planned investment, the aggregate demand curve will be vertical, or nearly so, as was shown in Exhibit 8.5 (page 214). This means that the economy has no built-in ability to recover from a depression.

Second, a weak transmission mechanism means that expansionary monetary policy will do little or nothing to help recovery. The reason is shown in part (c) of Exhibit 14.7. A shift in the money supply curve from MS_1 to MS_2 has almost no effect on the interest rate. To the extent that there is some small decline in the interest rate, the effect on planned investment is, in any event, negligible.

We see, then, that a weak transmission mechanism means both that the economy has no power to recover from a depression of its own accord and that expansionary monetary policy will not aid recovery. The conclusion is that only expansionary fiscal policy can save the economy from lasting depression.

The Monetarist Response

After World War II many of the early Keynesians forecast a new depression and economic stagnation. They thought that private investment would dry up with the end of wartime government spending. They were wrong: The postwar recovery of the United States and Western Europe was rapid. Central banks in most of the major economies pursued easy monetary policies during those years, and inflation was more widespread than depression. The countries that were able to control inflation did so only by using standard policies of monetary restraint. Economists began to take renewed interest in the role of money in the economy.

During the 1950s and 1960s there was a reaction against the tendency of Depression-era Keynesians to downplay the role of money. The response came most prominently from a group of economists led by Milton Friedman (see **Who Said It? Who Did It? 14.2**). Friedman's research led him to think that movements in the money supply had a much greater effect on economic events, even under depression conditions, than the early Keynesians had been willing to admit. Because of the emphasis Friedman and his followers placed on monetary policy, their school of thought came to be known as **monetarism.**

Monetarism
A school of economics that emphasizes the importance of changes in the money stock as determinants of changes in real output and the price level.

Reinterpretation of the Great Depression.   Friedman's research led to a reinterpretation of the Great Depression. In *A Monetary History of the United States*, Friedman and Anna J. Schwartz pointed to the 33 percent decrease in the broadly defined money supply that the Fed had allowed between 1929 and 1933 (see **Applying Economic Ideas 12.1,** pages 322–323). The 1930s gave no evidence that expansionary monetary policy was ineffective, said the monetarists, because such a policy was not tried. On the contrary, the fact that the Fed permitted the money stock to collapse emerged as a major reason for the severity of the Depression.

The economics profession was slow to convert to monetarism. In fact, in some ways the 1960s were the heyday of Keynesian policy. Many leading Keynesians left their university posts to join the Council of Economic Advisers under Presidents Kennedy and Johnson. Even so, however, the monetarists' ideas proved influential in persuading the Keynesians to pay more attention to money and monetary policy. A central issue in the debate of the 1950s and 1960s was the nature of the transmission mechanism for monetary policy.

Who Said It? Who Did It?   14.2
Milton Friedman and Monetarism

In October 1976 Milton Friedman received the Nobel Memorial Prize in economics, becoming the sixth American to win or share that honor. Few people were surprised. Most people wondered why he had had to wait so long. Perhaps it was because Friedman has built his career outside the economics establishment, challenging almost every major doctrine of that profession.

Friedman was born in New York in 1912, the son of immigrant garment workers. He attended Rutgers University, where he came under the influence of Arthur Burns, then a young assistant professor and later chairman of the Federal Reserve Board. From Burns, Friedman learned the importance of empirical work in economics. Statistical testing of all theory and policy prescriptions became a key feature of Friedman's later work. From Rutgers, Friedman went to the University of Chicago for an M.A. and then east again to Columbia University, where he received his Ph.D. in 1946. He returned to Chicago to teach. There he and his colleagues of the "Chicago school" of economics posed a major challenge to the economists of the "eastern establishment."

If one could single out a recurrent theme in Friedman's work, it would be his belief that the market economy works—and that it works best when left alone. This can be seen in his best-known work, *A Monetary History of the United States*. Written with Anna Schwartz, this book attacks two major tenets of Keynesian economics: (1) that the market economy is unstable without the guiding hand of government and (2) that monetary policy was tried and found useless as a cure for the Great Depression. Friedman and Schwartz found both beliefs to be far from the truth. "The Great Depression," Friedman later wrote, "far from being a sign of the inherent instability of the private enter-

prise system, is a testament to how much harm can be done by mistakes on the part of a few men when they wield vast power over the monetary system of the country."

Friedman strongly favors a hands-off policy by government in almost every area. In his view, the problem is not that government is evil by nature but that so many policies end up having the opposite of their intended effects: "The social reformers who seek through politics to do nothing but serve the public interest invariably end up serving some private interest that was no part of their intention to serve. They are led by an invisible hand to serve a private interest." Transport regulation, public education, agricultural subsidies, and housing programs are among the many policy areas in which Friedman believes that the government has done more harm than good and that a free competitive market would do better.

Today Friedman continues to take on new challenges. He promotes his ideas before congressional committees, in professional journals, in the press, and in face-to-face debates with colleagues. Economics has never had a more respected heretic.

The monetarist view of the transmission mechanism.   In the Keynesian theory the transmission mechanism through which monetary policy affects the rest of the economy is narrow and indirect. As we have told the story, it begins when an increase in the money supply causes households and firms to readjust their portfolios of assets. In the process of adjusting to the larger money stock, they drive up the prices of bonds and other securities and force down nominal and real interest rates. This, in turn, is supposed to encourage real planned investment, which, finally, stimulates aggregate demand.

Monetarists challenged the Keynesian view that this transmission mechanism is weak. Their statistical studies dispelled the notions that the economy had experienced a "liquidity trap" in the 1930s and that investment was unresponsive to interest rates. They claimed that there was simply no evidence to support the elasticities of the money demand curves and planned-investment schedules shown in Exhibit 14.7. In addition, monetarists, as well as many other economists, came to see the interest rate–investment linkage as only one aspect of a more complex transmission mechanism for monetary policy.

The Keynesian version of the transmission mechanism begins when people adjust their portfolios in response to an increase in the money stock. Keynesians tend to stress the trade-off between money and fixed-interest securities such as bonds. In the real world the choices are much broader. Besides bonds and money, people own common stocks, real estate, commodities, consumer durables, and even stocks of consumer nondurables. In the monetarist view, an excess supply of money is likely to affect the implicit and explicit returns on a wide variety of assets, both financial and nonfinancial. It is likely, therefore, to spill over into spending on goods as well as on securities. As it does so, aggregate demand is stimulated in many ways. An increase in stock prices can spawn new investment by making it less costly for corporations to issue new shares. Increases in the demand for real estate can stimulate new construction. Increases in the prices of commodities—wheat, gold, rubber, and so on—can stimulate production of those goods. Even consumption spending can respond directly to a change in the money supply as the increase in real money balances adds to real wealth.

In the monetarist view, then, the effect of an injection of money spreads through the whole economy. People become content to hold the newly issued money as a result not just of a change in interest rates but also of a broader change in the composition of their portfolios.

Looking Ahead

The monetarists' broader view of the transmission mechanism played a key role in rehabilitating the classical view of a downward-sloping aggregate demand curve that shifts in response to changes in monetary policy. This form of the aggregate supply and demand model—rather than the Depression-era Keynesian form with a vertical aggregate demand curve—is now widely accepted as standard. However, although the monetarist view of the importance of money as a determinant of aggregate demand is shared to a substantial degree by most economists, their views have by no means come to dominate the economics profession in all respects. Chapter 18 will show that other aspects of the Keynesian-monetarist debate are still very much alive.

To understand these ongoing aspects of the debate, however, we must leave the depression scenario that preoccupied economists of a generation ago. The next two chapters will use aggregate supply and demand analysis to strengthen our understanding of inflation and economic growth—the issues on which macroeconomics has focused in the 1970s and 1980s.

Summary

1. **How do changes in the money stock affect real output, the price level, and unemployment?** An increase in the money stock initially lowers interest rates. The resulting increase in real planned investment shifts the aggregate demand curve to the right. As the economy moves up and to the right along the aggregate supply curve, in the short run real output increases, the price level increases, and the unemployment rate falls. A decrease in the money stock has the opposite effects in the short run: Interest rates rise, real planned investment falls, and the aggregate demand curve shifts to the left. As a result, real output and the price level fall and the unemployment rate increases.

2. **What is meant by the neutrality of money?** A one-time increase in the money stock can cause real output to rise above its natural level in the short run but can-

not hold it there over the long run. As input prices rise, the economy returns to the natural level of real output at a higher price level than initially. In the new equilibrium the prices of both final goods and inputs will have changed in proportion to the increase in the money stock, but the values of all real variables—interest rates, planned investment, real output, and employment—will be unaffected. This proposition is known as the *neutrality of money*. Lasting changes in the rate of growth of the money stock, as opposed to one-time changes, are also neutral with regard to real output and may be neutral with respect to real interest rates. However, lasting changes in the rate of money growth will have a lasting effect on the inflation rate and, hence, affect nominal interest rates.

3. **How does fiscal policy affect interest rates and planned investment?** Expansionary fiscal policy shifts the aggregate demand curve to the right. Real output and the price level rise in the short run, as does nominal national income. The increase in nominal national income shifts the money demand curve to the right, causing both real and nominal interest rates to increase. This rise in interest rates *crowds out* some real planned investment. As the economy returns to a long-run equilibrium at the natural level of real output, a further rise in the price level causes nominal national income to rise still higher, putting additional upward pressure on interest rates. Thus, there is a further depressing effect on real investment, and the crowding-out effect intensifies in the long run.

4. **What are the international implications of fiscal policy?** In a closed economy, assuming no change in the saving rate, an increase in the government budget deficit will lead to a change in investment—the crowding-out effect. In an open economy, the economy may compensate for an increase in the budget deficit through an increase in the current account deficit and a corresponding rise in net capital inflows. This appears to have happened in the United States in the 1980s, when the economy experienced twin deficits—a federal budget deficit and a current account deficit, both of which reached record levels.

5. **What role did money play during the Great Depression, according to Keynes?** Keynes and his early followers saw money as playing a relatively minor role during the Great Depression. They thought that under depression conditions, a shift in the money supply or demand curves would have little effect on the interest rate, and that any interest rate change that did occur would have little impact on planned investment. These views implied both that the economy would be unable to recover from a depression on its own and that expansionary monetary policy would be of little help. In the Keynesian view, only expansionary fiscal policy could do the job.

6. **How have monetarists influenced economic thought?** After World War II, *monetarists*, led by Milton Friedman, argued that monetary policy is an important determinant of aggregate demand even under depression conditions and all the more so in normal times. They saw the Fed's failure to prevent a contraction of the money stock as a major factor in the length and severity of the Depression. Although by no means were all economists converted to monetarism, the monetarists' analysis helped all economists understand the role that monetary policy plays in determining the price level, real output, and employment.

Terms for Review

- transmission mechanism
- neutrality of money
- crowding-out effect
- monetarism

Questions for Review

1. In the short run, what happens to interest rates, real planned investment, real output, the unemployment rate, and the price level as a result of an increase in the money stock? What are the results of a decrease in the money stock?

2. Why does a one-time increase in the money stock have no long-run effect on interest rates whereas an increased fiscal stimulus does? How do the effects of a lasting increase in the rate of growth of the money stock differ from those of a one-time increase in the money stock?

3. Can the crowding-out effect extend to expenditures other than planned investment? Explain.

4. Why did Keynes and his early followers think that money played a relatively small role in the Great Depression?

5. Why do monetarists think that the Depression would have been less severe if the Fed had prevented the money stock from falling as it did from 1929 to 1933?

Problems and Topics for Discussion

1. **Examining the lead-off case.** Using government data sources such as the *Economic Report of the President* or current news sources, determine what has happened to inflation, the unemployment rate, the rate of growth of real GNP, and the federal budget deficit since 1989. Have the goals of the Bush administration as expressed in the 1990 *Economic Report* been realized?

2. **Long-run effects of contractionary monetary policy.** Use a set of diagrams similar to Exhibits 14.1 and 14.2 to trace the long-run effects of a one-time contraction of the money stock beginning from equilibrium at the natural level of real output.

3. **Effects of a tax increase.** Use a set of diagrams similar to Exhibit 14.4 to trace the effects of a contractionary fiscal policy such as a tax increase. What happens to real output, unemployment, the price level, interest rates, and real planned investment in the long run and in the short run?

4. **Crowding out and the money supply curve.** Use a set of diagrams similar to Exhibit 14.3 to investigate how

the crowding-out effect is influenced by the shape of the money supply curve. First use a positively sloped curve and then a horizontal curve. Discuss the policy implications of your results.

5. **The twin deficits.** Using data sources such as the *Economic Report of the President* or the *Survey of Current Business*, determine what has happened to the current account deficit and the federal budget deficit, both expressed as a percentage of GNP. Have the two deficits moved in the same direction or in opposite directions? Discuss in terms of the theory presented in this chapter.

Case for Discussion

Reaganomics, RIP

As the Congressional Budget Office observes in its latest *Economic and Budget Outlook,* published in January [1987], a verdict on Reaganomics boils down to the question of justice between generations. Our fiscal policy since 1981 has allowed people living today to enjoy higher consumption at the expense of those who will be living tomorrow. It is not clear whether President Reagan actually meant to throw this party or whether things simply got out of hand. . . .

Will the party soon have to end? Actually, we may go on for a while. As long as other nations are willing to add dollar-denominated American IOUs to their portfolios, we can continue to live happily beyond our means. . . .

An alternative would be to go back to square one and to balance the government's books. During 1980–1986, net private savings—roughly, the amount of investable funds available after replacement of worn-out capital—has averaged 6.2 percent of GNP (down from 8.1 percent in 1970–1979). Savings by state and local governments brought the total available savings pool to 7.5 percent of GNP. The federal deficit alone drained 4.1 percent of GNP from the pool—that is, more than half of it—leaving only 3.4 percent of GNP for net private capital formation beyond the replacement of worn-out capital. We did, as noted, supplement that meager pool by tapping the savings of foreigners through borrowing and the sale of real assets. If that is to cease, we must either bring the federal budget closer into balance or start saving a lot more—that is, start consuming less—as individuals.

Source: Uwe Reinhardt, "Reaganomics, RIP," *New Republic,* April 20, 1987, 24–27.

Questions

1. Leaving aside the issue of borrowing from foreigners, explain, in terms of what you learned in this chapter and in Chapter 10, how the policies of the Reagan administration might be said to have increased consumption by people alive today at the expense of future generations.

2. A counterargument to the position taken by Reinhardt goes like this: "If net taxes were raised or government purchases cut to balance the budget, the economy would be thrown into a recession. That would certainly cut consumption by people alive today, but it is not clear that it would benefit future generations." Discuss. Is there a way that the budget could be balanced without causing a recession? What does this argument assume about monetary policy?

3. Reinhardt thinks that people alive today are consuming too much and not investing enough. How does one determine the proper distribution of income and consumption between generations? Should we consume less today so that tomorrow's generations can consume more, even though they will probably have higher incomes than we do? Do you think your own parents should save more and consume less now so that you can consume more in the future when you inherit from them? Discuss.

4. Why did the large Reagan budget deficits cause U.S. borrowing from foreigners to increase? Given that the government decides to borrow to finance its expenditures, is it worse to borrow from foreigners than from U.S. citizens? Would we be better off today if we had the same deficit but no capital inflow from abroad? Would future generations be better off? Discuss.

Suggestions for Further Reading

Friedman, Milton, and Walter J. Heller. *Monetary vs. Fiscal Policy.* New York: Norton, 1969.

This book presents an overview of the debate between monetarists and Keynesians as conducted in the 1960s.

Tobin, James. "The Monetarist Counter-Revolution Today." *Economic Journal* 91 (March 1981): 29–42.

An appraisal of monetarism by a leading Keynesian thinker. The article by David Laidler in the same issue is also of interest.

PART FIVE

Price Stability, Employment, and Economic Growth

Inflation
and Policies
for Its Control

**Before reading this chapter,
make sure you know the meaning of:**

Indexation (Chapter 4)

Price level (Chapter 6)

Base year (Chapter 6)

After reading this chapter, you will understand:

The characteristics of inflation that arises from excessive growth in aggregate demand.

How inflation can arise from shifts in the short-run aggregate supply curve.

What contributions the new classical economists have made.

What types of policy can be used to combat inflation.

Why the rate of inflation slowed rapidly in the early 1980s.

The Great Inflation of the 1970s

If the 1930s were the decade of the Great Depression, the 1970s perhaps should be called the "Great Inflation." Like the Great Depression, the Great Inflation brought lasting changes to economic thought and policy. What went on in this turbulent decade?

The seeds of the Great Inflation were sown in the late 1960s. Under President Lyndon Johnson, federal outlays for the Vietnam War rose steadily, but because the war was unpopular at home, Johnson was reluctant to raise taxes. Many economists see the resulting fiscal stimulus as a key factor in the inflation that followed. In 1968, the inflation rate rose to 4.2 percent per year; in 1969, it reached 5.4 percent.[1] In comparison with what was to come, 5.4 percent inflation was moderate—but it was more than three times the 1.7 percent average rate for the decade 1958 to 1967.

In 1970 and early 1971, the inflation rate continued to creep upward. Then, in August 1971, President Richard Nixon announced a dramatic new economic program. The centerpiece was a 90-day freeze on all prices and wages. This attempt to control prices administratively worked for a time. The inflation rate fell in late 1971 and during 1972. Prices and wages were subject to some degree of control under three presidents for the rest of the decade.

However, in 1973, when the power of wage and price controls to restrain inflation was already waning, the world received a major inflationary shock. In the aftermath of a war with Israel, the Arab members of the Organization of Petroleum Exporting Countries (OPEC) doubled the price of oil—a major U.S. import and a key component of the consumer price index. Inflation was under way again, with the added complication of retail price controls on gasoline, which led to long waiting lines at gas stations.

Photo source: UPI/Bettman Newsphotos.

[1]All figures for inflation given here are year-to-year percentage changes in the consumer price index.

In 1974, the inflation rate reached 11 percent and the United States discovered an unpleasant new fact. In the past, inflation had been thought to have a silver lining in the form of low unemployment. Now the nation learned that it could suffer from both high unemployment and high inflation at the same time. In the 1974 to 1975 recession, the unemployment rate rose to nearly 9 percent while the inflation rate fell only slightly. A new concept was born: the "misery index," which is the sum of the rates of inflation and unemployment. The misery index hit a value of 18 during the 1974 to 1975 recession and, throughout the subsequent recovery, never fell below 13. This was miserable indeed compared with the under-6 values to which people had grown accustomed in the 1960s.

Despite the fiscal stimulus of the Vietnam War and the inflationary shock of the oil crisis, the Fed could have curbed inflation by restraining growth of the money stock. However, just as it had failed to prevent a drop in the money stock from 1929 to 1933, thereby worsening the Great Depression, during the 1970s the Fed failed to prevent rapid growth of the money stock, thus adding fuel to the Great Inflation.

Finally, in October 1979, the Fed put on the brakes and the economy went through the windshield. In 1980, as the economy entered a brief recession induced by President Carter's credit controls, both inflation and unemployment rose. The misery index soared to an all-time high of 20. On top of this, OPEC chose 1979 to 1980 to more than double the world oil price for the second time. After a temporary recovery from the 1980 recession, in 1981 the economy entered its most severe downturn since the Great Depression of the 1930s.

Inflation receded during the 1980s, and the misery index returned to single digits. But it will be a long time before Americans can again read about inflation abroad and think complacently that "it can never happen here."

At several points in this course, we have examined the Great Depression and the economic theories to which it gave rise. We have seen how Keynesian economics arose in reaction to classical views that seemed to deny the possibility of a depression such as that experienced in the 1930s and how monetarism emerged to counter the views of Keynes and some of his early followers. In this and the next four chapters, we will look at some aspects of economic theory that are an outgrowth of the "Great Inflation" of the 1970s.

This chapter develops the theory of inflation in terms of the aggregate supply and demand model and uses that model to examine a variety of policies for controlling inflation. Chapter 16 adds an optional dynamic model of inflation. Chapter 17 introduces economic growth into the model. Chapter 18 examines the ongoing debate over the proper strategy for economic policy. Chapter 19 presents a model of the international economy that takes inflation into account.

15.1   Inflation in the Aggregate Supply and Demand Model

Chapter 7 introduced the basic aggregate supply and demand model. Since that time we have refined our understanding of sources of shifts in the aggregate demand and supply curves. What we have learned about sources of such shifts can be summarized as follows:

1. Shifts in the aggregate demand curve may originate in its real consumption, planned investment, government purchases, or net export components. The position of the aggregate demand curve depends, among other things, on the money stock and policies determining fiscal policy. Expansionary monetary or fiscal policy shifts the aggregate demand curve to the right; contractionary monetary or fiscal policy shifts it to the left.

2. The long-run aggregate supply curve is a vertical line drawn at the level of natural real output. A change in the level of natural real output shifts the curve.

3. The positively sloped short-run aggregate supply curve is drawn on the assumption that the expected level of input prices adjusts only gradually to changes in aggregate demand and in final goods prices. The height of the intersection of a short-run aggregate supply curve with the long-run aggregate supply curve indicates the expected level of input prices on which that short-run curve is based. An increase in the expected level of input prices shifts the short-run aggregate supply curve upward; a decrease in the expected level of input prices shifts it downward.

Much can be learned about the relationships among inflation, real output, and unemployment simply by applying these rules for shifts in the aggregate supply and demand curves to specified changes in economic conditions.

Demand-Pull Inflation

We begin with the case of **demand-pull inflation,** by which we mean inflation caused by an upward shift in the aggregate demand curve while the short-run aggregate supply curve remains fixed or shifts upward at no more than an equal rate. We have already encountered the simplest form of demand-pull inflation, which occurs when there is a one-time rightward shift in the aggregate demand curve beginning from an initial state of equilibrium. The source of the shift may be an increase in the money stock; an increase in the government budget deficit; or an autonomous change in real consumption, planned investment, or net exports. Whatever the source of the shift, the response is a movement up and to the right along the short-run aggregate supply curve to a new short-run equilibrium. In the process, real output and the price level of final goods increase while the unemployment rate decreases. After a lag, the expected level of input prices will begin to catch up with the increase in prices of final goods. When this happens, the short-run aggregate supply curve will begin to shift upward. If the aggregate demand curve remains in its new position, the economy will move up and to the left along it to a new long-run equilibrium in which real output returns to its natural level.

However, such a one-time expansionary policy action is not the only possibility. Instead, lasting expansionary fiscal or monetary policy may allow aggregate demand to keep growing. In this case, as the short-run aggregate supply curve is driven upward by firms' expectations of higher and higher input prices, the aggregate demand curve keeps pace with it. Real output does not fall back toward its natural level; rather, it is kept above that level by ongoing demand-pull inflation.

This possibility is illustrated in Exhibit 15.1. There rising aggregate demand and rising inflationary expectations keep up with each other. The aggregate demand and supply curves both shift upward at the same rate, and the

Demand-pull inflation
Inflation caused by an upward shift of the aggregate demand curve while the aggregate supply curve remains fixed or shifts upward at no more than an equal rate.

Exhibit 15.1   Demand-Pull Inflation

Demand-pull inflation begins when a rightward shift in the aggregate demand
curve pulls the economy up and to the right along the short-run aggregate supply
curve, as from E_0 to E_1 in this exhibit. Subsequently the short-run aggregate
supply curve will begin to shift upward as increases in final goods prices filter
through to cause expected increases in wages and other input prices. If
expansionary policy continues to shift the aggregate demand curve upward, as
shown here, real output can be kept above its natural level, which corresponds to
the long-run aggregate supply curve N, for a sustained period. However, the cost
of maintaining this high level of real output is inflation.

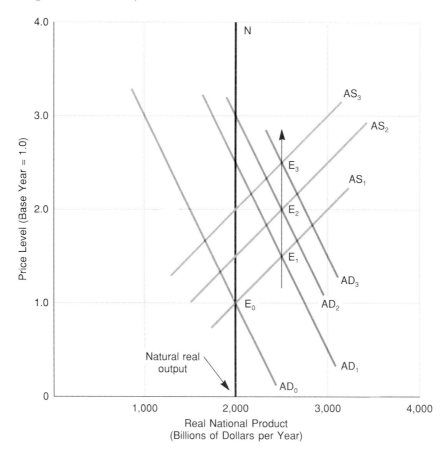

economy follows a path from E_1 to E_2 to E_3 and so on, as the arrow shows.

The scenario shown in Exhibit 15.1 has major implications for economic
policy. It says that in the short run, starting from a state of long-run equilibrium,
an expansionary fiscal or monetary policy is initially effective in stimulating real
economic growth and lower unemployment. The initial cost of such a policy is a
small amount of inflation. However, according to this interpretation, the initial
gains in real output can be sustained only at the cost of ongoing demand-pull
inflation.

Once the initial benefits of the expansion have been enjoyed, policymakers
will face a dilemma. One choice is to stop the stimulus. If they do this, inflation

will cease but output will fall back to its natural level, represented by the long-run aggregate supply curve N, and unemployment will rise to its natural rate. The other alternative is to continue the expansionary fiscal or monetary policy. In that case, according to the above theory, real output can be held above its natural level for some time and unemployment kept below its natural rate. Choosing this path, however, will mean year after year of inflation. Although it is not directly apparent from Exhibit 15.1, a rate of inflation that is steady in percentage terms from year to year may not be enough to hold unemployment below its natural rate. Chapter 16 will show that under certain plausible assumptions regarding the way expectations of inflation are formed, inflation must accelerate to a higher percentage rate each year to keep unemployment below its natural rate for an extended period.

Cost-Push Inflation and Supply Shocks

Demand-pull inflation occurs when the aggregate demand curve shifts upward while the aggregate supply curve remains fixed or shifts upward at no more than an equal rate. However, inflation can also occur as the result of an upward shift in the aggregate supply curve while the aggregate demand curve stays in place or shifts upward more slowly. This type of inflation is known as **cost-push inflation,** because upward shifts in the aggregate supply curve are linked with increases in firms' expected costs of production.

Supply shocks are one source of cost-push inflation. A supply shock is an event independent of changes in aggregate demand that raises the average level of input prices that firms expect. The sudden increases in the cost of imported oil that hit the U.S. economy in 1974 and 1979 to 1980 are examples of such events. The rise in the price of oil increases expected input prices through several channels. First, petroleum products themselves are inputs to many production processes in such forms as heating fuel, motor fuel for transportation, and chemical feedstocks. Second, firms anticipate that prices of substitute energy sources, such as natural gas and electric power, will rise when oil prices rise. Finally, firms anticipate that increased prices for oil and other energy sources will affect the cost of living and that nominal wages will sooner or later have to be adjusted to reflect those changes.

The oil price increases of the 1970s were particularly dramatic examples of supply shocks, but lesser supply shocks occur frequently. The effects of the weather on farming, construction, and transportation may increase firms' anticipated costs of doing business. Natural disasters, such as earthquakes or hurricanes, raise costs of doing business in the affected areas and may affect input prices in wider areas via changes in demand for such key inputs as construction materials. Finally, changes in the foreign-exchange value of the dollar can affect the prices of inputs that are traded on world markets. A fall in the value of the dollar relative to foreign currencies makes imported inputs (say, imported cotton used by a U.S. textile mill) more expensive; it may also increase demand for U.S. exports of intermediate goods such as chemicals that are traded on the world market, thereby driving up their prices.

Supply shocks can work both ways, however. The increases in world oil prices in the 1970s raised input prices expected by U.S. firms, but the subsequent decreases in oil prices during the early 1980s reduced expected input prices. Similarly, unusually good weather leading to bumper crops or an increase in the foreign-exchange value of the dollar would tend to cause a decrease in expected input prices.

Cost-push inflation
Inflation that is caused by an upward shift in the aggregate supply curve while the aggregate demand curve remains fixed or shifts upward more slowly.

Supply shock
An event, such as an increase in the price of imported oil, a crop failure, or a natural disaster, that raises input prices for all or most firms and pushes up workers' costs of living.

Exhibit 15.2   Effects of a Supply Shock

A supply shock is said to occur when an event external to the workings of the domestic economy—say, an increase in the price of imports or bad weather—raises the expected level of input prices. In this exhibit, a supply shock shifts the short-run aggregate supply curve upward from AS_0 to AS_1 while the aggregate demand curve initially stays at AD_0. The result is a cost-push inflation. The price level rises, real output falls, and the unemployment rate rises. If aggregate demand remains unchanged, the economy will eventually return to E_0. Alternatively, expansionary policy can be used to shift the aggregate demand curve to AD_1. This will move the economy to E_2 and hasten the recovery of real output, but it will worsen the inflationary consequences of the supply shock.

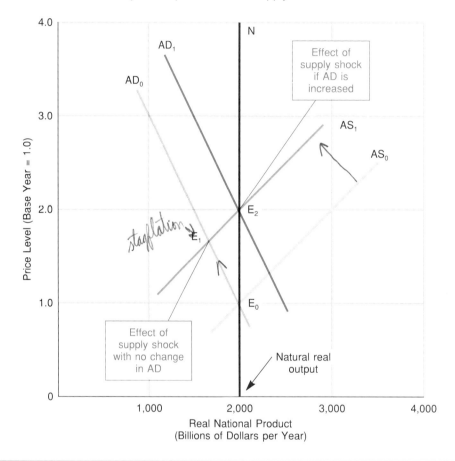

Exhibit 15.2 illustrates the effects of a supply shock in terms of aggregate supply and demand. There the economy begins in long-run equilibrium at E_0. The price level for final goods and the expected level of input prices are equal at 1.0, and real output is at its natural level of \$2,000 billion. At this point, something, say an increase in world oil prices, causes an increase in the average expected level of input prices. As firms adjust their expectations, the short-run aggregate supply curve shifts upward from AS_0 to AS_1, as shown in Exhibit 15.2. With the higher expected level of input prices but no matching increase in aggregate demand, firms must revise their plans. They find it is no

longer profitable to produce as much as before. As they cut back their output, each industry moves up and to the left along its industry demand curve. As this happens, the economy as a whole moves upward and to the left along aggregate demand curve AD_0 to a new short-run equilibrium at E_1. E_1 cannot, however, be a position of long-run equilibrium because real output is below its natural level and unemployment is above its natural rate.

Recovery via downward price adjustment.   What happens next depends on what happens to the aggregate demand curve. If there are no policy changes, the aggregate demand curve will stay at AD_0. In this case, unplanned inventory accumulation, excess capacity of firms, and excess unemployment will tend to put downward pressure on wages and prices. Some unemployed workers will accept jobs at lower wages than they had hoped for. Firms will find that although energy prices remain high, the average level of prices for final goods has not risen as much as they initially expected input prices to increase. (In graphical terms, this is shown by the fact that the intersection of AS_1 and AD_0, which marks the short-run equilibrium level of final goods prices, is lower than the intersection of AS_1 with the long-run aggregate supply curve, N.) Because firms will expect the level of input prices to adjust downward, with a lag, toward the prevailing price level of final goods, the short-run aggregate supply curve will begin to shift downward from AS_1. In time, as it does so, still assuming no change in the aggregate demand curve, the economy will move back down along AD_0 from E_1 all the way back to E_0. The price level will fall back to where it was before oil prices rose, and output will return to its natural level.

This path to recovery from a supply shock is likely to be slow, however. To follow it, the average price level of both inputs and final goods must fall while energy prices, the assumed source of the supply shock, remain high. For this to happen, there must be a major adjustment in relative prices. Real wages and the prices of goods and services other than energy must fall more than the average in order to bring the average down. This is likely to be a painful process for everyone—and until it is completed, unemployment will remain above its natural rate and output below its natural level.

Recovery via a shift in aggregate demand.   There is, however, another way to recover from a supply shock—through expansion of aggregate demand. If expansionary monetary or fiscal policy is used to shift the aggregate demand curve from AD_0 to AD_1, the economy can move to a new long-run equilibrium at E_2. In fact, if the expansion of aggregate demand follows the supply shock quickly enough, the economy may be able to avoid any major loss in real output. Instead of moving first to E_1, it will move straight up along the long-run aggregate supply curve, N, from E_0 to E_2.

Recovery from a supply shock through expansion of demand is likely to be faster than recovery through adjustment of relative prices. Also, the cost of recovery in terms of lost real output will probably be lower. But the cost in terms of increases in the price level will be greater. If policymakers respond to the supply shock by boosting aggregate demand, the price level will end up permanently higher, whereas if they keep the lid on aggregate demand, the impact of the supply shock on the average price level will be only temporary. Furthermore, there is a danger that the expansion of aggregate demand may be excessive, leading to an overshoot of the long-run equilibrium and a bout of demand-pull inflation.

There is no consensus on the best way to react to supply shocks. The response depends partly on the extent of one's dislike for inflation on the one hand and for unemployment on the other. Some economists have suggested that temporary supply shocks, such as crop failures or natural disasters, should not be accommodated by raising aggregate demand. They reason that the aggregate supply curve will soon shift back down as the damage is repaired. However, they suggest, a long-lasting supply shock such as the oil price increases of the 1970s might best be at least partially accommodated by raising aggregate demand. It may be worth suffering the resulting permanent increase in the price level to avoid a prolonged transition period of low real output and high unemployment.

Inflationary Expectations as a Source of Cost-Push Inflation

Supply shocks are not the only source of cost-push inflation. Cost-push inflation can also be caused by rising inflationary expectations fueled by past experiences of demand-pull inflation. To get this result, we must modify our assumptions regarding how firms form their expectations about the level of input prices. Up to this point, as a working assumption, we have supposed that firms expect input prices in the current year to be at a level consistent with that of final goods prices in the previous year. However, this assumption may not be realistic in an economy that has experienced inflation for several years in a row. Under conditions of ongoing inflation, firms more likely will expect the level of input prices to increase this year by a percentage equal to last year's inflation rate. Put another way, when firms have seen inflation in the past, they will expect more inflation in the future and will make their plans accordingly.

Exhibit 15.3 shows what happens when inflationary expectations become established in the economy. We begin from a situation of ongoing demand-pull inflation similar to that shown in Exhibit 15.1. An expansionary fiscal or monetary policy has held output above its natural level for some time. The economy is moving upward along the arrow through E_1 and E_2. After several years of inflation firms and workers expect more inflation in the future and have adjusted their plans to cope with it as best they can. Their plans are reflected in a series of upward-shifting short-run aggregate supply curves that keep pace with the upward-shifting aggregate demand curve.

What happens now if the government decides to stop inflation by halting the growth of aggregate demand? (We are talking not about reducing the level of aggregate demand but only stopping its growth.) In terms of Exhibit 15.3, the effect will be to stop the upward shift of the aggregate demand curve, leaving it in the position AD_2.

Halting the growth of aggregate demand, however, will not stop inflation in its tracks. Firms and workers have grown used to inflation and expect it to continue. Workers expect their costs of living to rise and will have made contracts with their employers giving them offsetting wage increases each year. Firms expect their input prices to rise and will have become used to passing the increases along to their customers. As long as firms expect their input prices to rise and set their prices and output plans on that basis, the short-run aggregate supply curve will continue to shift upward.

Inflationary Recession

With the aggregate supply curve moving upward while the aggregate demand curve stays put, real output starts to fall and unemployment begins to rise.

Exhibit 15.3   Inflationary Recession

An inflationary recession occurs when aggregate demand slows or stops growing following a period of sustained inflation. In this exhibit, the aggregate demand curve stops shifting after the economy reaches E_2. Firms expect the level of input prices to continue to rise; thus, the short-run aggregate supply curve moves on up to AS_3 in the next year and to AS_4 in the year after that. As it does, the economy enters a recession during which the price level continues to rise. For a time the inflation rate may actually increase as real output falls.

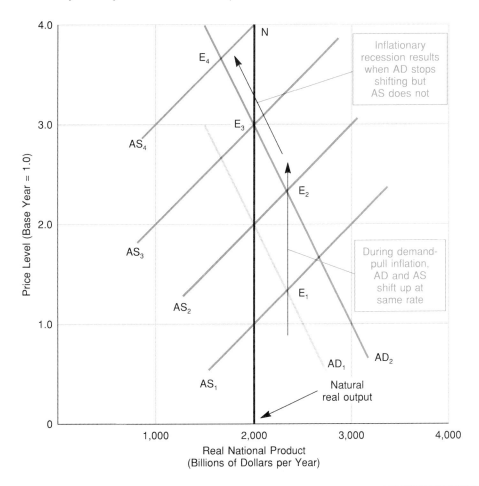

Meanwhile the price level keeps going up. The economy will soon reach E_3 in Exhibit 15.3. There real output and unemployment have returned to their natural levels. This is not the end of the story, however. Because firms experienced continued inflation as the economy moved from E_2 to E_3, they are not likely to expect inflation to stop now. As long as they anticipate that the prices of final goods will keep on rising, firms will continue to form their expectations regarding input prices on that basis. As a result the aggregate supply curve will keep drifting upward, as shown by AS_4 in Exhibit 15.3. As the economy moves along the aggregate demand curve toward E_4, the economy experiences an

Inflationary recession
An episode in which real output falls toward or below its natural level and unemployment rises toward or above its natural rate while rapid inflation continues.

inflationary recession. This is an episode in which inflation, rising unemployment, and falling real output all occur at the same time.[2]

What can be done to bring the economy out of an inflationary recession? A "cold turkey" approach would be to sit tight and keep the lid on aggregate demand. Rising unemployment, declining sales, and an unplanned inventory buildup would, in time, cause firms and workers to revise their expectations about the rate of inflation for both inputs and final goods. Prices of raw materials would begin to fall. Workers, seeing a moderation of the cost of living, would accept lower nominal wages. Lower levels of expected input prices would cause the aggregate supply curve to begin shifting downward. Slowly the economy would slip back down along the aggregate demand curve toward an equilibrium at E_3. But the experience would be a painful one.

A more moderate approach would be to slow the growth of aggregate demand gradually rather than stopping it cold. With luck, this could bring the economy to a "soft landing" at the natural level of real output. It might take longer to slow inflation this way, but a severe inflationary recession might be avoided.

In practice, though, there is a danger that policymakers will overreact to an inflationary recession. Instead of easing the economy to a soft landing, they may first react to pressures to "do something" about inflation (by stopping the growth of aggregate demand altogether) and then react to pressures to "do something" about unemployment by renewing the rapid growth of aggregate demand before inflationary expectations have been broken. Such a "stop-go" policy will result in a highly unstable path for the economy over time.

The truth is that no one knows a quick, painless way to stop inflation once it has become part of public expectations. As we will see, many economists think the best preventative is to keep inflation from getting started in the first place. This is a theme to which we will return in the last section of this chapter and in Chapter 16, which presents a more complete analysis of inflationary recession.

The Long-Run Price Level and Changes in Inflation

This section has discussed demand-pull inflation, cost-push inflation, supply shocks, and inflationary recession. All of these situations lead to a change in the rate of inflation. To round out the section, we can draw some generalizations from the various situations we have analyzed.

1. For any given position of the aggregate demand curve, as determined by the money stock and other variables, and for any given long-run aggregate supply curve, as determined by the natural level of real output, there is a unique long-run equilibrium price level for final goods, as determined by the intersection of the two curves.

2. Whenever the short-run equilibrium price level for final goods is below the long-run equilibrium level, the price level will rise toward the equilibrium level. Such a situation prevails whenever the aggregate demand curve inter-

[2]This situation is sometimes called *stagflation*, but the term is not apt. The term *stagflation*—a combination of "stagnation" and "inflation"—was coined in the 1970s to describe a situation of slow or zero growth in real output, high inflation, and unemployment in excess of its natural rate. The term *inflationary recession* is more suitable for periods that combine high inflation rates with actual drops in real output. The 1974 to 1975 and 1980 recessions were inflationary recessions in this sense.

sects the short-run aggregate supply curve to the right of the natural level of real output. Under certain plausible assumptions regarding the way expectations are formed, the larger the gap, the more rapidly the rate of inflation will rise.

3. Whenever the short-run equilibrium price level for final goods is above the long-run equilibrium level, the price level will eventually fall toward the equilibrium level. Such a situation prevails whenever the aggregate demand curve intersects the short-run aggregate supply curve to the left of the natural level of real output. Under plausible assumptions regarding the way expectations are formed, the greater the gap, the more rapidly inflation will slow, or the more rapidly prices will fall if inflation becomes negative.

These generalizations are supported by empirical evidence from recent U.S. experience, as discussed in *Applying Economic Ideas 15.1.* Chapter 16 will provide further theoretical and empirical support for them.

15.2   Rational Expectations and the New Classical Economics

The theory presented in this chapter is built on the idea of an upward-sloping short-run aggregate supply curve along which the economy initially moves when aggregate demand rises or falls. We have explained the upward slope of the short-run aggregate supply curve by saying that when demand rises firms do not—at least at first—expect the prices of their inputs to rise. As a result, each firm behaves as though the increase in aggregate demand were an isolated increase in market demand affecting its industry alone. Firms move up along their respective industry supply curves, and real output rises along with the price level.

Is it reasonable for firms to behave this way? Is this in fact how they do behave? These questions are a matter of debate in economics today. The debate hinges on how people form their expectations.

The Adaptive-Expectations Hypothesis

The simplest view of expectations is that people expect the future to be like the recent past and adapt their plans accordingly. The theory presented so far in this chapter is based on this view, which has come to be known as the **adaptive-expectations hypothesis.** Earlier in the chapter, we assumed that firms expect the level of input prices this year to be consistent with the level of final goods prices last year. In our discussion of inflationary recession, we modified the hypothesis by assuming that firms expect this year's inflation rate for input prices to be the same as last year's inflation rate for final goods prices. More complex economic models often assume that expectations are based on a weighted average of inflation rates over several prior years. But all these assumptions are variations on the theme that people form their expectations of the future primarily on the basis of past experience.

There is a good deal of common sense to this view. To the extent that it simply means that people learn from experience and adjust their plans on that basis, it is hard to disagree with it. Further, the U.S. economy's experience in the 1970s seems to bear out this hypothesis, at least in general terms. When

Adaptive-expectations hypothesis The hypothesis that people form their expectations about future economic events mainly on the basis of past economic events.

Applying Economic Ideas   15.1
The Price Gap and Changes in Inflation

The aggregate supply and demand model suggests that the direction and rate of change in the price level vary according to the gap between the current level of prices of final goods and the long-run equilibrium level. If the long-run equilibrium price level is above the current level, the price level and rate of inflation will be increasing. If the long-run

equilibrium level is below the current level, the rate of inflation will be slowing, and under some circumstances, the price level may actually fall. Recent research by Jeffrey J. Hallman, Richard D. Porter, and David H. Small, all on the staff of the Board of Governors of the Federal Reserve System, provides empirical support for this view.

The current level of final goods prices, corresponding to the intersection of the short-run aggregate supply curve and the aggregate demand curve, can be observed directly. The long-run equilibrium price level cannot be directly observed, however. Instead, Hallman, Porter, and Small suggest an indirect way of estimating the long-run equilibrium price level. Their approach is based on the equation of exchange, MV = Py, in which M stands for the money stock, V for velocity, P for the price level, and y for real output.

Source: Jeffrey J. Hallman, Richard D. Porter, and David H. Small, *M2 per Unit of Potential GNP as an Anchor for the Price Level* (Washington, D.C.: Federal Reserve Board Staff Study 157, April 1989), Table 1, updated through the end of 1989.

(a) Levels of P and P*, 1955–1989

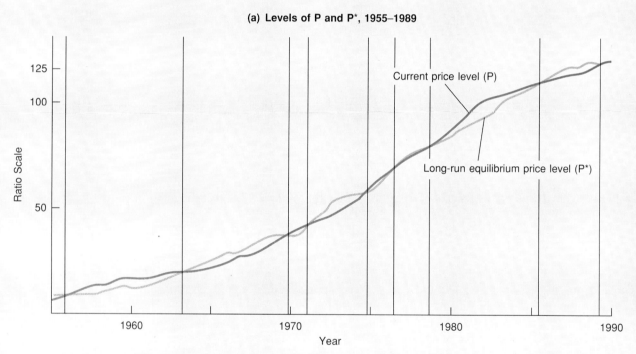

Note: The current price level (P) is the implicit GNP deflator, which is set to 100 in 1982. Inflation is the percentage change in the implicit GNP deflator from four quarters earlier. P★ uses the mean of the GNP velocity of M2 from 1955Q1 to 1988Q1.

inflation first began to get serious in the early 1970s, people were caught off guard; they did not know how to react. As inflation continued, however, people began to expect more of it. They changed their plans and ways of doing business. When inflation slowed in the early 1980s, they did not go right back to the old ways of doing things; their memory of high inflation rates influenced their plans for a time even after inflation slowed.

M2, which is viewed as the most suitable measure of the money stock, can be observed directly. Although the natural level of real output is not directly observable, well-established methods exist for estimating it. M2 velocity varies considerably from quarter to quarter as M2 opportunity cost varies, but smoothing through such variations over the last 35 years as a whole, the trend of M2 velocity has remained remarkably flat, with an average velocity of about 1.65. That is taken to be the long-run equilibrium value for M2 velocity. Given the values of these variables, then, the long-run equilibrium price level P* associated with any given stock of M2 can be estimated from the equation

$$P^\star = (M2 \times V^\star)/y^\star,$$

where $V^\star$ is the equilibrium value of M2 velocity and $y^\star$ is the natural level of real output.

On the basis of observations of the current price level P and estimates of the long-run equilibrium price level P* (pronounced "P-star"), Hallman, Porter, and Small produced the accompanying two-part chart. Part (a) shows levels of P and P* from 1955 to 1989. Vertical lines mark each point at which the two Ps cross. Part (b) shows the rate of inflation as measured by the percent rate of change of the GNP deflator. Comparing the two confirms that during periods such as the late 1960s through the early 1970s, when P* is above P, the rate of inflation tends to accelerate. On the other hand, during periods such as the mid-1970s and early 1980s, when P* is below P, the rate of inflation tends to slow.

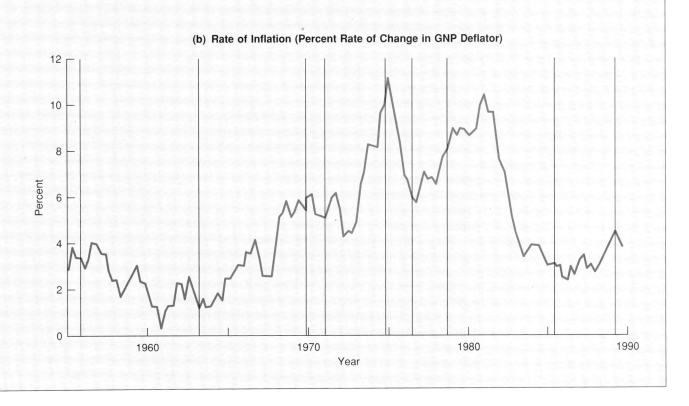

(b) Rate of Inflation (Percent Rate of Change in GNP Deflator)

The adaptive-expectations hypothesis produces the kind of aggregate supply curve that we have used—one that slopes upward in the short run and shifts upward in the long run. Adaptive expectations thus provide a basis for a plausible theory of recession and inflation. Even so, however, many economists are unhappy with this hypothesis.

The Rational-Expectations Hypothesis

The main challenge to the adaptive-expectations hypothesis has come from a group of economists who see past experience as only one of a number of factors that affect people's expectations. In forming their expectations about the future, they say, rational people should look forward as well as backward. In particular, they should examine what government policymakers are saying and are likely to do, and they should take into account the probable effects of current and future policy on future economic events. This view, promoted by economists such as Robert Lucas, Thomas Sargent, and Robert Barro, has come to be known as the **rational-expectations hypothesis.**

Rational-expectations hypothesis
The hypothesis that people form their expectations about future economic events on the basis of not only past events but also their expectations about economic policies and their likely effects.

Suppose, for example, that the economy has experienced an inflation rate of 10 percent for the last year or two and that political pressure has built up to do something about the situation. The president responds with a hard-hitting television speech claiming that the government is going to whip inflation now. The president vows to insist that the budget be balanced and to urge the Fed to pursue a restrictive monetary policy regardless of the political consequences. What do people expect will happen?

The adaptive-expectations hypothesis assumes that people will expect inflation to continue in the future just as it has in the past, regardless of the president's new program. The rational-expectations hypothesis takes a different view: It assumes that people are not simpleminded; they will listen to the president and then try to find out what policies are being undertaken to back up the president's statements.

On the one hand, suppose they conclude that the president has no influence on Congress and will be unable to control the federal deficit. They also think that the Fed shows little concern about inflation and will continue to pump up the money supply at a rapid rate. As they rationally analyze the implications of their beliefs concerning the future course of economic policy, they are unlikely to conclude that inflation will slow. Firms therefore will base their plans on the expectation of continued inflation. Unions will negotiate contracts protecting their members against future inflation. Households will take inflation into account when buying houses or cars. It would be irrational for people not to act this way.

On the other hand, say backers of the rational-expectations hypothesis, people might listen to the president's speech and conclude that it will be followed up with strong action. Suppose that congressional leaders applaud the president's statements and promise to restrain the deficit. Also suppose that the Fed joins the anti-inflation campaign by slowing the growth of money. In this case, according to the rational-expectations theory, firms, workers, and households will modify their plans to prepare for a slowdown in inflation.

Policy Implications of Rational Expectations

The rational-expectations hypothesis has strong implications for economic policy. It suggests that the effects of policy moves that the public anticipates will be quite different from the effects of those that are unexpected. Look at Exhibit 15.4, for example. This exhibit deals with the effects of a one-time increase in aggregate demand. Under the adaptive-expectations hypothesis, firms will initially respond to the shift in the aggregate demand curve by moving upward from E_0 along AS_0 to E_1. As this happens, the price level will rise. As

Exhibit 15.4 Effects of a Policy Change with
Adaptive and Rational Expectations

With adaptive expectations, an expansionary policy
causing the aggregate demand curve to shift from
AD_0 to AD_1 will cause the economy to move from E_0
to E_1 in the short run. Later the aggregate supply
curve will shift up to AS_1, and the economy will reach
a long-run equilibrium at E_2 after traveling the path
shown by the curved arrow. In contrast, with rational
expectations, an expansionary policy change that is
fully anticipated by firms and households will cause
the aggregate supply curve to shift up immediately to
AS_1. The economy will move straight up along line N
to E_2. There will be no intermediate period during
which real output rises above its natural level.

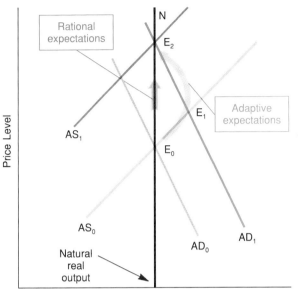

firms adapt their input-price expectations to the higher price level for prices of
final goods, the short-run aggregate supply curve will shift upward, and in time
the economy will move to a long-run equilibrium at E_2. Meanwhile, however,
the economy will have gained something in return for the experience of inflation.
From the time of the initial increase in demand until the economy finally reaches
E_2, real output will have been above its natural level and unemployment below
its natural rate.

Supporters of the rational-expectations hypothesis say that this sequence of
events will take place only if the cause of the increase in aggregate demand is
unexpected—say, an unforeseen surge in consumer spending or investment.
But if the increase in demand is caused by a shift in fiscal or monetary policy that
firms and households already expect, the outcome will differ. This might be the
case, for example, if the Fed announced an increase in its target for the money
stock for the coming year or Congress passed a budget for the coming fiscal year
with a larger deficit and higher spending than the year before.

An expected change in policy, according to the rational-expectations hypothesis, will affect the way firms plan to deal with the increase in demand. They
will know that an expansionary policy will soon cause a rise in the prices of all
final goods, and they will know that input prices in general must ultimately be
consistent with final goods prices. Workers will understand that the coming
expansionary policy will raise the cost of living. Expecting this, they will not
wait to feel the effects on their household budgets, but will instead demand
higher nominal wages immediately, so that their standard of living will be protected in advance. Firms, in turn, will be willing to grant such nominal wage
increases, knowing that the coming shift in aggregate demand will make it possible for them to pass the higher wages along to their customers in the form of
higher prices.

If everyone anticipates the effects of expansionary policy in advance, they will no longer react as though their respective industries were the only ones affected by the increase in demand. They will know that the whole economy will be affected simultaneously and modify their plans accordingly. As a result of the immediate change in expected input prices, the short-run aggregate supply curve will shift upward to AS_1 as soon as the expansionary policy goes into effect. Instead of moving from E_0 to E_1, the economy will move directly from E_0 to E_2. The expansionary policy will have little or no effect on real output; instead, it will only push prices up—and very promptly.

In sum, say supporters of the rational-expectations hypothesis, the economy will follow a positively sloped short-run aggregate supply curve only when shifts in aggregate demand come as a surprise. If they are expected, the positively sloped aggregate supply curve will not apply; instead, the shift in demand will affect the prices of inputs and final goods, but real output and unemployment will remain at their natural levels. In effect, under the rational-expectations hypothesis the economy's aggregate supply curve in the case of anticipated policy changes is the same in the short run as in the long run—a vertical line that coincides with the natural level of real output. Thus, expected changes in macroeconomic policy will not have even transitory effects on real output or employment.

The same mechanism would work during a contraction of aggregate demand, provided the causes of the contraction were fully expected. In that case, the economy would move straight downward to a new equilibrium at the natural level of real output. There would be no adverse effect on real output or employment. This possibility is the opposite extreme from the position taken by Keynes in *The General Theory* that the economy would never return to the natural level of real output on its own following a contraction of demand. If the rational-expectations hypothesis holds, so does the classical result of an economy that stabilizes itself at the natural level of real output. However—at least when changes in aggregate demand are fully anticipated—the speed of the stabilization process is even more rapid than the classicists would have thought. Similarly, the rational-expectations hypothesis not only vindicates the neutrality of money but makes it a short-run as well as long-run proposition, at least when changes in the money stock are fully anticipated. Because of these similarities with the classical economists' views, proponents of the rational-expectations hypothesis are often referred to as the school of **new classical economics.**

New classical economics
A school of economics stressing the role of rational expectations in shaping the economy's response to policy changes.

Doubts about Rational Expectations

The new classical economics has had an important impact on macroeconomic thinking. Still, most economists do not accept in full the policy implications that some new classicists draw from the rational-expectations hypothesis.

Some think it asks too much of firms, workers, and consumers. Do people really pay that much attention to what fiscal and monetary policymakers are doing? Do they understand what policy shifts imply for prices, interest rates, and so on? Can "ordinary" people form rational expectations about the future course of the economy when even professional forecasters so often disagree?

Supporters of the rational-expectations hypothesis claim that they do not require every farmer and shopkeeper to have a Ph.D. in economics. They just say that people do not ignore what they read in the papers and see on the television news. Such information has an impact on their economic decisions—a greater one than the adaptive-expectations hypothesis acknowledges. Also, many key economic decision makers—big corporations, stock market traders, banks, union leaders, and so on—do in fact act on the basis of professional economic advice.

A more telling criticism focuses on the policy implications of the new classical economics rather than on the way in which expectations themselves are formed. The critics point out that in practice shifts in economic policy seem to affect more than just the price level. On the average, according to one estimate, a one-percentage-point change in the growth rate of aggregate nominal demand has a first-year effect on prices of only .44 percent; the remaining .56 percent takes the form of a movement in real output.[3] In part this estimate may reflect the result of averaging episodes of expected demand shifts with episodes of unexpected ones. But economists who are not hard-line new classicists think there are reasons why even expected shifts in demand have major effects on real output and unemployment, at least in the short run. We have mentioned a number of these reasons before, but it is worth reviewing them here.

First, not all prices respond immediately to every change in demand because it is often costly to adjust prices. True, there are some markets, such as the commodity exchanges on which grain and metals are traded, in which prices respond to demand minute by minute. But in other markets, price responses are more sluggish. For example, it tends to be more costly to change prices in markets for goods that have many styles and sizes, such as clothing and auto parts; catalogs and price tags for such goods are changed only every now and then. In other markets, sellers are reluctant to change prices too often for fear of offending steady customers. In still other markets—unionized labor markets being a case in point—prices are subject to long-term contracts and are rarely changed before the contracts expire.

A second reason for gradual price changes is that inventories slow the rate at which demand shifts are transmitted from one sector of the economy to another. Any increase in aggregate demand tends to be felt first by sellers of final goods. It is transmitted to producers of intermediate goods only with a lag as inventories are depleted and restocking orders placed.

Finally, firms get information about demand for their own products more quickly than they do information about changes in aggregate demand for the economy as a whole. When a shoe store sees its sales rise and its inventories drop, it does not know at first whether this is an isolated piece of good luck or whether demand is booming throughout the economy. If the firm thinks the demand increase is a local phenomenon, it is less likely to expect the increase to push up its input prices. It initially responds simply by ordering more shoes from its suppliers. Only when the price increases of other firms have passed through to affect input prices does the firm revise its pricing plans.

This kind of reasoning leads to a middle ground between the rational-expectations and adaptive-expectations hypotheses. In this view the rational-expectations hypothesis is seen as correct in stressing that people take available information into account when they make their economic plans. It is agreed that the new classicists are right in saying that the response to expected policy changes may not be the same as for unexpected ones. Even so, there are many frictions, imperfections, and lags in the economy that keep people from responding imme-

[3]Robert J. Gordon, "Output Fluctuations and Gradual Price Adjustment," *Journal of Economic Literature* 19 (June 1981): 493–530.

diately to every bit of news that comes their way. In practice, then, an economy with rational expectations but also with many frictions, imperfections, and lags does not work much differently than one in which expectations are formed adaptively. In both cases, the economy will follow a positively sloped aggregate supply curve in the short run.

15.3   Strategies for Ending Inflation

In the first section of this chapter, we looked at the mechanisms that get inflation started; these include both demand-pull and cost-push elements. Now we turn to strategies for ending inflation once it has gotten under way.

Demand Management

All economists agree that management of aggregate demand via fiscal and monetary policy can slow inflation. There are costs of doing so, however. As we explained in the first section of this chapter, inflation can gain momentum as expectations of more inflation push the aggregate real supply curve ever higher. Stopping inflation by slowing the growth of demand will then cause an inflationary recession. The momentum of inflation will be broken but only at the cost of a period of high unemployment and low real output.

It is little wonder, then, that economists have looked for ways to reduce the cost of stopping inflation. The suggested strategies include demand management as a necessary element, but they aim to reduce the costs of applying restrictive monetary or fiscal policy. In this section we will look at some of these strategies. After we have done so, we will discuss the end of the Great Inflation of the 1970s.

Wage and Price Controls

Wage and price controls are any of a group of policies that range from mild guidelines to mandatory wage and price ceilings. The United States has tried using such controls a number of times, and they have been used even more widely abroad. Let us see how these policies work and why they are controversial.

The case for controls. The case for wage and price controls is strongest when they are used in conjunction with restrictive demand management as a temporary measure to fight an inflationary recession. When policymakers apply the brakes to aggregate demand after a period of rapid inflation, firms and workers do not expect inflation to stop right away. Their inflationary expectations for final goods and input prices push the aggregate supply curve upward, causing cost-push inflation, as shown in Exhibit 15.3. In effect, the expectation of more inflation becomes a self-fulfilling prophecy. The result is an inflationary recession.

Now suppose that just as the growth of aggregate demand is slowed the government imposes a program of strict wage and price controls. It does this with great fanfare and a show of firm resolve to lick inflation once and for all. It is hoped that workers and firms will believe that the controls are really going to stop inflation, for if they do they will lower their inflationary expectations much sooner than they would if they had to learn from experience.

This reduction in expected inflation—if it happens—will remove the cost-push element from the inflationary recession. Knowing that they need not push for higher wages to beat inflation, workers will continue to find their current wages acceptable. Knowing that their input prices will not be rising, firms will be less inclined to reduce output and raise the prices of the final goods they produce. A larger part of the reduction in the growth of nominal GNP will take the form of a slowdown in price increases than would otherwise be the case. The drop in real output and the rise in unemployment will be smaller than otherwise. As a result, the transition to price stability will be quicker and less painful than it would be without controls.

Problems with controls.   So much for theory. The problem is that wage and price controls often are used as a substitute for demand management policy rather than as a supplement to it. The government either tries to use wage and price controls to fight inflation without simultaneously slowing the growth of aggregate demand or leaves controls in force after the transition is over and a new boom is under way. Therefore, wage and price controls will either be ineffective or lead to shortages, rationing, and black markets.

There have been several experiments with wage and price controls in the United States. One took place during World War II. The high level of wartime government spending made it hard to control aggregate demand. Strict price controls were used to suppress inflation. The results were predictable: Rationing was introduced for gasoline, tires, sugar, and many other goods, and widespread black markets emerged.

Another experiment with wage and price controls took place from 1971 to 1974 during the Nixon administration. This episode is described in *Applying Economic Ideas 15.2.* As indicated there, the Nixon controls were a mixed success at best. They were first introduced when inflation already was falling and may have helped to speed the decline somewhat. But they were left in place after prices began to rise again in mid-1972. At that point, they proved useless or worse.

Despite the dubious success of Nixon's controls President Carter continued to experiment with controls throughout his four years in office. Carter's guidelines, as he called them, were voluntary, but they were backed by the threat to withhold government contracts to firms that refused to follow them. Because aggregate demand continued to grow strongly, the controls did nothing to prevent the inflation rate from doubling during Carter's term in office. One of President Reagan's first acts upon taking office in 1981 was to end the last vestiges of the Carter controls.

Because of their failure in the 1970s, controls have temporarily fallen out of favor. They conceivably could be revived, however, if rapid inflation returns to the United States. Controls allow politicians to take a "get-tough" stance against big business and big labor, which the public often sees as the villains of inflation—and in politics, appearances are sometimes more important than results.

Indexation

As explained in Chapter 4, indexing means making wages, taxes, debts, interest rates, and a host of other things inflation-proof by adjusting nominal payments in response to price-level changes. Indexing is sometimes used just to make it easier to live with inflation. It has been used this way in countries such as Brazil and Israel during their years of experience with double- and even triple-digit

Applying Economic Ideas 15.2
Nixon's Wage and Price Controls

On August 15, 1971, President Nixon announced a dramatic new economic policy. The part of the program that drew the most attention was a strict 90-day freeze on all wages and prices. The freeze later became known as Phase I of what proved to be a long-drawn-out experiment with wage and price controls. Phase I was followed by Phase II, in which firms could raise their prices to cover higher costs but not to increase their profit margins. Wage increases were limited to 5.5 percent except under special conditions.

Phases I and II of the Nixon controls came when controls could be expected to work best. As the accompanying chart shows, inflation was already slowing down. Phase I caused the inflation rate to fall more quickly. Some of this gain was lost in a price bulge when the strict controls of Phase I were lifted, but after that inflation continued to fall through mid-1972.

According to a study by Alan S. Blinder and William J. Newton, the combined effect of Phases I and II was to hold the price level 1.22 percent below the level it would have reached in the absence of controls. This modest but measurable reduction in inflation was achieved at the cost of only a few shortages, mainly in lumber. No widespread disruptions of the economy were felt.

Believing that Phases I and II had done their job, Nixon began to put controls back on the shelf. In January 1973, Phase II was replaced by Phase III. This phase imposed slightly looser standards and stressed self-enforcement by firms and unions. By the time Phase III came into effect, a strong recovery of aggregate demand was under way and the inflation rate had turned upward. According to Blinder and Newton, during Phase III prices rose slightly faster than they would have had controls never

been imposed. This indicates that there was a small "catch-up" effect during that phase.

As the inflation rate increased, political pressure to "get tough" mounted. Nixon responded in August 1973 with a renewed freeze on wages and prices that came to be called "Phase III 1/2." During this phase, inflation was temporarily stabilized, but this time, with demand booming, there were serious shortages. Firms began to hoard raw materials for fear of more shortages.

These distortions were judged to be too high a price to pay for keeping the inflation rate down. The freeze was soon dropped in favor of Phase IV, which was a phaseout. In April 1974, Congress let the controls for most products expire. According to Blinder and Newton, catch-up inflation then began in earnest. By August 1974, prices had reached the level they would have attained had controls never been in force. Even after that, however, catch-up inflation persisted for many months. By 1975, the price level was about 1 percent higher than it would have been had controls never been tried.

Source: Alan S. Blinder and William J. Newton, "The 1971–1974 Controls Program and the Price Level: An Econometric Postmortem" (Working Paper No. 279, National Bureau of Economic Research, September 1978). The chart is based on data from President's Council of Economic Advisers, *Economic Report of the President* (Washington, D.C.: Government Printing Office, various issues).

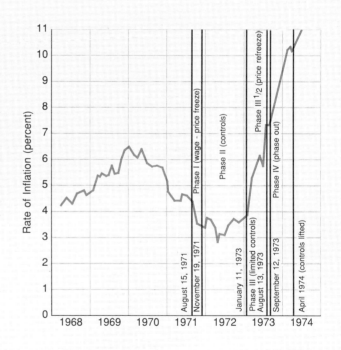

inflation. However, some economists, including Milton Friedman, have suggested that indexing can contribute to controlling inflation as well as easing its pain.

The argument is that indexing, like wage and price controls, can help squeeze the cost-push elements out of inflationary recessions. During a period of inflation all long-term contracts—union wage contracts, contracts for industrial supplies, loan contracts, and so on—must provide for protection against price increases. If they do this simply by setting higher nominal wage rates, prices, and interest rates, these contracts will continue to push up costs even after inflation has slowed elsewhere in the economy. However, if wages, prices, and interest rates in long-term contracts are tied to the inflation rate, they will slow down in step with the general price level. Thus, if indexing is widespread, the rate of inflation may slow more quickly in response to a slowdown in the growth of aggregate demand.

However, indexing can make matters worse instead of better when inflation is caused by a supply shock rather than by excess demand. As explained in the first section of this chapter, adjustment to a supply shock—say, an increase in the price of imported oil—requires a change in relative prices. The price of oil has to rise more rapidly than the inflation rate while other prices rise more slowly. Indexing tends to lock all prices and wages to the average, making the adjustment of relative prices more difficult. The highly indexed Israeli economy is often cited as a case in point. The oil shocks of the 1970s touched off an inflationary spiral in Israel that approached a rate of 1,000 percent per year by the mid-1980s. In the U.S. economy, where indexing is much less widespread, the oil price shocks added only a few percentage points to the inflation rate.

Changing the Policy Regime

At best, indexing and controls only ease the task of taming inflation. When inflation really gets out of control, something more basic is needed. Monetarists and, even more so, the new classicists like to say that what is needed is a change in *policy regime*. By this they mean a change in the basic rules underlying the conduct of economic policy.

Thomas Sargent, a leading member of the new classical school, has developed this line of thought in detail.[4] In Sargent's view, the policy regime of the post-World War II U.S. economy has been one of stop and go, with an inflationary bias. Under this regime, the government has alternately fought unemployment (with expansionary policies) and inflation (with contractionary policies). On average, however, the expansionary periods have been longer-lived and stronger than the contractionary ones.

Sargent points out that conventional estimates of the high costs of stopping inflation are based on the record of this policy regime. It should be no surprise, he says, that prices respond slowly to a contractionary policy in such a regime. After all, people know that the contractionary policy will not last long. They therefore resist price and wage controls to position themselves for the inflation that they know will return.

But, says Sargent, think what would happen if, during a period of rapid inflation, there were a credible change in policy regime. What if the government convinced everyone that it would never again—no matter what—allow aggregate demand to outpace the growth of natural real output? Believing this, firms and workers would expect the inflation rate to fall to zero. Their changed expectations would alter their short-run response to a contractionary policy. The short-run aggregate real supply curve would promptly stop drifting upward. As

[4]Thomas J. Sargent, "The Ends of Four Big Inflations" (Working Paper No. 158, Federal Reserve Bank of Minneapolis, May 1981).

Economics in the News   15.1
Curbing Hyperinflation in Bolivia

JANUARY 1984. The scene is a large bank in La Paz, Bolivia. A courier stumbles in, struggling under the weight of a huge bag of money he is carrying on his back. He announces that the sack contains 32 million pesos, and the teller slaps on a notation to that effect. The courier pitches the bag into a corner.

"We don't bother counting the money any more," explains Max Loew Stahl, a loan officer standing nearby. "We take the client's word for what's in the bag." Pointing to the courier's load, he says, "That's a small deposit."

At that moment, the 32 million pesos—enough bills to stuff a mail sack—are worth only $500.

Outside the bank, prices are rising by the day, the hour, or the customer. Julia Blanco Sirba, a vendor on the capital city's main street, sells a bar of chocolate for 35,000 pesos. Five minutes later, the next bar goes for 50,000 pesos. The two-inch stack of money needed to buy it far outweighs the chocolate.

In the month in which the above scenes took place, the inflation rate in Bolivia was 116,000 percent per year. Tons of paper money were printed to keep the country of 5.9 million inhabitants going. Planeloads of money arrived twice a week from printers in West Germany and Britain.

Source: Sonia L. Nazario, "When Inflation Rate Is 116,000 Percent, Prices Change by the Hour," *The Wall Street Journal*, February 7, 1985, 1; Eric Morgenthaler, "Bolivia Quickly Halts Hyperinflation, but It Does So at Heavy Cost," *The Wall Street Journal*, August 13, 1986, 1.

Purchases of money cost Bolivia more than $20 million in 1983, making it the third-largest import, after wheat and mining equipment.

In the midst of this hyperinflation, a new president, Victor Paz Estenssoro, took charge. His answer to the crisis: a radical change in policy regime. Within a month, he announced a harsh back-to-the-market approach to the economy. The government lifted controls on prices, interest rates, imports, and exports. It freed the official exchange rate. To cut the cost of government, it froze public sector wages and set about dismantling some big state-owned enterprises. It gave companies the right to fire workers. To increase government revenues, it raised the price of gasoline, a state monopoly, tenfold to market levels, and it pushed through Congress an overhaul of the tax system. The airlift of money was curtailed.

Within two months, inflation fell to zero and then averaged 20 percent over the next six months. But there were major costs. The crunch on government jobs came just as forces beyond the government's control were punishing Bolivia's main export industries. World prices of tin and natural gas crashed. At the same time, under pressure from the United States, a major campaign was undertaken against cocaine production, the source of half the country's foreign exchange earnings. Bolivia entered a period of depressed economic activity that lasted several years.

Said Javier Lopo Gamarra, the president of the National Chamber of Industries, "It isn't easy to erase a period of hyperinflation with a few months of stability. The economy is very fragile." But, he added, the program "has to have positive results because the alternative is chaos."

---

it came to rest, the economy could make a quick, painless transition to price stability.

Although this sounds too good to be true, Sargent claims there is evidence that it can work. The evidence comes from cases in which **hyperinflation** has been brought under control, such as that of Germany in the 1920s.[5] In late 1923, inflation in Germany reached a rate of 35,000 percent per month. Yet at the end of that year a sharp change in fiscal and monetary policy, accompanied by a pledge to make the German mark convertible to dollars (which at that time were convertible to gold) stopped inflation cold.

In recent years several countries that have experienced hyperinflation have attempted similar changes in policy regime, with mixed success; the experience of one country—Bolivia—is discussed in ***Economics in the News 15.1.*** In 1990 sharp changes in policy regime were initiated in Brazil and Poland, both of which had experienced hyperinflation in the previous year. Although these re-

Hyperinflation
Very rapid inflation.

[5]Ibid.

cent cases do not support the notion that there are ways to end inflation cost-lessly, they do indicate that a change in policy regime can be a significant element in a disinflation program.

Supply-Side Policies

We have seen that anything that slows the upward shift of the short-run aggregate supply curve or causes it to shift downward relative to the long-run aggregate supply curve will moderate the rate of inflation associated with any given increase in aggregate demand. Wage and price controls, indexing, and a change in policy regime all aim to have such an effect. A similar effect could be achieved if the long-run aggregate supply curve itself could be shifted to the right, and the short-run aggregate supply curve shifted along with it. A set of policies intended to produce such shifts were advocated by certain influential policy advisers early in the Reagan administration. These policies became known as **supply-side economics.**

Exhibit 15.5 shows how supply-side policies could help fight inflation. In this figure the economy is initially in long-run equilibrium at E_0. The long-run aggregate supply curve N_0 that passes through E_0 assumes a natural level of real output of $2,000 billion. Starting from that point, suppose that expansionary monetary policy shifts the aggregate demand curve to AD_1. Assuming no shift in the aggregate supply curve, the economy would move to a new short-run equilibrium at E_1. In the process the price level of final goods would increase substantially.

Suppose, however, that at the same time the aggregate demand curve shifts there is also an increase in the natural level of real output to $3,000 billion. An

Supply-side economics
An approach to economic policy that focuses on efforts to increase natural real output through the incentive effects of cuts in marginal tax rates and other means.

Exhibit 15.5   Supply-Side Anti-inflation Policy

Supply-side economic policies aim to increase the level of natural real output. Among the possible benefits of such policies is a reduction in the rate of inflation associated with a given rate of growth of aggregate demand. To see why, suppose that the economy is initially in long-run equilibrium at E_0, with a natural level of real output of $2,000 billion. If there is no change on the supply side of the economy, a shift in the aggregate demand curve from AD_0 to AD_1 would move the economy to a new short-run equilibrium at E_1. The economy would experience inflation. However, suppose that at the same time the aggregate demand shifts, supply-side policies succeed in boosting natural real output to $3,000 billion. That would shift the long-run aggregate supply curve from N_0 to N_1; if there is no change in expected input prices (adjusted for any changes in the productivity of inputs), the short-run aggregate supply curve will shift as well, to the position AS_1. Given those shifts of the supply curve, the economy will reach a new equilibrium at E_2 without any increase in the price level.

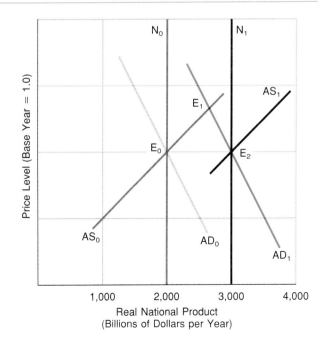

increase in natural real output would shift the long-run aggregate supply curve from N_0 to N_1. If we make the assumption that there is no immediate change in the expected level of input prices (adjusted for any changes in the productivity of inputs), the short-run aggregate supply curve will shift to the right along with the long-run curve. It will do so because the unchanged expectations regarding productivity-adjusted input prices imply no change in the costs of inputs per unit of output. Hence the intersection of the short- and long-run aggregate supply curves will remain at the level 1.0. If both aggregate supply curves shift to the right at the same rate that the aggregate demand curve shifts, the economy will reach a new equilibrium at E_2 rather than E_1. The rightward shift in the supply curves will have offset the rightward shift in the demand curve, and there will be no inflation of final goods prices.

Supply-side tax cuts.   The question now is how to bring about the desired increase in the natural level of real output. The Reagan administration's supply-side advisers saw changes in tax policy as one means to accomplish this end. Their argument ran something like this: During the 1970s, they noted, growth of natural real output stagnated. A major reason for the slowdown, in the supply-siders' view, was the U.S. tax system, which was biased against saving, investment, and work effort. Inflation worsened the problem. Taxes on interest and capital gains pushed the inflation-adjusted after-tax rate of return on an added dollar of investment below zero in many cases. Depreciation allowances based on historical costs of business equipment rather than on costs adjusted for inflation drained companies of funds needed to replace worn-out equipment. Although taxes discouraged investment in productive plant and equipment, tax loopholes encouraged wasteful investment in tax shelters ranging from luxury condominiums to racehorse breeding partnerships. And it was not just corporations and the wealthy who were hit by high taxes. Inflation, the progressive income tax, and the rising social security payroll tax combined to push ordinary wage earners into ever higher tax brackets. Marginal tax rates of 30 or even 40 percent on the incomes of clerks and factory workers discouraged them from improving their skills, working overtime, or even showing up regularly at their jobs.

The centerpiece of the supply-side program was to be a carefully designed set of cuts in marginal tax rates. First, these would improve work incentives by lowering the tax paid on each added dollar of earned income. Second, they would remove the bias against saving and investment by reforming capital gains taxes and depreciation allowances. Finally, they would index the tax system so that tax rates would not be pushed back up again by inflation.

The tax cuts passed by Congress in 1981 included many of the items on the supply-siders' wish list: lower personal tax rates, saving and investment incentives, and a reduction in capital gains taxes. (Some supply-siders were also calling for large cuts in government spending, but Congress was less willing to go along with that part of the program.) The 1986 tax law included further cuts in personal income tax rates and broadened the tax base by eliminating many loopholes, to the supply-siders' satisfaction. However, the law also contained many provisions that displeased them. High on their list of problems were increases in capital gains taxation and reduction of business investment incentives.

Other aspects of the supply-side program.   Tax cuts were the most publicized part of the supply-side program, but there was more to it. Other measures were also planned to boost the growth rate of natural real output. Regulatory reform in transportation, communications, and financial services was intended to spur competition and productivity. Environmental regulations that were viewed as burdensome were to be eased. The welfare system was to be reformed in ways that would increase work incentives for the poor. In short, wherever the productivity slowdown of the 1970s could be blamed on public policies, those policies were to be changed.

Meanwhile the Fed was urged to support the expected speedup of the growth of natural real output. To avoid inflation, supply-siders did not want to let aggregate demand outrun the growth of real output. However, they expected natural real output to grow by as much as 5 percent per year over an extended period, in contrast to more conventional estimates of 3 percent or so even with productivity gains. Expecting more real growth, the supply-siders urged the Fed to adopt a somewhat easier monetary policy than the restrictive anti-inflationary stance of the early 1980s.

Why Did Inflation Slow in the 1980s?

By the end of the 1970s, with inflation hitting double-digit rates, many economists had become pessimistic about the prospects of quickly bringing it to an end. Conventional restrictive monetary and fiscal policies could eventually do the job, they thought, but only at a substantial cost. In a 1978 paper, Arthur Okun examined six studies of this cost.[6] These studies found that reducing the inflation rate by just one percentage point would, on average, require real output to drop 10 percent below its natural level for a full year. Such a decline in real output would mean an unemployment rate of 10 to 11 percent compared with a natural unemployment rate that is now probably in the range of 5.5 to 6 percent, and evidently was higher at that time.

However, the cost of stopping the double-digit inflation rate of the late 1970s, although not trivial, turned out not to be as great as Okun's pessimistic estimate. Inflation reached an annual rate of more than 13 percent by the end of 1979. At that time the unemployment rate was 6.3 percent—not far from its natural rate. Restrictive monetary policy then slowed the growth of aggregate demand. The economy went through back-to-back recessions in 1980 and 1981 to 1982 with only a brief recovery in between. Unemployment rose to 10.6 percent by the end of 1982. Real output on balance hardly grew at all; thus, by the end of 1982 it was at least 10 percent below its natural level. Although Okun's estimate suggests that three years of a 10 percent shortfall of output would have cut only about three percentage points off the inflation rate, in practice, the inflation rate fell by almost ten percentage points, to less than 4 percent per year by 1983. During the remainder of the 1980s, the inflation rate mainly stayed within one percentage point of this 4 percent rate.

Why was the end of the Great Inflation of the 1970s less costly than some economists had thought? As might be expected, the Reagan administration was quick to claim credit for the accomplishment, but many economists outside the administration remained skeptical of those claims.

Claiming credit. Supporters of the Reagan administration claim that its policies, aided by the Fed, deserve the credit. They cite two factors in particular.

The first factor is the *credibility* of the administration's and the Fed's anti-inflation campaign. As we have seen, under a rational-expectations hypothesis,

[6]Arthur Okun, "Efficient Disinflationary Policies," *American Economic Review* 68 (May 1978): 348–352.

credibility is crucial. During the 1960s and 1970s, the argument goes, people could rationally expect each recession to be followed by renewed inflation—after all, that is what had always happened in the past. Their expectations of renewed inflation prevented a downward shift of the short-run aggregate supply curve even during periods of substantial unemployment. Okun's pessimistic estimate of the cost of stopping inflation was based on the experience of such a stop-go policy regime, and under such a regime, it was no doubt valid.

In contrast, the team of Ronald Reagan in the White House and Paul Volcker at the Fed convinced people that the government was serious about fighting inflation. With everyone expecting the inflation rate to fall, the short-run aggregate supply stabilized more rapidly than adaptive expectations alone would have predicted. Hence, the cost of slowing inflation from 1980 to 1983 was lower than had been estimated.

The second factor cited by many supporters of the Reagan administration is its program of supply-side policies. As they point out, for any given growth rate of aggregate demand, the higher the rate of growth of natural real output, the lower the rate of inflation. Faster growth of natural real output during the early part of the recovery from the 1981 to 1982 recession helped the anti-inflation effort, they say, crediting the improved growth to supply-side tax cuts, deregulation, and other policies. In sum, supporters of the Reagan administration claim that there was a change of policy regime.

The skeptics.   Not everyone buys the argument that the early 1980s represent a complete break with the past. The skeptics include not only political opponents of the Reagan administration but also many economists who claim that the recent progress in the battle against inflation is not all that remarkable. Let us look at their arguments.

First, say the skeptics, any analysis of inflation during the 1980s must take into account the role played by supply shocks. Two major supply shocks were at work during this period.

The first supply shock involved energy prices. In one year—from 1979 to 1980—the producer price index for energy products rose by a stunning 40 percent. This pushed costs and prices up in every sector of the economy. Then energy prices did not merely stop rising—they started to fall. From 1982 to 1986, producer prices for energy dropped by 24 percent. This downward supply shock depressed costs and prices in other sectors of the economy.

The second supply shock concerned the international value of the dollar. In 1980, the dollar was at a low point; it would buy only 4.2 French francs, 1.8 West German marks, or 227 Japanese yen. By early 1985, the dollar had rebounded to historic highs—equal to more than 10 francs, over 3 marks, and more than 250 yen. A low value for the dollar, as was the case in 1980, makes imports expensive. High prices for imported finished goods and raw materials push up prices directly. A low value for the dollar also shields domestic firms from import competition and gives them more room to raise their own prices. In contrast, a high value for the dollar makes imports cheap—and low-priced imports mean stiff competition for domestic firms, which find it hard to raise their own prices.

Describing the rise of the dollar and the fall in oil prices as supply shocks is in one sense misleading. The term *shock* seems to imply something that affects the economy from the outside, independently of any policy actions taken. This is not entirely true of the favorable supply-side developments under discussion here. The rise in the international value of the dollar was intensified by the strength of the 1982 to 1984 economic recovery and the high level of real interest rates in the United States. The strength of the dollar, in turn, raised the price of oil, which is quoted in dollars on world markets, to unsustainably high levels in terms of other currencies, and thereby triggered a fall in the dollar price of oil. Nonetheless, in evaluating the claims made by supply-side economists for the success of the Reagan policies, it seems fair to treat these developments as though they were true supply shocks. Although they were related to U.S. economic policies, they were not brought on specifically by supply-side elements of those policies, that is, by either the credibility effect or the incentive effect of tax cuts.

Whether we choose to call these events supply shocks or something else, the changes in world oil prices and the international value of the dollar accounted for a large part of the slowdown in the inflation rate. Higher oil prices and a lower dollar pushed the inflation rate to a peak of 13 percent in 1980. Without these developments, that year's rate probably would have been no higher than 10 percent. Also, falling oil prices and a soaring dollar pushed inflation down in 1983 and 1984. Without these factors, the inflation rate very likely would have been 5 percent or so in those years.

In short, favorable developments in the world economy not connected with the supply-side elements of the Reagan administration policy appear to account for about half of the nearly 10-percentage-point drop in the inflation rate in the early 1980s. Most of the remaining five percentage points can be explained by high unemployment. Even under Okun's assumptions, unemployment during the 1981 to 1983 period was high enough to cut 3.5 percentage points from the inflation rate. Many economists today believe the remaining 1.5-percentage-point reduction in the inflation rate actually can be attributed to an underestimate by Okun of the extent to which unemployment can slow the rate of inflation each year.

Looking Ahead

This chapter has applied the aggregate supply and demand model to many aspects of inflation and anti-inflationary policy. The topic has by no means been exhausted, however. For those readers who are interested, the following chapter provides another model that complements the view of inflation developed in this chapter and adds many useful details. However, the basics have now been covered. Readers who advance directly to Chapter 17 will experience no essential loss of continuity.

Summary

1. **What are the characteristics of inflation that arises from excessive growth in aggregate demand?** Inflation caused by an increase in aggregate demand is known as *demand-pull inflation.* In the short run, an increase in aggregate demand will move the economy up and to the right along its short-run aggregate supply curve. As increases in final goods prices come to be reflected in expected input prices, the aggregate

supply curve shifts upward. If continued expansionary policy shifts the aggregate demand curve upward at the same rate, the economy can be held above its natural level of real output for an extended period, but at a substantial cost in terms of inflation.

2. **How can inflation arise from shifts in the short-run aggregate supply curve?** If the short-run aggregate

supply curve shifts upward while the aggregate demand curve stays in place or shifts upward more slowly, the economy will experience *cost-push inflation*. Real output will fall, and the economy will enter an *inflationary recession*. One source of cost-push inflation is a *supply shock*, such as an increase in the price of a key input such as petroleum. Another is the momentum of inflationary expectations generated by previous demand-pull inflation.

3. **What contributions have the new classical economists made?** Under the *adaptive-expectations hypothesis*, people form their expectations about the future primarily on the basis of their experience in the recent past. But according to the *new classical economists*, households and firms form expectations rationally, taking into account probable impacts of present and future economic policies as well as past experiences. It is an implication of this *rational-expectations hypothesis* that changes in monetary or fiscal policy that are fully anticipated by firms and households will have no effect on real output or employment even in the short run. Critics of this view, however, think that various frictions and lags in the economy will cause policy changes to affect output and employment even when they are anticipated.

4. **What types of policies can be used to combat inflation?** Conventional methods of stopping inflation by restricting the growth of aggregate demand are able to stop inflation only at the cost of an inflationary recession. Several unconventional policies for reducing the cost of stopping inflation have been suggested. These include indexing, wage and price controls, a change of policy regime, and *supply-side* policies aimed at increasing natural real output.

5. **Why did the rate of inflation slow rapidly in the early 1980s?** From 1980 to 1983, the rate of inflation in the United States dropped from more than 13 percent per year to less than 4 percent per year. The inflation rate remained within a 3 to 5 percent range for most of the remainder of the decade. The reduction in inflation was accompanied by back-to-back recessions, during which the unemployment rate peaked at 10 percent of the labor force. The drop in inflation is attributable in large part to restrictive demand management policies. Still, the drop in inflation was more rapid than some economists had expected, and the cost in terms of unemployment was somewhat less than had been expected. Supporters of the Reagan administration attribute the rapid slowdown of inflation to supply-side policies and a change to a more credible policy regime. Skeptics note the role played by favorable supply shocks and argue that the remaining reduction of inflation is attributable to high unemployment brought about by restrictive demand management.

Terms for Review

- demand-pull inflation
- cost-push inflation
- supply shock
- inflationary recession
- adaptive-expectations hypothesis
- rational-expectations hypothesis
- new classical economics
- hyperinflation
- supply-side economics

Questions for Review

1. What are some of the reasons why firms might expect input prices to remain constant in the short run when demand for their output increases?
2. How can the expected level of input prices be determined given an aggregate supply curve and the natural level of real output?
3. How is demand-pull inflation distinguished from cost-push inflation?
4. What are two possible sources of cost-push inflation?
5. Under what circumstances is it possible for the price level and the unemployment rate to rise at the same time?
6. How does the rational-expectations hypothesis differ from the adaptive-expectations hypothesis?
7. Why do new classical economists think that anticipated changes in economic policy have less effect on real output than unexpected ones?
8. Under what circumstances are wage and price controls likely to be effective in slowing inflation? When are they likely to be ineffective?
9. Why is indexing likely to be beneficial as an aid to slowing demand-pull inflation but harmful when the economy is trying to adjust to a supply shock?
10. What is meant by a "change in policy regime"? How can such a change reduce the cost of slowing inflation?
11. What is meant by "supply-side economics"? What contribution can supply-side policies make to reducing inflation?

Problems and Topics for Discussion

1. **Examining the lead-off case.** Given the information provided about the "Great Inflation" in the opening case for this chapter, would you describe the nature of that inflation as demand-pull, cost-push, or a mixture of the two? Discuss.
2. **Expected input prices.** Three aggregate supply curves are shown in Exhibit 15.1. What is the expected level of input prices associated with each?

3. **Favorable supply shocks.** Supply shocks are not always bad. Use aggregate supply and demand curves to explain the short-run and long-run effects of a favorable supply shock, such as a decline in world oil prices.

4. **Price expectations and real output.** Use the aggregate supply and demand model to show that real output can be above its natural level only when the current level of final goods prices is above the level corresponding to expected input prices. Show too that real output can be below its natural level only when the current level of final goods prices is below that corresponding to expected input prices.

5. **Publicity and policy changes.** Assume that the economy has been going through a long period of demand-pull inflation. The government decides to try to stop the inflation by means of restrictive monetary and fiscal policies. Should it make the required policy changes with as little fanfare as possible, or should it publicize them widely? Will it make any difference? Why or why not?

6. **Forecasting inflation.** What do you expect the inflation rate to be next year? Do you know what it was last year? Last month? On what sources do you rely for information about past and present inflation and for forming your expectations about the future? Do you think this course will affect your ability to forecast future inflation? Discuss.

7. **Rational and adaptive expectations in choosing what to wear.** Each morning, you choose appropriate clothing from your wardrobe depending on your expectations regarding the weather. Consider the following two approaches to making this daily choice.

   a. Each day you choose your clothing on the assumption that today's temperature will be the same as yesterday's. If it was hot yesterday, you wear a T-shirt today; if it was chilly yesterday, you wear a wool sweater.

   b. Each day before dressing, you turn on the television and watch a weather report. When choosing what to wear, you make use of the general weather forecast for your part of the country together with your own experience regarding special factors that affect the local weather.

   Characterize these two rules in terms of the concepts of adaptive and rational expectations. Do you think either or both rules will result in your being more appropriately dressed, on average, than a strategy of wearing exactly the same medium-weight clothing year around?

8. **The current rate of inflation.** Inflation data given in this chapter refer to year-to-year percentage changes in the consumer price index. Use the most recent *Economic Report of the President* to determine the rate of inflation for 1990 (and later years, if applicable). Has inflation remained relatively steady, in the 3 to 5 percent range experienced throughout the later 1980s? If not, can you suggest any reason for the change based on the theories presented in this chapter?

Case for Discussion
Greenspan's Waiting Game

Alan Greenspan has a kinder, gentler way of dealing with inflation. The chairman of the Federal Reserve Board wants to eliminate it gradually without pushing the economy into a recession. Good luck. Everyone should hope that he succeeds. But you have to rate his prospects somewhere between poor and nonexistent. Since World War II, the only proven way of reducing inflation significantly has been a recession.

Greenspan's plan to curb inflation has been simple: raise interest rates just enough to slow the economy's growth and create a bit of "slack"—a euphemism for higher unemployment and more spare industrial capacity. The "slack" relieves wage and price pressures, and inflation gradually subsides. But the economy's slowdown isn't so severe as to qualify as a "recession." Greenspan has deftly pursued this strategy since succeeding Paul Volcker as chairman of the Fed in 1987.

But even if conducted flawlessly, his strategy wouldn't be painless. The Congressional Budget Office estimates that civilian unemployment (now 5.2 percent) would have to rise to at least 7.5 percent and stay there for three years to cut inflation to 1 percent [from its current rate of 4.5 percent]. You can quibble with the estimates, but the basic logic is sound.

Are we making a fetish of inflation? Some economists think so. The process of reducing it is too painful, the argument goes. We should be content to keep it in its current 4 to 5 percent range. No one suffers, because wages and interest rates compensate for the inflation.

Most Americans and politicians intuitively agree. Otherwise, there'd be an outcry against today's inflation. There isn't.

So to avoid a recession, a bit more inflation is rationalized. If 4.5 percent is all right, what's wrong with 5.5 percent? Sooner or later, inflation's upward creep begins to feed on itself.

The job of controlling inflation without harsh recessions would be easier if people actually believed that the government was determined to stop inflation. Companies and workers wouldn't feel they had to raise wages and prices aggressively to offset an expected erosion of their money. There are rich ironies in this logic. Every time the Bush administration suggests the Fed ease up, it subtly raises inflationary expectations and thereby increases the long-term odds of a deeper recession. This is the exact opposite of what it intends.

Source: Robert J. Samuelson, "Greenspan's Waiting Game," *The Washington Post*, April 25, 1990, A27. Also in *Newsweek*, © 1990 Newsweek, Inc. All rights reserved. Reprinted by permission.

Questions

1. Do you agree that the only proven way to cut inflation is to trigger a recession? Why or why not? Do you think the Congressional Budget Office estimates of the cost of reducing inflation are reasonable, assuming a natural rate of unemployment in the range 5.5 to 6 percent? How does this trade-off compare with Okun's estimate?

2. At the time this article was written, the unemployment rate had been below 5.5 percent for most of a year. Taking that as the lower limit of the natural rate, does the aggregate supply and demand model support the conclusion that "sooner or later, inflation's upward creep begins to feed on itself"?

3. Why would the job of controlling inflation without a harsh recession be easier if people actually believed that the government was determined to stop inflation? Explain in terms of the model presented in this chapter. Why does advising the Fed to "ease up" have unintended consequences in the long run?

Suggestions for Further Reading

Barro, Robert J. *Macroeconomics*. New York: Wiley, 1984.

An intermediate-level macroeconomics text written by one of the leading new classicists.

Gordon, Robert J. *Macroeconomics*, 3d ed. Boston: Little, Brown, 1984.

Chapters 6 through 9 of this intermediate text parallel the discussion in this chapter.

McCallum, Bennett T. "The Significance of Rational Expectations Theory." *Challenge* (January/February 1980): 37–43.

A nontechnical discussion of rational-expectations theory.

CHAPTER

16

The Accelerationist Model of Inflation[1]

Before reading this chapter, make sure you know the meaning of:

Okun's law (Chapter 4)

Adaptive- and rational-expectations hypotheses (Chapter 15)

Supply shocks (Chapter 15)

Inflationary recession (Chapter 15)

After reading this chapter, you will understand:

How inflation and unemployment are related.

How accelerating inflation affects the economy.

How the rates of inflation and unemployment can both rise during an inflationary recession.

Why the U.S. economy followed a pattern of alternating inflation and recession from the 1950s to the early 1980s.

How the behavior of the U.S. economy in the 1980s differed from that during earlier post–World War II years.

[1]In an abbreviated course, this chapter may be omitted without loss of continuity.

Breaking the Pattern

In 1981, when I first assumed the duties of the Presidency, our Nation was suffering from declining productivity and the highest inflation of the postwar period—the legacy of years of government overspending, overtaxing, and over-regulation.

We bent all of our efforts to correct these problems, not by unsustainable short-run measures, but by measures that would increase long-term growth without renewed inflation. We removed unnecessary regulations, cut taxes, and slowed the growth of Federal spending, freeing the private sector to develop markets, create jobs, and increase productivity. With conviction in our principles, with patience and hard work, we restored the economy to a condition of healthy growth without substantial inflation.

Although employment is now rising, business opportunities are expanding, and interest rates and inflation are under control, we cannot relax our economic vigilance. A return to the policies of excessive government spending and control that led to the economic "malaise" of the late seventies would quickly draw us back into that same disastrous pattern of inflation and recession. Now is the time to recommit ourselves to the policies that broke that awful pattern: policies of reduced Federal spending, lower tax rates, and less regulation to free the creative energy of our people and lead us to an even better economic future through strong and sustained economic growth.

Photo source: AP/Wide World Photos.

Source: Ronald Reagan, *Economic Report of the President* (Washington, D.C.: Government Printing Office, 1985), 3.

As we have seen in preceding chapters, the eight years of the Reagan administration did in many respects see a break in the "awful pattern" of accelerating inflation and recession that marked the earlier post–World War II period. Whatever the extent to which the break in the pattern can be attributed to Reagan administration policies, as he claimed in this passage from his 1985 economic report to Congress, or just to good luck, as some critics would have it, the economy did enjoy relative stability throughout the mid- and late 1980s. In this chapter, we examine both the pattern of accelerating inflation and recession that prevailed from the 1960s to the early 1980s and the break in that pattern that occurred following 1983. Although this chapter makes no attempt to forecast the future, it does discuss the conditions under which stability could be maintained.

16.1   The Accelerationist Model of Inflation

Chapter 15 treated many aspects of inflation, but the aggregate supply and demand model used there has one important limitation: it focuses on the extent of changes in the price level rather than on the speed at which those changes occur. A complete theory of inflation must show not only how the price level changes but *how quickly* it does so. After all, no one would think twice these days about a doubling of the price level that took 25 years to occur, as was the case in the United States from 1948 to 1973. But a doubling of the price level in eight years, as took place from 1974 to 1982, is another matter.

The model of inflation presented in this chapter addresses this shortcoming of the aggregate supply and demand model. It is based on the idea that the economy behaves differently in periods in which the inflation rate is accelerating or slowing down than it does in periods when it is holding steady. Because of the model's emphasis on changes in the inflation rate, it is known as the **accelerationist model of inflation.** In this section, we look at the foundations on which this model is constructed.

The Phillips Curve

Chapter 15 indicated that expansion of aggregate demand could be used to hold real output above its natural level and unemployment below its natural rate only at the cost of sustained inflation. This association between low unemployment and demand-pull inflation can be represented in the form of a graph called a **Phillips curve.** The curve is named after the British economist A. W. H. Phillips, who first described it in a 1958 paper[2] (see **Who Said It? Who Did It? 16.1**).

The Phillips curve as a policy menu.   A sample Phillips curve is drawn in Exhibit 16.1. During the 1960s, when the Phillips curve first attracted economists' attention, it was viewed as a menu of policy choices. Political liberals sometimes argued that we should choose a point such as L on the Phillips curve; this point would "buy" full employment and prosperity at the price of a modest inflation rate. Conservatives expressed horror at the thought of any degree of

Accelerationist model of inflation
A theory according to which changes in the inflation rate affect unemployment and real output.

Phillips curve
A graph showing the relationship between the inflation rate and the unemployment rate, other things being equal.

---

[2]A. W. H. Phillips, "The Relationship between Unemployment and the Rate of Change of Money Wage Rates in the United Kingdom, 1861–1957," *Economica*, new series, 25 (November 1958): 283–299.

Who Said It? Who Did It?   16.1
A. W. H. Phillips and
the Phillips Curve

A. W. H. Phillips was an economist whose reputation was based largely on a single paper on the right topic published at the right time. In the late 1950s, the connection between inflation and unemployment ranked as a major unsolved problem of macroeconomic theory. The curves that Phillips drew in his famous article in *Economica* suggested a simple, stable relationship between inflation and unemployment. Phillips' paper did not present a theory for explaining the relationship, but his curves became the peg on which all future discussion of the problem was hung. Every subsequent article on inflation and unemployment discussed the shape of the Phillips curve, the point on the Phillips curve that best served as a policy target, how the Phillips curve could be shifted, and so on. Today the term is so familiar that Phillips' name enjoys a sort of immortality even though his own interpretation of the curve has fallen into disfavor.

Phillips was born in New Zealand, but he made Lon-

don his base for most of his academic career. He taught at the London School of Economics during the 1950s and 1960s, moving to Australian National University in 1967. Phillips' training in electrical engineering seems to have influenced his approach to economic problems, which has been described as "scientist." In the mid-1950s, he was suggesting the use of an "electric analog machine or simulator" as an aid to the study of economic dynamics. This idea seems to have foreshadowed the widespread use of electronic computers in modern economic research.

inflation and argued for a point such as C, which would achieve price stability at the expense of some jobs.

However, the problem with viewing the Phillips curve as a policy menu was that the choices it offered kept changing while the meal was in progress. As the 1960s unfolded, economists began to notice that inflation-unemployment points for recent years did not fit the curves they had plotted using data from the 1950s.

Exhibit 16.1   The Phillips Curve
as a Policy Menu

When A. W. H. Phillips first drew attention to the inverse relationship between inflation and unemployment, his "Phillips curve" was treated as a policy menu. Liberals argued that a point such as L should be chosen; this would "buy" a permanent reduction in unemployment at the cost of a little inflation. Conservatives seemed to favor a point such as C, which would offer stable prices at the cost of more joblessness.

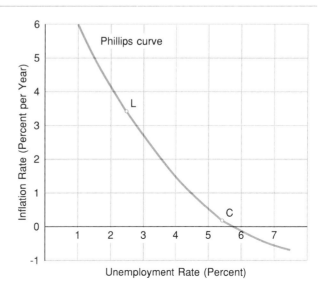

It became common to speak of an upward drift of the Phillips curve; a given level of inflation would "buy" less and less of a reduction in unemployment.

The menu was getting less appealing as time went by. Still, had the upward drift of the Phillips curve been caused by factors outside their control, policy-makers could have chosen their preferred point from a new, higher Phillips curve. With the advent of the 1970s, however, economists' perception of the Phillips curve started to change. It began to appear that shifts in the Phillips curve were caused by the very policies that had sought to move the economy along it.

The Phillips curve and the natural rate of unemployment. The distinction between the long-run and short-run effects of aggregate demand on prices, output, and unemployment provides the key to this new view of the Phillips curve. As Chapter 15 showed, a once-and-for-all rise in the level of aggregate demand leads to only a temporary reduction in unemployment. The reason is that the expected levels of wages and other input prices adjust to changes in the level of final goods prices, thereby pushing up the aggregate supply curve. Thus, real output can rise above its natural level only as long as the short-run aggregate supply curve does not completely catch up with the shifting aggregate demand curve.

In Chapter 4, we defined the natural rate of unemployment as the rate that prevailed when the economy was experiencing neither accelerating nor decelerating inflation. We can also say that the natural rate of unemployment is the rate that prevails when the expected inflation rate equals the actual inflation rate. This can happen with real output at its natural level and the expected and actual inflation rates both equal to zero. However, unemployment can also be at its natural rate when the economy is in a moving equilibrium with a constant inflation rate to which everyone has become accustomed.

This modern view of the Phillips curve is illustrated in Exhibit 16.2. Two short-run Phillips curves are shown, each corresponding to a different expected inflation rate. If no inflation is expected, the Phillips curve takes the position Ph₁. The intersection of this Phillips curve with the horizontal axis indicates the natural rate of unemployment, here taken to be 6 percent. If the actual inflation

Exhibit 16.2 Short-Run and Long-Run Phillips Curves

In the modern view, there is an inverse relationship between unemployment and inflation only in the short run. Unexpected inflation lowers the unemployment rate, but only until people's expectations adjust to the new inflation rate. Any change in the expected inflation rate shifts the short-run Phillips curve. The long-run Phillips curve is a vertical line drawn at the natural rate of unemployment, here assumed to be 6 percent. The long- and short-run curves intersect at the expected inflation rate for which the short-run curve is drawn.

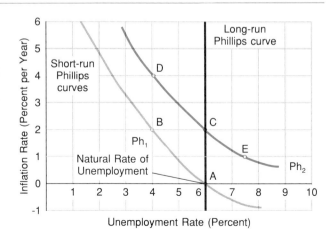

rate unexpectedly goes up to 2 percent per year, the economy will initially move upward and to the left along this Phillips curve from point A to point B. This will correspond to a movement upward and to the right along the economy's short-run aggregate supply curve; real output and the price level will rise as inflation gets under way and the unemployment rate falls.

If the inflation rate remains at 2 percent per year, people will, sooner or later, adjust their expectations accordingly. In terms of the diagrams of Chapter 15, the rising short-run aggregate supply curve will catch up with the aggregate demand curve. As this happens, real output will return to its natural level and unemployment to its natural rate. From that point, the intersection of the shifting aggregate demand and short-run aggregate supply curves moves upward along the vertical long-run aggregate supply curve at a constant 2 percent rate. In Exhibit 16.2, this is shown as an upward shift of the short-run Phillips curve to Ph₂. As a result, the economy moves to point C.

From point C, the economy can move upward or downward along the new short-run Phillips curve depending on what happens to the actual inflation rate. If inflation increases to 4 percent while people expect it to remain at 2 percent, the economy initially will move to point D. If inflation slows to 1 percent while people expect it to remain at 2 percent, the economy at first will move from point C to point E. However, these movements along the short-run Phillips curve will not represent new long-run equilibrium points. As soon as people get used to the new inflation rate, the short-run Phillips curve will shift again.

The long-run Phillips curve.   A final implication of the newer view of the Phillips curve is that it must be vertical in the long run. This follows from the notions that unemployment attains its natural rate whenever the actual and expected inflation rates are equal and that any given steady rate of inflation will be expected to continue. Such a long-run Phillips curve is shown in Exhibit 16.2 as a vertical line drawn at the natural rate of unemployment. Each short-run Phillips curve intersects the long-run Phillips curve at the expected inflation rate for which the short-run curve is drawn. Thus, unemployment will be at its natural rate only when the actual and expected inflation rates are equal.

Other Elements of the Accelerationist Model

The Phillips curve is one key element of the accelerationist model of inflation. Our version of the model has two other elements as well: Okun's law and a nominal national income target for monetary policy.

Okun's law.   In Chapter 4 we stated Okun's law in terms of the connection between the level of real output and the level of unemployment. Here it is more useful to restate that law in terms of rates of change in real output and unemployment: The unemployment rate will remain unchanged in any year in which actual real output grows at the same rate as natural real output. For each two percentage points by which growth of real output exceeds that of natural output in a given year, the unemployment rate tends to fall by about one percentage point. For each two percentage points by which the growth rate of real output lags behind the growth of its natural level, the unemployment rate tends to rise by one percentage point.

A nominal national income target for monetary policy.   In Chapter 13 we discussed a variety of possible targets for use in guiding monetary policy—a money stock target, a nonborrowed-reserves target, and an interest rate target.

In discussing the accelerationist model, it is convenient to assume still another form of target for monetary policy. Under this approach, the Fed chooses a target rate of growth for nominal national income. If nominal national income lags behind the target growth rate, the Fed uses open market purchases to expand reserves and the money stock, thereby lowering interest rates and stimulating aggregate demand until nominal national income catches up with the target growth rate. If growth of nominal national income runs ahead of the target rate, the Fed uses open market sales to restrain aggregate demand and rein in nominal income growth. As Chapter 18 will explain, a number of economists see important substantive benefits in a nominal national income target. Here, we assume such a target primarily because it simplifies the presentation of numerical and graphical examples.

A given target growth rate for nominal national income can be achieved through any combination of growth of real output and inflation that adds up to the target rate. For example, suppose the target growth rate of nominal income is 10 percent per year. This target can be achieved with a 3 percent growth rate of real income and a 7 percent inflation rate, zero growth of real income and 10 percent inflation, 12 percent inflation and a 2 percent drop in real income, and so on.

Other assumptions.   We will incorporate two other simplifying assumptions into our version of the accelerationist model.

First, we will assume that the growth rate of natural real GNP is zero. This assumption simplifies the application of Okun's law. That law relates changes in unemployment to the difference between the rates of growth of actual and natural real GNP. With the growth rate of natural real GNP assumed to be zero, a simplified form of Okun's law can be written as follows:

$$\Delta U = -(\dot{y}/2),$$

where ΔU stands for the percentage point change in the unemployment rate over a year's time and $\dot{y}$ stands for the growth rate of real output over the same period. The minus sign indicates that a positive growth rate of real output is associated with a *decrease* in the unemployment rate, and vice versa.

Second, we will make a simple assumption about inflationary expectations: The expected inflation rate in any year equals the actual inflation rate in the previous year. This will be recognized as a form of the adaptive-expectations hypothesis discussed in Chapter 15. In a more advanced treatment, other hypotheses concerning the formation of expectations could also be introduced into the accelerationist model.

16.2   The Effects of Accelerating Inflation

With these assumptions in hand, we can begin discussing the model by examining the effects of accelerating inflation. Because our simplifying assumptions do not fit the U.S. economy exactly, we will base our discussion on a hypothetical country. Like the United States, this country is a democracy dominated by two political parties, which we will call the Blues and the Grays. As we will see, electoral politics play a key role in our story.

Expansionary Policy from a Standing Start

We begin our analysis in year 0 with the economy in a "standing-start" position. This means that both the actual and expected inflation rates are zero; the growth rate of actual real GNP equals the growth rate of natural real GNP, which in this case is also zero; and unemployment is at its natural rate, here assumed to be 6 percent. In year 0, an election is held. The Blues base their campaign on a promise to "get the country moving." They convince the voters that a 6 percent unemployment rate is too high and that a little economic growth would be a good thing. Upon taking over the machinery of government in year 1, they reset the dials of fiscal and monetary policy so as to raise the growth rate of nominal national income from zero to, say, 6 percent per year. What happens next?

Exhibit 16.3 shows how the economy will react to this dose of expansionary policy in year 1. It shows a vertical long-run Phillips curve drawn at the natural rate of unemployment and a negatively sloped short-run Phillips curve labeled Ph_1. In year 0, the economy is at point A. As the expansionary policy takes hold in year 1, a familiar chain of events unfolds. Increased aggregate demand causes inventories to fall throughout the economy. Some firms react by raising their output, others by raising their prices, and still others by doing some of both. In terms of the diagrams in Chapter 15, at this point the economy is moving upward and to the right along its short-run aggregate supply curve.

Effects on the labor market. Soon the effects of the expansionary policy will be felt by the labor market. Firms that are stepping up their output will be recruiting new workers. Some will offer higher wages, expecting that improved demand conditions will allow them to pass along at least part of the higher labor costs to their customers. Job seekers will find both the quantity and the quality of job opportunities better than before. Acting without full knowledge of current and future economic trends, each job seeker will be likely to view the improved labor market conditions as mere good luck. The newly offered jobs will be quickly snapped up. The average length of unemployment spells will fall, and the unemployment rate will drop with it.

Exhibit 16.3 Effects of an Expansionary Policy from a Standing Start

This exhibit shows the effects of an increase in the growth rate of nominal national income to 6 percent from a standing start. As the economy moves from A to B, the unemployment rate drops by two percentage points. Following Okun's law, this means a 4 percent rate of growth of real output. The remaining 2 percent of the 6 percent growth in nominal GNP is accounted for by a 2 percent inflation rate. The 6 percent growth rate of nominal national income is more than enough to reach point B′ but not enough to reach point B″. No inflation-unemployment combination other than B is possible under these conditions.

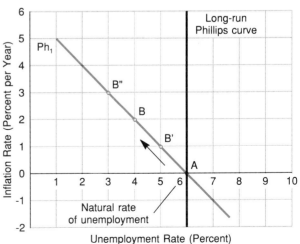

Moving up the Phillips curve.   At this point the economy is moving up and to the left along the Phillips curve, with the unemployment rate falling and the inflation rate rising. How far it will climb in year 1 can be determined by combining two of the elements of the model described earlier. First, the economy must move to a point at which the inflation rate plus the growth rate of real output equals the 6 percent growth rate of nominal GNP. Second, according to Okun's law, the rate of increase of real output must be equal to two times the drop in the unemployment rate. (This is the simplified form of Okun's law, using zero growth of natural real output.) Putting the two together, we conclude that the economy will move to a point on the Phillips curve at which the inflation rate plus two times the drop in the unemployment rate equals the rate of increase of nominal GNP. This occurs at point B in Exhibit 16.3, where the inflation rate is 2 percent and the two-percentage-point drop in the unemployment rate (from 6 to 4 percent) produces a 4 percent increase in real output for a total of 6 percent.

No other point on the Phillips curve satisfies the required condition. Consider point B', for example. There the inflation rate is 1 percent and the unemployment rate has fallen by 1 percent, giving a 2 percent real growth rate. The 1 percent inflation plus the 2 percent real growth sum to only 3 percent—far short of the assumed 6 percent growth rate of nominal GNP. Now consider point B''. There the inflation rate is 3 percent and unemployment has fallen by three percentage points, giving a 6 percent real growth rate. Adding the inflation rate to the real growth rate tells us that point B'' could be reached only if nominal GNP grew at 9 percent rather than at the assumed 6 percent rate.

In short, once the growth rate of nominal output, the initial unemployment rate, the slope of the short-run Phillips curve, and the expected inflation rate are given, only one combination of inflation and unemployment rate is possible.

Effects of Repeated Expansionary Policy

The Blues have every reason to be proud of the economic record of their first year in office. From the stagnation of the standing-start position, a little dose of expansionary demand management in year 1 has cut unemployment by a third and boosted the growth rate of real output to 4 percent at the cost of only a 2 percent inflation rate. These results are so encouraging that the Blues try more of the same. They raise the target growth rate for nominal national income to 7 percent in year 2. Exhibit 16.4 shows what happens.

The most noticeable difference between Exhibit 16.4 and Exhibit 16.3 is the shift in the short-run Phillips curve to the position Ph_2. The Phillips curve shifts because firms and workers, after experiencing 2 percent inflation in year 1, expect a 2 percent inflation in year 2 and firms expect a similar increase in input prices. In terms of the aggregate supply and demand diagram used in Chapter 15, this would be represented by an upward shift in the short-run aggregate supply curve. In terms of the present diagram, it means an upward shift of the short-run Phillips curve to a point at which it intersects the long-run Phillips curve at the new expected inflation rate of 2 percent.

Having concluded that in year 2 the economy will move to some point on the new Phillips curve, Ph_2, we next must determine to which point it will move. The same reasoning can be used as before: In year 2 the economy must move to a point at which the inflation rate plus the rate of increase in real output equals the rate of growth of nominal GNP.

Exhibit 16.4   Effects of a Second Year
of Expansionary Policy

If the target rate of growth of nominal national income
is increased to 7 percent in the second year, the
trade-off between inflation and unemployment will
become less favorable. As a result of the 2 percent
inflation experienced in year 1, the short-run Phillips
curve for year 2 shifts to the position Ph_2. The
economy moves from B to C. The one-percentage-
point drop in unemployment causes a 2 percent rate
of increase in real output. The remaining 5 percent of
nominal income growth is accounted for by inflation.

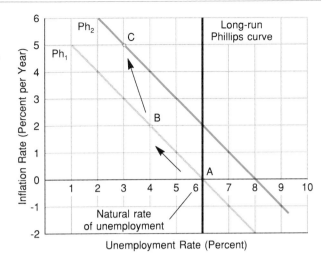

As before, the growth rate of real output can be calculated using Okun's
law, but now the starting point is the 4 percent unemployment rate reached in
year 1 rather than the 6 percent natural rate. Real output will grow in year 2 only
to the extent that the unemployment rate falls further. If it stays at 4 percent, no
real growth will occur. A little trial and error clearly shows, then, that the
economy must end year 2 at point C. There a further one-percentage-point drop
in the unemployment rate—from 4 to 3 percent—will yield a 2 percent rate of
growth of real output. That plus a 5 percent inflation rate equals the assumed 7
percent growth rate of nominal GNP.

Effects of Continued Acceleration

The Blues' record clearly is not quite as good in year 2 as in year 1. The growth
rate of real output has slowed to 2 percent, and the inflation rate has risen to 5
percent. On the plus side, though, unemployment has dropped to just 3 percent.
All in all, the campaign promise to get things moving has been kept. Let us
suppose that to keep up the momentum, the Blue policymakers decide to nudge
the target growth rate for nominal national income just a bit higher, this time to
8 percent per year.

As Exhibit 16.5 shows, in year 3 the economy will be operating on a new
short-run Phillips curve, Ph_3. This curve's upward shift reflects firms' and
workers' expectation that the inflation rate in year 3 will be the same 5 percent
that was actually experienced in year 2. (Thus, Ph_3 intersects the long-run Phillips curve at a 5 percent inflation rate.) To find the point on Ph_3 at which the
inflation rate plus the growth rate of real output equals 8 percent, we must now
move straight up from point C to point D. There is no room for any further
decrease in unemployment or any growth in real output. The entire 8 percent
growth rate of nominal GNP is absorbed in an 8 percent inflation rate.

This result leaves the Blues little to brag about except a continued low
unemployment rate. Clinging to this one remaining achievement, the Blue policymakers decide that in year 4 they will maintain the 3 percent unemployment

Exhibit 16.5   Effects of Continued
Expansionary Policy

An increase in the target for growth of nominal
national income to 8 percent in the third year results
in no further reduction in unemployment. The short-
run Phillips curve shifts to Ph_3, and 8 percent inflation
is required merely to keep unemployment from rising
(point D). To keep unemployment at 3 percent for a
fourth year, the growth rate of nominal GNP must
increase to 11 percent (point E).

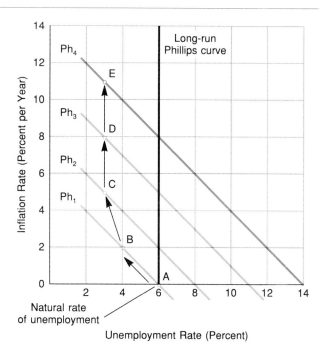

rate at all costs. Turning again to Exhibit 16.5, we can easily see what is needed.
In year 4 the short-run Phillips curve will shift upward to Ph_4 as a result of the
inflationary expectations brought on by the 8 percent inflation rate experienced
in year 3. To keep unemployment at 3 percent in year 4, then, the economy must
move straight up from point D on Ph_3 to point E on Ph_4. Point E corresponds to
an 11 percent inflation rate and zero real growth, so keeping the target for
nominal income growth at 8 percent, as in the previous year, will not be enough.
Instead, an even more expansionary monetary and fiscal policy will have to be
used to raise the growth rate of nominal national income to 11 percent per year.
The cost of maintaining the low unemployment rate is, therefore, accelerating
inflation.

Some Generalizations

Let us leave the world of the Blues and Grays for a moment and draw some
generalizations from our example.

1. Starting from the natural unemployment rate and zero inflation, expansion-
    ary policy initially produces falling unemployment and rapid real growth
    with only moderate inflation.

2. As firms and workers begin to adjust their expectations to the inflationary
    effects of the expansionary policy, the trade-off between inflation and unem-
    ployment becomes increasingly unfavorable.

3. The unemployment rate can be kept below the natural rate for a prolonged
    period only at the cost of a constantly accelerating inflation rate, which
    keeps the actual inflation rate always above the expected rate.

The last conclusion lies at the heart of the accelerationist theory of inflation
—indeed, it is the conclusion that gives the theory its name. The early treatment

Applying Economic Ideas   16.1
Acceleration in the Kennedy-Johnson Era

John Kennedy came to the presidency in 1960 with the stated intent of getting the country moving again after two recessions in the late Eisenhower years. Lyndon Johnson, his successor, was equally determined to pursue an expansionary policy. Economists are still debating the relative impact of the Kennedy tax cut, heavy defense spending, and accelerating monetary growth. But there is no doubt that this combination of policies was as expansionary as anyone could have wished. The result was a sustained period of growth and low unemployment.

The accompanying diagram shows the unemployment-inflation record for the economy during the Kennedy-Johnson era. The pattern is just what the accelerationist theory would lead us to expect. At first, the expansionary policy produced major gains in employment with little additional inflation. But starting in 1964, the

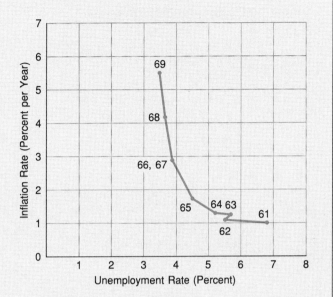

Source: President's Council of Economic Advisers, *Economic Report of the President* (Washington, D.C.: Government Printing Office, 1987), Tables B-35 and B-58. Civilian unemployment rate and changes in annual average CPI.

year of the tax cut, each successive drop in unemployment was accompanied by a bigger jump in prices. By the end of Johnson's term in office, inflation was rising higher and higher each year just to keep unemployment from growing.

---

of the Phillips curve as a policy menu suggested that a low unemployment rate could be bought at the cost of a steady, moderate inflation rate. What led to the demise of this view more than anything else was the U.S. macroeconomic experience in the 1960s, as discussed in *Applying Economic Ideas 16.1.*

16.3   Inflationary Recession and the Stop-Go Cycle

Given our assumption of adaptive expectations, there is no limit to the number of years that unemployment can be held below its natural rate by accelerating inflation. In practice, though, political pressure builds up to a point where something must be done about inflation. Let us suppose that this happens in the land of the Blues and the Grays. In year 4, another election is held. The Blues have a record of 11 percent inflation and stagnant real output. They point proudly to the low unemployment rate they have achieved, but the Grays' promise to do something about inflation wins the day. True to their pledge, once in office the Grays put on the monetary and fiscal brakes.

Effects of Deceleration

Let us assume that the growth rate target for nominal national income is cut from 11 percent in year 4 to just 8 percent in year 5. Exhibit 16.6 shows what happens as a result. First, in year 5 the Phillips curve is still shifting upward as people adjust to the inflationary experience of year 4. In year 5, then, the economy must

Exhibit 16.6   An Inflationary Recession

If the growth rate of nominal GNP is cut back from 11 percent in year 4 to, say, 8 percent in year 5, the result will be an inflationary recession. The Phillips curve continues to shift upward from Ph$_4$ to Ph$_5$, catching up with the actual inflation rate in year 4. Unemployment rises by two percentage points, resulting in a −4 percent rate of real output growth. With such a large negative real growth rate, the inflation rate must increase to 12 percent in order to account for the entire 8 percent nominal growth rate.

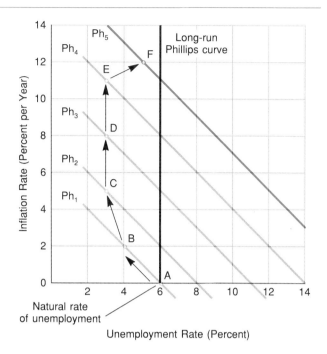

end up somewhere on short-run Phillips curve Ph$_5$, which intersects the long-run Phillips curve at an 11 percent inflation rate. To keep unemployment from rising, inflation would have to accelerate to 14 percent in year 5, but this is impossible given the Grays' restrictive demand management policy. Unemployment therefore rises. Each one-percentage-point increase in the unemployment rate will, according to Okun's law, produce a negative 2 percent growth (that is, a 2 percent decline) in real output. As real output falls and unemployment rises, the economy will move toward a point at which the inflation rate plus the rate of real growth (which is now negative) equals the assumed 8 percent growth rate of nominal GNP. This happens at point F on Ph$_5$. There the economy experiences a 4 percent drop in real output as a result of the two-percentage-point rise in unemployment and a 12 percent inflation rate. The sum of 12 percent inflation and negative 4 percent real growth is the required 8 percent growth rate of nominal output.

We already have a name for the events of year 5: *inflationary recession.* Every possible bad thing is happening at once. Real output is falling; unemployment is rising; and inflation, instead of slowing down, is still accelerating because of inflationary expectations. Economists used to think that such a combination of events was impossible. President Eisenhower's chief economic adviser supposedly promised to eat his hat if accelerating inflation and rising unemployment ever struck in the same year. Luckily for him, hats had gone out of style by the 1970s.

To ensure that we clearly understand the mechanics of inflationary recession, we can relate the events of Exhibit 16.6 to the aggregate supply and demand model used in Chapter 15. There an inflationary recession was shown to occur when inflationary expectations push the short-run aggregate supply curve up while the aggregate demand curve remains fixed or (as in this case) rises less rapidly. The aggregate supply curve shifts upward because firms expect a continued rise of input prices. But with aggregate nominal demand rising relatively slowly, there is not enough real purchasing power to absorb a constant level of real output at a higher price level. Inventories pile up, and firms react by cutting back their output. The economy moves upward and to the left along its aggregate demand curve.

The events of the inflationary recession can also be viewed in terms of what happens in the labor market. Because workers are expecting ever higher prices they will be reluctant to take jobs that do not pay proportionately higher nominal wages. However, the new, more restrictive, monetary policy means that labor demand is no longer increasing as rapidly as before. Workers find it harder and harder to find the jobs they want. Because they lack complete information, they attribute their problems to bad luck. They go on looking for work, stretching out the average duration of unemployment. The unemployment rate therefore rises.

Turning the Corner

Although the events of year 5 win no praise for the Grays, let us suppose that they remain committed to their policies. In year 6 they decide to cut the inflation rate back to 10 percent regardless of the cost in terms of jobs and output. What target should they set for nominal GNP growth to achieve this goal?

As Exhibit 16.7 shows, in year 6 policymakers are still fighting against the momentum of inflationary expectations, which continue to push the short-run Phillips curve upward. Under our assumption of adaptive expectations, because the actual inflation rate in year 5 was 12 percent, people will expect 12 percent

Exhibit 16.7 Turning the Corner on Inflation

To cut the inflation rate to 10 percent in year 6, the growth rate of nominal GNP must be slowed further. Because the actual inflation rate in year 5 was 12 percent, the Phillips curve will shift upward again in year 6 to Ph$_6$. For the economy to reach point G on Ph$_6$, where the inflation rate is 10 percent, unemployment must rise by three percentage points; that, in turn, will produce a −6 percent rate of real growth. Thus, if inflation is to be limited to 10 percent in year 6, nominal GNP can be allowed to increase by only 4 percent.

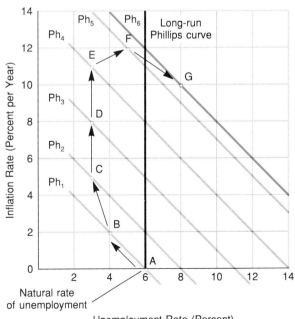

inflation to continue in year 6. That will put the Phillips curve in the position Ph$_6$. In the short run, then, policymakers must pick some point along that curve. The point on Ph$_6$ that meets the 10 percent inflation goal is point G.

To get to point G, the unemployment rate must rise by three percentage points, from 5 percent at point F to 8 percent at point G. According to Okun's law, a three-percentage-point rise in the unemployment rate (with no growth in natural GNP) will produce a 6 percent drop in real output. As always, the rate of change of real output plus the inflation rate must equal the rate of growth of nominal GNP. Inflation of 10 percent plus real growth of negative 6 percent gives 4 percent as the required target for nominal income growth in year 6. Thus, the Grays must press even harder on the brakes in year 6 than in year 5.

After year 6, things get a bit easier because the momentum of inflationary expectations has finally been broken. As Exhibit 16.8 shows, the short-run Phillips curve begins to drift slowly downward. For year 7 the expected inflation rate drops to the 10 percent rate experienced in year 6, putting the Phillips curve at Ph$_7$. Inflation can be cut by two more percentage points if the economy moves straight down from point G to point H. (Such a move calls for an 8 percent growth rate for nominal national income—a moderate easing of aggregate demand policy.) In year 8 another two percentage points can be trimmed if the nominal income growth is cut to 6 percent and the economy moves to point I, and so on.

In short, the Grays' deflationary policy is the mirror image of the policy of accelerating inflation pursued by the Blues. The Blues used accelerating inflation to hold the unemployment rate below its natural level. At first the trade-off between unemployment and inflation was very favorable, but it became less so over time as expectations were adjusted. The Grays, on the other hand, have

Exhibit 16.8   Continued Deceleration

In a mirror image of the initial acceleration, inflation can be slowed steadily each year by holding unemployment above its natural rate. Each year the short-run Phillips curve shifts downward as the expected inflation rate falls. In principle, the deceleration could be continued until a "soft landing" is reached back at point A.

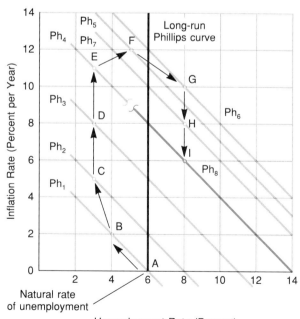

Exhibit 16.9   Reflation

If the growth rate of nominal GNP is again increased after a period of deceleration, the result will be falling unemployment with a minimal increase in inflation. For example, increasing the nominal growth rate from 6 percent in year 8 to 13 percent in year 9 will move the economy from point I to point J. The initial expansion will capitalize on the continued downward drift of the Phillips curve from Ph$_8$ to Ph$_9$.

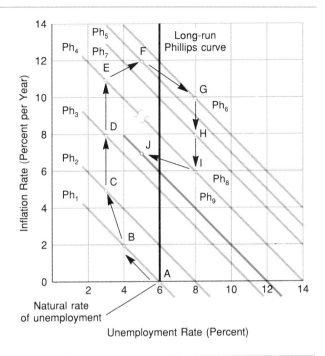

pushed the unemployment rate above its natural level to bring inflation down. At first the trade-off between unemployment and inflation was terrible, but over time it became more favorable as expectations adjusted. Thus, the accelerationist theory of inflation works both ways: Unemployment below the natural rate is linked with a rising inflation rate, and unemployment above the natural rate is linked with a falling inflation rate.

Reflation

After year 8, the Grays' game plan calls for three more years of continued high unemployment and falling inflation. Then the economy can be coaxed to a "soft landing" back at point A, with zero inflation and unemployment back at its natural level. However, year 8 is an election year. What kind of record do the Grays have? In year 4 they took over an economy with 11 percent inflation. By year 8 they had cut that figure almost in half to 6 percent. But the reduced inflation rate has been won only at the cost of a major recession. The unemployment rate is five percentage points higher than it was four years before, and real output is a full 10 percent lower. By this time voters are likely to remember the Blue era more as one of prosperity than as one of excessive inflation.

Further, the Grays' program offers the Blues a tempting opportunity: If the Blues win, for the first year after the election they can pursue an expansionary policy while still taking advantage of the downward momentum of inflationary expectations. Exhibit 16.9 shows how such a **reflation** program could work.

By year 8 the economy will have reached point I, with 6 percent inflation and 8 percent unemployment. In year 9 the short-run Phillips curve will shift to the position Ph$_9$, reflecting the previous year's inflation. Now consider what will

Reflation
An episode in which policy becomes more expansionary while the expected inflation rate is still falling.

happen if at this point the Blues have been elected and push the growth of nominal national income upward from 6 percent per year in year 8 to, say, 13 percent. Because firms will still be expecting input price increases to moderate further, they will react to the renewed burst of demand almost entirely by increasing their real output. Prices will be pushed up only a little more rapidly than in the previous year. Because workers are expecting a more moderate rate of increase in the cost of living, they will snap up the newly created job opportunities with little increase in nominal wages. As a result the economy will move almost horizontally to the left from point I to point J. Real output will grow by 6 percent and unemployment will fall by three percentage points at the cost of only one additional percentage point of inflation.

The Stop-Go Cycle

Compared with the prospect of continued belt tightening under a reelected Gray government, the Blues' promise of prosperity has won them the election. However, the reflation trick works for only one year. After that the inflationary price that must be paid for keeping unemployment below its natural rate will rise each year. The economy will enter a new upswing until political pressure to do something about inflation leads to another policy reversal.

Alternating periods of expansionary and contractionary demand management policy produce the stop-go policy cycle already noted in the preceding chapter. If the political system is, on the average, more sensitive to the evils of unemployment than it is to those of inflation, an inflationary bias will be added to the stop-go cycle, with each upswing lasting longer than each downswing. Without pursuing the matter in detail, we can say that the result is an upward spiral of the economy, as shown in Exhibit 16.10.

Exhibit 16.10   The Stop-Go Cycle with an Inflationary Bias

The so-called stop-go cycle means alternating acceleration, inflationary recession, deceleration, and reflation as political pressure builds up to do something first about inflation and then about unemployment. If the pressure to reduce unemployment is on the average stronger than the pressure to control inflation, the stop-go cycle will become an upward spiral, as shown in this exhibit.

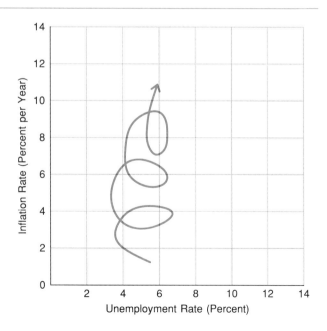

Applying Economic Ideas   16.2
The U.S. Experience with Unemployment and Inflation, 1954–1980

The accompanying chart presents data on inflation and unemployment in the U.S. economy from 1954 to 1980. We have already discussed one part of this record—the Kennedy-Johnson expansion. Now we will explore some other features.

The overall impression one gets from the figure is of a series of clockwise loops. The lengths and strengths of successive expansions and contractions are irregular, but it takes little imagination to see an upward spiral in them.

Although the inflation rate drifted upward over these years, it did not do so over every single cycle. Consider the period following the recession of 1957. The recovery from this recession was very weak. The vertical line between the points for 1959 and 1960, which forms the upward portion of the next loop, is shorter and further to the right than most. This weak recovery seems to have happened because President Eisenhower had been frightened by the inflation of 1956 and 1957 and did not want to repeat the experience. Restrictive policies cut the recovery off before the previous peak of inflation was reached.

During the 1970s, in contrast, the loops in the stop-go cycle resumed their upward drift and became more elongated. The acceleration of inflation from the 1972 rate to the high 1974 rate was especially abrupt, owing in part to the first oil price shock, and was followed by the sharp recession of 1974 to 1975. Beginning from 1976 and continuing throughout the Carter administration, inflation took off again, reaching a 30-year high in 1980.

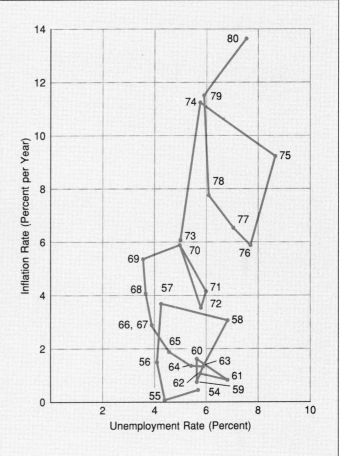

The assumptions that produce the stop-go policy cycle in the world of the Blues and Grays are highly restrictive. The actual U.S. economy is far more complex, as is the accompanying political system. But even so, as *Applying Economic Ideas 16.2* shows, the path followed by the U.S. economy from 1954 through 1980 is very similar to the spiral pattern of Exhibit 16.10.

The U.S. Experience Since 1980

This chapter began with a quotation from President Reagan's 1985 economic report to Congress, in which Reagan stressed the need to break the "disastrous pattern of inflation and recession" of the post–World War II period. As we saw in Chapter 15, that pattern was broken in the 1980s. Let us now use the accelerationist model of inflation to obtain a more precise look at the pattern of inflation and unemployment in the 1980s.

Exhibit 16.11   Deceleration of Inflation, 1980–1989

Between 1980 and 1983, the economy experienced back-to-back recessions. Unemployment reached a post–World War II high, and inflation fell by about 10 percentage points. In 1983, for the first time in 30 years, the low point reached by inflation dropped below that of the previous cycle. Although the inflation rate increased slightly in 1984, the second year of recovery, it turned downward again in 1985 and hit a 22-year low in 1986. From 1986 to 1989, however, the rate of inflation rose again as the unemployment rate fell. Some observers feared that this pattern might represent the beginning of another stop-go policy cycle.

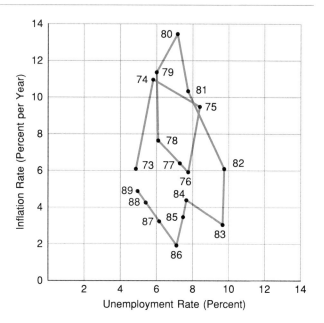

The slowdown of inflation.   Exhibit 16.11 adds the record for the years 1981 through 1989 to the inflation-unemployment chart and removes points before 1973. The added years include the back-to-back recessions of 1980 and 1981 to 1982 and the following expansion, which, already by the end of 1989, was longer than any other peacetime expansion on record. The chart indicates a break with the past pattern in several respects:

- In each of five previous inflation-recession cycles, the low point of inflation (1955, 1959, 1961, 1972, and 1976) was higher than the low point of the previous cycle. In contrast, the inflation rate reached in 1986 was the lowest in 22 years.

- The deceleration phase of the cycle from 1980 to 1983 was longer than it had been in any previous case.

- Although the inflation rate edged up a bit in 1984, the second year of the recovery, it fell again in 1985 and 1986 despite continued improvement in the unemployment rate. Such a "left turn" in the spiral is the first observed in the post–World War II period.

Interpreting Recent Data

We need not repeat everything that was said in Chapter 15 regarding the controversy over the causes of the 1980 to 1983 slowdown in inflation. As we saw there, supporters of the Reagan administration claim credit for the disinflation, pointing to the supply-side elements of administration policy and the greater credibility of its (and Paul Volcker's) commitment to ending inflation. Skeptics outside the administration attribute a considerable part of the slowdown to favorable supply shocks. The rest they attribute to the conventional effects of restrictive

Exhibit 16.12   Recent Inflation and Unemployment, Adjusted for Supply Shocks

The food and energy sectors of the economy are thought to be especially prone to supply shocks. A rough way of adjusting the data to eliminate the effects of supply shocks is to remove the food and energy components of the consumer price index when calculating its year-to-year rate of change. Such an adjustment is made here. Comparing this exhibit with Exhibit 16.11, we see that the general inflation-unemployment pattern from 1973 through 1982 is not greatly affected by removal of the food and energy sectors. The pattern from 1982 to 1989, however, is changed significantly. The big dip of inflation in 1986 turns out to be almost entirely due to a 13 percent drop in energy prices that year. Also, the upturn of inflation in 1989 almost disappears when food and energy components are removed from the CPI. If one optimistically assumes a drop in the natural unemployment rate to the bottom of the 5.5 to 6 percent range, the pattern from 1983 to 1989 suggests the possibility of a soft landing near a 4 percent inflation rate.

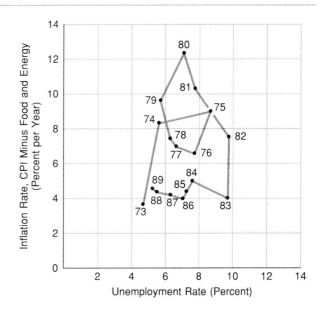

Source: President's Council of Economic Advisers, *Economic Report of the President* (Washington, D.C.: Government Printing Office, 1990), Tables C-39 and C-61. Civilian unemployment rate and year-to-year change in CPI less food and energy components.

demand-management policy and the resulting high unemployment. Next we turn to the more recent record. This record can be read in more than one way.

On the one hand, the points for 1986 to 1989 in Exhibit 16.11 can be read as the ominous beginnings of a new inflationary policy cycle. The critical signs are there: Three years of falling unemployment accompanied by three years of accelerating inflation. The 5.3 percent unemployment rate attained in 1989 is, for the first time, below the lower limit of the 5.5 to 6 percent range often cited for the natural rate of unemployment. When the rate of increase of the consumer price index spurted to an 8 percent annual rate in the first quarter of 1990 and the March 1990 unemployment rate dipped to 5.2 percent, some forecasters began to warn of inflationary recession ahead. On this reading of the data, the break in the "awful pattern" of stop-go cycles might turn out to be only temporary.

On the other hand, a less alarming interpretation is also possible. If the period from 1983 to 1989 is taken as a whole, there is little upward trend in the inflation rate. The year-to-year variations in inflation shown in Exhibit 16.11 may result from transient supply shocks rather than fundamental trends, a possibility that finds some support in Exhibit 16.12. Exhibit 16.12 differs from Exhibit 16.11 in that the food and energy components have been taken out of the consumer price index in calculating the year-to-year inflation rate. Food and energy prices are thought to be much more susceptible to supply shocks than the services and manufactured goods that dominate the remainder of the market basket used in calculating the consumer price index. Because changes in food and energy prices are to some extent passed through to other elements of the consumer price index, the adjusted index does not entirely remove the effects of supply shocks, but it does so at least partially.

The adjustment to the data has only a moderate effect on the general pattern of inflation and unemployment prior to 1982. However, it makes a considerable difference in the years 1982 to 1989. Those years now show a steady decline in the unemployment rate with relatively little year-to-year variation in the underlying rate of inflation. The sharp dip in inflation for 1986 that was shown in Exhibit 16.11 turns out to be largely attributable to a 13.2 percent drop in consumer energy prices that year—a genuine supply shock originating in world market forces beyond the control of U.S. economic policy. Also, the worrisome upturn in inflation as measured by the unadjusted CPI from 1987 to 1989 almost disappears. When a 5.6 percent increase in energy prices is removed from the 1989 data, along with a 5.8 percent increase in food prices (the aftermath of the 1988 drought in the Midwest), the rate of inflation increases by only .1 percentage point from 1988 to 1989.

Furthermore, trends in the composition of the labor force may be making a positive contribution by lowering the natural rate of unemployment. Certain signs point in this direction. In particular, the labor force is maturing. In 1980, 7.6 percent of the labor force was in the 16-to-19-year age range that has always exhibited a relatively high unemployment rate. By 1989 that percentage had dropped to 5.6 percent. Meanwhile, members of the "baby boom" generation born just after World War II were entering their prime working years, when unemployment rates are characteristically low. Also, the labor force is steadily shifting away from manufacturing toward service employment, which has more stable employment characteristics. No precise year-to-year measure of the natural unemployment rate is possible. But the 5.3 percent unemployment rate of 1989 might well be closer to the natural rate than was the 5.8 percent rate experienced in 1979, when the rate of inflation was high and accelerating.

Looking Ahead

Uncertainty in interpreting the inflation and unemployment pattern of the late 1980s makes it particularly difficult to hazard a guess at what lies ahead. Without attempting to foretell the future, however, it is not hard to identify the issues that will merit particular attention in the early 1990s.

First, it should become increasingly apparent which of the two interpretations of the late 1980s is more nearly correct. Further acceleration of inflation would tend to confirm a return to the old stop-go cycle. On the other hand, continued moderate inflation would suggest that the economy has achieved a "soft landing," if not at zero inflation, then at least at a rate that is tolerable by standards of the past two decades.

If the latter, more optimistic outcome materializes, we can expect renewed debate over the appropriate long-run inflation target. If relative stability is possible at an inflation rate near 4 percent per year, is it worth risking recession and much higher unemployment to bring the rate to zero? Or can a sufficiently credible anti-inflationary monetary policy, ideally carried out as the federal budget moves toward balance, ease the economy nearly straight down along its long-run Phillips curve to a point of true price stability? We can only watch and wait.

Summary

1. **How are inflation and unemployment related?** The short-run relationship between inflation and unemployment is shown by the *Phillips curve*. This is a negatively sloped curve that shows that for a given expected inflation rate, lower actual inflation rates tend to be linked with higher unemployment rates. The intersection of the short- and long-run Phillips curves corresponds to the expected rate of inflation; an increase in the expected inflation rate tends to shift the short-run Phillips curve upward. The long-run Phillips curve is a vertical line at the natural rate of unemployment. Unemployment will be at its natural rate only when the actual inflation rate equals the expected inflation rate. The relationship between the short- and long-run Phillips curves forms the basis for the *accelerationist theory of inflation*.

2. **How does accelerating inflation affect the economy?** If an expansionary policy is pursued from a standing start, it at first drives unemployment below its natural rate with only a moderate increase in inflation. As time goes by, however, the trade-off between inflation and unemployment becomes less and less favorable. Inflation must accelerate to a faster rate each year just to keep unemployment from rising back toward its natural rate.

3. **How can the rates of inflation and unemployment both rise during an inflationary recession?** Slowing the growth of aggregate nominal demand after a period of accelerating inflation will cause an inflationary recession. Until the momentum of inflationary expectations is broken, the inflation and unemployment rates may both rise while real output falls. After the expected inflation rate begins to fall, the actual rate can continue to decelerate as long as unemployment remains above its natural rate. The deceleration may continue until the economy reaches a "soft landing" at zero inflation and the natural unemployment rate, or it may be interrupted by a renewal of expansionary policy, or *reflation*.

4. **Why did the U.S. economy follow a pattern of alternating inflation and recession from the 1950s to the early 1980s?** Alternating expansionary and contractionary demand management policies creates a stop-go policy cycle. On the inflation-unemployment chart, the economy moves in clockwise loops around the vertical long-run Phillips curve. If the political system is, on the average, more sensitive to the problem of unemployment than it is to that of inflation, the loops may become an upward spiral. U.S. experience from the 1950s through the 1970s fits such a pattern.

5. **How did the behavior of the U.S. economy in the 1980s differ from that during earlier post–World**

War II years? From 1980 to 1983, the economy went through severe back-to-back recessions during which the inflation rate dropped about 10 percentage points. Backers of the Reagan administration's policies claim that this represents a complete break with the earlier stop-go policy cycle. Other economists attribute much of the slowdown to favorable supply shocks combined with traditional monetary restraint. From 1983 to 1989, the average rate of inflation changed relatively little, especially if the data are adjusted to remove the effects of volatile food and energy prices. Meanwhile the unemployment rate has declined substantially. By 1989, unemployment may have fallen below its natural rate, although the natural rate itself may have declined in recent years.

Terms for Review

- accelerationist model of inflation
- Phillips curve
- reflation

Questions for Review

1. Under what conditions will the economy move up or down along a Phillips curve? Under what conditions will the Phillips curve shift?

2. What are three elements on which the accelerationist theory of inflation is based?

3. Use an inflation-unemployment chart to trace the economy's response to accelerating inflation over a period of years according to the accelerationist model. Has this pattern ever been observed in the U.S. economy?

4. Use an inflation-unemployment chart to trace an inflationary recession. Why is it possible for both the inflation rate and the unemployment rate to rise in the same year?

5. Under what conditions will the stop-go policy cycle turn into an upward spiral?

6. What explanations have been given for the rapid slowdown of inflation in the United States between 1980 and 1983? For the pattern of inflation and unemployment from 1983 to 1989?

Problems and Topics for Discussion

1. **Examining the lead-off case.** Using the latest *Economic Report of the President* or another source, find the rates of inflation (year-to-year change in the CPI) and unemployment for 1990 and later years, if available. Add them to Exhibit 16.11. Does it continue to

appear that the "awful pattern" of the stop-go cycle was broken by the Reagan administration's policies?

2. **Setting policy targets.** Turn to Exhibit 16.4. If the Blues want only to keep the unemployment rate at 4 percent in year 2, what target rate of growth for nominal national income should they set? What target should they set if they want to keep the inflation rate at 2 percent?

3. **Effects of slowing nominal GNP growth.** Turn to Exhibit 16.5. If the rate of growth of nominal national income stays at 8 percent in year 4 instead of accelerating to 11 percent, what will happen to unemployment? To inflation? To real output?

4. **Effects of a rapid halt in inflation.** Turn to Exhibit 16.6. What rate of growth of nominal national income would be needed to keep the inflation rate at 11 percent in year 5? What would happen to the unemployment rate in that case?

5. **Aiming for a soft landing.** Turn to Exhibit 16.8. Suppose the Grays decided to aim for a "soft landing" at a 6 percent inflation rate and a 6 percent unemployment rate instead of zero inflation and a 6 percent unemployment rate. Beginning from point I, what target for nominal national income would they need in order to do this? Could they keep the economy at 6 percent inflation and 6 percent unemployment indefinitely? If so, what policy would be required?

Case for Discussion

A Very Good Year

From President Richard Nixon's economic report for 1972:

As predicted, 1972 was a very good year for the American economy.

From the end of 1971 to the end of 1972, total output rose by about 7 1/2 percent. This is one of the largest 1-year increases in the past 25 years. This growth took place in a largely peacetime economy; it was not achieved by a war-fed, inflationary boom. In fact, real defense spending declined 5 percent during the year. More important is the fact that the big increase in production of the year just ended was accompanied by a reduced rate of inflation. Consumer prices increased a little more than 3 percent from 1971 to 1972—a far cry from the runaway inflation rate of 6 percent that confronted us in 1969.

A year ago, looking ahead to 1972, I said that the great problem was to get the unemployment rate down from the 6-percent level where it was in 1971. During 1972 the rate was reduced to a little over 5 percent. We should get this down further, and expect to do so, but what was accomplished was gratifying. . . .

The general prediction is that 1973 will be another very good year for the American economy. I believe that it *can* be a great year. It can be a year in which we reduce unemployment and inflation further and enter into a sustained period of strong growth, full employment, and price stability. But 1973 will be a great year only if we manage our fiscal affairs prudently and do not exceed the increases in Federal expenditures that I have proposed. This is the practical lesson of the experience from 1965 to 1968, when loose fiscal policy turned a healthy expansion into a feverish boom followed by a recession. I am determined to live by this lesson. And I urgently appeal to the Congress to join me in doing so.

Source: President's Council of Economic Advisers, *Economic Report of the President* (Washington, D.C.: Government Printing Office, 1973), 3–7.

Questions

1. These passages from Nixon's 1973 economic report discuss the course of the economy from 1965 to 1972. Is the story given consistent with the accelerationist model of inflation?

2. Assuming a natural rate of unemployment of about 5.5 to 6 percent for the early 1970s, do you think it was realistic to predict further declines in both the unemployment rate and the inflation rate in 1973? Explain your answer in terms of the accelerationist model.

3. In retrospect, do you think that 1972 possibly was *too* good a year? What policies could have been used to bring the economy to a "soft landing" more gradually?

4. As expressed in this report, Nixon's only worry about the coming year concerned government spending. In fact, federal defense spending fell, in real terms, another 9 percent in 1973, and nondefense purchases of goods and services edged downward slightly. Thus, runaway government spending would not appear to account for the renewal of inflation in 1973. The first oil-related supply shock did not occur until the very end of the year. What else might have accounted for the renewal of inflation in 1973?

Suggestions for Further Reading

Friedman, Milton. "The Role of Monetary Policy." *American Economic Review* 58 (May 1968): 1–17.

Friedman's presidential address to the American Economics Association is considered to be the first statement of the accelerationist theory discussed in this chapter.

Gordon, Robert J. *Macroeconomics.* 3d ed. Boston: Little, Brown, 1984.

Chapter 8 of this book provides a more advanced treatment of the accelerationist theory.

Phelps, Edmund S. *Inflation Policy and Unemployment Theory.* New York: Norton, 1972.

A readable statement of the accelerationist theory by another of its pioneers. The theory is sometimes known as the Friedman-Phelps theory of inflation.

CHAPTER
17

Economic Growth, Productivity, and Saving

Before reading this chapter, make sure you know the meaning of:

Leakages and injections (Chapters 5, 14)

Cyclical and structural deficits (Chapter 10)

Crowding-out effect (Chapter 14)

Demand-pull and cost-push inflation (Chapter 15)

Supply-side economics (Chapter 15)

After reading this chapter, you will understand:

How the economy can grow while maintaining price stability.

How insufficient growth of aggregate demand can cause a *growth recession.*

How expansion of aggregate demand beyond the growth rate of natural real output can cause inflation.

What may have caused the slowdown in productivity growth in the U.S. economy beginning in the 1970s.

What policies are available to promote economic growth.

Why the national saving rate has declined in the United States and what policies could be used to raise it.

"I Want to Be Prepared When It Gets Here"

YPSILANTI, MICHIGAN. Lavester Frye works at an assembly table eight hours a day building automobile horns, setting a metal plate on a metal dish with one hand, adding a tiny ring with the other.

In the 22 years he has worked at the Ford Motor Company, it never really has mattered that he didn't finish high school. He always has had jobs like this one, jobs that depend more on his hands than his mind.

But Frye has been told that his job soon will become more complicated. To improve productivity, the company is phasing in an intricate statistical system of quality control.

The news made Frye feel nervous and unprepared, and when he looked at the charts he would be expected to keep under the new system, he was even more troubled by what he saw: decimal points. "A long time ago at school, I had decimals, but it faded out of my mind," he says.

On this factory floor, amidst the assembly lines, the huge hulking furnaces and the din of metal on metal, the ability to put a decimal point in the proper place suddenly has become a ticket to a job.

Les Walker came to work at the plant four decades ago as a 17-year-old high school dropout. "If you could read or write a little bit, you could get a job," he said of the booming postwar period when he was hired. "Now there's so much change. . . ."

Walker inspects the valves on shock absorbers that will be built into Ford bumpers. Soon, "statistical process control," which is designed to pinpoint and correct defects in manufacturing, will be introduced to his section of the plant.

Photo source: Courtesy of Ford Motor Company.

Source: Barbara Vobejda, "The New Cutting Edge in Factories: Education," *The Washington Post*, April 14, 1987, A1.

He'll need to use math skills he hasn't needed before and never learned in school: fractions, division, averaging, and decimals.

When Frye and Walker complete their afternoon shift at 3, they and several others gather in a converted office off the factory floor, hunching over high school books around a cafeteria table. They have volunteered for free courses, arranged under a 1982 United Auto Workers–Ford agreement, to prepare for the high school equivalency test. They also have taken instruction in computers and basic reading and math.

These workers, most of whom could retire in a few years, would not lose their jobs if they failed to learn statistical process control. But they know job promotions depend on their ability to adapt, and many of them believe that they will be better, more productive workers if they learn the new systems. They don't want to be left behind.

"I want to be prepared when it gets here," one of them says of the new technology.

Frye and Walker are at the forefront of a massive effort to improve the productivity of U.S. industry. In an increasingly competitive world economy, enhanced productivity—more output per worker—is the main source of increases in living standards. Ford Motor Company's efforts are typical in that some of the increased productivity comes from new equipment but a lot of it results from people finding better ways to work together to get things done. The example is being duplicated, with variations, in thousands of plants around the country.

In this chapter, we will look at the issue of productivity using the same aggregate supply and demand tools that we applied in Chapter 15. We will begin by discussing the policies required for long-run economic growth without inflation. Next we will look at the record of productivity growth in the U.S. economy and likely future trends. Finally, we will discuss policies for promoting economic growth.

17.1 Economic Growth with Price Stability

As we saw in earlier chapters, real output can, in the short run, rise above its natural level in response to an increase in aggregate demand. It can also fall below its natural level during a recession. Long-run growth, on the other hand, deals not with these short-run ups and downs relative to the natural level of real output but with growth in natural real output itself.

Growth in the natural level of real output can be broken down into growth of total worker-hours and increases in output per worker-hour, that is, gains in average labor productivity. The growth of total worker-hours depends on the growth of the labor force and trends in the average workweek. Increases in productivity stem from a variety of sources. Increases in the amount of capital and natural resources available per worker are one. Improvements in technology are another; the use of robot welding machines on an auto assembly line would be an example. Finally, enhancements to human factors such as education, motivation, organization, and quality of management also lead to productivity gains; the introduction of statistical process control at Ford Motor Company is a case in point.

Effects of the Growth of Natural Real Output

Exhibit 17.1 shows the effects of the growth of natural real output in terms of aggregate supply and demand. The economy starts out in equilibrium at E_0 with a natural real output of $1,500 billion per year, represented by the long-run aggregate supply curve N_0. Over time the labor force grows and productivity increases. The result is a rightward shift in the long-run aggregate supply curve to N_1.

As natural real output grows, the economy does not move upward along its short-run aggregate supply curve as it does when aggregate demand shifts with natural output constant. Instead, as we saw in Chapter 15, the short-run aggregate supply curve shifts to the right along with the long-run curve. So long as there is no change in the expected level of productivity-adjusted input prices, the intersection of the long-run and short-run curves will remain at the same price level, 1.0 in this case.[1] This happens because the conditions causing the growth of real output—more workers, more capital, better technology, improved management, and so on—make it possible for output to grow with no increase in input costs per unit of output.

---

[1]To understand why input prices must be adjusted for changes in productivity, imagine that nominal wages and other nominal input prices remained constant, but output per worker-hour doubled throughout the economy. In that case, a typical firm's cost of producing any given level of output would decrease, thereby shifting the firm's individual supply curve downward and increasing the quantity of output the firm would be willing to produce under any given conditions of market demand. For the economy as a whole, this would produce a downward shift of the short-run aggregate supply curve relative to the long-run aggregate supply curve. However, if nominal wages doubled at the same time output per worker-hour doubled, unit costs of production would remain unchanged, and there would be no such shift. In that case, we would say that productivity-adjusted wages were constant. The same kind of adjustment can be made for any input.

Exhibit 17.1 Growth with Stable Prices

Over time, growth of the labor force and of output per worker-hour causes natural real output to rise. As an increase in natural real output shifts the long-run aggregate supply curve from N_0 to N_1, the short-run aggregate supply curve also shifts to the right. If aggregate demand is allowed to grow at the same rate, the economy will move smoothly from its initial equilibrium at E_0 to a new equilibrium at E_1. Prices will be stable, and unemployment will remain at its natural rate.

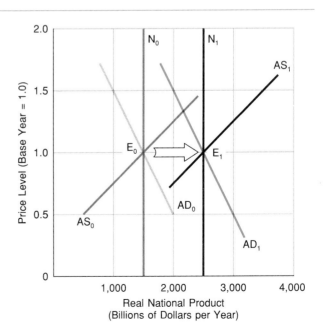

In Exhibit 17.1, the economy at first is able to produce $1,500 billion of goods and services at a price level of 1.0. The shift in natural real output means that it now can produce $2,500 billion of goods and services at the same price level. As we will see shortly, movements of real output above or below the new natural level would be linked with changes in the price level. These would be shown as movements upward or downward along the new aggregate supply curve, AS_1. However, a movement of the economy from one natural level of real output to another does not require a change in the price level.

Finally, Exhibit 17.1 shows the aggregate demand curve also shifting to the right by the same amount as natural real output. With such an increase in demand, firms will be able to sell all the output produced at the new natural level without cutting their prices. If the demand curve does shift as shown, the economy will move smoothly from E_0 to E_1. At these points, as well as all points in between, the economy will remain in long-run equilibrium. Prices will be stable; productivity-adjusted input prices will remain at the level expected by business managers; real output will keep up with its rising natural level; and unemployment will be steady at its natural rate.

Managing the Growth of Demand

Exhibit 17.1 shows the ideal condition of steady economic growth with no inflation or excessive unemployment. However, the economy does not always run smoothly; a number of things can go wrong. One possibility is that steady economic expansion may be thrown off course by autonomous swings in aggregate demand originating in consumption, investment, or net exports. Alternatively, fiscal and monetary policy may be mismanaged in a way that disturbs the smooth growth of the economy. In this section, we will look at what happens when demand grows too rapidly or too slowly.

Growth recession.   Exhibit 17.2 shows what happens when aggregate demand fails to keep up with natural real output. As before, the economy starts from an equilibrium at E_0. Natural real output then rises from $1,500 billion to $2,500 billion, as shown by the shift of the long-run aggregate supply curve from N_0 to N_1. The short-run aggregate supply curve also shifts rightward, to the position AS_1. This time, however, tight monetary and fiscal policy keep the lid on aggregate demand. With the aggregate demand curve stuck at AD_0, the economy cannot reach the intersection of AS_1 with N_1.

What will happen? If real output increases in line with the growth of hours worked and productivity while aggregate demand remains unchanged, unplanned inventory buildup will take place. Firms' managers are disappointed; they are producing more than before, but they cannot sell all their output at the prices that had previously prevailed. To keep stocks of unsold goods from building up, firms cut their prices, hoping to boost sales. At the same time, they cut back their production plans. They increase output somewhat, but not by as much as they otherwise would given the change in their potential real output, as shown by the position of the long-run aggregate supply curve. Thus, as the long-run aggregate supply curve shifts from N_0 to N_1 and the short-run aggregate supply curve shifts with it, firms' price and output cuts are moving them downward and to the left along the new aggregate supply curve, AS_1. Throughout this process, aggregate demand is assumed to be unchanged at AD_0. The economy thus moves to E_1, where AD_0 intersects AS_1.

Exhibit 17.2   A Growth Recession

In the case shown here, natural real output grows while aggregate demand remains fixed. Thus, as the long- and short-run aggregate supply curves shift to the right, the aggregate demand curve remains still. The economy moves downward and to the right along the aggregate demand curve and at the same time moves downward and to the left along the new short-run aggregate supply curve, AS_1, as it shifts to the right. The economy ends up at E_1, where unemployment is higher than its natural rate even though real output has grown. This is called a *growth recession.*

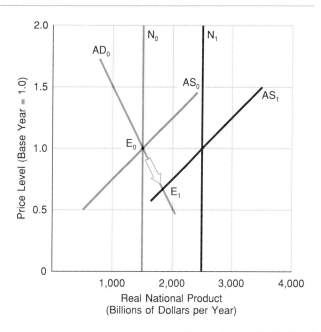

Now look at what happens to employment as the economy moves from E_0 to E_1. Firms have increased their output, but not by as much as natural real output has grown. Given the new investment that has been made and other productivity gains, the economy could produce \$2,500 billion in real output; but at E_1, output is only about \$1,800 billion. Some firms may need a few new workers, while others may lay off a few. Total employment may rise a little or fall a little. Nevertheless, the feeble growth in real output means that not enough jobs will be created to absorb all the new workers entering the labor force. Thus, the unemployment rate will rise.

A situation in which real output grows, but not by enough to keep unemployment from rising above its natural rate, is called a **growth recession.** The experience of the U.S. economy in recent decades suggests that real output has to grow by about 2.5 to 3 percent per year just to keep the unemployment rate from rising. If the growth of real output is too slow, the unemployment rate tends to rise. Because real output is growing, employed workers' real incomes continue to rise during a growth recession. However, they do not rise by as much as they would if demand were keeping up with the growth of natural real output.[2]

Growth recession
A situation in which real output grows, but not quickly enough to keep unemployment from rising.

---

[2]Exhibit 17.2 is an extreme case in that aggregate demand does not grow at all and the price level actually falls. A milder form of growth recession can occur when aggregate demand does grow, but not as rapidly as natural real output. In still other cases, a growth recession can be combined with cost-push inflation. For example, expected inflation, based on past experience, may push the aggregate supply curve upward at the same time that productivity growth is raising natural real output. When that happens, the economy can go through a period in which real output grows, but too slowly to hold unemployment at its natural rate, and the price level rises at the same time. This situation might appropriately be called "stagflation." (See also footnote 2 of Chapter 15, page 398.)

Growth with inflation. A growth recession results from overly cautious economic policy. The economy has the capacity to grow, but policymakers—perhaps fearing inflation—do not give it the room it needs. This has happened from time to time in the United States, but more often policymakers have made the opposite mistake: They have pushed the economy beyond the ability of natural real output to grow. The result has been growth with inflation.

The situation of growth with inflation is another form of the demand-pull inflation discussed in Chapter 15. The difference, as Exhibit 17.3 shows, is that growth of natural real output is now shifting the long-run aggregate supply curve to the right. As it does so, the short-run aggregate supply curve shifts with it. But while natural real output grows from \$1,000 billion to \$2,000 billion, an expansionary policy boosts the level of aggregate demand even more forcefully. The new aggregate demand curve, AD_1, intersects the new short-run aggregate supply curve, AS_1, at E_1. The actual level of real output grows by more than its natural level. As it does so, firms begin using their standby capacity and unemployment falls below its natural rate.

In moving from E_0 to E_1, the economy experiences demand-pull inflation. This inflation will affect expectations. In the following period, if productivity-adjusted input prices are expected to increase in step with the previous period's inflation rate, the aggregate supply curve will be pushed upward at the same time that growth in natural real output carries both the short- and long-run aggregate supply curves further to the right. On balance, the short-run curve will end up in the position AS_2. To keep real output above its natural level, the aggregate demand curve will have to shift to a position such as AD_2. In moving from E_1 to E_2, output stays exactly the same distance above its natural level, keeping unemployment from falling further, and prices will rise by more than they did during the move from E_0 to E_1.

Exhibit 17.3   Growth with Inflation

In this example, aggregate demand is allowed to grow more rapidly than natural real output. As the economy grows, it also experiences demand-pull inflation. As the economy moves from E_0 to E_1, the unemployment rate falls and there is only mild inflation. In later years, the inflation rate must increase just to keep unemployment from rising again. As a result, the inflation-unemployment trade-off worsens.

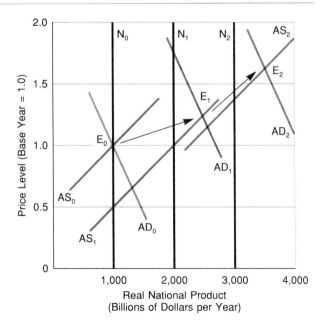

The policy implications of growth with inflation can be summarized as follows. In the short run, pushing the growth of aggregate demand to a faster rate than the growth of natural real output can speed the growth of real output and cut unemployment. The price of doing so is a moderate amount of demand-pull inflation. After this initial gain, however, the trade-off between output and inflation becomes less favorable as firms and workers come to expect further increases in final goods and input prices. Then aggregate demand must grow faster and faster just to keep real output from falling back to its natural level and unemployment from rising back to its natural rate. The growth rate of real output slows, and the inflation rate speeds up.

17.2 Recent Trends in U.S. Economic Growth and Productivity

Up to this point, we have treated the growth rate of natural real output as a given. Until the 1970s, this seemed like a reasonable assumption for the U.S. economy. To be sure, fiscal and monetary policy did not prevent a number of recessions during this period, and other years experienced low unemployment and rising inflation. But on the average, natural real GNP increased by about 3.4 percent per year in the period 1949 to 1973, as shown in Exhibit 17.4. This exhibit shows estimates of the growth of natural real output and its components over three subperiods of the years 1949 to 1989.

Of the 3.4 percent annual growth in real output in the period 1949 to 1973, growth of total worker-hours contributed 1.2 percent per year. The growth of

Exhibit 17.4 Estimated Growth Rates of Natural Real GNP and Components, 1949–1989, Selected Periods

This table shows estimated growth rates of natural real GNP for the U.S. economy and breaks that growth down into its components for selected periods. During 1949 to 1973, natural real output grew at a 3.4 percent rate, of which 1.2 percent was accounted for by growth of total worker-hours and 2.2 percent by increases in productivity. The growth rate of natural real GNP slowed to 2.5 percent in the 1974 to 1981 period. During this period, a decrease in productivity growth more than offset an increase in the rate of growth of worker-hours. The period 1982 to 1989 represents a partial recovery to the situation before 1974.

	1949–1973	1974–1981	1982–1989
Natural real GNP	3.4	2.5	2.7
Total worker-hours	1.2	1.8	1.4
Labor force	1.5	2.4	1.7
Population	1.4	1.8	1.3
Labor force participation	.1	.6	.4
Average workweek	−.3	−.6	−.3
Labor productivity (output per worker-hour)	2.2	.7	1.3

Source: Estimates by the authors based on a variety of data sources.

worker-hours, in turn, was largely the result of population growth, with labor force participation showing a small increase and the average workweek a small decrease. Increases in output per worker-hour (productivity) accounted for the remaining 2.2 percent annual growth of real output from 1949 to 1973. Research by Edward F. Denison of the Brookings Institution attributes the 2.2 percent productivity growth to increases in the quality of labor inputs, growth of the capital stock, and improvements in technology, organization, and the quality of business management.[3]

Productivity growth in the 1949 to 1973 period was generally considered satisfactory; it represents only a slight slowdown from the 2.75 percent rate experienced over the 50-year period beginning in 1920. In the period 1974 to 1981, however, problems developed. As the exhibit shows, the growth rate of natural real output fell to 2.5 percent. More troubling still was the fact that this happened despite substantial increases in the growth trends of the labor force and total worker-hours as younger workers and women entered the labor force in greater numbers. As Exhibit 17.4 shows, growth of output per worker-hour slowed from a trend of 2.2 percent per year to .7 percent per year. In this section, we first look at the productivity slowdown of the 1970s. Then we examine policies designed to promote the growth of natural real output.

The Productivity Slowdown of the 1970s

Exhibit 17.5 charts the productivity slowdown of the 1970s. The 2.2 percent trend shown for 1955 to 1973 dropped to about .7 percent in the period 1974 to 1981 and appears to have recovered only partially—to about 1.3 percent—through the rest of the decade. What went wrong? Over the last ten years, economists have spent a lot of time trying to answer this question. The blame has been placed on many different factors. The following are among those most often cited.

Changes in the labor force.   Many accounts of the productivity slowdown point to the entry of millions of women and young people into the labor force during the 1970s. These new workers were, on the whole, skilled and motivated, but they tended to have less experience than those who already held jobs. At the same time, by their sheer number they pulled down the ratio of capital to labor.

However, Denison found that the shift in the age and gender mix of the labor force could explain only a small part of the productivity slowdown. For one thing, that mix was already shifting against productivity before 1973. In addition, it was more than offset after 1973 by improvements in education.

Supply shocks.   Chapter 15 explained how supply shocks, such as the oil price increases of 1974 and 1979 to 1980, can push real output below its natural level. Some economists believe that the oil price shocks of the 1970s also reduced natural real output. The assumed reason was that higher oil prices rendered much of the economy's capital stock obsolete. Many older trucks, planes, furnaces, generators, and so on had to be retired or placed on standby because high oil prices made them too costly to operate. The effect was almost the same as if the equipment had been destroyed by fire or flood.

---

[3]Edward F. Denison, *Accounting for Slower Economic Growth* (Washington, D.C.: The Brookings Institution, 1979), Table 8-1.

Exhibit 17.5   The Productivity Slowdown of the 1970s

From 1955 to 1973, productivity in the United States increased at a rate of 2.2 percent per year, close to the average rate that had prevailed for half a century. Then, from 1974 to 1981, the rate of productivity growth slowed abruptly. Among the hypothesized causes were changes in the composition of the labor force, supply shocks, inflation, a slowdown in research and development, and increased regulation. Productivity growth recovered somewhat in the 1980s in part due to the reversal of several of these adverse factors, but it has still not reached the rate of increase of earlier years.

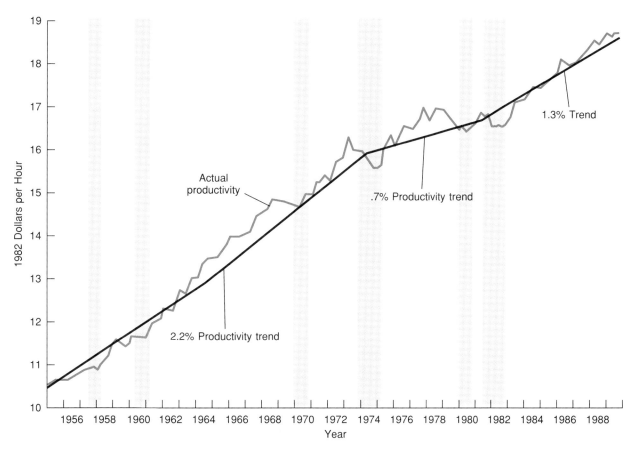

Note: Shaded bars represent recessions.
Source: Federal Reserve Board of Governors.

Moreover, it is argued, the oil price shocks made it necessary to rechannel much investment and research into finding ways of getting by with less oil, either through the design of more energy-efficient equipment or the production of energy substitutes. The resources devoted to this effort would have made a positive contribution to real GNP growth in their previous uses. If energy conservation had previously been the most productive use of these resources, they would already have been devoted to that purpose. Hence, it can be argued, the oil price increases diverted resources from uses that were more highly valued (measured at pre-oil-shock prices) to uses that were less highly valued.

Research and development.   At the same time that much research and development (R&D) spending had to be diverted to energy conservation, total R&D spending lagged during the 1970s. It fell from a high of 3 percent of GNP in the mid-1960s to a low of 2.2 percent in 1977. Some economists have seen the R&D slowdown as a major culprit in the stagnation of productivity. However, other economists have pointed out that most of the change in R&D spending was in its military component. R&D financed by private firms for their own uses did not change much. And it is private, rather than military, R&D that should be expected to have the greatest impact on promoting real economic growth.

Inflation.   The productivity slowdown of the 1970s occurred at the same time as the speedup of inflation. In part, the productivity decline can be seen as a factor contributing to the inflation; for a given growth rate of aggregate demand, any slowdown in the growth of aggregate supply will cause prices to rise more rapidly. But some economists think that cause and effect worked both ways. Inflation disrupted business planning and labor-management relations. Inflation also distorted the impact of taxes on business and investment income. This not only reduced total investment but also tended to channel investment toward uses that did little to enhance productivity, such as housing and tax shelters, and away from more productive projects.

Regulation.   The 1970s saw an upsurge in government regulation of business. Regulations dealing with health, safety, the environment, and discrimination in hiring and promotion are just a few examples. Firms had to spend vast sums to comply with these regulations. Although the regulations produced some welcome benefits, such as cleaner air and safer highways, they did not contribute to the growth of real output as conventionally measured. As a result, they pulled down measured productivity growth. Denison's data suggest that regulation and related factors cut about .2 percent from real growth in the period 1973 to 1981. The effect, however, is hard to determine exactly.

Why Productivity Remains a Puzzle

Despite all the studies on these possible causes, the full reasons for the productivity slowdown remain hazy. There are so many possible contributing factors that it is difficult to judge their relative importance. Moreover, some of the proposed causes of the productivity slowdown seem to miss the point altogether.

The worldwide nature of the slowdown.   One of the puzzling facts is that the productivity slowdown of the 1970s was not confined to the United States. Rather, it affected most of the major industrialized countries of the world simultaneously. For example, the rate of increase of output per worker-hour in manufacturing, one frequently cited measure of productivity, fell from 3.2 percent per year in the period 1960 to 1973 to 1.4 percent per year in 1973 to 1979 in the United States. However, over the same period the annual rate of growth of manufacturing output per worker-hour fell from 10.3 percent to 5.5 percent in Japan; from 6.4 to 4.6 percent in France; from 6.4 to 2.6 percent in Sweden; and from 4.2 to 1.2 percent in the United Kingdom.[4]

---

[4]U.S. Department of Labor, Bureau of Labor Statistics, "International Comparisons of Manufacturing Productivity and Labor Cost Trends," USDL 89-322, June 30, 1989, Table 1.

The worldwide nature of the productivity slowdown casts doubt on several of the explanations offered above that are peculiar to the United States, such as changes in the labor force, inflation, the drop in R&D spending, and changes in regulation. Oil price shocks remain as the only possible cause of the slowdown that had a worldwide impact. Even here there are some puzzles, however. For example, one might expect those industrialized countries that produce much or all of their own oil, such as the United States, the United Kingdom, and Norway, to have been less affected than such non-oil-producers as Japan, Germany, and Sweden, but instead, all were affected. Moreover, why were some countries hit harder by the first oil price shock and others by the second? Productivity growth dropped by half in Japan after the 1973 shock and actually rose a bit after the shock of 1979. On the other hand, productivity growth in Germany dropped from 5.8 to 4.3 percent after 1973, one of the smaller changes among the major industrialized countries in that period, but then fell further to 2.6 percent after 1979, when productivity growth in other countries was recovering. These patterns are not easily explained.

Measurement problems.   A major reason that productivity is so hard to understand is that the whole field is plagued by extraordinary measurement problems. Productivity numbers attempt to measure output per unit of input. That is simple enough when the output is a tangible good of unchanged quality over time, such as coal or lumber. But much of the economy does not fit this pattern.

For one thing, an increasing portion of the economy is devoted to producing goods where quality changes are more important than quantity changes. Computers are the classic example, but quality changes in such areas as pharmaceuticals, aircraft, and even automobiles are hardly less striking. National income statisticians try to capture some of these quality changes in their measures of output, but their efforts are not fully successful. Economist John Kendrick of Georgetown University, a leading productivity expert, thinks that failure to adjust fully for quality changes leads to a 0.36 percentage point understatement in the annual growth rate of real GNP.[5] This, in turn, reduces estimates of productivity growth.

Moreover, the measurement problems get worse when we turn from goods-producing industries to services, which now account for some two-thirds of GNP. As Exhibit 17.6 shows, services are where most of the productivity slowdown is concentrated. But what do the numbers pertaining to service-industry productivity actually mean?

In much of the service sector, they turn out to mean nothing at all. In the government sector and in much of the private service industry, ranging from finance to entertainment, output measures are simply based on the quantities of inputs used. If a government maintains the same staff, output is assumed to remain constant; if a private consulting firm maintains the same staff, its output is assumed to remain constant, too. But what if the use of word processors and computers allow the consulting firm to serve twice as many clients, while competition with other similar firms holds its profit margin to the same markup over labor costs as before? Surely by any reasonable measure, there has been a productivity increase, but one that does not appear at all in the national statistics. Even in service industries where output is measured more directly, such as transportation, there are problems of adjustment for output quality. For exam-

[5]"Are GNP Estimates Understated?" *The Margin* (January/February 1990): 13.

Exhibit 17.6   Productivity Growth:
Goods versus Services

The productivity slowdown of the 1970s affected both goods-producing and service industries. In the 1980s, measured productivity growth in goods-producing industries recovered but that in service industries did not. Negative productivity growth in service industries thus dragged down overall productivity growth. The reasons for the productivity slowdown in service industries are poorly understood, but a number of observers think they stem in considerable part from measurement problems.

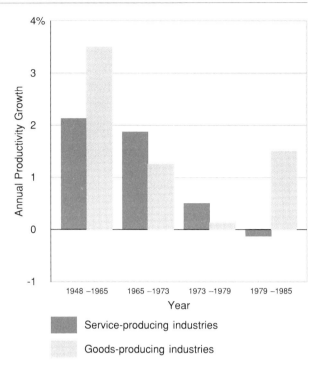

Source: American Productivity Center; Allan Murray, "The Service Sector's Productivity Problem," *The Wall Street Journal*, February 9, 1987, 1.

ple, the value of faster air travel and improved telephone service do not show up in the official accounts.

In short, official data, which, among other oddities, show negative productivity growth throughout the post–World War II period in the finance and insurance industries, are simply not believable. They fly in the face of everyday experience. Kendrick thinks that when understatement of service-industry output and quality changes are combined, the annual rate of productivity growth is understated by three-quarters of a percentage point. And, he argues, the degree of understatement is getting worse all the time.

17.3   Policies for Promoting Economic Growth and Saving

Throughout this course, we have listed growth of real output as one of the fundamental goals of macroeconomic policy. The idea that economic growth is good commands wide agreement among economists. Keynesian economists, monetarists, new classicists, and supply-side economists all see growth as important both to improvements in material welfare and to maintenance of national security. Accordingly, a variety of policies designed to promote growth have been advanced.

One element of growth policy commands widespread agreement: As we saw in the first section of this chapter, policymakers must allow a growth rate of aggregate demand that will at least roughly match that of natural real output. If demand is permitted to grow too rapidly, higher inflation rates will return—and rapid inflation, as we have seen, may have been one of the villains of the productivity slowdown of the 1970s. On the other hand, if demand grows too slowly, the economy may slip into a growth recession or worse.

Many policies other than those designed to match the growth of actual and natural real output have been proposed that are intended to promote the growth of natural real output itself. First we will consider the use of conventional monetary and fiscal policy tools to promote growth. We then consider policies that aim to increase growth by encouraging saving and investment. Some of these proposals command wider agreement than others.

Economic Growth and the Fiscal-Monetary Policy Mix

The basic macroeconomic model developed in the preceding chapters suggests that the mix of fiscal and monetary policies is important to long-run economic growth. This was shown explicitly in Chapter 14, where we saw that there is more than one way to achieve a given level or rate of growth of aggregate demand. A policy objective can be reached through an expansionary fiscal policy combined with a tight monetary policy or via a tight fiscal policy and an expansionary monetary policy, but the two policy mixes have different effects on interest rates. An easy monetary/tight fiscal policy mix, according to the model, leads to lower real and nominal interest rates than a tight monetary/easy fiscal policy mix.

Because the easy monetary/tight fiscal policy mix yields lower interest rates, it also results in more real investment. With lower interest rates, firms move further down and to the right along their planned-investment schedules. While low interest rates are used to encourage investment, tax and spending policies are used to keep the consumption and government spending portions of aggregate demand from growing too quickly.

This principle was understood already by the economists that President Kennedy brought to Washington in the early 1960s to help fulfill his campaign pledge to "get the country moving again." Those economists, influenced by the Keynesian tradition, saw no problem with federal budget deficits as a means of pulling the economy out of a recession. But they firmly believed that the deficit should disappear as the economy approaches its natural level of real output. The existence of a high budget deficit when the economy is operating near capacity, as explained in Chapter 14, would crowd out private investment. In so doing, it would, over time, tend to crowd out economic growth.

But shifting the policy mix toward tighter fiscal and easier monetary policies to promote growth is by no means an idea confined to liberal Democrats. In the 1990s, the same approach is a centerpiece of the Bush administration's policies. In his 1990 *Economic Report*, Bush declared that "the primary economic goal of my Administration is to achieve the highest possible rate of economic growth." A key part of that strategy consists of a planned elimination of the federal budget deficit by 1993 and a move to budgetary surplus after that. As the budget deficit disappears, the administration supports a more expansionary monetary policy to reduce real interest rates and encourage investment.

Growth and Saving

According to Denison's research cited earlier, accumulation of capital accounted for about .6 percentage points of the average growth of natural real output in the 1949 to 1973 period. Although this measure of the contribution of capital to growth is substantial in itself, it may understate the importance of capital investment in the growth process, because advances in knowledge, a larger source of growth, often can take effect only when embodied in new capital equipment.

Because of the role that capital investment plays in the growth process, economists concerned with growth have noted with alarm a sharp decline in net national saving in the United States. One measure of net national saving is net private saving less the government budget deficit. By this measure, net national saving fell from 7 percent of GNP in the 1971 to 1980 period to 3.2 percent in the 1981 to 1985 period and just 2.1 percent in the 1986 to 1989 period. As explained in Chapter 14, the decline in net national saving has been partly balanced by a reduction in domestic investment and partly by an increase in net capital inflows. Such is the logic of the leakages-injections equation. To the extent that there has been a decline in domestic investment, there will be a decrease in the future capital stock and hence lower future growth of productivity and real output. To the extent that net capital inflows have increased, an increased share of future output will have to be paid to foreign owners of capital or foreign creditors. Either way, low saving translates into reduced living standards in the future.

The components of national saving.[6]   There is no single cause of the saving shortfall. The net national saving rate is made up of three components: personal saving by households, business saving in the form of corporate retained earnings, and government saving in the form of budget surpluses. All three of these have declined:

- Personal saving averaged around 7 percent of disposable income for the period 1950 to 1980. By 1987, it had fallen to 3.2 percent of disposable income.

- Business saving fell from 4.5 percent of GNP in the 1960s to 2.75 percent by the late 1970s and to 1 percent by the late 1980s. An alternative measure of business saving constructed by the Federal Reserve Board showed negative saving in 1987 and 1988.

- Government saving, equal to the consolidated budget deficit of federal, state, and local governments, has made a negative contribution to total saving in every post–World War II decade. As the federal deficit rose, negative government saving increased from −1.0 percent of GNP in the 1960s to a peak of −5.3 percent of GNP in 1986.

Sources of the saving shortfall.   The growth of the government budget deficit has been discussed in preceding chapters. The reasons for the decline in personal and business saving remain more obscure. Popular accounts of the decrease in saving often place the blame on an increased appetite for consumption

---

[6]The data and analysis in this section are based on William D. Nordhaus, "What's Wrong with a Decline in the National Saving Rate?" *Challenge* (July/August 1989): 22–26, and Barry P. Bosworth, "There's No Simple Explanation for the Collapse in Saving," *Challenge* (July/August 1989): 27–33.

on the part of American consumers, but this explains nothing: Because saving is defined as the part of income not consumed, to say that consumption increased is just another way of saying that saving decreased. More serious attempts at explanation have ranged from the growth in the share of personal income derived from transfer payments to changes in wealth to changes in laws governing corporate pension fund contributions. Other studies have claimed that part of the change in measured saving may be accounted for by a shift in household budgets in favor of expenditures on consumer durables and education. If these are counted as saving rather than consumption, as many economists argue they should be, the saving figures do not look so bleak. Finally, a number of observers point to the changing age structure of the population. It is natural, they say, for saving to have fallen while the "baby boom" generation passed through its early years in the labor force. As that same generation enters middle age, when income and saving both tend to peak, the national saving rate should rise again.

Policies to Promote Saving

Not everyone is content to wait for the problem to solve itself with the graying of the baby-boomers. Government policymakers and independent economists have recommended a variety of policies to promote saving. These fall into two categories: those designed to raise the rate of return on saving and those relying on the tax system to reallocate national income between saving and nonsaving components.

Policies affecting the rate of return.   One way to encourage saving is to raise the rate of return that households receive on a dollar saved. More precisely, what counts is the *after-tax real rate of return*—the return on saving adjusted for the effects of both taxation and inflation.

Suppose, for example, that a household can earn a 10 percent nominal interest rate on a time deposit in the local savings and loan. If that household is subject to a marginal tax rate of 50 percent for income, including interest income, the after-tax nominal return on saving falls to a nominal 5 percent. If, on top of this, the country is experiencing 7 percent inflation, that rate is subtracted from the after-tax nominal rate of return to get an after-tax real rate of return of -2 percent. Suppose instead that the time deposit yields only a 9 percent nominal rate, but that the marginal tax rate is cut to 33 percent and the rate of inflation falls to 4 percent per year. The after-tax nominal rate is then 6 percent and the after-tax real rate a positive 2 percent.

It follows, then, that the after-tax real rate of return on saving can be raised either by policies that raise the nominal interest rate relative to the rate of inflation or by reductions in the marginal tax rate applied to nominal interest income from saving. As we have seen, changes in the fiscal-monetary policy mix may have some effect on nominal interest rates and the rate of inflation, although these variables are not under the government's direct control. However, marginal tax rates can be directly manipulated. One approach is to cut income tax rates across the board. Another is make income earned on certain types of savings partly or wholly tax exempt. Examples of such policies are Individual Retirement Accounts, tax-sheltered retirement saving plans for the self-employed (Keough accounts), and reduced tax rates on capital gains earned on certain types of investment.

Unfortunately, evidence from the 1980s does not support great optimism regarding the effects of such measures. During the early 1980s, the rate of inflation fell, although nominal interest rates also declined. At the same time, marginal tax rates were reduced across the board and eligibility for tax-exempt saving plans was widened. All told, the real after-tax rate of return on saving rose from −2.5 percent in 1979 to 3 percent in 1988. Yet, as we have seen, the personal saving rate declined. Evidently, any positive effect of a higher after-tax real rate of return on saving was more than offset by other considerations.

Other prosaving tax policies.   Cutting marginal tax rates on income from savings is one way to increase net national saving. However, some economists propose using tax increases to accomplish the same goal. They argue that the federal budget deficit is the largest single cause of the saving shortfall. Eliminating the deficit by raising taxes would thus raise the overall national saving rate.

If the tax increase took the form of increases in marginal income tax rates, the gain from reducing the budget deficit would be partly offset by a reduction in the after-tax real rate of return on savings. Therefore, many economists favor increased reliance on taxation of consumption. Some favor raising federal excise taxes on such items as tobacco, alcohol, and gasoline. Others favor some form of national sales tax.

Economists of the new classical school have expressed skepticism about the possibility of increasing the national saving rate by increasing taxes. As discussed in Chapter 10, they argue that tax changes are offset in whole or in part by opposite changes in saving. Empirical evidence suggests that at least a partial offset does take place. However, most economists doubt that tax increases are wholly offset by reductions in saving in the long run.

How Much Saving Is Enough?

In the debate over the saving shortfall and policies to deal with it, one question is almost never asked: How much saving is enough? Participants in the debate are almost universally agreed that more saving is better. What is more, they do not always limit themselves to positive economic arguments regarding the effects of saving on capital accumulation and growth. Many commentators are given to sweeping normative declarations to the effect that low savings "cheat the future" and to condemnations of an American culture that allegedly "bombards us with messages to buy things—not save." In short, a low saving rate is perceived as a sign of moral weakness.

But there are some counter arguments to be made. First, the primary reason that saving is valued is because it promotes more rapid economic growth. Yet there is a long tradition in economics that questions the unlimited desirability of economic growth itself. (Recall, for example, the views of John Stuart Mill as reported in **Who Said It? Who Did It? 4.1,** page 115.) This antigrowth tradition is manifested today in certain parts of the environmental movement, who see excessive growth of material output, combined with inadequate attention to nonmaterial sources of human welfare, as the root of many current problems.

Second, the welfare of future generations is constantly evoked in the debate over saving. But as long as growth of per capita real income does not come to a stop altogether (and it has not done so), future generations will be richer than our own. Saving is thus a transfer from the relatively poor present to the relatively rich future. Why is such a transfer so desirable, considering that most people favor transfers from the rich to the poor rather than from the poor to the rich within our own generation? This question is never asked and never answered by the proponents of a higher saving rate.

Finally, why is it that the private component of national saving should be a matter of public policy in the first place? After all, personal and business saving are not the result of decisions reached in some big town meeting—they are the outcome of millions of individual decisions by households and business managers. In the case of households, we are willing to leave people free to choose whether to eat better (consumption) or live in a better house (saving), and free to choose how much of their lifetime income to enjoy themselves and how much to leave to their children. In the case of firms, we are content to leave stockholders, acting through their agents in corporate management, free to choose between reinvestment of earnings and distribution of dividends. If we are content to leave all these micro-level choices up to individuals, why should we not be content with whatever national saving rate results from adding together their outcomes?

The debate over the saving shortfall would be more enlightening if the question of how much saving is enough were at least considered.

Summary

1. **How can the economy grow while maintaining price stability?** Over time, natural real output grows as a result of increases in total hours worked and increases in average output per worker-hour, that is, labor productivity. As growth of natural real output shifts the long-run aggregate supply curve to the right, the short-run aggregate supply curve will shift with it, provided there is no change in the expected level of productivity-adjusted input prices. If aggregate demand is allowed to grow at the same rate as natural real output, the aggregate demand curve will shift along with the others. Under these conditions output will grow smoothly, the level of final goods prices will be stable, and unemployment will remain at its natural rate.

2. **How can insufficient growth of aggregate demand cause a growth recession?** If aggregate demand does not keep up with the growth of natural real output, firms will be unable to sell all the output they are able to produce at an unchanged price level. Unplanned inventory buildup will put downward pressure on prices and cause the actual level of real output to grow more slowly than the natural level. The economy will move downward and to the left along the short-run aggregate supply curve at the same time that the curve is shifting to the right. This is called a *growth recession.* During such a recession, real output grows but the unemployment rate rises.

3. **How can expansion of aggregate demand beyond the growth rate of natural real output cause inflation?** If aggregate demand grows faster than natural real output, demand-pull inflation will result. In the short run, pushing the growth of aggregate demand to a rate faster than the growth of natural real output will speed the growth of real output and cut unemployment at the cost of only moderate inflation. After the initial gain, however, the trade-off between inflation and unemployment will worsen. The inflation rate will have to speed up just to keep the unemployment rate from rising.

4. **What may have caused the slowdown in productivity growth in the U.S. economy beginning in the 1970s?** During the 1970s, the rate of productivity growth fell from about 2.2 percent per year to about .7 percent. Explanations for this decline include changes in the age and gender composition of the labor force, supply shocks caused by oil price increases, inflation, a slowdown in research and development spending, and an increase in regulation. No one of these factors seems to fully explain the slowdown.

5. **What policies are available to promote economic growth?** In the 1960s, Keynesian economists called for expansionary fiscal policy to aid recovery from recession, but advocated a mix of macroeconomic policies that will include a balanced budget as the economy approaches the natural level of real output and a monetary policy that will permit relatively low interest rates. A similar policy mix is now favored by the Bush administration, which sees promoting economic growth as its highest policy priority. Economic growth can be promoted by other policies encouraging saving and investment, as well.

6. **Why has the national saving rate declined in the United States and what policies could be used to**

raise it? The decrease in the national saving rate in the United States can be traced to all three of its components—personal, business, and government savings. One approach to promoting increased saving is to increase the after-tax real rate of return on income from savings. Another approach is to use taxes, especially taxes on consumption, to channel income away from consumption toward saving and, at the same time, to reduce the government budget deficit.

Term for Review

- growth recession

Questions for Review

1. If natural real output is growing, what must happen to aggregate demand for prices to remain stable?

2. Under what conditions can the unemployment rate rise and the price level fall while real output is growing?

3. What are the short-run effects on inflation and unemployment if aggregate demand grows faster than natural real output? What are the long-run effects?

4. What factors contributed to the slowdown of productivity growth in the United States in the 1970s?

5. How can a change in the fiscal-monetary policy mix be used to promote economic growth?

6. If the nominal rate of return on saving is 8 percent, the marginal tax rate is 15 percent, and the rate of inflation is 5 percent, what is the after-tax real rate of return?

Problems and Topics for Discussion

1. **Examining the lead-off case.** Use aggregate supply and demand curves to illustrate what happens to the economy as a result of a general improvement in the education of the labor force. In what ways does such an improvement affect real output, the price level, and economic growth? What policies regarding aggregate demand would be appropriate in response to a general improvement in the educational level of the labor force?

2. **Stagflation.** Footnote 2 (page 449) describes an episode of what could be called "stagflation." Draw a set of aggregate supply and demand curves to illustrate this situation.

3. **Growth with inflation.** Exhibit 17.3 illustrates growth with inflation. What would happen to the economy if, starting from the situation represented by point E_2, policymakers were to stop the growth of aggregate demand while natural real output continued to grow? Use aggregate supply and demand curves to illustrate your answer.

4. **Personal saving.** Most people have negative saving when they are young (that is, they consume more than their income), have positive saving during their prime working years, and then have negative saving again in retirement. Do you expect your own saving to follow this pattern? Why or why not?

Case for Discussion
The Great American Saving Shortfall

President Bush thinks we need to save more. His first Economic Report to Congress emphasized economic growth as the primary goal of his administration and identified saving as a key to achieving that goal. The issue cuts across the lines of political parties. Barry Bosworth, a top economic adviser to the Democratic Carter administration, argues that "a country that doesn't save can't compete."[7]

There is less agreement regarding what to do about the saving rate. The Bush administration advocates traditional economic incentives, including a cut in capital gains taxes, tax-favored family savings plans, and reforms to Social Security. But some critics see the savings shortfall differently. Frank Levy of the University of Maryland and Richard C. Michel of the Urban Institute maintain that the problem is less about tax incentives than about culture—a culture, they

---

[7]Barry P. Bosworth, "A Country that Doesn't Save Can't Compete," *Fortune*, March 26, 1990, p. 116.

say, that "bombards us with messages to buy things—not save—every day." In this context, they see the key to increased saving as "a change in national outlook."[8]

Levy and Michel suggest that we think of saving as cholesterol. "Both are the byproduct of immediate gratification, neither involves short-run cost, both accrue slowly with real dangers for the future." If the president is serious about the saving shortfall, they say, he should talk as plainly about it as doctors talk about cholesterol. Why not publish national guidelines on what people ought to save? A simple schedule that relates annual savings to family income and age? "In a word, with guidelines on everything from salt intake to safe sex, a problem without guidelines is not seen as a problem," Levy and Michel conclude.

---

[8]Frank Levy and Richard C. Michel, "Why America Won't Save," *The Washington Post*, February 4, 1990, p. C1.

Questions

1. How would you define "undersaving"? Are you yourself undersaving? Is the country as a whole? How would you go about determining the ideal rate of national saving? Or is more saving always better, without limit?

2. The article suggests that saving, like eating a healthy diet, involves a trade-off between present and future gratification. Use a production possibility frontier to illustrate this trade-off. Label the horizontal axis "saving" and the vertical axis "consumption." First draw a frontier that is based on a fixed current income. Mark a point A on the frontier that represents a relatively low saving rate and a point B that represents a relatively high rate. Next draw two frontiers that represent future income levels—one based on saving rate A and the other on saving rate B. Why will the two future frontiers not be the same? Is it possible to draw the frontiers in such a way that the higher current saving rate will permit both higher saving *and* higher consumption in the future?

3. Do you think Levy's and Michel's proposal for national saving guidelines would have a significant impact on the national saving rate? How would you go about determining the proper guidelines? Would you favor voluntary guidelines, compulsory guidelines, or none at all? Discuss.

Suggestions for Further Reading

Bosworth, Barry P. "There's No Simple Explanation for the Collapse in Saving." *Challenge* (July/August, 1989): 27–33.

Analyzes the sources of the savings shortfall and assesses policies designed to raise the national saving rate.

Fink, Richard H., ed. *Supply Side Economics: A Critical Appraisal.* Frederick, Md.: University Publications of America, 1983.

Supply-side economists place a high priority on growth. This volume contains papers on all aspects of supply-side economics by authors with a wide range of views.

Fisher, Stanley, et al. "Symposium on the Slowdown in Productivity Growth." *Journal of Economic Perspectives* (Fall 1988): 3–98.

Argues for policies to increase the national savings rate to boost long-term growth.

Nordhaus, William D. "What's Wrong with a Decline in the National Savings Rate?" *Challenge* (July/August, 1989): 22–26.

Contributions by five leading experts look at the productivity slowdown from a variety of viewpoints.

Reich, Robert B. *The Next American Frontier.* New York: Times Books, 1983.

A liberal lawyer at Harvard's Kennedy School of Government makes a case for promoting economic growth and suggests ways of doing so.

CHAPTER

18

Strategies for Economic Stabilization

**Before reading this chapter,
make sure you know the meaning of:**

Business cycle (Chapter 4)

Budget process (Chapter 10)

Cyclical and structural deficits (Chapter 10)

Velocity and money demand (Chapter 13)

After reading this chapter, you will understand:

Why Keynesian economists favor active use of fiscal and monetary policy to stabilize the economy.

What are the implications of lags and forecasting errors for the conduct of discretionary policy.

Why politics may interfere with the conduct of stabilization policy.

What kinds of rules have been proposed for the conduct of monetary policy.

What kinds of rules have been proposed for the conduct of fiscal policy.

It Is Now within Our Capabilities . . .

Two decades of economic analysis and policy experience have shaped the development of a revised economic policy. By some, current policy has been labeled the "new economics." . . .

An industrial economy is vulnerable to cumulative upward and downward movements in activity, so evident in our long-term record. . . . In the future as in the past, policies to avert recession cannot wait until imbalances develop and the signs of a downturn are clear. The fact that economic activity is rising cannot be an assurance of continued growth if the expansion is too slow to match the growth of productive capacity. Nor can a strong level of investment be relied on to sustain expansion if it threatens an excessive growth of productive capacity. Recognizing these tasks, government must apply its fiscal and monetary policies continuously to sustain and support a balanced expansion, sometimes by moderating the strength of an excessive investment boom, sometimes by adding to the strength of lagging final demand. The best defense against recession is a policy to sustain continued expansion. . . .

The ability of economists to diagnose and forecast on the basis of current facts and to evaluate the impact of alternative policy measures is a key determinant of what policy can do to maintain stable balanced growth. Our economic knowledge has made great advances in the past generation, but many important questions remain, answers to which should be and can be improved through further research. . . .

But while much remains to be learned about our economy, it would be a disservice to understate the power of economic analysis, and to underrate the

---

Photo source: UPI/Bettmann Newsphotos.

Source: President's Council of Economic Advisers, *Economic Report of the President* (Washington, D.C.: Government Printing Office, 1966), 180–186.

substantial contribution of the profession to the successful course of our economy in the postwar period. . . .

While important problems remain, we are nonetheless at an historic point of accomplishment and promise. Twenty years of experience have demonstrated our ability to avoid ruinous inflations and severe depressions. It is now within our capabilities to set more ambitious goals. We strive to avoid recurrent recessions, to keep unemployment far below rates of the past decade, to maintain price stability at full employment, to move toward the Great Society, and, indeed, to make full prosperity the normal state of the American economy. It is a tribute to our success . . . that we now have not only the economic understanding but also the will and determination to use economic policy as an effective tool for progress.

These words are from the 1966 report of the President's Council of Economic Advisers. The report was signed by three of the most distinguished professionals ever to sit on that body: Gardner Ackley, its chairman, Otto Eckstein, and Arthur Okun. The 1960s marked the high-water mark of post–World War II Keynesianism—what was then called the "new economics." In this chapter, we examine the approach to economic policy outlined in these passages in the light of the U.S. economic experience of the 1970s and 1980s. We also discuss the different approach to policy recommended by the monetarists and new classical economists and the influence economists of all these schools have had on the conduct of policy today.

18.1   The Debate over Policy Activism

Chapter 4 called attention to the fact that the economy does not grow steadily year after year but tends to go through a business cycle. Growth is halted from time to time by recessions. When the economy recovers from a recession, it often overshoots its natural level of output. The resulting boom periods are followed by new recessions. This pattern has been observed for more than a century.

Nobody really likes the business cycle. It is disruptive and wasteful in both dollar and human terms. Almost all economists agree that the right policy could moderate the swings in the business cycle. But behind this general agreement lies one of the major debates in economics today: Just what kind of policy is right for dealing with the business cycle?

Keynesians, Monetarists, and New Classicists

On the one hand, there are the heirs to the Keynesian tradition. These are *policy activists* who see the business cycle as a flaw in the capitalist system that the government must try to correct. They perceive the source of the problem as unpredicted ups and downs in consumer confidence, investment plans, the foreign trade balance, and the demand for money and credit. These cause shifts in aggregate demand that are amplified by the multiplier effect.

To moderate the business cycle, government should actively use monetary and fiscal policy to offset disturbances arising in the private sector. Whether the business cycle is on an upward or downward swing, government should lean against the wind to shorten recessions and restrain booms.

On the other hand, there are the monetarists, joined today by many economists of the new classical school and others who do not identify closely with any one school of thought. They tend to see mistakes in government policy behind all but the mildest swings of the business cycle. To be sure, they say, there are unpredicted ups and downs in the spending plans of households and firms. But the private economy has built-in stabilizers that prevent serious depressions, prolonged unemployment, and persistent inflation. The really bad episodes—the Great Depression, the double-digit inflation of the 1970s—can be traced to policy errors. In this view, things got out of hand in these cases because attempts to fine-tune the economy only made things worse.

Over the years, the issue of policy activism versus policy rules has come to dominate the long-standing debate among Keynesians and monetarists, now joined by new classicists. The issues of the power of fiscal and monetary policy and the nature of the transmission mechanism discussed in Chapter 14 have taken a back seat; in fact, the gap between Keynesians and monetarists on these issues has narrowed greatly. However, Keynesians tend to argue that fiscal and monetary policies should both be used actively, whereas monetarists and new classicists claim that both should be guided by stable, long-term *policy rules*.

The Case for Policy Activism

The case for policy activism rests on three assumptions that are clearly set forth in the passages quoted at the beginning of the chapter. Although they might be expressed somewhat more cautiously today than they were in 1966, these assumptions are still shared by many economists.

First, modern Keynesians share the view that the private economy is inherently unstable: "An industrial economy is vulnerable to cumulative upward and downward movements in activity, so evident in our long-term record." Because of rigidities and unresponsiveness, the economy's powers of self-stabilization are weak. Put in terms of our model, modern Keynesians would say that although there is always a theoretical long-term equilibrium where aggregate supply and demand curves cross at the natural level of output, the economy cannot be counted on to move smoothly or rapidly to that point following a disturbance.

Second, proponents of policy activism are confident of economists' ability to forecast the future course of the economy and the effects of policy within at least a workable margin of error: "The ability of economists to diagnose and forecast on the basis of current facts and to evaluate the impact of alternative policy measures is a key determinant of what policy can do. . . . It would be a disservice to understate the power of economic analysis." Further, policy activists are certain that answers to remaining questions can be found through ongoing research.

Third, they are confident that those who wield political authority in the White House and on Capitol Hill will heed the technical advice given to them by economists: "It is a tribute to our success . . . that we now have not only the economic understanding but also the will and determination to use economic policy as an effective tool for progress."

Given these assumptions, the policymaker's job involves continuous application of policy to keep the economy on a course of balanced expansion. As an analogy, think of yourself as the captain of an ocean liner. You are steering your ship through waters in which treacherous winds and currents threaten to push it off course at every moment. Your tools for controlling the ship are the engine telegraph, which regulates the ship's engine speed, and the wheel, which controls the ship's rudder.

You can predict the effects of any movement of the controls. For example, calling for full speed ahead will cause the ship to reach its maximum speed of 30 knots; turning the wheel to the right will swing the rudder and cause the ship to turn; and so on. Your ship is not a sports car—it takes a long (but predictable) time to stop or turn it. Because of the time it takes the controls to act, you must look and plan ahead. Fortunately, you have satellite reports that warn you of changes in wind speed and radar to tell you the course and location of other ships in your area. You are ultimately responsible for the ship, but you would not think of disputing the technical judgments of your navigator, engineer, and harbor pilot.

So it is in the policy activists' world if you are the president or the chair of the Federal Reserve Board. You have at your command levers and wheels labeled "taxes," "government spending," and "money supply." You have computerized models of the economy that, combined with the judgments of professional forecasters, predict what will happen to real output, employment, the price level, and interest rates when you pull any of these levers or turn the wheels. Your staff economists give you frequent updates warning you of trends in investment, money demand, and other factors that you may have to offset with policy actions. You agree with other policymakers and congressional leaders that prices should be kept stable, unemployment at its natural rate, and real output growing in step with increases in its natural level. Also, you are willing to draw on the technical judgments of your economic advisers.

To be sure, there is more uncertainty in running the economy than in steering an ocean liner. Even the most ardent policy activists admit that the appropriate policy stance is not always clear and that mistakes will be made. These will cause the economy to drift off course now and then; the business cycle will be moderated but not eliminated. Even so, policy activists believe that the best way to stay on course is to adjust the controls quickly at the first sign of impending trouble.

Are Policymakers' Tools Adequate?

Monetarists and new classicists find fault with all of the activists' assumptions. They have more faith in the economy's powers of self-stabilization and see policy errors as the most serious source of instability. They do not think the tools and forecasts available to policymakers are good enough to do the job, even with the best of intentions. They also doubt the ability of the U.S. political system to focus on consistent long-run economic goals. Let us look at the case against policy activism, beginning with the second of these issues: whether policymakers have adequate tools for the job.

The activists assume that the government has a set of tools that can directly affect aggregate demand and indirectly influence real output, employment, and the price level. Their critics wonder how adequate these tools really are. Monetarists agree that monetary and fiscal policy affect aggregate demand, but they argue that changes in aggregate demand have only short-term effects on real output and employment. In the long run, they say, the economy always returns to the natural level of real output and the natural unemployment rate. On this point the new classicists are even more skeptical than the monetarists: They doubt the ability of anticipated changes in monetary and fiscal policy to affect real output and employment even in the short run.

Applying Economic Ideas 18.1
The Accuracy of Economic Forecasts

Economic forecasts—predictions of GNP, inflation, unemployment, and interest rates for the months or years ahead—are regular items of business news, and for good reason. Knowledge of future demand conditions, prices, and credit market conditions is of great value to decision makers in business and government. The thirst for knowledge about the future is a multi-million-dollar business for such forecasting firms as Data Resources Incorporated. Government agencies, including the Federal Reserve System, the Office of Management and Budget, and the Congressional Budget Office, also have large budgets for forecasting.

But despite all the money spent, the track record of economic forecasting leaves much to be desired. A study by two economists at the Federal Reserve Bank of Boston pinpoints some forecasts that were especially bad:

Source: Stephen K. McNees and John Ries, "The Track Record of Macroeconomic Forecasts," *New England Economic Review* (November/December 1983): 5–18.

- In 1973 to 1975, forecasters missed the surge in inflation and unemployment rates. They underestimated inflation by three to four percentage points and unemployment by more than two percentage points. At the same time, they underestimated the severity of the recession.
- In 1978 to 1979, they again failed to forecast a surge in inflation.
- In 1981, they underestimated the speed of the recovery from the short recession of the previous year. Just as they adjusted their forecasts to show strong growth, the economy fell back into recession. This left the GNP forecasts of five of the leading forecasters as much as four percentage points too high—the worst errors of any recent period.

In the forecasters' defense, the Federal Reserve Bank study points out that the forecasters did fairly well in the tranquil periods of 1970 to 1972 and 1975 to 1978. But that is not always good enough for decision makers in business and government. What they want is the ability to foresee turning points and unusual changes in the behavior of the economy. This the forecasters seem unable to deliver.

Then there is the related problem of predictability. Unless the effects of monetary and fiscal policies can be predicted, policy activists will not know how hard to pull their levers and twist their dials. They depend partly on large-scale computer models to predict the effects of any given policy. These models, although very elaborate, have the same basic structure as those used in this course. They will make accurate predictions only if the correct values are used for the marginal propensity to consume, the expenditure multipliers, the crowding-out effect, the money multiplier, and so on. However, different computer models give widely varying values for these constants. How can policy activists fine-tune the economy, ask the critics, if they cannot be sure about how much of a policy change is needed to produce a desired effect?

Policy activists consult the same computer models to forecast where the economy is headed in order to decide what corrections are needed. As *Applying Economic Ideas 18.1* shows, the record of forecasting in the past couple of decades has been mixed at best. During tranquil periods, the forecasting models have not done badly. However, they missed crucial turning points in 1973 to 1975, 1979 to 1980, and 1981 to 1982. The average of the various forecasts is often significantly far from the mark, and the forecasts typically encompass a wide range of policy outcomes as well.

The Problem of Lags

In addition to challenging the assumptions on which the case for fine-tuning is based, the critics make much of the problem of delays, or *lags,* in the policymaking process. Two kinds of lags deserve attention. The delay between the time

Inside lag
The delay between the time
a policy change is needed
and the time a decision is
made.

Outside lag
The delay between the time
a policy decision is made
and the time the policy
change has its main effect on
the economy.

when a policy change is needed and the time when a decision is made is called the **inside lag.** The delay between the time when a decision is made and the time when it has its main effect on the economy is known as the **outside lag.**

Lags in monetary policy.   For monetary policy, the inside lag is fairly short. Financial information is available most rapidly and monetary data within one to a few weeks. Data on inflation and unemployment are available to the Federal Reserve within a month. Data on changes in real output are available in estimated form within three months. Once the Fed has data on changes in the economy, it can quickly decide to make whatever policy changes are needed. The Federal Open Market Committee—the chief monetary policymaking body of the Federal Reserve System—meets at least eight times a year. If discretionary action is needed between meetings, the committee has authorized the open market desk in New York to make small adjustments in the stance of operating policy in consultation with the chair. If newly arriving data indicate a need for more substantial policy changes between FOMC meetings, the committee can hold a telephone conference.

The outside lag for monetary policy is a good deal longer than the inside lag, and it also varies. Studies based on both monetarist and Keynesian approaches indicate that slowing the rate of money stock growth in the post–World War II period has slowed the rate of growth of real output some 3 to 12 months later and has lowered the inflation rate only with an even longer lag. An increase in the rate of money stock growth appears to behave with a similar lag.

Lags in fiscal policy.   Overall lags for fiscal policy seem longer but harder to measure. The long inside lag for fiscal policy is a result of the budget process, in which the administration must first decide on the need for a policy action and then submit a proposal to Congress (see Chapter 10). Consider some examples:

· President Kennedy's advisers began urging him to ask for a tax cut soon after he took office early in 1961, but a proposal was not submitted to Congress until 1962. Congress did not pass the tax cut until 1964, some three years after the need for it had become clear. In the late 1960s, during the Vietnam War, President Johnson resisted his economists' advice to raise taxes for almost two years. In that case, Congress acted quickly on the call for a tax surcharge once it was submitted.

· During the 1974 to 1975 recession, President Ford called for tax cuts, including a one-time tax rebate. Congress again acted swiftly. Even so, however, the rebate was not paid out until the month in which unemployment hit its peak. The rebate thus came in time to help speed the recovery but not in time to shorten the recession.

· Congress also acted fairly promptly (within nine months) on President Reagan's call for tax cuts in 1981. However, the cuts were phased in over three years. Only the first phase of the tax cuts came while the economy was still in recession; the rest went into effect after the recovery was already under way.

On the basis of these examples, the inside lag for fiscal policy appears to range from about six months to more than three years. Also, there is a fairly long outside lag from a change in fiscal policy to a change in aggregate demand. This is the length of time it takes the expenditure multiplier to work itself out once a change has been made in taxes or government spending. Some effect on aggregate demand is felt very quickly, but various computer models differ widely in their estimates of how long it takes for the bulk of the effect to be felt. Some models show the bulk of the effect coming only six months after policy action has been taken. Others indicate that most of the effect is not felt for two years. All the models agree that a fiscal policy action continues to affect the aggregate demand to some degree as long as three years later.

The total lag for fiscal policy is the sum of the inside and outside lags. At best, the total lag is no less than a year. This allows the president only six months to make a proposal and Congress to act on it and six more months for the multiplier effect to be carried out. However, a total lag of several years is quite possible for real GNP, with the ultimate effect on the price level taking even longer to work itself out.

Interaction of lags and forecasting errors.   Lags mean that policymakers cannot wait until a problem develops before taking action. If they do, the measures they take to boost the economy during a recession will not take effect until the recovery is already under way. The result may be the turning of a normal recovery into an inflationary boom. Actions intended to restrain the inflation might take effect only after the economy is already plunging into the next recession.

To avoid this problem, policymakers must act on the basis of forecasts. If they know that a recession will begin in a year or two, they can take action now. If they know when inflation will begin to develop, they can adjust money growth or taxes in time to prevent it. But what if the forecasts are faulty, as they often are to at least some degree? A policy of stimulus or restraint based on a faulty forecast is as likely to make things worse as it is to make them better.

Political Problems of Policy Activism

Many activists would agree that lags and forecasting errors are good reasons to proceed with caution. However, they claim that following their advice, even if not perfect, is better than doing nothing and letting the business cycle run its course. At this point, their critics bring up the third assumption on which the case for policy activism is based. The problem, they say, is that even when economists are able to offer valid advice, policymakers may not follow it. They see two main reasons for this.

First, policymakers must respond to the political signals reaching them through the apparatus of democratic politics and not just to the technical advice of their staffs. When things go wrong with the economy, there is great political pressure to "do something." For example, as the economy slides into a recession, there is pressure to create jobs. However, the political pressure reaches a peak not at the time when the recession is forecast or when it first begins; instead, it peaks around the time the recession reaches its trough, which is after the time for action has passed. A spending program or tax cut that is undertaken at the trough of a recession, when unemployment is at its highest, will not create jobs when they are needed most. Instead, it will be adding to inflationary pressures six months to two years later, after a recovery is already under way.

Second, there is the tendency of politics to stress the short run. This is a problem because the short-run effects of economic policies often differ from their long-run effects. Take, for example, the effects of an expansionary fiscal or monetary policy. If an expansionary policy is applied when real output is at its natural rate, the short-run effects will be an increase in real output and a reduction in unemployment as the economy moves upward along its aggregate supply curve. Only moderate inflation will result at first. However, the long-run effects of a sustained expansionary policy are less positive. To keep real output high and unemployment low, policymakers must be willing to accept ongoing inflation, probably at an ever increasing rate. Reversing the expansionary policy to get rid of the inflation is likely to cause an inflationary recession.

In the U.S. political system, the next congressional or presidential election is never more than two years away—not a long time when compared with the lags in macroeconomic policy. As a result, critics of policy activism say, fiscal policymakers who will soon be running for reelection are under pressure to produce short-term results. They will want it to look as though they are doing something to help the economy as the election approaches. If the policy has negative long-term effects . . . well, those will not be felt until after the election.

The critics do not see the problem as one of bad intentions on the part of politicians. Instead, they perceive it as the result of intelligent, well-intentioned people's reaction to the pressures of the system in which they operate. In their view, the case for fiscal fine-tuning, already weakened by lags and forecasting errors, should be thrown out of court because of these political problems.

The Fed and the Time-Inconsistency Problem

What about Federal Reserve officials? New-classicist critics believe that monetary policymakers, despite their 14-year terms, also face a problem of inconsistency between their long-term and short-term goals.

To understand this so-called time-inconsistency problem, suppose that the Fed announces a long-term intention to keep the money stock from expanding more quickly than needed in order to keep aggregate demand growing at the same rate as natural real output. If carried out, this policy will eliminate inflation in the long run. If firms and workers believe the Fed's announcement, they will base their plans on the expectation of zero inflation, and the economy will avoid cost-push pressures having their origins in inflationary expectations. The economy will tend toward the natural level of real output with price stability.

Once this happy state of affairs is established, however, the Fed will face a temptation: Why not speed up money growth for a time, causing the aggregate demand curve to shift rightward more rapidly than natural real output? If this is done at a time when people still expect long-term price stability, there will be only a little inflation and a relatively big gain in real output. Then, before expectations have fully adjusted to the faster money growth, the Fed could issue another reassuring policy announcement claiming that its goal is still consistent with long-term price stability.

The trouble with this policy, say the critics, is that the temptation to depart from announced long-term goals to achieve desirable short-term results will cause both the expected and actual inflation rates to drift upward over time. New classicists think that under the assumption of rational expectations, the public would see through the policymakers' temptation from the beginning and, as a result, expect higher inflation all along. In this case, the surprise element in more expansionary policy would be lost. Indeed, monetary policy would have to become more expansionary, meeting the public's expectation of more rapid inflation, simply to avoid a drop in real output as the short-run aggregate supply curve shifted upward. The long-term result—persistent inflation with unem-

Applying Economic Ideas   18.2
The Professor's Dilemma

A professor at a certain university always tells his class at the start of the semester that grades will be based on a final exam. The purpose of the exam is to give students an incentive to study hard and learn all they can about economics. One semester, as exam time approaches, the professor thinks to himself, "My students have studied hard and learned everything they should. My job is done. Why go to the trouble of giving the exam?" He gives everyone an A and cancels the exam.

The next semester, he again announces that he will grade on the basis of the exam and again cancels it at the last minute. But by the end of the third semester, he notices something amiss. Even though he announced a final exam at the start of the semester, no one has studied at all. They didn't believe him. Now he thinks to himself, "Too bad. But what is the point of giving the exam now? They don't know a thing. It would just be a lot of work for me to grade the things." Again he cancels the exam.

Source: Based on a suggestion by Gary Gorton.

One day during vacation, there is a knock on our professor-hero's office door. There stands the head of his department. "What are you going to do about this?" she demands. "Your students aren't learning a thing anymore!"

"I know it's a problem," he replies, "but I don't know what to do. If I announce the exam and everyone believes me, then at the end of the semester the optimal strategy is not to give the exam. But if I announce the exam and no one believes me, then at the end of the semester it is still the optimal strategy to cancel the exam. You can't really blame me for what has happened. After all, every semester I'm doing what is best under the circumstances I'm faced with."

The department head walks out without saying a word. The next morning, there is a big notice on the department bulletin board for both faculty and students to see: BY ORDER OF THE DEPARTMENT HEAD, ALL PROFESSORS MUST GIVE FINAL EXAMS OR THEY WILL BE FIRED. Our friend reads this notice and breathes a sigh of relief. Now he can start giving exams again and be certain that his students will study for them.

ployment no lower than the natural rate—would not be optimal even though each short-term departure from the long-term goals was made with the best intentions given the circumstances. *Applying Economic Ideas 18.2* illustrates the time-inconsistency problem in another sphere of decision making that has been invoked as an analogy with the Fed's policy dilemma.

Implications for Stability

The combination of lags, forecasting errors, and political problems leads critics of activism finally to challenge the first of the activists' assumptions—that the economy is inherently unstable. They look at the same historical record of instability and see not an inherent vulnerability to cyclical disturbances but a record of policy errors that have transformed mild cyclical disturbances into serious ones. Exhibit "A" is the Great Depression. As we have seen, monetarists especially see policy errors—above all, the Fed's failure to resist the collapse of the money stock—as a key cause of the Depression. Exhibit "B" is the Great Inflation of the 1970s. In the critics' interpretation of events, the attempts of the "new economists" to "set more ambitious goals" and "keep unemployment far below" rates of the 1950s and 1960s did not usher in an era of stable growth; instead, the economy was subjected to erratic swings of policy. This not only raised the inflation rate, but also made the damage from various supply shocks, especially the oil price increases, worse than it needed to be.

Although they admit that mistakes have been made, believers in discretionary policy point to the relatively placid 1950s and 1960s as evidence of reasonably successful stabilization policy. They also cite the long economic expansion following recovery from the 1981 to 1982 recession—a period during which the rate of inflation was stabilized in the neighborhood of 4 percent per year—as an example of successful discretionary policy. Even in the case of the turbulent 1970s, at least some of them would say that actions that turned out to be inflationary accurately reflected public sentiment that it was better to take the pain of oil price shocks in the form of higher prices than in the form of still higher unemployment rates.

Who is right? There is reason to believe that the question cannot be answered simply by looking back at the record. The problem is that the question of whether activist policies worked better or worse than the alternatives requires assessing how the alternative nondiscretionary policies would have done. And it is inherently difficult to assess how the alternative policies would have worked on the basis of historical data that were generated entirely under an activist regime.

18.2   The Search for Policy Rules

The difficulty of proving their case against activism has not kept the critics from developing alternatives of their own. These alternatives propose that activist policy be replaced by some form of long-term policy rule. In view of lags and forecasting errors, they say, it is better to follow rules that are correct on the average than to follow an activist policy that is just as likely to do harm as good. They claim that as an added benefit, strict policy rules will prevent decision makers from bowing to short-run political temptations regardless of the long-term effects.

However, the argument that policy rules are safer than activists' fine-tuning is only part of the case. To complete it, critics of policy activism need to spell out in detail the rules they wish policymakers to follow and to give an indication of their effects. The fact that the rules have never been tried means that proof is hard to come by; thus, arguments in their support must be based on theory and inferential evidence. Under these circumstances, it is not surprising that there is not full agreement even among those who favor policy rules in principle. In the following sections, we will look first at some proposed rules for monetary policy and then briefly at some proposed fiscal policy rules.

Rules for Monetary Policy

A monetary growth rule.   The original monetarist proposal for a policy rule was to have the Fed peg the growth of the money stock to a preannounced constant rate. If the money stock grew faster than that rate, the Fed would slow it down with open market sales of securities; if it grew too slowly, the Fed would speed it up with open market purchases.

According to the original version of this rule, the growth rate of the money stock would be set at 3 percent per year—about equal to the long-run average growth rate of natural real output in the first 25 years after World War II. Thus, as growth of natural real output shifts the economy's aggregate supply curve to the right, the monetarist rule is supposed to let the aggregate demand curve shift just enough to keep up on the average. Such a policy would permit steady growth of real output without inflation.

The money growth rule avoids problems of lags and forecasts. The Fed receives data on changes in the money supply within a week or two and can adjust open market operations within a few hours. However, it has a potential flaw: Stabilizing money supply growth will stabilize the overall economy only if velocity is constant. (Recall that *velocity* is the ratio of nominal national income to the quantity of money.) If velocity rises, aggregate demand will grow at a rate greater than 3 percent even if money is held to its 3 percent target. Assuming constant growth of natural real output, a sustained rise in velocity will cause inflation. Likewise, if velocity falls, aggregate demand will grow by less than 3 percent even with the money supply on target. This could result in a recession or at least a growth recession.

How stable has velocity been? Exhibit 18.1 shows the behavior of velocity of M1 and M2. Before the 1980s, economists tended to view M1 as the single most

Exhibit 18.1   The Income Velocity of M1 and M2

As part (a) of this exhibit shows, the income velocity of M1 rose along a trend of about 3 percent per year from the late 1950s to the early 1980s, with some quarter-to-quarter variations. By the mid-1980s, the trend had been broken by a pronounced decline in M1 velocity. As shown in part (b), M2 velocity has exhibited no upward or downward trend since the late 1950s, but over the whole period it has demonstrated quarter-to-quarter and year-to-year variations comparable to those experienced by M1 velocity in the 1980s.

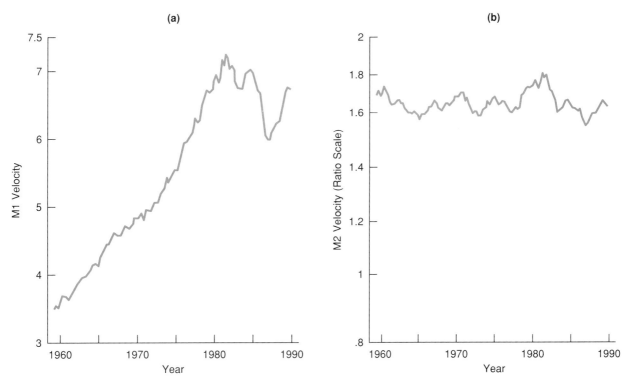

Source: Federal Reserve Board of Governors.

appropriate measure of the money stock and, hence, as the focus of a potential money growth rule. M1 velocity turned out to be far from constant, however. From the late 1950s to 1982, as shown in part (a) of the exhibit, M1 velocity rose at an annual rate of about 3 percent per year. By the mid-1980s, the trend had broken and M1 velocity had dropped sharply. Deregulation of transactions balances had effects on M1 behavior. Some of these were temporary, such as the shift of funds previously held outside M1 into newly authorized interest-bearing NOW accounts. Other effects were permanent, notably a substantial increase in the elasticity of demand for M1 with respect to market interest rates. Throughout the 1980s the rate of change of M1 velocity varied considerably from year to year and quarter to quarter.

By comparison, M2 velocity, as shown in part (b) of Exhibit 18.1, has exhibited no upward or downward trend over the past 30 years, although it has shown short-term variations comparable to those that M1 has experienced in the 1980s. The short-term volatility of M2 velocity severely limits its suitability as an anchor for a rigid short-term money growth rule. This volatility reflects the fact that M2 opportunity cost is strongly affected in the short term by changes in market interest rates. Over a time horizon of a year or so, however, offering rates on important components of M2 adjust to changes in market interest rates. Such adjustment cushions the impact of interest rate changes on M2 opportunity cost and reduces the interest sensitivity of M2 to a level well below that of M1. Over a somewhat longer term still, research indicates a strong link between M2 and the price level, as explained in ***Applying Economic Ideas 15.1*** (pages 400–401). Hence, M2 is attractive as a guidepost for monetary policy over a longer term.

Monetarists still say that had the Fed maintained a stable rate of money growth throughout the post–World War II period, the extremes of inflation of the 1970s would have been avoided. To be sure, there still would have been disturbances caused by various shocks to the economy, but there would have been no buildup of inflation to the double-digit levels that pushed short-term nominal interest rates near 20 percent at times during the early 1980s. Nor would it have been necessary to endure the wrenching process of disinflation in the early 1980s, which abruptly lowered nominal interest rates and velocity. Without these policy-induced disturbances, nominal interest rates would have varied less, and velocity itself would therefore have shown more short-term stability. Thus, instability of velocity is at least in part a result of past policy mistakes.

A nominal national income rule.   Thinking that troublesome variations in velocity are inevitable even if discretionary policy is replaced by a policy rule, a number of economists, including some former monetarists, have concluded that the Fed should use nominal national income instead of the money stock as a policy target. The Fed should aim for a constant 3 percent growth of nominal GNP, in the process automatically offsetting variations in velocity with changes in money growth. They claim that this would do a better job of holding the economy to a course of inflation-free growth. Given a fixed growth path for nominal GNP, consider what would happen if, for example, inflation accelerated. Real output would be squeezed, unemployment would rise above its natural rate, and inflation would start to decelerate. When price stability returned, real output could once again resume growing in step with the 3 percent trend of nominal GNP.

However, a nominal national income target has its own problems. One is that data on national income do not become available as quickly as data on the money supply. A second is that a variety of factors other than monetary policy—fiscal policy, for one—also affect nominal national income. A third is that the Fed can control nominal national income only indirectly, by adjusting the money supply. But changes in the money supply act on aggregate nominal demand only with a lag. Therefore, to stabilize the growth of nominal national income, the Fed would have to rely on forecasts of velocity. As with discretionary policy, this would raise the problem of possible destabilization due to actions that aim at stabilizing the growth of nominal GNP but take effect only after the conditions that necessitated them have passed. In short, the problems of lags and forecasting errors creep in through the window after having been thrown out through the door.

There is yet another problem: A fixed growth rate for nominal GNP will not work well unless natural real output grows at the same fixed rate. During a productivity slowdown such as that of the 1970s, a nominal national income rule would produce inflation. During a period of faster than expected productivity growth, such a rule could lead to a growth recession.

A price level rule.   These problems have led some other economists to propose yet another rule for monetary policy—one that sets its sights on a stable price level. Under such a rule, the Fed would drain reserves from the banking system if the price level rose and inject new reserves into the system if it fell. This rule would keep aggregate demand synchronized with natural real output even if the growth rate of natural real output varied from year to year.

Unfortunately, a price level rule raises the same problems of lags and forecasting errors as does a nominal national income rule. Also, a price level rule works poorly when a supply shock shifts the aggregate supply curve upward. To keep the price level from rising in the face of a supply shock, the Fed would have to reduce the money supply, shifting the aggregate demand curve to the left. This would cause a substantial loss of real output and a sharp rise in unemployment. But as we pointed out in Chapter 15, many economists think it is better to respond to a supply shock with some increase in aggregate demand, at least if the shock is likely to be long lasting. This would allow the price level to rise, but a supply shock would hurt the economy in some way no matter what was done. In this case, the pain of a little inflation probably would be less severe than that of a major recession.

The Fed's position.   To date, the Fed has adopted none of the proposed policy rules. The Fed agrees that a systematic monetary policy is needed. As required by law, it announces target ranges for various measures of money and credit growth each year, although these targets are not binding. It also announces projections of nominal and real GNP, the GNP deflator, and the unemployment rate that FOMC members think would be consistent with the projected growth paths for monetary aggregates. The Fed concurs that lags and forecasting errors make fine-tuning a dangerous game. But it also insists that macroeconomic stability can be enhanced by making adjustments in operating policy in response to new information that suggests that price and real output trends are departing from previous projections. The Fed doubts that any one policy rule can work well under all circumstances. An inflexible money growth rule would not let the Fed respond to unexpected changes in velocity as in the mid-1980s. Attaining a nominal income rule would be beyond the Fed's power and would risk instability over time. Further, the price level rule would not let the Fed respond flexibly enough to supply shocks, such as the oil price rises of 1974 and 1979 to 1980. For these reasons, the Fed emphasizes the need for policy feedback, judgment, and discretion in conducting monetary policy. It believes judgment and discretion must be combined with a credible commitment to the long-term goal of price stability; nonetheless, the Fed reserves the right to depart from its announced guidelines, as permitted by law, when unexpected developments warrant doing so.

Rules for Fiscal Policy

Fiscal policy rules raise a different set of issues than do monetary policy rules. One reason is that, as we have noted, there is no single set of policymakers in charge of fiscal policy. Instead, policies regarding taxes, government spending, and the deficit are the outcome of a political process in which not only Congress and the executive branch of the federal government but also state governments and state legislatures are involved. In the process by which these various bodies set fiscal policy, macroeconomic goals are often overshadowed by issues of social policy, defense policy, and vote trading. Even when tax cuts or job programs focus on macroeconomic issues, political factors such as elections are likely to affect their timing.

Another difference between fiscal and monetary policy is that fiscal policy deals with more types of policy actions. Discussions of monetary policy come down to decisions about how large open market operations should be or at what level the discount rate should be set. In the case of fiscal policy, it is not enough just to determine overall targets for taxes, transfers, and government purchases. Instead, decisions must be made regarding the thousands of expenditure programs and countless provisions of federal tax law, their relationship to state and local government fiscal policies, and so on. Any changes will have microeconomic and political impacts quite apart from their effects on aggregate demand.

Given these complexities, most proposed policy rules do not call for active use of fiscal policy as a tool of economic stabilization. Instead, they have the more modest aim of making fiscal policy less likely to be a source of instability. The greatest need, in many economists' view, is that of setting up a firm link between spending and taxes, that is, a set of rules regarding the federal deficit.

An annually balanced budget.   The most drastic proposal for a fiscal rule— sometimes proposed in the form of a constitutional amendment—would require the federal government to balance its budget each year. Any revenue shortfall would have to be made up right away by either raising taxes or cutting spending.

Proposals for an annually balanced federal budget score high in public opinion polls. Many people think that the government should be forced to live within its means just as they themselves are. But an annually balanced budget is not favored by many economists. The principal reason is that, as explained in Chapter 10, tax revenues tend to fall during a recession while transfer payments tend to rise. To maintain an annually balanced budget, then, taxes would have to be raised or spending cut during a recession. But these actions would cut aggregate demand just when output was already declining, tending to worsen the recession. Thus, an annually balanced budget might well make the economy not more but less stable than it is now.

A balanced structural budget.   To overcome this problem, some economists suggest that the budget should be balanced only over the business cycle. During recessions, a cyclical deficit would be permitted. When the economy was well into the expansion phase, the budget would be required to show a cyclical surplus. At all times the structural deficit would be held at zero.

A balanced structural budget would strengthen the economy's automatic stabilizers. However, it is not clear how the proposal could be put into practice. It does not lend itself to a simple constitutional amendment. In making spending decisions, the president and Congress would have to be guided by technical assessments of the economy's natural level of real output—a controversial matter. Also, policymakers would have to rely on technical forecasts of the levels of tax receipts and spending if the economy were at the natural level. Who would be punished and how if the forecasts or technical assessments turned out to be wrong? Answers to these questions are far from obvious.

Lessons of the Gramm-Rudman-Hollings experiment.   Congress struggled with these issues in 1985 when it formulated the Gramm-Rudman-Hollings law. The result was an elaborate system of triggers and automatic adjustment rules. The basic aim of the law, as Chapter 10 explained, was to force across-the-board cuts in federal expenditures (with important politically protected exceptions) sufficient to meet a scheduled set of reductions in the federal deficit. The size of the required cuts was to be determined by averaging the forecasts of the Office of Management and Budget (OMB), an executive branch agency, and the Congressional Budget Office (CBO), part of the legislative branch. The Supreme Court later invalidated the CBO's role in the process, and subsequent legislation left forecasting responsibilities to the OMB.

The Gramm-Rudman-Hollings law contains two safety valves for dealing with the problem of recessions. If the OMB forecasts a recession, the House and Senate would be required to vote on a joint resolution temporarily discarding the deficit limits. Also, if actual real growth fell below 1 percent for two successive quarters, such a vote would be triggered. However, even these safety valves left open the possibility that automatic spending cuts could be required during a period when growth had slowed to just over 1 percent per year. In such a situation, the cuts might turn a mild growth recession into something more serious.

The danger that a balanced budget rule would prove destabilizing would be reduced if the Fed were able to offset automatic fiscal restraint with discretionary monetary expansion. If both fiscal and monetary policy were "tied to the mast" by rules, however, there would be more cause for concern.

The State of the Debate

What can we conclude from the current state of the debate over policy activism versus policy rules? Over the years, the two sides have come closer together on many points. For example, both agree that stopping inflation is not easy; it is better to have a strategy that will keep inflation from getting out of hand in the first place. Policy activists recognize that forecasting errors and lags are serious problems. Those who favor policy rules admit that there may be no one rule that works perfectly all of the time. And both sides agree that a credible commitment to long-term goals will result in better outcomes than a policy that is perceived to be at the mercy of shifting short-term political winds. Given these points of agreement, what differences remain?

Technical differences.   The technical differences that remain revolve around how best to deal with lags and forecasting errors and whether any policy rule would be adequate under all of the various circumstances that the economy encounters. On these issues, some economists see a middle ground: If activists are unwilling to see human policymakers replaced with rigid rules, why not at least develop a somewhat more flexible set of rules to guide policymakers' actions? To return to the ocean liner example, this approach would not put the ship on automatic pilot, but neither would it leave the course entirely up to the captain's moods. Instead, the captain would be required to announce the chosen course in advance and react to unforeseen events according to the guidelines contained in a navigational manual.

The Fed has already moved in this direction in that it now announces target growth ranges for money and credit for the coming year. The next step, say supporters of this middle ground, would be to announce a set of rules for adjusting money growth within those ranges and adapting the ranges themselves when macroeconomic conditions develop differently than expected. For example, the target growth range for money might be adjusted upward or downward each quarter according to whether nominal national income is running above or below some target value or velocity is moving above or below its predicted trend. For example, monetarists Bennett McCallum and Allen Meltzer, both of Carnegie Mellon University, have concluded that changes in velocity trends or deviations of nominal GNP from a target growth path need to be taken into account in the conduct of monetary policy. With this in mind, they have devised adaptive rules for money growth rates that adjust for these factors. They argue that such sophisticated money growth rules can add the necessary element of policy activism without resorting to unbridled discretion.

McCallum, Meltzer, and others argue that the rules need not work perfectly. The important thing is that firms, workers, stock market traders, and everyone else would know the rules. In that case, the rules would become a stable framework for expectations. They would build in some room for policy activism but would reduce the scope for discretionary changes in policy compared with the present situation. Adaptive rules could, in effect, discourage policymakers from turning the ship's rudder violently from one side to the other and at the same time allow them to react flexibly to supply shocks, changes in financial institutions, and other unforeseen events.

Policy activists have their doubts about even this middle ground. They believe that in a complex real world, no set of rules fixed in advance, even adaptive rules, could cover all possible contingencies. Thus, any reasonable policy regime needs to allow some scope for human judgment even if that sometimes means throwing the "navigational manual" overboard.

Political differences.   Aside from these technical matters, the various schools of thought also differ on political issues. Monetarists and new classicists simply do not trust policymakers to use their power in a responsible manner. "Money is too important to be left to central bankers" is how Milton Friedman has put it. It is no help that policymakers are, for the most part, honest and well intentioned. The system forces them to stress the short run at the expense of the long run, to mask their true intentions from the public, and to change courses frequently. This being the case, macroeconomic policy will inevitably have an inflationary bias. In the monetarist view, even an imperfect set of rules would be better than leaving economic policy to the politicians.

Policy activists are less pessimistic. They think that just as economists have learned more about the inflation process from the experience of the 1970s, policymakers have learned to take a longer-term view of things. The case for a policy that combines credible commitment to long-term goals with cautious, systematic use of discretionary policy in the short run has been enhanced by the relative stability of the economy after the early 1980s. In the case that leads off this chapter, we saw that the "new economists" of 20 years ago dared to assert that they had attained "not only the economic understanding but also the will and determination to use economic policy as an effective tool for progress." The hope of someday reaching this state of affairs has not died.

Summary

1. **Why have Keynesian economists favored the active use of fiscal and monetary policy to stabilize the economy?** Economists have long disagreed over the best strategy for economic stabilization. Keynesians have favored the active use of fiscal and monetary policies to try to fine-tune the economy, keeping it on a path of relatively steady growth without inflation. The case for policy activism rests on three propositions: (1) that the private economy is inherently unstable; (2) that the future course of the economy and the effects of policy actions can be predicted well enough to guide policy decisions; and (3) that policymakers will follow economists' technical advice.

2. **What are the implications of lags and forecasting errors for the conduct of discretionary policy?** Monetarists and other opponents of policy activism draw attention to lags in the policy process. The *inside lag* is the delay between the time a policy change is needed and the time a decision is made. The *outside lag* is the delay between the time a decision is made and the time it has its main effect on the economy. Lags in fiscal and monetary policy range from as short as three months to several years. Because of lags, policymakers must act on the basis of forecasts. However, if the forecasts turn out to be seriously in error, their decisions may make things worse rather than better by the time they take effect.

3. **Why may politics interfere with the conduct of stabilization policy?** Even when economists offer valid technical advice, policymakers may not follow it. One reason for this is that there is great political pressure to "do something" when things go wrong with the economy. However, because of policy lags, it may be too late to do anything useful by the time this pressure reaches its peak. Also, more expansionary policy has favorable effects on real output and employment in

the short run but unfavorable effects on the price level in the long run. Politicians facing reelection may place undue stress on the short-run effects. Monetary authorities too may be tempted to seek short-term benefits by departing from announced long-term policy goals. In this way, an inflationary bias may creep into stabilization policy over time. Critics of policy activism see political and time-inconsistency factors as major problems.

4. **What kinds of rules have been proposed for the conduct of monetary policy?** A number of rules have been proposed for conducting monetary policy. One is to let the money supply grow at a steady rate equal to the long-term rate of growth of natural real output. A second is to let nominal national income grow at a steady rate equal to the long-term growth rate of natural real output. A third is to use a stable price level as a policy target. None of these policy rules work perfectly all of the time.

5. **What kinds of rules have been proposed for the conduct of fiscal policy?** The most often proposed rule for conducting fiscal policy is to require the federal government to balance its budget. An annually balanced budget would require the government to raise taxes or cut spending during a recession. However, this might lead to less rather than more stability. Many economists favor a budget that would be balanced on a structural basis but allow cyclical deficits and surpluses over the course of the business cycle.

Terms for Review

- inside lag
- outside lag

Questions for Review

1. What is the main cause of the business cycle according to economists who favor a strategy of policy activism? According to those who favor policy rules?

2. What three propositions underlie the case for policy activism?

3. What are the sources of the inside and outside lags for monetary policy? For fiscal policy?

4. According to critics of policy activism, what features of the U.S. political system interfere with attempts to stabilize the economy?

5. Describe three possible rules for the conduct of monetary policy.

6. Which is more likely to contribute to economic stability—a federal budget that is balanced every year or one that is balanced, on the average, over the course of the business cycle? Why?

Problems and Topics for Discussion

1. **Examining the lead-off case.** Review the events of the "Great Inflation" of the 1970s as described in the lead-off case in Chapter 15. Compare the actual events of the 1970s with the hopes expressed by the president's economic advisers in 1966 as given at the beginning of this chapter. Why did economic policy fail to achieve the objective of balanced growth with price stability?

2. **A game.** Here is a game that will give you a feeling for the effects of policy lags and forecasting errors. In your classroom or another large room, arrange a dozen chairs to form a "slalom course." The course should consist of pairs of chairs placed about three feet apart to form "gates." The gates should be laid out to form a path of S-shaped turns. The goal is to walk through the gates without bumping into them or wandering off the path. When your slalom course is set up, form teams of three and compete to see who can finish the course the fastest. Whoever hits a gate is disqualified.

   a. For practice, select one team member—A—to walk through the course. Note the time it takes to complete it.

   b. Next, blindfold team member A. Team member B watches and tells A when to turn to the right or left.

   c. With A still blindfolded, B watches A and writes directions to turn left or right on a memo pad. The directions are passed to team member C, who reads them aloud within A's hearing. C must sit facing away from the course so that he or she cannot see B's progress.

   d. Conditions are the same as in part c except that now B also sits facing away from the course. B is allowed to view the course only by looking over his or her shoulder using a hand-held mirror. B thus must check on A's progress using the mirror and then write instructions for C, who reads them to A.

   What does this game teach you about strategies for steering the economy through the "gates" of the business cycle? Discuss.

3. **A money growth rule.** Draw an aggregate supply and demand diagram to illustrate the use of a policy rule calling for a fixed rate of money growth equal to the growth rate of natural real output. Show what will happen to real output and the price level when velocity rises or falls unexpectedly while the rate of growth of natural real output stays the same.

4. **Nominal national income rule.** Draw an aggregate supply and demand diagram to illustrate the use of a monetary policy rule calling for a fixed rate of growth of nominal national income equal to the expected growth rate of natural real output. Show what will happen to real output and the price level if the growth of natural real output unexpectedly slows down or speeds up.

5. **Policy rules and supply shocks.** Use an aggregate supply and demand diagram to compare the effects of a supply shock when the Fed (a) follows a rule calling for a fixed price level; (b) follows a rule calling for a fixed level of nominal national income; and (c) accommodates the supply shock in order to keep real output equal to its natural level. What are the advantages and disadvantages of each policy?

6. **Project stockpiles and the fiscal policy lag.** Policy activists have long been aware that the process of getting the approval of Congress adds a long and uncertain period to the inside lag for fiscal policy. As a solution to this problem, it has often been proposed that the federal government "stockpile" a number of projects, such as highway improvements, bridges, post office buildings, and so on. All planning and design work for the projects would be completed and the projects kept "on the shelf" until needed. When the economy entered a recession, the president could order that the projects be started. Work on them could begin in a matter of weeks.

   Do you think this strategy would reduce the inside lag for fiscal policy? What problems of lags and forecasting would remain? How would the proposal affect the political problems of fine-tuning?

7. **Monetary policy and the professor's dilemma.** Review *Applying Economic Ideas 18.2* (page 473). Suppose the Fed has announced a low target for the growth of the money stock. Everyone believes the Fed

will stick to it. How does the Fed's situation compare with that of the professor who has reached the end of the semester and must decide whether to give the exam? What will happen if the Fed decides to exceed its money growth target one time only? What will happen to expectations of inflation if the public comes to suspect that the Fed will habitually exceed its target?

If the Fed then surprises people by sticking to its initial, low target after all, what will happen to real output? Why would a policymaker ever prefer to be bound by a rule rather than be left free to make discretionary changes in policy? What light does the story of the professor's dilemma shed on the time-inconsistency problem?

Case for Discussion
The Importance of a Credible Monetary Policy

A high degree of monetary policy credibility will often lead to superior economic performance compared with the situation where a policy is not perceived to be very credible.

Suppose monetary policymakers announced their intention to lower the rate of inflation over a specific time interval and, to achieve this goal, slowed the growth of the money supply and allowed interest rates to rise. If the policy was not viewed as credible—for example, if the public thought that the policy would not be maintained—households and firms would continue to set wages and prices as they had previously, at least for a time. Meanwhile, the increasingly restrictive monetary policy would restrain demand and production. Thus, the lack of policy credibility would result in a worsening of the economic situation, as inflation remained high and unemployment rose. This outcome would persist until the public's expectations of the rate of inflation fell.

Suppose, on the other hand, that the public believed that the policy of reduced inflation would be achieved. In these circumstances, the more restrained monetary policy would be accompanied by a drop of inflationary expectations. . . .

Policy credibility is also valuable during a period of falling inflation, because a temporarily higher rate of monetary growth may appear to contradict the stated policy of lower inflation. As the rate of inflation falls, the public will likely wish to hold a larger quantity of money, because the opportunity cost of doing so will be smaller. The Federal Reserve could accommodate this increased demand by allowing the money stock to grow more rapidly for a time. Ideally, the public will recognize that the increased rate of money growth is temporary and a natural consequence of the disinflationary policy. Even if the public does not understand this process but finds the policy of disinflation to be credible, inflation expectations will not rise in response to the pickup in money growth. If the policy does not have much credibility, on the other hand, the public might become concerned that the higher money growth is permanent, signaling an inflationary monetary policy.

Source: President's Council of Economic Advisers, *Economic Report of the President* (Washington, D.C.: Government Printing Office, 1990): 86–87.

Questions

1. Compare this excerpt from the 1990 *Economic Report* with those from the 1966 *Economic Report* that are given at the beginning of the chapter. What general differences in philosophy do you note?

2. Use aggregate supply and demand diagrams to show the effects of a slow-down in the rate of monetary policy under the suppositions that the commitment to lower inflation is and is not credible, as discussed here.

3. The point is made here that as inflation slows, money demand will increase and, by implication, velocity will decrease as interest rates fall. It is suggested that the Fed should respond with a temporary increase in the growth rate of the money stock. What would happen if the Fed instead adhered to a strict 3 percent money growth rule during such a period?

4. Does a credible monetary policy require adherence to a formal policy rule of some kind? Or is it compatible with a certain degree of discretion? Discuss in the light of the examples given here.

Suggestions for Further Reading

Darby, Michael R., et al. "Recent Behavior of the Velocity of Money." *Contemporary Policy Issues* (January 1987): 1–33.

A panel discussion devoted to the implications of changes in money velocity for the conduct of monetary policy. Milton Friedman, in contributing to the panel, restates the case for a money growth rule. David Lindsey argues for presumptive monetary targets but ones that are subject to change if warranted by unexpected developments.

Mayer, Thomas. "Replacing the FOMC by a PC." *Contemporary Policy Issues* (April 1987): 31–43.

A nontechnical discussion of monetary policy rules. Contains many useful references.

President's Council of Economic Advisers. *Economic Report of the President*. Washington, D.C.: Government Printing Office, 1985.

The 1985 edition of the report leans toward the monetarist position in its discussion of economic policy for the late 1980s.

Sheffrin, Steven M. "Fiscal Policy Tied to the Mast." *Contemporary Policy Issues* (April 1987): 44–56.

A good discussion of the lessons of the Gramm-Rudman-Hollings experiment.

**Before reading this chapter,
make sure you know the meaning of:**

Elasticity (Chapter 3)

International economic accounts (Chapter 6)

Foreign-exchange markets (Chapter 12)

Intervention in foreign-exchange markets
(Chapter 12)

After reading this chapter, you will understand:

How current account supply and demand interact
in foreign-exchange markets.

The considerations that determine the capital
account net demand for dollars.

How changes in rates of real economic growth
affect exchange rates.

How changes in real interest rates affect exchange
rates.

What actions governments take to influence
exchange rates.

How the international monetary system has
evolved since World War II.

Rude Awakening

The terrible U.S. trade gap has caused pain and disruption at home and abroad.

Now the gap is closing. The outlook: More pain and disruption at home and abroad.

Sure, the trade deficit symbolizes a profligate America, consuming more than it produces and spending more than it has. But it also represents the biggest gravy train ever for U.S. trading partners, who have been selling America all that stuff and lending the money to pay for it.

Suddenly reality is sinking in. If, as many think possible, America's trade books are finally brought into balance over the next five years, the train will stop. Other countries will be forced into a stunning $200 billion trade turnaround. That's how much more they will be buying from America and how much less they will be selling the United States or collecting in interest payments.

"After years of shouting for a quick fix, the world is staring the implications of this right in the face," says an international monetary official.

Those implications may have been obvious to economists. Still, they aren't going to be welcome. "Every one of our trading partners is going to feel real pain," promises Robert D. Hormats, a director of Goldman Sachs International Corp. in New York. So will the United States. Affordable imports will disappear, and more production will go for export instead of home use.

Photo source: AP/Wide World Photos.

The four emerging "tigers" of Asia—South Korea, Taiwan, Hong Kong and Singapore—could face a $20 billion swing in trade with the United States, slowing their export-led development. Lesser-developed countries may be forced into a $15 billion adjustment and Eastern Europe perhaps a $5 billion change. The remaining $160 billion will be divided between Japan and Western Europe, and many people figure Europe will feel its hit the hardest.

The job cutbacks have already begun. Last month, Dutch electronics giant NV Philips said it would slash 20,000 jobs this year and move or close 80 of its 200 European factories during the next five years. Porsche AG will cut output 39 percent in the model year ending next July 31 and put as many as 6,100 of its 8,500 employees on short workweeks.

Europe's problem is one of history confronting simple mathematics. In order to absorb their "share" of the deficit reversal, proud companies built on exports may have to change tracks, fast.

The effects of the foreign trade balance always seem to be in the news. In the early and mid-1980s, with the U.S. current account deficit soaring, U.S. exporters were suffering while overseas firms such as NV Philips, Porsche, and the clothing workshops of Hong Kong were riding high. More recently their roles have reversed. The future course of trade patterns cannot be predicted with complete accuracy, but one thing is certain: When exchange rates and trading balances undergo wide swings, as they did in the 1980s, they touch lives in towns and cities around the globe.

At several points in this book, we have raised the topics of imports, exports, capital flows, and exchange rates.[1] In this chapter, we explore those topics further. We begin with a review of supply and demand in foreign-exchange markets, adding a number of new details. Next we examine the ways in which current and capital account international transactions respond to changing conditions. Finally, we examine the international monetary system and policy related to it.

19.1 Foreign-Exchange Markets

Foreign-exchange markets were first introduced in Chapter 12. There we saw that supply, demand, and equilibrium exchange rates were influenced by both current account transactions (trade in goods and services and international transfer payments) and capital account transactions (international borrowing, lending, and exchange of assets). In this section we look more closely at each of these sets of transactions. First we will consider current account transactions by themselves and then capital account transactions by themselves. When each set of transactions is understood in isolation, we will put them back together to get a more complete picture of foreign-exchange supply and demand than was given earlier.

---

[1]Sections on international topics, identified by the world map symbol, appear in Chapters 5, 6, 9, 12, and 14. This chapter builds on those earlier sections. It may be useful to review them before proceeding.

Exchange Markets: Current Account Only

Imagine a world in which international transactions are limited to imports and exports of goods and services and transfer payments on current account. There are no net capital flows, because exchanges of bank deposits and currency in payment for a country's imports and net transfers are just balanced by payments for its exports.

The current account demand curve for dollars.   Assuming these conditions, suppose that a German clothing importer wants to buy a shipment of Levis. The importer has German marks in a Frankfurt bank account, but the U.S. manufacturer wants to be paid in dollars, which it can use to pay workers and buy supplies in the United States. The importer's bank sells the necessary number of marks on the foreign-exchange market and receives dollars in return. The dollars are then sent to the manufacturer to pay for the Levis.

The German importer's transactions create a demand for dollars in the foreign-exchange market where marks are exchanged for dollars. Together with the transactions of thousands of other buyers of U.S. goods and services, they can be represented in the form of a *current account demand curve* for dollars, as in both parts of Exhibit 19.1.

To understand why the current account demand curve has a negative slope, as shown, consider how German demand for U.S. goods and services varies as the exchange rate changes, other things being equal. Suppose, for example, that Levis sell for $20 a pair in the United States. At an exchange rate of 3 marks per dollar, German consumers will have to pay 60 marks per pair. They may buy a total of, say, 1,000 pairs a day, thereby creating a demand for $20,000 per day in the foreign-exchange market. If the exchange rate falls to 2.5 marks per dollar while the U.S. price remains unchanged, German consumers will be able to buy Levis more cheaply—for 50 marks a pair ($20 a pair $\times$ 2.5 marks per dollar). At the lower price, German consumers will buy a larger quantity—say, 1,250 pairs a day. The demand for dollars created by these sales will thus increase to $25,000 per day.

The current account supply curve for dollars.   The situation with the current account supply curve for dollars is somewhat more complicated. In a world limited to current account transactions, dollars are supplied to the foreign-exchange market by U.S. citizens who want to buy German goods. The slope of the supply curve thus depends on how their demand for German goods varies as the exchange rate changes. Two possibilities need to be considered: those of *elastic* and *inelastic* demand for German goods on the part of U.S. buyers.

Whenever the U.S. demand for German goods is elastic (that is, whenever a 1 percent change in the U.S. price of German goods causes a greater than 1 percent change in the quantity demanded), the supply curve for dollars will have a positive slope, as shown in part (a) of Exhibit 19.1. An example will show why this is the case.

Suppose that a certain model of the German BMW automobile has a price of 60,000 marks. At an exchange rate of 3 marks per dollar, the car will sell for $20,000 in the United States (ignoring shipping costs and other charges). If 500 BMWs a day are sold at that price, U.S. buyers will have to supply $10 million per day to this foreign-exchange market to get the 30 million marks needed to

Exhibit 19.1   Supply of and Demand for Dollars on Current Account

This exhibit shows the supply and demand curves for dollars in the foreign-exchange market in which dollars are exchanged for German marks. Only current account transactions—exports, imports, and transfer payments—are assumed to take place. The demand curve for dollars reflects the German demand for U.S. exports. The supply curve for dollars reflects U.S. demand for German imports. The slope of the supply curve depends on the elasticity of demand for imports. If demand for imports is elastic, the supply curve for dollars will have a positive slope, as in part (a). If demand for imports is inelastic, the supply curve for dollars will have a negative slope, as in part (b).

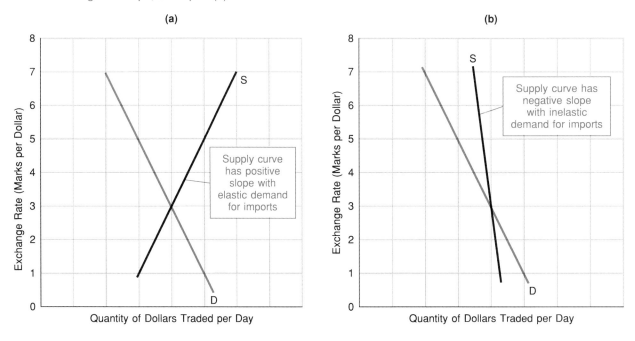

pay the German manufacturer. Suppose that the exchange rate then rises to 4 marks per dollar, enabling U.S. buyers to get the car for just $15,000 (a 25 percent decrease in the dollar price). Because we are assuming an elastic demand for BMWs, the number of BMWs imported will rise more than in proportion to the decrease in the dollar price—say, by 50 percent, to 750 a day. To obtain 750 cars at 60,000 marks per car and an exchange rate of 4 marks per dollar, U.S. buyers will have to supply $11.25 million per day to the foreign-exchange market (750 cars per day × 60,000 marks per car × .25 dollars per mark). The number of dollars supplied to the market will have increased in response to a rise in the price of the dollar in terms of marks.

If, on the other hand, U.S. demand for foreign goods is inelastic rather than elastic, the supply curve for dollars on the foreign-exchange market will have a negative slope. An inelastic demand means that a 1 percent change in the U.S. price of German goods will cause a less than 1 percent change in the quantity demanded. The BMW example can easily be changed to illustrate this. Suppose that when the exchange rate rises from 3 to 4 marks per dollar (bringing the U.S.

price of BMWs down by 25 percent—from $20,000 to $15,000), only 50 more cars are sold each day (only a 10 percent increase). To get the German marks needed to buy 550 cars at 60,000 marks per car at an exchange rate of 4 marks per dollar, U.S. buyers need supply only $8.25 million per day to the foreign-exchange market. An increase in the price of dollars in terms of marks will thus reduce the supply of dollars. However, as long as the negatively sloped supply curve is steeper than the demand curve, as shown in part (b) of Exhibit 19.1, the market will achieve a stable equilibrium at the point at which the curves cross.

For the time being, we will assume a positive slope for the supply curve, but this assumption is not always justified in practice. Later in the chapter we will consider the implications of different elasticity assumptions.

Appreciation, Depreciation, and Parity

As we saw in Chapter 12, changes in economic conditions can cause shifts in the supply and demand curves for foreign-exchange markets. For example, an increase in U.S. demand for imported goods resulting from expansion of the U.S. economy will cause the current account supply curve for dollars to shift to the right. On the other hand, an increase in German demand for U.S. goods resulting from expansion of the German economy would cause the current account demand curve for dollars to shift to the right. As the curves shifted, the exchange rate of the dollar, expressed in marks, would vary.

In the terminology of foreign-exchange markets, the dollar is said to **appreciate** when its price stated in terms of a foreign currency rises, and to **depreciate** when its price in terms of a foreign currency falls. Seen from the German point of view, an appreciation of the dollar is equivalent to a depreciation of the mark, and a depreciation of the dollar is equivalent to an appreciation of the mark.

According to one theory, in a world limited to current account transactions the dollar would tend to appreciate or depreciate until a point was reached at which a given amount of money, converted at the market exchange rate, would buy the same "market basket" of goods and services in the two countries. This state of affairs is known as **purchasing power parity.** For example, suppose 3 marks per dollar is the exchange rate corresponding to purchasing power parity for Germany and the United States. That would mean that a typical market basket of goods and services (so many raincoats, so many airline tickets, so many apples, and so on) that cost $1,000 in the United States would cost 3,000 marks in Germany so that a person would be no better off, on the average, by purchasing the whole market basket in one country rather than the other. Purchasing power parity provides an interesting reference point in discussing exchange rates. However, as *Applying Economic Ideas 19.1* shows, in practice exchange rates need not correspond to purchasing power parity at any given time, and rates of exchange between some currencies depart from purchasing power parity for long periods.

The Capital Account Net Demand Curve

Now that we have discussed the current account supply and demand curves for dollars, it is time to consider the capital account. In Chapter 12, we combined current and capital account demand for dollars into a single curve. We will do so again shortly, but for a moment, let us look at capital account demand in isolation.

Appreciation (of a currency)
An increase in the value of a country's currency relative to another's.

Depreciation (of a currency)
A decline in the value of a country's currency relative to another's.

Purchasing power parity
A situation in which a given sum of money will buy the same market basket of goods and services when converted from one currency to another at prevailing exchange rates.

Applying Economic Ideas   19.1
Exchange Rates and Purchasing Power Parity

Is the dollar, at any moment, overvalued, undervalued, or about right? In one sense, the answer is always "just right": The dollar is worth whatever people are willing to pay for it in exchange for marks, yen, pounds, or whatever. However, according to another view, the dollar tends, in the long run, to move toward the level of *purchasing power parity*. Under the purchasing power parity theory, the dollar's exchange rate is said to be appropriate when it is possible to buy the same basket of goods and services in various countries for the same amount of money when that money is converted at the prevailing exchange rates.

To illustrate, we can first apply the purchasing power parity concept to individual goods. As shown in the accompanying chart, in the spring of 1987 it was possible to buy a dozen eggs in the United States for about $1. In London, a dozen eggs would have cost 1.23 British pounds, the equivalent of $1.89 at the then current exchange rate. Thus, in terms of eggs the dollar could be said to have been below the purchasing power parity level at that time. As the chart shows, by the purchasing power parity standard, the dollar in early 1987 was undervalued relative to the currencies of six major U.S. trading partners in terms of several common goods and services.

A closer look at the chart reveals, however, that the degree of undervaluation relative to a given foreign currency differs from one good to another because of differences in relative prices. For example, at that time a dozen eggs cost about twice as much in Tokyo as in the United States, whereas a pound of beef cost about four times as much. Further, in terms of toothpaste in London and Seoul and beef in Rome, the dollar was actually above the parity level. To allow for variations in relative prices, economists commonly base purchasing power parity calculations on the average price of a broad-based market basket of goods and services. For example, a study conducted in late 1986 by the Organization for European Cooperation and Development confirmed undervaluation relative to purchasing power parity for a broad-based market basket of goods and services. According to that study, at that time the purchasing power parity exchange rate for the Japanese yen would have been 223 to the dollar compared with a

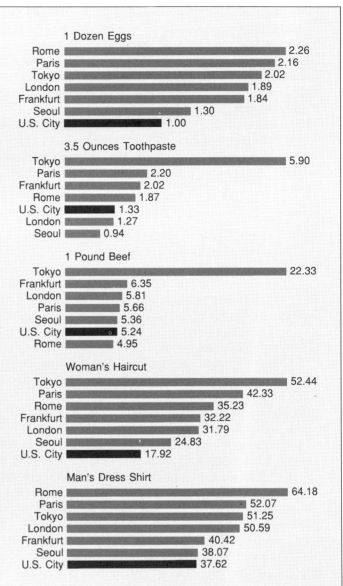

market rate of 169. For West Germany, the purchasing power parity rate would have been 2.48 marks per dollar compared with a market rate of 2.17 marks. For France, the purchasing power parity rate would have been 7.48 francs per dollar compared with a market rate of 6.93. At that time, however, the broad-based comparison showed the dollar to be slightly overvalued relative to purchasing power parity in the case of the Italian lira and the British pound.

The purchasing power parity concept does not allow for capital flows, transportation costs, or international differences in buying habits. However, it provides an interesting, if rough, benchmark for interpreting movements of market exchange rates.

Source: Alfred L. Malabre, Jr., "By One Measure, Dollar Rebound Is Due," *The Wall Street Journal*, April 15, 1987, 6. Reprinted by permission of *The Wall Street Journal*, © Dow Jones & Company, Inc., 1987. All Rights Reserved Worldwide.

A graphical representation of the capital account is given in Exhibit 19.2. It contains a downward-sloping line, which we will call the **capital account net demand curve,** that shows the net demand for dollars arising from capital account transactions. If capital inflows to the United States exceed capital outflows, the net demand for dollars on capital account will be positive. If capital outflows from the United States exceed capital inflows, the net demand for dollars on capital account will be negative. To allow for both positive and negative net demand, the vertical axis is drawn in the middle of the graph.

Several factors affect the slope and position of the capital account net demand curve. The most important of these can be grouped under factors affecting expectations and factors related to interest rates. Let us look at each of these in turn.

Capital account net demand curve
A graph that shows the net demand for a country's currency that results at various exchange rates from capital account transactions.

Expectations Regarding Future Exchange Rates

We begin by looking at how the capital account net demand for dollars is affected by changes in the exchange rate relative to that expected to prevail in the future. Put yourself in the position of a person with $1 million to invest. You are trying

Exhibit 19.2 The Capital Account Net Demand Curve

The negatively sloped curve in this graph represents the net demand for dollars on capital account. The zero point on the horizontal axis is placed at the center of the diagram because current account net demand can be either positive (indicating a net capital inflow) or negative (indicating a net capital outflow). Assuming interest rates in the two countries to be equal, the curve crosses the central vertical axis at the level of the future exchange rate expected by the average investor. The capital account net demand curve has a negative slope because investors are attracted to assets denominated in currencies that they think are undervalued relative to the expected future exchange rate and tend to avoid assets denominated in currencies that they believe are overvalued relative to that rate.

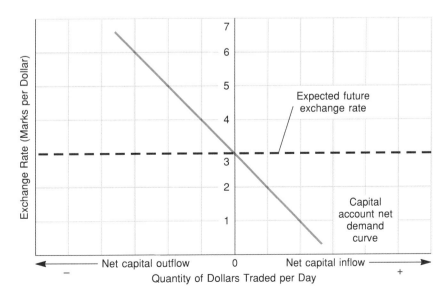

to decide whether to use the funds to buy bonds issued by the U.S. government or comparable bonds issued by the German government.

To keep things simple, we will initially assume that the U.S. and German bonds you are considering have identical 10 percent nominal interest rates and mature one year from now. We will also assume for the moment that no change is expected in the average price level for goods and services in either country. Finally, we will assume that you expect the exchange rate one year from now to be 3 marks per dollar.

Given these expectations, suppose that today's exchange rate is 2 marks per dollar. If you trade your $1 million for marks now, you can buy 2 million marks of German bonds. When the bonds mature a year later, you will have 2.2 million marks, including the interest you have earned at the 10 percent rate assumed in our example. However, you expect the exchange rate to have risen to 3 marks per dollar by then. At that exchange rate, you will get only $733,000 for your 2.2 million marks. You would have done better to buy U.S. government bonds; then you would have come out with $1.1 million at the end of the year, including interest.

Suppose, however, that today's exchange rate is 4 marks per dollar, but you expect it to fall to 3 marks per dollar over the next year. In that case, you will come out better buying 4 million marks of German bonds for your $1 million. At 3 marks per dollar, the 4.4 million marks you will have at the end of the year will get you $1,466,666 in the foreign-exchange market—more than the $1.1 million you would have had you invested in U.S. bonds.

The moral of the story is: Given the same interest rates in two countries, you should invest in assets of the country whose currency you think is more likely to appreciate and avoid those of the country whose currency is likely to depreciate. The same reasoning applies in reverse if you are a borrower: If interest rates on loans are the same in two countries, you will want to borrow from the one whose exchange rate you expect to fall. That way you will be able to repay the loan in "cheap" marks, dollars, or whatever when the loan comes due.

The effects of expected changes in exchange rates account for the negative slope of the capital account net demand curve. In Exhibit 19.2, the curve intersects the vertical axis at the future rate of 3 marks per dollar that is, on the average, expected by participants in foreign-exchange markets. In this example, the exchange rate that the average investor expects one year hence is 3 marks per dollar. As the current exchange rate falls below the benchmark, other things being equal, more investors will expect it to move up over the lives of their investments. Given this majority expectation of a rising exchange rate, those investors will want to switch their mark-denominated assets to dollar-denominated ones. At the same time, borrowers who expect the dollar to appreciate over the lives of their loans will want to switch their borrowing from U.S. to German sources. The actions of both investors and borrowers will increase the net quantity of dollars demanded on capital account. The further the exchange rate of the dollar falls in the present, the greater the proportion of investors who will expect it to rise later and switch to dollar-denominated assets and the greater the proportion of borrowers who will switch out of dollar-denominated borrowing. In Exhibit 19.2, the result is shown as a movement downward and to the right along the capital account net demand curve.

When the current exchange rate rises above the 3-mark-per-dollar average expected rate, the reactions will be reversed. As the dollar rises, more and more investors and borrowers will anticipate that the dollar will fall back toward the average expected rate over the lives of their investments or loans. Hence, they will switch their investments out of dollar-denominated assets and their borrowing into dollar-denominated loans. The net quantity of dollars demanded on capital account will then become negative, moving them upward and to the left along the capital account net demand curve.

Real versus Nominal Exchange Rates

If we relax the assumption of no change in price levels, things become a bit more complicated. In a world in which inflation takes place and at different rates in different countries, it becomes necessary to distinguish between nominal and real exchange rates. The **nominal exchange rate** is the exchange rate expressed in the usual way: in terms of current currency units. The **real exchange rate** is adjusted to allow for changes in the price levels of both countries relative to a chosen base year. The nominal rate can be converted to the real rate by applying the formula

$$E_r = E_n(P_d/P_f),$$

where E_r is the real exchange rate, E_n is the nominal exchange rate, P_d is the domestic price level, and P_f is the foreign price level, with both price levels expressed in terms of the same base year.

For example, suppose that in the base year, 1980, a given market basket of goods costs \$1,000 in the United States and 3,000 marks in Germany. The 1980 nominal exchange rate is 3 marks per dollar. By 1990, the price level in the United States has risen by 50 percent—from 1.0 to 1.5—while the price level in Germany is unchanged at 1.0. This means that the market basket now costs \$1,500 in the United States. To maintain a constant real exchange rate, the 1990 nominal exchange rate must fall to 2 marks per dollar (2 marks per dollar nominal × 1.5/1.0 = 3 marks per dollar real). If the nominal rate had remained unchanged at 3 marks per dollar, the real rate would have risen to 4.5 marks per dollar (3 marks per dollar nominal × 1.5/1.0 = 4.5).

Other things being equal, nominal exchange rates tend to respond to inflation in a way that keeps real exchange rates constant. If the capital account net demand curve were expressed in terms of real exchange rates, changes in expected future nominal exchange rates that matched differences in inflation rates would have no effect on the volume of capital inflows or outflows.

Differences in Real Interest Rates

Now that we have seen how changes in the current exchange rate relative to its expected future value cause movements along the capital account net demand curve, let us return to the subject of interest rates. Exhibit 19.3 sets the stage. As before, we will assume that nominal interest rates initially are equal in the United States and Germany and that there is no inflation. We will also assume that the initial exchange rate of 3 marks per dollar is equal to the average expected future rate. This puts the capital account in balance at E_1.

Now suppose that the nominal interest rate rises in the United States and falls in Germany. Other things being equal, this difference in nominal interest rates will encourage people to buy U.S. assets and discourage them from borrowing from U.S. sources. The resulting increase in the net demand for dollars

Nominal exchange rate
The exchange rate expressed in the usual way: in terms of current units of foreign currency per current dollar.

Real exchange rate
The nominal exchange rate adjusted for changes in the price levels of both countries relative to a chosen base year.

Exhibit 19.3   A Shift in the Capital Account Net Demand Curve

This exhibit shows the effects of a rise in the U.S. interest rate relative to the German interest rate. An increase in the U.S. interest rate makes dollar-denominated assets more attractive to investors, shifting the curve upward. This causes the exchange rate to rise. At a higher exchange rate, some investors then again become unwilling to buy dollar-denominated assets because they think the dollar is overvalued relative to the exchange rate they expect in the future. Leaving effects on current account transactions out of the picture, the shift in the demand curve moves the market from its equilibrium at E_1 to a new equilibrium at E_2.

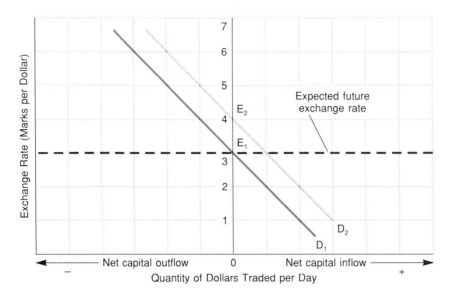

on capital account is shown by an upward and rightward shift in the capital account net demand curve from D_1 to D_2.

The shift in the demand curve that results from the relative increase in U.S. interest rates creates an excess demand for dollars in the foreign-exchange markets. The excess demand causes the exchange rate to rise above the average expected future level. As it does, investors must begin to consider the possibility that it will fall again at some time during the life of their investments. Leaving any effects on current account imports and exports out of the picture for the moment, the market will reach a new equilibrium at E_2. At that point, the appeal of the relatively higher U.S. interest rate for the marginal investor will be exactly offset by the expectation that the exchange rate will fall. The capital account will be restored to balance.

The example just given is simplified by the assumption of fixed price levels in both countries, but the model can be extended to the case in which inflation is possible at various rates in different countries. To make this extension, we can express both exchange rates and interest rates in real terms. In principle, a stable relationship prevails between real interest rates and real exchange rates even when inflation rates differ from one country to another. For example, beginning from the case illustrated in Exhibit 19.3, consider no change in Germany but an increase in the nominal interest rate that is associated with an equal increase in the expected U.S. inflation rate, thus leaving the expected real U.S. interest rate unchanged. This development would make dollar-denominated assets neither more nor less attractive to German investors. The reason is that the anticipated increase in the U.S. price level will be expected to cause a proportional depreciation in the nominal mark-dollar exchange rate. The higher nominal return on U.S. assets will thus be exactly offset by the expectation of a lower future nominal exchange rate and will be associated with an unchanged net quantity of dollars demanded on capital account.

However, a full development of real exchange rate determination under conditions of differential inflation is beyond the scope of this book. To keep things simple, we will now return to the assumption of fixed price levels in both countries. Under these conditions, real exchange rates are equal to nominal exchange rates and real interest rates to nominal interest rates.

Combining the Current and Capital Accounts

Having looked at the current and capital accounts separately, we will now combine them. Exhibit 19.4 shows how this is done. Part (a) shows the current account supply and demand curves; as we have seen, these reflect imports and exports of goods and services, plus transfer payments. Part (b) shows the capital account net demand curve, which reflects international purchases and sales of

Exhibit 19.4   Combining the Current and Capital Account Demand Curves

This graph shows how the current account demand curve for dollars and the capital account net demand curve can be added together to get a total demand curve for dollars. Total demand at each exchange rate equals current account demand plus the net capital inflow to the United States. If there is a net capital outflow from the United States, the total demand curve will lie to the left of the current account demand curve. Here the market is assumed to be in equilibrium at an exchange rate of 3 marks per dollar, which is also the average exchange rate expected in the future. At that point, both the current and capital accounts are in balance.

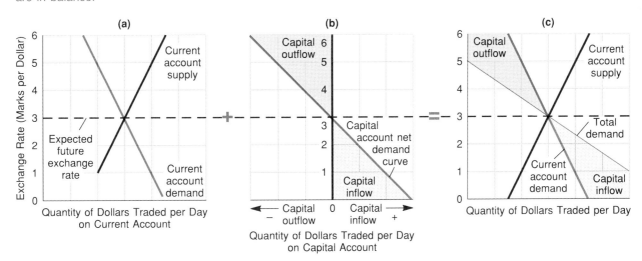

assets and international borrowing and lending. In this exhibit, the net quantity of dollars demanded in capital account transactions is positive when the exchange rate is below the expected future rate of 3 marks per dollar, indicating a net capital inflow. Above 3 marks per dollar, the net quantity of dollars demanded in capital account transactions is negative, indicating a net capital outflow.

Part (c) combines the two demand curves. The horizontal distance from the vertical axis to the total demand curve for dollars equals the sum of the current and net capital account demands. The total demand curve for dollars intersects the current account demand curve at the exchange rate for which the capital account is in balance, that is, at the point where the capital account net demand curve in part (b) intersects its vertical axis. Thus, at exchange rates below 3 marks per dollar, the total demand curve for dollars is greater than it would be if only current account transactions were considered. Above 3 marks per dollar, where the total demand curve lies to the left of the current account demand curve, the total demand for dollars is less than it would be if only current account transactions were considered.

In Exhibit 19.4 the market is in equilibrium at 3 marks per dollar, the exchange rate that corresponds to the average expected future rate. At this exchange rate, both the current and capital accounts are in balance. The value of imports plus net transfers equals that of exports, and capital inflows equal capital outflows. This position of the foreign-exchange market provides a useful benchmark for discussing policy issues—and, in a general sense, it is a position toward which foreign-exchange rates tend. However, in practice exchange rates may depart from expected future rates and the current and capital accounts can show surpluses or deficits, not only in the short run but often over periods of many years. In the next section, we examine some of the reasons for this.

19.2   Sources of Changes in Exchange Rates

This section will interpret changes in exchange rates in terms of the interaction of the current and capital accounts. As we will see, even when movements in exchange rates originate from changes in current account supply and demand, the capital account will be affected. Likewise, when movements in exchange rates originate from changes in capital account net demand, the current account will be affected. In the first case, the dog wags the tail; in the second, the tail wags the dog.

Exchange Rates and Economic Growth

As we have mentioned before, differences among countries in rates of economic growth are a key factor affecting exchange rates. We can now use our expanded supply-and-demand model to show the effects of differential growth rates in detail.

Exhibit 19.5 provides an illustration. At first, the foreign-exchange markets are in equilibrium at point E_1. The exchange rate is at 3 marks per dollar, which corresponds to the average expected future rate. Growth rates and interest rates in Germany and the United States are assumed to be equal, and both the current and capital accounts are in balance.

Starting from this situation, suppose that the rate of growth of the U.S. economy increases. To keep things simple, we will assume that this happens without affecting interest rates or upsetting the price stability assumed to prevail

Exhibit 19.5   Effects of an Increase in the U.S. Rate of Economic Growth

An increase in the rate of growth of the U.S. economy increases the demand for imports by U.S. households, firms, and government units. This shifts the current account supply curve for dollars to the right. In the process, an excess supply causes the dollar to depreciate. As the exchange rate depreciates below the average expected future rate of 3 marks per dollar, some investors shift out of mark-denominated assets into dollar-denominated ones. The resulting net capital inflow, shown as a movement downward and to the right along the total dollar demand curve, brings the market back into equilibrium at E_2. There the United States experiences a current account deficit, which is shown by the arrow between the current account demand curve and the current account supply curve for dollars. This deficit is offset by a net capital inflow.

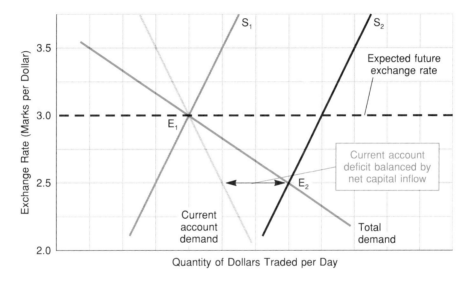

in both countries. As the economy grows, U.S. households and firms increase their spending on consumer goods, investment goods, and raw materials. Much of this spending is directed toward goods and services produced at home, but a certain fraction goes for goods and services imported from Germany. To get the marks they need to buy these imported goods, U.S. households and firms bring dollars to the foreign-exchange market. The result is a rightward shift in the current account supply curve from S_1 to S_2.

Given the position of the total demand curve, the increased supply of dollars puts downward pressure on the exchange rate. As the exchange rate begins to fall, both the current and capital accounts are affected. On the current account, the lower exchange rate makes U.S.-made goods cheaper for buyers in Germany. U.S. exports increase, as shown by a movement downward and to the right along the current account demand curve. On the capital account, investors see that the dollar has depreciated to a level below the expected future rate. This makes dollar-denominated assets more attractive. We assume that U.S. interest rates remain unchanged and international investors now face better odds that U.S. assets bought with marks now, when the dollar is low, can be converted back into marks later at a profit. Thus, the net quantity of dollars demanded on capital account also increases; this is shown as a widening gap between the current account and total demand curves for dollars as the exchange rate falls.

When the exchange rate falls to 2.5 marks per dollar, the foreign-exchange market reaches a new equilibrium at point E_2. Here the total quantity of dollars demanded has increased by enough to equal the quantity of dollars supplied. Note, however, that although the foreign-exchange market is back in equilibrium, the current and capital accounts are no longer in balance. As the arrow in Exhibit 19.5 shows, the current account demand for dollars falls short of the current account supply. This indicates that the value of imports exceeds the value of exports—a current account deficit. The remaining supply of dollars is absorbed by the net demand for dollars on capital account. Thus, the current account deficit is just offset by a net inflow of capital.

To summarize, when a country's rate of economic growth increases, other things being equal, its imports increase, its currency depreciates, and a current account deficit develops, offset by a net capital inflow. When a country's growth rate slows down relative to those of its trading partners, the opposite effects take place: Imports fall, the currency appreciates, and a current account surplus develops, offset by a net capital outflow.

Exchange Rates and Interest Rate Differentials

Changing real interest rate differentials among countries are another major factor affecting exchange rates. The relationship between interest rates and exchange rates was discussed in a preliminary way in Chapter 13. Exhibit 19.6 tells the interest rate story using our model of the foreign-exchange market.

At first, the market is again in equilibrium at 3 marks per dollar, which corresponds to the expected future rate. Growth rates and interest rates are the same in Germany and the United States, and both the current and capital accounts are in balance. Now we assume that interest rates increase in the United States but remain unchanged in Germany. To keep things simple, we will assume that this happens with no change in the U.S. or German rates of economic growth and with stable price levels in both countries.

An increase in U.S. interest rates relative to German rates makes dollar-denominated assets more attractive to investors. At the same time, it makes borrowing from U.S. sources less attractive. These developments are shown in Exhibit 19.6 by an upward and rightward shift in the total demand curve for dollars from D_1 to D_2. The current account demand curve remains in place, as the entire shift arises from the capital account.

Investors' increased demand for dollars puts upward pressure on the exchange rate. As the exchange rate rises, imports become cheaper for U.S. buyers. They supply more dollars to obtain the marks they need to buy additional imports, thereby moving upward and to the right along the current account supply curve. At the same time, U.S. exports become more expensive for German buyers. They demand fewer dollars, thus moving upward and to the left along the current account demand curve.

The capital account is also affected by the rising exchange rate. The higher the rate rises above the average expected future rate of 3 marks per dollar, the more widespread is the expectation that it will fall again during the time period affecting investors and borrowers. If it were to fall, holders of dollar-denominated assets would suffer a loss. This expectation of an exchange rate loss just offsets the attractiveness of relatively high interest rates on dollar-denominated assets for the marginal investor.

Exhibit 19.6   Effects of an Increase in the U.S. Interest Rate

This graph shows the effects of an increase in the U.S. interest rate relative to Germany's. The increase in the interest rates causes investors to switch to dollar-denominated assets and borrowers to switch to mark-denominated borrowing. The result is an upward shift in the capital account net demand curve for dollars and, hence, a shift in the total demand curve from D_1 to D_2. The shift in the demand curve causes an excess demand for dollars, and the dollar appreciates. As it does, U.S.-made goods become more expensive for German buyers and German-made goods become cheaper for U.S. buyers. The result is a current account deficit, as shown by the arrow. This is offset by a net capital inflow into the United States.

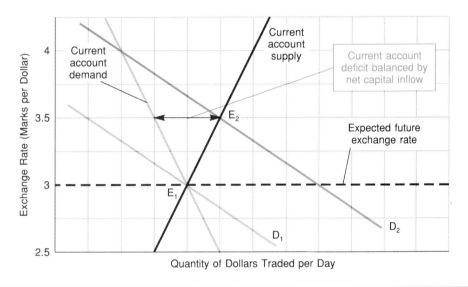

As the higher exchange rate reduces the number of dollars demanded on both current and capital account, the market moves upward and to the left along the new total demand curve for dollars. When it reaches point E_2, equilibrium is restored at an exchange rate of 3.5 marks per dollar. Note, however, that neither the current account nor the capital account is in balance. As the arrow in Exhibit 19.6 shows, the current account demand for dollars falls short of the current account supply, indicating a current account deficit. This deficit is offset by an equal net capital inflow.

It is useful to compare the results of an increase in the domestic growth rate (Exhibit 19.5) with those of an increase in domestic interest rates (Exhibit 19.6). In both cases, the United States develops a current account deficit accompanied by a net capital inflow. The effects on the dollar's value are in no way the same, however. In the case of relatively faster U.S. economic growth, a rightward and downward shift in the current account supply curve for dollars produces a current account deficit. It is this deficit that causes the exchange rate to fall. In the case of a higher U.S. interest rate, an upward and rightward shift in the capital account net demand curve for dollars causes the exchange rate to rise. It is this change in the exchange rate that causes a current account deficit.

Applying Economic Ideas 19.2
Interest Rates and the Dollar, 1973–1989

According to a standard model of foreign-exchange markets, an increase in U.S. interest rates relative to those of trading partners will, other things being equal, cause the dollar to appreciate. Similarly, a fall in U.S. interest rates relative to those abroad will cause the dollar to depreciate.

In the case in which inflation proceeds at different rates in various countries, the underlying relationship predicted by the model is most clearly brought out when expressed in terms of real rather than nominal interest rates and real rather than nominal exchange rates. In this chart, the real exchange rate is represented by a weighted average of the dollar's value relative to the currencies of 10 major trading partners, adjusted for movements in consumer prices both in the United States and its trading partners. The interest rate differential is the real interest rate on long-term U.S. securities minus the real rate on a weighted average of comparable long-term securities in the same 10 trading partners. Real interest rates for each country are the country's nominal interest rate minus a moving average of its inflation rate, which serves as a rough measure of the inflation rate that investors on the average expect.

The chart shows that movements in exchange rates do reflect movements in the interest rate differential during

several key periods. In the late 1970s, real interest rates in the United States fell because the U.S. inflation rate rose more rapidly than nominal interest rates. In this situation, foreign investors avoided dollar-denominated assets, and the dollar's real exchange rate hit record lows. In the early 1980s, the real interest rate differential rose substantially. This happened as nominal U.S. interest rates rose relative to the average rate of inflation. Many economists think that the high U.S. real rates of this period resulted from sizable increases in the federal budget deficit combined with disinflationary monetary policy. During these years, the dollar rose to record highs.

The fit between exchange rates and interest rates is not always exact, however. For example, the real interest rate differential began to fall early in 1984, but for a time, the real dollar exchange rate continued to rise—in fact, it rose at its most rapid rate of the entire period. Some observers have attributed the rise in the value of the dollar during this period to "safe haven" motives—foreign purchases of U.S. assets motivated by the relative political stability of the United States rather than by the financial return on those assets. Others interpret the peak of exchange rates in early 1985 as a "speculative bubble" that defies explanation in terms of economic fundamentals. By late 1985, as the real interest rate differential between the United States and its trading partners continued its downward course, the dollar began a rapid descent.

From 1987 to 1989, the real interest rate differential moved within a narrower range than in earlier years, as did the real exchange rate. As in the period 1973 to 1975, the variations in exchange rates that did occur do not closely follow the path of the interest rate differential. Evidently exchange rate movements were dominated by other considerations during these periods.

Sources: Federal Reserve Board macro database; Peter Hooper and Catherine Mann. Also see, Jeffrey A. Frankel, "Chartists, Fundamentalists, and Trading in the Foreign Exchange Market," *NBER Reporter* (Winter 1989–90), Figure 1. Reprinted with permission from the National Bureau of Economic Research.

An understanding of the effects of changes in interest rates and growth rates is useful in interpreting the dramatic changes in the international value of the dollar during the 1980s, as *Applying Economic Ideas 19.2* demonstrates.

The J-Curve Effect

The preceding examples suggest that other things being equal, a depreciation of a country's currency will move the current account toward surplus. By "other things being equal" in this case, we mean an appreciation or depreciation that

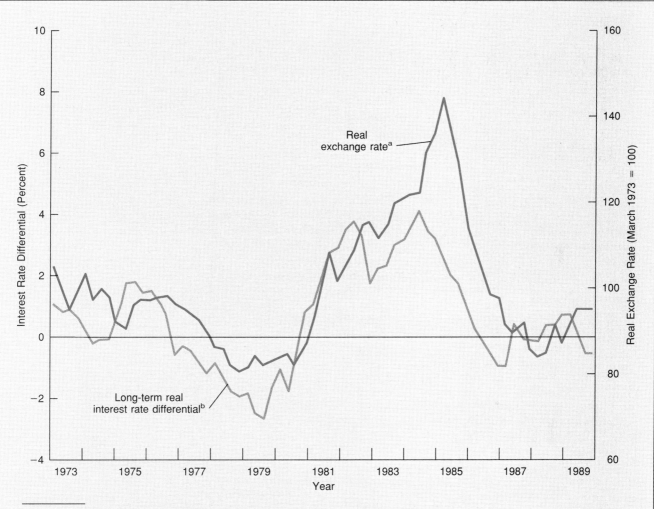

aThe CIP-adjusted dollar is a weighted average index of the exchange value of the dollar against
the currencies of the foreign G-10 countries plus Switzerland, where nominal exchange rates are
multiplied by relative levels of CPIs. Weights are proportional to each foreign country's share in
world exports plus imports from 1978 through 1983.
bLong-term real U.S. interest rate minus weighted average of long-term real foreign-country interest rates.

does not arise from a shift in either the current account supply curve or the
current account demand curve. This situation is illustrated in part (a) of
Exhibit 19.7. There, beginning from an equilibrium at E_1, a drop in the U.S.
interest rate shifts the total demand curve for dollars from D_1 to D_2. The economy moves to a new equilibrium at E_2, where D_2 intersects the current account
supply curve. At that point, the exchange rate is 2.5 marks per dollar. Because
the current account supply and demand curves have "normal" slopes, the quantity of dollars demanded on current account exceeds the quantity supplied, indicating a current account surplus. This current account surplus is balanced by a
net capital outflow.

Exhibit 19.7   The J-Curve Effect

This exhibit shows the effects of a downward shift in the total demand curve for dollars, caused by a decrease in U.S. interest rates, under two elasticity assumptions. If the demand for imported goods is elastic, the current account supply curve for dollars will have a positive slope, as shown in part (a). The shift in the demand curve from D_1 to D_2 will then move the foreign-exchange market to a new equilibrium at E_2, where there is a current account surplus balanced by a net capital outflow. In part (b), the demand for imports is assumed to be inelastic. The current account supply curve is negatively sloped and cuts the current account demand curve from below. The supply curve therefore lies to the right of the current account demand curve below their intersection at E_1. In this case, a downward shift in the total demand curve will move the economy to a new equilibrium in which there is a current account deficit balanced by a net capital inflow. If import and export demands are inelastic in the short run and more elastic in the long run, a downward shift in the total demand curve will cause the nominal current account to move first toward deficit and then toward surplus. This is known as the *J-curve effect*.

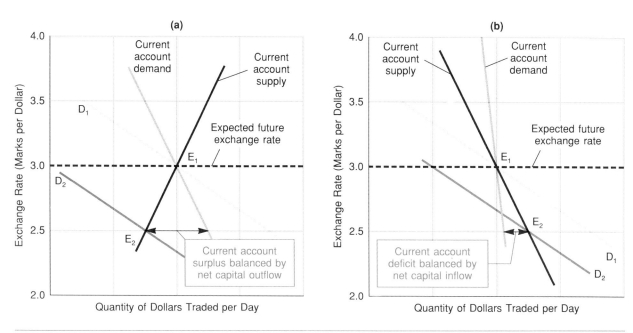

As we saw earlier in the chapter, however, the slopes of the current account supply and demand curves depend on the elasticity of demand for imports and exports. As we saw in Chapter 3, there are a variety of reasons to believe that the demands for most goods and services are less elastic in the short run than in the long run. This applies to goods traded in international markets just as to any other goods.

In the case of industrial goods, one reason why demand for both imports and exports tends to be less elastic in the short run than in the long run is the long order times that are often required. Aircraft, machine tools, oil rigs, and the like are not sold "off the shelf." On the contrary, commitments to buy these goods are made months or even years in advance of shipment. Thus, when exchange rates change, they affect shipments of such goods only after a considerable lag. Demand is also less responsive to price in the short run than in the long run for consumer goods. One reason is that it takes time for tastes and preferences to shift. For example, in the 1960s relatively few U.S. drivers bought imported cars, and those who did were attracted largely by the low prices. By the mid-1980s, however, imported cars had developed a reputation for quality and styling among U.S. buyers. Thus, after 1985 sales of imported cars fell only a little at first, even when the fall of the dollar drove their prices sharply higher. Finally, for both industrial goods and consumer goods, the full adjustment of demand to changes in prices may require replacement of durable industrial or consumer capital. For example, demand will not fully respond to an increase in imported fuel prices until firms and households have replaced transportation equipment, built new energy-efficient factories and houses, and so on.

Part (b) of Exhibit 19.7 shows the result of inelastic short-run demand for imports and exports. There the current account demand curve is steeper than in part (a), reflecting less elastic short-run demand in Germany for goods exported from the United States. As explained earlier in the chapter, inelastic demand for imports gives the current account supply curve a negative slope. However, here, in contrast to part (b) of Exhibit 19.1, the current account supply curve has a slope low enough to cut the current account demand curve from below rather than from above. Even so, it cuts the total demand curve for dollars, D_1, from above. This insures a stable equilibrium in the foreign-exchange market.

Given these curves, we can trace out what happens when falling U.S. interest rates shift the total demand curve downward from D_1 to D_2. The exchange rate, as usual, falls. As it does, the volume of exports rises. Although the increase is only slight, with the dollar price of U.S. exports unchanged, the quantity of dollars demanded on current account increases slightly, indicated by a move downward along the current account demand curve. At the same time, the falling exchange rate raises the dollar prices of imported goods, even though their prices in marks are unchanged. The rising dollar price reduces the physical volume of imports; fewer BMWs, fewer cases of German beer, and so on are imported than before. However, the physical volume of imports falls by a smaller percentage than the dollar prices increase; thus, more dollars than before must be supplied to purchase them. Hence, the foreign-exchange market moves down and to the right along the current account supply curve.

As the figure is drawn, the quantity of dollars supplied on current account increases more rapidly than the quantity of dollars demanded on current account. This indicates a deficit in the current account, which must be balanced by a net capital inflow.

The implication for policy is as follows. When a reduction in domestic real interest rates (or something else) causes the domestic currency to depreciate, the volume of imports and exports will change only slightly in the short run. Thus, the current account balance will move in the direction of deficit, as in part (b) of Exhibit 19.7. Over time, consumers and firms will adjust more fully to the change in the exchange rate. If the exchange rate remains at its new, lower level, the volume of exports will continue to rise and the volume of imports to shrink. As this happens, the current account will move toward surplus. The final outcome will look more like part (a) of Exhibit 19.7.

A curve showing the current account balance over time—first falling toward deficit, then rising toward surplus—is somewhat like the letter J. Accordingly,

Applying Economic Ideas 19.3
The J-Curve Effect and the Decline of the Dollar, 1985–1989

In the mid-1980s, the dollar rose to record highs on foreign-exchange markets (see part (a) of the accompanying chart). As it did, U.S. net exports, measured in both real and nominal terms, moved ever further into deficit (see part (b) of the chart). This surprised no one: The dollar's high value had made imported goods very cheap for U.S. buyers while at the same time making it very difficult for U.S. exporters to compete in world markets.

Beginning in the spring of 1985, the dollar's exchange rate fell sharply, in part because of changes in interest rate differentials and in part because of coordinated policy initiatives of major trading nations. Some observers expected an immediate improvement in the nominal trade deficit. Instead it began to turn upward only in the second half of 1987. Why?

The J-curve effect appears to be part of the explanation. The decline in the exchange rate made imports more costly for U.S. buyers and lowered the price of U.S. exports in world markets. As a result, by mid-1986 real U.S. exports were rising rapidly and the growth of real imports began to slow. As a result, real net exports began to rise in the second half of 1986, as shown in the chart. However, because short-run demand for imports is inelastic, the decline in the exchange rate at first forced up the current-dollar price of imports faster, in percentage terms, than the rate of growth of the real volume of imports decreased. Hence, nominal imports continued to grow rapidly for a

time even after growth of real imports had begun to slow. Just as the J-curve model predicts, nominal net exports turned upward later than real net exports—a full year later, in this case.

It might also be asked why the upturn in real net exports was delayed for six quarters after the exchange rate began its decline. It appears that during 1985 and 1986, several factors beyond the usual elasticity considerations operated to bolster the J-curve effect. For one thing, although the value of the dollar fell rapidly during 1985 and 1986 relative to the average of currencies of the "Group of 10" industrial countries, as shown in the chart, it changed little relative to the currencies of important trading partners such as Korea, Taiwan, and Canada. Accordingly, these countries were able to increase their share of the U.S. market at the expense of Japan, West Germany, and others whose currencies had risen sharply relative to the dollar.

Also, the textbook model of exchange markets assumes that changes in exchange rates are immediately passed on to buyers in the importing country as price changes. This was not what happened in many markets, however. During the early 1980s, when the dollar's value was rising, foreign firms widened their profit margins as well as increasing their volume of exports. When the dollar began to fall again, many of these firms at first absorbed the movement in exchange rates through reduced profit margins. This lessened the impact of the falling dollar on relative prices; thus, U.S. import prices in fact rose much less rapidly than they otherwise would have.

[a]Nominal weighted average exchange value of the dollar against G-10 plus Switzerland.
[b]Net exports, national income accounts basis (in billions and seasonally adjusted).

Source: Federal Reserve Board of Governors.

J-curve effect
A situation in which a country's nominal current account balance moves at first toward deficit and later toward surplus following a decrease in its currency's exchange rate.

this curve has come to be called the **J-curve effect.** *Applying Economic Ideas 19.3* discusses the operation of the J-curve effect as the value of the dollar fell in 1985 and 1986.

19.3 International Monetary Policy

Every change in exchange rates, whether upward or downward, helps some firms and individuals and hurts others, as illustrated by the news item that opened the chapter. When a country's currency appreciates, its export industries suffer, as do industries that compete with imports. However, consumers benefit from the availability of low-cost imports, and they profit from efforts by domestic producers to cut costs and improve quality in response to foreign competition. Also, profits rise and the number of jobs increases in sectors that use

(a)

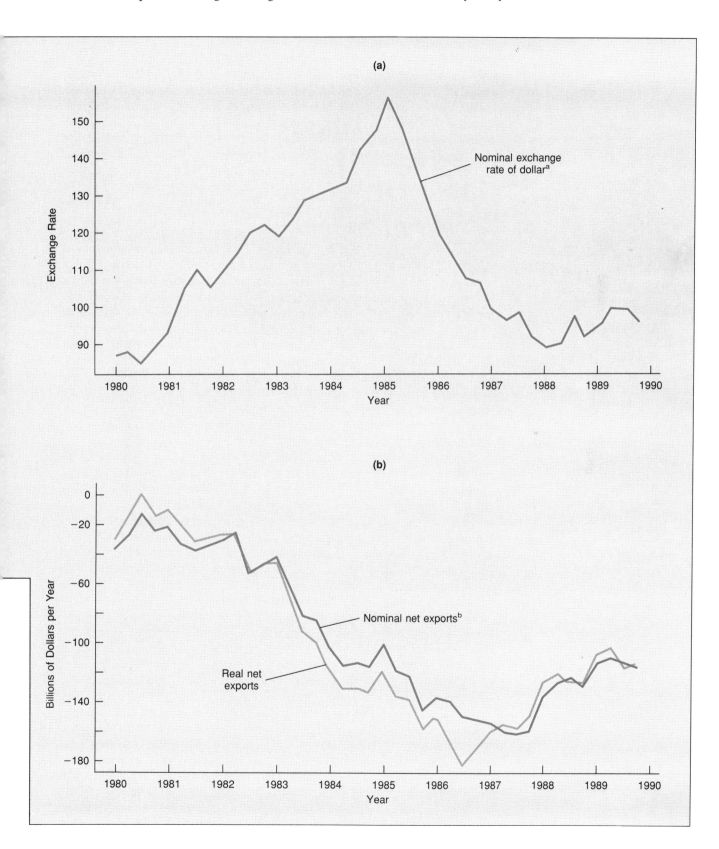

(b)

imported raw materials and in those devoted to marketing and servicing imported goods.

When a country's currency depreciates, the effects are reversed: Consumers face higher prices; people who sell and service imported goods suffer; but export industries boom, and import-competing industries enjoy a respite from international competition. The former winners become the losers, and vice versa.

These effects ensure that exchange rates are a matter of constant concern for policymakers. In preceding chapters, we saw several ways in which domestic and international economic policies interact. Now we will use our model of foreign-exchange markets to take a closer look at these phenomena.

Effects of Intervention

As we saw in Chapter 12, one option open to governments that wish to raise or lower exchange rates is to intervene in the exchange markets. Suppose, for example, that the Fed buys foreign currencies and sells dollars in an attempt to counter upward pressure on the exchange rate of the dollar. These transactions appear as a net outflow in the official reserve account section of the balance of payments statistics that were introduced in Chapter 6. The immediate impact of the sales of dollars would shift the demand curves for dollars to the left as the dollars sold by the Fed partially offset other net capital inflows. The reduced total demand for dollars would relieve the upward pressure on the exchange rate. Compared with what would have been, the lower exchange rate would eventually cause the value of exports to be higher and the value of imports to be lower, although the nominal deficit might temporarily be higher due to the J-curve effect.

However, as we know, the initial shift in the demand curve is not the only result of an official reserve account sale of dollars. The dollars sold could end up as new reserves in the U.S. banking system. The increase in the U.S. banking system's total reserves, in turn, would permit the U.S. money supply to expand.

To the extent that the government's goal is to get the exchange rate down, such an increase in the money supply is helpful. An increase in the money supply would depress U.S. interest rates at least temporarily. This, in turn, would cause a further downward shift in the capital account net demand curve for dollars. This further shift in the net demand curve would reinforce the initial shift and add downward pressure on the exchange rate.

However, the changes in reserves and the money supply resulting from intervention in the foreign-exchange market may conflict with the goals of domestic economic policy. The Fed can, and routinely does, *sterilize* the impact of official reserve transactions on domestic bank reserves by using domestic open market sales of government securities. The sterilization sales of securities will absorb reserves at the same time that intervention purchases of foreign currencies for dollars are creating reserves. Similarly, the Fed routinely uses domestic open market purchases of securities to create reserves at the same time that intervention sales of foreign currencies in exchange for dollars are absorbing reserves. However, sterilized intervention has far less impact on exchange rates than simple, unsterilized intervention. The volume of foreign-exchange-market transactions and the world stock of dollar-denominated assets are huge—more than $500 billion per day, by one estimate. Relative to this enormous daily volume of transactions, the impact of central banks' official reserve transactions is slight. Trying to stop or reverse fundamental market forces with a few billion dollars' worth of sterilized intervention is like trying to hold back the tide with a teacup.

Other Policies for Affecting the Exchange Rate

Because sterilized intervention gives only limited control over the exchange rate, governments in many countries have looked for alternatives. Pressure to find other means of controlling the exchange rate tends to be especially strong when a country's currency is depreciating and the government lacks the foreign-currency reserves necessary for sustained sterilized intervention.

One option is to use tariffs, import quotas, and other *protectionist* methods to restrain imports. If successful, these will shift the current account supply curve to the left, thus limiting downward pressure on the currency. However, this approach, though often tried, has drawbacks. It can raise import prices, contributing to domestic inflation. The inflation, in turn, can create expectations of future depreciation of the nominal exchange rate, thus sparking a capital outflow that will offset any gains on current account. Also, there is a distinct danger that trading partners will retaliate with protectionist measures of their own, thus harming exports.

Another option is to use export subsidies in an attempt to shift the current account demand curve for dollars to the right. Such policies are used by many countries, although only to a limited extent by the United States. They have drawbacks similar to those of import restrictions.

Still another option is to impose **exchange controls,** which are regulations that restrict the right to exchange the domestic currency for foreign currency. For example, countries may restrict the amount of currency that citizens can take abroad as tourists or allow access to the foreign-exchange markets only to those with "essential" import needs. If controls become so extensive that they permit no access whatever to exchange markets without government permission, the country's currency is said to be **inconvertible.** The currency of the Soviet Union as well as those of many third world countries are inconvertible.

All these policies—protectionism, export subsidies, and exchange controls—impose major costs on the domestic economy. They damage efficiency by distorting relative prices and prevent realization of gains from comparative advantage. The fact that these measures are nonetheless frequently employed reflects the political activities of those firms and workers that benefit from the reduction in international competition.

Exchange controls
Restrictions on the freedom of firms and individuals to exchange the domestic currency for foreign currencies at market rates.

Inconvertibility (of a currency)
A situation in which a country's currency can be exchanged for foreign currency only through a government agency or with a government permit.

Exchange Rate Management Systems

How should governments use their powers to intervene in foreign-exchange markets? This much-debated question has received varying answers in the post–World War II period. Sometimes central banks have actively intervened in the foreign-exchange markets on an almost daily basis. In the early 1980s, the U.S. Treasury and the Federal Reserve System followed a largely hands-off strategy. Then, in 1985, the United States joined with Japan, Britain, France, and Germany (the so-called Group of Five) in a coordinated effort to bring down the value of the dollar. In this section, we will look briefly at various systems for managing foreign-exchange rates.

Bretton Woods and the fixed-rate system.   After World War II, the major trading nations of the world met under United Nations auspices at Bretton Woods, New Hampshire, to forge a new world monetary system. That system, administered by the newly created International Monetary Fund (IMF), was based on a set of fixed exchange rates—four West German marks to the dollar, five French francs to the dollar, and so on. The member nations of the IMF agreed to maintain these rates through systematic intervention in foreign-exchange markets.

For example, suppose rapid growth of the French economy caused the value of the franc to fall relative to the dollar. The French central bank would support its currency by buying francs in the foreign-exchange markets. To be fully effective, these purchases would have to be unsterilized. As a result, they would drain francs from the domestic money supply at the same time that they propped up the exchange rate. Sooner or later, slower monetary growth would retard the growth of the French economy as a whole, which would remove the source of the downward pressure on the franc. Intervention could then stop, and the franc would be back in equilibrium at the agreed-upon level.

This system had both strengths and weaknesses. On the plus side, it controlled variations in exchange rates. Importers and exporters tended to like this situation, because it created a stable framework for business planning. However, the Bretton Woods system deprived national governments of a great deal of control over economic policy. They could not use domestic monetary policy to expand and contract their economies, control inflation, or create jobs; instead, domestic economic policy was constrained by the need to maintain exchange rates at a fixed level. Countries whose exchange rates tended to fall below the agreed-upon level had to accept lower growth rates than they wanted. Also, those whose currencies tended to push upward could be forced to take unwanted inflationary steps. To avoid these consequences, it was not uncommon for governments to resort to exchange controls, protectionism, and export subsidies.

In the early 1970s, the Bretton Woods system collapsed. Since then, most countries' currencies have been free to fluctuate, or "float," in foreign-exchange markets according to supply and demand.[2] What has been the experience with floating rates since 1973?

Experience with floating rates.   During its lifetime, the fixed-rate Bretton Woods system was criticized by many economists. They viewed it as a brake on world economic growth and free international trade. They especially resented the fact that many countries used protectionist measures and exchange controls, in addition to simple intervention, as a way of keeping their currencies at the agreed-upon exchange rates. The critics thought that if currencies were left free to respond to the forces of supply and demand, they would gravitate toward a set of natural exchange rate relationships. These would remain sufficiently stable over time to provide a basis for an efficient and growing world economy.

For the most part, the international monetary system has worked well since 1973. Few of the former critics of the Bretton Woods system have concluded that floating rates are a mistake. Even so, however, there have been some disappointments.

[2]There are exceptions. A group of countries in Western Europe have attempted to maintain exchange rates within a narrow range for their group. Also, some small countries have pegged their currencies to the U.S. dollar, the French franc, or some other major currency.

One of these was the worldwide spread of inflation during the 1970s. Fixed exchange rates help restrain inflation by forcing countries with weak currencies to intervene in foreign-exchange markets and thereby slow the growth of their domestic money supplies. Floating rates leave each country's government open to inflationary pressures from within its own political and economic systems. However, inflation among the major industrial countries has moderated since the early 1980s; thus, the worst of this problem may have passed.

The volatility of exchange rates has been another disappointment. In the short run, exchange rates have proven to be highly sensitive to every bit of new information that might bear on the expected future levels of exchange rates. Further, as shown in *Applying Economic Ideas 19.2*, the value of the dollar relative to other currencies and the value of other currencies relative to one another have also fluctuated over the longer run in the years since 1973—more widely than many Bretton Woods critics expected. These exchange rate fluctuations have produced boom-and-bust cycles in import and export industries such as those described in the article at the beginning of the chapter. It is hoped that steps toward greater international policy coordination will damp exchange rate fluctuations in the years ahead—but only time will tell.

Finally, floating rates have not brought an era of free world trade. Although it is true that many governments used Bretton Woods as a rationale for pursuing protectionist policies in the early postwar years, since 1973 governments have found many other excuses for doing so. The danger of a slide back into world-wide protectionism, which did so much damage to the world economy during the 1930s, persists despite floating rates.

Presently there is no realistic alternative to a floating-rate system. At every international conference on the subject, some speakers urge a return to a fixed-rate system. But the fact remains that national governments are not inclined to give up the control over their domestic economic policies that fixed exchange rates imply, nor do most economists think that fixed rates are superior to floating rates despite some disappointments with the latter.

The future, then, will almost certainly see a continuation of the present mixed system. The basis for the system is exchange rates that float against one another. However, the system is modified by exchange rate intervention (used more actively by some countries than by others), the existence of some currency blocs within which exchange rates are linked to one another, and protectionist policies that are often inspired by imbalances in current or capital accounts.

Summary

1. **How do current account supply and demand interact in foreign-exchange markets?** In the world of current account transactions, the demand for dollars arises from foreigners' demand for U.S. exports. The supply of dollars arises from the demand for imports by U.S. firms and households. The supply curve will have a positive slope if the demand for imports is elastic and a negative slope if the demand for imports is inelastic. A shift in either the supply curve or the demand curve will cause the exchange rate of the dollar for foreign currency to rise (*appreciate*) or fall (*depreciate*). In the long run, the exchange rate tends to-

ward *purchasing power parity*—a situation in which it reflects differences in price level between countries. However, exchange rates may depart substantially from purchasing power parity for many years.

2. **What are the considerations that determine the capital account net demand for dollars?** Capital account transactions can be represented by a *capital account net demand curve* for dollars. The negative slope indicates that, other things being equal, investors are attracted to assets denominated in currencies that they think are

likely to appreciate and avoid assets denominated in currencies that they believe will depreciate. An increase in the U.S. real interest rate relative to real interest rates abroad will shift the U.S. capital account net demand curve upward. The current and capital account demand curves can be added together to get a total demand curve for dollars in the foreign-exchange market.

3. How do changes in rates of real economic growth affect exchange rates? Other things being equal, an increase in the U.S. growth rate will increase the demand for imports. This will shift the supply curve for dollars to the right and put downward pressure on the exchange rate. As the exchange rate falls, the number of dollars demanded on both current and capital account will increase, as shown by a movement downward and to the right along the total demand curve for dollars. In the new equilibrium, the exchange rate will be lower and there will be a current account deficit offset by a net capital inflow.

4. How do changes in real interest rates affect exchange rates? Other things being equal (including fixed price levels), an increase in U.S. interest rates will cause an upward shift in the capital account net demand curve for dollars and, hence, in the total demand curve for dollars. This will put upward pressure on the exchange rate, and the dollar will appreciate. As it does, the value of U.S. imports will increase and the value of U.S. exports will decrease. In the new long-run equilibrium, the exchange rate will be higher and there will be a current account deficit offset by a net capital inflow. Similarly, a drop in U.S. interest rates will result in a lower exchange rate and a current account surplus. However, if the demand for imports and exports is inelastic in the short run, the *J-curve effect* will result in a short-run movement toward a nominal current account deficit following a depreciation of the currency, followed by a longer-run swing toward surplus.

5. What actions can governments take to influence exchange rates? Official reserve account transactions by central banks can be used to influence foreign-exchange rates. For example, the Federal Reserve System can sell dollars and buy foreign currency in foreign-exchange markets, shifting the dollar demand curve to the left and causing the dollar to depreciate. However, intervention can also upset plans for domestic monetary policy. To neutralize the impact of intervention on the domestic money supply, the Fed may sterilize the intervention by using domestic open market sales to soak up the dollars created by its official dollar sales in the foreign-exchange market. However, sterilized intervention has much less impact on the exchange rate than unsterilized intervention. Govern-

ments can also try to affect exchange rates through protectionist measures such as tariffs and import quotas, export subsidies, and *exchange controls.*

6. How has the international monetary system evolved since World War II? After World War II, the major trading nations met at Bretton Woods, New Hampshire, to set up a new international monetary system. That system featured fixed exchange rates. If supply and demand tended to push the value of a country's currency above or below the agreed-upon exchange rate, the country was supposed to intervene with official reserve sales or purchases. The Bretton Woods system was abandoned in the early 1970s. Since then, the world has operated with a system of floating exchange rates.

Terms for Review

-   appreciation
-   depreciation
-   purchasing power parity
-   capital account net demand curve
-   nominal exchange rate
-   real exchange rate
-   J-curve effect
-   exchange controls
-   inconvertibility

Questions for Review

1. What determines the slope and position of the demand curve for a country's currency when only current account transactions are considered? What determines the slope and position of the supply curve for its currency? Under what conditions can the supply curve have a negative slope?

2. Why does the capital account net demand curve for a country's currency have a negative slope? How is the curve affected by a change in the interest rate?

3. How does an increase in a country's rate of economic growth, other things being equal, affect its exchange rate, current account balance, and net capital flows?

4. How does an increase in a country's interest rate, other things being equal, affect its exchange rate, current account balance, and net capital flows?

5. How can official reserve transactions be used to affect a country's exchange rate? What is meant by *sterilization* of official reserve account transactions?

6. What kind of exchange rate system was established at the Bretton Woods conference after World War II? What kind of system has prevailed since 1973?

Problems and Topics for Discussion

1. **Examining the lead-off case.** The dollar underwent a dramatic depreciation from early 1985 to late 1986. Why did the U.S. current account deficit not close immediately? Why was the reduction of the current account deficit just getting seriously under way in 1988? Why do both widening and narrowing of the U.S. current account deficit cause "pain and disruption at home and abroad"? How, if at all, can such pain and disruption be avoided—or should an effort be made to avoid it?

2. **Exchange rates and currency reform.** In the mid-1980s, the Italian lira has traded at times at an exchange rate of as much as 2,000 lire per dollar. The Italian government from time to time has discussed the possibility of establishing a new unit of currency, a "strong lira," that would be worth 1,000 old lire. New currency would be issued to replace the old; all bank accounts would be changed over to the new unit; and so on. If the Italian currency reform were carried out, how would it affect the purchasing power parity of the dollar compared with the lira? How would it affect the nominal exchange rate? The real exchange rate?

3. **Growth abroad and the exchange rate.** Rework the graph presented in Exhibit 19.5 for a case in which the German growth rate speeds up while that of the United States stays the same. What happens to the supply curve? The current account, capital account net, and total demand curves? The exchange rate? The current account balance? Net capital flows?

4. **The J-curve effect.** Using the *Survey of Current Business* or another government statistical source, update the data given in **Applying Economic Ideas 19.3.** Is the pattern you observe consistent with the J-curve effect? Discuss.

5. **Exchange market intervention.** Every day *The Wall Street Journal* carries a column entitled "Foreign Exchange," which discusses the reasons for exchange rate changes during the previous trading day. Read a sample of these columns from recent issues of *The Wall Street Journal.* What countries' central banks, if any, have recently intervened in foreign-exchange markets, and why? What sources of changes in exchange rates other than central bank intervention have influenced exchange rates?

Case for Discussion

Leave the Trade Deficit Alone

To say that the United States has a trade deficit is to use a figure of speech. It is like saying that New York won the World Series when we really mean that the New York Mets, a team of young men who mostly live elsewhere, won it.

The fact is that a certain (unknown) number of Americans bought more abroad than they sold abroad and a certain other (unknown) number of Americans sold more than they bought abroad. The trade deficit is the excess of the net foreign purchases of the first group over the net foreign sales of the second group. It is a statistical aggregate.

My interest here is not simply in verbal precision. I am raising the question why any of us should worry about this particular statistic, and why the U.S. government should take any responsibility for it. The people who have the trade deficit—who are buying more abroad than they are selling—are doing so voluntarily. If they were worried much they would stop. I had a trade deficit in 1986 because I took a vacation in France. I didn't worry about it; I enjoyed it.

A cliche of these days is that the trade deficit of the present size cannot go on forever. That is not axiomatically true, but it is probably true. That does not, however, give any guidance. As I have said before, if something cannot go on forever it will stop. Government action to stop it is not required.

The trade deficit will end when Americans are no longer willing to borrow enough or foreigners are no longer willing to lend enough to finance it. These borrowers and lenders have a lot of their own money at stake and are at least as well informed and as well motivated as the government to decide when the deficit has gone too far.

A great source of confusion today is the common association of the term "trade deficit" with the term "competitiveness." The term "competitiveness" raises all kinds of images that give the trade deficit a popular emotional force that the mere economist's term does not have. Competitiveness evokes the spirit of a game, and suggests that the United States is losing. National pride is involved. Politicians are inspired to promise that they will make America "No. 1" again.

But the fact of the trade deficit does not mean that the United States is losing anything, and it is not a sign of economic weakness. Total output in the United States and total per-capita output are both higher now than when we last had a trade surplus (1982). We have a trade deficit because although we produce much, we use more, including what we invest for the future and use for the defense of the entire Free World. The United States can have a trade deficit only because the rest of the world has confidence in the U.S. economy and U.S. policy and is willing to invest here. No one has to hold dollars. Willingness of foreigners to do so is a sign of the strength of the United States, not of its weakness. Taiwan and South Korea have large trade surpluses. That does not make them stronger economies or countries than the United States.

Anyway, the belief that the United States is in economic competition with the other industrial countries that are our principal allies and trading partners is a mistake. To have high real output per capita in the United States is a good thing, but there is no advantage for us in its being higher than that of our friends. This is important to realize, because we cannot expect to have more output per capita than our friends forever.

Knowledge and capital move around the world with increasing ease. There is a strong tendency for levels of output per capita to converge—for the difference between the lowest and the highest to diminish. We will have to get used to living in a world in which we are no longer No. 1 in that sense, or at least not No. 1 by much.

There must be something more serious to worry about.

Source: Herbert Stein, "Leave the Trade Deficit Alone," *The Wall Street Journal*, March 11, 1987, 36. Reprinted by permission of The Wall Street Journal Editorial Department.

Questions

1. It is common for a balance of payments surplus to be called a "favorable" balance of payments and for a deficit to be called an "unfavorable" balance. In view of the points raised in this editorial, do you think this terminology is appropriate?

2. Suppose that a massive earthquake devastated the Japanese consumer electronics industry. What do you think would happen to the U.S. trade balance as a result? Who in the United States would benefit from this disaster? Who would suffer? In what sense, if any, would the United States "as a whole" be made better off?

3. When foreign firms sell goods and services to buyers in the United States, they earn dollars. They can use these dollars to buy goods and services produced in the United States, make loans to U.S. borrowers, or buy U.S. assets. How does their choice affect the U.S. balance of payments on current account? Who in the United States gains or loses as a result of their choice?

Suggestions for Further Reading

Grennes, Thomas. *International Economics.* Englewood Cliffs, N.J.: Prentice-Hall, 1984.

Chapters 14 through 24 review the economics of foreign-exchange markets and the international monetary system.

Melton, William C. *Inside the Fed.* Homewood, Ill.: Dow Jones-Irwin, 1985.

Chapter 11 of this book by a former Federal Reserve System official covers the relationship between domestic and international monetary policy.

President's Council of Economic Advisers. *Economic Report of the President.* Washington, D.C.: Government Printing Office, annually.

Each year's economic report contains a chapter on international economic policy.

Schwartz, Anna J. "Prospects for an International Monetary System Constitution." *Contemporary Policy Issues* (April 1987): 16–30.

Schwartz briefly reviews experience with Bretton Woods and the floating-rate system and then discusses several alternative proposals for a new international monetary system.

Appendix
Careers in Economics*

The General Value of an Economics Degree

In describing the qualities essential to being a good economist, John Maynard Keynes, himself a master at the profession, remarked:

> He must study the present in the light of the past for the purpose of the future.
> No part of man's nature or his institutions must lie entirely outside his regard.[1]

As you begin the study of economics, you will quickly become aware of the breadth to which Keynes refers. There seem to be no limits to the reaches of economic inquiry. Your first exam may include a question that applies to today's newspaper headlines. At the same time, economics is very much a part of your everyday life. A discussion with a local merchant concerning the price of an item may lead you to conclude that an understanding of economics is a matter of common sense. However, economics is not a subject to be left to common sense alone, since what is "common sense" to one person may well be "nonsense" to another.

The trained economist is a valuable and respected member of many organizations, be they private businesses, public utilities, governments, or colleges and universities. The career opportunities open to an economist are limited only by the resourcefulness of employers and employees. The following two sections will show you how an economics major can prepare you for a wide variety of careers in economics and will also briefly comment on the employment outlook for economists between 1987 and 1995. Every effort has been made to provide you, the beginning economics student, with the latest information concerning career opportunities in economics. Major assistance was provided by the National Association of Business Economists (NABE) through its secretary-treasurer, David L. Williams. In addition, the attitudes, opinions, and experiences of successful, currently employed business and government economists were solicited by means of a questionnaire sent to a significant number of randomly selected members of the NABE and the Society of Government Economists. (This will be referred to below as the *Dryden questionnaire* to distinguish it from the NABE publications used.)

Even if your career interests lie in other directions, the analytical training emphasized in an economics major generally can make you more adaptable to changing employment opportunities after graduation. As one member of the

---

*This appendix was written by Keith D. Evans, chairman of the Department of Economics at California State University, Northridge. It was prepared with the cooperation of the National Association of Business Economists and the Society of Government Economists.
[1] John Maynard Keynes, *Essays in Biography*, ed. Geoffrey Keynes (New York: Norton, 1963).

NABE puts it, "Some theoretical micro and macro concepts proved useful; however, more often than not my training in analyzing and researching subjects was used." Further, there are definite benefits in having a thorough understanding of how our private enterprise economy works and a basis for comparing it with centrally planned economies. Often people report that in their first career jobs they literally got lost in a maze—they had no sense of where they fit in and how their jobs pertained to a larger picture. A background in economics can ease that shock. The analytical training, with specific applications to real-life situations, makes it easier to come to grips with the events of the world around us.

One respondent to the Dryden questionnaire put it this way: "My work in economics prepared me well for career advancement and flexibility because of the emphasis my economics study placed on cause-and-effect relationships, on the link between incentives and resultant actions, all of which have helped me develop a rational and productive way of generating results-oriented thinking." Another replied that the most useful part of his training in economics was "flexibility, perspective, and ability to deal with intangibles and uncertainty." Still another successful career economist reflected on the importance of his economics degree as follows: "It taught me the ability to think and to reason."

You cannot possibly learn all you will need to know in four years of college; but in pursuing a degree in economics, you can learn how to think better. With that ability, your opportunities are immensely varied and exciting.

Career Opportunities Available to an Economics Major

It is not enough to tell yourself that you will study economics because in doing so you will learn how to think better and thinking better is essential to a career as an economist. Choosing a course of study in college is more likely to lead to a successful career if you discover which subjects interest you and in which you do well. Thus, it follows that if you enjoy and do well in courses in economics and business administration, you will very likely enjoy a career as an economist.

But what are your opportunities as an economics major? What type of work might you actually do as an economist? In general—and depending on the amount of education you ultimately receive—your future lies in one of three areas: working in one of a wide variety of positions in private business; serving in a local, state, or national government agency; and teaching economics at the college and university level. In fact, many economists combine their primary work in one of these fields with part-time work in another. It is not unusual for a business economist to teach part time or for a professor to also be a consultant to business or government.

Economics as an academic subject goes back more than 150 years. In practical terms, economists found that their theories increasingly influenced federal government decisions as the Depression of the 1930s occupied worldwide attention. It was not until after World War II, however, that private businesses began to realize the extent to which economic theory might be applied in solving business problems and formulating business policies. Despite this relatively late start, about 23,000 of the people identified as economists by the Bureau of Labor Statistics in 1984 work in private business.[2] They are employed by manufacturing firms, banks, insurance companies, securities and investment companies, economic research firms, management consulting firms, and others.

---

[2] U.S. Department of Labor, Bureau of Labor Statistics, *Occupational Outlook Handbook*, 1986–1987 ed. (Washington, D.C.: Government Printing Office, April 1986), 102.

Business organizations that are large enough to warrant having their own economists employ them directly. Smaller firms hire the services of economic consultants as needed. Regardless of their size, all businesses are aware that government policies and subsequent actions have economic effects. A major function of the business economist, therefore, is to analyze and interpret government policies in light of their effects on the economy in general and the specific firm in particular.

According to the same 1984 Bureau of Labor Statistics report, another 15,000 economists are employed by government agencies, including a wide range of federal agencies. In addition, approximately 22,000 hold economics and marketing faculty positions at colleges and universities.

Certainly the primary function of the business economist is to apply economic theory to problems faced by the firm. This requires the ability to understand the economic implications of events taking place throughout the world; to project how those events might affect the firm; to prepare guidelines for decision makers in the organization; and to communicate concepts, principles, and conclusions in a clear, effective, and concise manner.

In a booklet entitled *Careers in Business Economics*, the National Association of Business Economists stresses that business economists follow no set patterns. The most successful, established economists have high job mobility because their ability to interpret national and international events in light of their economic impact on a particular sector of business makes them especially adaptable to changing business requirements.

Following are descriptions of the activities of several kinds of business economists based on *Careers in Business Economics*.

Bank Economist

> The primary function of our bank's economics department is to analyze how changes in economic and financial market conditions affect the banking business and to suggest—to the extent possible—appropriate strategies and policies to protect or enhance the bank's earnings. Obviously, this is an assignment of tall order and presents great challenges as well as opportunities.[3]

An essential analytical tool that the *bank economist* must develop is the macroeconomic forecast. Such a forecast forms the basis for anticipating changes in the bank's volume of business—primarily its loans and investments. Even more important for the bank economist is a firm grasp of the underlying forces that determine interest rates. Changes in interest rates directly affect the spread between the yields the bank earns on its investments and the cost of acquiring investment funds. Hence, the profitability of a bank's operations hinges on correctly anticipating interest rate changes.

A bank also manages and invests money for customers through its trust department. Thus, the bank economist's expertise can be highly valuable, since sound investment strategies depend on expert judgment of economic and financial trends. In addition, the bank economist represents the bank in interviews with financial reporters and is likely to be quoted in newspapers and magazines. Further, the bank economist may write newsletters for the bank and make numerous presentations both within and outside. Hence, good communication skills are essential.

---

[3] National Association of Business Economists, *Careers in Business Economics* (Cleveland, Ohio, 1986), 10.

As you can see, the bank economist's job responsibilities are very important. The bank economist constantly interacts with high-level managers and is often a member of the senior management team.

Consulting Economist

The following quote from *Careers in Business Economics* indicates the nature of the duties performed by the *consulting economist:*

> Within our firm, we conduct research and advise clients of developments affecting financial institutions, trends in economic activity, and interest rates in money and capital markets—with special emphasis on the monetary policy of the Federal Reserve. The firm has carried out a number of assignments—including the preparation of estimates of the cost of capital for public utilities, assessments of the impact of alternative tax measures on the volume of investment, the impact of research and development expenditures on technology and innovation in American industry, the economic cost of restrictions on a range of imports, excise taxes and the demand for distilled spirits, monetary policy and the housing sector, and the economic benefits of lease financing.[4]

Like a bank economist, a consulting economist may also do macroeconomic forecasting. The results of research done by consulting economists are usually given to their clients as private reports. Some of the findings of economics consulting firms, however, are made public in the form of reports, congressional testimony, and publications in professional journals.

Industrial Economist

An *industrial economist* employed by a large, widely diversified manufacturing company writes:

> The most important part of my job is meeting with our management committee every month to discuss economic and political developments in the countries where we have operations, and the likely impact of such developments on our businesses. Preparation for these meetings involves maintaining contacts with a large number of economists, business analysts, and academic experts around the world. This means that I'm usually on an airplane about four out of every five weeks and am physically out of the office about 60 percent of the time.[5]

The industrial economist also does macroeconomic forecasting, but on an international level. It is common for industrial economists to participate in preparing forecasts of their firms' operations for as much as 10 years in advance. Some industrial economists also engage in "structural analysis," which involves "the basic econometric analysis of the relationships among various businesses with a variety of external series as well as internal data, such as advertising expense, research and development programs, capital expenditures, and so on. The results are used to evaluate strategic plans of individual businesses, to determine the relative impacts of various external policy changes, and to determine strategies for improving profitability."[6]

---

[4] Ibid., 13.

[5] Ibid., 17.

[6] Ibid.

Like the bank economist, the industrial economist usually represents his or her firm in interviews requested by the news media, might prepare a newsletter, and may make numerous presentations to groups outside the company.

Government Economist

The *government economist* may perform essentially the same tasks as business economists as far as forecasting the outcome of economic conditions is concerned. However, the emphasis may be on formulating policy rather than reacting to policy changes, since the government agency can be in a position to initiate economic changes. The government economist may be called upon to do research on major policy issues, draft speeches for legislators and government officials, and help determine the purpose and scope of congressional hearings.

Academic Economist

The *academic economist* concentrates on the understanding and improvement of economic theory. In teaching theory, he or she stresses how economies function and how a knowledge of economics applies to decision making by business and government as well as individuals. In addition, the academic economist may devote some time to research, writing, and consulting with business firms, government agencies, or private individuals.

Advice from Practicing Economists

The Dryden questionnaire asked members of the National Association of Business Economists and the Society of Government Economists to reflect on the value of their college education and to offer advice for people just beginning the study of economics. Of those whose major was economics, more than two-thirds from each group reported that their college studies had been very useful to them in their first full-time jobs. From the vantage point of their ultimate careers, more than half felt that their college education was useful in performing the duties of their present occupations. What courses did they feel had such lasting value? Both business and government economists most frequently mentioned courses in microeconomic and macroeconomic theory, econometrics (the application of statistical techniques to obtain quantitative estimates of relationships suggested by economic analysis), money and banking, forecasting, and international economics and courses that provided specific applications of economic theory to the decision-making process or to public policy.

Respondents also emphasized the importance of courses involving economic and business applications of statistics and accounting, as well as the study of related business institutions, especially financial ones. Important too were courses on using and programming computers. Mathematics courses were emphasized as having been helpful. Along with the references to applied statistics, there was continual mention of such courses as analytical geometry, calculus, and linear algebra.

One necessary skill for an economist, whether academic, business, or government, cannot be overemphasized: the ability to make the results of one's work understandable to a wide range of people. To be useful, economic analyses and forecasts must be understood by those who make the decisions for the business or government agency involved. Therefore, an economist must be able to write and speak clearly and to state sophisticated economic ideas in a way that people with little economic knowledge can understand. Recognizing this need to make their work clear and usable for others, both government and business economists placed high value on courses that improved their written and oral communication skills.

The NABE advises potential business economists to strive to be generalists rather than specialists. Its *Careers in Business Economics* booklet recommends some familiarity with as many of the major fields of economics and business administration as possible. In addition to the areas mentioned by the Dryden questionnaire respondents, economics and business administration deal with economic and business history, national income and public finance, business cycles and government stabilization policies, corporate finance and industrial organization, marketing and consumer behavior, labor and collective bargaining, purchasing and personnel policies, and economic development and comparative economic systems.

Some respondents to the Dryden questionnaire had not majored in economics at the undergraduate level. Many of them said they had benefited from the broad-based liberal arts education they acquired before earning advanced degrees in economics or business. It was generally agreed, however, that any liberal arts major would be well advised, considering the current job market, to take courses in economics, accounting, statistics, and computer science.

Interestingly, in the last three to four years many major corporations have begun to look increasingly favorably on candidates who have earned an undergraduate liberal arts degree, especially if they have done well at universities that are held in high academic regard at least regionally, if not nationally. Such individuals, however, are expected to have taken relevant courses in economics and applied statistics, as well as business courses such as accounting fundamentals and principles of finance. Moreover, business and government recruiters have become increasingly insistent that students be exposed to a variety of "hands-on" computer applications, ideally including some programming. All of the fields of economics profiled earlier require extensive use of computers.

June Hillman, associate director of the Office of Career Planning and Placement at California State University, Northridge, summarized this recent change in attitude on the part of recruiters as follows: "Recruiters are tending to be attracted to the well-educated university graduate with some business-related courses and work experience rather than the specific, vocationally oriented majors. This continues to be a trend in recruiting criteria."[7]

For further support of the recent change in attitude by many recruiters toward liberal arts graduates, refer to the references at the end of the *Study Guide* career section.

It should be added that the guidelines presented here must be taken in the spirit in which they have been given—as suggestions from practicing economists. When you are planning your particular course of study to fulfill the requirements of your college or university and to satisfy your unique interests, you cannot expect these guidelines to replace the need for personal faculty advice.

How important is an advanced degree? For an academic economist, it is a must. A master's degree is the minimum qualification for teaching at the community college level, and a Ph.D. is required for most university teaching.

[7] Interview given September 30, 1987.

Eighty percent of the government economists who responded to the Dryden questionnaire indicated that they consider an advanced degree very important, and 11 percent consider one moderately important. Of that number, 56 percent specified a Ph.D. while an additional 25 percent emphasized a master's degree. The business economists surveyed placed less importance on an advanced degree. Only 57 percent rated it as very important, and 25 percent considered it moderately important. Those responses were much more evenly distributed regarding which advanced degree is more important. Almost 30 percent favored the M.B.A., while another 30 percent suggested pursuing either an M.A. or an M.S. degree in economics or business administration. Only 35 percent considered a doctorate essential.

These differences undoubtedly reflect the attitudes of various employers in different businesses and government agencies. Again they are presented here as guidelines that can be one source of help to you as you make your own career decisions.

Employment Outlook for Economists, 1987–1995

Before launching into some "fearless forecasts" for the employment outlook for economists in the 1990s, *caveat emptor:* Let the buyer, whether of tangible goods or intangible ideas, beware. Keeping in mind this recognition that all forecasts are fallible, let's look at the current thought regarding the employment outlook for economists in the decade ahead.

The U.S. Department of Labor offers the following job outlook for economists:

> Employment of economists is expected to grow about as fast as the average for all occupations through the mid-1990's. Most job openings will result from the need to replace experienced economists who transfer to other occupations, retire, or leave the labor force for other reasons.
>
> Overall, economists are likely to have more favorable job prospects than most other social scientists. Opportunities should be best in manufacturing, financial services, advertising agencies, research organizations, and consulting firms, reflecting the complexity of the domestic and international economies and increased reliance on quantitative methods of analyzing business trends, forecasting sales, and planning purchasing and production. The continued need for economic analyses by lawyers, accountants, engineers, health service administrators, urban and regional planners, environmental scientists, and others will also increase the number of jobs for economists.[8]

The U.S. Department of Labor projects little change in the employment of economists in the federal government. Average growth is expected in the employment of economists in state and local government.[9]

The National Association of Business Economists agrees that job prospects are by far the brightest for various types of business economists. Besides the reasons given in the above quoted passage, the NABE points out that more and more firms are becoming aware of the contribution that business economists can make in day-to-day decision making. This greater awareness is due partly to the

---

[8] U.S. Department of Labor, *Occupational Outlook Handbook*, 103.

[9] Ibid.

growing number of middle and top managers who have master's degrees in business or similar training that equips them to understand and utilize the professional work of economists.[10]

> Finally, the career of business economics is increasingly recognized as one of the routes to top management. In recent years, business economists have become presidents or senior officers of banks, insurance companies, trade associations, investment houses, and industrial companies. Although not all business economists are capable or even desirous of advancing to a top management position, it is clear that economics is a business function of central importance and thus can be a pathway to the top.[11]

Because of the relative difficulty of obtaining satisfactory employment in an academic setting, many people who might otherwise have directed themselves toward a career in higher education are now accepting nonacademic jobs. That puts graduates with bachelor's degrees in a position of competing not only with others of similar academic background and level but also with candidates who have more advanced degrees. However, through the mid-1990s graduates with bachelor's degrees in economics should compete well if they have training in applied mathematics, statistics, and computer use.

These indicators are in harmony with the comments of several respondents to the Dryden questionnaire, who believe that the best preparation for many of today's careers in economics begins with an undergraduate degree in economics and continues with acquisition of an M.B.A.

---

[10] National Association of Business Economists, *Careers in Business Economics*, 28.
[11] Ibid.

Dictionary of Economic Terms

Accelerationist model of inflation
A theory according to which changes in the inflation rate affect unemployment and real output.

Adaptive-expectations hypothesis
The hypothesis that people form their expectations about future economic events mainly on the basis of past economic events.

Aggregate demand
The value of all planned expenditures.

Aggregate demand curve
A graph showing the relationship between real planned expenditures on final goods and the average price level of final goods.

Aggregate supply
The value of all goods and services produced in the economy; a synonym for national product.

Aggregate supply curve
A graph showing the relationship between real output (real national product) and the average price level of final goods.

Appreciation (of a currency)
An increase in the value of a country's currency relative to another's.

Assets
All the things that the firm or household owns or to which it holds a legal claim.

Automatic fiscal policy
Changes in government purchases or net taxes that are caused by changes

in economic conditions given unchanged tax and spending laws.

Automatic stabilizers
Those elements of automatic fiscal policy that move the federal budget toward deficit during an economic contraction and toward surplus during an expansion.

Autonomous
In the context of the Keynesian income-expenditure model, refers to an expenditure that is independent of the level of real national income.

Autonomous consumption
The part of total real consumption expenditure that is independent of the level of real disposable income; for any given consumption schedule, real autonomous consumption equals the level of real consumption associated with zero real disposable income.

Autonomous net taxes
Taxes or transfer payments that do not vary with the level of national income.

Average propensity to consume
Total consumption for any income level divided by total disposable income.

Balance sheet
A financial statement showing what a firm or household owns and what it owes.

Base year
The year that is chosen as a basis for comparison in calculating a price index or price level.

Bond
A certificate that represents a promise, in return for borrowed funds, to repay the loan over a period of years, with interest, according to an agreed-upon schedule.

Business cycle
A pattern of irregular but repeated expansion and contraction of aggregate economic activity.

Capital
All means of production that are created by people, including tools, industrial equipment, and structures.

Capital account
The section of a country's international accounts that consists of purchases and sales of assets and international borrowing and lending.

Capital account net demand curve
A graph that shows the net demand for a country's currency that results at various exchange rates from capital account transactions.

Capital inflows
Net borrowing from foreign financial intermediaries and net funds received from sales of real or financial assets to foreign buyers.

Capital outflows
Net lending to foreign borrowers and net funds used to purchase real or financial assets from foreign sellers.

Change in demand
A change in the quantity of a good

that buyers are willing and able to purchase that results from a change in some condition other than the price of that good; shown by a shift in the demand curve.

Change in quantity demanded
A change in the quantity of a good that buyers are willing and able to purchase that results from a change in the good's price, other things being equal; shown by a movement from one point to another along a demand curve.

Change in quantity supplied
A change in the quantity of a good that suppliers are willing and able to sell that results from a change in the good's price, other things being equal; shown by a movement along a supply curve.

Change in supply
A change in the quantity of a good that suppliers are willing and able to sell that results from a change in some condition other than the good's price; shown by a shift in the supply curve.

Circular flow of income and product
The flow of goods and services between households and firms, balanced by the flow of payments made in exchange for goods and services.

Closed economy
An economy that has no links to the rest of the world.

Commercial banks
Financial intermediaries that provide a broad range of banking services, including accepting demand deposits and making commercial loans.

Common stock
A certificate of shared ownership in a corporation that gives the owner a vote in the selection of the firm's management and the right to a share in its profits.

Comparative advantage
The ability to produce a good or service at a relatively lower opportunity cost than someone else.

Complements
A pair of goods for which an increase in the price of one results in a decrease in demand for the other.

Conditional forecast
A prediction of future economic events in the form "If A, then B, other things being equal."

Consumer price index
An average of the prices of goods and services purchased by a typical urban household.

Consumption function
See Consumption schedule.

Consumption schedule
A graph that shows how real consumption expenditure varies as real disposable income changes, other things being equal.

Corporation
A firm that takes the form of an independent legal entity with ownership divided into equal shares and each owner's liability limited to his or her investment in the firm.

Cost-push inflation
Inflation that is caused by an upward shift in the aggregate supply curve while the aggregate demand curve remains fixed or shifts upward more slowly.

Crowding-out effect
The tendency of expansionary fiscal policy to raise the interest rate and thereby cause a decrease in real planned investment.

Currency
Coins and paper money.

Current account
The section of a country's international accounts that consists of imports and exports of goods and services and unilateral transfers.

Current account balance
The value of a country's exports of goods and services minus the value of its imports of goods and services plus its net transfer receipts from foreign sources.

Cyclical deficit
The difference between the actual federal deficit and the structural deficit.

Cyclical unemployment
The difference between the observed rate of unemployment at a given point in the business cycle and the natural rate of unemployment.

Demand curve
A graphical representation of the relationship between the price of a good and the quantity of that good that buyers demand.

Demand-pull inflation
Inflation caused by an upward shift of the aggregate demand curve while the aggregate supply curve remains fixed or shifts upward at no more than an equal rate.

Depository institutions
Financial intermediaries, including commercial banks and thrift institutions, that accept deposits from the public.

Depreciation (of a currency)
A decline in the value of a country's currency relative to another's.

Discount rate
The interest rate charged by the Fed on loans of reserves to banks.

Discount window
The department through which the Federal Reserve lends reserves to banks.

Discouraged worker
A person who would work if a suitable job were available but has given up looking for such a job.

Discretionary fiscal policy
Changes in the laws regarding government purchases and net taxes.

Disposable income
See Disposable personal income.

Disposable personal income
Personal income less personal taxes (particularly income taxes).

Economic efficiency
A state of affairs in which it is impossible to make any change that satisfies one person's wants more fully without causing some other person's wants to be satisfied less fully.

Economic rent
Any payment to a factor of production in excess of its opportunity cost.

Economics
The social science that seeks to understand the choices people make in using scarce resources to meet their wants.

Efficiency in distribution
A situation in which it is not possible, by redistributing existing supplies of goods, to satisfy one person's wants more fully without causing some other person's wants to be satisfied less fully.

Efficiency in production
A situation in which it is not possible, given available knowledge and productive resources, to produce more of one good without forgoing the opportunity to produce some of another good.

Employed
A term used to refer to a person working at least 1 hour a week for pay or at least 15 hours per week as an unpaid worker in a family business.

Employment-population ratio
The percentage of the noninstitutional adult population that is employed.

Entitlements
Transfer payments governed by long-term laws that are not subject to annual budget review.

Entrepreneurship
The process of looking for new possibilities—making use of new ways of doing things, being alert to new opportunities, and overcoming old limits.

Equation of exchange
An equation that shows the relationship among the money stock (M), the income velocity of money (V), the price level (P), and real national product (y); written as MV = Py.

Equilibrium
A condition in which buyers' and sellers' plans exactly mesh in the marketplace, so that the quantity supplied exactly equals the quantity demanded at a given price.

Excess quantity demanded (shortage)
A condition in which the quantity of a good demanded at a given price exceeds the quantity supplied.

Excess quantity supplied (surplus)
A condition in which the quantity of a good supplied at a given price exceeds the quantity demanded.

Excess reserves
Total reserves minus required reserves.

Exchange controls
Restrictions on the freedom of firms and individuals to exchange the domestic currency for foreign currencies at market rates.

Expenditure multiplier
The ratio of the resultant shift in real aggregate demand to an initial shift in real planned investment (or other expenditure).

Externalities
The effects of producing or consuming a good whose impact on third parties other than buyers and sellers of the good is not reflected in the good's price.

Factors of production
The basic inputs of labor, capital, and natural resources used in producing all goods and services.

Federal funds market
A market in which banks lend reserves to one another for periods as short as 24 hours.

Federal funds rate
The interest rate on overnight loans of reserves from one bank to another.

Final goods and services
Goods and services that are sold to or are ready for sale to parties that will use them for consumption, investment, government purchases, or export.

Financial intermediaries
A group of firms, including banks, insurance companies, pension funds, and mutual funds, that gathers funds from net savers and lends them to net borrowers.

Financial markets
A set of market institutions whose function is to channel the flow of funds from net savers to net borrowers.

Fiscal policy
Policy that is concerned with government purchases, taxes, and transfer payments.

Fiscal year
The federal government's budgetary year, which starts on October 1 of the preceding calendar year.

Fixed investment
Purchases by firms of newly produced capital goods, such as production machinery, office equipment, and newly built structures.

Flow
A process that occurs continuously through time, measured in units per time period.

Foreign exchange market
A market in which the currency of one country is traded for that of another.

Frictional unemployment
The portion of unemployment that is accounted for by the short periods of unemployment needed for matching jobs with job seekers.

GNP deflator
A weighted average of the prices of

all final goods and services produced in the economy.

Goods
All things that people value.

Gross national product (GNP)
A measure of the economy's total output of goods and services; the dollar value at current market prices of all final goods and services produced annually by a nation's factors of production.

Growth recession
A situation in which real output grows, but not quickly enough to keep unemployment from rising.

Hyperinflation
Very rapid inflation.

Income-expenditure model
The Keynesian model in which the equilibrium level of real national income is determined by treating real planned expenditure and real national product as functions of the level of real national income.

Income-product line
A graph showing the level of real planned expenditure (aggregate demand) associated with each level of real national income.

Inconvertibility (of a currency)
A situation in which a country's currency can be exchanged for foreign currency only through a government agency or with a government permit.

Indexation
A policy of automatically adjusting a value or payment in proportion to changes in the average price level.

Inferior good
A good for which an increase in consumer incomes results in a decrease in demand.

Inflation
A sustained increase in the average price level of all goods and services.

Inflationary recession
An episode in which real output falls toward or below its natural level and unemployment rises

toward or above its natural rate while rapid inflation continues.

Injections
Flows of funds into domestic product markets that do not begin with the consumption expenditures of domestic households; included are investment, government purchases, and exports.

Inside lag
The delay between the time a policy change is needed and the time a decision is made.

Inventory
A stock of a finished good awaiting sale or use.

Inventory investment
Changes in the stocks of finished products and raw materials that firms keep on hand; the figure is positive if such stocks are increasing and negative if they are decreasing.

Investment
The act of increasing the economy's stock of capital, that is, its supply of means of production made by people.

J-curve effect
A situation in which a country's nominal current account balance moves at first toward deficit and later toward surplus following a decrease in its currency's exchange rate.

Labor
The contributions to production made by people working with their minds and muscles.

Labor force
The sum of all individuals who are employed and all individuals who are unemployed.

Law of demand
The principle that an inverse relationship exists between the price of a good and the quantity of that good that buyers demand, other things being equal.

Leakages
The parts of national income that are not used by households to buy

domestic consumer goods; included are saving, net taxes, and purchases of imports.

Liabilities
All the legal claims against a firm by nonowners or against a household by nonmembers.

Liquidity
An asset's ability to be used directly as a means of payment, or to be readily converted into one, and to retain a fixed nominal value.

M1
A measure of the money supply that includes currency and transaction deposits.

M2
A measure of the money supply that includes M1 plus money market mutual fund shares, money market deposit accounts, savings deposits, small-denomination time deposits, overnight repurchase agreements, and certain other liquid assets.

Macroeconomics
The branch of economics that studies large-scale economic phenomena, particularly inflation, unemployment, and economic growth.

Marginal propensity to consume
The proportion of each added dollar of real disposable income that households devote to real consumption.

Marginal propensity to import
The percentage of each added dollar of real disposable income that is devoted to real consumption of imported goods and services.

Marginal tax rate
The percentage of each added dollar of real personal income that must be paid in taxes.

Market
Any arrangement people have for trading with one another.

Market failure
A situation in which a market fails to coordinate choices in a way that achieves efficient use of resources.

Merchandise balance
The value of a country's merchandise exports minus the value of its merchandise imports.

Microeconomics
The branch of economics that studies the choices of small economic units, including households, business firms, and government agencies.

Model
A synonym for theory; in economics, often applied to theories that are stated in graphical or mathematical form.

Monetarism
A school of economics that emphasizes the importance of changes in the money stock as determinants of changes in real output and the price level.

Money
An asset that serves as a means of payment, a store of purchasing power, and a unit of account.

Money multiplier
The ratio of the equilibrium money stock to the banking system's total reserves.

Multiplier effect
The tendency for a given shift in real planned investment (or another component of real aggregate demand) to cause a larger shift in total real aggregate demand.

National income
The total income earned by households, including wages, rents, interest payments, and profits.

National product
The total value of all goods and services produced in the economy.

Natural level of real output
The level of real output that is consistent with the natural rate of unemployment.

Natural rate of unemployment
The sum of frictional and structural unemployment; the rate of unemployment that persists when the economy is experiencing neither accelerating nor decelerating inflation.

Natural resources
Anything that can be used as a productive input in its natural state, such as farmland, building sites, forests, and mineral deposits.

Net exports
Exports minus imports.

Net national product (NNP)
Gross national product minus an allowance (called the *capital consumption allowance*) that represents the value of capital equipment used up in the production process.

Net taxes
Taxes paid to government minus transfer payments made by government.

Net tax multiplier
The ratio of an induced change in real aggregate demand to a given change in real net taxes.

Net worth
The firm's or household's assets minus its liabilities.

Neutrality of money
The proposition that in the long run a one-time change in the money stock affects only the price level and not real output, employment, interest rates, or real planned investment.

New classical economics
A school of economics stressing the role of rational expectations in shaping the economy's response to policy changes.

Nominal
In economics, a term that refers to data that have not been adjusted for the effects of inflation.

Nominal exchange rate
The exchange rate expressed in the usual way: in terms of current units of foreign currency per current dollar.

Nominal interest rate
The interest rate expressed in the usual way: in terms of current dollars without adjustment for inflation.

Normal good
A good for which an increase in consumer incomes results in an increase in demand.

Normative economics
The area of economics that is devoted to judgments about whether economic policies or conditions are good or bad.

Okun's law
A rule of thumb according to which each 2 percent by which real output rises above (or falls below) its natural level results in an unemployment rate one percentage point below (or above) the natural rate.

Open economy
An economy that is linked to the outside world by imports, exports, and financial transactions.

Open market operation
A purchase (sale) by the Fed of government securities from (to) the public.

Operating target
A financial variable for which the Fed sets a short-term target, which it then uses as a guide in the day-to-day conduct of open market operations.

Opportunity cost
The cost of a good or service measured in terms of the forgone opportunity to pursue the best possible alternative activity with the same time or resources.

Outside lag
The delay between the time a policy decision is made and the time the policy change has its main effect on the economy.

Owners' equity
See Net worth.

Partnership
An association of two or more people who operate a business as co-owners under a voluntary legal agreement.

Personal income
The total income received by households, including earned income and transfer payments.

Phillips curve
A graph showing the relationship between the inflation rate and the unemployment rate, other things being equal.

Planned-expenditure schedule
A graph showing the level of total real planned expenditure associated with each level of real national income.

Planned-investment schedule
A graph showing the relationship between the total quantity of real planned-investment expenditure and the interest rate.

Positive economics
The area of economics that is concerned with facts and relationships among them.

Price index
A weighted average of the prices of goods and services expressed in relation to a base year value of 100.

Price level
A weighted average of the prices of goods and services expressed in relation to a base year value of 1.0.

Price stability
A situation in which the rate of inflation is low enough that it is not a significant factor in business and individual decision making.

Privatization
The turning over of government functions to the private sector.

Producer price index (PPI)
A price index based on a sample of goods and services bought by business firms.

Production possibility frontier
A graph that shows possible combinations of goods that can be produced by an economy given available knowledge and factors of production.

Public good
Goods that (1) cannot be provided for one person without also being provided for others and (2) once they are provided for one person can be provided for others at zero cost.

Purchasing power parity
A situation in which a given sum of money will buy the same market basket of goods and services when converted from one currency to another at prevailing exchange rates.

Rational-expectations hypothesis
The hypothesis that people form their expectations about future economic events on the basis of not only past events but also their expectations about economic policies and their likely effects.

Real
In economics, a term that refers to data that have been adjusted for the effects of inflation.

Real exchange rate
The nominal exchange rate adjusted for changes in the price levels of both countries relative to a chosen base year.

Real interest rate
The nominal interest rate minus the rate of inflation.

Realized expenditure
The sum of all planned and unplanned expenditures.

Realized investment
The sum of planned and unplanned investment.

Real output
A synonym for real gross national product.

Recession
A cyclical economic contraction that lasts six months or more.

Reflation
An episode in which policy becomes more expansionary while the expected inflation rate is still falling.

Repurchase agreement (RP)
A short-term liquid asset that consists of an agreement by a firm or person to buy securities from a financial institution for resale at an agreed-upon price at a later date (often the next business day).

Required-reserve ratio
Required reserves stated as a percentage of the deposits to which reserve requirements apply.

Required reserves
The minimum amount of reserves that the Fed requires depository institutions to hold.

Reserves
Cash in bank vaults and non-interest-bearing deposits of banks with the Federal Reserve System.

Saving
The part of household income that is not used to buy goods and services or to pay taxes.

Saving schedule
A graph showing the relationship between the total quantity of real saving and the interest rate.

Savings deposit
A deposit at a bank or thrift institution from which funds can be withdrawn at any time without payment of a penalty.

Say's law
The proposition that real aggregate demand will automatically be sufficient to absorb all of the output that firms and workers are willing to produce using given technology and resources.

Scarcity
A situation in which there is not enough of a resource to meet all of everyone's wants.

Securities
A collective term for common stocks, bonds, and other financial instruments.

Sole proprietorship
A firm that is owned, and usually operated, by one person, who receives all the profits and is responsible for all the firm's liabilities.

Sterilization
The Fed's use of open market operations to offset the effects of exchange market intervention on domestic reserves and on the money stock.

Stock
A quantity that exists at a given point in time, measured in terms of units only.

Structural deficit
The budget surplus or deficit that the federal government would incur given current tax and spending laws and a 6 percent unemployment rate.

Structural unemployment
The portion of unemployment that is accounted for by people who are out of work for long periods because their skills do not match those required for available jobs.

Substitutes
A pair of goods for which an increase in the price of one causes an increase in demand for the other.

Supply curve
A graphical representation of the relationship between the price of a good and the quantity of that good that sellers are willing to supply.

Supply shock
An event, such as an increase in the price of imported oil, a crop failure, or a natural disaster, that raises input prices for all or most firms and pushes up workers' costs of living.

Supply-side economics
An approach to economic policy that focuses on efforts to increase natural real output through the incentive effects of cuts in marginal tax rates and other means.

Thrift institutions
A group of financial intermediaries that operate much like commercial banks; they include savings and loan associations, savings banks, and credit unions.

Thrifts
See Thrift institutions.

Time deposit
A deposit at a bank or thrift institution from which funds can be withdrawn without payment of a penalty only at the end of an agreed-upon period.

Transaction costs
The costs, other than production costs, of carrying out a transaction.

Transaction deposit
A deposit from which funds can be freely withdrawn by check or electronic transfer to make payments to third parties.

Transfer payments
Payments to individuals that are not made in return for work they currently perform.

Transmission mechanism
The set of channels through which monetary policy affects real output and the price level.

Unemployed
A term used to refer to a person who is not employed but is actively looking for work.

Unemployment rate
The percentage of the labor force that is unemployed.

Value added
The dollar value of an industry's sales less the value of intermediate goods purchased for use in production.

Velocity (income velocity of money)
The ratio of nominal national income to the money stock; a measure of the average number of times each dollar of the money stock is used each year for income-producing purposes.

Index